A HISTORY OF
ROMAN BRITAIN

Peter Salway, formerly a Fellow of Sidney Sussex College, Cambridge, and subsequently of All Souls College, Oxford, is an Emeritus Professor of the Open University and Chairman of the Academic Committee of the Oxford Archaeological Unit. He is a Fellow of the Society of Antiquaries and has served on the Council of the National Trust. He has also written reviews for the *Times Literary Supplement* and the *Times Higher Education Supplement*, and has appeared in television and radio broadcasts.

A HISTORY OF

ROMAN
BRITAIN

PETER SALWAY

OXFORD
UNIVERSITY PRESS

OXFORD

UNIVERSITY PRESS

Great Clarendon Street, Oxford OX2 6DP

Oxford University Press is a department of the University of Oxford.
It furthers the University's objective of excellence in research, scholarship,
and education by publishing worldwide in

Oxford New York

Athens Auckland Bangkok Bogotá Buenos Aires
Cape Town Chennai Dar es Salaam Delhi Florence Hong Kong Istanbul
Karachi Kolkata Kuala Lumpur Madrid Melbourne Mexico City Mumbai
Nairobi Paris São Paulo Shanghai Singapore Taipei Tokyo Toronto Warsaw

with associated companies in Berlin Ibadan

Oxford is a trade mark of Oxford University Press
in the UK and in certain other countries

British Library Cataloguing in Publication Data

Data available

Library of Congress Cataloging in Publication Data

Data available

ISBN 0-19-280138-4

1 3 5 7 9 10 8 6 4 2

Printed in Great Britain by
Cox & Wyman Ltd
Reading, Berkshire

PREFACE

When the volume entitled *Roman Britain* was published in 1981 as part of the Oxford History of England series, I thought it necessary to explain why I had chosen to treat Britain in that period as an integral part of the Roman world, reacting in its own way to events and trends observable across the known world, but always within the orbit of an empire that encompassed the greater part of it. 'Roman Britain' as a field of study or a leisure interest was still often regarded by its devotees—and from outside—as a self-contained entity whose study was a traditional craft handed down from scholar to scholar. Prehistorians (particularly those without a background in Greek and Roman classical literature) were inclined to find it alien. Sometimes they dismissed the Roman centuries in the history of Britain as a transient phase with a superficial culture imposed by a foreign occupation. They were reinforced in this by an overall impression conveyed by much of the scholarly work on the period following the collapse of Roman imperial rule at the beginning of the fifth century AD. Studies of the Celtic tradition that survived and flourished in western and northern Britain—and most of all in Ireland, where there had been no Roman occupation—seemed to reveal an indigenous tribal society with apparently close social and artistic similarities to what was known of pre-Roman Iron Age Britain. This suggested that, even in the areas of Britain that had been most heavily marked by the remains of Roman material culture, the natural 'trajectory' of development of the native population had been only temporarily nudged off course by the Roman presence. The fact that these areas were also those most intensely affected by a blanket of subsequent Anglo-Saxon settlement, which seemed to have submerged whatever preceded it very swiftly after the end of Roman rule, reinforced the notion that Roman Britain had been a fragile and transient aberration in the natural evolution of these islands. Even students of Classics themselves could often go along with this picture, since Britain seemed to them to be so peripheral to the essentially Mediterranean civilization that was at the centre of their interests.

In adapting for the *Oxford Illustrated History of Roman Britain* what I wrote a decade earlier for the Oxford History of England, it became obvious that advances in the studies of both the pre-Roman and the post-Roman periods made it largely unnecessary to restate the case for regarding the relationship between Britain and Rome as critical to understanding the development of the island for many centuries. That relationship was now clearly accepted as starting long before the Claudian conquest in the middle of the first century AD, and as archaeologically demonstrable in Britain and from the Mediterranean to the Channel. Study of the historical sources had highlighted the remarkable place that Britain occupied in Roman thought and politics from Julius Caesar to the last years of Roman rule and possibly beyond. Similarly, recent scholarship was beginning to show Britain more clearly playing an intelligible part in the origins of modern Europe that arose out of the fusion of Roman and barbarian in the fifth and sixth centuries, processes always better understood in Britain's Continental neighbours and now themselves the subject of important new discoveries and reappraisals on both sides of the Channel.

In Britain itself the pace of discovery and research has not slackened during these decades. In almost all aspects, the effect of recasting my 1981 text for the present book has been to sharpen the view of Roman Britain and to provide depth and detail to opinions that were tentative or part-formed. Some hypotheses have fallen by the wayside, but fewer than I had expected. The text is broadly based on that of the Oxford History of England, condensed and revised to take account of the advances in knowledge of the past ten years. Opportunity has been taken for substantial rewriting, particularly in the narrative chapters. As this book is aimed at a wider public, footnotes have been avoided. Instead, the appendices and ancillary material follow the Oxford Illustrated Histories in aiming to provide the general reader with background information in a convenient form. Compiling the section on further reading emphasized, perhaps more than any of the other work on this book, the continuing vigour of Romano-British studies and their central place in the understanding of the early history of this country.

PETER SALWAY

ACKNOWLEDGEMENTS

In a book of this sort it is impossible to acknowledge adequately the enormous but unseen contribution of the many people who, in conversation or in answer to specific queries, provided information, criticized ill-founded notions, and suggested new lines of enquiry. Others supplied material for the pictures that accompany the text, with a degree of helpfulness that made the task of illustration an unexpected pleasure. I hope they will accept that I recognize my debt to each of them. Interpretations of what they provided—and with which they may not agree—are my responsibility, not theirs, as are any errors inadvertently introduced.

The publisher's support for this book has been outstanding. It would have proceeded nowhere without the backing of Ivon Asquith. From the time they inherited the project, Tony Morris and Sophie MacCallum have treated it with an enthusiasm that is much appreciated. Sandra Assersohn deserves special thanks for handling the complex picture research with professionalism and good humour. It is easy for an author to overlook the contribution of the desk-editing team: my thanks go to Peter Momtchiloff, and to Nicola Pike who copy-edited the text. Finally my thanks are due to Sue Tipping for the page layout.

PETER SALWAY

1993

In preparing this paperback edition of the text of the *Oxford Illustrated History of Roman Britain* opportunity has been taken to make a few minor corrections and amendments. I am very grateful to Angus Phillips and Caroline Cory-Pearce of OUP for seeing it through the press, and particularly to the latter for overseeing the choice and production of the maps with which it is illustrated.

P.S.

1997

CONTENTS

x Contents

LIST OF MAPS

These maps, in common with most other maps of the ancient world, should be used with caution. Many details are approximate or conjectural, particularly ancient political boundaries. Present coastlines have been adopted throughout, in view of continuing uncertainty about changes during and since the Roman period. Place-names for Roman sites here and in the text are given in modern rather than ancient form, except for a few, such as Verulamium, that are in common use. Similarly, the modern place-names themselves are given in whatever spelling seems most likely at the present time to be recognized readily by non-specialist English-speaking readers.

I

THE FIRST ROMAN
CONTACTS

1
THE BRITISH
BACKGROUND

In this book we shall be looking at as long a stretch of time as from the Wars of the Roses to the present day. It is the first age for which we have contemporary or near-contemporary written sources. It is also the age for the greater part of which Britain was absorbed into an empire based on the Mediterranean, subject to the direct impact of classical culture, and closely involved with the fortunes of Europe at one of the most formative periods of its history. 'The toga was often to be seen among them': with these words the Roman historian Tacitus described the Britons adopting the Roman way of life at an early stage of their long career as Roman provincials. The purpose of this book is to chart this process and to see how far it went, to examine Britain as a part of the Roman empire. Out of this will emerge its own particular character.

Rome herself never underestimated Britain. For Julius Caesar's first expedition across the 'Ocean' the Roman senate decreed a lengthy period of thanksgiving. To a people used to the tideless Mediterranean, and in an age when travel by sea was regarded as exceedingly hazardous, the Channel presented a mental barrier of formidable proportions. Augustan propaganda constantly foretold the subjection of Britain to imperial control, or claimed it as virtually accomplished. That Virgil used Britain poetically to denote the furthermost parts of the world reflected popular ideas of the island that persisted to the end of antiquity. Even after centuries of incorporation into the empire, it suited Roman emperors anxious for prestige that this stereotype survived alongside everyday experience of Britain as one among the many and varied pieces in the jigsaw of empire.

The Emperor Claudius' splendid triumphal ceremony in Rome for the British conquests of the armies under his command performed a vital role in confirming him on the throne to which he had been elevated in an unexpected and undignified manner. His eccentric predecessor Gaius' last-minute cancellation of the invasion had seemed all the more striking because of the magnitude of the enterprise in Roman eyes. Claudius, in emulating the deified Julius, had exceeded him by turning victories across the Ocean into permanent augmentation of the empire. Britain's importance to Rome and to emperors and would-be emperors was rarely overlooked. Command in Britain was time and time again felt to require the appointment of Rome's greatest generals. Hadrian authorized the construction across the island of the most elaborate of all Roman frontier defences. Septimius Severus led his armies in person in what was perhaps the last real attempt to conquer the whole island for the empire. The forces stationed in Britain were exceptionally large, powerful, and sometimes notorious. On several occasions they intervened in imperial politics in a major way, and in proclaiming Constantine the Great as emperor, they made their greatest impact on world history. It is a measure of the weight that Rome attached to Britain for century after century that, so long as it could physically maintain control, the central imperial government thought it worth tying down substantial forces in its defence—for long periods as much as a tenth of the entire Roman army. Scarce resources were expended on successive restorations after civil wars and barbarian incursions. Even after the remnants of the imperial government in the west had lost political control of Britain, there is reason to think that Roman interest in it was not dead—and Britain remained within the orbit of the late Roman world after the western empire as a political organization was extinct.

The framework on which the Roman province was constructed has customarily been defined by reference to the geographical division of Britain into highland and lowland zones, differentiated by relief, soil, communications, and, to some extent, climate. Broadly speaking, the lowland zone is that part of Britain which lies south and east of a line drawn from the mouth of the

THE ISLAND OF BRITAIN. A broad division into highland and lowland zones is reflected in the general character of its conquest and evolution under Roman rule—with greater civil development in the lowland parts—but there are many local exceptions.

River Tees to the mouth of the Exe, geologically characterized by comparatively young rocks and a countryside marked by relatively low hills and large areas of flat ground, much of it gravelly river valley highly suitable for settlement and agriculture. The highland zone to the north and west is characterized by the bleak hills of Dartmoor, Exmoor, and Bodmin Moor in the south-west, by the mountains of Wales, the Lake District, the Peak District, the high moors of the Pennines and Cheviots—and most of Scotland, 'Lowlands' as well as 'Highlands'. There are, of course, patches of the opposite sort of landscape in each zone, and some highland land is better for agriculture than contiguous lowlands. All in all, however, there is a broad distinction between the two. The lowland zone was particularly suitable for settled, arable agriculture; and the relative ease of communications made both the spread of new ideas and actual conquest relatively easy. The highland zone was more naturally pastoral country, with communities comparatively isolated and resistant to change.

There were factors that could override this divide. In the Roman period we have to take into account the intervention of men whose decisions might be determined by considerations that had nothing to do with the conditions of a particular locality, and who had the physical resources, the technology, and the organization to carry out projects that would have been impossible or unrewarding for a local community. Romans were capable of overcoming natural difficulties to an extent that few of their predecessors could approach. If they failed to exploit certain areas, we may confidently assume that they did not think the probable return worthwhile (measured, of course, in their terms, not ours). Roman occupation sometimes spread into areas sparsely inhabited in the late Iron Age. One such area was the Fenland of East Anglia, where, seizing opportunities offered by a change in relative sea-level, they opened up lands largely empty of recent occupation, engineered drainage and communications, and introduced new population.

A factor of great importance, at least in the early stages of provincial development, was the character and existing culture of the various peoples brought under Roman rule. The degree of material prosperity of each had depended to a large extent on location —both in respect of the sort of terrain on which they were

situated and how it might be exploited, and in their geographical position in the island in relation to communications with the
Continent. But by the time of Caesar's expeditions in 55 and 54
BC, the cultures of nearly all the inhabitants of Britain had been
formed to a greater or lesser extent under the influence of what
was happening among the later Iron Age peoples on the Continent, though prehistorians disagree on how much independent
development occurred in Britain itself. In some areas change
probably resulted from the arrival of strangers—whether individually or in large groups, and whether arriving peaceably or as
invaders—in others from the exchange of material objects by way
of trade or gift and from the spread of ideas. It seems most unlikely that we shall ever be certain to what extent there had been
significant changes of population in the immediate pre-Roman
centuries, but opinion among prehistorians tends now to discount
the once-dominant line of thinking that attributed the major
changes observable archaeologically to successive large-scale invasions by Continental peoples. A much greater willingness to see
Britain as part of an overall European Iron Age picture is now
coupled to an acknowledgement among some prehistorians that
the position was complex and constantly changing, susceptible to
no single theory of development.

It is now clear that Britain was profoundly affected by Roman
activities for at least three-quarters of a century before Caesar's
expeditions. Rome had long had an interest in the Mediterranean
region of Gaul, at first largely because of the routes from Italy
to the possessions in Spain that she had acquired during and after
the epic struggle with Carthage in the third and second centuries
BC. Alliance with Marseilles, the most important of the Greek
city-states long established on the Mediterranean coast of Gaul,
drew Rome into military intervention in wars between the
Massiliots and Celtic neighbours, and soon into a permanent
presence. It is not at all clear when this developed into a regular
province (a concept that, in any case, is somewhat different in
this earlier period from the sense it acquired under the early
Empire), but the catalyst was probably the great victories won by
the Roman populist general Marius over the Cimbri and Teu-
tones, Germanic tribes whose vast folk movements threatened both
Gaul and Italy in the last years of the second century. However,

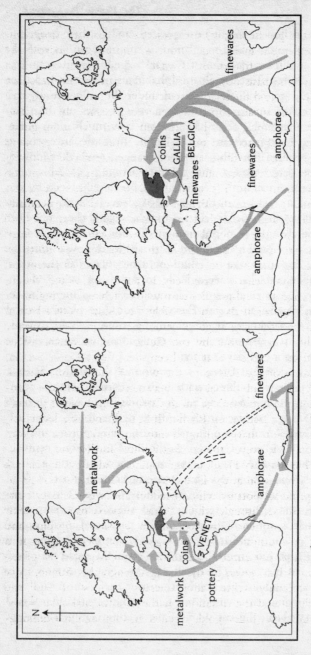

CAESAR'S CONQUEST OF GAUL and expeditions across the Channel dramatically altered the pattern of contact between the Continent and Britain. The Continental sources of imports from the third to mid-first century BC (*left*) contrast with those from Caesar to Claudius (*right*).

whatever the precise details, the presence of Roman armies and Roman settlement in Provence from around 125 BC enormously increased the penetration of Roman culture northwards into Gaul. Since the basis of archaeology is the physical remains that people leave behind them, it is inevitably trade (or exchange) that seems to us the spearhead of this penetration, since the distribution of archaeological finds had revealed a trail of Roman goods through central France and on to Britain. There is no reason to doubt, however, that these archaeological patterns do faithfully reflect important cultural and political changes in Britain in the period between about 125 BC and Caesar, and that the traffic between the Continent and Britain that originated in the Roman-dominated Mediterranean had much to do with them.

In this period the principal routes to Britain ran westward from the Mediterranean via Toulouse to the Gironde, then north to Brittany along the Atlantic coast of France. Trans-shipment on towards Britain seems to have been in the hands of the Veneti, the chief tribe of southern Brittany who inhabited the region of Vannes and Quiberon Bay, and possibly the Osismi, with a base at Quimper. Final shipping of goods across the Channel seems mainly to have been carried out by the Coriosolites of north-eastern Brittany from a harbour that has been identified at Saint-Servan, at the mouth of the Rance to the west of Mont-Saint-Michel. In earlier periods substantial trade between Britain and the Continent, linked to extraction of tin in Cornwall, had passed through a port at Mount Batten, on Plymouth Sound, and, at a lesser volume, this seems to have continued into the Roman period. From around 100 BC, however, the emphasis shifted further east, to Portland and Hengistbury Head, on the southern side of Christchurch Harbour. Excavation at the latter has revealed that this was probably the principal port by which Mediterranean goods now came into Britain and through which British exports passed on their way to the Continent. Wine-containers (*amphorae*), fig pips, and ingots of glass indicate some of the goods that were coming into the island. It is not entirely safe to use a much-quoted list of exports from Britain given by the Roman geographer Strabo, since that was certainly written after Caesar's conquest of Gaul had profoundly altered the situation on the Continental side. Strabo listed grain, cattle, hides, gold, silver, iron, thoroughbred hunting-

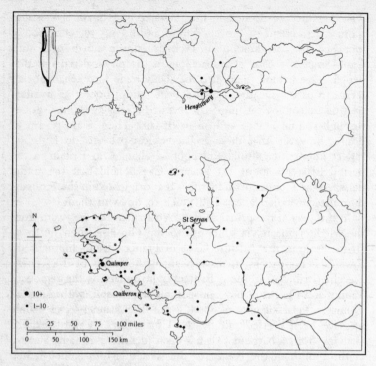

TRADE in Mediterranean goods between Gaul and Britain before Julius Caesar's conquest of Gaul is reflected in the pattern of finds of Italian pottery containers (*amphorae*) of a type manufactured from the second century BC to the middle of the first. Three principal ports in Brittany were in contact with the Iron Age settlement on Hengistbury Head, Dorset, overlooking Christchurch Harbour.

dogs, and slaves. Nevertheless, the archaeology already confirms the presence of all except the last two items at Hengistbury in this earlier period, and it would not be surprising to find traces of the slave-trade, like the chain-gang fetters from an Iron Age sacred site on Anglesey, appearing here too.

Hengistbury was not just a place of trans-shipment or exchange. Iron-smelting, extraction of silver from British ores, working of bronze, and some form of gold-processing occurred alongside cattle-slaughtering, accompanied probably by the curing of meat or hides using native salt. This suggests a population profiting

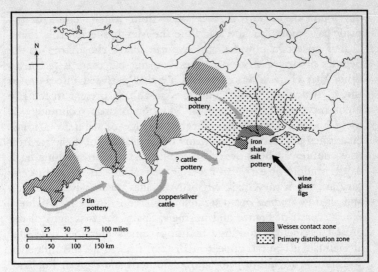

IRON AGE BRITISH EXPORTS met Continental imports on Portland Bay, where there was direct and mutually profitable contact between Britons and Gauls, possibly, too, with Roman merchants from the Mediterranean. A broad zone in Wessex benefited from this trade, controlling access to it by communities beyond.

both through the straightforward handling of goods and also through the added value that could be gained by using skilled labour to process raw materials into finished or part-finished products. It would not be wholly unexpected to find evidence of Romans directly involved at Hengistbury, but Caesar does remark on the lack of direct information about Britain before his expeditions. It is more certain that the north-western Gauls themselves were involved on the spot, judging by the amount of imported pottery from that region and the number of Coriosolitan coins. Indeed, the excavator of Hengistbury has suggested that there was a resident group of Coriosolites, and it is not impossible that the settlement was primarily Gallic rather than native British. Whoever controlled Hengistbury itself, however, the stimulating effects on the culture and prosperity of Britons in the districts around the port and the region immediately beyond are clear, and the activities at Hengistbury are likely also to have influenced developments in areas further afield from which certain of the principal exports, such as lead from the Mendips, eventually came.

It is uncertain how far back we can follow the history of the peoples of Britain known to the Romans, but there is reason to think that characteristic ways of life that persisted into Roman times, particularly in agriculture, were already present in the late Neolithic period. The eventual adoption of iron technology in the island may simply have been a change of habit by a long-established population, since many of the features of their late Iron Age culture can be shown to belong to a tradition reaching back to the middle or early Bronze Age or beyond. In the sixth century BC, when the Greek city at Marseilles was newly established and already sending out daughter-foundations along the Mediterranean coasts of France and northern Spain, the first signs of the great Continental Iron Age tradition named after the 'type site' at Hallstatt in Austria appear in Britain. By 500 BC this influence was starting to spread throughout southern and eastern England, with outliers to the north-west. In the fourth and third centuries distinctive changes based on the Continental developments labelled 'La Tène' after another type site, in Switzerland, appear in the south of England and begin to penetrate north and west.

While the Continental Iron Age was in its 'La Tène I' phase, there appeared in east Yorkshire the so-called 'Arras Culture'. This culture is characterized archaeologically by burials containing wheeled vehicles, and by burial mounds or 'barrows' and funerary enclosures with square-plan ditches. The culture's origin has been attributed to the Marne region of northern France, but it, too, seems to have affinities further east. The part of Yorkshire in which it appears was known in Roman times as the district of the Parisi, a tribe whose name has its parallel in Gaul. While the British version is not an exact reproduction of its Continental relative, these burials do introduce us to the practice of conspicuous consumption as a means of proving status—by lavish provision of feasts, by giving away, ritually breaking, dedicating to the gods, or, as here, depositing in graves objects of value to demonstrate that the donor did not need to care about the cost. This practice was a major feature of the Iron Age society that the Romans encountered right across Europe and to which they themselves were in some ways related.

The settlement patterns of British Iron Age society were broadly established in the crucial period from about 600, with certain important developments in the last century BC, to which we shall return. Some prehistorians have identified two main patterns, which they think derive from different forms of social organization, and which they have labelled 'chiefdoms' and 'tribes'. This ethnographical terminology is not altogether convenient in the present context, as it has long been conventional to refer to the peoples outside the Roman empire collectively, as the Greeks and Romans themselves did, as 'barbarians', and individually as 'tribes'.

There are several distinctive settlement patterns on the ground. In southern and western England the dominant form is the large defended earthwork generically known to archaeologists as the hill-fort (though not always on a hill), often demonstrably lying at the centre of a number of small family-sized settlements. It is now known that many hill-forts were themselves intensively settled, in some cases displaying substantial signs of organization, including street systems, that on occasion suggest the beginnings of an urban life. The fact that the distances between neighbouring hill-forts tend to be not dissimilar has led to the idea that they represent the centres of chiefdoms, in which a single person or family dominated a substantial territory. It is not yet clear whether the local chief would normally have resided in the hill-fort like a medieval lord of the manor, or whether it served chiefly as a centre at which various communal functions—such as feasting and religious ritual—were carried out, and as a refuge in time of war. In either case, the system as a whole probably indicates authority based on the holding of land, and implies an interest in the maintenance of relatively settled conditions.

In eastern and central England and areas of eastern Scotland there is visually a different pattern, in which undefended villages are complemented by single farms. It has been suggested, however, that in fact these represent a social system not entirely unlike the hill-fort chiefdoms of the west and south, and certainly closer to it than what we shall see in the highland zone. An intermediate version appears in some districts, for example, in the Upper Thames region, where a limited number of relatively small but apparently defended (or at least enclosed) sites located on the higher ground are accompanied by larger numbers of humble farming sites on the easily farmed gravel terraces and alluvium of the river plain. The latter are of several types, which correspond to variations in soil and drainage, and demonstrate an accurate local knowledge of suitability for different forms of agriculture and a surprising degree of specialization from farm to farm. Such sophistication supports the notion of an ordered landscape, and may very well reflect a similar system of lord and dependant as suggested above. Overall, the picture is emerging of a broadly similar arrangement of society, given different physical expression in different parts of southern Britain, whether from local tradition, or from terrain, or a combination of such factors.

The predominant pattern in the north and west, however, is fundamentally different. There are few sites that might have been centres controlled by individual chiefs, and the population seems to have been scattered, inhabiting large numbers of small settlements. Compared to lowland Britain, there are far fewer signs of settled husbandry, whether arable or of livestock grazed on relatively small and well-defined tracts of land. Instead, the agricultural economy seems to have been largely a matter of herding beasts over very large areas of landscape. Politically, it is suggested that a loose organization within the tribe took the place of the closely managed territorial lordships postulated for southern Britain as a whole.

The spread of La Tène III culture over large areas of southeastern Britain has generally been coupled with Julius Caesar's statement that the tribes of the seaward part of Britain were recent 'Belgic' arrivals who had come as raiders and subsequently settled, retaining the names of the peoples from whom they had originated. However, before Caesar's expeditions, there are difficulties in dating characteristics in the archaeological record that are clearly Belgic, in the sense of being identical or very similar to finds from the parts of northern Gaul recognized as 'Belgic' in Caesar's and later times. It is true that some of the same tribal names occur on both sides of the Channel, though in some cases they may not have appeared in Britain until after Caesar's expeditions. It is also true that the recurrence of names of tribes and of places in districts far apart from one another is not that uncommon in the Celtic world—the Veneti of Brittany, for example, are paralleled by the Veneti of north-east Italy, a case in which no recent migration is suggested. One may suspect that this phenomenon generally had more to do with language than actual kinship. While it is always highly dangerous to reject a contemporary account without very good reason, it is also always appropriate to consider the circumstances in which the statements were written. It is not at all clear whether Caesar here, in his description of Britain, is reporting what he knew, or had been told, or had deduced from what he had observed, in much the same way as we have to deduce.

There is one specific area of central southern Britain for which a good case can be made from the written evidence, rather than from the archaeology, for an actual arrival of a substantial group of incomers from Gallia Belgica. In the developed Roman province Winchester was the administrative centre of one of the civil authorities (*civitates*) of the sort that were often given the names of the native tribes that preceded them, and from reliable members of whose aristocracies their governing councils were generally formed. In the Roman period Winchester was called Venta Belgarum, signifying 'market of the Belgae'. There is reason to think, as we shall see later, that this particular *civitas* was created out of an earlier, larger grouping. As such, it may have had no usable native tribal name: the Roman adoption of 'Belgae' at the least indicates that, when the *civitas* was formed in the first century AD, they thought the people were recognizably Belgic. It is perhaps no coincidence that in Roman times the *civitas* immediately to the north of Winchester bore the same name as the Atrebates of Gallia Belgica, of whose political affinity with their namesakes in Britain Caesar was to be made very aware. It would have been entirely reasonable for Caesar to put information about a relatively small settlement of Belgic Gauls together with knowledge of the fact that the name 'Atrebates' occurred in the same general area and expand it into an explanation for the wider occurrence of similar tribal names.

The modern need to explain similarities between the Iron Age cultures of Britain and the Continent in terms of invasions perhaps really lies in our insular acceptance of the Roman view of the Channel as a formidable barrier to be crossed only by determined invaders. To the tribes of Gaul and Britain, it may rather have been regarded as a stretch of water inside the Celtic world, like a river or a lake, across which movement to and fro was a matter of course and which was not thought of as differentiating Britons and Gauls in any important sense. Rivers in the ancient world were frequently unifying rather than dividing factors between the peoples on either side, not to mention being often the easiest means of communication. We ought, perhaps, to be thinking of tribes and individuals reacting to one another across a single north-western Celtic region rather than within Britain or Gaul alone.

Many Iron Age settlements in Britain continued to be used into the Roman period, or can be distinguished from Roman sites only by their datable small finds. In places there seems to be continuity of settlement boundaries, and by the late first or early second century AD under Roman rule some Iron Age farmsteads were replaced on the same site by modest Roman villas, as if only the ownership or simply the standard of living had changed, but the unit of farming remained constant. Sometimes, as on one of the sites at Stanton Harcourt in Oxfordshire, an Iron Age farm on one side of a boundary ditch is replaced by a Roman one on the other, with the boundary remaining unchanged. Evidence has been accumulating in the Thames Valley—where some of the most intensive research has been conducted—that the decisive changes in land-use occurred not with the Roman conquest in the 40s of the first century AD, but in the hundred years or so before it. This is marked not only by alterations in the shape and appearance of the farmsteads themselves, but, more importantly, by a switch from agriculture based on the grazing of livestock over uninterrupted pasture between farms to the development of enclosed meadows and to the relatively intense exploitation of arable within fields with fixed boundaries. It is not surprising to find the same sort of pattern emerging elsewhere. At Odell in Bedfordshire we can again note the employment of fixed boundaries in the years just before the conquest, and excavations there have shown no distinction in types of activity that can be equated with the arrival of the Romans. Positive developments do not occur at Odell until considerably later in the first century AD. It is becoming clear that there was a major change relatively late in the pre-Roman Iron Age in

Britain, at least in these densely populated agricultural river valleys. The Roman conquest accelerated the development of this new way of life, rather than initiated it.

The overall pattern of labour, too, was changing in the later pre-Roman Iron Age. In the archaeology there is a much higher proportion of wheel-made pottery, for example, instead of the generally handmade wares of earlier periods. There are signs of a professional pottery industry emerging, making some excellent products that strongly influenced Roman factory production in Britain when it got under way. Life was becoming more specialized and more organized. Slave-chains from the hoard of pre-Roman metalwork at Llyn Cerrig in Anglesey and from the Iron Age site that preceded the villa at Park Street in Hertfordshire may relate to the slave-trade from Britain to the empire already referred to, but they may also reflect a local slave-using society, as in the classical world. The beginnings of urbanization have been noted, with its implications of incipient specialization as some people cease to spend all their time on the land, but there is also an apparent division between a tribal aristocracy chiefly interested in the arts of war and a farming peasantry. This is reflected in the surviving visual art of late Iron Age Britain. It is of a patently aristocratic genre. It is marked by splendid weapons, mirrors, and personal ornaments of the highest artistic merit and technical achievement, but the material occurs in small quantities only, as is characteristic of an art essentially confined to a restricted class in society. The tribes in Gaul were to prove admirably suited to Roman ways, however politically unreliable they might sometimes be. They, too, were tribal societies comprised essentially of nobility and commons, and by Caesar's time these were not only being governed by their local upper classes, but loose intertribal organizations of leading Gauls had emerged. Out of the scholarly controversies that surround the British Iron Age, we can at least be confident that by the time Claudius came to form the Roman province, and perhaps already before Caesar, influential contacts existed between the aristocracies on both sides of the Channel. We shall encounter named individuals active in Britain and Gaul later, but we may suspect much larger interchange across this Gallo-Britannic region. The way of life of the southern and eastern Britons in this period probably had more in common with their nearest counterparts in Gaul than with their western and northern neighbours in Britain, and they were to become among the most successfully Romanized under imperial rule.

It is easy, however, to overemphasize the differences within Britain. It is, in fact, clear that a culture with more common elements than divisions had spread over most or all of Britain by the time of the Roman conquest of Gaul, and that it broadly resembled that which had come to dominate Continental Europe from the Danube to the North Sea. We have so far avoided defining the terms 'Celt' and 'Celtic'. They have modern and misleading overtones, but there are no other convenient words with which to describe this remarkable phenomenon, and the area in Europe is so vast, and the peoples with which we are dealing are so varied that, like the ancient writers, we can only use the terms with a vague idea as to their geographical and broadly cultural limits. They can, however, be applied with some precision to the language spoken by the Britons. In the post-Roman period two main versions of the Celtic language were spoken in the British Isles, and from these the modern Celtic languages of Britain and Ireland are descended. They were distinguished by the use of a *p* sound in one where a *q* sound occurred in the other. The first ('Brythonic' or 'Brittonic') is now represented by Welsh and Cornish, the second ('Goidelic') by Irish, Gaelic, and Manx. Since Scottish Gaelic derives from late immigration from Ireland, it is clear that historically these versions represent two blocks, one centred on mainland Britain, the other on Ireland. Except where explicable by subsequent Irish immigration, Celtic place-names in England and Wales fall wholly into the Brythonic group. Goidelic was, it seems, an Irish variant of the common tongue; it can be ignored for the present purposes as beyond the area that ever came under Roman rule. It has been argued that Celtic remained in general use as the everyday language in Britain throughout the Roman period. This is almost certainly true of much of the countryside, where the bulk of the population continued to live. The widespread occurrence of Celtic place-names in Romanized forms, and the virtual absence of any obviously derived from an earlier language, strongly support the hypothesis that by the time of the Roman conquest almost all of Britain was speaking Celtic. In Caesar's account we find that all personal and place-names are Celtic, and there is no sign that the conquering Roman armies a century later encountered anything else, even when they penetrated far into the north of Scotland.

2

THE EXPEDITIONS
OF CAESAR

By the middle of the first century BC the old Republican system of governing the Roman state was in an advanced state of decay. Theoretically, the Republic was still governed by annual magistrates, elected by the citizen body and advised by the senate. The latter was a body whose legal powers were limited but which had exercised enormous authority by virtue of its composition, since it was made up of men who had held major public office and led by those ('consulars') who had occupied one of the two annual consulships, the supreme office of state. Most of those elected to office came from families that had produced previous office-holders, and it was this 'senatorial' class that had come to dominate the state for generation after generation. Competition was keen, but there had been certain conventions within the game, and there was much intermarriage for political reasons. Poorer relations and lesser families attached themselves to greater ones, and in a network of patronage the great commanded the allegiance of their 'clients'. The size and composition of the *clientela* thus formed themselves became symbols of status. Landed property was central to the position of the senatorial aristocracy. Not only were high property qualifications required for office, but the acquisition of vast holdings of land by the great families brought with it a web of obligation and influence. Some families dominated whole regions—Pompey the Great boasted that he had only to stamp his foot in his home district and legions would spring from the ground to follow his command—and as public lawlessness increased, these senatorial clans began to become states within the state, to whom lesser men looked for protection and advancement rather than to the public institutions.

Magistrates' powers were theoretically unlimited within their sphere of competence, but in Rome the holders of office had been controlled not only by the pressures of public opinion, but also by the principle of collegiality, under which magistrates were appointed in pairs or greater numbers, each having the power of veto over his fellows. Military command normally went to former holders of the highest offices, and as Rome's foreign wars gradually brought her an empire piecemeal in the second and first centuries BC, provincial governorships followed suit. Opportunities for glory in war—the greatest of spurs to an ambitious Roman—and for enrichment overseas under the Republic's very lax control made these commands much sought after. By the first century BC the principal senatorial families were making a normal practice of manipulating the electoral system, by corruption of the common electorate and violence on the streets of Rome as well as through the traditional use of their *clientelae*.

At the same time a new element had entered politics with the creation of a permanent professional army. Until the appointment of the populist general Marius, armies had normally been raised as and when they were required, theoretically by conscription of ordinary citizens who returned to normal life after the emergency. By the end of the second century BC there were so many landless peasants and unemployed city-dwellers that it was not difficult to attract men to serve in one campaign after another for pay. Marius reformed military tactics and welded these men into a professional army; and the Republic made the crucial mistake of failing to attach the troops to the Roman state rather than to their generals, largely through senatorial unwillingness to commit the treasury to regular provision for soldiers discharged after a campaign or retired after long service. These professionals therefore had to look to their own old commanders for support. Rome now not only had the best army in the world, but also one that would follow individual generals rather than the legitimate government if it came to a choice. This extremely dangerous extension of the principle of patron and client was a fatal error on the part of the Republic that constituted a major element in its downfall. Subsequently, Rome made excellent provision for its veterans, but the pattern of loyalty set by the Republic was to contribute significantly to the long-drawn-out failure of the Roman state under the emperors.

The fall of the Republic had its immediate origins in the upheavals of the latter part of the second and the early part of the first century BC. By the 50s BC the traditional curbs on political behaviour were largely ineffective. Magistrates' colleagues were intimidated, courts were bribed or overawed by force, and every constitutional trick was played. Power had largely fallen into the hands of three men—Caesar, Pompey, and the immensely wealthy Crassus—who jockeyed for power, sometimes in uneasy alliance, sometimes near to civil war. Caesar himself came comparatively late to military command, but he had shown a natural genius for it in Spain. Command in Gaul gave him the opportunity to display a capacity for large-scale conquest that he proceeded to demonstrate by overrunning that vast country with extraordinary speed and reaching the Rhine. His combination of daring and attention to detail brought success in the field and the devotion of his troops. Good fortune (*felicitas*), whether the product of luck or the taking of carefully calculated risks, was of immense importance to a Roman commander, since it demonstrated that the favour of the gods shone upon him. In times of wavering loyalties, a notably lucky commander tended to be a secure one.

There is unresolved debate as to whether Caesar had long-term plans in life, always intent eventually on supreme power, or was essentially an opportunist. In 55 BC, however, use of his troops to seize power in Rome was not feasible, even if he wished it. Instead, Germany and Britain lay outside the commission of any other Roman commander, and arguably he might extend his operations in either direction. He reported a threat from the Germans to the new Roman conquests in Gaul, and a request from one German tribe for assistance. Britain presented a very similar picture. We are never likely to know his precise intentions, and it is probable that in his account of the expeditions he consciously avoids telling us whether he aimed at conquest or punitive action. He does state that in most of his Gallic campaigns he had found British contingents fighting against him, but even this he cites as a reason for hastening his first invasion, not for deciding on it in the first place.

To Romans, the notion of a common culture between those tribes Caesar had already subdued and the unconquered barbarian tribes immediately beyond them would not have caused surprise. He noted that within living memory one Diviciacus, 'the greatest man in Gaul', had held sway not only amongst Gallic tribes, including the Suessiones (around Soissons), but also in Britain. In 57 BC those nobles of the Bellovaci (Beauvais), also Belgic, who had unsuccessfully urged an anti-Roman policy on their tribe fled to Britain. Moreover, the most powerful political force among the Gauls, Druidism, had, according to Caesar, originated in Britain and spread to Gaul. True or not, what matters in this context is what Caesar thought at the time—or chose to let be believed in Rome.

It is not possible to say when Caesar first conceived the idea of invading Britain. The revolt of the Veneti may have been due to fear that Roman presence on the Channel—even more, an invasion of Britain—would bring their lucrative sea-trade to an end, though the immediate cause was a dispute over hostages. If he had the idea by the beginning of 56, it was probably much strengthened during that year by successes that seemed to have procured the total pacification of Gaul. He was almost obliged to look for further opportunities for conquest by the extension of his provincial command following the Conference of Luca in 56. At that meeting Pompey, Crassus, and Caesar had joined in uneasy alliance, and in 55 Pompey and Crassus were to hold the two consulships in Rome. Caesar needed spectacular new victories to keep his name before the Roman public. It has also been argued that Caesar could have been recalled if the purpose for which he had been sent to Gaul had been completed. A Roman magistrate enjoyed something analogous to diplomatic immunity while he retained office, and this applied to provincial governors as well as to magistrates in Rome. Once he laid down his command, Caesar would both lose his troops and become vulnerable to prosecution on real or trumped-up charges brought by political enemies. An extension of the war to Britain, particularly if it could be presented as necessary for the security of Gaul, would be good reason for retaining his commission.

It seems likely that Caesar had decided on invasion in time for the campaigning season of 55. A disturbance on the Rhine

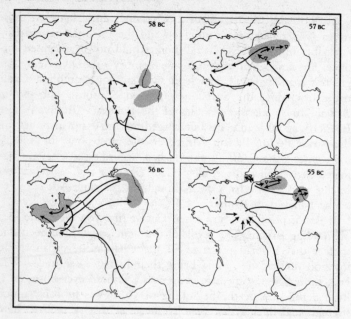

JULIUS CAESAR'S EXPEDITIONS TO BRITAIN (55 and 54 BC) occurred in the interlude when Gaul seemed to have been conquered, before the great uprisings that were not finally crushed till 50 BC.

delayed him until the end of summer was close, leaving little time for an expedition to Britain. Ancient armies were rarely able to mount campaigns in winter, even by land, and the transport of men and supplies by sea was normally halted for long periods of the year. That he decided not to wait for the following season emphasizes the urgency of the operation in his eyes.

An essential preliminary was the discovery of a suitable landing-place. Caesar had been unable to obtain this intelligence from traders, probably reflecting the difference between the requirements of single merchant ships and an invasion fleet rather than an exclusive control of cross-Channel travel by secretive Gauls in the immediately previous period. A four-day reconnaissance from the sea by an officer whose powers of observation Caesar respected revealed open beaches and a good anchorage at Deal, but general lack of information about coastal conditions was to prove nearly

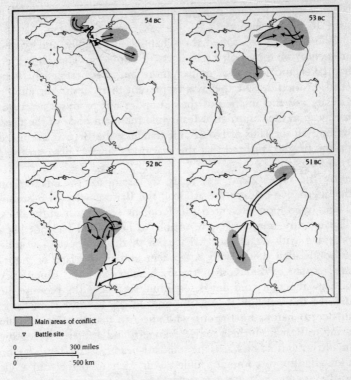

Main areas of conflict

▽ Battle site

0   300 miles

0   500 km

fatal both this year and the next. For this first expedition, about eighty transports and a number of warships were assembled, probably at Boulogne, and a further eighteen transports, detained by a contrary wind, loaded cavalry at another port. The main force consisted of two legions, Roman regulars, and some native auxiliary troops, sufficient for a powerful reconnaissance but hardly intended for conquest.

These preparations, however, seemed formidable enough from the other side of the Channel. Several tribes sent envoys across offering submission. Caesar, accepting their offers, sent back with them a Gaul named Commius, whom he had made king of the Gallic Atrebates in the Pas-de-Calais and who commanded great respect both with Caesar himself and in Britain. Commius was to contact as many tribes as possible, spread news of the impending Roman arrival, and encourage adherence to the Roman side.

Neither these Britons nor, in the long run, Commius himself were to prove reliable.

The main force crossed the Channel successfully, and waited at anchor for the cavalry transports to come up. They, however, had taken too long over embarkation, and were carried back to Gaul on the tide. Weather was to prevent them from ever joining Caesar, and the absence of their support was to prove a serious handicap in the campaign. Meanwhile the main body of the fleet, waiting off the cliffs of Dover and watching the Britons assembled on the heights, realized that this was not a suitable place to force a landing.

By the time Caesar was ready to disembark his infantry on the alternative landing-site at Deal, the Britons were in position. Their opposition presented the Romans with grave difficulties. The infantry transports were unable to beach and had not been provided with assault boats. Faced with the prospect of wading inshore, laden down with equipment and in the face of vigorous resistance, the Roman troops hesitated. In this emergency Caesar's ingenuity did not desert him. To relieve the pressure, he ordered the warships to run aground on the enemy's right flank, thence to harass the Britons with the fire that they could then bring to bear from their archers, slingers, and artillery. Seeing the infantry still holding back, the standard-bearer of the Tenth legion shouted: 'Jump, comrades, unless you wish to betray our eagle to the enemy: I, at any rate, intend to do my duty to my country and my commander,' and promptly leapt from the ship, clutching the legionary standard. Thus encouraged, the others from his own vessel followed and the men from the rest did the same. This heroic action did not, however, immediately win the success it deserved: the men were unable to form up correctly in their units, and the Britons surrounded them as they disembarked in small groups. Caesar now had the warships' boats and his scout vessels filled with soldiers, and, by sending them to the points where reinforcement was needed, he gradually brought the situation under control. Immediately the legions were formed up on the beach, they charged, routing the Britons at once. This, however, was the point at which the absence of Roman cavalry first made itself felt: Caesar was unable to follow up his success and turn it into complete victory.

The Britons nevertheless were overwhelmed by their reverse, and sent envoys to ask for peace. With them came Commius, bearing the Britons' excuses for having arrested him when he first arrived. Caesar, reproaching them for opposing him after sending an embassy to Gaul offering friendship, pardoned them, but demanded hostages. The Britons produced some of these immediately, dispersing their own troops back to their homesteads. 'From all parts', as Caesar says, chiefs were now coming into his camp, suing for peace. For two or three days it looked as if Caesar had achieved total victory with a single battle.

On the fourth day after Caesar's landing, disaster occurred. First the transports making a second attempt to bring the cavalry to Britain were caught by a violent storm, scattered, and forced to return to the Continent. The same storm struck the fleet that had brought the main force over, and, combined with the exceptionally high tide at full moon—a phenomenon that Caesar says was unknown to the Romans—wreaked havoc. Not one ship was left seaworthy. The army was now in a very serious situation. They had brought no stores for the winter with them, the intention having been to return to Gaul, and—perhaps more frightening—they were now isolated beyond the limits of their known world. The Britons reacted immediately. The chiefs in Caesar's camp were aware of how small his army was, they realized the magnitude of the disaster, and they saw a possibility of finishing with Rome once and for all if they prolonged the war into the winter. Secretly they renewed their vows of alliance and slipped away from the camp one by one, recalling their men from home to war.

Caesar guessed what was going to happen from the cessation of the supply of hostages, but not how soon. By salvaging equipment from the most badly damaged ships and by sending to Gaul for naval supplies, he was able to save all but twelve of his vessels. He tackled the problem of food by sending out soldiers daily to collect corn from the fields of the nearby farms, to be prepared for whatever might occur. In this latter operation he all but lost one of his two legions, which suffered a sudden attack while cutting corn. The Britons, now in good heart, spent the next few days of bad weather assembling an army from far and wide. Eventually, Caesar, assisted now by a very small cavalry contingent that

Commius had brought across, was able to bring them to battle in front of his camp. This was the paramount aim of a Roman commander fighting a barbarian enemy, since his best hope of securing victory was to use his armoured and disciplined troops in the dense, hand-to-hand combat for which they were specially trained. On this occasion, though the weight of the legions soon overwhelmed the enemy, the pursuit had to be on foot and was once more incapable of clinching the victory.

This time when the Britons came suing for peace, Caesar demanded twice the number of hostages and ordered them to be brought to the Continent. He had already decided to sail back as soon as possible so as not to expose his patched-up ships to the winter seas, and we may assume that he announced his intention of returning the following year, since otherwise his demands would have had no force.

During the winter, while Caesar was in northern Italy and Illyricum holding assizes and ordering the affairs of those parts of his vast command, his legionary legates in Gaul were engaged in building new ships and repairing the old ones. When Caesar returned, he found 600 new transports and 28 warships. The transports were constructed to a special design, low and broad, workable by sail or oar. Caesar had learnt the lesson of the first landing, that it was essential to get his men ashore rapidly and in good order. These new ships were easy to manœuvre and could be run right on to the beach. The new expeditionary force, too, was much more formidable than the old. This time Caesar had 5 legions and 2,000 cavalry, a force that could hit hard and follow up its successes.

Though 60 of the new ships were prevented from joining the invasion fleet, Caesar eventually sailed with over 800 vessels. He tells us that these included some private ships, implying the presence of camp-followers. Clearly it was no longer reckoned an expedition of extreme danger beyond the confines of the known world. The safe return of the previous year's expedition and the magnitude of this year's force must have reassured these civilians. Some may have intended to trade with the natives or exploit conquered lands; others, one may be sure, meant to live off the Roman soldiery, after the manner of their kind. An active campaign, too, promised spectacular profits through the purchase of booty from troops fresh from battle. But there is no need to assume that all the civilians were petty adventurers. It was normal practice for a Roman magistrate to be accompanied by a group of respected friends on whom he would draw for advice, and some of these may have had their own ships, whether for comfort or with an eye to profit. War was expected to confer not only the glory of military success to the victors, but also a handsome financial return. The greater the latter, the higher the prestige. Writing about Britain, the historian Tacitus was later to employ the memorable and revealing phrase 'the wages of victory', *pretium victoriae*.

It is surprising that, after the experiences of the previous year, Caesar's landing was followed again by serious storm damage to his fleet, left at anchor in an unprotected roadstead. This time he reacted by building a fortification on the shore large enough to allow the beaching of the fleet within its rampart and to enclose his base-camp as well. It is tantalizing that neither this nor any of his marching camps has yet been positively identified by archaeology. It was certainly substantial, since its construction occupied his troops day and night for ten days. The delay, too, encouraged the Britons, who now assembled a larger force under a new leader, Cassivellaunus. The acquisition of an effective leader made the Britons formidable opponents. It was not until Caesar was able to draw them into a pitched battle, in which his Roman infantry repelled a thrust that reached the legionary standards, and his cavalry charged to shatter the retreating Britons, that he broke the British confederacy. Defeated again at the Thames, where Caesar got his infantry and cavalry across in one assault that took the heavily manned British position at a rush, Cassivellaunus abandoned all hope of winning a battle and retained in his army only four thousand charioteers to harass Caesar's line of march.

This might well have been stalemate but for one of those diplomatic incidents that often favoured Rome. A young prince of the Trinovantes of Essex, one of the most prominent of the southern British tribes, had come to Caesar in Gaul as an exile. The story of the Trinovantes was certainly later closely connected with that of the Catuvellauni, who were centred in Hertfordshire and subsequently became, if they were not already, the most powerful

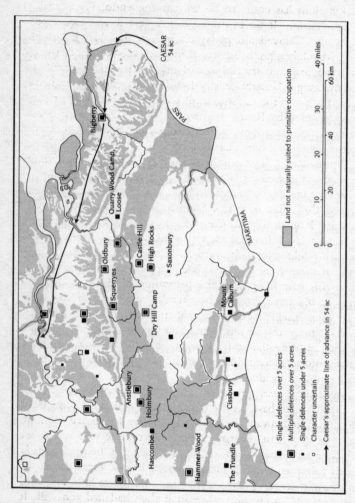

CAESAR'S ADVANCE TO THE THAMES in 54 BC was probably along a route north of the North Downs, bypassing all of the principal strongholds that might have been defended by the Britons (except Bigberry), minimizing costly assaults and avoiding sieges for which he did not have the time.

tribe in southern Britain, though the exact relationships are unclear. In the ensuing period these tribes were eventually linked in a single kingdom, though who annexed whom is obscure. This kingdom has come to be known conventionally as that of the Catuvellauni. It seems quite possible that it was recent pressure by the Catuvellauni and their friends that had led to the prince, Mandubracius, being exiled to Gaul. Cassivellaunus (whose own tribal origin is the subject of debate) had, Caesar tells us, killed the king, Mandubracius' father. Roman territory frequently provided a haven for such political refugees. They, in their turn, were often used by Rome as pawns in her relations with neighbouring states, sometimes, when it suited her book, as an excuse for direct intervention. The Trinovantes now saw their chance and appealed to Caesar for help against Cassivellaunus and the return of Mandubracius as king.

In exchange for hostages and grain for his troops, Caesar approved this alliance, which had the added advantage of placing a pro-Roman tribe in Cassivellaunus' rear. This action of the Trinovantes, doubtless linked with Cassivellaunus' failure against Rome, brought over other tribes. These included the 'Cenimagni': if these were the Iceni later well known in Roman East Anglia, this may have been the beginning of their pro-Roman stance. In the mean time, the surrender of these tribes brought Caesar vital intelligence of the whereabouts of Cassivellaunus' base. This may now be represented by the Iron Age fortifications surviving at Wheathampstead or those at Prae Wood near St Albans, both in Hertfordshire, but the identification is uncertain. It was captured by direct assault.

Cassivellaunus was not taken, but the failure of a final British attack on Caesar's base on the Kentish coast persuaded him, faced with the falling away of his allies, to sue for peace through Commius. The least surprising feature of these events is Caesar's acceptance of these overtures: he tells us that he had already decided to return to Gaul for the winter in case there should be an uprising there, and that the Britons could have held out until the end of the campaigning season if they had had the will. It looks as if he would have withdrawn—or at least kept no more than a token force in Britain—whatever the outcome. His terms were moderate: hostages, an annual tribute (we do not know if it was paid or, if so, for how long), and an undertaking not to attack Mandubracius or the Trinovantes.

Whether Caesar would have withdrawn if he had not scented Gallic rebellion in the air is a moot point. Certain elements of the technical language he uses in describing the surrender of the Britons and the terms imposed on them recall the first steps in setting up a new province. That impression, however, was probably precisely what he meant to leave with his reader. His actual withdrawal was providential for Rome, since total victory by the Gauls under Vercingetorix would not only have wiped out the enormous gains that Caesar had made in central and northern Gaul, but it might also have threatened her hold on the Rhone valley and the Mediterranean coast. But we may be looking too hard with modern eyes for Caesar's motives in Britain. To Roman observers, it may have seemed obvious that the glory to be gained by such a prestigious foray across the Ocean was an objective that needed no explaining. If it was also intended to deter the Britons from sending reinforcements to rebellious Gauls, then, in the medium term at least, Caesar's strategy was successful, and his British expeditions would fall into line with the aims of his two German campaigns—the weakening of hostile tribes and the strengthening of friendly ones in consolidation of the conquest of Gaul.

It is possible to argue that conquest and occupation had been expected in Rome. The senate decreed no thanksgiving for the second expedition, but this may well have been due to the influence of Caesar's many political enemies rather than to public disappointment at a victory apparently thrown away. The writer and politician Cicero may provide a hint of the arguments that could have been used in the senate. On two occasions in 54 BC he reported having received letters from Caesar and from his own brother Quintus who was serving as an officer in Caesar's invasion force. The first time he records these letters as registering a complete lack of silver in Britain and no hope of booty except slaves; the second, he confirms the failure to acquire booty and reports that the army is returning home only with hostages and the imposition of tribute. It looks as if Caesar's expedition had failed to come up to the financial expectations that had been widely put about.

Caesar's actions in Britain can be interpreted as the probable reaction of almost any leading Roman of the period given the chance of military success, let alone such a spectacular one. Caesar's later biographer Suetonius emphasizes that in Gaul he missed no pretext for war, however dangerous or unjust. What Caesar did in Britain fits his character as a tactical opportunist, but tells us nothing of any deeper intentions. The real importance for Rome and Britain of the terms that Caesar imposed on the Britons was not their doubtful effectiveness, but the simple fact that he had been able to dictate them.

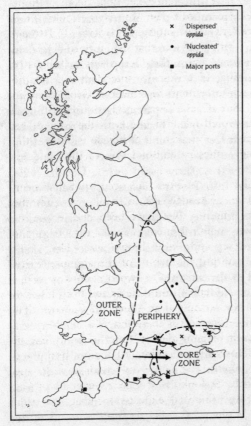

BRITAIN AFTER CAESAR. Analysis by prehistorians of imports from the Continent suggests that after the expeditions of Caesar the peoples of Britain can be divided into (1) a core zone in direct contact with Rome; (2) a periphery supplying trading goods to the core in exchange for Celtic coins or Roman products; (3) an outer zone exploited by its neighbours, particularly for slaves (perhaps chiefly obtained by raiding).

3

FROM CAESAR TO
CLAUDIUS

When we compare our picture of the country that Caesar found
with the state of knowledge about Britain just before the Claudian invasion a century later, we must be struck by the fact that
we can construct a reasonably complete map of the tribes for the
later period, and people it with the names of a substantial number of rulers at whose relations with one another we can in some
cases make guesses. However, the apparent clarity of our picture
of the Britain that emerged in the period between the invasions
must not cause us to forget that our knowledge rests on foundations that may be radically modified or eroded by future
advances in scholarship. It is partly based on the fact that when
they were transformed into Roman *civitates* tribes often maintained their identities under Roman rule, and so are known from
literary sources and inscriptions. But this is an uncertain guide to
the pre-Roman pattern, since tribes were divided or amalgamated
by the Romans, centres were often shifted, boundaries were altered
for administrative and political reasons, and territories were carved
out for new elements in the landscape, such as colonies of veterans
from the Roman army settled in cities deliberately founded for
the purpose (*coloniae*), or estates belonging to the emperor. This
source is a retrospective one, and no substitute for contemporary
evidence. There is another source, however, in the British coinage
and its distribution. There are undoubtedly basic uncertainties in
this form of evidence. We cannot be sure to what extent the areas
of contact represented by the spread of coins correspond to tribal
boundaries. Indeed, it has been suggested that the manner in which
densities of particular types of coin diminish with increasing

distance from central points indicates a form of distribution that was not greatly restricted by political boundaries. Moreover, we know little about the way in which coins were used in pre-Roman Britain—whether as the internal currency of a tribe, as a means for interstate trade, or as precious objects chiefly employed as gifts between princes, for symbolic disposal in display of wealth, or as offerings to deities. Nevertheless, blocks of coins on a distribution map may produce a blurred approximation to a tribal picture. It cannot tell us whether this means political power or a spread of influence, but it should help to indicate where the effective centres of a tribe lay, and from which districts its influence spread out to be felt by others.

Further information about the changing tribal scene between the invasions of Caesar and Claudius can emerge from studying the successive personal names that appear on coins, and possibly, too, the adoption of particular coin types by individual British rulers. Sufficient evidence exists to indicate dynasties of rulers, though precise family relationships are insecurely recorded. It is not safe to attempt to derive a detailed political history from these coins, but when we find persons appearing in Roman literary sources whose names are recorded on British coins, we know that the archaeology of Britain is emerging from the prehistoric world.

Another approach to understanding the map of Britain between the invasions—and the interrelationships between its peoples—emerges from the study of settlements and artefacts against the background of this numismatic and literary evidence. The 'dynastic' coinages, the probable existence of settlements that were centres of power, and the substantial presence of imported Roman goods have combined to suggest a 'core' area of tribes in the east and central southern regions of Britain whose similarities were greater than their differences and which had reached a broadly comparable stage of development under the influence of their nearness to the Continent. An outer ring of powerful but, as yet, not so developed tribes is seen as the 'periphery' that was affected by the trade and cultural movements that passed through the core on their way to and from the Continent. Differences in the way in which the economies of the inner and outer tribes operated are perhaps reflected in the coinages they were developing at this time. Both groups were producing coins in precious metals—and

THE PRINCIPAL TRIBES OF BRITAIN. This map broadly represents the situation
in the first century AD. Larger groupings formed north of the part of Britain
under Roman rule from the third century onwards, as on other frontiers of the
empire.

therefore presumably of high value—but only the core communities issued lower-value pieces, suggesting money-based trade at something more like an everyday level. The presence of Roman traders and envoys in person after the country had been opened up by Caesar's expeditions is unproven but highly likely. Communities of Roman merchants resident in particular settlements on a fairly long-term basis (*consistentes*) are well attested outside other Roman frontiers, and may well be reflected in Britain by such finds as the quantities of Roman material of this date unearthed in the Iron Age occupation areas between Puckeridge, in Hertfordshire, and Braughing. Sooner or later, houses in Roman style must turn up on a pre-conquest site somewhere in southern or eastern Britain. Magnificent Roman silver plate of this same early period found at Welwyn probably originated as a diplomatic gift to (or a major trading deal with) a Briton of power or influence within this core area, and a similar group of silver of the highest quality from Hockwold in Norfolk, previously interpreted as the property of a Roman officer buried for safety during a revolt in that area after the Claudian conquest, is much more likely to have originated as a similar exchange, possibly directly from Romans who had penetrated to a potentate in a peripheral region, but perhaps more likely at one remove, between a British power in the primary area of contact with the Continent and a neighbour in Britain beyond. It can be assumed that the peoples of the south and east benefited greatly from the traffic passing through their territories, and that they themselves acquired luxury goods and other items from the Roman empire. In this way the members of their upper classes were drawn into the cultural and economic orbit of Rome, however inimical they may have felt individually towards Roman power.

From the course of the Roman invasions of Britain, it is likely that one route into Britain was through Kent. Caesar considered the people of 'Cantium' to be the most civilized of the Britons (*humanissimi*). In Caesar's time, there were four kings in that area, which may indicate a multiple magistracy, as was sometimes known in Gaul, but alternatively may reflect four small kingdoms. Westward there was a group of peoples over the area broadly known as the Weald who, in their forested region, seem to have escaped conquest or even much influence from their neighbours and to have been centred on hill-forts to a greater extent. West of the Weald was a large area, extending over west Sussex, west Surrey, Hampshire, Berkshire, and north-east Wiltshire, which was to play an important part politically in the early years of the Roman province. In the fully developed province this territory was divided between three Roman *civitates*. The northern part bore the name of the Atrebates, with which we are already familiar; the southern and eastern parts became the *civitates* of the Belgae, discussed earlier, and the Regini, centred on Chichester.

Proceeding northwards and crossing the Thames, a Roman traveller would enter the broad territories of the Catuvellauni. They had originally been concentrated in Hertfordshire, but in the period between the invasions they seem to have expanded outwards to dominate Cambridgeshire, Northamptonshire, Bedfordshire, that part of Buckinghamshire east of the Cherwell, the old Middlesex, and north-east Surrey. Their coins appear in Kent, and they seem to have gained influence in the kingdom of the Atrebates. The nature of their society, and the degree of the power and prosperity of their ruling élite are graphically illustrated by the series of rich 'warrior graves', burials containing both Celtic artefacts of high quality and Roman luxuries. The impact of these graves is the more startling as Iron Age burials in southern Britain are extremely rare, to such an extent that it has been surmised that most of the dead were disposed of by 'excarnation', exposing the body to the elements and natural scavengers, or in sacred rivers. Difficult though it is to extract political information from the coins and pottery, it does appear that the history of this period must be centrally concerned with the growth of this Catuvellaunian kingdom, until the early part of the first century AD, when merger with, or annexation by, the Trinovantes created a state that could effectively take over the south and east of England.

Outside the core group of southern and eastern British tribes, the ascendancy of the Catuvellauni has been detected in the territory of the Dobunni to the west, in the part of Oxfordshire west of the Cherwell, Gloucestershire, north Somerset, Avon, parts of Hereford and Worcester, and Warwickshire. These Dobunni were, unlike their eastern neighbours, organized around a series of massive hill-forts. North of the core lay the Corieltauvi, based on Dragonby, Old Sleaford, and possibly Leicester, and inhabiting Leicestershire, Nottinghamshire, Lincolnshire, and perhaps part of south Yorkshire. An interesting feature of their coinage is that it was regularly struck by two rulers at once, and at one time by three, apparently colleagues. A similar state was situated to the east of the Corieltauvi. This was the Iceni of Norfolk and north-west Suffolk, who may well have been divided into two parts, centred on the southern Fens and the Norwich district respectively. It is certain that none of these peoples could ignore their Catuvellaunian neighbours.

Along the south coast of Britain, outside the core area and out of Catuvellaunian reach, were tribes with their own direct contacts with the Continent. Immediately to the west were the Durotriges of Dorset, on whose coast lay Portland and Hengistbury, where they maintained a mint. Their possession of a quite unusual density of hill-forts, and the apparent lack of a clearly dominant centre suggest a state based on a number of powerful baronies.

Beyond the ring of peoples that were in direct contact with the south-eastern core of tribes—and who produced their own local coinage—were communities that even the most ingenious find it difficult to divide into neat categories. Bordering the Durotriges to the west were the Dumnonii, probably concentrated along the River Exe. Continuity of culture from the Bronze Age seems to have been a particular feature of theirs, and externally they had an even longer tradition of direct contact with the Continent than the Durotriges and other peoples further east. In the eastern half of their territory they had hill-forts of the common type, with some alien elements from further west, but across the Tamar these are replaced more or less entirely by fortifications whose parallels are to be found in Brittany and Spain. Diodorus Siculus, writing after Caesar and before 30 BC (but probably incorporating material gathered by Pytheas of Marseilles, who sailed to Britain in the late fourth century BC), stated that the inhabitants were friendly to strangers, having become used to them through the Cornish tin trade. By about 800 BC the port of Mount Batten at the mouth of the Tamar was in contact with south-west France —and possibly with the Mediterranean direct. With varying fortunes, the trade links persisted through to the Roman period, and in the late Iron Age Mount Batten was probably feeding the ports further east along the coast.

North of the Dobunni was another tribe, the Cornovii, who were like the Durotriges in possessing many hill-forts and no obvious centre. They spanned a significant area, chiefly Shropshire, but also extending into Staffordshire, Cheshire, Clwyd, and the eastern part of Powys. West of them, and of the Dobunni, lay Wales, where tribal boundaries are even more problematic than in England. Broadly speaking, the Deceangli occupied the extreme north, comprising north-west and north-east Clwyd and northern Gwynedd; the Ordovices were chiefly situated in southern Gwynedd; the Demetae spread over south-western Dyfed; and the Silures were settled in the Glamorgans and Gwent, and perhaps extended into southern Powys. Hill-forts were fairly common throughout most of Wales, and in the territory of the southern tribes these show affinities with south-west England.

The whole of the north of England except Humberside was occupied by a people known as the Brigantes. Humberside itself was occupied by the Parisi, whose distinctive culture has already been mentioned. Politically, the latter, though relatively small, may have been divided into four sections. It is not safe, however, to assume that the vast Brigantes must have been composed of a federation rather than a single tribe; the known presence of factions among them at a later date is no certain evidence of this. The apparent existence in Roman times of named entities in north Northumberland, in the South Tyne valley, and in Cumbria suggests that, as with several of the tribes already mentioned, there were subdivisions or clans among the Brigantes, but these were not necessarily separate peoples. The vast earthworks at Stanwick in north Yorkshire were formerly thought to represent fortifications hastily thrown up in the last stage of resistance to the Romans. It now seems likely that Stanwick had been a well-established tribal centre of the Brigantes, perhaps the principal one.

The literary evidence for the political history of Britain and its relations with the Roman world in this period consists of tantalizingly brief references in a number of classical authors. The tribal coinage fills some of the gaps with further names of rulers otherwise unattested, but as political evidence it has to be used with considerable caution. The first event about which we have any information after the expeditions of Caesar is that in 52 BC Commius, the Gallic Atrebatian who had been Caesar's envoy in

Britain, fell out with him and led a powerful contingent to join the forces of Vercingetorix. Efforts were made to capture or assassinate him, but he escaped across the water to Britain. The appearance of coins struck with his name by the British Atrebates strongly suggests that he became their king, though whether by invitation or war we do not know. His apparent successor Tincommius (now apparently more correctly 'Tincomarus') is described on coins as 'son of Commius'—natural or (as was common in the contemporary Roman world for reasons of politics and inheritance) adoptive we cannot tell—who held the Atrebatic leadership until about the end of the century or a little beyond. It is very likely indeed that he was eventually driven out, for it is probable that he was the suppliant king at Rome whose name is imperfectly preserved in an incompletely surviving part of the *Res Gestae*, the official account of his own reign that the Emperor Augustus had displayed in great public inscriptions across the empire.

Around 15 BC coinage of one Tasciovanus appears in the territory described above as Catuvellaunian and beyond, especially in Essex, and it may be that the merger with the Trinovantes had now happened. In the same period coins of a king named Dubnovellaunus are recorded in Kent (though, as in Caesar's day, his name appears with other rulers). Around the end of the century they appear for a while in Essex as well, as if this Kentish ruler's influence had spread across the Thames Estuary in some manner. It was not well received. Dubnovellaunus' entire coinage disappears altogether at about the same time as that of Tincommius from among the Atrebates. It is a reasonable assumption that he was the 'Dumnobellaunus' or 'Domnoellaunos' named with 'Tim . . .' as suppliant kings in the Augustan record. It was, of course, a matter of considerable prestige for Augustus to be able to represent such distinguished foreign visitors as suppliants at his doors, in no better a position than the merest petitioner among his humblest clients, but there is no particular reason to doubt the fact that these two Britons appealed to Rome for assistance. Reflected in the Roman mirror, we are surely seeing the expulsion of kings from two of the principal tribes that bordered on the expanding Catuvellaunian power.

Roman policy towards Britain in this period falls into three distinct phases. For twenty years after Caesar's second expedition no action seems to have been taken to follow it up. Yet in the nine years from 34 BC there were no less than three occasions on which preparations for invasion proceeded some way before being cancelled. By 34 BC it was a very different Roman world from that to which Caesar returned from Britain in 54. The split between Caesar and the dominant party in the senate, which eventually won over a reluctant Pompey, had become irreparable. Caesar's overwhelming series of victories in the subsequent civil war put him into supreme power, with the permanent position of *dictator*, a post previously only used as a temporary appointment in moments of national emergency. The Roman Republic was effectively dead. Even Caesar's murder in 44 brought only a flicker of life, for renewed civil war almost immediately put power back into the hands of the Caesarian party. By 34 BC the Caesarian magnates had been reduced to two, with his old lieutenant, Mark Antony, commanding the eastern half of the empire, and his great-nephew and adopted heir, the youthful but utterly ruthless Octavian, the west. Octavian had so far won no real military reputation, while Antony's was uncomfortably brilliant. A campaign in Illyricum, however, went well, and Octavian was free to seek further military glory. Despite plans for following up the Illyrican success with conquests on the Danube, Britain was a feasible interlude. The later historian Dio tells us that Octavian intended to emulate Caesar, the first context in which we find the potent imperial motif that links conquest in Britain with emulation of Julius Caesar. In the case of Caesar's own first campaign, we noted the extraordinary recognition by the senate of the success represented by an expedition across the Ocean. Now Octavian, whose political position rested on being Caesar's heir, could see an ideal opportunity at one and the same time to exploit the traditional notions of maintaining the family eminence and to enlarge his recently acquired military reputation. In the event, the expedition was postponed and, as we shall see, eventually shelved. The immediate cause was a series of dangerous revolts inside Roman territory, followed by a rapid deterioration of relations with Antony. In the great battle of Actium the latter was deserted by Cleopatra and decisively defeated. By the summer of 30 Octavian was the undisputed (if unconstitutional) master of the Roman world.

There was now a critical problem to be faced, and out of its solution sprang the political system (the 'Principate') on which the Roman emperors of the next three hundred years based their rule, and which provided the essential forms and framework for the absolutism of the late Roman Empire and Byzantium. Octavian's power essentially lay in the loyalty of Roman troops to a victorious commander. Yet Romans, however much they might break the law, had a deeply rooted need to find constitutional forms for the exercise of authority. Octavian's offer to give up power in 27 BC, and his assumption of new authority at the hands of Senate and People, were essential parts of his consolidation of his own position and a prerequisite for any return to stability. The Republic was, on the surface, restored: Octavian himself, henceforth accepting the name Augustus, was ostensibly no more than the leading citizen, *primus inter pares*. In practice, his concurrent holding of the key offices of state, including the command of practically all the armies, meant that his power was irresistible if he chose to exercise it. He possessed legal authority (*imperium*) over many aspects of state by virtue of the offices and grants of specific powers that he held at a particular time; he held unchallengeable sway over any area in which he chose to intervene because of his personal 'weight' (*auctoritas*), the respect traditionally given to men of great seniority and reputation in public life. From now on there is no doubt that Rome had an emperor.

By 27, therefore, Augustus was obviously sufficiently free from worries about the Roman state to think about fresh conquests abroad. What, moreover, could better mark the restoration of the Republic than a spectacular victory by its armies under the supreme command of its first citizen? In the event, the enterprise was called off that year because, according to Dio, not only was Gaul still in an unsettled state, but also the Britons seemed likely to propose a treaty. The prestige of a success without loss of Roman life is a theme we shall encounter again, and something that could be represented as capitulation merely at the name of Augustus was even better. Presumably nothing came of the rumoured agreement, for in 26 we hear that the Britons had refused to come to terms. What the emperor had demanded is not recorded—possibly the tribute that had been imposed by Caesar. Revived, the expedition was cancelled again, this time because of uprisings in the Alps and the Pyrenees. After that, no further plans for an invasion seem to have been made public during the reign of Augustus.

Into this account of Augustan policy towards Britain we have to fit two undated passages in Strabo. The first says that though they could have taken Britain, the Romans scorned to do so, because they saw that the Britons were too weak to cross the Channel and harass them, and because the cost of holding the country and collecting tribute would be more than was already brought in by taxes on commerce. The second passage from Strabo makes the same point. He tells us that the Britons submitted to heavy duties on the import and export trade with Gaul, and that if Britain were occupied, the tribute would be fully offset by the minimum cost of an occupying army, and, moreover, the customs duties themselves would have to be lowered. In this passage Strabo also mentions that some of the leading Britons had paid court to Augustus and had dedicated offerings on the Capitol in Rome—indeed, that 'they had practically made the whole island Roman property'. Even allowing for slanted exaggeration in either source, it is difficult to identify these with the fugitive kings described by Augustus himself in the *Res Gestae*: they are clearly persons still carrying weight at home. The Strabo passages must have been written during a period when Rome and Britain as a whole were not overtly hostile, and therefore either before the first recorded plans for invasion in 34 or after the last in 26.

Though Augustus seems to have made no more plans for direct military intervention in Britain, there is a slight literary hint of diplomatic activity when he visited Gaul in 16 BC, and it is at about this time that Tincommius started to strike coins of a distinctly Romanizing type. Achieving friendly relations with the kingdom of the 'son of Commius' might well have gained much of what Augustus had earlier intended to seek by invasion. Diplomatic success was almost as good as victory in war.

But why did the Romans have this obsession with conquest? As well as concentrating attention on the concept of Roman invincibility and its immediate embodiment in himself, Augustus also illustrated an abiding strand in Roman tradition when he erected statues of great Roman commanders of the past alongside his own in Rome, 'in order that the lives of these men should be, as it were, a standard that would be required by their fellow citizens both of himself and of the emperors of succeeding ages'. Cicero summarized the public face of the Roman aristocracy, old and new alike: 'Glory in war exceeds all other forms of success. This is the origin of the Roman people's reputation, this is what ensures our city will have eternal fame, this has compelled the world to submit to her rule.' Cicero had studied the ways in which success was gained in the political arena he had entered: 'Who can doubt that, for a man who hopes to achieve the consulship, the possession of a military reputation is much more useful than a successful practice at the Bar?' In addition, it is, he says, more advantageous to have been engaged in enlarging the bounds of Roman rule than in administering territories already won. This ordering of priorities is fundamental to understanding Roman actions and the motives behind them.

The tradition that carried these attitudes from the Republic to the Empire was based on foundations largely alien to the modern western mind. Central to Roman religion was the cult of the family, living and dead, and this was at its most intense among the oldest senatorial clans. The holding of the highest offices in the state by successive generations was an act not only of personal ambition, but also of piety, and the acquisition of military glory shed added lustre on the family name and did honour to the ancestors by recalling their own achievements and keeping their reputations alive in the public eye. Even those who privately scorned religion and publicly misused it for political ends moved in a society imbued with this tradition, and where they acted in the crudest self-interest, they could appear to be following the highest path of honour. Augustus hoped to restore stability by encouraging the readoption of the ancient restraints, but this was never more than partially successful. Loyalty to the state—and to the emperor as embodying the state—could never be relied upon above loyalty to self and family.

Though these traditions had their origins and centre in the aristocracy, there is no evidence of substantial variation by class or gender. Indeed, the unusual degree of social mobility in Roman society (compared with most past societies of which we have sufficient knowledge) must have greatly assisted the formation and perpetuation of a relatively uniform outlook on the world. The basic weakness in Roman society was never overcome, and the more the empire assimilated other peoples and imbued them with its attitudes and ideals, the wider this fault extended. It might, indeed, seem surprising that Rome did not collapse from within centuries before the actual disintegration of the empire in the west. But there were two factors that sustained her. One was that the overriding spirit of competition was at its worst—or at least most effective—among a relatively small group of people, those in a position to hope for high office or supreme power—in other words, chiefly in the senatorial order under the early Empire, and, as the older nobility was gradually excluded from military careers, among the professional officer-class of the later Empire. Though the Roman army gained an evil reputation for indiscipline in the ranks, a reputation cultivated by ancient historians mostly drawn from the upper classes, relatively few army revolts started with mutinies of ordinary soldiers. Most were generated by dissatisfied middle or senior officers, often by feuding members of the imperial house itself. Troops were prepared to follow their commanders when someone appealed to their personal loyalties and interests, but for the most part the initiative came from above.

The second factor was the Roman genius for organization. Something in the Roman character enabled them to create systems that continued to work effectively despite the political instability. To understand the Romans, it is necessary to draw a distinction between their innate sense of order when they were engaged in any professional activity and their political indiscipline. This explains how they were able both to forge the army into an unparalleled military force by the imposition of strict order in its everyday affairs and to retain acceptance of that discipline by the troops almost without break, yet be prepared to use those troops for personal ends. Similarly, the legal system could from time to time be misused shamelessly for political and personal ends, yet the normal processes of justice were maintained by the very same men in the daily round of cases that came before the courts. Throughout the empire and over the centuries enormous numbers of people at every level of public and private business carried on a conscientious and reasonably competent administration of the affairs of everyday life. Indeed, from the topmost levels of society downwards, there were many who believed that public service was an absolute duty, however bad the current emperor and whatever the depth of corruption amongst the immediate holders of power. In this, they were able to appeal to the better side of the old Republican tradition, contributing enormously to the survival of the empire despite the not infrequent incompetence and occasional criminality of its leading citizens.

While Rome's military attention was diverted elsewhere in the last years of Augustus' rule and during the reign of Tiberius, the political pattern in Britain underwent further development. The first sign is the minting of coins at Colchester by a prince generally regarded as one of the house of Tasciovanus, named Cunobelinus, better known to English readers as Shakespeare's Cymbeline. This appears as Dubnovellaunus' coinage disappears, around AD 7, and it is likely that it was Cunobelinus who supplanted his influence in Essex and drove him out of Britain. It is not clear whether this represents an independent movement among the Trinovantes or direct Catuvellaunian intervention, but shortly afterwards Cunobelinus started striking coins at Verulamium (St Albans) as well, and had clearly succeeded to the whole Catuvellaunian kingdom. That this may, in fact, have been in the nature of a reverse take-over is not impossible, since henceforth the consolidated kingdom had its principal centre at Colchester. In due course such coins also appear in Kent, and coins of this state are found in the northern part of the Atrebatic kingdom as well, perhaps in both cases indicating temporary dominance or, alternatively, the purchasing of influence by means of princely exchange. The power of Cunobelinus certainly made sufficient impact for Suetonius, looking back a century, to be able to describe him as 'king of the Britons' (*rex Britannorum*).

In the Atrebatic lands south of the middle reaches of the Thames, formerly held by Commius, the coins of Tincommius were replaced by coins struck by kings named as Epillus and then Verica, both employing the Latin word *rex*. It has been suggested that Epillus and Verica were the British rulers who dedicated offerings on the Capitol, and that they were in a regular relationship with Rome as 'client kings'. This would certainly justify

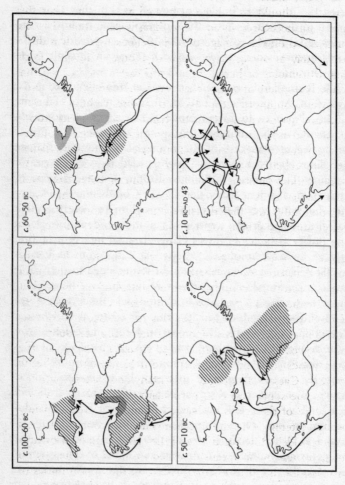

CROSS-CHANNEL CONTACTS between Britain and Gaul: the changing archaeological pattern down to the Claudian invasion as it has been tentatively summarized.

Strabo's description of them as virtually Roman, but it is equally possible that Epillus and Verica were simply adopting Roman fashions. Moreover, the fact that written Celtic is extremely rare, even in Gaul, makes it more likely that, if titles needed to be written, they should have been translated into Latin. That the title need not necessarily mean a *client* king is demonstrated by its appearance also on the coinage of Cunobelinus, whom it is difficult to portray as owing his position to Rome. The finds from the famous tumulus or burial-mound at Lexden near Colchester show how the rulers of a state that was sometimes strongly anti-Roman were coming to accept Roman culture. Fashion and politics did not necessarily go hand in hand in the ancient world, and it is most unsafe to assume that political or religious affiliation can automatically be deduced from style or taste. The leaders of the Catuvellaunian kingdom never showed any disinclination to import either amphorae, whether of wine or other delicacies, or other luxury items of Roman origin, however far they were moving politically in a direction likely to incur Roman hostility.

A more substantial basis for hypothesis on changes in the balance of power in Britain is offered by a remarkable shift in the pattern of distribution of goods from the Continent. It is very noticeable that, after Caesar, the bulk of Roman goods in Britain no longer seems to be coming in through Hengistbury Head, but is found in the central and eastern kingdom. One cannot help wondering whether one reason for this lay in Caesar's contacts with the Trinovantes and his support of their king Mandubracius. Was it followed by a transference of a virtual monopoly of the traffic in goods from the Continent from Hengistbury—already disrupted by Caesar's campaigns in Brittany and victory over the Veneti—to the south and east, particularly Essex?

The nature of the goods exchanged points to a predominantly aristocratic interest. On the Roman side, of course, material goods were widely distributed among the classes, and even ownership of slaves was by no means confined to the rich. There is no reason to doubt that private enterprise took the opportunities of profit offered, and we may be sure that this included individual merchants, some probably in a relatively modest way of business. But we may also suspect that the involvement of leading personages of the Roman state was not confined to the lucrative official operation of taxing the passage of goods. The commodities that Strabo mentions as being derived from Britain are of two kinds. The first—gold, silver, slaves, and hunting-dogs (used not only for the chase but also the arena)—were exactly the sort of spectacular booty that a victorious Roman general flaunted. To suggest that they might represent the tribute imposed by Caesar and perhaps momentarily revived by Augustus is probably going too far. Nevertheless, they certainly fell into the category of goods particularly attractive to members of the Roman upper classes, led by the imperial family itself. The bulk of exchange in these commodities was probably between aristocrats on each side, even though we are ignorant of the actual mechanism. It is certainly likely that the richest objects of Roman manufacture found in Britain arrived as diplomatic gifts from Rome, and that some of the commodities in this first category of Strabo's included presents sent to Rome by British leaders.

The second category suggests a rather different area of contact between Rome and Britain. Grain was always a political commodity in the Roman world: control of the corn supply to the capital, for example, was at all times politically vital. It is improbable that any British grain reached Rome itself, but it is not unreasonable to suspect that, as in later centuries, a major customer was the Roman army. This supposition is strengthened when one adds in the remaining goods in Strabo's list: hides, cattle, and iron, all essential military supplies. It is not too fanciful to imagine British princes such as Cunobelinus paying for their luxuries by supplying the procurement agents of the Roman army. Control of the Thames and the east coast estuaries would have become critical once Roman forces were permanently stationed in large numbers on the Rhine, from 12 BC onwards, while expansion of influence into Kent would give access to the short crossings to Gaul as well. It is a reasonable conjecture to detect some of the changes in the pattern of agriculture in southern Britain as representing a response by farmers and landowners to the demands and opportunities of this vast new market. The wider the leaders of the central and eastern kingdom spread their influence, the more vital the existence of reasonable working relationships between them and Rome must have become. By the early years of the first century Cunobelinus may have been in a position to supply or withhold more or less at will the luxuries or status symbols desired by the notables of a number of other British tribes.

It has been argued that there was a strong movement in western Britain against any alignment with Rome. The Durotriges' hostility at the time of the Claudian campaigns may well have originated in resentment at the shift in trade from Hengistbury to the east coast, and all that that implied for the wealth and influence of its hinterland. At about 25 BC the Dobunni were striking coins very similar to those of their Atrebatic neighbours, but they failed to follow when Tincommius changed over to a Romanized type at the time of his putative understanding with Augustus. Their centre and mint at Bagendon, in Gloucestershire, has many characteristics, including large quantities of Italian, Gallic, and Gallo-Belgic pottery, that indicate that their rulers could tap the same sources of imports as the Catuvellauni, and most likely were supplied through the latter. Such possessions, however, do not—as we noted earlier—automatically imply political alignment with Rome, nor do they prove subservience to the Catuvellauni. The Dobunni probably benefited from good relations with the kingdom of Cunobelinus, but at a safe distance at first, since his coins stop at the Cherwell. A smaller group, of similar culture, seems to have settled in west Oxfordshire, acting as a buffer between them. But from around AD 20/25 Dobunnic coinage had spread eastwards to the supposed Catuvellaunian border.

It may seem surprising that Augustus made no attempt to assist Tincommius and Dubnovellaunus back on to their thrones. This was doubtless partly due to the long pause in Roman imperial expansion that followed the disaster of AD 9, when Augustus' general Quinctilius Varus was ambushed and his army of three legions was totally destroyed in the Teutoberger Wald, resulting in the loss of the embryonic province of Germany across the Rhine. But it was also common Roman policy not to intervene when rulers of friendly neighbouring states were expelled by their own compatriots, provided their successors were not hostile to Roman interests. Cunobelinus' reign of more than thirty years is strong evidence that he did not pick unnecessary quarrels with Rome.

The influence of his kingdom was approaching its peak when,

nearly two decades later, the first of a series of events occurred that drew the attention of Rome and led to its destruction. In AD 39/40 Cunobelinus expelled one of his sons, Adminius. The latter fled to the Continent with a small band of followers and surrendered to the Romans. The eccentric Emperor Gaius (Caligula) treated this as a famous victory, and conceived the idea of an expedition across the Channel.

It is impossible to disentangle the truth about Gaius' abortive expedition from the ridicule of the historians. Assembling his army on the Channel shore, he is alleged to have given the order for battle and then suddenly commanded the troops to collect sea shells, subsequently sent to Rome as spoils of war. Unbalanced as he was, sound assessment of the poor state of military discipline may nevertheless have influenced his decision to call off the invasion. Three years later, his successor Claudius was to have a hard time persuading the troops to embark. The only concrete mark of Gaius' attempt was the lighthouse he had erected as a monument of victory, but the real legacy was the preparations for a full-scale operation across the Channel. The presence of troops on the coast of Gaul indicates that the actual movement of units required had been carried out, serving as a dress rehearsal. What is known archaeologically of Roman military supply bases in the first century indicates that extensive construction work will have been carried out in Gaul, and intense naval activity must have accompanied the preparations on land for transporting troops and supplies. Two or three years later, all this may not yet have been dismantled. The planning and paperwork had certainly been done. Most of all, public attention had been drawn to a great venture that had lain dormant for so long.

II

THE ROMAN CONQUEST

4

THE CLAUDIAN
INVASION

While it is not really true that the Romans acquired their empire in a series of fits of absent-mindedness, much of it came as the incidental result of wars whose causes were very varied, or of the absorption of foreign peoples in other ways, including the bequest of kingdoms in the wills of their rulers or involvement in nominating princes to their thrones. It has been doubted whether Roman emperors can be said to have had 'policies' in the modern sense, due to the enormous burden of daily response to immediate problems that fell on them personally. Certainly, within particular reigns or periods, emperors and their advisers did sometimes attempt specific objectives. However, much more important than policy were the trends that consistently underlay Roman action, which were remarkably persistent through the centuries. Some we have already seen. Others need identifying before we can understand much of what Rome and individual Romans did or did not do.

Virgil, poet of Augustan power, has the supreme god of the Roman state, Jupiter, declare: 'I set upon the Romans bounds neither of space nor of time: I have bestowed on them empire without limit.' Again, the Romans' special genius is to rule, 'to impose the ways of peace, to spare the defeated, and to crush those proud men who will not submit'. If you were a non-Roman people, you were either dependent or recalcitrant: absolute moral right was felt to be on Rome's side. This doctrine explains why, for example, the Romans felt that they could treat client kingdoms exactly as they wished, or why it was permissible to exterminate whole tribes who proved intractable. Ruthlessness

—even unhesitating breach of faith—was justifiable under this divine mission, whether applied to barbarians outside the current limits of Roman rule or to rebellious non-Roman communities within it. Indeed, the divine gift of empire without limit ensured that Romans did not recognize areas of the known world where there was no legal or moral right for Roman writ to run if they could physically enforce it. Even when the western empire was failing—and the old gods whose divine authority had been invoked in support of the doctrine had been replaced by Christianity as the state religion—examples of total disregard for non-Romans occurred, not least towards barbarian allies. It was a tradition that was to become a serious liability when Rome no longer had the overwhelming military strength to back it up.

In the days of the late Republic and early Empire, however, there was a very good chance of success for any Roman general who sought glory within these principles by victory and conquest in foreign lands. In the first half of the first century AD Britain was undoubtedly classified as one of the fields in which a major campaign would be required for success, and where the reward in terms of glory would be commensurately great. The prospects in the period immediately following Gaius' abortive attempt became more and more promising as the political situation in the island altered. The most important of these changes were set off by the death of Cunobelinus somewhere between 40 and 43. The nearest Cunobelinus seems to have come to a quarrel with the Romans was when his son Adminius had taken refuge with them, but Gaius' failure saved him from confrontation. Under his other sons, Togodumnus and Caratacus, the story was to be different. Togodumnus seems to have succeeded his father in the lands north of the Thames, and may have been involved in an extension of Catuvellaunian pre-eminence towards the Humber. Caratacus may have ruled south of the Thames. Further west, the Dobunni seem, by 43, to have been divided between two rulers, Bodvoc and Corio, and at least part of the tribe was now under Catuvellaunian control. Togodumnus had probably extended his influence westwards.

Within the Roman empire, Gaius' behaviour encouraged conspiracy and an answering reign of terror. Early in AD 41 a plot engineered by a group of army officers and senators succeeded.

Briefly it seemed as if the Republic might be restored, but the praetorian guard, the élite troops who, until the third century, represented the only major garrison in or near Rome, elevated the surprised and, for the moment, terrified Claudius. The assassinated emperor's uncle, physically handicapped and, from his youth, mistakenly regarded as mentally retarded, nevertheless possessed the magical membership of the imperial family that had been the sole focus of the army's loyalty since the days of Augustus. The soldiers had now demonstrated that their allegiance was to the imperial house, not to the Senate and People. In successive struggles in the subsequent course of Roman history, the issue of which contender could most legitimately claim to represent the imperial line was a vital one. Claudius found himself having to execute some of those who had murdered his predecessor, to demonstrate family piety and retain the allegiance of the army as a whole. He set out on a course of reform, to restore stability and to raise the prestige of the imperial family from the low point to which it had sunk. To stay alive he required respect, and that meant seeking success in the most prestigious field of endeavour.

Claudius was given little time to reflect. In 42 an attempted coup by the governor of Dalmatia received substantial backing among his colleagues in the senate. It collapsed because support within the two legions under his command faded away in a matter of days. The lessons were clear. The senate could not be relied upon. The troops in the provinces, on the other hand, were not yet ready to march against an emperor from the established imperial house or to put up a candidate of their own, but had wavered far enough to set the alarm ringing. Claudius had somehow to win personal credibility with the army.

Britain provided not only the ideal opportunity, but also a positive reason for immediate intervention. The excuse was a fresh outbreak of the endemic strife among British princes, and yet another fugitive. The spur was a real threat that Britain would be united under one power, entirely contrary to the perpetual Roman interest of keeping barbarians at loggerheads with one another. Verica had been driven out of his Atrebatic kingdom by internal opponents, perhaps with the aid of Caratacus, and there was uproar in Britain when Claudius refused to send back the political refugees sheltering on Roman soil. Whether or not Togo-dumnus and Caratacus had direct control, what concerned the Romans was that the part of the island that immediately affected them was being closed off by newly hostile British states. First the access from the Rhine through the eastern ports into Cunobelinus' former kingdom had been threatened by the succession of these two sons, now the older route from western Gaul to the south coast had fallen. Verica is said to have urged invasion, but Claudius may have needed little persuasion.

Additional factors may have added force to the argument. To set up an effective defence against disturbance in Gaul from British tribes kept from internal raiding by a centralizing dynasty and owing nothing to Rome would both be expensive and upset the balance of power inside the empire by concentrating an undue number of troops in the north-western provinces, already un-comfortably large. Gaius, it seems, had recently added two new legions to the Rhine garrison. If this new frontier force were stationed in Britain, however, it might pay for itself from the proceeds of new conquest rather than being a burden on exist-ing resources. More certainly, the Channel would make it much more difficult for a usurper to link up these forces with the army on the Rhine. Augustus had deliberately reduced the number of legions to the absolute minimum, and the concentration of too large a number of troops in the hands of commanders became a matter of constant concern to later emperors.

A further need was money. Gaius had been wildly extravagant, yet it was necessary to maintain the loyalty of the soldiers with cash. An even more simple desire for booty from Britain may also have played an important part. A cardinal difference between the ancient world and the modern is that victory in an external war usually brought a handsome profit to the victors, especially when prisoners could be sold as slaves. Tacitus includes gold, silver, and other metals in the 'wages of victory', and comments on British pearls, though deprecating their quality. Irrespective of whether the Claudian invasion brought an immediate profit, what matters is what the Romans thought they might gain. The grow-ing prosperity of Britain, and the much wider knowledge of the island brought through increased trade could have greatly modi-fied the opinions formed in Rome during Caesar's campaigns and soon after. British exiles doubtless exaggerated their country's wealth to Claudius, but it may well have been another element in a decision already largely assured.

The backbone of the force was probably four legions of citizen troops: II *Augusta* and XIV *Gemina* definitely took part in the invasion, while IX *Hispana* and XX are attested early in Roman Britain. All except the Ninth came from the Rhine army. Under the early Empire the commander of a legion, the legionary legate (*legatus legionis*), was a senator who had already held the praetorship at Rome. He was therefore a man of considerable seniority. The legates were by no means all primarily military men, but all would have served at an earlier stage in their public careers as staff officers in a legion with the rank of military tribune. These young senatorial tribunes (*tribuni laticlavii*, so called from the broad purple stripe on the senatorial toga) were distinguished from the *tribuni angusticlavii*, 'narrow-striped' military tribunes, who were officers of equestrian (middle-class) status. In the ranks, the legions of this time still contained a very substantial proportion of Italian-born soldiers, though the extension of the franchise to selected individual provincials—even to whole communities—as well as the establishment of citizen colonies outside Italy, meant that an increasing number of legionaries came from the provinces. A legion had a nominal strength of something over 5,000 men, and was divided into ten cohorts, each of 480 men except the first, which probably had 800. Each ordinary cohort comprised 6 centuries of 80 men. Immediate command within the legion was exercised by the centurions, some originating in the ranks, who could rise through an elaborate structure of promotion to high levels of responsibility. The bulk of the legion was infantry. There were a few mounted men who acted as scouts and messengers, but not yet sufficient to make up a substantial cavalry wing. Many of the legionaries were specialists—engineers, architects, masons, clerks, medical staff, and other trades. Except when legions had to be brought up to strength hurriedly in an emergency, these soldiers were highly trained long-service professionals whose skills were as important to the Roman administration in peace as in war.

The personal equipment of the legionary underwent some evolution during the first century, though a fairly wide range of variation at any one time is known. The simple bronze helmet was being replaced by a more elaborate headpiece, and the strengthened leather corslet was giving way to flexible body-armour made of strips of metal. Under his armour the soldier wore a sleeved tunic. Below the waist he had a group of metal-bound thongs like a sporran, and on his feet he wore studded boots like heavy sandals. His shield, generally rectangular and curved to fit the body, was made mostly of wood, but it was fitted with a metal boss that could be used to throw an enemy off balance by being thrust into his face. As offensive equipment, the legionary carried a pair of javelins, and as his main personal weapon, the short sword. Legionary tactics were based on in-fighting, with closely packed disciplined ranks, where the stabbing sword was more effective than the long slashing weapon used by the Celts. The infantryman was backed up with an assortment of catapults and other missile-throwing machines, some on wheels and fully mobile, and, for attacking fortifications, with all manner of ingenious devices.

The 'auxiliaries' had originated under the Republic as non-Roman troops, often unreliable. The acquisition of immense provincial territories, and the surrender of whole warlike tribes, created vast new sources for recruitment within the empire. Under Augustus these men were organized into regular units, increasingly commanded by Roman officers. Many retained national differences of equipment and mode of fighting. They supplied the Roman army for the first time with satisfactory forces of cavalry and archers, but there were many infantry as well. In Claudius' time they were organized in units of about 500 men, some entirely mounted, some part, and some all on foot. It may have been under Claudius himself that the automatic reward for an honourable career in the auxiliaries became the grant of Roman citizenship, with sons becoming eligible for service in the legions. The Claudian army for Britain may have had approximately the same number of auxiliaries as legionaries, bringing the total force to perhaps 40,000 men.

A notable product of the discipline of the Roman army was the regularity of its encampments. Each soldier carried two stakes that were used for a palisade inside the ditch that was dug at each overnight stop on campaign. Within this, the tents were drawn up according to a fixed pattern. As regular garrisons developed, these patterns, in adapted form, became the standard fort whose classic playing-card shape evolved during the first century AD. At first, it still had tents, then it was furnished with wooden buildings, and eventually with stone. Even in garrison the troops were sometimes set to dig practice works, or to assist the civil authorities with building projects. Such exercises made it possible for Roman armies in the field to build bridges, lay roads, and construct siege-works at remarkable speed. To achieve such operations and to carry out its routine tasks, the army evolved a complex organization for stores and transport. Indeed, the whole working of the Roman military machine depended on its capacity to produce systems for recording and utilizing information, and those systems in their turn would have been useless but for the theoretical knowledge and practical experience of the long-serving men in the ranks and their career officers.

On the British side, there were no standing armies, only the levies of tribes who might or might not join a common cause. Lengthy campaigns were more or less impossible for them, since the vast majority of the troops were farmers. It will be recalled that when Cassivellaunus had been faced with a protracted war against Caesar, he had dismissed the main body of his army and kept only his chariots. The latter force was manned by aristocrats, who, like medieval landed knights, could afford constant practice at arms and took their greatest pleasure in personal prowess in combat. The chariots themselves were light vehicles, intended for carrying warriors rapidly into and out of battle. They were not armoured or heavy enough to crash through determined infantry. On the contrary, one of their favourite stratagems was the feigned retreat, to draw off small parties of the enemy who could then be tackled by chariot-borne retainers leaping down to fight hand to hand.

The equipment of the individual Briton was fairly scanty. His basic weapon was the long Celtic sword, for fighting in open order. Hardly any wore body-armour, most going into battle dressed only in loose trousers. This was not necessarily through poverty, but as likely associated with notions of careless bravery. An élite few were equipped with helmets and elaborately decorated shields, as much for show as protection. Little is known of the cavalry, but in status they were probably closer to the nobility than the foot-soldiers, belonging to a class that could afford the freedom from everyday manual labour that enabled regular practice, and possessing sufficient means to supply their own horses.

Scarcity of opportunities for bringing large numbers of men together, lack of daily training, and absence of the discipline conferred on the Roman army by drill and a permanent structure of command meant that the Britons could not carry out complicated manœuvres in battle. Roman troops could execute prearranged movements at the command of the trumpet, could be detached and sent to different parts of the field as required, and could operate either *en masse* or as trained individuals. The deficiencies of British armies make it remarkable that they presented the Romans with so much hard fighting.

This is the more noteworthy in that the power confronting the Britons now was much more formidable than in Caesar's day. The organization of the Roman empire had made immense strides. Gaul and that part of Germany west of the Rhine were no longer half-conquered tribal lands watched over by scattered Roman forces in temporary quarters, but Roman provinces, possessing powerful garrisons in permanent bases on their borders and advanced civil administrations. From the Alps to the North Sea, north-western Europe was united under Roman rule. At a word from the emperor, the whole empire could mobilize its resources to launch an invasion across the Channel.

The Roman government now had at its command the administration to support the military operations and to organize the lands won by military conquest. It could, indeed, be argued that there was now a 'government' where, under the late Republic, there had been no more than a series of shifting alliances between senatorial factions, alliances that had become deadly at a level that went far beyond the politics of Rome and Italy when individual senatorial politicians gained the allegiance of armies. By Claudius' time the system of administration out in the provinces was already well developed, and a central civil service that would enable the man at the centre to keep control of the system was evolving out of the imperial household. From Augustus' assumption of power, the emperors had extended what was in origin the normal domestic and estates' administration of a great Roman family to take on more and more public business. Indeed, in this as in other aspects, they never quite lost the tendency to treat the empire as if it were part of their own private domain. They were only following on a greater scale the practices of the sen-atorial magnates of the Republic.

The emperor's household was now no longer adequate to the task. Claudius, through his secretaries, took the process of con-structing a full-scale civil service much further. Under Claudius, however, it still retained the appearance of a private establish-ment. The immense powers wielded by the former slaves who headed the departments created deep resentment among Romans whose dignity would never have allowed them to take instruc-tions from freedmen in their own households, yet were now expected to take orders from such men in the emperor's. It took reforms later in the century to complete the process of turning the Claudian system into something approaching a true civil ser-vice, when freedmen were largely replaced in the top positions by men of the second rank in the state, the equestrians or 'knights', who were more acceptable to the senatorial aristocracy and from among whom their own ranks were increasingly being replenished by imperial intervention. Nevertheless, direct respon-sibility to, and dependence on, the emperor, was always retained, which meant that he kept in his hands an increasingly effective means of ensuring that his will was carried out. At the same time the new system established posts and procedures that enabled continuity of administration by professionals, something that had hardly been possible under the Republic or within the ad hoc arrangements of the earliest years of the Empire.

In another way, too, the Roman empire had become more formidably organized, though many would have said at the ex-pense of liberty. As the emperor had always directly controlled almost all the armies and most of the principal appointments, his patronage was immense. Progress in a public career for a mem-ber of the senatorial order now meant retaining the favour of the emperor. Emperors had found themselves obliged to influence elections to the magistracies, from which the holders of military commands and provincial governorships continued to be drawn, in order to get the men they needed. Both at senatorial and, to some extent, equestrian level, there was an ordered succession of posts, and under the early Empire the same men would occupy in turn military and civil appointments. There was a continuous process by which emperors were on the look-out for promising young men to provide the next generation of senior officers, and devices to accelerate promotion were frequently employed. There was an increasing tendency to specialization according to aptitude, and some emperors deliberately kept good men in particular posts well beyond the normal tour of duty. In effect, the vast majority of men with any ambition were clients of the emperor. Under Augustus himself, the affront to senatorial dignity was largely contained, partly through the emperor's undeniable personal *auctoritas* as the greatest aristocrat of the age, and partly through his deliberate pretence of restoring the Republic. The succession of Tiberius to Augustus' position in AD 14, however, had made it clear that there was a permanent throne and that the Empire was not a passing phase; and a series of plots and treason trials exposed the powerlessness of the senate. When Gaius followed Tiberius, who had at least been a distinguished general and a serious administrator before distaste for public life drove him into self-appointed seclusion, the youthful emperor's excesses alienated the senatorial class even further. Nevertheless, the development of a career structure at every level in the public service continued, and there seems to have been no shortage of men to fill the posts.

It is clear that many of those in public life were men not only of great ability, but also of personal dignity. Some, indeed, were never reconciled to the existence of the emperors; some spoke out against the system and from time to time paid the extreme penalty for it, but even these were not entirely inhibited from following a public career. It is important to understand a strong element in the Roman character here. From the letters they wrote to one another and from Latin poetry, the Roman upper classes reveal that they set great store on the opportunity to cultivate the arts considered suitable for a gentleman in dignified leisure (*otium cum dignitate*). Yet, at the same time, they were driven by a restless urge to activity in both private and public affairs (*negotium*). This tension permeated the Roman way of life, and helps to explain why even those who could well afford to rest on their laurels were frequently unable to resist the labours and perils of public affairs, even under emperors they despised.

From across the Channel, the British aristocracy could observe the life-style of the Roman upper classes being adopted by their Gallic counterparts. As peace took the place of tribal warfare, Gauls who had co-operated with the Roman administration had achieved wealth, influence, and, in a few cases, high rank in Roman society. Some prominent Britons had seen Rome itself, as envoys or suppliants to the imperial court. At a more ordinary level, by the middle of the first century AD the material comforts of the Roman way of life were there for all to see across only a few miles of water, and the dazzling products of Mediterranean art and fashion, which were already entering Britain in small quantities, were readily available on the Continent. The interests of individual British nobles were not necessarily the same as those of the kings whose wealth came from control of the means of contact with the Continent, nor were the objectives of the princelings of smaller tribes the same as those of the dominant ones. There may have been more Britons ready to welcome the Romans than ordinary Romans keen to go adventuring in the strange land beyond the Ocean.

It was, indeed, on this point that the Claudian campaign of AD 43 ran into trouble at the very outset: the troops, feeling they were being sent beyond the known world, refused to embark. An appeal to Claudius from their baffled commander Aulus Plautius was answered in the person of the imperial freedman Narcissus, one of that group which had already risen very high in the emperor's personal administration. At first the soldiers were outraged when an ex-slave dared to address them from the commander's tribunal. Then, seeing the funny side of it, they greeted him with cries of 'Io, Saturnalia!', because at the festival of Saturn it was customary for slaves to change clothes with their masters and give the orders. Whether because they had been put into a good humour, or out of shame at having to be given courage by a freedman, or out of respect for the direct communication from the emperor, the troops now obeyed orders without further trouble.

The crossing was made in three divisions, to make opposition to the landing less easy. In fact, the delays had led the Britons to disperse the forces on the coast, believing that the Romans would not come and doubtless needing to send the men home for the harvest. One section of the Roman army almost certainly made its base at Richborough, where the Claudian camp is witness to it and where there was the haven Caesar had lacked. Another probably landed near Chichester, perhaps to link up with elements loyal to the exiled Verica. The position of the third landing is quite unknown: it may have been a mere feint, with disembarkation at one of the two other points.

Once ashore, Plautius had considerable difficulty in making contact with the enemy. In the hope that the Romans would exhaust their supplies, the Britons retreated into swamps and forests. They were evidently not assembled into a single host, for when Plautius finally flushed them out, he defeated first a force under Caratacus, then one led by Togodumnus. At this point a section of the Dobunni surrendered, either by envoys or as part of the British army in the field. The influence of the Catuvellaunian princes was beginning to wane.

The Britons, however, were not yet beaten. A substantial force disputed the crossing of a river usually identified as the Medway in a prolonged battle. The river was first crossed by Roman auxiliary troops described as 'Celtic', who took the Britons by surprise and caused chaos by attacking the horses of the British chariots. But it took two days of bitter fighting for the Roman army finally to secure the position, in the course of which the future emperor Vespasian and his elder brother acquitted themselves with distinction. But it was another officer, Hosidius Geta, who snatched the final success from near disaster. For that service he was to be awarded the high honour of triumphal insignia, rare at any time and very unusual for one who had not yet been a consul.

The retreating Britons made their way across the Thames. At first the Romans had difficulty in following them, but eventually the Celtic auxiliaries again swam across, and another detachment made use of a bridge further upstream. When Togodumnus himself was killed shortly afterwards, it might have been thought that the war was over. The contrary was the case; Aulus Plautius was so alarmed at a new spirit of unity among the Britons, brought together by desire for revenge, that he halted his forces to hold what he had won and sent for the emperor, as he had been instructed to do if he ran into particularly stiff resistance. Modern historians have played down the seriousness of the military situation, and have assumed that Plautius had been ordered not to make a triumphant entry into the enemy's capital before Claudius could arrive merely so that the emperor might enjoy the glory. This is not what our chief source, Dio, says. He emphasizes that a considerable armament, including elephants, had been made ready to accompany Claudius on just such an occasion. Nor would it have been entirely out of character for Plautius to ask for assistance in the face of a new combination of forces against his advance. He had already appealed to the emperor in the case of the embarkation mutiny. He may, too, have been under orders not to take too much responsibility upon himself if circumstances took an unexpected turn.

It must have been very late indeed in the campaigning season when Claudius arrived to take direct command of the expeditionary army. He advanced across the Thames, and there is the intriguing possibility that the unusual Roman name for Chelmsford (Caesaromagus) reflects something founded by imperial authority to record the momentous and auspicious presence of the emperor among his troops. It is also possible that he chose to do this at a place that had previously witnessed the submission of the Britons to Julius Caesar. Whether or not these speculations are close to the mark, the formality and solemnity of Claudius' arrival must have been enhanced even further by an unusual circumstance. It was normal practice for a Roman magistrate to be accompanied by a group of friends (*amici*) who acted as an informal consultative council, but Claudius—doubtless chiefly because he distrusted many of them—brought with him an exceptionally large number of distinguished senators. However involuntary on their part, this direct experience of Britain by those who constituted the topmost circles of the senate is a factor that should not be overlooked, either in judging the genuineness of Claudius' claimed successes in the field, or the effect on future metropolitan interest in Britain. Half a century later, Suetonius belittles the brief campaign that followed. He describes it as 'of little importance', saying that the emperor fought no battles and suffered no casualties, but received a large part of the island into submission.

The Jewish historian Josephus, a younger contemporary of Vespasian, cannot be relied upon when he gives all the credit for the successes in Britain to the latter, stating that Claudius gained his triumph without effort on his own part. Josephus owed his own life and his prosperity in his later years to the clemency and favour of Vespasian and his family, and cannot be regarded as an independent witness, much as Vespasian contributed in Britain. Dio's account is clearly based on a different source. He makes Claudius defeat a British army that had assembled at his approach, capture Colchester, and go on to gain the surrender of other tribes, some by diplomacy and others by force. This was perhaps based on the official account that justified the splendid triumph celebrated on Claudius' return to Rome, but he adds a further scrap of information that supports his version of the emperor's part in the war. He tells how, against precedent, Claudius was hailed as *imperator* several times. It was traditional for a victorious general to be hailed in this way by his troops: he had to win the acclamation by fighting a successful action. The unusual feature was that Claudius received this acclaim several times in one campaign. This indicates that there were a number of incidents that could be represented as victories, a record that it would have been peculiarly difficult to fake, since, exceptionally, so many leading senators were eyewitnesses.

The contemporary line was undoubtedly to emphasize the magnitude of the gain and the smallness of the price paid in Roman lives. Of the two triumphal arches voted by the senate— one in Gaul and one in Rome—fragments of the latter survive. This proclaimed that it was erected 'by the Roman Senate and People because he [Claudius] had received the surrender of eleven British kings, defeated without loss, and for the first time had brought barbarian peoples beyond the Ocean under Roman rule'. While the reference to absence of loss probably does refer to Claudius' own short period in Britain, it would have had much greater impact if he were known to have commanded his troops in real action. Indeed, it falls into that special category of praise given to Roman commanders who won victories without losing Roman troops, of which we shall encounter further examples.

It is probable that Claudius planned much of the organization of the conquered territory himself, and laid down guide-lines for the rest. We have Dio's statement that he disarmed the tribes that had surrendered and handed them over to Aulus Plautius. Tacitus, probably writing in 97/8, tells us:

The first of the men of consular rank appointed as governor was Aulus Plautius, and after him Ostorius Scapula, both excellent at war. Little by little the part nearest [to the Continent] was reduced into the usual form of a province (*in formam provinciae*), and a colony of military veterans was added [Colchester]. Certain of the tribes (*civitates*) were given to Cogidumnus as king. The latter survived, ever most loyal, to within our own memory. This was in accordance with the long-accepted Roman habit of making even kings instruments for the imposition of servitude.

Under the Republic, when the situation in a new province had been sufficiently stabilized, its organization was given legal form in a set of statutes (*lex provinciae*). We do not know whether this practice was generally maintained, but the senate certainly ratified any agreements made by Claudius or his lieutenants in Britain, 'as if they had been undertaken by the Senate and People of Rome'. The arrangements adopted in Britain were in line with other provinces. In those directly responsible to the emperor (broadly speaking, those, like Britain, with significant military garrisons), the main division under the early Empire was between local administration and imperial administration. The latter was represented by two main arms, the governor himself (in Britain an ex-consul, in deference to the size of its garrison and the importance of the province) with a considerable staff, and the financial secretary (*procurator provinciae*), drawn from the equestrian class. The equestrians were at this time strengthening their position as the second tier in the Roman state (we have already seen how, after Claudius, they were to take over the principal posts in the central imperial secretariat). They had traditionally been men of business, as opposed to the land-owning senatorial nobility, but were now coming to include many regular army officers, administrators, and the lesser landowners who tended to make up the governing class in the cities of Italy outside Rome and in the provinces. Socially, they were regarded as inferiors by many senators. The procurator of an imperial province had his own staff and was directly responsible to the emperor, not the governor, a potential cause of friction within the province, but also a means by which an emperor could keep his governors under surveillance.

Not all of Britain within the area under Roman control in these early days was, however, included in the part 'transformed into a regular province'. The ultimate intention would certainly have been to transfer as much of the burden of administration as possible on to local shoulders, but Claudius must have been well aware that over-hasty imposition of provincial institutions in that part of Germany between the Rhine and the Elbe had contributed to the rising that destroyed Varus' legions and caused Augustus to abandon most of the territory won. At Colchester the symbolic heart of Cunobelinus' former kingdom was immediately obliterated by a Roman fort that incorporated earthworks that had formed the entrance to the royal compound and the tribal sacred enclosure. But it was six years before Claudius founded the ostentatious city nearby that was to act as a memorial of victory and the capital of the new province: in the mean time the site that was subsequently used for that purpose was occupied by a base for the Twentieth legion.

In the short term, therefore, large parts of the conquered territory probably remained under direct military rule. Other areas were entrusted for the time being to Tacitus' 'instruments of servitude'—client kings—and it is quite likely that, but for later events, they would have been left permanently in those hands. The client kingdoms play a very important part in the story of Britain's first quarter-century within the empire. North of the area immediately conquered, the great tribe of the Brigantes showed by their subsequent actions that they considered themselves independent, though they were liable to Roman intervention, like any other state bordering on Roman territories. They may well, however, have had some treaty arrangement already. The kingdom of the Iceni in Norfolk was more directly accountable to Rome. It is possible that they may temporarily have remained technically outside the province: geographically, the Iceni were on the fringe, with only the sea beyond, and for the time being they were permitted to retain their weapons. Suetonius, however, makes it clear that the realms of allied princes (*reges socii*) were considered by Rome to be integral parts of the empire (*membra partesque imperii*). We do not know whether Prasutagus, husband of Boudicca and friend of Rome, was already their king. Nevertheless, the initial friendship of the Iceni was important. Not only were they near neighbours to Colchester, but they also controlled the sea routes into the Wash and the estuaries on the Norfolk coast.

It was also important to ensure that the south coast routes into Britain remained secure, without tying down large numbers of Roman troops better employed in the forward areas or watching recently defeated communities. The shortest sea crossing itself was guarded by the invasion base at Richborough, but the vital entries along the south coast required a large area of central southern Britain to be in safe hands. It will be remembered that Verica of the Atrebates had played an important part in the decision to invade. Surprisingly, there is no sign that he returned to the Hampshire domains from which he had been expelled. Perhaps he was dead by now, or had been discarded in favour of other policies better suited to the times. Victory had been achieved: reconciliation was desirable. The origins of Cogidumnus—or Cogidubnus, as he has become better known and as we may for convenience call him—are quite unknown. He apparently was, or was made, a Roman citizen. He may well have been a Gaul rather than a Briton, possibly a member of one of the Gallic families that Claudius wished to bring into the Roman senate. The imperial patronage that installed him as ruler of the 'certain tribes' must also have been responsible for the title of 'great king' (*rex magnus*) that appears on an inscription in Chichester. Grandiloquent though it may sound, it is a title that is also found in this period in the eastern part of the empire, applied to client kings who had been given rule over more than one people.

The realm of Cogidubnus probably consisted of the territories that were administered in later days from Roman towns at Chichester and Winchester (when they became known as the *civitates* of the Regini (or Regni) and Belgae respectively), and possibly at first Silchester (*civitas Atrebatum*). The discovery of early military structures in the Chichester area strongly suggests that the initial object was to secure the loyalty of this vital base area without tying down troops on surveillance or officers in civil administration. It is possible that the kingdom was intended to be a short-term arrangement. Though Tacitus makes it clear that Cogidubnus remained loyal for a long time, neither this nor the 'palace' at Fishbourne that was probably his prove that the kingdom as such survived equally long. The Roman government became increasingly disillusioned with client states after the reign of Nero, and was inclined to replace them with direct rule. Nevertheless, the kingdom of Cogidubnus seems to have been a success. Politically, its support was probably crucial during the rebellion of Boudicca and so many of the other British tribes. Economically, the early development of a string of fine country houses or 'villas' in the coastal area of the kingdom, quite exceptional for first-century Britain, suggest an unusual initial impetus and the presence of persons in high favour with the authorities or able to take particular advantage of the opportunities afforded by the Roman peace.

While Claudius was still in Britain, the future emperor Vespasian was campaigning separately towards the west. Suetonius tells us that he conquered the Isle of Wight, fought thirty battles, subjugated two warlike tribes (*validissimae gentes*), and captured more than twenty native centres (*oppida*). From later history, it seems likely that the backbone of his force was the Second legion. The 'warlike tribes' pose some problems. One may be assumed to have been the Durotriges of Dorset. The other may have been the part of the Dobunni that had not surrendered earlier. We may perhaps visualize him fighting his way westward from hill-fort to hill-fort, supported along the coast by the fleet. Vespasian's personal success was rated very highly, and, like Hosidius Geta, he too received great rewards; he was granted triumphal insignia, elected to two of the priesthoods that were ranked at Rome like orders in an honours list, and subsequently, in AD 51, was advanced to the consulship, thus qualifying his family for inclusion among the leading senatorial houses. It must be admitted that Claudius was lavish with honours for this, his only campaign—granting them even to the senators, some of doubtful loyalty, who had accompanied him—but the case of Vespasian was different. For a man whose origins were equestrian, he had already achieved remarkable eminence by AD 51. Although he undoubtedly owed much of his preferment to the great imperial freedman Narcissus, there is no question that his brilliant performance in Britain confirmed Narcissus' judgement of him in the eyes of the emperor, and won for Vespasian the respect that was to stand him in good stead later in the struggle for the throne.

We have no literary evidence for the operations carried out in other sectors in the four years of Aulus Plautius' governorship after Claudius' departure. We have already noted the Twentieth legion stationed at Colchester, and an early fort is recorded at Verulamium, thus securing both centres of the old kingdom. From its later appearance at Lincoln, it seems probable that the Ninth operated northwards, perhaps halting at the Nene before entering the territory of the Corieltauvi. Tombstones of the Fourteenth at Wroxeter in Shropshire suggest an early drive north-westwards through the outlying territory of the Catuvellauni and their dependents. By 47 the greater part of the lowlands of south and east England were under Roman control, either garrisoned or in the hands of friendly kings.

A dominant concept in the thinking of modern scholars on Britain in its early years has been that of a 'Fosse Way Frontier', sometimes formulated in the slightly different guise of a 'Severn–Trent' line. The Fosse Way is the major Roman road that runs diagonally across Britain from the sea at Topsham in Devon to Leicester and Lincoln, and whose line can be taken on by another road from Lincoln to the Humber. Romano-British specialists fell into the habit of speaking of it as a deliberate frontier, delimiting the early province more or less from sea to sea. The discovery of more and more forts in the south and Midlands (including a number of legionary appearance but part-legion size, known to archaeologists as 'vexillation fortresses', because they probably often housed vexillations, or detachments, from legions) has combined with the difficulties of precise dating to make it clear that the situation is much more complicated. This is in addition to the fact that, even apart from the extension of the line to the Humber, it is certain that the road itself was not constructed in one piece. The actual idea of a linear frontier is itself distracting and anachronistic. Modern notions of guarded national boundaries join with Hadrian's Wall and other physical barriers that were erected for military purposes, but were not introduced in Britain for another three-quarters of a century. It may well be that the Fosse Way indicates the general limit of secure control

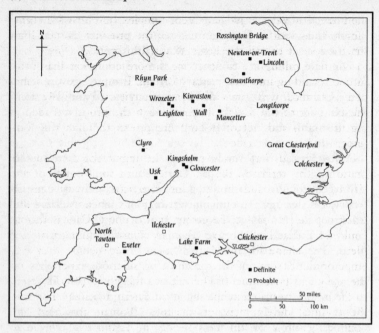

N

Rossington Bridge

Newton-on-Trent
■Lincoln

Rhyn Park
Osmanthorpe

Wroxeter Kinvaston
Leighton Wall Longthorpe
Mancetter

Clyro
Great Chesterford

Kingsholm
Colchester
Usk Gloucester

North Ilchester
Tawton Lake Farm Chichester
Exeter

■ Definite
□ Probable

0   50 miles
0   50   100 km

THE MAIN UNITS OF THE ROMAN ARMY in the early years of the conquest were
not provided with strategic bases big enough to take one (or two) full legions,
except initially at Colchester, the provincial capital and former British centre of
power. The legions were divided into large detachments and (perhaps brigaded
with auxiliaries) distributed, indicating lack of apprehension of attack in force.

in this early stage, but in essence it is much better to think of it
as a cross-country link that eventually connected the various lines
of communication radiating from the south-east. Its construction
and safe operation must have required the presence of strong
forces to the north and west of it, as well as posts on the road
itself and behind. At this period, in the first half of the first century, the word *limes* (which archaeologists conventionally apply to
a Roman frontier) meant a road. It only later came to signify a
boundary, and later still expanded to apply to whole frontier regions, but never specifically a physical, fortified border. The political arrangements in that part of Britain to the south and east of

the Fosse Way were, as we have seen, complex, and included client kingdoms as well as the beginnings of the province proper. It is strictly correct to call the Fosse Way in this period a *limes*, but to continue calling it a frontier causes more confusion than gain in understanding mid-first-century Britain. It represents the spine of a very broad, well-garrisoned band of territory, eventually from the Humber to the Severn, behind which the process of reducing the south and east of Britain into provincial form was well under way.

Aulus Plautius had surely earned the tribute of a triumphal oration on his return to Rome. The emperor went out from the city to meet him, and showed him other extraordinary signs of favour. But we have to remember two things when assessing the extent of the Roman achievement at this point. One is that it could very nearly all be lost again by Roman stupidity under Nero. The blame for that lay on many more people than the emperor alone, some of them men of considerable experience in the army and government. The other is that the area conquered so far by no means encompassed all of lowland Britain, nor was the eventual development of successful Roman provincial life confined entirely to this section of the island. Whether the Romans might not better have remained content with what was won under Claudius is another matter, and lies in the profitless historical realm of the 'might have been'.

5

RESISTANCE AND REVOLT

If the later years of Aulus Plautius' governorship seem to be a period of military consolidation within which a new province could be shaped, the period following is marked by violent reaction from the Britons. The Romans were manifestly here to stay, but one may wonder from subsequent events whether there would have been internal resistance but for Roman policy itself. In the mean time, the change of governor in 47 was marked by an attack by hostile tribes from outside the conquered territory, thinking that, with the onset of winter, they would take a new commander by surprise. Publius Ostorius Scapula, however, was not the man to hesitate. He marched at speed at the head of a number of lightly armed cohorts, and stamped out all opposition.

His next action, however, may have appeared to show military sense, but lacked political judgement. An attractive emendation of an apparently corrupt text of Tacitus, if correct, tells us that Ostorius 'prepared to tame everything this side of the Trent and Severn'. It is likely to refer both to the establishment of some of the later Claudian forts and to the disarming of tribes within the south and east that had so far been allowed to keep their weapons. The decision may have stemmed from the intention to move more troops forward in preparation for further conquest, but it can also be envisaged as part of the general policy of 'reducing the nearest part of Britain into the form of a province'. It proved a costly mistake, for this was the point at which the Iceni rebelled for the first time, bitterly resenting the governor's action, since they had voluntarily acceded to the Roman side. With them they took certain neighbouring tribes who are not specified in the record. This native alliance was defeated by Ostorius after a stiff fight, in which he once again used auxiliary troops rather than heavily armed legionaries. The battle was probably at Stonea Camp, the fortified island in the peat fens near March, in Cambridgeshire, difficult of access in a maze of watercourses and meres, which had probably been the political focus of the western half of the Iceni. Ostorius had scored an unusual success for a Roman general operating against such an opponent, for he had defeated a British foe without forcing him to fight a pitched battle in open country or being obliged to employ the full effort of Roman siege tactics and heavy equipment to storm a major fortress. His political acumen, however, had not equalled his military resourcefulness, since it had been the disarming that had made the fighting necessary in the first place. Romans had a dangerous propensity for making this sort of mistake, which caused them to fight unnecessary wars out of insensitivity for the emotions of other peoples.

For the moment, Ostorius' victory persuaded other tribes who had been contemplating rebellion to desist, and he was left free to campaign beyond the borders that his army currently held. His first drive was against the Deceangli of north-east Wales. He again fought no pitched battles, but defeated the enemy whenever they tried to harass his column, ravaged their territory, and collected extensive quantities of booty. This profitable operation, however, was broken off when an outbreak of violence among the Brigantes demanded his attention. Peace in the vast territories that stretched north from the current limits of Roman-occupied Britain was a prerequisite to its security. With the execution of the few who had taken up arms, this revolt against friends of Rome subsided, but the existence of a hostile party in what was already amounting to a client kingdom had been revealed. The omens for the future were bad.

At this point Cunobelinus' pugnacious son Caratacus comes back into the picture, first as a leader among the Silures of south Wales, and then, a little later, as general commander of the opposition to Rome, centred on the territory of the Ordovices of central Wales. The great earthworks on Minchinhampton Common on the western edge of the Cotswolds may represent one of his strongholds in the years following his defeat in the initial invasion, a period for which we have no documentary evidence. There is certainly some reason to think that this was in the territory of an anti-Roman section of the Dobunni, and an intended stand here by Caratacus seems quite likely. He cannot have remained at Minchinhampton until he reappeared among the Silures, since it is almost certain that this district was occupied or overseen by the Roman army by that time.

The rising of the Silures had important consequences. To release the legion based at Colchester for stationing in the forward area, a colony of military veterans was founded at that site, to act, as Tacitus says, as a bulwark against revolt and to familiarize the natives with the ground rules and procedures of Roman government. This gives us a date—AD 49—for the foundation of the first Roman *colonia* in Britain. Many legionaries must by now have been due for discharge, and this was an appropriate and prestigious way of providing for them. Under the early Empire, a colony was a deliberate foundation, all of whose members were Roman citizens, generally time-expired soldiers. It was at the head of the hierarchy of provincial cities, and, in conquered territory, it was a symbol of the permanence of Roman power. It was frequently accompanied by land allotments to the colonists, and the provision of these from the lands of a defeated enemy was straightforward. The confiscated estates of the house of Cunobelinus will automatically, like all such captured royal domains, have been added to the private property of the emperor, and could now be given to Claudius' legionary veterans in the continuing tradition of calculated generosity that had once bound soldiers to their generals under the Republic.

Meanwhile, the troops released by the foundation of the colony found themselves transferred to a major theatre of war. Caratacus had by now a supranational authority among the opponents of Rome, switching the war from the lands of the Silures to those of the Ordovices, and attracting all who dreaded a Roman peace to his side. The exact site of the culminating battle remains uncertain, though it is probable that it was fought on the Severn in the region of Newtown. The Britons had stationed themselves on a steep ridge above the river, and had fortified the places where the gradient was easiest. Ostorius, uncharacteristically, is reported as being dismayed at the difficulties of crossing the river and taking such a position from the formidable warriors he saw in front of him. In the tradition of heroic literature, Tacitus tells us of the general's doubts being overcome by the eagerness of the soldiers and their officers. The crossing proved easy, and the tactics and equipment of the legionaries and auxiliaries combined to give them overwhelming superiority. Caratacus' wife and daughter were captured, his brother surrendered, and he himself fled to the Brigantes.

The respite gained by Caratacus was a short one. The pro-Roman queen Cartimandua, conscious of her status as a Roman ally and of the rebellion amongst her own subjects that the governor had recently put down, promptly handed him over. This was treated as a very special success at Rome. Not only did the senate equate it with the most famous captures of kings in ancient days, but Claudius staged a great display of the captives in front of the barracks of the praetorian guard in Rome. The speech of Caratacus as reported by Tacitus is one of those set pieces by kings and commanders that are a familiar device in the pages of the Roman historians, but whatever he did or did not actually say, his bearing so impressed the emperor that, with a show of clemency, the latter pardoned both the Briton and his family. This was something Julius Caesar had not done for Vercingetorix, despite his reputation for mercy. Claudius had once again outdone his great predecessor. Living up to the destiny that Virgil had proclaimed for Rome in Augustus' time, the emperor had 'put down those barbarians who would not submit to Roman rule, and shown mercy to the defeated'.

Ostorius himself was honoured with triumphal insignia, but this was to bring him little pleasure. Injudiciously announcing that the Silures must either be annihilated or transplanted, he drove them to desperation. A series of successful attacks provided the latter with booty and prisoners which they used to bind other tribes to them. A new British confederacy was in the making. Ostorius' death, 'worn out with care', saved the Silures from extinction, but left Rome a half-pacified province and a turbulent frontier.

A new governor was appointed with unusual speed. There was a danger that the image gained by the Claudian victories would be tarnished. A man with an impressive record was chosen: Aulus

Didius Gallus, who had recently been decorated for a successful campaign in south Russia. Tacitus, probably unfairly, accuses him of leaving the action in Britain to his subordinates. The Silures had defeated a legion by the time Didius reached the province, and were ranging far and wide. Yet his arrival seems to have been sufficient to restore order, implying more energy and skill than Tacitus would allow.

No sooner were the Silures restrained than Didius, fresh from placing a Roman nominee on the throne of the troubled client kingdom in the Crimea, found himself facing similar problems with the Brigantes. Venutius, husband of Queen Cartimandua and inheritor of the mantle of Caratacus as the best military leader among the Britons, had been one of those confirmed in power by the Romans after the previous Brigantian upheaval. Now, however, he was alienated from his wife, retaliating by invading her kingdom when she seized his brother and other relatives. Didius tried a measured response, sending in auxiliary cohorts and then committing a legion. Successful actions confirmed Cartimandua on her throne, but Venutius was to cause further trouble in the future.

In AD 54, perhaps while these events were happening in Britain, the Emperor Claudius died in suspicious circumstances, and his stepson Nero came to the throne. Suetonius states that Nero considered abandoning Britain at one stage, and it is possible that this was the occasion, rather than after the rebellion of Boudicca. With the death of Claudius came the fall of most of his leading advisers, including the freedman Narcissus, who had been so publicly associated with the British adventure. It is typical of the ambivalent attitude of the regime to the late emperor and his policies that it arranged for his deification, but permitted literary fun to be poked at the new god. It is, however, indicative of the importance that the imperial house attached to the military reputation that Claudius had won in Britain that the reason given for the young Nero's decision not to withdraw was that it would have reflected on Claudius' glory.

The next governor, Quintus Veranius, had been marked out early for promotion, and had acquired a distinguished reputation by his conduct of a war in the Near East, in the mountains of Lycia and Pamphylia. Campaigns in Wales, and perhaps into the

Brigantian Pennines, seem to be implied. Veranius, however, had time only for a few minor raids against the Silures before he, like Scapula, died in office. A death-bed claim that he could have conquered the province given two more years (the balance of a normal tour of duty) attracted the scorn of Tacitus, but it seems likely that Veranius was referring to the pacification of the existing province by the defeat of the Silures rather than to the conquest of the whole island.

C. Suetonius Paullinus, Veranius' successor, was again a man of high military reputation, with outstanding experience of mountain warfare as the first Roman general to cross the Atlas mountains of Mauretania. Two highly successful years in the field were coming to a climax in AD 60 with preparations for an all-out assault on the island of Anglesey. It is often claimed that this was in order finally to extirpate the Druids: more certainly, we have the statement of Tacitus that Anglesey was 'heavily populated and a sanctuary for fugitives' and 'a source of strength to rebels'. A further reason imputed by Tacitus is entirely believable in its Roman social context. Paullinus is alleged to have been driven by jealousy of the foremost of his peers, being 'a rival general to Corbulo, both in fact as a professional soldier and in popular belief (in which every prominent man has to have a rival), and therefore longing for a victory to set against Corbulo's reconquest of Armenia'. Tacitus has left us a dramatic picture of the savage force that defended the shores of Anglesey—fierce warriors, wild women, and praying Druids. The countervailing savagery of the Roman assault, sketched in a few words by the historian, cannot be doubted. Yet while Paullinus was engaged on this operation, the bloodiest episode in Romano-British history was taking shape behind him.

Winning and maintaining the co-operation of the provincial upper classes was crucial to the peace, administration, and financial structure of the empire, for the relatively small Roman army could not possibly have controlled the provinces without it. The Boudiccan rebellion arose from the disastrous failure of the early governors to get these relations with the local inhabitants right. Until the advantages of being within the empire were clear to a large proportion of men of influence within the local communities, there could be no real security. This had not yet come about. On the contrary, friends were being turned into enemies, and the initial advantage of the Britons being divided against themselves was being lost. Worse, the Romans seem to have had no inkling of what was happening. The acute and original mind of the Emperor Claudius was no longer there to interpret the reports coming back. Nor, as we shall see, was the government in Rome likely to have had alternative intelligence from the provincial procurator, for his own cupidity and foolishness were among the immediate causes of the uprising.

By AD 60 we may expect a number of British tribes to have been formally recognized as *civitates peregrinae*, non-citizen ('peregrine') but regular local authorities on the Roman pattern, to whom various functions were delegated. It is likely that the kingdoms of Prasutagus of the Iceni, Cogidubnus, and perhaps others were similarly regulated, with individual arrangements set out for each. The governor's main administration was perhaps briefly at Colchester, but it may have moved from there when the Claudian colony was founded in 49. It is not certain that the provincial procurator's office was ever at Colchester, and the foundation of London around AD 50 may have been accompanied by a move of officials or even whole departments. It was certainly in the most convenient place for financial and other administration, a port with access to the sea, placed at the hub of the developing road system of the new province. It rapidly became a hive of commerce, and may from the outset have been intended to become the eventual seat of government. For historical reasons, however, Colchester was the centre of imperial prestige in this period, containing the focus of the Imperial Cult, and probably in these early days providing the meeting-place of the provincial council, the loyal assembly of provincial aristocracy that seems later to have met in London.

Many towns were now developing on comfortable but, as yet, fairly irregular lines. Amenities for civilians—even defences in the few places provided with them under the early Empire—were almost always expected to come out of the pockets of private citizens, usually at their own initiative, either collectively or individually. Indeed, until the upheavals across the empire in the middle of the third century, competition for status among the upper classes was centred on conspicuous benefactions to their home towns or to other places with which they had connections. This 'munificence', as it is termed, was the driving force behind the blossoming of the cities of the early Empire. Public works therefore usually originated with members of the local council or with some great magnate with an interest in the district, often because estates in the locality formed part of his landed property. The role of government was a matter of permissions and occasional supervision, perhaps with the provision of skilled advice, but much less commonly with money. 'Romanization', in the sense of a conscious spreading of Roman amenities at Roman expense, is a misunderstanding. Pressurizing local men of influence and offering them advantages were the methods employed to secure loyalty. It was as these leading provincial families came to identify themselves with Roman political and social culture, and to strive with one another within its terms, that the Romanization of the provinces that we can recognize archaeologically followed. The merging of these people with the Roman official classes, military and civil, and the creation of a unified substructure of urban society to serve this establishment were the mainsprings of the provincial cities now developing, which in their turn influenced the economies and expectations of the countryside around them. But it all depended on the native aristocracies being convinced, and remaining convinced, that their interests lay with Rome. By AD 60 in Britain pacification seemed to have reached the critical point at which the south and east could largely be trusted, and it was judged that massive concentrations of troops in those parts were no longer needed. Paullinus had ambitions for spectacular conquest in Wales, and the distribution of legionary vexillations, supported by auxiliary forts where still deemed necessary, should have been enough to deal with any local difficulty.

The reasons given by the ancient historians for the rebellion of Boudicca are revealing of the conditions that could prevail under Roman rule when those in charge had lost sight of its basic principles. The seat of the fire was again the Iceni. Now their king, Prasutagus, had died and the land was wide open to the worst elements in Roman provincial administration. That these were not restrained must be laid in large measure at the door of Paullinus. Tacitus states that Prasutagus had left the emperor co-heir with his two daughters, hoping thereby to keep his kingdom and household safe. It is quite clear that the whole kingdom was not left to Rome outright, in the way that Attalus III had bequeathed the kingdom of Pergamum in Asia Minor in 133 BC. Probably, the king had left the emperor a share of his personal possessions and royal estates, a common device by which wealthy Romans ensured the carrying-out of their wills. Under such an arrangement, part of the Icenian territory should have become imperial estate, and the emperor would have received a proportion of the royal treasure.

The local officers of the governor and of the provincial procurator, Decianus Catus, took a different view. They treated the whole territory as if it had been surrendered by a defeated enemy. The Iceni and their friends complained that the governor tyrannized over their persons, the procurator over their possessions. Centurions from the governor's staff were plundering the kingdom. Icenian nobles were being evicted from their ancestral properties. Members of the royal house were being treated as slaves, at the same time as slaves serving the procurator were looting the king's household. The royal family put up some resistance; the late king's widow, Boudicca, was flogged, and his daughters were raped. The result was rebellion, led by the formidable queen. She was joined by certain tribes, unspecified in the sources, 'who had not yet been broken by servitude', and by the Iceni's southern neighbours, the Trinovantes.

The Trinovantes had developed a special hatred for the veterans settled at Colchester. These had driven native inhabitants from their homes and lands and were treating them like captives or slaves, encouraged by serving soldiers who hoped for similar opportunities in the future. The original land allotments may indeed have been taken chiefly from the royal domain of the house of Cunobelinus, but it would seem that the colonists were now expanding beyond these. Another source claims that the procurator was demanding the return of money that had been given to influential Britons by Claudius, and that the prominent statesman, playwright, and moralist Seneca was recalling, *in toto* and in an unfeeling manner, huge loans that he had previously forced on unwilling Britons. The nature of these sums of money is unclear, though it is possible to speculate that some were cash grants that Claudius had given to individual British nobles so that they could meet the property qualifications required for municipal council or even senatorial eligibility. Another possibility is that the money was loaned to enable the payment of taxes in cash, since it must have been difficult for Britons to raise cash by the sale of land—for most local aristocrats probably their largest asset—before a Roman-style property market had had time to develop.

If the allegation concerning Seneca is true, then a lead in the exploitation of the provincials was being given at the highest level. Seneca, formerly Nero's tutor, had dominated the young emperor since he came to the throne, in collaboration with his friend, the praetorian prefect Burrus. Their influence is generally considered to have been a moderating one. It gradually waned: it finally came to an end in 62, but not until after the Boudiccan rebellion. Considerable doubt has been cast upon the reliability of the source, but even if only part of this is true, then we may have both an explanation for the conduct of the governor and the procurator, and a contributory cause in the decline of Seneca.

The exact date of the outbreak of rebellion is the cause of some debate. Though Tacitus places it firmly in the consulship of Caesennius Paetus and Petronius Turpilianus (AD 61), we have to fit into this year not only the rebellion itself and its complicated aftermath, but Turpilianus completing his term of office at Rome and arriving as Suetonius Paullinus' successor in Britain. Modern historians differ, therefore, with opinion now tending to favour 60.

In true Roman fashion, the ancient authors build up the atmosphere with prodigies and portents. A 'fifth column' inside the colony at Colchester, doubtless native residents, successfully confused the colonists and prevented any serious measures for the defence of the city. Though well provided with public buildings —council chamber, theatre, and the huge temple of the Imperial Cult—the ramparts that had surrounded the legionary fortress before AD 49 had been levelled. The temple was a particular object of hatred to the Britons, not only because it symbolized their servitude, but also because 'those chosen as its priests found themselves obliged to pour out their whole fortunes in its service'. A prime purpose of the cult was to bring together influential provincials and to encourage their loyalty to the emperor and their integration into the Roman governing class, yet it seems to have been so mismanaged as to have had the opposite effect. Some of these individuals were probably among those privy to the conspiracy, and their prominent position would have rendered them particularly able to spread uncertainty within the city.

No attempt was made by the colonists to evacuate the non-combatants, though they had enough warning to ask the procurator for assistance. All they received was two hundred 'semi-armed' men. There were also a few regular troops in the neighbourhood, but the city was overrun and destroyed almost immediately. Only the small band of soldiers was able to barricade itself into the temple, where it held out for two days. The British horde was soon on its way towards London.

Before they could fall on London, however, Boudicca had to deal with a force that was marching to the rescue under the command of the legate of the Ninth legion, Petillius Cerialis, a mercurial individual whose career is remarkable for the number of times he escaped from the brink of military disaster. Though it seems likely that he had with him only one of the vexillations into which his legion was probably divided at this time, he did not hesitate to meet the Britons in battle. His infantry was cut to pieces, and he escaped with only his cavalry to take shelter behind the defences of his base, the vexillation fortress at Longthorpe, near Peterborough, where hasty work of this period probably records the desperate attempt by the remnants of this force to put themselves into a position of defence if Boudicca came after them.

The effects of this disaster on the governor and the procurator were dramatic but different. The latter, now thoroughly terrified by the intensity of the hatred directed against him, wisely fled to Gaul. Paullinus made for London with all speed, apparently without the bulk of his troops. He may have expected the other legionary vexillations to be gathering there, and he appears to have had ideas of defending it until news of the defeat of Cerialis arrived. He made the unpalatable decision to regroup elsewhere, deciding to sacrifice one town to save the overall situation. Tacitus describes what followed:

Undeflected by the prayers and tears of those who begged for his help, he gave the signal to move, and took into his column any who could join it. Those who were unfit for war because of their sex, or too aged to go, or too fond of the place to abandon it, were butchered by the enemy. A similar massacre took place at the city of Verulamium, for the barbarian British, happiest when looting, and unenthusiastic about real effort, bypassed the forts and garrisons, and headed for the places where they knew the largest amounts of undefended booty lay. Something like 70,000 Roman citizens and other friends of Rome died in the places mentioned. The Britons took no prisoners, sold no captives as slaves, and went in for none of the usual trading of war. They wasted no time in getting down to the bloody business of hanging, burning, and crucifying. It was as if they feared that retribution might catch up with them while their vengeance was only half-complete.

Paullinus' march brought him back to his main force, which numbered about 10,000 men and comprised the Fourteenth legion, detachments of the Twentieth, and auxiliaries drawn from the nearest garrisons. A shock was the non-arrival of the Second, then under the temporary command of its camp commandant Poenius Postumus, who refused to move. It is possible that he was afraid to leave the west unguarded, rather than that he acted out of terror of Boudicca. He may also have remembered too vividly a *praefectus castrorum* who had been caught unawares and killed by the Silures during Scapula's governorship. In the event, his disobedience probably pinned down some of the most dangerous tribes, but this does not seem to have been taken into account subsequently. Meanwhile, Paullinus, ever a cautious man in war, was preparing to give battle on ground of his own choosing somewhere in the Midlands, perhaps near Mancetter or Towcester on Watling Street.

Paullinus drew up his legionary troops in close order in a defile, protected in the rear by dense forest. Auxiliaries were stationed on the flanks, with cavalry on either wing. Boudicca's enormous force assembled in loose array. Behind it were its wagons, loaded with women and children, like grandstands at a Roman spectacle. That the Britons were still using chariots suggests either that the Romans had dropped the disarmament policy after the trouble in AD 47, or that these weapons had been supplied from outside the area under Roman control. The critical features of the engagement seem to have been the shock effect of the rain of javelins that descended upon the Britons after they had been lured into attacking up a slope, followed by the disciplined charge of the heavy infantry in wedge-formation, backed by the lighter units. This broke up the British army and forced it back upon the wagons. These turned into a trap when the draught animals were slaughtered by the Romans. From that moment the battle became a massacre, with the women being killed with the men; and Tacitus, without committing himself as to their accuracy, quotes figures of 80,000 British dead as against 400 Romans. As he says, it was a victory to set alongside those of former days.

Boudicca herself escaped from the field, but her death followed soon after—by poison according to Tacitus, from sickness in Dio's account. Poenius Postumus also killed himself when he heard of the victory. The Second legion, together with the surviving part of the Ninth, now joined Paullinus in the field. The Fourteenth legion received the triumphant title of 'Martia Victrix', and a reputation for pride and invincibility. The men of the Twentieth who took part in the battle won for their legion, which until then had not had any name attached to its unit number, the right to be called 'Valeria Victrix'. Reinforcements were received from Germany, consisting of 2,000 legionary infantry to bring the Ninth back up to strength, 8 cohorts of auxiliary infantry, and 1,000 auxiliary cavalry. The auxiliaries were placed in new winter quarters; the legionaries apparently remained on active operations. The nature of those operations shows Paullinus at his most active and unpleasant. With fire and sword, he set about laying waste the territory of all the British tribes that had joined the rebellion or just stayed neutral. Bodies, weapons, and signs of violent destruction by fire at the hill-fort of South Cadbury in Somerset may be traces of Paullinus' consuming vengeance, and the same may be true of evidence of destruction at other native sites formerly assigned archaeologically to the initial conquest. Among the officers carrying out Paullinus' orders may have been Vespasian's elder son, the future emperor Titus, who served as a legionary tribune in Britain at about this time. The historian Suetonius tells us that many busts, statues, and inscriptions were erected in the province in honour of Titus' diligence and modest bearing in that post. It is politically improbable that these were dedicated until a decade later at the earliest—probably not before he had been publicly designated co-emperor by Vespasian in 71, and possibly not until his own reign as sole ruler commenced in 79. Nevertheless, it must have been unusual for a young *laticlavius*, at the most barely 22 years of age, to have made such an impression on the provincials, and the fact that, as the commander of his father's praetorian guard, he subsequently acquired a reputation for harsh treatment of dissidence—not to mention the ferocity of his suppression of the Jewish revolt in 70 and his destruction of Jerusalem—may raise the suspicion that his popularity in Britain had originated among pro-Roman communities that had been delivered from the fury of the Boudiccan rebels and had seen those who had taken the other side being crushed.

Despite all the odds, Dio says, there were Britons who were ready to fight again after the battle, and they now received support for their resistance to the governor from an unexpected quarter. They were in desperate straits, having failed to sow their crops earlier in the year, while they prepared for war, because they expected to capture the Roman military granaries. Now they were being pressed hard by Paullinus, and faced a winter without supplies that promised famine for those who survived the punitive actions of the governor. Yet they were heartened in their resistance by a new figure on the scene, Julius Classicianus, the provincial procurator sent out to replace the runaway Decianus Catus. He encouraged them to hold out in the hope that Paullinus might be replaced by a less harsh governor. He was almost certainly a Celt himself by ancestry, and he was the son-in-law of Julius Indus, a Celtic nobleman from the region around Trier on the Moselle, who had raised a cavalry regiment and supported the Roman authorities at the time of a dangerous rebellion there in the reign of Tiberius. Classicianus is likely to have had considerable insight into the motives of such rebellions and the consequences of their repression. Tacitus alleges that his support for the Britons was due to dislike of Paullinus; yet even in the absence of more generous motives, he may at least have seen the disastrous consequences to his own tax-collecting department if the continued devastation of the tribal lands was allowed to continue. His intervention was of the highest importance for the future of Britain.

Classicianus' adverse report to Rome on the governor provoked a commission of inquiry, in the person of the imperial freedman Polyclitus. Tacitus does not bother to conceal the prejudices of his own senatorial class, yet it is difficult not to conclude that Polyclitus carried out a very delicate mission with success. Paullinus was not immediately recalled, his success in battle was celebrated as a victory, his future career was assured, and, after a short but decent interval, the accidental loss of a small number of ships in his command was taken as a convenient moment for the hand-over of the province to his successor.

Tacitus is scornful of the lack of action under this new governor, Petronius Turpilianus. It may fairly be argued, however, that quiescence on the part of the provincial government was just what was required at this point. Turpilianus possessed the prestige of being related to the first governor, Aulus Plautius, and the reputation of being the son or grandson of a man who had been a notably kind governor of Syria. Certainly, Turpilianus and Classicianus achieved such a satisfactory settlement that the south never rose again.

6

RECOVERY AND
ADVANCE

A picture is now beginning to emerge of the progress of material Romanization and the development of Roman institutions immediately after the pacification of the province. In due course archaeology may tell us more about how quickly the cities struck down by the rebels recovered, and about the manner in which other towns developed in this period. Structural evidence for new public buildings comes from London and Bath. In London a building detected under the first phase of the forum may date from this period. It seems to have been of civil type, in contrast to the buildings of military appearance that Boudicca destroyed on the site which may have housed the governor's administration before the great rebellion. At Bath, some time in the fifteen years after the rebellion, a start was made on the grand complex of baths and temple, in which a deliberate attempt seems to have been made to do spectacular honour to a native cult by amalgamating it publicly with one of the greatest Roman deities in the new worship of Sulis Minerva, rather than to obliterate or downgrade the British element.

It is not fanciful to trace archaeologically the changed style of government under Petronius Turpilianus and Julius Classicianus. The experience of Colchester had made the imperial government and its legates chary of pressing British aristocrats to take on new public burdens while old grievances were fresh in their minds. London and Bath—and the rebuilding of the temple at Colchester itself—are sites where direct Roman financing of public development are perhaps most likely to have occurred. We have also to remember that the war and the reprisals carried out by Paullinus must have left many areas with a decimated and impoverished native upper class. Neglected farms, a whole year's harvest lost, and a sizeable proportion of the agricultural labour force either killed in battle, wounded, sold as slaves by their Roman captors, or simply run away in the confusion must have damaged the fortunes even of families who had escaped personal retribution.

A possible pointer to the state of the countryside is the history of the site at Gorhambury, near Verulamium. A villa replaced Iron Age round-houses, arguably in the years before the Boudiccan war, but the site seems to have reverted to a hutted settlement for a period before eventually being rebuilt again on Roman lines. The literary record, which for all practical purposes is that of Tacitus, presents almost total silence on the achievements of the new administration. Tacitus himself was eager to give the credit for civil development in Britain to his father-in-law's governorship nearly twenty years later, and we would expect anything done in the years immediately after the rebellion to be played down. Despite the fact that archaeology is likely to give us only the inherently inconclusive accumulation of negative evidence, the period is a vital one for understanding Roman Britain.

There can be no doubt that winning the general support of the native aristocracy in these years was crucial to the recovery of the province. Without it, the problems of security and administration would have been, as long-term propositions, extremely difficult to bear. A substantial number of Britons had favoured Rome in 43, but we have seen how many were alienated in the years that followed. A hint of how the Britons were won back is contained in Tacitus' reference to the way in which, under Trebellius Maximus, who was governor from 63, the Britons learnt the pleasures of peace and civilization, even though the historian chose to regard it as degeneracy. More can be learnt of Roman methods in a remarkable speech that Tacitus puts into the mouth of Petillius Cerialis, the occasion being an appeal to the Gallic Treviri and Lingones at the most critical moment in the great revolt on the Rhine that was stirred up during the civil wars of AD 68–9. It has special interest, in that it is attributed to Cerialis just before he was sent back to Britain as governor, and, whether or not it was delivered in the words reported—and disingenuous as it is about Roman motives for intervention—it undoubtedly represents a well-informed Roman view of the factors that swayed provincials in the second half of the first century AD:

The reason why Roman generals and emperors came into your territories and those of the other Gauls was not a desire for gain, but at the invitation of your forefathers. They had become so exhausted by internal strife that they were close to collapse, and the Germans whom they had called in to help had seized power over friend and foe alike. . . . We did not occupy the Rhineland to protect Italy, but so that another German leader like Ariovistus should not impose his rule on the peoples of Gaul . . . Until you conceded to us the right to govern you, there were wars constantly among you, and local despots in control all over Gaul. Yet, though we have often been provoked, we have used our victories to impose only those burdens that are unavoidable if peace is to be preserved. Peace between nations cannot be maintained without armies; armies need paying, and that means taxes. Everything else is shared with you. You and your fellow countrymen frequently command our legions and govern these and other provinces of the empire. You are not excluded from anything. In fact, in one way you benefit especially: the good that flows from popular emperors reaches everyone, far and near, but the evil wreaked by tyrants falls on those closest to them. Just as you put up with natural disasters such as too much rain or poor harvests, so should you look upon extravagance and greed among those who are in power over you. There will be faults as long as there are men, but they are not with us all the time, and better times compensate for bad. But do you really expect a milder regime if [the rebels] Tutor and Classicus take over? Or that they will reduce the taxes necessary to support the army that protects you from the Germans and the Britons? If the Romans are expelled—which Heaven forbid!—what else can follow but world-wide conflict, in which each people will fall on its neighbours? Good fortune and discipline have gone hand in hand over the past eight hundred years to build this structure [the Roman state], which destroyed will bring down all together . . . At present, victor and vanquished enjoy peace and the imperial civilization under the same law on an equal footing. Let your experience of the alternatives prevent you from preferring the ruin that will follow on revolt to the safety that is conferred by obedience.

Cerialis drove the points home by pointing out that his audience, prosperous and by now extensively Romanized, was in particular danger from the very fact that it was so well off. This was at the heart of the matter: the more that provincials became Romanized, acquired Roman amenities, and became identified with Roman rule, the more they needed the protection that only Rome could give them. At one point Germans hostile to Rome appealed to their kinsmen living in the Roman city of Cologne to make common cause with them, as Britons seem to have done in Boudicca's day at Colchester. The native inhabitants of Cologne, however, replied that they were now so intermingled with the Romans that they were one population. While it was at the citizens' own expense that they developed their local manifestations of Roman culture, Cerialis was surely correct in pointing out that it could not have happened, and would not continue, without the existence of the Roman system or the presence of the Roman army.

The success of the work of Trebellius Maximus and his colleagues can be measured by what happened—or rather did not happen—in Britain when news came of the shattering events of AD 68 that led to the deposition and suicide of Nero and to the civil wars that followed. Britain itself was on the sidelines throughout, but troops from the Roman army in Britain took significant part in some of these upheavals, and there were political repercussions amongst the Romans in the province. Although every Roman's attention must have been on the news from the Continent, no Britons inside the province seized the opportunity that this represented. This reflects great credit on the despised administrators who succeeded Paullinus. Indeed, probably in 66 or 67 the emperor had been able to withdraw the famous Fourteenth legion, victors in the final battle against Boudicca, for service elsewhere. It is also extremely likely that, both after Boudicca's rebellion and when the civil wars actually broke out, this continuing and steadfast loyalty played a powerful part in maintaining peace among the native population.

The upheavals that deposed Nero, drove him to suicide, and replaced him in quick succession with Galba, Otho, Vitellius, and finally Vespasian, started in the provinces and were decided by provincial armies. Britain's apparent lack of involvement was not due to remoteness, but to the fact that different sections of the army had different sympathies. During the struggle between Otho and Vitellius, military sympathy in the province lay broadly with

the latter, though the former governor Paullinus and his old comrades of the Fourteenth legion (whose overweening pride may
have made them unpopular) were in the Othonian army. The
governor in office, still Trebellius Maximus, had for a long time
been at odds with the commander of the Twentieth, Roscius
Coelius, and this now came to a head. Coelius complained of
the impoverished state of the British troops, which suggests that
Trebellius had been continuing his policy of peaceful reconstruction by restraining their natural tendency to despoil the natives.
In the end the auxiliaries joined the legions, and the unfortunate
Trebellius was forced to flee to Vitellius, leaving his province in
the hands of a committee of legionary commanders dominated by
Coelius. This committee, however, still adhered to the Vitellian
cause. Nevertheless, though the support of the army of Britain
was held to have strengthened this cause immensely, a force of
8,000 men drawn from the Second, Ninth, and Twentieth legions
arrived on the Continent too late to take part in the decisive
battle at Bedriacum, near Cremona.

Trebellius Maximus was now replaced as governor by Vettius
Bolanus, at that time at the imperial court. The state of the
Fourteenth legion, still in Italy, constituted a serious problem.
Living up to its proud reputation, it refused to acknowledge that
it had been defeated on the Othonian side, saying that only an
advance party had shared in the débâcle at Bedriacum. At one
point the legionaries picked a quarrel with some Batavian auxiliaries with whom they had long had bad relations, possibly since
service together in Britain. They also burnt part of the city of
Turin. Vitellius took the only possible course and sent them back
to Britain, where they are hardly likely to have been greeted
with enthusiasm by their old colleagues who had supported the
other side.

Vitellius then made a fatal mistake. The brutal execution of
Othonian centurions sparked off alarm among the legions that had
sympathized with Otho, initially in the Balkans. Concurrently,
Vespasian, the same Flavius Vespasianus who had served so successfully in Britain under Claudius, was proclaimed emperor in
Egypt, Syria, and Palestine. His supporters on the Danube were
already in correspondence with the Fourteenth legion, now back
in Britain. To meet a lightning march on Italy from the Danube,

Vitellius called for reinforcements from Gaul, Spain, and Britain. Vettius Bolanus in Britain hesistated, considering his province to be insufficiently pacified and in genuine doubt. Amongst his considerations must have been that, of his four legions, one was the Fourteenth and another was II *Augusta*, which Vespasian had commanded with great distinction in the original invasion. They were also seriously depleted: the detachments, 'the flower of the army of Britain', were still in Italy. Indeed Vespasian's supporters were well aware of the fact that the Vitellian army might draw further troops from Britain.

Close to the site of the previous battle of Bedriacum, the two sides met. This time the detachments from the British legions formed the centre of the Vitellian army. The outcome of the battle was a crushing defeat for the Vitellians. There was little mercy shown, and it may be assumed that the troops from Britain suffered heavily. The victorious 'Flavian' army, by this time out of hand, went on to destroy the city of Cremona, which became a prime example of what Roman troops could do to Roman civilians in time of civil war. But the outstanding lessons of this 'Year of the Four Emperors' were that emperors could be made outside Rome, that it was no longer essential to be a member of the intertwined Julian and Claudian families, and that men of comparatively obscure family could hope for the throne. Henceforth, every provincial governor and army commander was a potential emperor, and the loyalty of the provincial armies became a precarious thing, assiduously to be cultivated by every emperor who wished for stability and a long reign. The British garrison had played its part, and had been shown to be a formidable reserve of military power that would have to be taken into account in any future calculations of this sort. It had yet to produce an imperial candidate of its own, but the possibility was now open.

Britain went over to the Flavian side when it finally became clear who had won the war. Vespasian's old Second legion was keen to support him, and it will be recalled that the conduct of his elder son Titus had won acclamation in the province when he had served as a military tribune a few years earlier. The Fourteenth, whose previous enmity to Vitellius had not been forgotten, had already been approached by the Flavian party in the province.

Nevertheless, the fact that many of the career officers and soldiers in the ranks of the army of Britain had been promoted by Vitellius caused some hesitation among them. The Twentieth and its commander Roscius Coelius were particularly doubtful quantities. Vespasian therefore decided to replace Roscius with Gnaeus Julius Agricola, the historian Tacitus' father-in-law, who knew Britain well from service on Paullinus' staff during the Boudiccan rebellion. He had recently proved his efficiency and political sympathies by raising levies in the Flavian cause. For the moment Vettius Bolanus, whose lack of positive action on the Vitellian side now stood him in good stead, continued as governor of Britain, administering with a light hand.

It was Bolanus' misfortune that serious discord broke out again among the Brigantes, possibly beginning before the victory of Vespasian was complete. Queen Cartimandua, who over a decade earlier had rejected her husband and been restored to her throne by the Romans after the mêlée that followed that action, now compounded the insult by replacing Venutius with his armour-bearer, Vellocatus. The infuriated Venutius replied by fomenting revolt within the scandalized kingdom, and summoned help from outside. News of the civil wars and the unsettled state of the Roman army in Britain encouraged Venutius' party to think that Rome would not intervene this time. Bolanus, however, did send in a force of auxiliary cavalry and infantry, but, despite some bitter fighting, it could do no more than rescue the queen herself. Venutius was left master of the Brigantian kingdom.

The situation in Britain was transformed. The province was no longer protected from the tribes of the far north by a powerful friendly kingdom, but immediately threatened by a determined foe who might provide a rallying-point for dissident elements in regions that had only recently been pacified after Boudicca. The policy of relying extensively on client kingdoms, already severely dented by the Boudiccan rebellion, had, despite the exceptional loyalty of Cogidubnus, finally collapsed. A complete reassessment of the Roman position in Britain was required.

The first sign that this had been carried out was the appointment of Petillius Cerialis to replace Bolanus. His speech to the provincials of the Trier region quoted earlier was made in the context of the great rebellion in the Rhineland, from the quelling of which he now came to Britain. Originally stirred up deliberately by the Flavian party to embarrass the Vitellians, it had got out of hand and become a most hazardous affair, in which Cerialis' extraordinary mixture of flair and foolhardiness had led him in and out of extreme danger, but had ended by much enhancing his reputation. There can be little doubt that his appointment to Britain was at least partly due to his family connections with Vespasian. It is not certain exactly what these were, though he may have been married to Vespasian's daughter, Domitilla. But beyond the everyday working of patronage and the political good sense of having a relative in this posting, which was both prestigious and militarily important, Vespasian needed someone in charge of Britain who could pull together the divided loyalties of the legions. And perhaps the most significant feature of Cerialis' campaign on the Rhine had been that he had welded together Flavian legions and former Vitellian troops, including the remarkable Fourteenth, summoned once again from Britain.

In Britain Cerialis was going to need all his energy and his genius for diplomacy. The army was in a poor state: Bolanus had declined to enforce discipline, and an attitude of unwillingness to act in the face of hostile incidents had grown up. The cure was going to be to get the army into the field, but much preparation and retraining must have been required before that could be risked. Now, to use Tacitus' phrase, began 'a succession of great commanders and excellent armies'. Tacitus may not have intended to include Cerialis himself here, but we have to ignore the historian's personal dislike and note Cerialis' rejuvenating effect upon the morale of the British army, ably supported in this new forward policy by Agricola, the commander of the Twentieth legion and sometimes of larger forces as well.

Cerialis brought with him a fresh legion to replace the Fourteenth. This was II *Adiutrix*, newly formed during the civil wars. It was put into garrison in Lincoln, while Cerialis took his own old command, the hardened Ninth, forward into Brigantian territory. There it was eventually established in a brand-new fortress at York. In the mean time it became the spearhead of Cerialis' campaigns. Traces are thought to have been identified at Brough-on-Humber, Malton, York, at the British fortification at Stanwick, near Richmond, in the marching camps in the Stainmore

Pass, and at Carlisle. We may imagine a strategy that moved the main force across the Humber, established a hold on eastern York-shire, and planned a pincer movement on the southern Pennines. Cerialis will have advanced up the Stainmore Pass to meet the Twentieth legion, under Agricola, moving up the western side of the country. The final stage would have been a probe at least as far north as Carlisle, with the whole army now united. At some point there may have been a major battle with Venutius, but whether or not this happened, we hear nothing more of him thereafter, and his power must have been broken. All this was not achieved without loss on the Roman side and on the British; Tacitus, treading a narrow path between intended praise of Agricola and denigration of Cerialis, curtly informs us of 'many battles, some not unbloody'.

On the recall of Cerialis after the more or less usual three years, Julius Frontinus was appointed in his stead. The latter was not only a versatile soldier, but also the author of several treat-ises on military and engineering matters. He clearly regarded the problems of the northern frontier as having been solved, at least for the time being—no mean compliment to Cerialis—for he turned his attention to the uneasy situation in south Wales. He followed Cerialis' example by pursuing a forward policy—with considerable difficulty, but in the end triumphantly—subduing the Silures and their rugged terrain. The history of the legionary fortresses at Exeter and Gloucester, and a new one now con-structed at Caerleon, in the valley of the Usk, are complex, and it is by no means certain that one was completely evacuated as another was built. However, Frontinus' establishment of a base for II *Augusta* at Caerleon, in direct contact with the Bristol Channel, meant easy communication both inland to central Wales and by land and sea to the fertile vale of Glamorgan, the best land of the Silures. Frontinus also seems to have established aux-iliary forts in central Wales itself, and Tacitus records a cavalry squadron operating in the territory of the Ordovices. In the later part of his governorship Frontinus started the construction of a fortress at Chester. If, as seems likely, his purpose was to trans-fer II *Adiutrix* here from Lincoln, then Wales was to face a remarkable concentration of legions.

It has been suggested that, under Frontinus, the Romanization

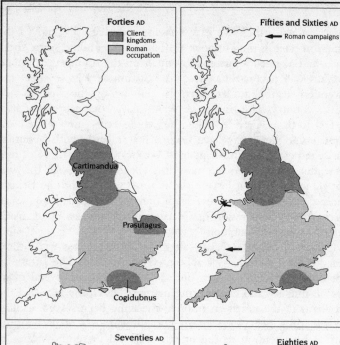

Forties AD

Client kingdoms
Roman occupation

Cartimandua

Prasutagus

Cogidubnus

Fifties and Sixties AD

⬅ Roman campaigns

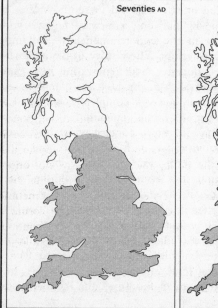

Seventies AD

Eighties AD

■ Inchtuthil

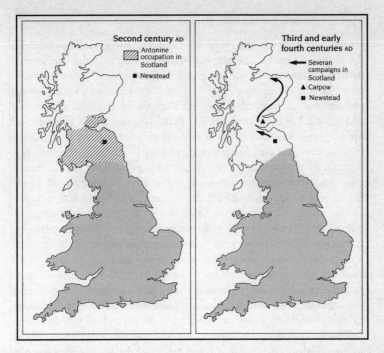

of the province went ahead as it may not have done under Cerialis. The movement of the centre of the Silures from their native fortress in Llanmelin Wood to a new Roman town at Caerwent has long been thought to belong to Frontinus' governorship, and it seems likely that, with his interest in administration, he rounded off his conquest by forming the Silures into the *respublica civitatis Silurum* known much later to epigraphy. It is at least certain that, unlike Ostorius Scapula, his policy towards them was not one of extermination. It is possible that we may detect Frontinus' hand elsewhere, too, in the surge of civic projects that is sometimes attributed exclusively to his successor Agricola. The forum at Verulamium was probably planned and started under Frontinus, and it is highly likely that the forum at Cirencester should also be assigned to him.

The exact year in which Frontinus' successor arrived has long been a subject of debate. We know that Julius Agricola was consul for part of the year 77, that he subsequently gave his daughter in marriage to the historian Tacitus, and that he arrived in Britain late in the campaigning season. There is no knowing whether the latter was in 77 or 78. We have serious historical problems with Agricola. The fact that Tacitus was his son-in-law and wrote his biography means that we have more material on his governorship than that of any other governor of Britain, but it also presents substantial difficulties of its own. Tacitus was anxious to present his father-in-law in a good light and to maximize his achievements, especially given the importance of family reputation to Romans of his class. But Tacitus also had a moral and political intent in his writing: to inculcate through example the proper behaviour of a Roman aristocrat. In particular, his intention was to show how the ancient Republican tradition of service to the state under the Empire could be carried on even under a bad emperor. Both Agricola and Tacitus himself may have been a little uneasy about their own careers—and one may feel that there is an element of self-justification in the attitude adopted—but the historian does seem to have thought that there was more value in loyally serving the public good than in the ruin and death that fell on the most obdurate martyrs to the old Republican cause. Agricola's governorship in Britain started under Vespasian, continued under Titus, but was brought to an end under Domitian, whom Tacitus was at pains to portray as the ogre he appeared to represent to the writer's own class and political faction at Rome. In employing the text of Tacitus as a source, we therefore have to take into account that his narrative can be coloured by these attitudes and aims, and that what he chose to report or emphasize is not always what we would like for our own purposes. Nevertheless, what he says is in itself always of first importance as an artefact of its time and environment.

Although Agricola arrived in Britain well into the season, he apparently surprised everyone by going into action straightaway to avenge the destruction of the cavalry squadron that had been operating among the Ordovices. He had commanded the Twentieth legion under Cerialis, when its home station was most likely Wroxeter, and during that command he had probably learnt much about the Welsh Marches and the tribes facing Rome in that region. Earlier, he had been a military tribune in Britain under

Suetonius Paullinus, and must have been well aware of the assault on Anglesey that was aborted when Boudicca's rebellion erupted. Like Cerialis, Agricola may have deliberately chosen to use his old legion as the prime instrument of his first field operation as governor. Indeed, a newly arrived governor, keen to make an immediate impression, may have preferred to rely on troops he knew well and who knew him. The location of that legion itself may also have influenced his choice of where to act first.

Agricola struck at once, against the advice of many who thought it better to wait and see how the situation developed. One may guess that this advice came from the group of friends who normally advised a Roman magistrate, as well as from senior officers. Tacitus would leave us with the impression that Agricola overrode opinion based on hidebound unwillingness to act rapidly and out of the normal campaigning season, but there may have been those who thought that the extermination of the Ordovices, and the likely commitment to a larger war, were unwise in view of past history in Britain. In the event, the near-annihilation of the Ordovices was carried out, duly followed by a spectacular assault on, and annexation of, Anglesey. Agricola had from the first gained a psychological advantage over the Britons. He had struck before anyone, including his own troops, had expected it, and he had made conscious use of terror. He had established his position with his army, his province, and his potential barbarian enemies. He had also, in a political climate in which Vespasian had so recently rehabilitated the name of Corbulo, strikingly completed the work that Suetonius Paullinus had been engaged upon while attempting to rival Corbulo's achievements, and had done it with the maximum economy of men and effort. Agricola had now joined that league of generals which Paullinus and Corbulo had represented in their day.

Unlike Paullinus, Agricola was not to throw away the advantages of military capability of a high order by inability to ensure just government or to understand when the application of terror was counter-productive. It is admittedly difficult to believe that the abuses in taxation that Agricola is said to have put down in his first winter were really rife under Frontinus. It is more likely that scattered instances of malpractice are being interpreted by Tacitus as a general malaise. Yet they give some idea of the disadvantages of Roman rule, and of the problems that a good governor might face on arrival. We hear, for example, of provincials having to buy back grain that they had already supplied as taxation in order to fulfil their quotas, and at inflated prices, and then being ordered to deliver it to military stations far away—often not served by adequate roads—doubtless to persuade them to bribe officials in order to avoid the burden.

The following summer Agricola again took the field, incorporating new territory, receiving hostages, and throwing a network of forts around the tribes whose surrender he accepted. The mention of 'estuaries and forests' in Tacitus' account may suggest the north-west of England, and it is likely that Agricola was following up the work he had carried out as a subordinate of Cerialis a few years earlier. The eventual pattern of garrisons in this area demonstrates the classic Roman method of control of areas with difficult terrain, whereby the native inhabitants were split up into relatively small units that could be supervised and prevented from making common cause. The surrender of many tribes was doubtless due to Agricola's complementary policies of harassment of the recalcitrant and display of the advantages of peace to those who co-operated.

In the winter of 78 or 79 Agricola can be observed in Tacitus' biography turning his attention to the extension of these policies:

The following winter was taken up with the soundest projects. In order to encourage rough men who lived in scattered settlements (and were thus only too ready to fall to fighting) to live in a peaceful and inactive manner, Agricola urged them privately and helped them officially to build temples, public squares with public buildings (*fora*), and private houses (*domus*). He praised those who responded quickly, and severely criticized the laggards. In this way, competition for public recognition took the place of compulsion. Moreover, he had the children of the leading Britons educated in the civilized arts, and openly placed the natural ability of the Britons above that of the Gauls, however well trained. The result was that those who had once shunned the Latin language now sought fluency and eloquence in it. Roman dress, too, became popular, and the toga was frequently seen. Little by little there was a slide towards the allurements of degeneracy: assembly rooms (*porticus*), bathing establishments, and smart dinner parties. In their naïvety the Britons called it civilization, when it was really all part of their servitude.

Agricola's true achievement seems to have been to obtain the right balance between persuasion and pressure. In local communities undergoing transformation, it was, as we have noted, normal practice to expect private individuals or the local aristocracy as a whole to bear the costs. We may imagine Agricola providing professional advisers and probably military architects and engineers for public works. The laying-out of town centres and street systems according to standard surveying techniques is increasingly being identified archaeologically in Britain. The Flavian tileworks discovered at Somerford Keynes near Cirencester may stand as an example of the planned supply of the necessary materials for one of these developments. Whether the local councils were also assisted with grants is less certain. This generally only happened when an emperor became interested in a project, either because of some personal connection or if persuaded by the envoys of a local community or friends at court. It is perhaps no coincidence that the Emperor Titus succeeded his father in 79, and that his service as a military tribune in Britain had been during the governorship of Paullinus, when Agricola had held the same rank in the same province. We noted earlier that the historian Suetonius tells us that there were many busts and statues of Titus in Britain, and that it is probable that the statuary was actually erected by the provincials while he was formally sharing the chief offices of state with his father or during his own reign. Even if he did not directly initiate Agricola's urbanization policies, it is not unreasonable to guess that he did intervene to support them with money as well as approval. It is a pleasing coincidence that we have sufficient extant fragments of the great inscription that records the completion of the basilica at Verulamium to make it reasonably certain that it dated from Titus' own first year as emperor and opened with his own name and titles.

The education of the heirs of Asiatic and African princes at Rome had long been a weapon of foreign policy. Now the nobility of the British tribes was also being educated in the Roman fashion, presumably in the new cities, though some may have travelled to Gaul or elsewhere in the empire. The regular medium of communication in Roman administration was the Latin language. A further essential ingredient was the study and practice of rhetoric. This was a training for public life as much as a cultural exercise, since it was an essential tool in the conduct of affairs. Despite the fall of the Roman Republic, public speaking retained real importance, particularly in the lawcourts. The latter were now a primary forum not only for the simple prosecution of maladministration, but also for the pursuit of politics. In its new role as a supreme court, the senate itself played a major part in this process, and provincial communities placed great importance on having influential senators as 'patrons' who could speak out for them at Rome, in the senate, in the courts, and to the emperor and those around him. In the provinces themselves the development of imperial and local administration under the early Empire brought a dramatic increase in the need for people capable of effective public speaking and skilled in the conventions of Latin oratory. The methods of teaching, based on the composition of practice pieces on set themes from history and mythology, meant that the Britons were learning the rudiments of classical culture at the same time. The acquisition of a common framework of ideas and ideals was central to the coming-together of Roman and native. Moreover, insomuch as language itself shapes attitudes as well as being shaped by them, the spreading of the Latin tongue carried with it a subtle means of absorbing subject populations into the Roman system. This education was, in short, an essential step in establishing the civil mechanism of a Roman province.

In the next campaigning season Agricola made a notable advance. It is emphasized that he was opening up and ravaging the territory of fresh nations. The pattern of roads established later would seem to suggest that he advanced in two columns, one through Corbridge across the Tyne and the Tweed, reaching the Forth at Inveresk, the other through Carlisle and Crawford, before swinging north-east to meet the first. When the two arms of the advance had met, the joint force pressed on to the Tay. At some point, it now seems likely, the Twentieth legion started to prepare a new fortress for themselves at Carlisle; and on the eastern line of march, the Agricolan base disovered at Corbridge on the Tyne must be associated with these campaigns. The placing of garrisons also made it possible to harass the enemy continually through the winter, still a powerful inducement to sue for peace among tribes used to regaining strength and ground during that part of the year.

The following summer was employed in consolidating the gains of the previous year as far north as the Forth–Clyde isthmus. Though Tacitus is emphatic that the isthmus was garrisoned, it is likely that long-range patrols were deployed from fewer bases than in later days, when the concept of continuous strings of forts and linear barriers was fully developed. Further south, the first period of occupation of such permanent sites as Newstead probably began. The emphasis of the fifth season was on a future conquest of Ireland, and we are told that the campaign started with a 'crossing' by ship, and that the whole coast facing Ireland was occupied. It seems certain that these operations were in south-west Scotland, where increasing numbers of Roman military sites are being found. The 'crossing' was most probably a preliminary sea-borne assault across the Solway Firth. Whether Agricola made any serious preparations for an invasion of Ireland, we do not know. In view of his belief that it could be conquered with one legion and a few auxiliaries, the fact that he did not proceed with the invasion was perhaps fortunate.

In the event, Agricola's attention was diverted to the more pressing problem of Scotland north of the Forth–Clyde line. In the summer of 82 or 83, to forestall a possible general rising, he launched a general advance by land and sea. He seems to have established bases as he went, for the first sign of enemy reaction was an assault on a fort somewhere beyond the Forth. Agricola's answer to an intended attack in several columns was to divide his army into three. This nearly proved disastrous, for the Britons promptly concentrated their forces on a night attack on the Ninth legion that all but succeeded. The Ninth was only rescued by the arrival of Agricola in the nick of time with the rest of his army. The particular camp involved in this action is not known, though aerial photography and excavation may eventually enable us to identify conclusively the marching camps of different periods beyond the Forth.

Where Agricola wintered is not certain, but there is some reason to think that a large camp at Carpow on the Tay was the point from which the next year's campaign was launched. In that

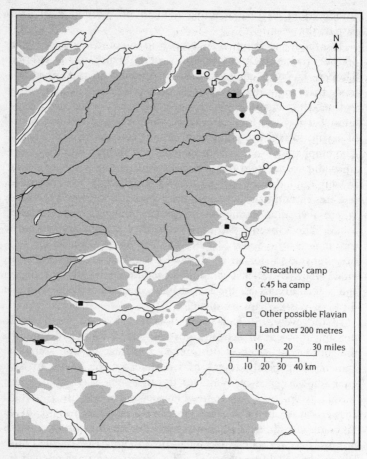

MARCHING CAMPS of the Roman army in north-east Scotland are of various sizes and designs. Of those identified by some as Domitianic, the huge camp at Durno (58 hectares: 143 acres) may have housed Agricola's army concentrated before the battle of Mons Graupius, though, being capable of holding a force much larger than that described by Tacitus, could date from one of the later expeditions led by emperors in person.

decisive summer he entered the field determined to force the enemy to give battle. Once again the fleet was sent ahead to raid the coast and spread terror, and this time the army was accompanied by British allies. They came up with the enemy at a place named Mons Graupius, where the Britons had at last clearly chosen to turn and fight, barring further Roman advance. The location of this battle has been the subject of endless debate, by no means over even now. Pending new evidence, we can do no more than say that it was somewhere in north-east Scotland. The British host, under a Caledonian named Calgacus, amounted to more than 30,000 according to the Roman account, though modern attempts to judge the size of crowds are so notoriously unreliable that the figure must remain subject to doubt. Agricola had 8,000 auxiliary infantry and between 4,000 and 5,000 auxiliary cavalry. The size and number of his legionary detachments are so uncertain that the full strength of his force has been variously estimated between 17,000 and 30,000. It was drawn up in battle order with the auxiliaries forming the front and their infantry in the centre. The legions were held in reserve in front of the camp: the glory would be the greater in Roman eyes if no citizen blood was shed.

The Britons had the advantage of the slope, as befitted the side that had chosen the ground, and placed their chariots in front of the main body. Agricola spread out his line and, sending away his own horse, led his auxiliaries into battle on foot. To lead in person was a gesture often made by generals in the past for the sake of morale. It emphasizes how little control a commander could exercise once a battle was under way. There was little point in holding back on occasions when real advantage could be gained from being seen to be in the van.

Tacitus reports Calgacus as giving a speech comparing British unity with what he likes to portray as the motley and unreliable nature of the Roman forces. He was right in pointing to the multi-ethnic character of the Roman army, but disingenuous in contrasting this with an alleged unity among his own forces, made up of Highland clans and, doubtless, fugitives from further south. He was wrong to assume no common cause, no merging of Roman and provincial, but he did point to a vital ingredient in the Roman army's effectiveness, its reputation for success. To some extent that success was based on fear, on a ferocious code of discipline, but, whatever the reason, revolts by units of non-Roman troops were rare. Discipline and training won battles and campaigns.

The battle of Mons Graupius fell into two stages. In the first, the preliminary exchange of missiles was followed by hand-to-hand fighting, ordered by Agricola so that the Batavian and Tungrian infantry, equipped, it would appear, in Roman fashion, could make use of their superior arms and training in close combat. At the same time the cavalry engaged and routed the British chariots and then turned to join the infantry. At this point the rearward sections of the British army slowly moved down the slope and began to encircle the Roman rear. This opened the second phase of the battle. On Agricola's orders, four squadrons of cavalry that had been held in reserve broke the British ranks and then rode round to take them from behind. The result was complete chaos on the British side. Tacitus wrote in triumph: 'Some 10,000 of the foe had fallen; our losses were 360, among whom was numbered Aulus Atticus, prefect of a cohort, whose youthful keenness for battle and the ardour of his horse had carried him deep amongst the enemy.'

It is perhaps more significant that two-thirds of the British army disappeared completely in the night, presumably back into the Highlands from which they had come. Next morning the Roman scouts could find no trace of them. These 20,000 angry men may have been the reason for the massive concentration of garrisons now to be established in that part of eastern Scotland north of the Forth. Alternatively, it may have been the prospect of being bottled up in the glens that had provoked the Britons to give battle in the first place, a battle that it was essential to Roman policy should be fought. It is difficult to estimate the point in the history of the Roman conquest of Britain at which long-term security made complete victory essential, if indeed it ever was. Certainly, Agricola's apparent intention to establish permanent occupation beyond the Tyne–Solway line must have made this battle vital, but it may go right back to the original decision not to stop with control of south-east England. Whatever the truth, Agricola's failure to destroy or capture such a large number of the fighting men of the northern enemy ought perhaps to be recognized as crucial in the history of Roman Britain.

Most of the elements by which the Highlands were to be controlled are now known. The system hinged on a new legionary fortress at Inchtuthil on the Tay. This was supported by auxiliary forts to the north-east at Cardean and Stracathro, and to the south-west at Fendoch, Strageath, Dalginross, Bochastle, and, south of Loch Lomond, on Drumquhassle Ridge. North of this was campaigning country. Agricola had continued his advance northwards after Mons Graupius, but despite Tacitus' assertion that all Britain had been conquered—*perdomita Britannia*—it is clear from his account that not all the operations Agricola had in mind were in fact carried out that season. Because it was late in the summer, the war could not be extended, and it is clearly implied that further operations in future years were a possibility. It was maybe in anticipation of these that Agricola now sent his fleet on a circumnavigation of Britain.

Perdomita Britannia et statim missa: 'Britain was completely conquered and immediately let go.' Tacitus is deliberately creating a picture of a province that was conquered and handed over safe and sound by Agricola to his successor, but was immediately let slip by the wicked Emperor Domitian. We have already seen that the description of total conquest was false—the truth of the second statement will bear examination. It should be noted that there is one complaint that Tacitus does not make. He does not say that Agricola was recalled too soon. It would spoil his picture if he implied that there was more to do. Agricola had had an unusually long run, and Tacitus' contemporary audience would know it. Instead, he implies that Domitian deliberately cheated Agricola of the coveted governorship of Syria that he had earned, and subsequently, out of malice, failed to appoint him to one of the great proconsulships, Africa or Asia. Tacitus' account of Agricola's death contains a hint of poisoning arranged by the emperor. For how long Agricola's dispositions in Caledonia were allowed to stand, however, there is an objective test in the archaeology. We know very little of the governors after the recall of Agricola to the death of Domitian in 96. He may have been succeeded by Sallustius Lucullus, to whom we shall return shortly. Whoever he was, it seems reasonably certain that Agricola's immediate successor had every intention of completing the permanent conquest of Scotland, and likely that the forts closing off the glens were actually constructed under him. Excavation has, certainly, demonstrated that Inchtuthil, Fendoch, and others were deliberately dismantled not long after construction. The numismatic evidence, however, proves that this did not happen *before* 86, whereas Agricola's governorship ended in 83 or 84.

The immediate reasons for the withdrawal of the legion stationed at Inchtuthil have been the subject of much discussion. Though it is not certain which legion occupied the fortress, it is most likely that it was the Twentieth that was beginning to move in when the order to dismantle came, which may not have been until as late as 88. Stationed at Chester, II *Adiutrix* had been transferred from Britain to Moesia by 92—probably in consequence of Domitian's Dacian problems (where the emperor faced a serious situation, two Roman generals having been defeated in quick succession)—possibly leaving as early as 85. It is not even certain that it left Britain directly from Chester (though the likelihood is that it did). The final withdrawal of II *Adiutrix* will have reduced the legionary garrison of Britain to three. A move back south by the Twentieth may have become imperative, even if at that time the reduction was not expected to be permanent. Equally, a shortage of auxiliaries may have been making permanent occupation of Scotland seem less feasible. In either case, the Twentieth probably moved into Chester at this point. Nevertheless, one factor indicates that military occupation north of the Forth–Clyde isthmus was not immediately surrendered. The concept of total occupation may have been given up or deferred, but a series of watch-towers discovered between Ardoch and Bertha—sometimes referred to as the 'Gask Frontier'—may still have been maintained for a time, perhaps as late as 90, though the dates of construction and abandonment are subject to debate. It is, indeed, not impossible that Agricola had done his work so well, that the Highlands were now so cowed, that larger numbers of troops appeared unnecessary. Under any interpretation of the evidence, therefore, it is not true to say that northern Scotland was given up immediately after Agricola's recall. When it did happen, moreover, there was no massive concentration of forces immediately to the south of the area from which the army had withdrawn. Pacification, we may presume, seemed sufficiently complete for control to be exercised at a distance, from a command centred probably on the large fort of Newstead in the Lowlands, as it was to continue to be into the early second century. Such peace in Scotland underlines the magnitude of Agricola's achievement in war, but it fails to support Tacitus' thesis against Domitian.

The withdrawal of the garrisoning legion from Inchtuthil is a certainty; the date of departure of II *Adiutrix*, as we have noted, is not. If the latter did not in fact occur until some time *after* the former, then there was a period, however short, when the concentration of legions in the main part of the province was restored to the same remarkably high level as before Agricola advanced into Scotland. It is not impossible that one consequence of such a concentration was to throw suspicion on to Sallustius Lucullus, for it is known he was executed around AD 90. The reason for his death was ostensibly that he had named a new lance after himself. This may have been the immediate cause, given the paranoiac atmosphere with which Domitian had by then surrounded himself, but the background was perhaps some imagined (or real) connection between troop movements in Britain and the unsuccessful conspiracy against the emperor in 89, led by Saturninus, legate of Upper Germany.

Early in the second century the long series of changes in the location of legions in Britain was over. Henceforth, for a century or more, there were three permanent fortresses, at Chester, Caerleon, and York, occupied at this time by the Twentieth, II *Augusta*, and the Ninth respectively. Two important developments in the last few years of the first century also had a bearing on the overall military situation: the foundation of two citizen colonies, almost certainly consisting of discharged legionary soldiers and indicating a period when immediate campaigning was not envisaged. The first was founded at Lincoln, on the site of the disused legionary fortress. Its precise date is uncertain, though it is certainly Flavian and subsequent to the transfer away of its legion by 78 at the latest. It is most unlikely that Tacitus would have failed to mention so prestigious a piece of work as the foundation of a colony if it had happened during Agricola's governorship.

It is therefore almost certain that it fell near to the end of Domitian's reign. It is possible that it took place in the governorship of Nepos (probably P. Metilius Nepos), who may have been appointed before Domitian's death, as he is mentioned as a recent incumbent of Britain on a *diploma*, an army veteran's certificate of citizenship, dated to AD 98.

At about the same time another colony was established, at Gloucester, also on the site of a former legionary fortress. It is noticeable that in both cases the new cities were established on land that had been within legionary territory. There is some evidence that such land normally reverted, perhaps unofficially, to the local civil authority when it was given up by the army, but this reoccupation by the state may have caused much less resentment than had the appropriation of the best tribal land by the colonists of Colchester half a century earlier. Moreover, there was riverine ground near Lincoln and Gloucester that could be reclaimed by Roman drainage methods, and may previously have been of little use to the locals. It is therefore quite possible that the bulk of the land redistributed to the colonists had not previously been settled by Britons. As a reserve of military strength and a centre of loyal influence, Colchester had been a failure, but this time the colonies were not only tactfully situated, they were walled. The imperial government had learnt its lesson.

It has seemed that a more precise date can be determined for Gloucester than for Lincoln, as this city bore the honorific title of 'Nervia' or 'Nerviana', referring to Domitian's short-lived successor Nerva. But we have to be cautious. Domitian was by then so unpopular that, after his death, his name was deliberately expunged from official records, following the formal process of *damnatio memoriae*. There is a distinct possibility that both Lincoln and Gloucester were planned, even if not actually inaugurated, as counterparts to the military changes in the north in the dozen or so years of Domitian's reign after Agricola's victories in the field. At Lincoln the fortress seems to have been kept on a care and maintenance basis after the removal of its garrison, probably early in Agricola's campaigns. At Gloucester the fortress seems to have been extensively refurbished for military use—according to numismatic evidence, after 87/8. This suggests an intermediate disposition of legions following the abandonment of Inchtuthil, but it would still leave some years of Domitian's reign for the foundation of colonies on sites that were in good order, perhaps as part of a broad plan to reorganize the province once final decisions about expansion or consolidation had been taken.

Until the conspiracy of Saturninus, the reign of Domitian had been stern but on the whole just. His provincial administration was particularly fair, and he vigorously suppressed abuses. Unfortunately, his personal inclination towards absolutism aroused opposition among the Roman aristocracy, and he had unwisely tended to ignore the senate as far as serious matters of state were concerned. At the same time, his use of his powers to draft into it many provincials and members of the equestrian order, an unpopular move, had important effects in accelerating the growth of an empire-wide senatorial class. From 88 he became more and more suspicious of individual senators, and from 93 this developed into a reign of terror. Finally, in 96 Domitian's own wife, Corbulo's daughter, in fear for her own life, led a conspiracy in concert with both praetorian prefects. This time the plot was real and the assassination successful.

The senate now came as close to restoring the Republic as they dared, by proclaiming the fairly elderly, but moderate and capable senator Marcus Cocceius Nerva as emperor. This marks the beginning of the period often known as 'the Five Good Emperors'. Lasting from AD 96 to 180, it is regarded, in many ways reasonably, as the golden age of the Roman empire. It is too simple a view to regard this solely as an outcome of a revulsion against the hereditary principle in choosing emperors, but it was a major element. The new pattern was for the emperor to mark out his successor during his lifetime, and usually for there to be an association between them in office. This allowed the measured choice of men of experience and moderation, likely to win acceptance among the upper classes, to whom they were personally well known. Yet even at the elevation of Nerva there were disquieting signs. The army was anything but happy at the loss of an emperor who had both shown military aptitude and raised their pay. The senate was unable to resist pressure for the execution of Domitian's murderers, and Nerva was more or less forced to indicate a military man as his successor at an early date. It was fortunate that his choice fell on Trajan, who had the confidence of the troops: it had been he who had suppressed the revolt of Saturninus. He bridged the parties of senate and army, and was careful to keep this balance. This was true, too, of his background. He was indeed patrician, but this had been due to his own father's rise to the consulship and appointment into the ranks of the patricians under Vespasian. Trajan himself had been born in Spain, where his father was a citizen of the Roman chartered town (*municipium*) of Italica, and his mother was Spanish. Vespasian had been the first emperor who, though Italian, had not come from one of the old senatorial families. Trajan, though Roman by citizenship and career, was the first with a provincial origin. This had been the background of Agricola, too: men like him could now aspire to the supreme position in the empire. The advantages of merging with the new imperial aristocracy were becoming increasingly obvious to ambitious provincials, and with the upward mobility that is an outstanding feature of Roman society, this attitude spread far beyond the leading families. In 98 the change became real, and Trajan unostentatiously but firmly assumed power, backed by army and civilians alike.

We can now see how Britain stood at the end of the first century, and assess the achievements of the Flavian regime in the island. From being a relatively small province encompassing only the south of England and part of Wales, and still shaken by the Boudiccan upheaval, Britain was now all but conquered. Quiet attempts had begun soon after the crushing of Boudicca to encourage Britons to settle down into Roman ways. By the time of Frontinus' governorship confidence was being reflected by major public works, and Agricola is credited with a programme to turn Britain into a region of the empire that would fully accept the Roman way of life. When one turns to the archaeology, it is possible to appreciate the monumental scale on which building construction was now proceeding, representing a real enlargement in the way in which people thought about public life.

Flavian propaganda liked to use architecture to depict a government devoted to the public, unlike the egocentric regime of Nero and his erratic predecessors. In Britain, while there may be doubts about attributing the Flavian flowering of 'temples, public squares, and private houses' to Agricola alone, the reality of the movement is clear. A few examples will show the pattern, and we may start with London. It is now clear that there were periods of intense building activity from about AD 70 to perhaps 130, much of it under the Flavian emperors. Some scholars have suggested that, by the mid-Flavian period, London's growth had caused it to be granted the status of a *municipium*, and its citizens had begun the construction of appropriate public buildings. Yet the scale and nature of the buildings may suggest something more. It is admittedly true that in the 70s London, like Verulamium and Cirencester, was provided with a forum, which was of modest size. Yet at some time after about AD 80 a governor's palace was built, and perhaps a little before the end of the century a military fort was added. The latter has generally been dated to Trajan's reign (98–117) or early in the reign of his successor, Hadrian. However, the discovery of an amphitheatre in 1987 that can almost certainly be associated with it and that is apparently of late first-century date strongly suggests that the origins of the fort itself go back at least to the beginning of Trajan's reign and quite believably as far as Domitian's. Indeed, the alignment of an early road towards the point at which the south gate of the stone fort was built has even suggested that the land had been in the possession of the army or some other official body for a very considerable time, perhaps even before London was sacked by Boudicca. Certainly, whatever their exact dates, both palace and fort were, by definition, imperial constructions, not civic. The fort, indeed, in being attached to a city, was a great rarity for the early Empire. It is just possible, but very unlikely, that it housed an 'urban cohort', one of the special units of gendarmerie otherwise only known outside Rome itself at Lyons and Carthage. Instead, its troops almost certainly included the legionaries and other men serving on the governor's staff and as his guard. It is clear that with the cessation of active campaigning in the north, the governor was normally going to be resident in the provincial capital. But other building was also under way in London. At around the same time a massive set of public baths was constructed near the palace, on Huggin Hill. But the most extraordinary development was the replacement of the recently completed forum by a vast new complex of forum and basilica, of which the latter is the largest yet discovered north of the Alps.

Outside London there were other spectacular developments

in the late first century. Before the end of Claudius' reign an early military establishment on the coastal site of Fishbourne, near Chichester, had already made way for a timber-framed villa. This was replaced in the 60s by the first stone villa, which was of an unusually high standard for that period in Britain. Sometime after AD 73 the enormous 'palace' itself was built, probably around 80, and its construction incorporated a great deal of expensive imported materials. It was bigger than the largest of the fourth-century villas found in Britain—the great age of the grand country house. In terms of the second half of the first century, it has been measured against other imperial houses and compared with Domitian's palace on the Palatine Hill in Rome, though perhaps the seaside villa attributed to Nero's wife Poppaea at the site known as Oplontis on the Bay of Naples is a better comparison for a house at that social level outside a city.

There is no doubt that, by the standards of the period, Fishbourne at its greatest extent would have been appropriate for a member of the imperial family or one of the great Italian senatorial clans. Whether it belonged, as has been vigorously argued, to the client king Cogidubnus, perhaps in his old age, is not proven but nor is it inherently unlikely. Alternatively, it is possible to think in terms of an official residence, perhaps matching the Flavian governor's palace in London. We know, for example, that two of the new grade of special legal commissioners introduced by Vespasian—*legati iuridici*—were on temporary assignments in Britain in the period immediately after AD 80. Both were senators of great distinction. One was Salvius Liberalis; the other was the outstanding jurist Javolenus Priscus. The latter had already held legionary commands by this time, and was to go on from this post to the consulship. Subsequently he held three major provincial governorships, including Syria and the most prestigious of all, the proconsulship of Africa, both posts of which Agricola himself was disappointed.

Fishbourne is so far *sui generis*, and we should not expect it to reflect a general trend in the countryside. Agricola's encouragement of the Britons to build houses in the Roman manner did not, at least as far as Tacitus' description goes, refer to the construction of villas, or 'country houses' in modern terms. Tacitus uses the word *domus*, the normal word for town houses, and we may be sure that this is what he meant. It reflects the stated objective of getting the Britons to come in from their scattered dwellings, become educated in Roman ways, and take part in public life, which in Roman terms was a city-based concept. It was important that leaders of the local communities should have a stake in the town, even if they retained houses on their country properties. No one would have dreamt of suggesting that they give up their country estates altogether, since the possession of land was an essential ingredient of being a Roman gentleman, but the city was the proper focus of life.

In the countryside of Roman Britain there are very many examples of farmsteads that changed very little from their pre-Roman appearance, and indeed continued thus throughout the Roman period. By far the largest part of the population was certainly engaged on the land throughout the period of Roman rule, and most people's lives were lived out in physical surroundings much like those of their Iron Age predecessors. On the other hand, there is a fair amount of archaeological evidence that, as the province recovered from the Boudiccan revolt, some country properties gradually began to be rebuilt in Roman style and to Roman standards of amenity, if in a fairly modest way. This was a process that seems to have gained considerable momentum in the Flavian period, and to be well established at the end of the first century and in the first half of the second. It has been suggested that, architecturally, developments occurred first in the country and only subsequently in the towns, but it is significant that such an indicator of wealth and taste as the provision of floor mosaics is confined almost exclusively to the towns in this period, not the villas. Even though many of the town buildings seem relatively simple in terms of structure, and many of them were primarily for trade and commerce, the very fact that British notables were becoming landlords of town properties, whether commercial or domestic, would mean that they were fulfilling the objectives of Roman policy by being drawn into urban life.

While it is important to see the last third of the first century and the beginning of the second as in many senses hanging together—as the period when conquest was largely completed and the province was organized on the broad lines that were to settle into the mould that determined its appearance for the next two centuries—the developments did not evolve, as we have seen, in an entirely steady progression. Indeed, there is one more point that needs examination before we leave the first century AD. It is noticeable how, within the margin of error of archaeological dating, it would be possible to place a substantial number of innovations just before the end of the century: the foundation of the colonies of Lincoln and Gloucester, for example; the settling of the pattern of legionary bases; the abandonment of permanent military occupation north of the Forth–Clyde line; and the primary phase of the replacement of the first forum and basilica in London by its vast successor. Something fairly big seems to be happening, and London perhaps gives us more than one clue. We have already seen how extraordinarily unusual the provision of a fort was in a city, even at the seat of a provincial governor. A further clue is to be found at Richborough, the site of the arrival of Claudius in Britain. At just the time we are now considering a massive triumphal arch was built there. There can be very little doubt that it was put up on the instructions of the Emperor Domitian to indicate that the conquest that had been started by Claudius was now regarded as completed. But if it is taken together with the unusual developments in London, it may also suggest more than the marking of successes in a distant province, even one in which Domitian's father, brother, uncle, and kinsman Cerialis had served with distinction. Domitian was only 45 when his rule was abruptly cut short. Richborough and London suggest an intended imperial visit: Domitian would have had every incentive to mark as publicly as possible that it was under his auspices that the enormously prestigious expansion of Roman domination across the Ocean started by Julius Caesar, revived by Claudius, and so strongly associated with his own family had been brought to a triumphant conclusion in his reign.

The probability that Domitian saw this stage in the history of Roman Britain in these terms must also make us wonder what effects his sudden demise had on the island. We have to remember here that we are trying to distinguish between short periods of time that are extremely difficult to determine archaeologically. Some of the developments that we have assigned to Domitian may in fact have occurred under Nerva or in the early years of

Trajan's reign. The latter was a great builder elsewhere in the empire, commissioning huge architectural and engineering projects notable both for the quality of their design and for the powerful sense of public utility that runs through them. Nevertheless, in Britain there is an overall impression of a pause, or at least consolidation. Certainly, we shall see widespread indications of renewed activity in the civil field at the time of the Emperor Hadrian's visit to Britain in 122. In the military sphere, the early years of Trajan's reign are marked by a general move to replace the timber buildings in forts and fortresses with stone. This was no doubt partly because the structures put up by Frontinus and Agricola now required extensive repairs, but it also implies the prospect of fairly stable military conditions. At Caerleon the process had already begun in AD 100, at Chester it was at least partly carried out after 102, and at York it took place either at the end of 107 or during 108. The same process is also observable at auxiliary forts. The army was settling down to be a garrison army, and in Britain campaigns were no longer the normal way of life. Military stations were not now to be thought of primarily as winter quarters, but as the year-round homes of permanent garrisons.

It is possible that the first of Trajan's appointments to the governorship of Britain was T. Avidius Quietus. P. Metilius Nepos had been governor in AD 98 under Nerva, having probably been appointed by Domitian, but he may have completed his term after Nerva's death. Quietus held the post until perhaps 100 or 101. His immediate successor was likely to have been L. Neratius Marcellus, who was certainly governor in 103. These men are of particular interest, for, like their contemporary Pliny the Younger, in whose letters they are recorded, they belonged to that group of prominent senators who were coming to terms with the permanence of the Principate and who supported Nerva and Trajan as the next best alternative to the restoration of the Republic. What we know of them characterizes exactly the spirit and practices of the governing class of their time. Their appearance in Britain, apparently one following the other, reflects the high prestige in which this governorship was currently held within the senatorial order.

The intellectual climate of the party now in power is typified by Quietus. In his youth he had been a member of the aristocratic

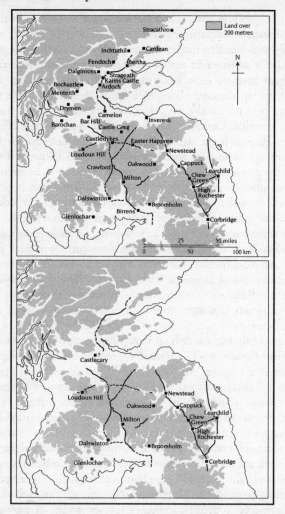

THE FIRST ROMAN WITHDRAWAL FROM SCOTLAND. By early in the second century all the military sites north of the Forth–Clyde isthmus (*above*) had been given up, and a smaller presence maintained in southern Scotland (*below*).

circle of Thrasea Paetus, the most distinguished representative of the traditionalist opposition to Nero and put to death by him. That circle had professed devotion to the old Republic, and their ideals were enshrined in the Stoic philosophy of the day, though many were ready to draw back from the extremes of open opposition in favour of survival or of a belief that the service of the state was best promoted by continuance in public life, however bad the emperor. Quietus' friendship with the historian Plutarch, and an apparent particular interest in Greece help to fill in the picture of this man. He was a personal friend of Pliny, in whose support he spoke in the senate when the latter was attempting to obtain justice for the surviving relatives of Helvidius Priscus, a family that had suffered much under the Flavians for continuing the senatorial opposition to the emperors.

Neratius Marcellus was also personally known to Pliny. The influence that the latter now wielded among the closest adherents of the new regime is clear. From Marcellus, Pliny was able to obtain a commission as a military tribune for his slightly younger contemporary Suetonius, the historian. Particularly interesting is the fact that this piece of patronage was not only clearly routine, but that, when Suetonius declined the opportunity to go to Britain, Pliny had no difficulty in transferring the post to someone whom Suetonius himself wished to advance. Thus we see a governor of Britain at this time not only able to make appointments in his army without prior reference to the emperor, but also quite content, as it were, to issue a friend with a blank cheque. It is, of course, true that such appointments often entailed little real responsibility, but in general the existence of such an apparently casual system only avoided causing the rapid military and administrative collapse of the Roman provinces because it was operated by a fairly close-knit ruling circle, made up of men of experience in government who could normally be relied upon not to promote hopeless candidates into positions of responsibility, if only to protect their own credibility. The weaknesses are obvious, and it is not surprising that imperial supervision of postings became tighter. However, so long as the emperors themselves continued to be drawn invariably from the same social group, the system was not unsuccessful in providing for the staffing of the empire.

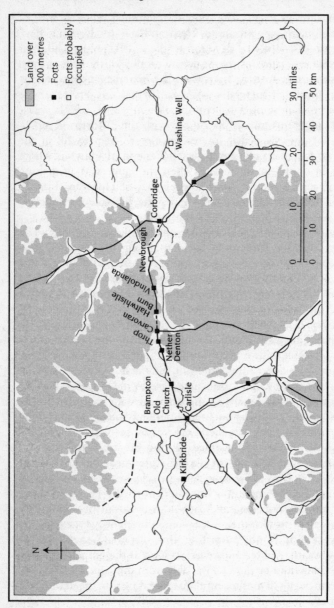

THE 'STANEGATE FRONTIER'. Under Trajan, after the abandonment of the already reduced military occupation of southern Scotland, the garrisons furthest north were those along the road known as the Stanegate between Corbridge and Carlisle, and to east and west of those places. However, the Stanegate was a defended link between the two main highways into Scotland, not a linear barrier.

It is a curious coincidence that among the fragments of writing-tablets found at the early fort at Chesterholm in Northumberland (generally referred to by its Roman name of Vindolanda) is one on which Marcellus' name occurs in what appears to be a draft of a private letter. Vindolanda, by a further coincidence, lay on the Stanegate, a road that took on new importance soon after AD 100. Indeed, it may well have been within Marcellus' governorship itself that a major change came over the northern frontier region. Some time in or around 100/5, Newstead was demolished and Cappuck, Glenlochar, High Rochester, Blakehope, and Corbridge forts were all burnt. It is possible that the burning of these forts was part of a strategic withdrawal precipitated by the need for troops for the great Dacian wars of 101-2 and 105-6. In excavation, the destruction of Newstead looked more like a military disaster than orderly withdrawal, but it has more recently been reinterpreted as evidence of systematic clearance by the military. Only at Corbridge does it still appear certain that the whole fort was fired, though we cannot be sure whether this was accidental, or a deliberate action by an enemy or a Roman commander forced to abandon his base in the face of hostile pressure. Opinion therefore remains divided on whether the abandonment of southern Scotland was due to enemy action or an imperial decision. Trajan's wars of conquest elsewhere, however, may well have been the reason why the ground that was lost or given up was not permanently reoccupied within his reign.

The Trajanic frontier thereafter seems in effect to have lain in the Tyne–Solway gap, through which the Stanegate ran. This east–west route had acted primarily as a link between the western high road to the north, through Carlisle, and the eastern one, Dere Street, where it crossed the road at Corbridge. Despite the uncertainties over the circumstances in which Scotland was given up by AD 100 or soon after, Roman Britain had attained what, in the long perspective of history, may seem like its natural boundary. This may not have seemed so at the time. Tacitus used the phrase 'statim missa', and left the reader with the impression that the recall of Agricola had allowed the total conquest of Britain to be thrown away by the jealous Domitian. Was he deliberately concealing the fact that Scotland had been finally evacuated in the reign of the hero-emperor Trajan under whom he was writing, whether through disaster or prudent withdrawal? The latter would not fit the image of an extender of the bounds of empire much better than the former. In the long run, however, the Tyne–Solway region was to prove the best location for a frontier that could be found.

7

HADRIANIC
BRITAIN

The death of Trajan in 117 marks a turning-point in Roman, indeed European, history. In Britain Trajan's reign had been a period of military withdrawal and consolidation, in sharp contrast to his expansion of the empire elsewhere. In Dacia and Mesopotamia his campaigns won whole new regions, and that alone is enough to explain why no forward policy was adopted in Britain. In many ways, Trajanic Britain foreshadows the general imperial strategy of Hadrian, who gave up the expansionist policy and abandoned Trajan's new territories in the east. In the military sphere, Hadrian concentrated on restoring order in the various parts of the empire where there was disaffection, and in consolidating the frontiers. A great part of his reign was spent in personal tours of inspection in the provinces. The renewed respect for the Principate that had been won by Nerva and Trajan permitted the new emperor to direct his energies away from Roman politics and towards the largest schemes of civil and military reconstruction. His constant presence among the frontier armies encouraged their loyalty. His keen interest in the provinces underlined the fact that he was the second provincial to come to the throne (from the same city as Trajan), and emphasized the oneness of the empire—or at least of its communities of Roman citizens, wherever they might be located within its territories. Italy was no longer to be regarded as mistress of the Roman world, with the provinces as her inferiors, and, though she always retained a special social status, she gradually lost her political privileges.

Hadrian was a very different person from Trajan. The latter had seemed a personification of all the old Roman virtues: a deliberately modest style of life; a devotion to the ancient ideals of the family; a grandeur in his public works, essentially based on utility; and a conviction that the glory of Rome was best served in the extension of the empire by wars of conquest. Hadrian shared Trajan's devotion to duty and his scale of vision, but broke away from the ideal of glory by military conquest. His personal tastes were for Greek culture, his character complex. His building works were as vast as Trajan's, but they were motivated as much by aesthetics as utility. His devotion to the Greek youth Antinous, and the extravagance of his grief at the young man's untimely death, reveal an emotional and restless nature. Though he did not share Trajan's affinity with the senate, a fact that soured his relations with society at Rome, he was probably the kind of ruler most suited to the needs of the empire at that time. Constant expansion and internal stresses in the recent past required that attention should now be concentrated on continuing and expanding the work of reforming the system, and welding the peoples within the Roman frontiers together into a single nation.

From this time forward the Roman empire effectively stopped expanding. From time to time there were limited movements that rationalized a frontier, but in practice the military emphasis was on defence. Looked at from the long perspective of history, it is sometimes argued that the loss of dynamism involved in the conversion from offence to defence was the first sign of 'decadence' in the empire. Yet it is important to note that the change was voluntary: it was half a century before serious pressure from barbarian peoples beyond the frontiers began to manifest itself. The immediate effect was three-quarters of a century of profound peace in most corners of the empire, and the consequent development of its prosperity and its institutions to their highest peak. The achievement of peace and restrained government over so huge an area for so long is something that few statesmen in world history have to their credit.

It should not be imagined, however, that there was any change of heart among Romans at large on their nation's role in the world. By his insensitivity towards the Jews, even Hadrian could show that he conceived Rome's task as the extension of the classical way of life to the whole empire, not the governing of the Roman world in terms of a multitude of nations with equally

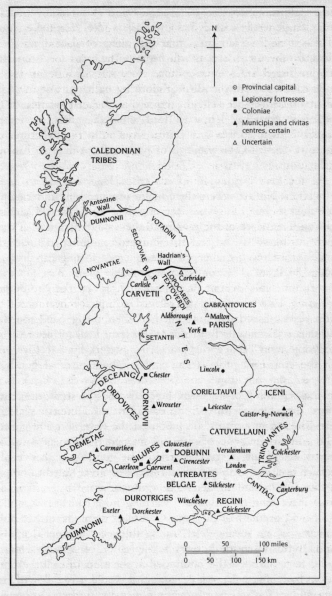

N

- ⊙ Provincial capital
- ■ Legionary fortresses
- ● Coloniae
- ▲ Municipia and civitas centres, certain
- △ Uncertain

CALEDONIAN TRIBES

Antonine Wall

DUMNONII

VOTADINI

SELGOVAE

NOVANTAE

Hadrian's Wall

B R I G A N T E S

Carlisle

CARVETII

LOPOCARES

Corbridge

TEXTOVERDI

GABRANTOVICES

Aldborough

△ Malton

York ■

PARISI

SETANTII

DECEANGLI ■ Chester

Lincoln ●

ORDOVICES

CORNOVII

CORIELTAUVI

ICENI

▲ Wroxeter

▲ Leicester

Caistor-by-Norwich ▲

DEMETAE

CATUVELLAUNI

▲ Carmarthen

SILURES

Gloucester ●

DOBUNNI

Verulamium ▲

TRINOVANTES

Colchester ●

Caerleon ■

Caerwent ▲

▲ Cirencester

London ●

ATREBATES

BELGAE ▲ Silchester

CANTIACI

Canterbury ▲

DUROTRIGES

Winchester ▲

REGINI

▲ Chichester

Exeter ▲

Dorchester ▲

DUMNONII

| 0 | 50 | 100 miles |
| 0 | 50 | 100 | 150 km |

SECOND-CENTURY BRITAIN (lesser towns and forts not shown).

valid cultures. Nor was carrying forward this task by glorious conquest generally regarded as an obsolete ideal. On the contrary, Britain itself saw Hadrian's immediate successor launching a new forward movement, and it will be important not to assume that this was merely to achieve a more economical frontier or to deal with a local difficulty with neighbouring barbarians. It was force of circumstance that kept the empire as the first quarter of the second century had left it. Indeed, one may question whether Hadrian's own decisions to retreat from military adventures did not owe more to the pressure of circumstance than to his own inclinations.

At the very beginning of his reign Hadrian was in severe difficulties. Not only were there major insurrections in the empire to suppress, but his own succession had been in odd circumstances. The peace of the empire in the second century has often been attributed to the fact that emperors nominated their own successors. However, there were suspicions that Trajan had not named Hadrian. The rumour was probably groundless, but there was considerable discontent, particularly among the late emperor's most senior generals. An alleged conspiracy by four of the most distinguished ex-consuls led to their being condemned in the senate and promptly executed. Hadrian had not yet returned to Rome, and blamed the praetorian prefect for excessive zeal. All the emperor's protestations and lavish gestures of goodwill, however, did not dispel the suspicions. This was a black mark on the beginning of his reign, especially for the senatorial aristocracy, the chief victim of the dark days of Domitian's closing years and the group that still produced the governors and generals who administered the empire and formed the society to which the provincial upper classes aspired. The good times that seemed to have returned with Nerva and Trajan were revealed to be precarious. Peace and moderate government were in fact to continue for a long time, but the warning note had been sounded.

The 'Conspiracy of the Four Consulars' reminds us that ambition was by no means dead among the most influential men in the empire, and raises the very real question of whether Hadrian could have afforded the continued acquisition of military reputations by leading senatorial generals that would have followed from continuing Trajan's expansionary policy by further unnecessary wars. Moreover, to deal with the widespread provincial disturbances and, at the same time, to launch new foreign conquests would have meant increasing the army very considerably. It is not surprising that Hadrian followed Augustus' advice to Tiberius to maintain the empire within its existing borders. Yet one remembers that Augustus' advice was quite contrary to his own ambitions and those of his class.

The political executions and the subsequent moves to placate public feeling were, however, sufficiently successful for Hadrian, unlike any emperor before him, to spend a very large part of his reign away from Rome. His protracted tours of inspection and reform in the provinces are of major importance, not least in Britain, where they left their mark on civil and military affairs alike. These absences also established that the *de facto* capital of the empire was wherever the emperor might be, that the empire could be run from outside Rome and Italy, not just for short periods but for years at a time. Combined with Hadrian's intense interest in the welfare of the provinces, this accelerated the process by which the provincials came to identify with the empire. A major step had been taken in creating a unified governing class, and, on a wider front, the changes looked forward to the almost universal extension of Roman citizenship to the free inhabitants of the empire at the beginning of the next century.

At the commencement of Hadrian's reign, however, Britain was one of the places where all was not well. When, in the course of one of his early tours, the emperor arrived in Britain in 122, the province had recently been the scene of serious warfare, probably during the governorship of Q. Pompeius Falco (118–22). This was probably caused by invasion from outside the province, though the epigraphic evidence is not entirely clear. It is also possible that there was collusion with rebels inside the province, of which a fourth-century description of Hadrian's Wall— that it was intended to divide the barbarians from the Romans —may be a distorted echo. The governor had brought the situation back under control, and the emperor bent his mind to seeing that this sort of trouble should not happen again.

In 122, the year of his visit, Hadrian appointed his friend Aulus Platorius Nepos governor, and it seems likely that emperor and governor were closely associated in the design of the new frontier.

It is almost certain that Hadrian brought a new legion with him, VI *Victrix*, since it is recorded on what was probably one of the first elements of the great building operations now put in hand. Whether the Sixth was brought specifically for the Wall project or as a replacement for IX *Hispana* is not known. It is no longer thought that the unlucky Ninth disappeared from the army lists while still in Britain, whether destroyed or disbanded, since there is some evidence pointing to its continued existence beyond the present date and to its presence on the Rhine. Whether there was a short period when the legionary establishment was reduced to two legions depends on the date accepted for the transfer of the Ninth. There is even a possibility that the Ninth returned for a while, temporarily restoring the legionary garrison to four during the period when there was great pressure on military resources from the building programme on the Wall. It has been conjectured that it was eventually lost in the east, long after its final withdrawal from Britain.

The new frontier works, on the construction of which the Sixth, the Second, and the Twentieth legions were employed, were the most elaborate in the Roman world, and were much modified in the course of building. It was a means of exercising physical control, not a line marking out Roman territory from barbarian. The presence of outpost forts shows that imperial authority went beyond the Wall. From the German frontier, we know that the law could recognize actual possession of land beyond the physical barrier, since imperial estates are recorded on both sides of the military line, and we may be sure that Rome claimed authority at least as far as the empire could actually exercise rule, whether directly or through client princes. Hadrian's innovation in military thinking was to add a linear barrier to the system of forts and watch-towers linked by a road that had been developed in Germany under Domitian. Hadrian had introduced a continuous palisade on that frontier immediately before coming to Britain, and subsequently constructed linear barriers in Raetia and probably, though the dating is uncertain, Africa. None would have withstood a determined attack, but all, when used in conjunction with patrols, would have allowed an effective degree of control on movement.

Hadrian's Wall took advantage of the fortunate configuration of the ground of the isthmus between the Tyne and the Solway. The valleys of the Tyne, Irthing, and Eden rivers form an almost continuous trough from sea to sea, near the bottom of which ran the Stanegate road on which the existing forts lay. The new line followed the northern edge of this Tyne–Solway gap; for about two-thirds of its distance a ridge gives a generally commanding view northwards, and at its centre the ground rises to the heights of the basalt cliffs known as the Whin Sill. Only at the western end of the Wall was it thought necessary in Hadrian's day to provide outpost forts to the north. It seems likely that these were not primarily outposts in the accepted sense, but garrisoned a part of the land of the conquered Brigantes that lay beyond what was physically the most convenient line for the Wall.

The order in which the various elements of the system were built and the modifications introduced has been deduced from excavation and from their relation to one another. Specialist opinion on the details changes from time to time as research on this intensely studied frontier continues, but the broad outline can be stated. The original scheme was to provide a lightly held line forward of the main garrisons. The Wall itself (the 'curtain', or continuous, wall) was begun at the eastern end, and was originally planned to be in stone, 10 feet (3.1 m.) wide and 12–15 feet (3.7–4.6 m.) high. It is not clear whether there was a continuous platform, or wall-walk, along the top, or any form of parapet. Beyond the River Irthing it was to be in turf. At the west end of the line sandstone replaces limestone as the local rock: the latter provided not only superior building stone but—probably more importantly—the lime mortar required in construction. The Turf Wall was 20 feet (6.2 m.) wide and perhaps 12 feet (3.7 m.) in height. In front of the Wall was a ditch, of varying width and depth. The patrolling garrison used small forts at intervals of one Roman mile, known today as 'milecastles', with two turrets between each pair. The turrets throughout were in stone from the beginning, the milecastles on the Turf Wall only being in earth and timber. The broad foundation of the stone wall was carried through to the Irthing, and the full height of the 'Broad Wall' was carried out as far as the crossing of the North Tyne. Stone bridges were to carry the Wall across the North Tyne and, at the Irthing, over the river to meet the beginning of the Turf Wall.

With one continuous base laid, the milecastles and turrets were constructed to provide shelter and look-out positions for patrols protecting the working parties at this early stage.

At their western end the frontier works were carried down the Cumbrian coast, where crossings to and from the shore of south-west Scotland were quite easy. There was no curtain wall, here, but the same scheme of forts and minor works, known nowadays as 'mile-fortlets' and 'towers' to distinguish them from the corresponding structures on the Wall proper, has been discovered. Though at least one of these forts was being built in or after 128, it is thought that the coastal stretch was part of the original plan. A pair of shallow parallel ditches has been noted at several points along the first section, beyond the end of the continuous curtain wall at Bowness-on-Solway, apparently connecting the towers and fortlets as far as Cardurnock on the River Wampool, and at one point associated with stakes or a palisade. Despite several attempts at repair, this particular work seems to have been abandoned within the Hadrianic period in the face of coastal flooding, but it suggests that there had been an intention to carry on the continuous barrier. Elsewhere in the empire, however, there were frontiers on which water was employed as the continuous line, supplemented by forts and other works, as on parts of the Rhine and the Danube.

The first major modifications were introduced while the central sector of the Wall was being built. The width of the curtain wall was reduced to 8 feet (2.5 m.), and—a much greater change of plan—the fighting garrisons were brought up on to the Wall. The forts of the Stanegate line were in some cases abandoned. At certain of the new forts, for example, Chesters and Housesteads, the foundations of the Broad Wall and the demolished remains of a turret have been found beneath the superimposed fort.

The reduction in gauge (the 'Narrow Wall') may have been made possible by a change in the composition of the core, giving a greater strength for a given thickness, but a direct design connection has not been satisfactorily demonstrated. It may rather have been due to a need for economy and speed of completion. Eventual replacement of the Turf Wall by stone may have been intended from the beginning: when it came, it was mainly to a gauge of 9 feet (2.8 m.) that has been called the 'Intermediate

Wall'. Beyond Newcastle, to the east, there was one more fort, which lay at Wallsend. On grounds of spacing between the forts, this fits in with the first decision to move the garrisons up to the Wall, but the curtain wall itself was constructed to the Narrow gauge and seems to have been built late in the sequence of construction. It was carried on beyond the fort and down to the Tyne.

Most of the modifications seem to have been decided upon, and substantially carried out, during the governorship of Platorius Nepos. It is reasonable to assume that the main purposes of moving the garrisons on to the Wall were to allow rapid deployment of troops along and in front of it, and to facilitate the everyday patrolling and maintenance of the works. The fact that the first series of forts to be added to the Wall were designed so that three out of four of their main gates opened on to ground to the north of the Wall line (other than where the lie of the land made this impossible) implies that actual fighting in close proximity to the Wall was now anticipated. The Wall was being converted from a simple patrolled barrier to a position from which forward attacks could be launched. The decision to move the garrisons was not one to be taken lightly. As well as major problems of redesign and rescheduling, it involved a substantial amount of demolition of work completed or half-done. Commanders of units in the Stanegate forts, however, must have realized very early in the first phase of the Wall that the situation was highly unsatisfactory. The day-to-day manning, supplying, and upkeep of the Wall itself must have been extremely awkward, and probably weighed much more heavily on the officers on the spot than distant prospects of battle conditions in some hypothetical war. If planning errors on the largest scale were not a commonplace of life in complex civilizations, it would be surprising that this was not realized when the Wall was first designed. On the other hand, we could perhaps give Hadrian and Platorius Nepos the benefit of the doubt, and assume that they had decided to tackle the task in stages—deliberately choosing to wait and see whether it was possible to avoid moving the garrisons, even if it meant expensive alterations if the gamble did not come off. One may wonder, too, whether they were avoiding trouble with the troops. Some everyday tasks may have become easier when the garrisons

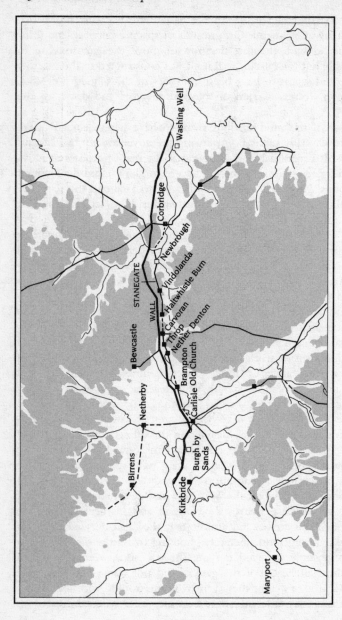

HADRIAN'S WALL. The first intention was to house most of the troops in existing forts on the Stanegate line, with the linear barrier only lightly held by milecastles and turrets. Outpost forts at the western end, however, indicate that difficulties were already anticipated there.

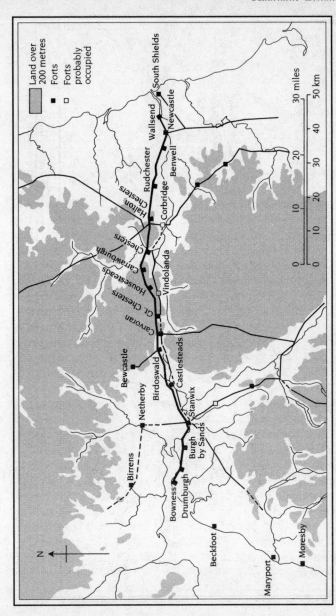

HADRIAN'S WALL. By the latter part of Hadrian's reign, the linear Wall itself had received its first permanent garrisons, and these had then been augmented by a second series of forts. Some garrisons still remained to secure the Stanegate and territory southwards.

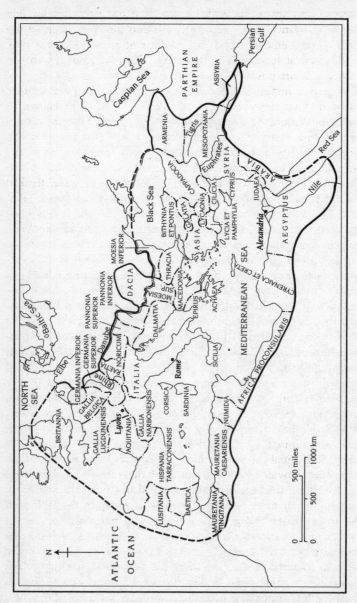

THE ROMAN EMPIRE AT THE ACCESSION OF HADRIAN.

were moved on to the Wall, but the men had been comfortably settled in relatively sheltered forts well into the valleys behind the Wall. In the end, however, the balance of advantage must have been clear, at least to senior officers. They, of course, were on relatively short postings.

A further modification, representing an enormous expenditure of labour, was the addition of the rearward earthwork known to us as the Vallum. It swerves from a direct route to avoid certain of the forts, and was therefore certainly constructed after the decision had been taken to move the main forces up on to the line. It was a continuous ditch 20 feet (6.2 m.) wide and 10 feet (3.1 m.) deep, with a flat bottom 8 feet (2.5 m.) wide, flanked on either side by 20-foot mounds set 30 feet (9.2 m.) back. This huge work cut a swathe 120 feet (36.9 m.) broad. It was constructed without breaks, unlike the ditch in front of the Wall, which was omitted where conditions made it difficult to cut or where a steep drop rendered it unnecessary. The Vallum was evidently deemed essential throughout its length. Its purpose has been much disputed, but the most likely is that it was to prevent unauthorized access to the military zone, reducing the risk of damage to official buildings outside the forts and the theft of bulky stores and equipment, such as wagons, which had to be left outside. It would also have provided safe camping grounds for units and supply columns in transit along the Wall, obviating the need to construct temporary camps for what must have been a very frequent event. Crossing from north to south and vice versa was, conversely, severely restricted. Apart from the major highways that traversed the Wall system just north of Carlisle and Corbridge, passages through the Vallum were only provided opposite the forts. Substantial gateways made strict control possible. Causeways were also provided south of some of the milecastles, but these gave only on to the south berm and did not penetrate the south mound. Their function was to provide access from the Wall itself for maintenance and perhaps for patrolling purposes.

The most extraordinary feature of the Vallum is undoubtedly its immense scale. It reflects the extravagant ideas abroad at the time in imperial circles, and there can be little doubt that it was intended to impress and overawe. If we may also assume that its purpose was connected with the day-to-day working of the Wall system, then it emphasizes the seriousness with which pressure from the south was viewed. There is no need to suppose a threatened assault—more the extreme nuisance value of harassment from a local tribal population with a tradition of raiding and disorder.

Platorius Nepos' record for expenditure on frontier works cannot often have been matched by a Roman governor anywhere. He eventually fell out of favour with the emperor, perhaps for this reason, though it may have happened some time after the end of his governorship. Expenditure on construction certainly grew and grew. The assessment of requirements seems consistently to have been faulty, and the magnitude of the modifications very considerable. Yet the errors of judgement may have been Hadrian's own, and he did not like his acumen in such matters to be questioned. Trajan's brilliant architect Apollodorus was exiled on a mere pretext—eventually executed—for doubting Hadrian's architectural abilities. Money was perhaps not at the heart of the displeasure that fell on Nepos: Hadrian was incredibly lavish on building projects, as the numerous new cities bearing his name, his enormous villa at Tivoli, and the elaborate monuments to his sorrow at the death of Antinous most emphatically testify. Nepos' tour of duty in Britain may have been cut short, but even that is uncertain, for his replacement (by a governor whose name we do not know) was not before the autumn of 124 at the earliest, and may have been considerably later.

The appointment of Sextus Julius Severus as governor in about 131 has been thought by some scholars to imply that there had been serious fighting that required the presence of one of Hadrian's most distinguished generals. This might have been provoked by the cutting of traditional routes between people to the north and south of the Wall. Reconsideration of the coin types of Hadrian's reign, and epigraphic references to a British expeditionary campaign suggest that the historian Fronto's reference to substantial casualties in Britain may refer to this period rather than to fighting at the beginning of Hadrian's reign. Nevertheless, a command of an army of the size of that in Britain is precisely what one would expect at the stage in his career that Severus had reached. What is certain is that in 132 or 133 he was transferred to deal with the extremely serious revolt of Bar Kochba in Judaea.

To succeed Severus in Britain, Hadrian drafted in P. Mummius Sisenna. It is possible that he was responsible for carrying out some of the latest stages in the development of the Wall under Hadrian. One large-scale change was the rebuilding in stone (to the Narrow gauge) of the Turf Wall from the Irthing to the 'Red Rock Fault' five miles to the west, where the limestone ends and red sandstone becomes the local rock. This reconstruction certainly occurred after the main garrisons were moved up on to the line, as is demonstrated at Birdoswald. There the new stone wall was carried on a fresh line in front of the old Turf Wall, which Birdoswald fort had already spanned and obliterated, and was taken up to the front corner of the fort, which had previously projected beyond the line of the curtain wall. This last fact also demonstrates that the rebuilding happened after the idea of having three of the main gates of a fort beyond the line of the curtain wall, clearly adopted when the fort garrisons were being moved up on to the Wall, had already been abandoned. But Birdoswald was not alone: the change in policy also affected the form another modification took. It had become apparent that there were sections that were still difficult to control. This was tackled by adding extra forts. That work on this had already started is demonstrated at Carrawburgh, which has yielded an inscription of Julius Severus, and whose position in the order of events is made clear by the fact that it overlies the filled-in Vallum, which here had run parallel to, and close behind, the Wall.

It will be clear by now that the history of the building of the Wall under Hadrian is extremely complicated and extends over a substantial period. We cannot be confident that we understand it all yet. In judging it, it is only fair to recall that much of the system represented ideas that were new and untried, at least on this scale. In the end it looks as if practical considerations of manning, operation, and administrative convenience forced reappraisal of many elements in the scheme. Nevertheless, the overall conception proved effective in the long run, and Hadrian's choice of a frontier here, despite the fluctuations over the centuries, proved decisive.

In the short run its primary effect was to divide native from native, for the better maintenance of order. It facilitated the establishment of settled conditions behind the Wall, allowing the economy of the tribal peoples to the south to expand. The development of a heavily settled agricultural area in the Cumbrian plain has long been recognized. The presence of so many troops, and in due course their families and a trading community, doubtless did much to stimulate the economy. The largest fort on the Wall was at Stanwix, a northern suburb of Carlisle, where the western route into Scotland ran through the Hadrianic line. The commander of this unit was the most senior on the Wall, though the relationship between the various unit commanders is uncertain, and it has not been proved, though it is often assumed, that they reported to Stanwix. Stanwix certainly lies not far off the centre of the system considered as a whole, from Ravenglass on the western sea to Wallsend in the east. The surrounding area certainly seems to have developed eventually into a civil *civitas*, with its own city at Carlisle.

While it is anachronistic to talk of the Wall as having an economic rather than a military purpose, the role of the army in the second century became, through force of circumstance, essentially the keeping of order, both internally and against foreign invaders. It was rarely used now to win new territory, but it still served to further the careers of the upper and, in many cases, the lower classes. From time to time it gratified the personal ambitions of emperors for glory. It had not yet evolved into a largely self-sufficient institution that could make its own interests paramount in the Roman state. Hadrian's decisions to eschew further conquest and to employ this loyal army to establish the strongest possible frontiers gave Roman Britain a crucial period of stability in which to consolidate the foundations already laid down.

The Flavian period in Britain had been marked by spectacular advances in Romanization, but the great public buildings and the widespread adoption of Roman fashions were mostly novel developments in a province of which much had until recently been in savage rebellion and was still in the process of being brought to heel. As a consequence, some Flavian initiatives may have been stillborn, for example (though the exact interpretation is uncertain) at Wroxeter. It was not until Hadrian's visit to Britain that a new start was made there: the great dedication inscription of AD 129–30 that the *civitas Cornoviorum* erected over the entrance to the newly completed forum leaves us in no doubt as to the purpose or date of that structure. It is reasonable to assume that Hadrian's visit was as much a spur to civil development in Britain as it was to military. It is also reasonable to observe that, just as it took most of the decade and many changes to complete the work on the Wall, much the same may have happened to the civil enterprises he set in motion. Indeed, even though we know that he sometimes directly assisted civil works, we may suspect that, with local supervision and at least partly local financing, construction for civil purposes could take longer than military. Thus it is necessary to be aware that the results of Hadrian's interventions in the affairs of Britain may not appear in the archaeological record until the end of his reign or after.

In the case of the great second forum basilica in London, where one may reasonably suspect direct imperial involvement, the sheer scale of the enterprise probably dictated a lengthy timescale for each phase of the construction. On the other hand, the presence or absence of official enthusiasm does seem to have affected progress. We have already seen that the dating of the first phase is consistent with a decision emanating from Domitian. This phase was completed, and the main hall and apse were brought into use. However, there then seems to have been a pause, and distinct signs that the remainder of the site was neglected for some time. We seem to be seeing the same phenomenon here as elsewhere at this period. It is significant that, when work resumed, there were substantial changes in plan, indicating something of a new start rather than simple continuation. The dating for this new phase indicates commencement at around AD 120 and completion in about 130. This is entirely consistent with a start linked to Hadrian's visit to Britain in 122—in anticipation of it perhaps, or as a consequence of his seeing the state of the site. One may at least note how unlikely it is that London showed no consequences of his presence. It is certainly believable that a massive masonry monumental arch found close to the Huggin Hill public baths and the governor's palace ought to be associated with Hadrian. Elsewhere, there is further evidence for renewed enterprise in the cities. Leicester's impressive forum was being built at the end of Hadrian's reign, and Caistor-by-Norwich also received its city centre under him, though on a much smaller scale, as befitted a *civitas* that had been severely retarded by its great rebellion in the previous century.

In the countryside villas flourished and increased, and a more uniform spread of Romanization can be observed. In both town and country the adoption of Roman ways and tastes and the increasing complexity of local and central administration meant a growth in service industries and occupations. This brought in more and more Romans on tours of duty to fill official posts at every level, and Romanized people from many corners of the empire came to do trade and business. It also opened up opportunities for larger numbers of locals from further and further down the social scale. The countryside was directly affected by industries that depended on natural resources—for example, iron deposits or potters' clay—for in many ways industry was a rural rather than an urban phenomenon in the ancient world, particularly in the case of those industries involved in large-scale production. There can be no doubt that the development of a monetary economy and the multiplication of opportunities for marketing output had a profound effect on rural economies and on the involvement of the rural population in the Roman way of life. Archaeologically, this is particularly noticeable in the immediate neighbourhood of towns and in rural settlements close to lines of communication such as roads, for the density of the material signs of Roman culture often tails off significantly the further away one proceeds from centres and routes of distribution.

There is at least one remote rural area, however, where direct intervention by Hadrian is highly likely to have occurred, and on a very large scale. Interestingly, it is a region where apparently simple rural settlements produce an exceptionally high yield of Roman pottery and other small finds. The emperor is known to have had a lively commitment towards solving the problem of cultivated land within the empire that had for one reason or another been abandoned. The same problem was to be particularly acute in the late Empire. Research in the Fenland of East Anglia has thrown light on an analogous situation, where land that had not been available for settlement for a long time because of flooding, but was potentially very productive, was becoming accessible again, probably due to natural changes in the relative level of land and sea in the region of the Wash. There is relatively little late Iron Age material from the area, and it was only in Flavian times that there was a trickle of Roman settlement, other than on one or two exceptional sites. In the second quarter of the second century, however, there was a very large influx of population, associated with 'straight-line' features—waterways, drove-roads, and some long-distance boundaries—that indicate public works. The settlements themselves seem at first sight haphazard, but their form and siting is largely dictated by the innumerable natural watercourses, and there are clear signs that at least the broad areas of settlement were determined by a central authority. The nature of the settlement was part farming (chiefly pastoral rather than arable), part industrial (largely salt production). The likelihood is that the Hadrianic government recognized the opportunity that small-scale private enterprise had seized in the latter part of the first century, and decided to exploit it on a grand scale, with the emperor's authority if not at his direct command. The probability of a government initiative has been much strengthened by the discovery of an extraordinary complex of buildings of Hadrianic date at Stonea Grange, on a gravel island in the peat near March. Its principal function was almost certainly as an administrative centre. It may have been intended to grow into a town, perhaps another deliberately founded 'Forum Hadriani', as in the Netherlands. However, architecturally, its most striking feature was a great tower-like building of Italian type that must have been visible from far across the Fens. It may be more than a coincidence that this was built at the most likely location of Ostorius Scapula's victory over the Iceni in AD 47. The Fenland development is certainly consistent with the breadth of vision possessed by Hadrian, and one could believe that the enormously elaborate and permanent new frontier of the Wall would require an equally permanent and regular source of supplies of just the sort that the Fens could provide. The fact that many of the settlements went out of use after only a short time was almost certainly caused by renewed drainage problems that it may have been impossible to foresee. On the other hand, the Wall has already shown how spectacular schemes of the Hadrianic period could require expensive modification, and leaves one with doubts about the judgement of the men responsible.

In a way, the early abandonment of many of these Fenland settlements is also symbolic of the attitude of the succeeding regime to Hadrian's work in Britain. The accession of a new emperor was almost immediately to bring changes that must have surprised the people who had spent two decades laboriously constructing what they must have assumed was to be the permanent framework within which the governors of Britain were henceforth to operate, the frontier and military system on which their administration would largely hinge, and within which the civil province would continue to develop. But a few might have had a suspicion that the death of such an unusual Roman emperor as Hadrian would bring a return to more conventional ways of thinking at the level where the highest policy decisions were taken.

8

THE ANTONINE
FRONTIER

In 136, two years before his death, Hadrian had prepared for the succession by adopting one of the consuls for that year, Lucius Ceionius Commodus, under the name of L. Aelius Caesar. However, the latter's own premature death forced a new choice on the emperor. This time he settled upon the man whom we know as Antoninus Pius, a distinguished member of the senate who had acquired a reputation for honesty and devotion to duty. He had been a consular since 120, and towards the end of Hadrian's reign he became a member of the emperor's *consilium*, the advisory committee that was analogous to the group of senior friends on whom Roman magistrates relied for counsel. Hadrian had made the *consilium principis* more formal than before, and there can be no doubt that Antoninus' long career in the public service, and his closeness to the emperor towards the end, gave him intimate knowledge of the workings of the empire and of Hadrian's own policies in matters of state. In the emperor's last year Antoninus had largely administered the empire on Hadrian's behalf. He thus came to the throne exceptionally well prepared. To extend the principle of adoptive succession further, Hadrian had also required Antoninus to adopt both Marcus Aurelius, nephew of Antoninus' wife Faustina, and Lucius Verus, son of the original intended successor, L. Aelius. Hadrian was making sure that there would be no repetition of the uncertainty over his own elevation.

It may, nevertheless, have been the respect in which Antoninus was held by the senate that ensured his untroubled accession in 138. This respect he retained throughout his life. The exact reasons for, and the significance of, the title of 'Pius' bestowed on him by that body are uncertain, but it reflects their recognition of his devotion to the Roman state, the quality that Roman moralists liked to think of as the mark of the ancient figures of the Republic. Though Antoninus, too, came from a provincial family, Gallo-Roman on both sides, his father and mother had been of consular stock, and he was himself a great landowner in Italy. He preferred to live in the villas on these estates as much as possible, and, unlike Hadrian, showed no sign of wanting to travel the empire.

The respect and affection in which he was held by the members of the senate—and the fact that he so clearly seemed one of them—allowed him unobtrusively to continue the policy of strengthening the grip of the imperial administration on the empire. The measures he took to stop abuses by equestrian procurators and by freedmen were doubtless popular with senate and provinces alike, while conducive to good government. His tendency to keep efficient provincial governors in office for longer periods was perhaps more difficult to reconcile with senatorial opinion, for it reduced the opportunities for promotion in the senatorial career. Yet it may have been welcomed by some individual senators, and undoubtedly assisted continuity in provincial administration.

Antoninus' foreign policy was deliberately unadventurous, and in general it followed Hadrian's line of resisting expansion of the empire. Unlike Hadrian, however, he largely avoided grandiose projects and he had a keen eye for financial economy, while at the same time engaging in considerable building operations. It was Hadrian's memory, indeed, that gave Antoninus some of his most difficult problems. It proved not at all easy to persuade the senate to proclaim the deification of his predecessor, a clear sign that the old resentments had not died with him. It may also help to explain Antoninus' surprising change of imperial policy in Britain, the one notable example in his reign of deliberate expansion by war. One might have expected that, even though Hadrian's Wall had been immensely costly to construct, with the modifications completed the expenditure would have been written off and the new system would have been allowed to settle down. In fact, Antoninus' decision on the British frontier was as dramatic and perhaps as sudden as Hadrian's own disavowal of Trajan's conquests in the east.

It may have been one of the new emperor's first acts in office to appoint to the governorship of Britain the energetic Q. Lollius Urbicus, previously governor of Lower Germany. He is found as early as 139 reconstructing the base at Corbridge, where Agricola's old road to the north crossed the Tyne. This is a sure sign of renewed interest in Scotland, for, as in Agricola's day, it made an ideal point from which to prepare for a campaign, and it permitted the preliminary work to be done without disrupting the routine of the Wall garrisons. Something large was afoot. The Greek topographer Pausanias, writing in the same century, says that Antoninus Pius never willingly made war: it is possible that the pressures that had led to the strengthening of the Hadrianic frontier had reached such a level by now that a drive into southern Scotland would have been justified on purely military grounds. In 140 Urbicus was still building at Corbridge; by the end of 142 or the beginning of 143 coins announced a victory in Britain. The reoccupation of southern Scotland therefore occurred between these dates. That this victory was in a Scottish campaign is supported by the statement in the fourth-century collection of imperial biographies known as the *Historia Augusta* that Antoninus Pius 'conquered the Britons through the agency of the governor, Lollius Urbicus, and having driven off the barbarians built another wall in turf'. It is to this turf wall across the Forth–Clyde isthmus, independently dated by building inscriptions to the reign of Antoninus, that we must now turn.

Two of these inscriptions record the involvement of Lollius Urbicus. We may therefore suppose that the project was started in 143 at the latest, for it seems likely that Urbicus was recalled soon after the end of the fighting. The work may have continued under an officer named Cornelius Priscianus, since it has been conjectured that his name should be read to fill an erasure on an inscription. If the conjecture is accurate, the latter would have been governor between 142 or 143 and about 145. He was followed by Cn. Papirius Aelianus, recorded in 146. The Antonine Wall was basically similar in conception to Hadrian's Wall after the garrisons had been moved on to it, but executed on more economical lines. This time the continuous barrier was constructed in turf throughout, on a stone base mostly about 14 feet (4.3 m.) wide and fronted by a ditch normally about 40 feet (12.3 m.) across and 10 feet (3.1 m.) deep. There is some reason to think that the Antonine Wall was originally planned to follow the developed pattern of Hadrian's Wall, with forts on the line, comparatively widely spaced and interspersed with smaller stations. Economy was further served by omitting the Vallum entirely, providing the forts with defended annexes instead, which might serve the same military purposes at less expense in construction and supervision. Subsequently, more forts were added, bringing the main garrisons much closer together than on the southern Wall. The length of the line itself was shorter, and the final result was a system held in considerably greater strength, since the forts were an easy march apart, and the concentration of troops was approximately double that on Hadrian's Wall. The new line was therefore more capable of resisting powerful thrusts than the old. In fact, by the time the second stage of the Antonine frontier had been completed, a significant step had been taken towards the concept of a static frontier held in great strength, though it is doubtful whether this was the result of a conscious decision of grand strategy. It is much more likely to have been dictated by immediate considerations of operational convenience and economy of effort, another step in the process that had brought the main garrisons up on to Hadrian's Wall from the Stanegate behind. The army was almost certainly expected to patrol continuously in the field and to meet any major enemy force in open battle. Now, however, the Antonine Wall could contain substantial enemy forces without being obliged to muster a large army, no longer depleting other parts of the line to deal with trouble at a single point on it.

The reoccupation of southern Scotland was intended to be permanent. This could hardly be demonstrated more dramatically than by the fact that on Hadrian's Wall sections of the Vallum were now deliberately cancelled by means of regular cuttings through the two mounds, with the material being thrown into the ditch to form causeways. Similarly, the gates were taken off the milecastles, so that free passage was restored. This gesture also suggests that sinister combination between the peoples immediately to the north and south of the Wall was no longer anticipated.

Indeed, that northern England now seemed generally peaceful is supported by the fact that the troops to garrison southern Scotland between the two Walls seem to have been obtained by evacuating forts in the Pennines. It is noticeable, too, that on the whole the military posts in the newly reoccupied area were smaller than those in the Pennines, so that some economy of troops may have been achieved.

Returning to the layout of the new frontier system, it was found expedient to place forts forward of the line in some sectors, as on Hadrian's Wall. In the east these reached as far as the Tay. However, the strategic intention of these forts on the eastern side of Scotland seems to have been different from that of the first-century series that blocked the mouths of the Highland glens. Now the chief purposes appear to have been the supervision of the Fife peninsula and some advance warning of hostile tribes gathering to the north. The flanks were protected by further forts on the Forth and the Clyde, but there is no evidence so far of a continuous system like that of Hadrian on the Solway coast.

The reconquest of southern Scotland may be the context for the appearance of inscriptions from 145–6 recording units of Britons, *numeri Brittonum*, on the Roman frontier in Germany. It was long argued that these units were raised in the newly conquered areas, at least partly to transfer a significant proportion of the fighting strength of the subdued tribes out of the area. Yet archaeological investigation of the native settlements of the period does not suggest that there was any wholesale movement of peoples or any depopulation. If there was any action, it did not go beyond conscripting young men into these units.

So far the Antonine advance in Britain had been a spectacular success, but it is so out of character with what we know of Antoninus Pius' reign that we cannot avoid asking what the motives really were. Economy can hardly be more than part of the answer. New recruiting grounds may well have been gained, but one cannot help feeling that this could have been attained by reoccupying some of the forts in southern Scotland alone. In terms of cash and manpower, the disturbance caused by abandoning one Wall system and building an entirely new one must have been very large, and the upheaval cannot but have spread wide through the province. Experienced administrators must have heard the plans with despair. In terms of Britain alone, the only reasonable explanation seems to be that the Roman government felt that the north would be more secure if the tribes of southern Scotland were brought back under direct control and a shorter line was held more intensively. The area between the two Walls was certainly more heavily garrisoned now than at other times. But one cannot help suspecting that that there was a much wider motive. Antoninus Pius, like Claudius, came to the throne without a military reputation, and he also needed to demonstrate that he was going to be a very different emperor from Hadrian by reviving memories of the reign of Trajan, when senate and emperor had seemed at one. Antoninus was a traditionalist, and there could be nothing more traditional than extending the empire by war. In Britain there was a chance of a tremendous propaganda victory: by winning back what had been lost under Trajan or before, and by abandoning Hadrian's grandiose Wall, which had seemed beset by poor planning, and replacing it by a simple but effective frontier system. It might, too, leave a hint of further advance to come: to regain all the territory that Tacitus had recently claimed had been thrown away in the recall of Agricola by Domitian. The effect would be all the greater if it could be achieved at once, and it looks as if Antoninus must have had this plan in mind at the very beginning of his reign.

Looked at from a Roman point of view, one might conclude that the British frontier was one of the few where military adventure, if it went badly wrong, would not threaten either the real security of the empire or the home districts of its more influential inhabitants. It has been suggested that before the Balkans became regular Roman provinces, parts of that region were used from time to time to give fighting experience to Roman armies and reputations to Roman generals. The Roman record in Britain sometimes seems to reflect such an attitude. It had particular advantages in being remote: failure could perhaps be concealed more easily, while success was undoubtedly enhanced by the aura of distance. Victory across the Ocean still had a special quality, while disaster on an island would not lay the empire open to unlimited barbarian penetration. Against this background, Antoninus' initiative paid off handsomely. In less than five years, all the propaganda victories he might need had been won. If the British units on the Rhine were indeed raised from the newly won territories, then he had added the ultimate traditional touch, doubtless greatly impressing opinion at Rome and among the important garrisons in Germany. It was an ancient custom dating from the Republic that Roman generals were only acclaimed as *imperator* after winning an actual victory in the field. Under the Empire, emperors had assumed the practice of accepting such a salutation themselves after any victory won in their name. Antoninus accepted this honour only once, and that was in 142. The point had been made, and the mild-mannered emperor had no further need to launch foreign wars during his reign.

He was not, however, able to avoid further fighting altogether. Externally, he was able to restrict Roman intervention largely to diplomacy, but there had already been serious risings inside the empire in two of the North African provinces, and also between Jews and Egyptians, before trouble broke out on a serious scale in Britain. In the years following the reconquest of southern Scotland, the process of military evacuation in the Pennines had perhaps been completed. This may have been premature, for coins of Antoninus Pius of 154–5 show Britain as subdued. A much disputed and somewhat obscure passage in Pausanias appears to refer to a serious disturbance among the Brigantes, for he says that Antoninus deprived them of part of their territory after they had launched an attack on 'the Genounian district'. There is good reason to think that Pausanias might have confused the British Brigantes with the Brigantii of Raetia and their neighbours the Genauni, but other evidence that something fairly serious had happened in the Pennines at this time suggests that Pausanias really was reporting an incident in Britain, and had merely made a mistake about the name of the people attacked. An inscription from Newcastle upon Tyne records the arrival of reinforcements for all three legions from the armies of Upper and Lower Germany under a new governor, Cn. Julius Verus. The exact date of his arrival is uncertain, but he was still in office in 158. It is quite likely that he came direct from the governorship of Lower Germany, possibly bringing these men with him to assist in the fighting or to replace losses after it was finished. It is conjectured that Julius Verus supervised a withdrawal from southern Scotland after the uprising had been finally quelled. Whatever the truth of the matter, it does now seem that something sufficiently serious happened in the 150s to cause an abandonment of the Antonine Wall and a refurbishing of the Hadrianic system.

On Hadrian's Wall the archaeological sequence shows a general recommissioning, and, under Julius Verus and later, many forts in the Pennines were reoccupied. Assuming that all this hangs together, the so-called 'Period Ib' on Hadrian's Wall began in the later 150s, and the frontier effectively lay on that line. The idea that both Walls were held together for a substantial period of their history is inherently unlikely and, from pottery studies, appears untenable. Which territory was taken from the Brigantes is unclear. It is probable that substantial tracts of land were taken back into military occupation with the refurbishment of Hadrian's Wall and the restoration of garrisons in the Pennines, while the wording used by Pausanias seems to hint at ownership passing to the imperial estates. It is not impossible that new *civitates*, based on Carlisle and perhaps Corbridge, were formed at this time or subsequently on confiscated lands that were never returned to the Brigantes.

In 158 or 159 Verus was succeeded as governor by someone whom we know only by the last four letters of his name. The latter was followed briefly in 161 or 162 by M. Statius Priscus, a man of considerable distinction in provincial and central affairs and shortly to win a victory on the eastern frontier of the empire. As in the first century, the emperors were continuing to send some of their best men to Britain. It has often been noted that this implies that military problems in Britain were still large enough to need the most experienced generals in command, and that Britain remained important enough in imperial eyes to warrant major effort. It might also be suggested that the governorship of Britain continued to be a significant item of patronage at the disposal of the emperor, and was still regarded in senatorial circles as a plum among postings.

III

IMPERIAL CRISIS
AND RECOVERY

9

MARCUS AURELIUS
AND COMMODUS

M. Statius Priscus was followed as governor of Britain in 162 or 163 by Sextus Calpurnius Agricola, well known to Romano-British specialists because of the number of his building inscriptions on Hadrian's Wall and further south. Before either was appointed, however, there had been a greater event. Early in 161 Antoninus Pius died and was succeeded by Marcus Aurelius, now known more widely for his reputation as a philosopher than for his acts as emperor. Yet in many ways the power of his *Meditations* is due to the personal stress caused by his intense devotion to the twin ideals of Stoicism as recognized by the aristocracy—service to the state and withdrawal into self. Marcus suffered the extreme condition of the characteristically Roman conflict between *otium* and *negotium*, having a passionate feeling for philosophy but conducting a reign tormented by almost continuous warfare. We tend to think loosely of the 'Antonine Age' (by which is generally meant the period from the death of Hadrian to the accession of Septimius Severus in 193) as a unity, in many ways the golden age of the empire. Yet the pressures on the imperial government were very different under Marcus from those that faced Antoninus Pius. The relatively peaceful frontiers of Antoninus' reign were now struck by major attack from outside: on the Rhine, in the east, and, by far the worst, on the Danube. Thereafter Rome was rarely to be free from serious pressure on her frontiers: the wars of the reign of Marcus were the harbingers of the imperial crisis that was to last for more than a century and transform the empire.

Marcus' reign continued the existing process of extending the hold of the imperial administration over local as well as central affairs, but the constant warfare had new and serious consequences for imperial finances. In other important ways Marcus' government foreshadows later developments. Marcus himself had been high in favour both with Hadrian and Antoninus, and was clearly intended as the successor to the latter. It will be remembered, however, that Hadrian had insisted on Antoninus also adopting L. Verus. The latter was retained as second choice throughout the reign of Antoninus, but on his accession Marcus compelled the senate to recognize Verus as emperor as well as himself. For the first time the empire had a pair of co-emperors, declared as such from the outset, not as on those occasions in the past when emperors had taken their favourite sons as colleagues in their formal powers and titles. In practice, Marcus remained the senior, and Verus died early, in 169. Yet precedents had been set.

Another precedent was set in the course of Marcus' military operations on the Danube. From 166 the position there was constantly difficult, sometimes critical. In 166 itself a German invasion had actually penetrated northern Italy, and at one stage Marcus was apparently contemplating a major war of conquest across the Danube. Antoninus' break with the Hadrianic approach to frontier policy had quite clearly restored the traditional Roman instincts. In the end Marcus made the interesting and important decision to transfer barbarians from outside the empire into abandoned lands south of the Danube, in return for an obligation on their part to provide military support for the frontier. This kind of resettlement by the Romans was nothing new (100,000 barbarians had, for example, been brought across the Danube in the reign of Nero), but the requirement to act positively as an internal military buffer for the frontier was a new device. It was employed frequently under the late Empire, but was something of a novelty in the second century.

In Britain Marcus seems to have been faced with problems at the outset of his reign. As late as 163 war was threatening in the island, but the appointment of Statius Priscus may indicate that there had already been important work to be done when Marcus came to the throne. It is true, as scholars have pointed out, that each of the emperors from Hadrian to Commodus is said in the ancient sources to have found a difficult situation in Britain that he subsequently solved. It may, therefore, have become part of the stock-in-trade of imperial biographers. Indeed, the fact that Priscus was transferred to the east in less than a year to take charge in an undoubted emergency should remind us of the very similar case of Julius Severus in 133, and reveals that, whatever the situation in Britain, it was more pressing elsewhere.

The reconstruction of forts in the region of Hadrian's Wall and elsewhere in northern England that began under Julius Verus is recorded again in the inscriptions of Calpurnius Agricola. At first sight this might suggest a continuing process, but the dates span a critical period. It is not until 213 that we can really be confident that we understand the northern frontier, but the short period at the end of Antoninus' reign and the beginning of Marcus' is crucial. It has been conjectured that Julius Verus' withdrawal to Hadrian's Wall was unpopular with Antoninus, whose one great military success had been the reconquest of southern Scotland and the establishment of the Antonine Wall. It is difficult to believe that Verus could have taken this step without imperial authority, but Antoninus may well have accepted its necessity with reluctance, and hoped to reverse it at the earliest opportunity. The reoccupation of the Antonine Wall, known to archaeologists as 'Antonine II', would then be the result of the emperor ordering a forward move once more, and should date from about 160. The archaeology indicates that any reoccupation was implemented to simpler standards than before, and may reflect both a more realistic appreciation of what was necessary and, with the passing of time, less pressure to rival the splendours of Hadrian.

The next stage perhaps coincided with the accession of Marcus or the transfer of Priscus. The new emperor had no known personal involvement with the Antonine Wall, but he did have a growing need for troops elsewhere. A second abandonment of the northern Wall by about 163 would be consistent with this, though it looks as if certain forts in Scotland, particularly Newstead, continued to be held at least until the 180s. Calpurnius Agricola could have been sent out to implement the new policy, recommencing the restoration of Hadrian's Wall where Julius Verus had left it. There were important differences from the frontier in Hadrian's time: significant forces were retained in southern Scotland, and the Cumbrian coast was held more lightly than before. Nevertheless, Hadrian's Wall, not the Antonine Wall, was the linear system that was used from now on.

Calpurnius Agricola was recalled by about 166, and we know nothing for certain of the governors of the next ten years, and little of events in Britain, except that there was a threat of war in 169. The imperial government is likely to have had little time to devote to Britain in this period. From 163 to 166 L. Verus was campaigning in the east, and his troops are said to have brought back the plague that went through Europe in 166–7. At about the same time or shortly after, the Germans broke through the Danube frontier and reached Italy. The withdrawal of the Germans was at length achieved, but Verus died in 169, leaving Marcus as sole emperor to face the problem of the Danube, which now appeared to threaten the security of Italy itself. It was a very long time since hostile barbarian armies had been seen in Italy, and Marcus was never to be free of this problem again. He hoped to counter-attack by reviving the old idea of the conquest of Germany and the part of central Europe to the north and east of the Danube. This was not to be. The plans for Germany were set back by a revolt in the east by one of his own senior generals, Avidius Cassius, and then by renewed German aggression. Subsequently, the eastern parts of the empire claimed his chief energies.

Sometime in the 170s Q. Antistius Adventus was governor in Britain, possibly around 173/6. It may therefore have been in his term of office that a particularly interesting incident took place. Marcus had been campaigning across the Danube against the Sarmatians, a tribe famous for their armoured cavalry and proving extremely troublesome to the frontier. It was Marcus' intention to solve this difficulty, like Julius Agricola and the Ordovices, by wholesale extermination. However, the proclamation in Syria and Egypt of Avidius Cassius as emperor in Marcus' place caused him to break off his campaign, which had been going well— from his point of view. In haste he made terms with the enemy, including the supply of 8,000 Sarmatian cavalry for enrolment in the Roman army. Of these, 5,500 were sent to Britain. They were doubtless no more enthusiastic about this than other units raised compulsorily and transferred to another part of the Roman world, but in being drawn from outside the empire, they, too, foreshadow late Roman practice. What was done with these Sarmatians when they arrived in Britain is not known. As veterans, they are found later settled near Ribchester, on the Ribble, still under special supervision and presumably remaining a doubtful quantity. Nevertheless, on arrival they represented a substantial reinforcement to the auxiliary forces in Britain.

In 177 war broke out again on the Danube. This time Marcus did not leave the rest of the empire unsupervised. It may have been the revolt of Avidius Cassius that persuaded him that he could not trust someone outside his own family and continue the policy of choosing an established figure as his successor. He may, too, have been disillusioned by the relatively unimpressive performance of his late colleague L. Verus. Possibly hoping that the benefits of a Stoic education would bear fruit if his own son actually assumed the responsibilities of empire, he made the disastrous decision to have the dissolute young Commodus invested with the full imperial titles.

Modern commentators have often expressed surprise that the Romans should have abandoned the system that had produced such a successful series of emperors. Yet in many ways the success had been accidental, and the system had not really worked as smoothly as a superficial look suggests. Moreover, the position of emperor was unique, and no amount of previous experience of high office or of apparent suitability could ensure that the candidate would rise to the task once installed. Marcus' decision was an error of judgement of the first magnitude, but it is more intelligible if we forget hindsight. He may reasonably have expected to shape his son to meet his responsibilities by sharing everyday duties with him. At the same time he would be set free to solve the terrible problems of the Danube once and for all by a final campaign. This was precisely what he proceeded to do, starting with great success. In 180 Marcus was on the point of making a major addition to the empire by incorporating some of the most dangerous of the barbarian people that constantly harassed this critical frontier. His death at this moment deprived Rome of a probable solution to a problem that was never to be settled hereafter. It also put one of the most worthless of her emperors on the throne.

In Britain Antistius Adventus had probably been replaced as governor in about 178; his successor may have been Caerellius Priscus. It is unfortunate that we know nothing for certain about his governorship, for major warfare occurred in Britain not long after the death of Marcus, said to have been the most serious war of the new reign. Dio states that enemy tribes crossed 'the Wall' that divided them from the Roman garrisons, ravaged widely, and cut down a 'general' and the troops he had with him. It seems very likely that this officer was Caerellius' unknown successor. Assuming that the sequence of frontier history that we have adopted until now is correct, then 'the Wall' will have been Hadrian's Wall. Signs of destruction recorded on a number of sites and previously, as we shall see, attributed to a hypothetical invasion in 197, are almost certainly to be placed here, around 182/3.

It would seem that the first reaction of the emperor was to appoint an acting governor, one M. Antius Crescens Calpurnianus, and then in 184 to replace him with the formidable Ulpius Marcellus, a man of austere incorruptibility and an extreme disciplinarian. Action against the barbarians was authorized, and, we are told, Marcellus exacted a terrible retribution from the enemy. This must imply a punitive campaign in southern Scotland, probably north of the Forth–Clyde isthmus as well. Coins suggest that the first major successes were in 184, with campaigning continuing into 185. The outpost forts of Birrens, Newstead, Risingham, and probably Cappuck and High Rochester, which had been retained after the Antonine Wall was given up, had been lost and were not reoccupied after the victory. It may have been felt that the successes themselves were enough, without assuming either the burden of permanently occupying a large part of Scotland or even of holding large outposts beyond the Wall.

This war seems also to have had far-reaching effects on the civilian population of the province. Only a very few urban centres in Britain had previously had walls. Their widespread appearance in the later second century requires explanation, and has been the subject of intense debate over dating and cause among students of Roman Britain. Permission to build defences had to be sought from the emperor, and was not easy to obtain. Emperors were unenthusiastic about the creation of strong points not under the control of their own armies. Moreover, they had frequently had trouble over public works in provinces where cities and individuals vied with one another over impossibly expensive and often grandiose but ill-planned projects.

We have seen the fearful havoc that was caused in the first century by the failure before the Boudiccan rebellion to provide defences for the new cities. After Boudicca's defeat had been followed first by revenge and then by reconciliation, there probably seemed no urgent need for wall-building. However, the notion of a total lack of town defences needs to be modified a little. Chichester, Winchester, and Silchester provide evidence for first-century defences, probably indicating special circumstances within the client kingdom of Cogidubnus. The *coloniae* of Lincoln and Gloucester were provided with stone walls, and Colchester followed their example; we should not entirely overlook Tacitus' statement about the original purpose of Colchester—'as a precaution against rebellion'. There was only a limited period for which the original military veterans could serve this purpose, and in only slightly more than a decade Colchester had proved singularly useless without defences in working order. Half-trained rebels could take an unwalled city by virtue of sheer numbers, but without siegecraft or siege-engines they were liable to find city walls impregnable, even when the defenders were comparatively few. Like a burglar faced by a burglar-alarm, such enemies usually preferred to try elsewhere, unless they could rely upon friends within the city to betray it. This was a cardinal fact of ancient warfare, and an essential ingredient in the rationale for urban defences.

At some stage in the second century something happened to make a substantial number of the urban centres without walls or with obsolete defences provide themselves with circuits of earthwork ramparts. This had nothing to do with civic status, since towns that were neither colonies nor the centre of a *civitas* were included. At Lincoln the walled area was extended down to the river with a new earthwork defence. In some cases construction started with the building of fine masonry gates and towers, notably at Verulamium and Cirencester, and there is no sign that the operation was in haste. By far the most likely cause is fear of a repetition of the war of the early 180s. The threat was clearly not felt to be imminent, but real enough to embark on a major programme. In the third century these defences were gradually reconstructed in stone and extended to many other centres. Thus this early scare fortuitously provided the British towns with a protection that was lacking across the Channel, where its absence was to prove disastrous during the great barbarian invasions of the second half of the third century.

The mood of the army in Britain in the reign of Commodus was rebellious. To what extent the governors, particularly Ulpius Marcellus, were responsible, we cannot judge, but we do know that Marcellus himself was dangerously hindered by the fact that he lacked that quality in a commander which inspires men to do out of affection and respect what they would otherwise be disinclined to attempt—and was constitutionally incapable of cajoling them into it. Despite his successes in battle, his behaviour towards his officers was judged to be intolerable. It may have been a consequence of information laid by some of them that Marcellus was recalled swiftly after his victory and accused of treason. We do not know the content of the charge (it could perhaps have had something to do with allowing the towns to fortify themselves), and it was as swiftly dropped. Nevertheless, a tone had been set that outlived his governorship, and at one point the disaffection reached such a point that the army in Britain attempted to put one Priscus, apparently a legionary commander, on the imperial throne. This candidate refused the perilous honour, but the temper of the troops is clear. They were prepared to revert to the old game of emperor-making. The revolt of Avidius Cassius under Marcus had shown that the tradition was not dead, even though several generations of soldiers had passed through the Roman army since there had been a successful military coup. The common soldier and his officers were deeply imbued with the ethic in which personal and family reputations were supreme, and loyalty was a matter of ties to patron and commander. The system held together as long as the current emperor was personally capable of maintaining the network of respect and obligation that bound his commanders to himself, and his troops to the imperial house, but it was a precarious unity into which a weak or neglectful emperor could introduce an almost immediately fatal flaw. Loyalty to the Roman state counted for little without the right man to personify it. Now, as units were stationed in particular provinces for very long periods, sometimes for centuries on end, and were recruited more and more from the local population, the likelihood of provincial armies backing their own candidates became stronger and stronger. The British army had shown it was prepared to enter the lists.

Like Nero, Commodus started his reign under moderating influences. He had gradually been associated with his father in government, and must have been well acquainted with the men and policies that Marcus had favoured. However, he soon fell out with the senate, where the men of greatest influence and experience in government and war were concentrated, and his own behaviour became increasingly eccentric. In 182 he had appointed a praetorian prefect named Perennis, to whom he proceeded to leave most of the government of the empire. One of Perennis' unpopular acts was to replace the senatorial commanders of legions by equestrians: given that revolts in the Roman armies tended to originate among the officers rather than the men, and that this threatened seriously to hinder the careers of young men from powerful families, it is not surprising that discontent was fuelled thereby. As part of the surge of protest against Perennis' measures, the army of Britain adopted the extraordinary manœuvre of sending a deputation of 1,500 men to Rome in 185. Even more extraordinarily, the move succeeded, and Commodus abandoned Perennis. The self-confidence that the British garrison had already demonstrated can only have been augmented.

After the fall of Perennis, Commodus recalled to public life a personal enemy of the late praetorian prefect, Helvius Pertinax, and sent him to take charge of the difficult situation in Britain. Pertinax had already served twice in the province, and started his governorship well. He quelled the disaffected ringleaders in the army, and prevented the troops from setting up yet another pretender, even though he himself was the favoured candidate. However, he does not seem to have avoided trouble for long, since a legion is reported to have mutinied, killing a number of people (perhaps Pertinax' bodyguard or his *amici*), and leaving him for dead. Having recovered, he punished this mutiny very severely. Acquiring a reputation as an extreme disciplinarian, he was in the end forced to resign, probably in 187, on the grounds that the legions were impossibly hostile to him. The delicate balance of forces that had kept the army in check since Trajan's reign—a well-judged degree of discipline, and personal respect for the emperor and the men that he appointed—was visibly breaking down, and the garrison of Britain was well to the fore.

The removal of one praetorian prefect from a position as effective ruler of the empire was followed by the elevation of others. The emperor, careless as he was of public duty, nevertheless did not keep out of the limelight. His personal behaviour became odder and odder. He directed a vicious attack towards the senate, and came to believe that he was divinely inspired as a reincarnation of Hercules. Finally, he went too far, even for the most tolerant, by announcing that he would appear publicly on 1 January 193 as Hercules returned, assume the dual roles of consul and gladiator, and prove his divinity by invincibility in the arena. The latest of his praetorian prefects successfully arranged his assassination, and proclaimed Pertinax, now prefect of the city of Rome, as emperor. The reactions of the army in Britain on hearing of the usurpation and the name of the new emperor are likely to have been mixed, but not difficult to imagine.

10

CIVIL WAR AND ITS
AFTERMATH

The name of the governor who succeeded Pertinax in Britain is unknown, but by the end of 192 the province was under the command of Decimus Clodius Albinus, another aristocratic Roman provincial, this time from North Africa. He was in post when the murder of Commodus set off a train of events that were to alter the life of the Roman world irrevocably, mostly, it must be said, for the worse. The first consequence, however, was a false dawn of reform, for Pertinax attempted too much too quickly at Rome. He treated the senatorial order with scrupulous courtesy, and restrained both the imperial freedmen and the praetorian guard. Unfortunately, he had already proved incapable of winning the support of the legions in Britain for the discipline he imposed there, and the praetorians, accustomed to even greater privileges, liked his approach no better. The same praetorian prefect as had arranged the murder of Commodus induced his men to assassinate the new emperor. In perhaps the most cynical act in their history, the praetorians put up the throne for auction, whereupon it was purchased by the immensely wealthy senator Didius Julianus. However, the chain reaction of mutiny could not now be stopped. The legions in Pannonia proclaimed their commander, Septimius Severus, as emperor, also of North African origin. At almost the same moment Pescennius Niger was proclaimed in Syria and Clodius Albinus in Britain. All the ingredients for prolonged civil war were now present.

The first move was a march on Italy by Severus, the nearest of the claimants to Rome, which provoked the praetorians into declaring for him. The senate condemned Julianus, who was forthwith murdered in the palace, only six months after the death of Commodus. Severus now had control of the central machinery of government as well as a powerful army. He had already shown Machiavellian shrewdness by offering Albinus the title of 'Caesar', an act that also has constitutional interest for the future in designating as 'Caesar' a junior emperor who was understood to be a working colleague. Albinus certainly seems to have been persuaded that he was to be a partner in government with Severus, and this prevented a flank attack while the latter dealt with Niger.

In the following year Severus defeated Niger's army in the east, pursued him, and killed him. Severus was no longer inclined to allow the title of Caesar to Albinus, who for his part was now aspiring to the supreme rank. It must at this point have become obvious that another civil war was inevitable. By 196 the discord had finally come to a head. Though the sources are unclear, the historian Herodian represents Severus as making the first military move, after dispatching agents on an unsuccessful mission to assassinate Albinus. Herodian implies that Albinus was in a poor state of readiness, but he nevertheless seems to have acted fairly rapidly in transferring himself to Gaul. Having induced the senate to pronounce Albinus a public enemy, Severus set out in person to bring him to battle, an act sufficiently unusual in him to excite remark.

Albinus won an initial success, an engagement in which he defeated a Severan commander named Lupus, almost certainly the Virius Lupus who was later appointed governor of Britain. The campaign culminated when the two main armies met near Lyons in 197. Dio claims that there were 150,000 men on each side, figures that it is difficult to credit, at least for Albinus' army: the whole army of Britain was not much more than a third of that number. If the figures are anywhere near right, then Albinus must have won over very substantial numbers of regular Roman troops stationed on the Continent, as well as raised some new forces from the territories he now controlled. The fight put up by his army indicates that it could not have been made up largely of raw recruits. Unlike the first century BC or even AD, Spain, Gaul, and even Britain no longer had a recent tradition of continuous native warfare from which to supply experienced warriors for new units. We do know that Albinus gained one legion,

VII *Gemina* from Spain, and the single urban cohort stationed at Lyons itself, but the Rhine armies are generally believed by modern scholars not to have supported him.

A more probable explanation is that the figures are considerably exaggerated. This is by no means unknown among ancient historians; inevitably, they often had to draw on the propaganda put out by the victors, and it was always very difficult to obtain reliable information, particularly in a civil war, where hurriedly raised units and temporary allies were involved. Yet the list of forces on Albinus' side conjectured above still seems too small to make up his whole army, even if the overall totals are exaggerated, and one cannot help suspecting that there was not absolute solidarity among the Rhine troops. Indeed, it is difficult to see how Albinus could have risked committing the bulk of his army at Lyons if the whole of the Rhine forces might move on his rear. Certainly, something like seven or eight years later, detachments of legions from both Upper and Lower Germany were still in action against 'deserters and rebels'. There is no doubt either about the fact that Albinus' forces were not easily overcome at Lyons, for the fortunes of battle wavered for a long time before they finally came down in favour of Severus. Whether Albinus managed to commit suicide, the honourable end for a defeated Roman, cannot be verified, but there is no question that he did not survive.

Despite the uncertainties about the size and composition of Albinus' forces at Lyons, there is little reason to question the assumption that the bulk of the British garrison supported him. It does not follow, however, that most of it accompanied him to the Continent. We have seen that Albinus could not have challenged Severus without recruiting on the Continent, even if he had taken the whole of the army of Britain with him. Until recently, it was generally accepted that hardly any of the auxiliary forts in Britain were occupied by the same unit both before and after 197, and that this indicated an upheaval at this time. This, however, is not true of the legions, and it seems that at least basic legionary cadres were left behind. Yet the fact of the matter is that we know hardly anything about the identity of the garrisons in the auxiliary forts between the 180s and the Severan occupation of Britain. Thus the changes could have occurred at any time in this period, which we have already seen was as turbulent in Britain as elsewhere.

Having accepted Albinus' alleged removal of the garrison of Britain to fight on the Continent, Romano-British historians long believed that the result was a disastrous invasion of the province from beyond the northern frontier. It was subsequently realized that this was not reflected by any consistent archaeological signs of damage in the north. There is, moreover, no literary report of frontier trouble on the scale implied. The alleged epigraphical evidence depends on disbelieving what at least one inscription actually says. All in all, it seems more likely that the widespread repairs indisputably carried out in the reign of Severus —and some of those thought to be so—were needed because there had been no large-scale reorganization for at least two decades. Hadrian's Wall itself was now three-quarters of a century old, and had twice been temporarily abandoned: it is not surprising that some sections needed rebuilding from the ground up. Moreover, we may reasonably surmise that there had been vandalism and looting during the temporary dislocations of civil war, particularly if some forts were left empty for a short period; nor is it unlikely that the new regime adopted a new broom.

It is perhaps significant that the first rebuilding inscriptions for the Pennines can be dated immediately after the Severan capture of Britain in 197, while those for Hadrian's Wall and further north are from 205 or later. The most urgent task seems to have been restoration in the Pennines. Damage may have been caused by locals who still nursed old grievances, or perhaps during operations by Severan troops to eliminate pockets of resistance among those who had been too deeply involved with Albinus to hope for clemency. On the other hand, restoration of the frontier region does seem to have proceeded from south to north, and the differences in date may reflect nothing more than a systematic programme of maintenance of installations that had been neglected but not destroyed. It is certainly difficult to believe that Severus would have left the Wall line itself untouched for several years if there had been the sort of wholesale damage that put it out of service.

The effects of Clodius Albinus' four years as emperor are most likely to have been felt in London, where one may assume that he had his imperial capital. Archaeologically, it is extremely difficult to disentangle those changes in the city that should be dated to the last decade of the second century from those that were perhaps consequences of the presence of Septimius Severus and his entire imperial family in Britain in the years 208–11. One example is the city wall. If it was started as early as the 180s, it can be seen as part of the general pattern across the country. The fact that it was built straightaway in stone, without any earthwork phase, may well be attributed to London's probable greater wealth, but it is equally possible that the presence of a would-be imperial government meant a direct input of cash. It is also possible that London had not been supplied with defences at the very beginning of the countrywide programme because of its unique possession of a fort, but that the new circumstances required the provision of walls, both for security and prestige. The fort was incorporated in the new defences. The Thames frontage, however, was not provided with a wall as early as this. The dating of the riverside wall has long been a subject for debate, but it now seems that the completion of the circuit occurred between about 250 and 270.

We do not know whether Albinus appointed a governor to take over the local duties when he himself assumed the purple. After his defeat, however, Severus put Virius Lupus into the post. This is almost certainly the man whom Albinus defeated early on in his campaign in Gaul. It is likely that one of Lupus' first tasks was to carry out a programme of confiscation of property and executions among the former supporters of Albinus, as in Gaul and Spain, though there is no literary evidence and not much archaeological sign of disruption. The evidence from amphorae, the large pottery containers in which wine, oil, and other liquids were transported, does indicate a major interruption in a trade route, but this was probably due to Severan measures against enemies with properties in Spain—the country of origin—rather than in Britain. Sending Sextus Varius Marcellus, an eastern equestrian who happened to be related to the new emperor, to Britain as provincial procurator was doubtless intended to ensure that the financial affairs of the province were in completely reliable hands, and that taxation would be exacted without mercy. The office was subsequently held by M. Oclatinius

Adventus, who had previously been commander of the emperor's secret police (*frumentarii*). A provincial procurator, with his control of the tax records, was in a particularly good position to carry out a programme of investigation and seizure, and his responsibility for the junior procurators in charge of crown properties in the province—landed estates and industrial enterprises of many kinds, including mines and, probably, salt production—must have reduced the administrative problems of absorbing confiscated property into the emperor's possessions. There are possible signs of changed ownership in some British villas at this time, and the Severan victory marks one of the larger steps forward in the process by which more and more of the property in the empire came into the hands of the emperors, weakening the upper classes and greatly strengthening the centralizing of power. Yet, overall, the comparatively small amount of evidence in Britain for punitive action suggests that Albinus received less support from civilians here than he did in parts of the Continent, and any slowing down of improvements to property archaeologically detectable in the early third century is probably due more to economic uncertainty, and indeed to the soundness of work done in the second century, than to political persecution of owners.

Externally, the new governor certainly had problems. The Caledonians are said to have been breaking treaty agreements and preparing to aid the Maeatae. These agreements were perhaps obligations that had been laid upon them by Ulpius Marcellus, but equally they might have been part of precautions taken by Albinus before his campaign in Gaul. Dio tells us that the various tribes of the Britons (he must be talking about those outside the province to the north) had by this time become subsumed into two main groupings, the Caledonii and the Maeatae. Lupus seems to have been facing a threatened attack on the Wall, and it appears that he did not think he had the strength to fight it off. As Severus was unable to send reinforcements, owing to commitments elsewhere, Lupus bought off the Maeatae with a very large bribe, clearly with the emperor's approval. In return, he obtained peace and the return of a few prisoners.

The order of the next two governors is not entirely certain, but it is clear that C. Valerius Pudens was in post in 205, and that he probably preceded L. Alfenus Senecio, who seems to have been governor between 205 and 207. The latter may have been responsible for military successes in 206, but he is noted for the inscriptions that record restoration on Hadrian's Wall and one of the outpost forts, in two cases in collaboration with the procurator Oclatinius Adventus. This collaboration suggests that the governor was occupied by some exceptional demand on his attention. Something out of the ordinary had indeed happened, for the governor appealed to the emperor for reinforcements 'or an imperial expedition'. Few governors can have welcomed an imperial visit, with the enormous burdens that they imposed, so a very serious situation must have threatened. It is too long after Severus' accession for it to have been staged by the emperor as an excuse for a campaign in Britain for the propaganda reasons suggested at the beginning of earlier reigns. Indeed, after Lyons Severus had no need to prove a capacity for military success. Lupus' bribe to the northern barbarians had probably only bought a few years' peace, though that had been well worth having in the disturbed period immediately after the civil wars. Herodian's account implies that Senecio now judged that the situation was out of control.

Both Dio and Herodian represent Severus as welcoming the opportunity to campaign, chiefly in order to provide employment for his unruly sons, Caracalla and Geta. Dio adds that indiscipline among the army was a factor, since it had been idle for some time. This cannot refer to the troops in Britain, unless the whole business of the barbarian uprising was a sham. In fact, Severus decided to use a substantial proportion of troops from other provinces on his campaign, for on his journey to the island the emperor collected forces from the areas through which he passed, and he must have crossed the Channel with considerable reinforcements. On arrival, he gathered together the troops already available in the island, and rejected offers of peace from an enemy alarmed by the size of the army now gathered. The emperor was accompanied by his empress, the formidable and learned Julia Domna, and his two quarrelling sons. Caracalla he took on campaign; Geta he left 'in the part under Roman control', to dispense justice and to administer the affairs of the empire. In these dispositions we can discern the politics of the imperial court being worked out in Britain. Caracalla, of whom

Severus was rightly suspicious, was kept where he could be observed. The concerns of the emperor over who should succeed him are apparent: Geta, previously hardly ever entrusted with responsibility, was allowed to demonstrate whether or not he was fit to govern, but under supervision. He was certainly left with an advisory council, though this may have been no more than an instance of the practice that we have previously noted of supplying experienced support for Roman magistrates. Much more significant is the presence of Julia Domna, who had regained her political influence after a period of eclipse. One might have expected that Severus would also have left the great jurist Papinian to advise Geta, rather than taking him on campaign. At first sight, the reason would seem to be that Papinian was currently praetorian prefect, and thus needed in the field. Yet he had had little military experience, and it is more significant that he was related to Julia Domna and that he supported Geta (his subsequent protest at the murder of the latter by his brother was to cause his own downfall). It was considered unwise to have too many people in one place who might form a faction while holding the reins of the imperial administration. It is thought that another great name in Roman law was also in Britain at this time: Ulpian, who, though assessor to Papinian as praetorian prefect, tended towards Caracalla, in whose reign he later prospered. We may suppose that his legal advice was available to the administration, and it is not impossible that Severus saw him as a potential political counterbalance at the imperial court.

It seems probable that the campaign did not start in earnest until Severus was beyond the Forth–Clyde isthmus. The literary sources are unclear, but Carpow, in Fife, was probably the real jumping-off point for the campaign. A Severan legionary base has been discovered there, but it is uncertain whether it was established at the beginning of this campaign or later. Once across the isthmus, Severus may have run into opposition before he could set about construction. Successes are recorded on the first campaign, and the accounts emphasize the engineering side of the operation, which the emperor prosecuted with great vigour, despite his own ill health. The literary phrases describing him as cutting through difficult terrain and approaching the extremity of the island are probably conventional, but some of the temporary

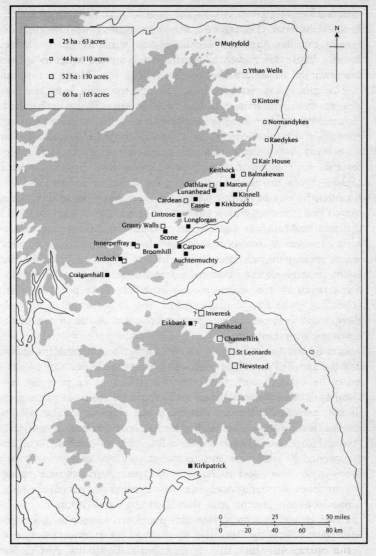

PROBABLE CAMPS of the Severan armies on campaign in Scotland.

camps extending far north on the eastern side of the Highlands
must be Severan. That terrain, however, assisted the Britons, for
Severus, unlike Agricola, was unable to tempt them out to a
decisive battle. He had to be satisfied with forcing them to agree
to surrender a considerable area.

This peace was not kept long. The Britons rose again, probably in the summer of 210, and Severus immediately ordered a
punitive campaign, with the intention of slaughtering every native
encountered by the expedition. This was carried out, and it may
have been at this point that command was given to Caracalla,
for the emperor was by now very ill. However, Severus seems
to have spent the winter preparing for a further major expedition that he would lead in person. By now the Caledonians had
joined the Maeatae, who seem to have been alone in revolt until
the punitive campaign had been carried out. Severus was perhaps considering total conquest now. If not, the punitive action
was a serious misjudgement that ensured long-term hostility to
Rome from both the great confederations of tribes in Scotland.
On 4 February 211 Severus died at York. His last reported words
characterize the new century. Addressing his sons, he urged on
them unity between themselves, enrichment of the troops, and
scorn for everyone else.

Immediately after Severus' death, Caracalla attempted to sub-
orn the army to recognize him as sole emperor. When this failed,
he made a treaty with the enemy, accepting their promises of
good faith, and evacuated their territory, returning south to meet
his mother and brother at York or possibly London. The political situation was too tense for him to risk staying in the far
north. Not only was Caracalla at odds with his brother, but the
emergence of rival claimants to the throne was only too likely
in view of the events that had put his father on it. Actual evacuation from Scotland does not, however, seem to have been
immediate, and it is possible that Caracalla carried out one further campaign. Dio does note that the new emperor abandoned
forts, but, even so, the decision to make the evacuation permanent and total may not have been taken straightaway. Part of II
Augusta was still undertaking building work at Carpow in 212.
But whatever the truth about this brief period at the beginning

of Caracalla's reign, abandonment of Scotland became a reality after a very short time.

It was probably as part of Caracalla's settlement of the affairs of Britain that the administration of the island was rearranged into two provinces. There are considerable uncertainties about precisely when this was done, and there are even more uncertainties about the identities of the last one or two governors of the undivided province. Not much more can be said than that one C. Junius Faustinus Postumianus should probably be put into this period, and that a second Ulpius Marcellus, possibly the son of the earlier man of the same name, may have been in office in 211 and 212, and C. Julius Marcus in 213. The latter is particularly interesting, as it seems that his name was erased from a number of dedications professing loyalty to Caracalla. Such erasure is a sign of disgrace, but whether this was political or military is unknown, though the former is more likely. It is possible that disturbances occurred after Caracalla had murdered his brother and co-emperor early in 212. As Geta had been acting emperor while his father and elder brother were campaigning in the north, he must have become exceptionally well known in Britain for a member of the imperial family. The loyalty inscriptions of 213 suggest that such unrest was not immediately quelled, and the erasure of Marcus' name leads one to think that his own conduct had raised suspicion, whether as an alleged friend of Geta or for lack of rigour in suppressing discontent.

The background to the division of Britain is Septimius Severus' attempt to reduce the risk of further attempts on the throne by cutting down the number of legions at the disposal of any one provincial governor. There are difficulties in accepting Herodian's statement that Severus divided Britain straightaway in 197, and on balance it is most likely that the definitive reorganization was introduced under Caracalla. Divided provinces were named on the basis of their distance from Rome; the 'upper' province (the south, or Britannia Superior) held legions at Chester and Caerleon, and was administered by a consular governor, probably from London; the northern, 'lower' province (Britannia Inferior), under a governor of praetorian rank, had only one legion but a large number of auxiliary troops, with its centre at York. It is highly likely that the large civil settlement that had grown up there in the previous century across the River Ouse from the legionary fortress had recently received the title of *colonia*, most probably as the temporary seat of the imperial court, but just possibly implying that it had supported the Severan side against Albinus. Some troops were removed to the Continent at this point, but these were probably chiefly men that Severus had brought over with him to use in Scotland. Overall, the military establishment was maintained, and the basic military and civil pattern for third-century Britain had been fashioned.

11

FROM CARACALLA TO DIOCLETIAN

As one contemplates the third century, the feeling that a real change has come over the Roman world is overwhelming. In the first half of the second century the empire was still expanding; in the second half, despite the pressure on the Danube that at times looked very dangerous, the empire stood triumphant and unshaken. In the third century all seems changed. Inflation, military insurrection, one murdered emperor following another, open autocracy, and the simultaneous breaching of the imperial defences in both east and west look like the beginning of the end. Yet we are powerfully conditioned by hindsight. We know that, under barbarian invasion and internal discord, the political and military structure of the western empire disintegrated two centuries later —though that was by no means the end of Roman society in the west, an important distinction—and it is easy but unreasonable to suppose that people should have been able to recognize in the third century the seriousness of events whose significance only appears in the light of later history.

It is, however, true that the revitalizing of Rome's old eastern enemy Parthia in the second half of the third century in the guise of the new Persian empire of the Sassanians, and the regrouping of the German barbarians into powerful confederations (with other barbarians behind them) represented fresh and dangerous versions of the old threats to the empire from without. These were joined, too, by northern peoples raiding by sea. Nevertheless, there was no reason at the time to believe that these were other than variations of the frontier problems that Rome had been used to facing and overcoming for centuries. It is tempting for us to see the movement of the barbarians westward as inevitable and irresistible, but the situation was constantly changing and highly complex. Many Romans still expected that there would be successful wars of conquest in the future, and few behaved as if the empire could fall.

It had often suited the Roman moralists to see the barbarian as the noble savage, struggling to save his native virtues against the corruption of Roman civilization. Even if this had ever been generally true of Rome's enemies in the west—and it is very doubtful—there are many pointers that indicate that later barbarians, far from rejecting Roman civilization, envied the comfort and wealth that it represented. In due course we shall observe the merging of Roman and barbarian in the west during the late Empire. Here we have to note the growing desire to share in the wealth of the Roman world, whether by raiding and piracy or by entering and dwelling in Roman territory. Inward movements of population were not always treated as hostile by the Romans, particularly not when it suited them to make use of the barbarians for their own ends. Moreover, many barbarians came as individuals to seek careers and riches within the empire. Overall, however, Roman attitudes to the barbarians were still based on the assumption that they were both a menace to be guarded against and fair game for generals ambitious to make their names and fortunes. This was to remain the dominant approach of Rome towards her neighbours, long after the realities of power had decisively changed.

In Britain we have already seen how a new confederation of old enemies joined the Highland grouping long known as the Caledonii. Well before the end of the third century Rome's northern foes have taken to the sea and are harassing provinces on both sides of the Channel and the North Sea, chiefly those two groups of Germanic peoples known as the Franks and the Saxons who were to play such an important part in the history of the west over the next few centuries. They are also joined by further sea-borne raiders from Ireland, less well known but equally dangerous. But this broad view of events is that of Romans long after the third century. As late as the 370s Roman frontier commanders were taking little serious notice of the vast movements among the barbarians caused by the defeat of the Goths by the

Huns, so used were they to conflict among the barbarians that in the past had generally worked to Rome's advantage, and that had never produced results that could not in the end be contained.

Behind many modern assessments of the changing policies of the Severan house in Britain lies the individual historian's attitude to the frontier question. Was it the right policy in the north, from Rome's point of view, to attempt complete conquest or to establish some kind of frontier defence that accepted that not all of northern Britain would ever be held by Roman garrisons? It is, of course, another question whether the choice was so clear to the Romans themselves. Certainly, it is not reasonable to judge Caracalla and his immediate successors on the basis of events that took place three-quarters of a century or even a century and a half later. Few defensive systems can be expected to be effective for more than a generation or so, and only a foreshortened view of history encourages wider judgements. The fact remains that Caracalla's dispositions in Britain were highly successful at the time. The northern frontier remained unbreached for at least seventy years or so, in an age when other frontier regions were being overrun, some never to be held again. Given the troubles of the third century, it is unlikely that it would have been possible to hold Scotland effectively while providing strong garrisons further south. Since the Roman government now deemed such garrisons necessary, it is difficult to avoid the conclusion that Caracalla was right to consolidate the Roman position in the north on a modernized and strengthened version of the Hadrianic frontier.

It is all the easier to give Caracalla the credit he deserves in this respect as it becomes increasingly difficult to sustain the older view that the third century was a period of universal stagnation in the civil life of Britain. Of course, given that the fostering of the arrogance of the army was a major factor in the disorders and disasters of the third century, then the Severans, as a result of their policy on the affairs of the empire at large, were responsible for the seeming inability of the administration to deal with major problems in individual provinces. Nevertheless, the evidence suggests that where civil life was bypassed by major disasters (and we may reasonably suppose that this was the norm), it continued in fair prosperity. There is little sign in Britain of the destructive inroads of barbarians that characterize this century in Germany and Gaul (to mention only the neighbouring areas of the empire), or of the frightful horrors of mutiny, brigandage, and civil war that broke out in many parts of the empire. We shall later have to account for a remarkable period of prosperity in the earlier part of the fourth century, and we shall find that it is much easier to understand if we assume that it was based on sound foundations that remained relatively undisturbed in the third century, rather than sprang up overnight from reforms instituted under the new imperial order imposed by Diocletian.

It is not, however, easy to form a general impression of the third century, due to a shortage of contemporary sources. Literary material is comparatively scarce, and many of the leading personalities of the age are consequently shadowy. In the middle of the century emperors came so thick and fast that it becomes more than usually difficult to associate such subdivisions of the period as we think we can detect archaeologically with historical figures and events. A reduction in Britain of the number of Roman inscriptions (paralleled elsewhere in the Roman world) combines with a decline in the import of samian pottery, a decline that reaches almost complete cessation sometime in the century. Coin hoards, though a notable feature of the period and generally indicative of political and military instability and monetary troubles, are subject to so many factors affecting their individual composition that they can be used for historical purposes only with extreme caution.

One cannot properly appreciate the remarkable phenomenon of a relatively undisturbed and moderately prosperous Britain without looking at the state of the empire in general in the third century, and of the neighbouring provinces in particular. Yet our evidence for the empire at large, scrappy though it is, allows considerably more chronological precision than is possible in Britain. In brief, four directly relevant broad periods can be distinguished in the western part of the empire. They are, first, the period that began with the departure of Caracalla from Britain in 213 to launch his great campaign in Germany and ended with the death of Severus Alexander, the last of the Severan emperors, in 235; next, the period of rapid turnover of emperors in the middle of the century; then the German invasions, together with the establishment of the 'Gallic Empire' (*Imperium Galliarum*) in 260; and finally, the restoration of strong central authority by Aurelian and Probus from 274, followed by the accession of Diocletian in 284, heralding major structural reform in the imperial system. These broad divisions will need some refinement, but they provide a usable framework. In Britain, however, it is extremely difficult to go much further than distinguishing between 'Severan' (though the consolidation from Caracalla to Severus Alexander does form a distinct feature in military affairs), 'mid-third century', 'later third century' or 'around 270', and 'late third–early fourth'. We shall also see that the second half of the century presents particular problems in Britain, since its inclusion in the Gallic Empire from 260 to 274 was followed by a second period of independence from the central government from 287 to 296, under Carausius and Allectus.

As usual in Britain, such chronology as we can construct historically has to be built largely on military events and military remains. On Hadrian's Wall, the restoration begun by Septimius Severus continued in many parts of the northern frontier area over the next quarter of a century or so. We can, for example, probably construe the refurbishment of the old outpost forts in the west at Netherby and Bewcastle as part of a gradual renewal of the system as occasion and convenience dictated. There is little sign of urgency or of any fear that the Caracallan arrangements might break down. At Bewcastle we can observe new ideas being implemented, when we see how the rigidly planned second-century fort was abandoned in favour of a shape better adapted to the terrain. This greater flexibility in the design of military works had already appeared elsewhere, and was now having its effect on the Hadrianic frontier. By the latter part of the first century a series of more or less standard plans had emerged from the very varied designs found earlier. There is a certain intellectual pleasure to be gained from contemplating the classic regularity then achieved—and Romans were rarely so stupid as to impose without modification solutions straight out of the textbook—and such standardization doubtless greatly simplified the problems of construction and supply, not to mention decision-making, with its difficulties and delays. However, it is not surprising to find this gradually giving way to experimentation and economy. The process was to accelerate in the third century, and one is justified in wondering whether this was not only a response to new military and economic problems, but also a reflection of the presence in the army of more and more officers in senior positions who had risen from the ranks or who came from families that had been producing career soldiers for generations.

The rebuilding of Bewcastle and the renovation of other forts were only part of the strengthening of the Wall system. In the Hadrianic period the Wall had lacked forward positions in the east. Under the Antonines, Risingham and High Rochester had first been built on Dere Street as hinterland forts on the vital route to Newstead and the Antonine Wall. Lost in the troubles of the 180s, they had been left empty ever since. Now, however, strong new forts were built on both sites, and the third-century Wall was thus provided with powerful forward garrisons in both the east and the west.

On the Wall itself, some of the turrets that can never have had much practical value were abandoned, most of the milecastle gateways were narrowed, bridges were enlarged and rebuilt, and sections of the curtain wall were reconstructed. It may well have proved extremely awkward to man all the turrets, and excessively uncomfortable as well as unnecessary on the central crags. It may also have been discovered that the double doors to the north on the milecastles were hardly ever used by cavalry or vehicles, and that when the wooden leaves decayed, it was cheaper and more convenient to reduce the apertures and provide a small postern door. Hadrianic regularity had been abandoned long ago in the design of the Antonine Wall, and by the early third century the consequences of the tidy mind were probably all too obvious.

In the third century substantial civil settlements developed on ground outside the forts, south of the curtain wall itself. Here and there along the Wall these had already begun to appear in the course of the second century, but the major expansion came in the third. It is difficult not to associate this change with Septimius Severus' permission for soldiers to have lawful wives. There is no reason to think that this impaired the fighting ability of the troops. They had been used to contracting permanent attachments in the provinces in which they served, and this had been recognized in the discharge documents available to auxiliaries.

It is not necessary to think that it implies a peasant militia, half soldier, half farmer. There is no evidence that the third-century troops were other than full-time soldiers, and none that civilians were settling into the forts themselves. The lessons of the past few years had been learnt. Pertinax's attempt to impose the strictest forms of military discipline had been a disaster, and on his death-bed Severus had, as we saw, charged his sons above all else to please the troops. There had been a decisive change of power in the direction of the soldier. The development of the civil settlements at this time is directly in line with Severan policy towards him.

One reason why it was now apparently deemed safe to allow the development of civil settlements (*vici*) close to the Wall forts may have been because the region was better patrolled. It was at this time that new units of auxiliary infantry and cavalry, known as *numeri* and *cunei*, were being added to the regular garrisons of some northern forts. These were perhaps more obviously semi-barbarian than the very long-established auxiliary units. There would have been little room to accommodate these extra troops in the forts if these were fully manned, but there would not have been a problem if some troops now lived with their families in the civil settlements. There is also a possibility that the actual strength of some units was reduced in the course of the century. These new troops may have been employed chiefly in patrols, southwards as well as to the north. There is little doubt that the *exploratores* and Raetian spearmen who appear at outpost forts north of the Wall were intended for patrol duties, and part of the duties of the men attached to the Wall itself may have been similar patrol work in the wild country to the south. The otherwise surprising reoccupation of Lanchester may have been connected with such a need.

Describing this reorganized frontier is easier than identifying the men who governed it. It will be recalled that Britain was now divided into two provinces. Despite the fact that Upper Britain ranked higher as a posting, information about the men who filled the governorships is rather more satisfactory for the northern province. The first to be recorded (there is some evidence for AD 216) would seem to be the elder Gordian, who was to be emperor for just under three weeks in 238. He may have been followed directly by Modius Julius, for whom there is an inscription that can be read as dating from 219, but of whom nothing more is known. For 220 it is a positive relief to find Tiberius Claudius Paulinus, who is documented both in Gaul and on an inscription at Caerwent in south Wales. At an earlier stage of his career he had been commander of the Second legion stationed locally at Caerleon, and, while he was subsequently governor of one of the Gallic provinces, the *civitas* of the Silures (a people, the reader will recall, noted in the first century as exceptionally hostile to Rome) set up an official inscription recording their gratitude to him. It seems likely that he had done them some service, perhaps by becoming their 'patron' and pressing their interests with the central government. Maybe they had heard that he was coming back to Britain (even if it was to the other province), or maybe they were just demonstrating their acquaintance with the great. The traditional connection between prominent Romans and the local community was still operating. Such bonds mitigated some of the effects of distance on provincial communities and individuals. One may suspect that the need for friends at court was felt more keenly than ever in the troubled times of the third century, even if one could not always be sure at which court they ought to be.

From this point the record of governors becomes a mere catalogue. For three periods of office the dating is reasonably close: Marius Valerianus in 221 and 222, Claudius Xenophon in 223, and one Maximus in 225. After Maximus the order and dating of the appointments become much less certain: Calvisius Rufus and Valerius Crescens Fulvianus between 225 and 235, and Claudius Apellinus perhaps in 235 itself. Apellinus may still have been in office at the beginning of the period of extreme confusion in the imperial government between the murder of Severus Alexander in 235 and the accession of Valerian and Gallienus in 253. There is a Tuccianus, if that is his name, in 237, Maecilius Fuscus and Egnatius Lucilianus between 238 and 244, and Nonius Philippus in 242. There is also an Aemilianus, probably sometime after 244.

Considerably later—and included here only out of convenience since we are listing governors of Britannia Inferior—we know of Octavius Sabinus from an inscription at Lancaster apparently dated between 263 and 268. There is a special interest in this inscription, as he is already called *praeses* (the term that was to replace *legatus Augusti* as the title of the governor of an imperial province), yet he was of senatorial rank. This is contrary to the politically significant third-century trend of putting equestrian career officers rather than senatorial gentlemen into important military commands. This policy became the norm under Gallienus (emperor from 253 to 268), and he was not loved by the senate for it, since it struck at their deepest traditions. It is relevant to note that Sabinus, though in office during the reign of Gallienus, is unlikely to have been appointed by him, since the usurpation of Postumus in Gaul occurred in 260. The adherence of Britain to the Gallic Empire meant that Britannia Inferior was already beyond the central emperor's control. Postumus may have been short of good equestrians: he may also have made such appointments quite deliberately with an eye to gaining support from the senatorial class.

There is another interesting feature of the third-century governors. The men in charge of the British frontier were in general much less distinguished than before, which may reflect the success of the new arrangements. Even Sabinus is not in the same class as the senators who were sent out in the first and second centuries, nor were conditions anything like normal when he was appointed. One may also reasonably point out that, whatever the pressures on Britain at this time, they are hardly likely to have loomed as large in the minds of Roman emperors as they had in more peaceful times for the empire at large. We ought not to forget, too, that, with Britain divided, the individual governors no longer commanded armies on the scale that they once had.

The comparative paucity of closely dated information from the more lightly garrisoned areas of Britain is not surprising. The new southern province of Britannia Superior, however, though never dominated by military installations in the way that the north was, possessed from its inception a substantial military establishment, including two of the three legions stationed in Britain, the Second and the Twentieth. In the course of the third century we shall see the governors of the new province reorganizing the forces under their command, doubtless taking account of the revised limits of their responsibility and the structure of their administration, and reflecting altered military thinking about security and defence. They may also have had to take into account reductions in the actual manning of units, in a world of increasing costs and, particularly, in a relatively peaceful province. It is in this overall context that new military installations appear in what in the second century had been the almost exclusively 'civil' part of Britain. These developments included new and strong military bases, representing at least to some extent a shift in the weight of garrisons from the west towards the south and east. We may be confident that the reasons for this included both changes in the external threats to the island and also internal factors, reflecting political instability, the demands of the troops for better conditions, and the worsening relationship in the empire between army and civilian populations.

Establishing the identity of the governors of Britannia Superior is made difficult not only by the shortage of literary sources for the third century, but also by the rarity of extant inscriptions in the south. This is true throughout the Roman period, but it is exacerbated by the general falling-off in the number of inscriptions from Roman Britain as a whole from the third century onwards, a phenomenon noted in many parts of the empire. It is significant that new discoveries recording otherwise unknown governors have come either from one of the new forts or from London. An inscription from the fort of Reculver on the north Kentish coast records a Rufinus. He is perhaps more likely to have been in Britain after its division than before it, but there is a choice of several candidates. Two others, Pollienus Auspex and C. Junius Faustinus Postumianus, may also have been governors of Britannia Superior rather than of the earlier undivided island. An inscribed stone altar that was reused in the later riverside defences of London records another third-century governor (or, rather, acting governor). Marcus Martiannius Pulcher, a senator, could also have been a second-century governor, but the probability is that he was in office in 221/2 or somewhere between 235 and the accession of Gallienus, or just possibly in the first years of the latter's reign. He records on this altar the repair of the temple of Isis, 'collapsed from old age', and it is interesting to see that restoration of a fairly routine sort was still being carried out by a governor clearly not so preoccupied by events elsewhere as to neglect civil management.

The military preoccupations of the governors of Upper Britain differed from those of the second century. In Wales the garrison had been gradually run down from the middle of the second century, and though the two legions of the new province still lay at Caerleon and Chester, it would seem that the internal security of Wales by now needed relatively few troops. It is likely, too, that detachments from the two legions were more often away, as in the third century the use of large detachments as task forces working away from their bases for long periods rather than for a single campaign was becoming more common, pointing the way towards the eventual development of standing field armies and to the reduction of the overwhelming importance in the military pattern of the legion barracked together in its permanent fortress.

There are signs that governors were concerned about other parts of the province in the middle of the third century. Our attention is drawn first to the new coastal forts of the south and east. If the fort at Reculver is correctly dated to the first half of the century, it may not be much out of line with the gradual reconstruction of the defences of the north, reminding us not to separate the two provinces too firmly in our minds. Reculver is one of the series of forts commonly known as the 'Saxon Shore'. This is a thoroughly unsatisfactory but completely entrenched term, which owes its existence to a list of forts eventually established on the south and east coasts that is contained in a document known as the *Notitia Dignitatum*. This document, which may have reached its present form by the early fifth century, lists the stations that were under the command of an officer called, in the traditional translation, the 'Count of the Saxon Shore' (*comes litoris Saxonici*). This officer's title, and almost certainly his command as well, have nothing to do with Britain before the *late* third century at the very earliest. The list and title have also made it very difficult to break away from the idea that these forts were from the beginning a coherent series. Moreover, so firmly is the name 'Saxon Shore' now ingrained, that it is frequently applied also both to a style of architecture and to other forts of the third and fourth centuries, irrespective of the part of the country in which they are found.

For a start, we can detach from this late third- or fourth-century context two of the named series: Reculver itself, and Brancaster on the north Norfolk coast. As examples of military architecture in Britain, they are both in the style of the second century. They have a broad earthen bank behind their stone walls, and are without external towers or bastions. This is in direct line with the tradition of the earth and timber forts and their immediate stone successors. They are both placed adjacent to major estuaries that allowed easy access by sea into Britain from the Continent. In the case of Reculver, the access was to London, the principal city of Britain and a major port, as well as being the hub of the British road system and the point from which a large part of the richest areas of southern Britain could be reached. Brancaster lies alongside the Wash, from which it would have been simple for a sea-borne enemy to penetrate deeply into a region of dense occupation that may have been largely imperial estate, and to enter and disrupt the system of waterways that was perhaps still of major importance. It is not entirely clear whether the existence of a second-century civil settlement at Brancaster derived from some previous military occupation, but there was clearly good reason to build a new fort there in the third century. It is reasonable to suspect that Brancaster was planned and probably built before the mid-third-century flood that wrecked much of the Fenland for a long time. Brancaster could both watch for raids from the sea and guard a vital exit to the sea, as well as offering protection to coastal shipping lanes. In other words, this fort, which it is reasonable to suppose lay within Britannia Superior (the boundaries remain conjectural), could command the routes for heavy transport between major agricultural and industrial regions of the Upper provinces and important centres in Lower Britain, including its capital at York. This has implications for the dependence of one province on another, and may not, in the light of Severan policy, be accidental. It is interesting, too, to note a third site that may fit into this context. This is Caister-by-Yarmouth, which commands two river-mouths and acts as the terminus of the Fen Causeway. That road linked the eastern coast to the Fen waterways and, furthermore, ran through to the great industrial area around Peterborough, including the Nene Valley potteries that came into full production in the third century.

How these forts operated is uncertain, but the fact that Reculver is too large for its attested garrison, *cohors I Baetasiorum*, raises the possibility that it also served units of the fleet, the *classis Britannica*. Are we justified in assuming that these forts were intended to cope with sea-borne raids by Saxons or other Germanic barbarians? It is odd that Dover, which had been an active base of the *classis Britannica* in the second century, seems to have been run down and hardly occupied, if at all, in the mid-third. It was not revived until the construction of a 'Saxon Shore' fort around 270. This would suggest that the problems in the early and mid-third century were northward from the Thames to the Wash, rather than in the Channel and on the south coast. It may also have been that, after Albinus, the central government was unenthusiastic about any future governor of Britain having too complete a military stranglehold on the route from London to Gaul. These possibilities ought to make us hesitate before accepting that in the first half of the third century these forts had the same function—guarding against sea-borne barbarian raids—as the coastal forts as a whole at a later date.

The fact that Brancaster and Reculver do not seem to be placed as garrisons for specific ports (as Dover could have been) suggests that their tactical purpose was to support patrols out to sea, possibly serving as supply bases for ships. On the other hand, the garrison of Reculver was an infantry unit, which could indicate that its principal function was coastal observation and perhaps interception on land, and it is interesting to note that in the later second century the First cohort of Baetasians had been at Maryport, in the Cumberland coast section of the northern frontier. It is easy to forget that ordinary piracy, rather than serious sea-borne invasion, could be a real menace. In the second century a principal function of the *classis Britannica* had been the control of the iron industry in the Weald and the export of its products. In the fourth century the traffic in grain between Britain and the Continent was so well established that it was possible to expand it greatly in an emergency. The implied importance of protecting the freight routes should not be overlooked. This must have been as great in the third century as it had been in the second or was to be in the fourth, since so much attention was focused on the German frontier from Caracalla onwards. At the same time, the ease with which Constantius was able to dispose of the defences of the usurper Allectus at the end of the third century, and relieve London by sea, perhaps supports the idea that these forts were not geared to opposing a real invasion, at least not by an organized fleet.

We can now begin to imagine how the overall security situation might present itself to a third-century governor of Britannia Superior. His regular troops are concentrated into units of medium size but big enough for fairly decisive action, distributed over a comparatively small number of bases. His headquarters in London perhaps still retained its unique fort, but was now provided with city walls, built in stone from scratch. One might imagine that, having secured the safety of the principal city, the instinct would be to demolish the defences of the other cities in view of the recent attempt on the throne from Britain. This did not happen. Instead, stone walls were gradually provided for those towns that were as yet undefended or were supplied only with earthworks. The political risk of leaving the towns of a recently rebellious province with defences that might be seized by their local aristocracies or by military usurpers was clearly overridden by recognition of a pressure sufficient to affect the interests of the imperial authorities. It is reasonable to suppose that the threat that had prompted the earthwork construction in the first place —the reader will recall that it was suggested that the earthworks were constructed after the fighting in the 180s—was still felt to be real. However, the fact that the third-century process of building stone walls seems to have continued over a period of perhaps fifty years suggests that it was not acute, and this leisureliness is in some ways reflected in the renewal of the other defences of the island. Nor is that likely to have been entirely coincidental. Without an acute threat, it is difficult to imagine that the imperial government would have sanctioned the town walls unless there was a direct advantage to be gained. One cannot help suspecting that governors were now beginning to see the existence of a large number of walled towns as a potential military resource to be put alongside the forts. This is not to suggest the creation of local militias, rather the presence of defendable circuits enclosing buildings and supplies that could, in case of war, be immediately requisitioned for the use of quite large bodies of troops.

In sharp contrast to the limited circuits of walls that were built in many cities in Gaul after the barbarian devastations of the second half of the third century, there is the very remarkable fact that these third-century British town walls generally consisted of long stretches enclosing all or a large part of the town area, as in the second century, not just strong points. It implies that local communities still felt that it was worth building on this scale, and still had the resources to do so, even if architecturally these new walls tended to be more utilitarian in style than the second-century gates of Verulamium or Cirencester. In the light of this, it becomes extremely difficult to believe in a sharp decline in town life, nor do the wide circuits suggest that we should expect to find large areas of derelict land or abandoned property within the former built-up areas, though the nature of the occupation may have changed. Local magnates were still presumably powerful enough in their own communities to ensure that land belonging to them was enclosed within the new circuits.

The small urban centres that developed around active military stations showed no general decline in the third century: indeed, this was the period when they especially flourished. It used to be possible to argue that they were an exception, caused by the deliberate courting of the troops by the Severans, and in particular by the official recognition of soldiers' marriages. It is now clear that much building work went on as usual in towns without a military presence. It can also be contended—for example for Verulamium—that the widespread replacement in stone in the second century of private buildings constructed in timber in the first meant that there was comparatively little requirement in the third century for total rebuilding because of structural decay. It is understandable that in a period of sharp inflation private citizens might not be inclined to rebuild unless strictly necessary. In the public sector the same factor could have inhibited the construction of those major works that were usually the product of private generosity or came out of the collective purse of the membership of the town council. Moreover, these same people are likely to have been heavily committed to paying for the new walls, willingly or unwillingly. In the early part of the century the inclination to spend private resources on public works is likely to have remained strong, though confiscations after the fall of Albinus probably affected the ability to do so. By the late third century sentiment had changed in many parts of the empire, and it is much less likely that we should find such benefactions. Solid private comfort could nevertheless still exist and increase along-side relative impoverishment in the provision of new or renewed public amenities.

The owners of the more substantial country properties are in many cases likely to be the same people whose role as magnates in the towns we have been discussing. The picture of third-century decline used to be as overstated for the villas as for the towns. There were certainly a few brand-new villas in the third century, and there was a very considerable surge of rebuilding and enlargement towards the end of the period. For most of the century, however, there was probably no more need to reconstruct than in the towns, and the same problems of financial stringency and of the after-effects of political upheaval applied. Confisca-tions are most likely to have resulted in the amalgamation of estates: abandonment of the main house need not imply any reduction in the working of the land. Few would suggest that this was an age of expansion, but this does not mean that it was one of catastrophic decline.

There was one rural area that had been densely populated that does display undoubted decline in the third century, and here we are perhaps moving into the age of chaos that followed the mur-der of Severus Alexander. Nevertheless, it was the culmination of a physical process that had already started in the second cen-tury. The peak of farming in the Fenland was undoubtedly in the first half of the second century, and the ambitious settlement of that period was fairly soon beset with drainage troubles. By the middle of the third century this was acute, at least in the southern Fenlands, with many settlements abandoned. It is likely that a slow process of worsening drainage culminated in a major flood, with at least one river changing course. These events were probably mainly due to natural causes associated with river silt-ing and changes in relative sea-level, but they may well have been aided by lack of maintenance. It is possible that shortage of money compelled estate owners to neglect local drainage. On the other hand, it is more than possible that ignorance on the part of Roman engineers about the long-term effects of cutting certain channels was an important factor in the disasters that now occurred.

The skirtlands of the southern Fens were the worst hit by these troubles, and these are the areas where private ownership has been suggested. The villas of the area were mainly on the high ground of the Fenland margin, but many of the humbler settlements situated on low rises at the edge of the fen itself were severely affected. This, in its turn, is likely to have reduced the incomes of the landlords, whether as private owners or as leaseholders from the crown (*conductores*) who either farmed the land themselves or, more likely, drew rents from subtenant smallholders. A circular process may have been created, whereby shortage of cash reduced maintenance of the drainage system, which led to further diminishing of returns and thus more serious problems. Confiscation here too may have caused temporary but very damaging disruption of estate routine. It is certainly clear that nothing serious was done for twenty-five years or more. In the chaos of the mid-third century neither time nor money are likely to have been available for large-scale public action. No real recovery occurred in the Fenland until towards the end of the century. Some settlements never recovered.

We have seen that the evidence for a dramatic decline in prosperity throughout Britain in the third century is not strong. On the contrary, things may have looked quite different by the standards of the age. To understand why one of the British provinces may still have been an attractive posting for a governor in the middle of the third century, and to appreciate the background to the two periods of independence from the goverment in Rome that occurred in the second half of the century, we need now to look in a little more detail at the state of the empire.

The accession of Valerian and his son Gallienus as joint emperors in AD 253 marks the end of nearly two decades of chaos at the centre, with usurper after usurper gaining and losing the imperial throne. Palace plot, mutiny, and murder had created a climate in which disorder raised no less than seventeen would-be emperors to the purple between the assassination of the last of the Severans in 235 and the accession of Valerian, and as quickly disposed of them. The installation of Valerian and Gallienus halted this appalling procession—at least for the time being—and it never again reached that level of chaos over such a long period. On the other hand, their joint reign also marks the point at which pressure on the Roman frontiers in both the west and the east turned into a series of massive invasions. Until now, the third-century changes in administration, and the deliberate fostering of professional leadership in the army by the Severan emperors had allowed the Roman military and civil machine to continue to function efficiently despite lack of direction from the top. In the end, however, concentration on the internal struggles for power can only have opened up the way for the external enemies of Rome. In Germany Caracalla seems to have won peace for a substantial period, though for a shorter time than in Britain. From the 230s, however, the Roman territory beyond the Rhine became subject to insecurity again. The comparison and contrasts with Britain are important. In many ways life in Roman Britain had been very similar to that in the large areas of Roman territory that lay between the Rhine, the Danube, and the outer frontier, an area conquered and Romanized by the Flavians in the last part of the first century, like much of Britain. Like Britain, the region not only had its garrisons and frontier line, but it also had flourishing Roman towns and a Romanized countryside. Direct connections with Britain existed in the troop movements between the two countries, which had a long history. A detachment from the Twentieth legion at Chester (and probably from the other British legions as well) which is known to have been on the Rhine at Mainz in AD 255 must have seen what was happening in Germany, and it is unlikely that soldiers or civilians in Britain itself were unaware of the situation that was developing across the Rhine.

This situation became acute when Germanic barbarians, the Alamanni, broke into the empire in strength, causing widespread damage. The impetus of their attack carried them right through to Italy, where they were halted at last by Gallienus, who defeated them at Milan in 258. The effect on the Roman public, particularly in those regions hundreds of miles from the frontiers, can be imagined. Even Milan, which was becoming increasingly important as a centre of government from which communications with the provinces were easier than from Rome itself, was now within reach of the barbarians. The psychological shock is likely to have been great. The northern barbarians were part of Roman folk-history. The ancient threat from the north went back to the sack of Rome by the Celts in 387 BC, when only the Capitoline Hill stood out. More recently, there had been the alarming moment in the reign of Marcus Aurelius when the semi-subject peoples across the Danube revolted and entered north-east Italy. This time the struggle was more desperate and more prolonged. Even under Marcus military revolt inside the empire had made it difficult to deal with the northern barbarians. In the third century civil war was to weaken Roman attention to external defence so much that the whole system almost collapsed.

It would be misleading to think of there being a revolutionary proletariat in the ranks of the Roman army or a revolutionary officer class. The Roman soldier, however strict the discipline imposed upon him, was already an unusually privileged person by the standards of the ancient world: he was paid a regular money wage, he had secure employment, and he could look forward to a comfortable retirement as a solid citizen even if he had not risen to superior rank during his service. Many retired soldiers founded influential families. In times of civil war promotion was often extremely rapid, and the elevation of families to positions of wealth and influence consequently accelerated. The army had long been a powerful instrument of social mobility, and produced men who expected to enjoy the fruits of the existing system, not to overthrow it. Very large numbers of non-Romans passed through the auxiliary units and swelled the ranks of Roman citizens with a vested interest in the empire. In the third century, when Caracalla's edict had granted citizenship to almost all those free inhabitants of the empire who still did not have it—the *Constitutio Antoniniana*—and when senior posts were going to equestrian officers, many of whom had climbed from the ranks, the limits of ambition were enormously extended. It is a commonplace that the success of the Roman empire was largely due to its ability to Romanize and absorb very large numbers of people of very differing origins. It is often noted that the Roman aristocracy, despite its devotion to family, tended not to propagate itself. Moreover, political upheaval eliminated many of the most prominent families, either entirely or from public life. Large gaps appeared at the top of the social scale, and were immediately filled. The successors adopted their predecessors' attitudes and way of life without doubt or delay. It is perhaps not perverse to suggest that Rome's enormous success in turning provincials into Romans was itself a major force in the eventual collapse of the Roman world, since part of what they acquired was the upper-class Roman devotion to family and ambition over state. By the middle of the third century disorder and military usurpation had become so frequent that Roman tradition must have been militating against the chances of the empire surviving in its established form.

The reign of Gallienus was marked by another event that was as striking in the context of Roman history as the invasion of Italy by the Alamanni. This time, however, the shock was not tempered by a subsequent victory. One of the worst blows ever suffered by Roman prestige had been the annihilation of an army under the politician Crassus by Rome's eastern enemy, the Parthians, in 53 BC at Carrhae. In AD 224 the Sassanians overthrew the rulers of the Parthian empire, and their revived Persian empire, governed by direct descendants of the men who had led the army that destroyed Crassus, henceforth pursued a more or less consistently aggressive policy against Rome. This was to last for no less than four hundred years, with varying fortunes.

Coming to the throne in 253, Valerian had left his son Gallienus to administer the west of the Roman empire while he himself tackled the problems of the eastern frontier. Soon after his accession Valerian had struggled to deal with attacks on the eastern territories of Rome from the north, in particular by the Goths, and from the east by the Persians. In 260 his not very successful attempts were brought to an end by his own defeat and capture by the Sassanian king, Shapur I. Carrhae had been repeated in dramatic fashion.

In the west Gallienus was putting down a rebellion on the Danube, in the frontier province of Pannonia, when, perhaps while he was still attending to this problem, his lieutenant on the Rhine, Marcus Postumus, murdered the praetorian prefect Silvanus and Gallienus' own son Saloninus, who were at Cologne. Under the weight of these national and family disasters, Gallienus' run of success ceased. In Germany Postumus declared himself emperor. The provinces and armies of Germany, Gaul, Spain, and Britain supported him. Thus began the curious phase known as the Gallic Empire, when for thirteen years the whole of the north-western part of the empire was run as an independent entity, with its own series of emperors. It was a fully Roman state, not a manifestation of nationalist separatism.

The sustaining of the Gallic Empire cannot have been easy. The large military forces of the north-west now had to be paid for solely by the north-west, not to mention the cost of supporting an imperial administration and an imperial court. It is uncertain to what extent in the third century the eastern provinces were still being tapped as the principal source of wealth for the Roman empire as a whole, but it is certain that the Gallic Empire had to exist on what had never been a rich part of the Roman world. The provincials of the north-west had to cope entirely alone with an army that had been taught to expect the best and to change its emperor if it did not get it. This might not have been so bad if the pressure from outside had not been so grave. Under Severus Alexander, the frontier garrison was gradually being run down, but in 233 a significant point in the history of the west was reached with the first of the Alamannic invasions. In 258, as we have seen, the Alamanni had poured through a land of unwalled cities until halted by Gallienus in Italy. But in 260 the frontier across the Rhine collapsed completely in the face of the same enemy. One might suppose that the end must have seemed imminent. Indeed, henceforth there seems to have been no permanent military presence across the Rhine, and parts of the region were probably already severely damaged by the earlier invasions. It is, however, not clear that the region was immediately and comprehensively taken over by Germanic settlement, and there are some signs that the Gallic emperors made attempts to restore the situation.

The first of the Gallic emperors deserves credit for preventing a much worse deterioration in the west, but his own rebellion must have weakened the empire seriously. Gallienus, after an abortive attempt in 263 to recover the north-western provinces, had to accept their loss to the Gallic Empire. This is an appropriate point at which to reflect on the situation in Britain. As long ago as the first century Roman legions had mutinied when they were being transferred from a comfortable province in which they had built up strong local ties to do service on a frontier that they regarded as dangerous and unpleasant. Now the local ties were much stronger, and we may guess that there were troops in Britain who did not want to follow the detachment we have already noted at Mainz in 255 and to obey summonses to join in the central empire's wars against distant barbarians. Britain seems to have been free from major attack: this can hardly have seemed true of many other parts of the empire. It is therefore perhaps not surprising that Britain fell in with the Gallic Empire, influenced also, no doubt, by the cutting of communications with Rome. When discussing the appointment of Octavius Sabinus to the governorship of Britannia Inferior, we noted the possibility that members of the senatorial order who were excluded from military command by Gallienus might have supported Postumus. There were probably few of that class in Britain, but those there were are likely to have been influential.

If there was any tendency for the programme of wall-building in British towns to slacken under the financial pressures of this period, there is no sign in the archaeology. It is likely that any such inclinations were overruled by the fact that the lack of walls was a major factor in the damage to cities in Gaul. Nor can it have been overlooked that barbarian raids into provinces in which Roman forces were concentrated on the actual frontiers had been remarkably successful. The need for protection in the inner areas of provinces was now clear. Despite all this, there is no sign of haste in the provision of defences. Britain must have seemed to the Gallic emperors to be among the healthiest parts of their dominions.

From AD 268 the gloom over the Roman world at large began to lift. A series of remarkable soldier emperors commenced the process of reunifying and restoring the empire. After Postumus had been murdered in 269 while putting down an insurrection, the *Imperium Galliarum* fell successively into the hands of the Gallic emperors Victorinus and Tetricus. The central government, however, was recovering. The accession of Aurelian, also in 269, had brought to the throne an emperor determined to restore the unity and security of the empire, and capable of doing so. By

274 he had defeated the barbarians who had crossed the Danube, crushed an attempt at another independent empire (in the east), and put an end to the military power of the Gallic Empire at the battle of Châlons. Tetricus surrendered to him after Châlons, ceased to be an emperor, and was permitted to pursue a useful and distinguished career in the public life of the reunited Roman empire. Britain came back into the mainstream of Roman affairs, and one may suspect that Aurelian's treatment of the Gallic emperor encouraged reconciliation and the continuation of normal life in the British provinces.

By the standards of the age, then, the middle of the century was not a depressed period in Britain. Two examples should reinforce the point. The Great Witcombe villa in Gloucestershire developed from a small establishment into a large one: the first phase of major extension appears to date from the period 250–70. Similarly, in the small town of Droitwich a very substantial urban house with painted plaster was started in this period, sometime after 250. Some property owners clearly had both money and confidence. On the other hand, there is some sign that public works requiring major expenditure were liable to be put off—for example, the restoration of the Fenland after its third-century inundation. Yet there is no reason to suppose that Britain lacked attention under the Gallic Empire. The presence of an imperial government in Gaul rather than in Italy may have meant more interest rather than less, particularly from an insecure regime that relied upon the unwavering support of Britain and its neighbours to survive. It is interesting to note that the *civitas* of the Carvetii, apparently based on the city of Carlisle, is first recorded under Postumus. This might reflect administrative development under the Gallic Empire. On the other hand, one might argue that the new *civitas* recognized the importance of the third-century expansion of the civil settlements dependent on the army in the frontier region. It would be a logical development of the Severan policy of favouring the troops. It would make good sense to involve soldiers and their families in a stable local community with its own local rights and sense of pride, and to give retired soldiers the traditional opportunity to gain prestige by being absorbed into a municipal *ordo* without having to move away from the district in which they had their roots.

Turning now to the last quarter of the century, we can begin to estimate what happened in Britain when the Gallic Empire finally collapsed. A substantial amount of building development in Britain is dated by archaeologists to around 270/5. Taking the last quarter of the century as a whole, there are signs of new prosperity. In the private sector, for example, the villa at Witcombe shows further major alterations after 275, and at Frocester Court, another large villa not far away, a formal walled garden was added at about the same time. In the public domain, Brough-on-Humber, which had developed as a reasonably important civil centre between 125 and 200, and showed signs of military use after 200, was now being rebuilt in stone. Was the reason solely the reunification of the empire? After Aurelian's victory over the Gallic emperor, there was one more Germanic invasion, in 276. Fifty to sixty towns are reported to have been captured by the barbarians and subsequently recovered by the Romans. Archaeology shows large numbers of villas in northern Gaul as apparently abandoned from the late third century. In consequence, it has been suggested that the remarkable flowering of villas in Britain from the 270s onwards reflects a 'flight of capital' from Gaul. It might more likely reflect a flight of *owners*, for there is no reason to suppose that land in Britain may not have belonged to rich men living elsewhere in the empire.

It may be significant in this context that the unwalled cities of Gaul were slow to respond to the invasions, and when they did at last begin to remedy their deficiency, they did not construct the great circuits that can be seen in Britain, but only relatively small citadels. Other reasons can be adduced for the need to have at least one part of the town secure, but the failure to provide full circuits may not simply reflect the extent of destruction and the lack of will to rebuild the whole of the former urban area. Indeed, it has been argued that the urban areas of Gallic cities did not shrink by anything like the extent usually assumed, nor had been so badly damaged. Another explanation may lie in the way in which wall-building was financed in the provinces in the absence of the imperial subsidies, which were probably comparatively rare. Responsibility essentially lay with individual property owners. At Godmanchester it has been shown that the town defences were completed where they ran at the back of a temple, and left unfinished in a stretch on private property. Owners may be divided into three broad categories: the private individual; the semi-public organization (such as temple guilds); and the municipal authorities themselves. The sacking of the Gallic cities will have been immediately ruinous for the first two groups, for we may be certain that individual houses and businesses were looted, and temple treasures—often built up from the gifts of the faithful over centuries—were carried off. The municipality, too, probably lost its ready cash holdings. More seriously, its fortunes could only be revived if the town's notables— the councillors and any private patrons that it might have had —were on hand to replenish the coffers. These people were the town's fundamental assets. If the local aristocracy had departed, then despite the undoubted fact that they could not legally escape their duties to their *civitas*, the possibility of actually raising cash from them must have been enormously reduced. The lack of response in the Gallic cities is therefore entirely consistent with a flight of their chief citizens abroad.

The argument has been taken further. The fact that in the region between Cirencester and Dorchester (Dorset) there are apparently no villas that can be dated earlier than the beginning of the third century, and that around Bath, eventually the district most densely occupied by villas, there seem to be none before about 270, has been taken to suggest that former imperial estates may have been sold off to raise cash. It will be suggested later, in another context, that an early third-century inscription from Combe Down outside Bath may relate to estates then in the hands of the emperor, perhaps after earlier confiscations. It is equally possible that at some stage imperial estates may have been given to supporters of the current emperor as rewards. Either way, it is possible that large areas of non-private land now fell into the hands of rich landowners from Gaul, who proceeded to build villas where there had previously been none.

Whatever their origins, the British villas of the late third century are an archaeological fact. Both their construction and the implied presence of rich households must have injected new vitality into the economy. There have been suggestions that estates in Britain were changing from arable cultivation to sheep-farming or other large-scale ranching, with possible reductions in farm labour and even evictions, but the sheer presence of upper-class households can only have stimulated many branches of trade and the manufacturing, construction, and service industries. This ought also to have increased activity in the urban centres and at the sites of major fairs, where markets were often associated with religious complexes and pilgrimage destinations. Nor is there any reason to assume that any transference of capital investment from the Continent would only affect landed property: commercial and industrial enterprise could also have benefited greatly.

A new interest in Britain on the part of people of importance and influence could also help to explain the renewal of official attention to the military security of the island. The next stage in the development of the Saxon Shore may be a sign. At Burgh Castle in Suffolk, for example, a new stone fort was commenced in an archaic style with rounded corners, but incorporating the more recent trend towards thick stone walls without an earthen backing. Before these walls had reached their full height, the plan was radically altered by the addition of massive external towers. At Richborough the venerable Domitianic triumphal monument first began to be converted into a small fort, and then the whole site was remodelled to take a brand-new large stone fort on modern lines.

It is certain that, even after the breaking of the Gallic Empire, political stability was not all that it might have been in the northeastern part of the empire. Of two risings in Gaul that were put down in the reign of Probus, who carried on Aurelian's tremendous work of military recovery, by far the more serious was the second, that of Bonosus. The latter's inefficiency had allowed the Roman fleet on the Rhine, based at Cologne, to be destroyed by barbarians, and he had rebelled to avoid the inevitable punishment. This revolt may have affected Britain. Certainly, there were alarming disturbances. Probus was obliged to send a Moorish officer named Victorinus to put down a rebellion by a governor in Britain whom Victorinus himself had recommended, and it is also recorded that Probus settled Burgundian and Vandal prisoners of war in the island, whom he was then able to employ against uprisings. These barbarians had been defeated in 277 and were transferred in 277 or 278 to new homes in Britain. One may guess that they were used on internal security operations in Britain because, unlike the regular garrison in Britain, they had not yet formed any local ties. The archaeological evidence of burning on several sites in Sussex in this period may reflect barbarian raids on the coast, but it might equally be explained by the internal situation in the reign of Probus. On the other hand, after Probus had been supplanted by his praetorian prefect Carus in 282, the latter's son Carinus, left as *nobilissimus Caesar* in charge of the western part of the empire, carried on the policy of vigorous action against the barbarians. A single inscription dedicated to Carinus (from the villa at Clanville, near Andover), dated from 282 or 283, must reflect an early recognition of his authority in Britain. His assumption of the titles 'Britannicus Maximus' and 'Germanicus Maximus' suggests that his continued control of the west after succeeding his father, when he ruled as joint emperor with his brother Numerian, was marked with military successes, and is much more likely to refer to victories over external enemies than suppression of internal disturbances. The enemies, moreover, that gave rise to the title 'Britannicus' may well have been defeated by the Channel fleet, and not in Britain itself nor by forces necessarily based in Britain: the *classis Britannica* had always had its principal—and, in recent years, perhaps only— headquarters on the Gallic side of the Channel at Boulogne. Even if the old *classis Britannica* had by now been dispersed or reorganized, the association of the name with the theatre of operations could well have persisted.

There undoubtedly were barbarians in the Channel in the late third century. Britain may have suffered actual or threatened raids, though Eutropius, our historical source, refers to the coasts from Brittany northwards to Flanders. At the same time there was a serious outbreak of disorder in Gaul caused by the 'Bacaudae', a name that first appears in the literature referring to this period and signifies bands of disaffected country people, refugees, deserters, and old soldiers who had been thrown into brigandage on a considerable scale by the barbarian invasions, civil wars, and financial chaos of the time. After a century of intermittent peasant upheaval, these elements broke into armed and organized rebellion in 284. Yet, interestingly, even these rebels could not escape from Roman tradition, but demanded their own 'empire'. The threat to authority and established order, however, was a real one, and it is likely that the eventual provision of town walls in Gaul was as much a response to this growing disorder in the surrounding countryside as to the recurrent barbarian invasions, themselves a contributory cause to the upheaval in rural life. The Bacaudae, therefore, are likely to have been a further factor in any flight of the upper class across the Channel.

Ironically, vigorous action by the restored central authority to strengthen the Roman military presence in the north-west rebounded on its initiators by producing the conditions for yet another army coup. The Roman problem was perhaps insoluble. Augustus had recognized that security from revolution required the smallest possible standing army. Severus refined this by combining a sharp reduction in the size of individual commands with maximum generosity to the troops themselves. On the other hand, increasing barbarian pressure and problems of internal security in the third century compelled larger concentrations of troops, which were accompanied by the transfer of commands to a professional officer class drawn from outside the traditional aristocracy. The vicious circle was completed by the fact that the consequent increases in taxation and military recruitment combined with the unpopularity of an arrogant and privileged army to intensify internal disaffection towards the Roman government. It is in the context of these fundamental faults that we find Britain in 287 once again embroiled in a *coup d'état*.

12

THE TETRARCHY

'Medieval history' traditionally starts with the accession of Diocletian in AD 284. It has become conventional to accept the subsequent 'reforms'—constitutional, political, military, social, economic,
and religious—as marking a decisive break between the ancient
and medieval worlds. Most of all, attention is drawn to the establishment of the 'Christian Empire' by Constantine (the Edict of
Milan conferring imperial favour on the Church was issued in
313), and the foundation of Constantinople by the same emperor
in 324. Nevertheless, the landmark date of 284 is of more convenience to the medieval historian and the Byzantinist than it is
to those studying the ancient world. Whatever the magnitude of
the changes in the forty years after the accession of Diocletian,
fourth-century Britain had much more in common with its own
history since the Claudian conquest than with its condition in
the centuries after the end of Roman rule. With Diocletian, we
are not entering the Middle Ages, but the 'late Roman' world.

Diocletian's elevation was a direct consequence of the mysteri-
ous death of Carinus' co-emperor and brother Numerian, whose
personal guard Diocletian commanded at the time. Diocletian
was of humble provincial origin, from Dalmatia. His fate has been
to be labelled as the arch-reformer, yet his work is notable for
intense devotion to Roman tradition. In personal terms, he marks
the total absorption of other peoples into the Roman way of life,
and his reforms were aimed throughout at restoring the integrity
of the Roman state, not at creating something new.

In 285 Diocletian's power became complete when Carinus was
assassinated and the western armies went over to his side. Diocletian appointed Marcus Aurelius Valerius Maximianus, one of

his officers, as his chief lieutenant, bearing (like Carinus himself earlier) the title of 'Caesar' and responsibility for the defence of Italy and the western provinces. In the same year Diocletian himself took the title of 'Britannicus Maximus', and it seems reasonable to suppose that a military success of some importance had been won in his name that concerned Britain, which lay within Maximian's command. At this stage, the latter was engaged in restoring order throughout the north-west of the empire, continuing the work of Aurelian and Probus, under both of whom he had served with distinction. In particular, he had to contend with the Bacaudae in Gaul. Maximian successfully dealt with these problems, and in 286 he was promoted by Diocletian to the rank of 'Augustus' to act as co-emperor, retaining responsibility for the west. There was nothing unusual about an emperor taking a colleague thus, nor was this out of line with Roman tradition generally—many magistrates had colleagues, from the consuls downwards. It had also, conversely, been part of Roman tradition as far back as the Republic for one magistrate to dominate his fellows through his personal *auctoritas*. Diocletian was unmistakably the senior Augustus, and had no difficulty in retaining the ultimate power. This principle remained broadly valid throughout the fourth century, and, despite increasing polarization towards east and west, we shall only confuse ourselves if we think in terms of 'eastern' and 'western' empires in the sense of separate states. Except for periods when eastern and western colleagues were at loggerheads, this was not even *de facto* the position until after the death of Theodosius the Great in 395, and that the separation was not reflected constitutionally even then is a key to much that happened subsequently.

The west was no easy assignment for Maximian. As well as internal disturbances, he faced other serious military problems. A little later he was obliged to put great efforts into the defence of the imperial frontier both on the lower Rhine and in Raetia. At this stage he was tackling swarms of Saxon and Frankish raiders who were descending on the coasts of Brittany and Gallia Belgica. In charge of his countermeasures, Maximian put an officer called M. Mausaeus Carausius, by origin a Menapian from the Low Countries. Carausius is said to have been of very humble birth but to have acquired an impressive reputation as a soldier. He was based at Boulogne, and had enjoyed frequent successes, capturing many barbarians. Unfortunately, a suspicion was growing that he had prior knowledge of the raids. He was alleged to turn this to his own advantage, letting the barbarians in and refraining from taking them until they were back at sea, laden with plunder. It was said that he returned the stolen goods neither to the provincials who owned them nor to the emperors (it is unclear which of these was thought to be the worse crime), but converted them to his own use. Maximian ordered his execution. Carausius replied by proclaiming himself emperor and seizing the provinces of Britain. From late 286 or 287 the island once again came under a Roman administration independent of the central government.

In Britain Carausius' safety from attack across the Channel was secured by the fleet that he already commanded, but he also had substantial land forces in Gaul, with which he was able to deny Maximian access to the coast. These forces probably included troops allocated to him to defend the coast itself and to work with the fleet, and perhaps others that joined him subsequently. In Britain, too, he must have had substantial support. One may assume that there were survivors from amongst those who had found themselves on the wrong side in one or other of the upheavals of the previous decades. The crucial role that the recent Burgundian and Vandal settlers had played in the subduing of revolt in the reign of Probus suggests strongly that the regular garrisons had been sympathetic to the rebellious governor. Past independence from the central administration in the days of the Gallic Empire may also have become an attractive memory by now: the people of the empire were faced with a central government dominated, in Diocletian, by a tough soldier obsessed with organization, determined to impose national discipline, and intent on collecting the resources for a vast overhaul of the defences of the empire, behind which order could be restored and maintained. Many communities and individuals, too, may have seen real advantages in having an emperor who was at hand, since so much depended on cultivating imperial favour. As private patronage declined, this was becoming of increasing importance. For the politically aware and well informed, recent Roman politics did not give much reason to suppose that Diocletian and Maximian would be any more secure in the long run than their predecessors, and there must have been much to be said for submitting unobtrusively to the nearest would-be emperor who seemed to have solid support from his troops. Finally, to the vast mass of common people, particularly in the more remote provinces, the niceties of legitimacy probably meant little. Many may have had little idea who was currently on the throne, and, even if they did know names, the emperor whose agents were encountered in the daily round and whose head was on the newest coins *was* the emperor as far as they were concerned.

Diocletian's reputation as a reformer rests on the totality of the measures during his reign, some of which were introduced while Britain was cut off from the central empire. To us the most spectacular change is the introduction of the 'Tetrarchy' in 293, when the empire was again under severe strain. It was a development of the delegation of authority to Maximian. In outline, this new scheme of government rested on the two senior emperors ('Augusti'), who ruled the eastern and western parts of the empire respectively, each with a junior or 'Caesar' acting as his deputy and taking particular responsibility for one geographical area within the half of the empire controlled by his Augustus. The system was to work as a college of four emperors. They normally ruled their own sectors more or less independently, but operations that were carried out when required in each other's territories show that no rigid geographical division was intended, and the fact that they were regularly addressed as a group of four confirms that Diocletian saw them as a team.

At its best, the Tetrarchy could cope with the administrative and security problems caused by the sheer size of the empire and the slowness of communications. It might also ensure a smooth succession to the throne, for Diocletian added a touch of real imagination in proposing that both senior emperors should retire at the same time and be succeeded by their Caesars, who would then have Caesars of their own. This was to be cemented, in traditional Roman fashion, by family alliances. Diocletian and Maximian had taken additional family names—Jovius and Herculius respectively, after the gods Jupiter and Hercules—emphasizing the exalted nature of their sovereignty. The two Augusti now adopted the Caesars and arranged marriage alliances, so that the two junior emperors became members of the Jovii and Herculii as well. The line between this and hereditary dynasties is a thin one, and it is not surprising that the next generation of troops (and the sons themselves) were not inclined to make anything of the distinction. In the first century it had been vital in retaining the loyalty of the armies to be a member of the Julian house or to be able to claim a connection. In the fourth century 'legitimate' imperial families established a similar advantage over their rivals. In truth, the question of the succession was, in the context of the Roman tradition of personal reputation and family rivalry, quite insoluble. Nevertheless, though Diocletian's quadripartite scheme did not last at the top, it was a framework on which to hang the major modifications of the administrative and military structure of the empire that did endure.

In the military field, it is doubtful whether Diocletian can be called a conscious reformer, in the sense of instituting major changes in the structure or methods of the Roman army. Rather, he seems to have pursued with great vigour a policy of strengthening it more or less as it was. Zosimus, comparing Diocletian favourably with Constantine, says that

by the foresight of Diocletian the frontiers of the Roman empire were everywhere studded with cities and forts and towers . . . and the whole army was stationed along them, so that it was impossible for the barbarians to break through, as the attackers were everywhere withstood by an opposing force. But Constantine ruined this defensive system by withdrawing the majority of the troops from the frontiers, and stationing them in cities which did not require protection.

As we have seen, a standing field army or armies had been emerging, more or less accidentally, from the system of *ad hoc* arrangements for specific campaigns. To some extent Diocletian seems to have reversed this trend, returning troops to frontier service and splitting up the substantial mobile force of cavalry that had existed since the time of Gallienus. However, he also raised new legions—calling them 'Ioviani' and 'Herculiani' after himself and his chief colleague—that came to be used in a more flexible way than the frontier garrisons, and he created new élite mounted regiments that were intended to be deployed centrally. By 295 the idea of troops being permanently attached to the central imperial court had become sufficiently entrenched to receive the description *comitatus*. The whole group had by now acquired some appearance of permanency, and must have profited from their proximity to the emperors they served. It is not impossible that there were also some units normally stationed elsewhere that were designated as part of a reserve that could be assembled quickly for field service with the emperors. There is no reason to think, however, that they were regularly brigaded together or stationed away from the frontiers as early as this. Indeed, when a permanent field army, formally constituted, did emerge clearly, it seems at first to have been a fairly small force.

In the course of the fourth century the military *comitatus* became firmly established, and there are already signs that its units were acquiring higher status from their privileged position, just as the praetorians had long enjoyed over the legions. Yet there are also indications that in Diocletian's reign the old primary distinction between legions and auxiliaries remained. His arrangements for veterans still differentiated between the legions (now joined by the special cavalry units) and the old auxiliary *cohortes* and *alae*. The distinctions of training, function, career structure, and pay had once reflected the differences between citizen and non-citizen, but the latter had been eroded, first by individual cases, and eventually by the wholesale extension of the citizenship under Caracalla. However, as we have seen, the old auxiliary units of the army had also been supplemented by newly raised *numeri* and *cunei*. At the beginning of the fourth century, therefore, the concept of an army with many levels of status and emoluments was of very long standing, and was thus capable of further development without offending tradition.

It had been the aim of Augustus—and, on the whole, of his successors—to keep the army as small as was consistent with the security of the empire. To work, the policy required that there should not be pressure on several frontiers at once, that there should be a reasonable degree of internal acceptance of imperial rule, and abstention from large-scale military adventure on the part of the emperor himself. It also assumed that the advantage of the state and not of the army itself was the prime consideration among the troops and their officers. All these conditions for success had broken down. There is much debate about how much Diocletian increased the actual size of the armed forces.

There is some indication that the army was seriously under strength by the late third century, and this he certainly remedied. There are real difficulties in discovering the actual size of units in the fourth century, and some reason to think that the overall picture was of many more separate units, with substantially fewer men in each. On paper, at least, the total number of soldiers may have been a third more than at the beginning of the third century —and, under Diocletian himself at least, the actual number may have been that great—but many uncertainties remain. Fresh legions were certainly being formed out of detachments from existing legions (some detachments had been away from their parent legions for very long periods), and others were raised from scratch. Conscription had to be applied very severely to produce the recruits. Diocletian's remedies tended always to include coercion of the individual and an expansion of numbers in the direct service of the empire. The strain on the economy, which he was also trying to put right by means of state control, must have been considerable.

Diocletian's genius was in the employment of organization as a cure for the ills of the state, adapting and expanding existing elements in the Roman scene on a grand scale. Unlike Constantine, he was not a revolutionary, in the sense of admitting of a radically different political, social, or religious pattern—very much the reverse. Nevertheless, like the reforms of Augustus, his measures created the conditions for a new framework for the Roman world. They were also achieved at the cost of a vast increase in public expenditure—one feature that we shall find repeated under Constantine. Of the Diocletianic period, the hostile writer Lactantius complained that this did not stop with the increased number of senior posts (probably unavoidable to cope with the expanding burden of administration). Referring to the latest division of provinces, he pointed out that every extra provincial governor meant an extra staff to go with him. We shall do well to remember this when considering the appearance of four, and then five, provinces in Britain in the fourth century —not overlooking the fact that a new tier of provincial administration was also added, the 'diocese' or group of provinces, which had its own head (*vicarius*) and staff. The new, smaller provinces of Britain formed such a diocese. And it was not very long before the armies in the provinces were to have their own quite separate commanders and accompanying headquarters. The opportunities for extending the tradition of patronage and placemen increased enormously. One may wonder how the empire could possibly stand it, especially after the ravages of the third century. It certainly had huge social effects. The old structure of society, in which the empire was composed of a vast network of communities kept vigorous by competition between its local notables, had declined to a very low point over large areas of the empire in the troubles of the third century. In the fourth century, except for a small number of very rich magnates, advancement and reputation were to be sought in areas of activity under the direct control of the emperor and his ministers. Hugely burdensome on the state as they may seem now, at the time the reforms of Diocletian may have looked cheap compared with the prospect of renewed internal decay, civil war, and barbarian invasion.

The revolt of Carausius was embarrassing and awkward for Maximian as the newly elevated Augustus. Up to that point he had been generally successful in restoring order in the west, and Carausius' naval operations had been a notable part of those victories. The blow was compounded when Maximian's decision to take drastic action against Carausius backfired. Diocletian can hardly have been pleased at the bungled handling of the affair. Nor can he have enjoyed the loss of provinces that were of considerable military importance and whose more or less undamaged economy contrasted strongly with the battered state of Gaul and Germany. It is a measure of just how serious the situation remained on the German frontier that Maximian had delayed preparing for military action against Carausius until the latter part of 288. Maybe he also hoped to negotiate a settlement, or to topple Carausius from his position by intrigue. Carausius, for his part, tried to consolidate his support by playing on local interests. Something of his propaganda remains on the coinage that he began to issue, which describes him as 'restorer of Britain' and the like. One of his issues is the only Roman coin with an (adapted) quotation from Virgil: 'Come, you who have been so eagerly awaited.' It presents Carausius as a political saviour, and tries to imply the existence of a general body of opinion that had awaited some such relief from unspecified troubles. There is an aura, too, of the supernatural or divine, which accords with the image of the emperor that Diocletian himself was developing. It might not be fanciful to think that in some people's minds echoes of the Messianic will have been aroused. Reference on other Carausian coins to the *genius Britanniae*, the personified spirit of the island, adds to the impression of an intelligent use of that blend of political and religious ideas which earlier emperors had employed in the interests of themselves and of the stability of the state.

We do not know the extent of Carausius' command under Maximian at the time of his revolt. The subsequent position can perhaps partly be inferred from his coin series, which lists a number of legions, including not only two of the regular garrison of Britain, but also various others. The inference is that he retained or managed to take command of legionary detachments in northern Gaul, perhaps originally allocated to work with him in the campaign against the pirates. An intriguing feature of this coin series is the presence of II *Augusta* and XX *Valeria Victrix*, but not of VI *Victrix*, whose fortress at York had been the pivot of the northern frontier since Trajan's reign, and the centre of the province of Lower Britain for the best part of a century. At some time during his reign Carausius was recognized in at least part of the northern frontier area, since a milestone with his name was found at Carlisle, but this need not mean that the loyalty of the Sixth was above suspicion. It seems possible that Britannia Inferior did not come over to Carausius as promptly as Britannia Superior, the south-eastern part of whose garrison may already have been under his command. The legions of Britain, as the reader will remember from the Year of the Four Emperors, did not always support the same party in times of civil war.

There does not, however, seem any reason to doubt that Carausius was in a strong military position. The fact that the coin series includes the names of six legions normally stationed on the Continent suggests that, even if he only had detachments from these, he nevertheless had substantial land forces at his disposal. Maximian certainly made little headway in 289, not only losing a naval battle, but also being unable to dislodge Carausius' forces from the powerful land and sea base at Boulogne, which he was still holding in 293. Success against such an opponent as

Maximian was proof to his troops that Carausius possessed the divine gift of good fortune in war, enhancing his personal *auctoritas* and inspiring confidence in a military future that must otherwise have looked decidedly unpromising.

It was equally important—with civilians as well as soldiers—to establish the trappings of legitimacy. Carausius had not hesitated to follow tradition by proclaiming himself emperor. The administration of his realm required an emperor as the fount of authority to confirm appointments and to legalize the actions of officials. A usurper, moreover, was only a usurper until he was firmly established. Carausius took the imperial names of M. Aurelius, and adopted the device of portraying himself on his coinage as a third colleague, sharing the throne with Diocletian and Maximian. Perhaps the best known of these coins is the issue that pictured the three of them with the legend 'Carausius and his Brothers'. The others did not respond, yet the events of the past century need have given him no cause to feel less legitimate than they did.

Carausius took care to issue a sound coinage, a sensible move in view of the disastrous state into which the imperial coinage had fallen during the third century. This had been just one aspect of the deep-rooted condition of inflation and financial chaos that had dominated many decades. Diocletian himself—after Carausius' death, but before the recovery of Britain by the central government—introduced a reformed coinage into the empire at large, and the regime in Britain in its turn adjusted its currency to the new values. We should not assume that Britain was economically as well as politically isolated, other than in the collection and destination of taxes. Britain's rulers would have had reason to encourage normality and the maximum flow of trade. Nor, with signs of returning stability and security on the Continent, would commercial interests and those landowners with properties on both sides of the Channel have thanked them if they had not. These were the people who kept the Roman system going and (particularly the provincial gentry of less than senatorial rank) supplied many of the administrators and army officers on whom the emperors depended. As the neighbouring provinces recovered, Carausius may have felt a fresh need to compete for loyalty, now that the central government was showing clear signs of being there to stay and of being capable of beating back the barbarians. Conditioned by hindsight and the immense reputation of Diocletian in later ages, it is difficult for us to appreciate the surprise with which the survival of an emperor for more than a short time will have been greeted.

We touched earlier on the dating of the Saxon Shore forts. It still looks likely that the series as we know it was the result of building and modification over a long period with forts serving different purposes at different times. This is not to deny that there were periods when scattered elements already in existence were probably drawn together and combined with new forts and features to form a coherent system for specific purposes. This, we might surmise, perhaps first happened under Probus or Carinus. However, it is unlikely that either the system as a whole or individual elements in it retained an identical purpose to the end of Roman Britain—or, for that matter, until their individual operational lives came to an end. We have seen that Reculver and Brancaster go back to the earlier part of the third century; the Saxon Shore fort at Dover dates from the latter part of that century; and the first evidence at a Saxon Shore fort from tree-ring dating indicates that the timber for foundation piling at Pevensey was cut somewhere between about 280 and 300. Their ends, too, need not be contemporary. It is important, also, not to see the forts in isolation from the fortified towns, since, as we have noted, the latter were probably being included in contemporary military planning. Indeed, if the completion of the London circuit with the riverside wall can be fixed as late as about 270, then this may suggest a direct link with the Saxon Shore forts. Nor is there any cause to think that defence from barbarian attack from outside the empire—generally assumed to be the purpose of these forts—excluded the functions of maintaining a watch for signs of internal unrest, and of controlling, for both political and fiscal reasons, movement and communications within the empire. Civil war is a circumstance in which these latter needs become particularly acute, and we may guess that some of the building works or modifications were initiated by Carausius and his successor Allectus. We are working without the precision of exact epigraphic evidence, and trying to tie these structures down by archaeological means is a tricky enterprise, particularly liable to reassessment.

As we have already noted, it was during the political separation of the territories controlled by Carausius from those of the central government that important changes took place in the empire at large. The Tetrarchic system was introduced in 293, and it is perhaps not insignificant that the next attempt to drive Carausius out of Boulogne occurred in the same year. It can be argued that his existence as a putative third Augustus interfered particularly with the new scheme of twin pairs of senior and junior emperors in east and west, and now required eradication even more than before. Yet Roman constitutional arrangements were rarely that neat, and it was the Roman capacity for local modification that made the imperial system work in practice. It could be argued instead that it was the existence of another separate and workable empire so soon after the Gallic Empire that underlined the need for a major attempt to tackle the structure of imperial government. One very important thing that the Tetrarchic system provided was the devolution of supreme power in a way that made it geographically accessible. We shall see later how the same principle ran through the reorganization of the lower levels of the civil and military hierarchy. For the moment, in the context of imperial power in relation to Britain, it is worth noting that it was felt necessary to establish one of the four emperors in the north-west of the empire.

The appointment of Flavius Julius Constantius, sometimes thought to have been Maximian's praetorian prefect, to the new post of Caesar to Maximian served to inaugurate the system in the west. Constantius had already put aside his unofficial wife Helena, the mother of Constantine the Great and a future saint, and married Maximian's daughter. In the east Diocletian chose as his Caesar an officer of peasant origin, Gaius Galerius Valerius Maximianus, known to history as the Emperor Galerius. The latter now divorced his wife in favour of Diocletian's daughter Valeria. Each of the four emperors had his own staff, and moved about with much of it in attendance. Like a medieval king, where the emperor was, there was the capital. This peripatetic tendency was of long standing: Hadrian's great tour of the provinces, which kept him away from Rome for nearly seven years, was an early example. It promoted the development of alternative centres of imperial administration that took on the character of imperial cities. It also seriously widened the gap between the imperial house and the most prestigious section of the senatorial aristocracy, still centred on Italy and the city of Rome, which the third-century exclusion of senators from military commands and the governorships of 'imperial' provinces had done much to establish.

In the north-west Constantius followed Maximian in using the city of Trier as a frequent base. This great city had been damaged during the recent barbarian invasions, but it took on a new lease of life as it became a regular imperial capital. It received much grand architecture, and its hinterland in the Moselle region witnessed the flowering of villa estates, including at least one probable imperial country residence. Centres such as Trier undoubtedly acquired extra importance and dignity as a result of Diocletian's deliberate cultivation of a style that emphasized the remoteness of the emperor's person and included the elaboration of court ritual and court magnificence. This was contrary to earlier imperial tradition, whereby an emperor was praised for accessibility and often pretended to the part of *primus inter pares*. But it was a logical development of increasingly open autocracy, it was supported by the long evolution of the religious cult of the imperial house, and it had political advantages in making it psychologically less easy for a Roman officer to imagine himself as a possible emperor. It doubtless widened the breach with the senatorial aristocracy, but the expenditure involved must have had considerable effect in stimulating prosperity in regions that housed an emperor. Constantius' upgrading to Caesar put an emperor with title, powers, and an imperial staff more or less permanently in the north-west who could give undivided attention to the restoration of order and prosperity there. To Constantius, the elimination of Carausius' regime, and the recovery of the lost provinces must have appeared as a major item of unfinished business. It is difficult to see how the new Caesar could hope to maintain order in northern Gaul with Carausius in control of part of it, backed up by Britain, let alone tolerate the ever-present affront to his authority. A show of power was needed, particularly as Maximian's own record in the north-west had fallen at the same hurdle. We are fortunate that we have contemporary and near-contemporary sources for the retaking of Britain. The countervailing difficulty is that much of the detail comes from panegyric, specifically written to flatter the victor. Just as with Tacitus' *Agricola*, one suspects the author of fitting the character and deeds of his hero to the ideal of a Roman officer and gentleman, so that one has an uncomfortable feeling of *déjà vu* when reading of the exploits of Constantius.

The account of the taking of Boulogne is sufficiently circumstantial to be convincing. Constantius' success followed the building of a mole to close the harbour, an operation in the best tradition of Roman military virtuosity. It seems to have dealt Carausius' prestige a desperate blow, and his assassination by one of his chief associates, Allectus, followed promptly. Yet even this did not lead to an immediate invasion of Britain by the victorious Caesar. Instead, Carausius' place was taken by Allectus, who seems still for some time to have held territory in Gaul, including Rouen. Overall, the central power in Gaul faced the sort of problems that had existed before the Claudian invasion of Britain, only to an increased degree. There were refuges for dissidents, and an ever-present threat of raids. The situation was made much worse by the fact that the hostile power was a Roman one, not a few barbarian tribes. Constantius also had to tackle the pirates, unfinished business left by Carausius. The high praise that Constantius received for dealing with marauding Franks who had penetrated the Low Countries shows how seriously these people were still regarded. Having defeated them, he took an action of considerable significance for the distant future, for after disarming them, he compelled these Franks to settle within Roman territory, 'giving up their savagery'. Two centuries later, the Franks of northern Gaul were to play a central part in the beginnings of the kingdom of France. More immediately, with the menace of piracy removed for the time being, the Roman navy—which Constantius augmented by constructing a new fleet in preparation for the eventual assault on Britain—had a new problem. With Boulogne taken, naval units in the Channel were under different commands and at war with one another. It is difficult to imagine that they could have combined effectively against pirates, and it was perhaps fortunate that Constantius had just defeated the Franks. Other Franks were to prove Allectus' most faithful supporters, and one may suspect that Allectus' fleet had an arrangement with at least some of the raiding peoples.

Allectus' position at the time of his assumption of power is obscure. The contemporary author Eutropius simply describes him as an associate or ally of Carausius. In the later fourth century Aurelius Victor uses a phrase (*summae rei praeesset*) that may mean that Allectus had been appointed by Carausius as the chief finance officer in charge of money taxes, mines, and the mints (*rationalis summae rei*), though we have no way of knowing to what extent the regime in Britain kept its administrative structure in line with that of Diocletian and his official colleagues, or whether Aurelius Victor had interpreted his lost source in terms of his own period rather than of the late third century. There is perhaps enough to suggest that Carausius fell to a palace plot rather than a military coup. The inability of Allectus subsequently to organize his regular troops into an effective stand against Constantius' invasion may point in the same direction.

It is still somewhat surprising that Constantius took another three years to launch an attack on Britain. We should probably not underestimate the difficulties presented by the Channel crossing. Caesar and Claudius had not found it easy, and Gaius had given up. The lesson that special ocean-going transports were required had perhaps been learnt from reading the accounts of those expeditions. To prepare them took time. Moreover, the ships and port facilities remaining on the Gallic side of the Channel may not have been in very good condition after the campaign of 293 and whatever fighting was required to drive Allectus from his positions on the Continent. The delay further suggests that Allectus was thought to have reasonably solid support from the army in Britain, whatever the truth of the matter. Neither Caesar nor Claudius had had to face making a landing that would be opposed by regular Roman troops, let alone in strength and on their own ground.

It is clear, too, that Gaul and Germany still presented problems. Maximian had been personally involved in heavy fighting on the lower Rhine and on the upper Danube from 288 to 292, and to release Constantius for the British expedition of 296 had necessitated his return to take personal command on the Rhine.

This is an illuminating example of the Tetrarchy at work, illustrating how territorial responsibilities were not regarded as mutually exclusive and how the emperors worked as partners. Constantius himself delegated a major part in the expedition to the praetorian prefect Julius Asclepiodotus. It was fortunate that, in Asclepiodotus, Constantius had an experienced professional soldier who had been a general under Probus. He may, indeed, have had previous knowledge of the coastal fortifications of Britain, if the conjecture is right that it was under that emperor that the Saxon Shore forts were first brought together as a coherent system. Constantius set out from Boulogne with one part of the invasion force; Asclepiodotus from the mouth of the Seine with the rest. The latter is a longer crossing, but has the advantage of a number of excellent landfalls in the Southampton region, where defenders would have had difficulty in guarding every haven in strength, and from which there is direct access into the heart of Britain. It is possible, too, that Constantius' use of the short crossing was a deliberate feint, particularly sensible if a substantial part of the Second legion was now garrisoning the new fortress at Richborough, where it is recorded in the *Notitia Dignitatum*.

Whatever he had planned, Constantius himself did not land in the early phases of the operation. Irrespective of the tactical intentions of each side, the weather seems to have played the major part. Allectus had stationed a naval force on the Isle of Wight to attack the invasion force from concealed positions. However, a thick fog enabled Asclepiodotus' ships to go past unnoticed, making a landfall that implies a considerable feat of navigation on the part of his fleet. Had it not been successful, it would surely have been judged foolhardy. Archaeological excavation at the Shore fort of Portchester has suggested that it was at this time out of commission. Certainly, Asclepiodotus seems to have landed unopposed, and, once ashore, promptly had his ships burned. This was the traditional gesture of confidence, no doubt, but he probably did not wish to leave a substantial force to prevent the ships augmenting Allectus' untouched navy as soon as his back was turned.

The panegyrist of Constantius says that Allectus, on sighting Constantius' ships, immediately abandoned 'his own fleet and port', preferring to face Constantius' generals than the Caesar himself.

Despite the obvious element of flattery, this does suggest that Allectus himself was somewhere in the south-east of England. He may have been at Richborough or Dover, or perhaps more likely at Canterbury, which, it has recently been suggested, took on a military aspect in the late third century and is the obvious point from which to command all four of the Shore forts that lie nearest to the short routes across the Channel. Whatever the truth of the intended slur on Allectus' courage, it need not have been foolish to head in the opposite direction. Allectus may or may not have assumed that his fleet and coastal forces, now alerted, could ward off Constantius. The account in the panegyric certainly seems to imply that he had warships available here as well as at the Isle of Wight. He may even have suspected that Constantius was not going to land at all. In the event, he was right: adverse weather is given as the reason for that, too. Equally important for Allectus was the fact that Asclepiodotus was now ashore—where, but for the fog, he should not have been. He was heading into a wealthy part of the province that was ungarrisoned, as far as we know. Moreover, he was now apparently cut off. Having literally burnt his boats, Allectus' undamaged fleet lay across his line of communication with the Continent. It would make a lot of sense for Allectus to concentrate all the available units of the army of Britain, other than those keeping watch on Constantius, on bringing Asclepiodotus to battle.

The panegyrist Eumenius' account is worth quoting in full, since, behind the rhetoric, we can glimpse what went wrong with Allectus' move:

Fleeing from you [Constantius], he ran straight into your forces. Overcome by you, he was put down by your army. What happened was that, seeing you behind him, the turn of events so overwhelmed Allectus that he rushed headlong to his death. He was, as it were, so deranged with shock that he neither drew up his troops into a proper order for battle nor organized all the units he was collecting together into an effective force. Instead, quite forgetting all the massive preparation just carried out, he hurled himself into battle, with only the old authors of the conspiracy and some regiments of barbarian mercenaries. Thus, Caesar, your good fortune once again furthered the happiness of our nation, since, while the Roman empire triumphed, hardly a Roman citizen was killed.

It is impossible to know how much of this is colouring. Unless we are putting too much weight upon the tense of one verb, the wording does seem to indicate that the forces that had been summoned had not all assembled at the time that Allectus gave battle. It may suggest, too, that Allectus came upon Asclepiodotus' army sooner than he expected. It has also been conjectured that Allectus could not trust his regular Roman troops not to change sides. This was not uncommon in Roman civil wars. On the other hand, it may have proved extremely difficult to organize the units that had actually arrived from their scattered garrisons into a field army fit to fight a battle straightaway. One may wonder how many of them had any experience of acting together in a large army, let alone engaging in a pitched battle. Asclepiodotus' troops, however, were presumably drawn from armies on the Continent that had fought in many campaigns over the past few years.

There has been speculation about the exact meaning of the phrase 'old authors of the conspiracy'. It has been suggested that these were the men from Carausius' original fleet; yet unless they were mainly barbarians, it is difficult to account for the boast that hardly any Romans were killed in the battle. It is perhaps reasonable to assume, while accepting that there really is insufficient evidence to confirm it, that these 'authors' were merely those who were privy to the 'conspiracy' in the beginning. This may have been only a small group—and even then we do not know whether the conspiracy referred to was Carausius' original rebellion or Allectus' seizure of power. Whatever the truth, it gave Eumenius the opportunity to employ a cliché of Roman rhetoric, and perhaps to associate Constantius in his audience's mind with another famous success in Britain: Agricola's triumph at Mons Graupius, 'the greater being the glory of victory if it could be won without the shedding of Roman blood'.

Despite the decisive defeat in battle of Allectus, there was nearly a major disaster at the hands of his supporters. The story is told by Eumenius, and, by an extraordinary chance, it is also dramatically illustrated by a superb gold medallion from the Trier mint that was found near Arras in northern France. The incident could not have been a better example of Constantius' *felicitas*. It was once again fog that played the decisive part. Some of Constantius' troops, themselves astray during the crossing and probably part of Constantius' division rather than Asclepiodotus', reached London. There they found that some of the Frankish warriors who had escaped from the defeat of Allectus were engaged in sacking the city, doubtless on their way homewards across the North Sea. Constantius' soldiers fell upon them and destroyed them. As Eumenius puts it with evident relish, Constantius' men 'not only rescued your provincials but gave them the pleasure of witnessing the slaughter, as if it were a public show'. This is an insight into the feelings of the citizens of Roman London, and one of those touches of the real world of the past that one so rarely experiences. The slaughter was a bonus added to deliverance. Constantius had acted like any proper Roman magistrate, providing his loyal people with, as it were, a fine gladiatorial show, complete with the execution of criminals.

There is no doubt that Constantius regarded this as a great propaganda victory. The details are important. Eumenius, in listing Constantius' glories, makes particular play with the claimed 'almost complete extirpation' of the Franks, with the imposition of his rule 'on many other people who had taken part in this criminal conspiracy', and with the establishment of peace and order at sea under Roman naval power. Although Allectus had been defeated on land, it was clearly felt important to emphasize the gaining of control of the sea. While the Franks were considered to be the worst of those defeated, it also seems that various other barbarian peoples were involved. It is impossible to deduce from the victor's propaganda whether there really was a general conspiracy. It was convenient to represent Allectus' support as largely barbarian-based. Nevertheless, a general concern about sea-borne barbarians does come through. On the other hand, it also reveals that those barbarians would take service under Roman commanders if the conditions were right. We are seeing here a foretaste of the future, when barbarians recruited from outside the empire would be paid to serve in late Roman armies. This is in real distinction both from the enrolment of non-citizens from inside the empire or from neighbouring regions effectively under Roman control, and from the long-standing practice of the incorporation of barbarian soldiers who had been taken as prisoners of war or who had been extracted from a defeated foreign enemy as part of the price of peace.

Archaeology has not yet produced any traces of Asclepiodotus' campaign. For Romano-British archaeologists, AD 296 had for long a rather different significance. R. G. Collingwood said of Allectus: 'It is evident that he had stripped the whole country of troops. For the first time since Clodius Albinus crossed to Gaul, the frontier was left undefended. The northern tribes took their opportunity: they broke in, and along the Wall we can trace the destruction they left behind them.' The year 296 thus became a landmark, like 197, and it, too, was widely attached to stratified signs of demolition and fire in forts, sometimes followed by reconstruction that, on the evidence of coins and pottery, can be dated broadly to this period. Yet it has been recognized on the one hand that the phenomenon scarcely extends outside the Wall region, and on the other that hardly a garrison on the Wall changed between the third and fourth centuries. Moreover, much of the dating evidence is relatively imprecise, pointing only to the third century after about 270, or the early fourth. There is also once again the important point that routine rebuilding and maintenance may well account for considerable traces of fire without hostile intervention, not to mention the ever-present hazard of accidental fire. There is, however, a circumstance that increases caution about 296 even further. Very few coins of Carausius or Allectus have been found on the northern frontier, and most of those come from Corbridge or South Shields, where much of the activity was civilian or was to do with military supply. Taken with the Carausian milestone already mentioned, which demonstrates that his regime was recognized in the north, and with general evidence about the size of the garrison at the time, the impression is gained that the frontier was relatively lightly held. One may perhaps surmise that, at least since whatever military action had caused Diocletian to take the title of 'Britannicus Maximus' in 285, there had been no serious land-based threat to Britain. The implication is that under Carausius and Allectus the frontier was regarded as safe, and that its garrisons had been removed or run down for a fairly long period rather than being suddenly withdrawn to repel invasion. Any barbarian invasion in 296 is thus likely to have been little more than opportunist looting of sites that had relatively little worth taking.

The widespread occurrence of rebuilding in the military installations of the north around the beginning of the fourth century
is more securely established. Tetrarchic building inscriptions from
Housesteads and Birdoswald date from before 305. The surviving fragment from Housesteads seems to record the names of
Diocletian and Maximian; the inscription from Birdoswald refers
to the garrison commandant's house as having collapsed and been
covered with earth, and records both its reconstruction and that
of other elements of the fort. This is renovation of a frontier
neglected in recent years, not wrecked by invasion. In fact, so
minor do the problems seem to have been that in 297 Constantius returned to Gaul, and it was almost a decade before he
came back to mount a campaign in the north. Instead, in 297/8
he is found drawing on Britain for skilled men (*artifices*) to restore
the great city of Autun in Burgundy, which had been severely
damaged in 269 by the army of the Gallic Empire. These *artifices*
were recruited from the British provinces because 'they had a
surplus of them'. This tells dramatically against Britain in general,
or the northern frontier in particular, having suffered recent
barbarian invasion on any scale. The panegyric of 297 claims that
following Constantius' recovery of Britain, the northernmost
peoples of the island were obedient to his every wish. This conventional flourish is perhaps more significant for what it does not
say. There is no reference to any defeat of northern barbarians
or to Constantius having driven them out of Roman territory.
It is not possible to believe that the orator would have omitted
to mention a successful war.

One may speculate that the northern barbarians did not like
the renewal of a strong barrier between themselves and the
Roman province. A willingness to fall in with Roman wishes in
297 may have become quite a different attitude a decade later.
People may also have suspected that Constantius was planning a
campaign. Another panegyrist, addressing Constantius' son Constantine around 310, found it necessary to deny a 'popular belief'
that the campaign of 306 was launched because Constantius
wanted the laurels of a victory in Britain. The orator ingeniously
insisted that Constantius had been summoned by the gods themselves to penetrate to the furthest limits of terra firma—not that
this is likely to have been much consolation to the tribes attacked.

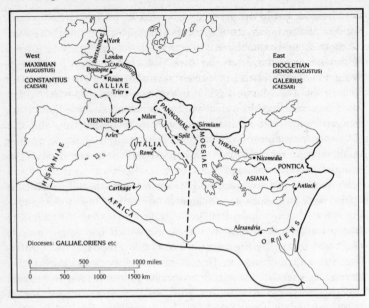

THE TETRARCHY: its arrangement under Diocletian, with the grouping of provinces into dioceses.

This decade was the period when Britain was exposed to the full force of Diocletian's reorganization of the empire. On 1 May 305, after a severe illness, Diocletian felt that he could retire and let the system take over. Maximian was required to abdicate at the same time. It was therefore as a full Augustus that Constantius returned to Britain to launch his campaign in 306, having succeeded Maximian in the west, while the Caesar in the east, Galerius, succeeded Diocletian. Galerius looked like acquiring Diocletian's commanding influence throughout the empire, as well as his territorial oversight, since not only was his nephew Maximin Daia appointed as his own Caesar in the east, but he managed to install a close friend in the equivalent post in the west, Flavius Severus. The latter proved to be an unfortunate error.

It is uncertain how soon the fourth-century pattern of administrative structure came into effect in Britain. Overall, the intention was institutionally to separate civil administration from military, though the army continued to have a large influence. Paradoxically, purely civil office and officials became much more military in form. The division was only at an embryonic stage by the end of Diocletian's reign, and only in a few instances does it seem that he had transferred the command of armies away from the governors of provinces to new, purely military officers. As in other fields, the beginnings of great changes are discernible under Diocletian, but their full development came under his successors, and were probably neither foreseen nor intended by him. The administration of the north-western group of provinces was to be headed by a praetorian prefect. As in the Severan period, there was multiplication of provinces by division. Britain was split into four instead of two. The provincial governor (*praeses*) became a civilian officer; normally without command of the troops, he bore an increasing load of administration. Co-ordination was achieved by the introduction of dioceses, the new level in the structure. The diocesan *vicarii* were, as their name implies, regarded as deputies of, and responsible to, the relevant praetorian prefect. Theoretically, since the praetorian prefect himself was a personal deputy to whichever Augustus or Caesar happened to be in control of a particular part of the empire at a particular time, this was a very changeable arrangement. Nevertheless, as the system settled down, the 'Prefecture of the Gauls' (which included Britain) became a permanent part of the structure of the Roman state. The four new provinces of Britain constituted one of the dioceses of this prefecture, and were headed by the *vicarius Britanniarum*. The provinces appear not later than 314, named as Britannia Prima, Britannia Secunda, Maxima Caesariensis, and Flavia Caesariensis. Where the centre of the diocese originally lay is not recorded, but it would be very surprising if it were not London. The *Notitia Dignitatum* certainly places the diocesan treasurer (*praepositus thesaurorum*) at London. It seems reasonable to suppose that the *vicarius* was also normally based at London, though we should remember that it was the officer, not the place, that was of prime importance. This was true even of imperial 'capitals': Diocletian, for example, did not pay his first visit to Rome until the celebration of his tenth year as Augustus, despite the city's enormous constitutional and political prestige.

In noting these reforms, we have probably moved somewhat

THE PROVINCES OF BRITAIN: likely (but not certain) form of the successive reorganizations down to the early fourth century (later fourth-century province of Valentia not shown).

ahead of the narrative. Even those changes initiated by Diocletian himself were not introduced at the same time throughout. Britain was, furthermore, in a special position, having been beyond his control for a decade. It is clear that the division of military from civil commands was not implemented immediately after Constantius' recovery of Britain, for the inscription from Birdoswald fort reveals a provincial governor, Aurelius Arpagius, in charge of the work.

It is not without significance that Constantius decided to conduct the British campaign in person, since to delegate it to his Caesar, Severus, would have been to offer the chance of success in this prestigious enterprise to a friend and supporter of the hostile eastern Augustus. Constantius was accompanied on the campaign by his own son, Constantine, already a considerable figure, whom Galerius had reluctantly allowed to join his father from the east. We do not know the size of the forces involved in the British campaign, nor do we know whether Constantius assembled an army from troops already in Britain or brought in units from the Continent. It is not impossible that some such Continental units had remained in Britain to ensure the island's loyalty after the defeat of Allectus.

The course of the campaign is unknown. The literary sources claim penetration to the far north of Scotland, and a victory over the 'Picts', the first time that the northern enemies of Rome are called thus. This included Caledonii and others, and therefore seems to have been a generic name that embraced the Highland tribes beyond the Forth–Clyde isthmus, and perhaps additional groups as well. One cannot help feeling that some of the Roman temporary camps identified in north-east Scotland ought to be Constantian, where they are not Agricolan or Severan. A process of elimination may eventually resolve this point, as the characteristics by which each of the earlier series of camps can be recognized become more and more reliably identified. The literary accounts once again provide intriguing parallels between the story of earlier campaigns and this one. Constantius is, for example, reported as making observations of the natural phenomena in the far north, just as Severus did. The crossing of marshes is similarly emphasized by the panegyrist, a feature that was said to have given Severus considerable trouble before he overcame it with the loss of many men. Indeed, one begins to be sure that, even if the fourth-century writer is not simply drawing on conventional material for such campaigns to add colour to his text, he is at least expecting his well-read public to see the parallels and credit Constantius with doing as well as, if not better than, the great generals of the past. To be fair, the parallels do go further than just the literary accounts. Pottery of this period has been found on the site of the old Severan legionary fortress at Carpow on the Tay and at Cramond on the Firth of Forth, the latter being one of the few Antonine frontier forts that also produces Severan pottery. This may suggest Constantius' use of a fleet. There is good reason to think that Severus had done so, and Tacitus reports Agricola's simultaneous use of land and sea forces, and the employment of ships to harry the elusive tribes of the Highlands into accepting battle. It is, of course, likely that a similar enemy on the same terrain would force successive Roman commanders to adopt the same tactics, even though there was a century or more between the wars. Nevertheless, we have noted before that an important factor in these situations must have been that the generals or members of their staffs had read the historians. It was a proper part of Roman education. We may also suspect that much additional information was available in Roman military records deriving from earlier campaigns over the same country, or that had accumulated over the centuries from innumerable sources, perhaps including the records of many minor actions in Britain about which we are completely ignorant.

13

CONSTANTINE THE GREAT

Some of the parallels between Constantius I and Septimius Severus in Britain were certainly not literary inventions. The last campaign of each was his war in northern Britain. And the coincidences went further: both had their sons with them; both returned to York after a victorious campaign, and there died. In the Severan case, however, the succession was clear, but the subsequent struggle between Caracalla and Geta inevitable. In 306 Diocletian's newly established constitutional system ought to have made the succession indisputable. Constantius' Caesar, Flavius Valerius Severus, should have become the western Augustus without question, and a new Caesar should have been appointed to replace him. Unfortunately, old traditions reasserted themselves. It is not clear that Galerius originally planned to have any western colleague at all in the same rank as himself, but the army at York forestalled whatever was intended. They proclaimed Constantine as Augustus, encouraged by a Germanic king, Crocus, who had been put in command of a cohort of Alamanni, a fact that may have influenced Constantine in his subsequent liking for German troops and officers. He certainly made much in later years of the origin of his rule in distant Britain, across the Ocean, and liked to dwell on the notion of a divine mission that had swept his power from the far west of the empire to its extreme east.

Galerius had already been reluctant to release Constantine from service at his court in the east to accompany his father on the Scottish campaign. By remaining in the east, he could have served as a hostage. Now that Constantine was independent, and had his father's victorious army behind him, the *de facto* control of the whole empire, which Galerius might have expected to fall into his own hands if his follower Severus were left without a rival, slipped away. The complexity of the situation was further enhanced by the intervention of the praetorian guard in Rome, who proclaimed in favour of Maxentius, the retired emperor Maximian's son, passed over in Diocletian's arrangements for the succession. The support of the senate for Maxentius underlines the division that had been developing between the emperors, rarely seen in Rome, and the ancient seat of authority.

For a while the situation was partially rectified by Constantine's acceptance of official appointment as Caesar—a step down in rank—while Severus seems eventually to have received recognition as Augustus. This will have made Constantine formally responsible to Severus. More importantly, it regularized his position. Legitimacy was still a very important element of power in the Roman world. On paper, the provinces of Britain, with the rest of the north-western provinces, now came under the authority of Severus. However, it is very difficult to imagine that he exercised any real power there. Diocletian's constitution had been shipwrecked on the same rock as previous reforms of the imperial system. Mutually suspicious multiple emperors, common in the century following the murder of Commodus, were now back, with the added element that they were now to be immensely strengthened by the gradual emergence of separate support systems of courts, civil services, and armies.

It took eighteen years of unstable arrangements, nominally respecting Diocletian's system and even once bringing him out of retirement to patch it up, punctuated by a series of civil wars, before Constantine finally emerged in AD 324 as sole emperor of an undivided empire. He had shown military and political ability of a high order, not to say skilfully applied ruthlessness, and peace was established for the rest of his reign. Immense changes were introduced under his rule, both before and after 324, but if Diocletian's great initiative to save the empire from its fatal flaw—the succession—had ever had a chance, it had none now. It can be argued that in his spectacular religious policy Constantine was following the logic of Roman tradition, since the failure of Diocletian's persecution of the Christians had demonstrated the greater power of the Christian god, particularly when taken with Constantine's victory over Maxentius at the Milvian Bridge under a Christian banner. But perhaps the only really traditional aspect of Constantine's reign was his extravagance. This was traditionally approved of in a Roman magistrate, when lavished on the populace and in public display. By the standards of the ancient world, too, his rise to power had not been unreasonable. Galerius' attempt to bend the Diocletianic constitution to his own ends had already made its collapse inevitable. We have noted the devotion of the Roman soldier to the hereditary principle, and it has been argued that even if the Diocletianic system had not been interfered with, this devotion would have made it unworkable once its originator had left the scene. The death of Constantius in a distant province in the presence of his victorious troops and of a son who was already an officer with a creditable military record had created the classic situation for the proclamation of an emperor by a Roman army in the field.

The tense situation in the empire that was created by Constantius' death at York raises the question of whether much of the military restoration and reorganization that has been loosely dated to about 300 was, like that of Caracalla a century earlier, the choice of an emperor now beset with greater problems. We cannot tell whether following up the successes in Scotland would have completed the conquest at last. But, like the Severan restoration of the northern frontier, what was done now seems to have ushered in an age of peace in Britain. Among the visible signs of reconstruction, pride of place must go to York. The walls for the fortress were extensively rebuilt, and in particular the great river-front was restored with a series of multangular towers that made it among the grandest examples in the west of the military architecture of its age. This splendour, directly overlooking the civil city across the river, must primarily have been intended as a demonstration of the power and studied magnificence of the new regime, whether the original order for the work came from Diocletian and Maximian, Constantius, or Constantine. Magnificence was deliberately used by Diocletian and his colleagues to elevate and protect the person of the emperor by seeming to put it out of human reach. It is an idea that sank very deep, becoming the origin of the lifestyle of the Byzantine emperors and their courts, and irregularly proclaimed emperors had as much reason to employ it as those more constitutionally appointed.

At Trier the exact dates of the enormous monuments of this period cannot yet be determined precisely, but it is reasonably certain that a major part should be attributed to Constantine himself, both on general grounds and with the support of a panegyric proclaimed in his presence in 310. At York one has to be cautious, since the dating evidence is even more ambiguous. It is just feasible that the remodelling of the fortress goes back as far as Probus and his possible work on the Saxon Shore, or more likely to the regime of Carausius and Allectus, with their particular need to assert their authority and stability, or to Constantius. An attribution to Constantine seems at present on archaeological grounds a little too late, but has some circumstantial support from a number of pieces of evidence that point to a long-term interest in Britain on the part of this emperor, beyond a single imperial visit. No fewer than nineteen milestones have been found in Britain bearing Constantine's name, six of them from the short period in 306–7 when he tolerated being a Caesar rather than Augustus. Coins from the London mint of the 'arrival' (*adventus*) type seem to record actual visits by Constantine in 307, 312, and 314. At some time in his reign, moreover, he took the title 'Britannicus Maximus', reflecting a victory gained by the emperor himself or in his name, somewhere between 315 and 318. All this evidence seems to come from before 324, when Constantine finally eliminated his last rival. Until then, there was an immediate need to maintain an absolute grip on the adherence of the west to his cause. Constantine was acutely conscious both of his divine mission and of the practical value of emphasizing it. Both factors are likely to have reinforced a continuing interest in reminding the world of the hand of destiny revealed in the events at York in 306. This is wholly consistent with what we noted earlier about his vision of himself as a divinely inspired force that swept over the empire from the remotest west, as represented by Britain.

York, nevertheless, was not just for show. In purely military terms, its refortification fits in with what is known of the pattern in early fourth-century Britain. The Wall was being refurbished,

and its garrison at least partially restored. In a number of forts
new types of accommodation may suggest that there were smaller
numbers of troops actually living inside the defences. At Housesteads, for example, barracks were reconstructed as rows of small
huts or 'chalets'. At Wallsend a substantial area of the fort seems
to have been cleared of buildings and left open. The fortress at
Chester was repaired at about this time, and the same phenomenon of open space within the walls is found. Other forts
were being reoccupied, and the completion of the main elements
in the coastal system could date from this period, with the same
feature of internal open space. The overall size of the fourth-
century garrison of Britain remains a matter of debate, but it
seems probable that we should not assume automatically that a reduction in intramural accommodation meant many fewer troops,
as we have to take into account that soldiers were now allowed
to live in the surrounding civil settlements, and that elements of
the new field army could have been billeted or stationed in towns
and cities. Open space inside the forts may well have been created in order to provide camping-grounds for mobile forces on
the move, since it must have been much more difficult to find
space for marching camps in the countryside of fully developed
provinces than it had been in earlier days.

It is pertinent to ask what the widespread signs of revived military activity in Britain may have reflected, other than imperial
megalomania. We have seen that the military, political, and economic crises of the third century had comparatively less effect in
Britain than elsewhere; that it was thought worthwhile to continue the process of fortifying the cities and towns of Britain in
the third century—an expensive process, at least for the provincials; and that there are substantial signs of renewed enthusiasm
for building, including private construction, from the 270s on-
ward. From around AD 300 there is a veritable epidemic of work
in Britain on country houses, ranging from simple improvements
in the amenities to vast extensions that converted relatively modest properties into grand mansions in the manner of the stately
villas of Gaul.

It is significant that, unlike some properties in Gaul, villas in
Britain did not fortify themselves. Towns, on the other hand, received elaborate additions to their defences in the fourth century,

or, in the case of some of the smaller ones, were fortified for the first time. The details of these works show great variety, suggesting either that the initiative was still largely local or that the townspeople were responsible for having the work carried out on orders from central government. The fact that, for example, adjacent towers in the north-eastern quarter of Roman Cirencester can be quite different supports the view that individuals could be responsible for separate parts of the work.

In this context we may return to Zosimus' criticism of Constantine for allegedly withdrawing troops from the frontier forts and stationing them in towns, and recall the evidence just cited for reduced accommodation in the garrison forts. We have to be cautious about putting too much weight on Zosimus, since he was probably influenced by events long after the Constantinian period. He criticizes the Emperor Honorius for failing to deploy all the forces available to him at the beginning of the fifth century, and for the year 409 he claims that troops (cavalry as well as infantry) were dispersed throughout the cities. Writing a century later still, Zosimus may have been repeating a criticism of Constantine that had become conventional but had little basis in fact, or he may have been exaggerating the beginnings in Constantine's reign of a practice that became prominent much later. Nevertheless, his account is not inconsistent with a significant transfer of troops from forts to towns in the course of the fourth century.

Such a change was doubtless popular with the soldiers. It is also likely to have made emperors much more willing to allow towns to have modern defences capable of withstanding anything short of a full-scale siege by an army trained and equipped to that end. The political risk was obviously much less if the emperors had their own regular troops inside the walls on a more or less permanent basis. We have already noted how some towns seemed to take on military aspects in the late Empire, and the garrisoning of substantial numbers of well-fortified towns makes sense if it was part of an official policy of defence in depth. It would provide a network of strong points, each of which could be held by a relatively small number of professional soldiers, and it would extend military protection to areas that had not been garrisoned for centuries. It could be argued that this, not the stationing of massive forces on the frontiers themselves, was the right way to deal with raids by bands of men looking for easy plunder, not conquest. The permanent presence of such troops in areas with a large civil population might be a much better way of securing public confidence than the knowledge that the main fighting units of the Roman army were far away. The army in general was not popular, but one can imagine that some pressure for protection would have come from the wealthy owners of the new villas, who are likely to have been in a better position than most to use influence to shield themselves from the requisitions and depredations of the soldiery.

The counterpart to the new pattern of civil government was the reorganization of the command structure of the army. Military and civil government had been so closely interlinked that radical alteration of the one must affect the other. Cessation of the arrangement by which provincial governors had been in charge of any military units stationed in their provinces automatically affected the whole system of command. The military structure that replaced it does not seem to have been the result of total reorganization under the Tetrarchy. Many of the army reforms seem to have been the work of Constantine, being either attested during his reign or known to us for the first time soon after his death. In this, as in other matters, Constantine was prepared to be much more radical than Diocletian.

Under the Tetrarchy, and perhaps under Constantine as well, the praetorian prefects continued to play the chief part in the supreme command of the armies, with their *vicarii* as their deputies. In AD 312 the praetorian guard itself was dissolved, having shared in the defeat of Maxentius. Under Constantine's sons, new commanders-in-chief of the armies make their appearance: the master of infantry (*magister peditum*), and the master of cavalry (*magister equitum*). These *magistri militum*, like the praetorian prefects of recent years, tended to be awarded with consulships. Constantine was accused subsequently of Germanizing the army and of raising barbarians to the consulship. It is likely that these allegations applied specifically to Germans who were appointed as *magistri militum*, which would imply that that office was introduced under Constantine.

The reformed office of praetorian prefect was of crucial importance in the new administration. Included in its responsibilities were the vital areas of supply and recruitment to the army. Under the late Empire supply became a major part of the machinery of imperial administration, one that was so critical to the functioning of the army and civil service as to justify a substantial part of the attention of an officer of state at the level of a praetorian prefect. This responsibility was exercised down the line by the diocesan administration and, below that, by the provincial governors and their men on the spot. It is likely, therefore, that the removal of the active command of armies from the prefects' work-load was as much due to their burden of administration as to their long history of military usurpation and the praetorians recent support of Maxentius. Diocletian's enormous increases in administration were probably making their jobs impossible. Nevertheless, from a political point of view, there must have been much to be said for separating the operational command of the armies from their supply.

It is perhaps at this point that the divorce of the military and civil structures became decisive. In the fourth century the two services were recruited largely from different groups of people. The tendency in the army to favour promotion from the ranks was intensified, and many more men of recent barbarian origin rose to the most senior commands. Yet it is an irony that underlines the prestige of the Roman army that, in form, civilian posts became more and more like military ones. In the civil service military titles were often used, military grades and pay structures were applied, and even the wearing of uniform insignia was increasingly adopted by holders of civil office.

An important consequence of the separation was that it became unnecessary to base the organization of the army on the arrangement of provinces, since provincial governors no longer commanded the troops in their territories. This doubtless had considerable advantages. The division and redivision of provinces must often have created areas that were highly inconvenient for military purposes. By setting up a formal military structure that spanned provinces, Rome was recognizing and regularizing a situation that had often been necessary as a military expedient. These new area commands were headed by generals with the title of *dux*. At what point of time these became directly responsible to the *magistri militum* is not known: it was certainly the arrangement in the later fourth century.

The responsibilities of the new generals can be observed running through several provinces. Thus in Britain we find a *dux Britanniarum*, whose command could clearly include units based in more than one of the fourth-century provinces, and was probably defined by the list of forces allocated to him rather than by geographical area. Such commands made good sense operationally, though one may guess that having to deal with more than one provincial governor on matters of supply must have been tiresome, not to mention the fact that the supplies were now coming from a department that had no operational responsibilities.

Under Diocletian himself, legionary detachments seem normally to have returned to garrison duty when their special tasks were completed, but in the course of the late Roman period many such detachments were formally constituted as legions in their own right. This can probably be attributed to Constantine. In the troubles of the third century the old practice of constructing campaign armies from such detachments had pointed in the direction of permanent mobile field armies, and we noted earlier that by 295 the notion of the *comitatus* as a body of troops that accompanied the emperor had already grown up. Constantine built on this practice by setting up, as a formal structural division of the Roman army, a distinction between the soldiers of the *comitatus* and the garrison troops of the frontier provinces (*limitanei*). The terms derived from those functions: the *comitatenses* were originally members of units that were 'companions' (*comites*) of the emperor; the *limitanei* were those stationed in the frontier regions (*limites*). But Roman conservatism retained titles for very long periods, even when function had changed, or reused them, so that it is unsafe to associate these titles with function at particular points in time. The *comitatenses* acquired higher status than the *limitanei*, but this should not mislead us into assuming that the latter were just border guards or militia. It is only necessary to note that *all* the units under the command of the *dux Britanniarum* were so classified to see that this is too simple a notion. It may also have been under Constantine that the new military post of *comes* was introduced, a commanding general of higher rank than a *dux*, though actual examples of *comites rei militaris* are lacking until the reigns of his sons.

There was nothing startlingly new in the idea of a central military force as it emerged between Diocletian and Constantine. From the time of Augustus, there had been elements of a standing army regularly stationed in or near Rome. In the early days this had been made up of the city troops—praetorian guard, urban cohorts, *vigiles*—plus the emperor's personal bodyguards. Septimius Severus made this into a substantially larger force, reforming and possibly doubling the size of the praetorian cohorts, and stationing his own favourite legion, II *Parthica*, close by. He also adopted the practice of moving this special legion around the empire as he needed it. The events of the later third century meant not only that the emperors and their courts became much more mobile, but that the former spent a great deal of their time actually in command of troops on the move. In line with Severus' adage to look after the troops, the developments in organization and status of the early fourth century made good political as well as strategic sense.

There were also changes in the relative importance given to cavalry as against infantry. In the old auxiliary forces cavalry had indeed been more highly rated than infantry, and the command of mounted units went to more senior men. But in the prestigious legions the infantry had been the major arm. Vexillations of legionary cavalry, however, as we have noticed, became more important in the third century, and although the old parent frontier legions remained in existence in the fourth, they were generally classed among the *limitanei*. Among the new *comitatenses* there were cavalry units of 500 men, which were called, interestingly, *vexillationes*, and *legiones* of infantry, which may have been of 1,000 men, like the cohorts of the old praetorian guard. The frontier legions may have been permanently reduced in size at the same time, by being drawn upon for the new units. Reduction in accommodation of the sort noted at Chester would be compatible with such a change, and the space left vacant would be used, as suggested earlier, when required for troops now serving in the *comitatus*. There were also new infantry units known as *auxilia*, apparently recruited initially from Germans living within and outside the empire. Though the old 'auxiliary' label was attached to them, they were granted high status and privileges. It is almost certain that these units were introduced by Constantine, and, along with others raised from the German settlers or *laeti* introduced earlier under agreements providing for military service, formed the core of Constantine's mobile striking-force in the west. The *auxilia* were amongst the best troops at Constantine's disposal, and their inclusion among the *comitatenses* in the army lists underlines their ranking in the late Roman army.

Later on we shall examine a further development of the fourth-century army, the separation of 'palatine' troops from the rest of the military *comitatus*, and other changes. For the present, this necessarily simplified outline of the reorganized military machine will suffice, provided that it is realized not only that much of the evidence is fragmentary and sometimes apparently contradictory, but that we are dealing with a long period, and one in which some desperate expedients must have been necessary from time to time. Much of the difficulty lies with that document known as the *Notitia Dignitatum*, the detailed but now incomplete list of civil and military commands in the eastern and western parts of the empire. Its date and purpose are hotly disputed, though it does seem reasonably clear that it was compiled from other documents, some of which pre-date the time that the list reached the form in which it has come down to us. For the western list, this was perhaps around AD 425. It is possible that it did originally come from the official registry of the *primicerius notariorum*, or one of the other central government departments. However, it has been suggested that what we have is an unofficial copy, which someone attempted to correct with insufficient recent information.

We have already noted that Diocletian's reforms were not confined to strengthening the constitutional and military institutions of the state by direct means. Concern over the ravages of inflation and the condition of the central currency led him to take initiatives that were the beginning of radical changes in the economic and social pattern of the empire. It will come as no surprise that Diocletian's propensity for seeing solutions in terms of close regulation by law and by elaborate administrative structures is just as evident in the economic field as elsewhere. An example is his unsuccessful attempt to set prices for a long list of commodities in his notorious 'Price Edict'. In one respect, however, his reforms had a brilliant simplicity. A fundamental problem of state finance had been that taxes had been cumbersomely expressed in terms of fixed amounts of money, which produced inadequate income in periods of currency inflation, or as percentages, where ignorance of the sums being taxed meant that the state could not predict how much a particular tax would bring in. Diocletian introduced a radically new principle, whereby taxpayers were assessed according to a system of units, partly based on land and partly per capita, so that the total yield from a given tax per unit could readily be calculated. The actual tax rate could thus be set to meet estimated expenditure for any particular period.

This reform was accompanied by a much wider use of payment in kind, both to the state and from the state. After a long period of inflation, allowances and benefits in kind seemed much more attractive to the holders of public office than in times of stable currency, and the state itself could be more certain of obtaining vital provisions for the army and other public services if actual supplies were specified. Not all such transactions were necessarily completed in commodities; in certain instances it is probable that sums expressed as quantities of goods were in fact translated into cash at whatever was the current local price. The method, however, prevented loss to the state or state employee through rapid currency fluctuations.

Great extensions were certainly made to the old method of direct victualling of the army as a levy on the taxpayer, abuses of which system Agricola was said to have stamped out in Britain two centuries earlier. Though assessments were fairer and less disputable under the new system, the sheer handling of material implies a larger administrative machine. The army's supply system was also vastly augmented by the development of a number of state-owned industrial concerns manufacturing such items of equipment as clothing, weapons, and armour. Diocletian did not shrink at the manning implications of his reforms. We shall find that it was a long time before the trend towards greater complexities in structures, and therefore in the number of men employed by the state, was given check.

The main branch of the central financial administration of the empire was retained, but it was reduced in importance by the movement towards payment in kind. The central offices of the chief secretaries who made up that branch—one in charge of taxation collected in cash, the other of imperial estates—were reorganized. The *rationalis summae rei* at the imperial court still controlled money taxes, and the new diocesan *rationales vicarii* were responsible to him. Provincial governors now answered to the *rationalis* of the diocese within which their provinces fell for the collection of these taxes. The same *rationalis* was also charged with the official issue of coinage, and with the administration of mines throughout the diocese. The imperial estates were now controlled by the emperor's *magister rei privatae*, who also had diocesan *magistri* under him, with local procurators responsible to them. There is evidence that these two financial departments often worked closely together at the diocesan level, to the extent of sometimes carrying out tasks strictly in the remit of the other department. Their work remained of substantial importance. Nevertheless, the greatest financial responsibility now fell to the praetorian prefect, who was in charge both of the assessments for, and the collection of, the tremendous new system of exactions in kind. This became the major finance department of the Roman state.

The Roman government was attempting to deal with crises that threatened the collapse of the imperial system, partly by a much greater control of everyday affairs through imperial edicts and rulings, and partly by replacing the older administrative systems that had left much to the provincials by new ones that required far more direct intervention. We have noted the obvious reason why the military and civil administrations had to be separated, that the load would have been impossibly great. There was a further reason—the type of men now commanding the troops. From the early days of the Principate, there had been a tradition of giving the provinces with major armies to imperial legates who had been selected early in their careers by the emperor, and had been directed into successive posts designed to give them serious military training as well as expertise in civil administration. Nevertheless, their background had been the senatorial class, whose education was in rhetoric and law, and whose social world was that of Rome, the senate, the courts, and the city administration. The third-century exclusion of senators from imperial governorships must have struck a heavy blow at the civil administration of the empire and the standard of justice in the provinces. Since this coincided with the more frequent advancement of able but unlettered men to senior military commands (and even to the throne itself), the need for a separate class of civil administrators must have become pressing. It is this latter class, men with a background of classical education and experience in law and administration but not military affairs, that we find holding important posts in the fourth-century civil administration.

Above the governor of a fourth-century province in Britain, the next level of authority was almost certainly centred in London. Beyond London, the perspective is likely for most of the period to have been to Trier, to the praetorian prefect in the main, but also to the financial secretaries of the current Caesar or Augustus. Beyond that, supreme authority might be in Italy, probably at Milan, or in Constantinople. The task of keeping all these upper tiers of the system happy must have been formidable, particularly when they themselves were in conflict.

For practical purposes, the fountain-head of authority for the senior administrators of Britain lay in Gaul. This was something they came increasingly to share with their military colleagues, and we shall observe the process by which the military command of the empire was regionalized. We shall see how, although the civil officers themselves did not necessarily come from the region, the very fact that the organization itself was evolving something of a unity in the north-western provinces makes it probable that there was a profound political and cultural effect on the British scene. More and more we have to see Britain in the light of its immediate Continental neighbours, its fellow dioceses in the Gallic prefecture.

Apart from the army, there was one further power structure that a fourth-century governor had to take into account: the bishops of the Christian Church. For a considerable period of time before the Tetrarchy, there seems to have been little real persecution of Christians in the empire. They had become increasingly accepted, and in places they were even ostentatious. The last great persecution, starting in 303, was intended as one of Diocletian's remedies for the ills of the empire, based on a belief that neglect of the traditional gods had been a major factor in the calamities of the third century. The Christians of Britain and Gaul were less affected than most. Constantius I was not anti-Christian, and as Caesar to Maximian he allegedly went no further in complying with the imperial edicts than demolishing existing churches. While it seems that the full fury was only unleashed in Egypt, for a while it was clearly much more unpleasant for Christians in many other parts of the empire than in Britain or Gaul. The possibility of Christian refugees in Britain is not to be discounted, if only as a few people unobtrusively transferring their residences or arranging a suitable posting for themselves or their friends.

Constantine's usurpation of the throne may have strengthened toleration, though he himself was not yet a Christian. It is ironic that it was his tremendous victory over Maxentius that turned him into an enthusiastic supporter, since Maxentius himself was equally tolerant. However, from the 'Peace of the Church', marked by the Edict of Milan, the Christian religion was legal in the empire, and in the west the Church was in high favour. From 324 Constantine's absolute supremacy extended this favour to churches throughout the whole empire. It is clear that Constantine believed that it was of paramount importance for the Roman state to retain the approval of the Christian god that had been made manifest at the Milvian Bridge.

There were immediate and immense political, social, and economic consequences. Constantine's own enthusiasms tended to make things happen fast and on a large scale. Even from Britain, which does not seem to have been very deeply penetrated by Christianity so far, three bishops appeared at the Council of Arles in 314, only two years after the Milvian Bridge, together with a priest and a deacon who may have been representing a fourth bishopric. This council was called to settle a dispute within the Church, and when it failed, the emperor himself arbitrated. It represented a change of the first magnitude that doctrine, schism, and the politics of the Church had now become matters of major concern to the emperors. This added a new dimension to Roman politics.

One important consequence was to sharpen the developing antagonism between the largely pagan and conservative senatorial class in Rome and the imperial house and its great officers, who were mostly recruited from outside the senate. However, it ought to be mentioned briefly here in Constantine's favour that he did try to reverse the trend of excluding senators from major offices. Moreover, many of those of lesser birth who were successful in the imperial service were eventually absorbed into the senatorial order. The Church, too, suddenly began to find that it was rich—and wealth was a prerequisite of respectability and influence in the Roman world. Not only did Constantine immediately begin to restore to the churches the property that had been confiscated from them, but also to add to this some very large sums from his own treasury. Throughout the eastern part of the empire after 324 Constantine allowed funds from the public purse to be used for the rebuilding of churches that had been destroyed. The future of Christian communities was put on a sound footing by massive grants of estates as endowments. At the same time individuals were encouraged to make gifts and bequests to the same end, reviving the old tradition of munificence that had largely died in the west in the third century, but diverting it away from the adornment of the local city and the provision of amenities and amusements for the community as a whole, and directing it towards the Church and, in particular, the poor. On top of this, substantial rights and privileges were granted to men in Christian orders.

While Constantine seems to have destroyed or closed few temples, he did carry out a programme of stripping them of their wealth. It has to be remembered that public and private donations to the innumerable temples of the Graeco-Roman world had been going on for centuries, and many of these institutions doubled as public treasuries. While the barbarian raids and civil wars of the previous century had doubtless reduced the amount of portable treasure and cash that they contained, the total must still have been immense. Moreover, many of the more famous pagan religious centres had become great property owners. Constantine's acquisition of this enormous wealth and his great gifts to the churches represent a shift in riches and power throughout the empire comparable to the dissolution of the monasteries in sixteenth-century England.

If individual churches became rich overnight, one may wonder what happened to individual churchmen and secular Christians.

Many a fortune in Tudor England was based on the spoils of the religious houses and the favour of the king. Respectability fell naturally on to the new Tudor landowner, and monastic estates and buildings formed the foundation of the rising gentry and new aristocracy. Many older established families did not hold back from this process, and merged with the others to become the Protestant upper classes of Elizabethan England. It should not, therefore, surprise us in Roman Britain to find Christian motifs displayed on the mosaics of the reception rooms in such fine villas as Frampton in Gloucestershire or Hinton St Mary in Dorset. Not all the wealth from the temples went to the Church: large sums were retained by the emperor to finance other projects. Overall, in such a large operation one cannot imagine that a good deal of wealth did not stick to various fingers. When we consider the remarkable prosperity of Britain in the fourth century compared with Gaul, we may perhaps reflect on the fact that its temples had not suffered the same disasters in the third century. We shall look at a good deal of evidence later for the continuance of pagan cults in Britain right through the fourth century, particularly local ones, and even of some new temples being built, but we do not know what financial losses they had suffered. We may suspect, however, that their treasures had survived relatively undisturbed until the reign of Constantine—except perhaps in southern coastal areas affected by the pirate raids that Carausius had originally been sent to stop—and that their lands and other property lay unpillaged and tempting.

As well as the status conferred on Christians by this transfer of wealth, imperial favour must have meant that many now received preferment in public office, especially since the enormous increase in the imperial services in Diocletian's reign had brought a vast new range of appointments in a world where the exercise of patronage by the influential was expected. What must have really shocked traditional Romans was Constantine's transfer to the Church of certain powers that had always been the prerogative of Roman magistrates. Even Constantine's own praetorian prefect, himself a Christian, was not sure that he had understood the emperor correctly when Constantine decided that either party in a legal action could have the case transferred out of the ordinary courts to the local bishop—and that, if necessary, the secular authorities were required to enforce the judgement. This extraordinary ecclesiastical privilege did not, admittedly, last, but it sheds an interesting light on how revolutionary Constantine was prepared to be. We have yet to come upon incontrovertible evidence for grand church buildings in fourth-century Britain, and the fact that three of the British bishops who went to Italy in 359 for the Council of Ariminum had to accept assistance with their travel may suggest that, as institutions, the churches in Britain were not well off, but, nevertheless, this sort of temporal power given to the Church, compounded with the presence of well-to-do Christian landowners and backed by the known favour of the imperial house, meant that a Roman governor had to take the wishes of the Church and its officers, however few in number, very seriously. This was a real revolution.

It was not, of course, revolutionary to find religious authority entwined with that of the Roman state, or to have a merging of religion with politics. For Augustus, the restoration of traditional Roman religion, particularly the ancient institutions and rituals of the Roman state, was integral to his restored Republic, and Diocletian had seen the strengthening of religion as an essential part of the renewal of the empire. Observance of the official sacrifices was considered to be a necessary display of loyalty both in the army and in civilian public life, and election to membership of the various priesthoods played an important part in binding together the provincial upper classes in the service of the empire. Such loyalty mattered more and more in the upheavals of the third century. Moreover, the troubles of that century brought an increased interest in personal religion, in personal belief and its consolations, that benefited both the older and the newer religions, and made the conflict between them, when it came, more intense.

A paradox of the attribution of public misfortunes to anger by the state gods at the rise of Christianity was that when the persecutions failed, the belief could be exactly reversed. The persecution of Christians had from the first embodied much of the perennial fear of the Roman state about secret societies and conspiracy. If so clear-headed an emperor as Trajan could refuse permission for a voluntary fire brigade on these grounds, it is not surprising that the Christians had so much trouble, particularly as they were for long confused with some of the groups of Jewish extremists. However, by the beginning of the fourth century the idea that personal religious belief was enough to force people to refuse the normal gestures of loyalty without intending any political disrespect was becoming intelligible. As far as the Imperial Cult is concerned, Constantine largely incorporated it: it was too important to do otherwise. What was new was to find a cult whose members had just been persecuted as dangerous revolutionaries and sources of offence to the gods of the state becoming the basis of a new state religion, with adherence to it a symbol of loyalty. Actual belief in a religion (or the pretence of it) became politically and socially important—and in a religion that was exclusive of all other religions. To be a Christian was like being a member of the Party in certain modern states.

Constantine's religious policy offended much of the Roman upper classes, but, as noted briefly above, he made real efforts to bring them back into public life. Some offices that had become equestrian in the third century were now upgraded: for example, certain provincial governorships were given the title *consularis*, which now indicated the lowest grade qualifying for senatorial status, and were reserved for senators. Governors of the other provinces continued to be known by the third-century title of *praeses*. Constantine was, it is true, extending the pool of experienced men that could be drawn on by substantially increasing the number of successful members of the imperial service who were admitted to the senate. The enormous funds at his disposal as the result of confiscations in the civil wars, new taxation, and seizure of temple property enabled him to raise the private fortunes of these men to the level of capital required for eligibility for senatorial rank. This was not popular with the older families, but the ancient process of assimilation in fact continued.

Constantine's redistribution of the temple treasures allowed him, with the mass of precious metal acquired, to establish a new currency based on a new gold coin, the *solidus*. It also, as we have seen, permitted unparalleled imperial expenditure. In addition, the vast increase in the numbers of officials must have brought much employment among the trades that looked after them. The beneficial effects in the short term, particularly in provinces that had not been so badly damaged in recent years as to be unable to take advantage of the opportunities, must have been very considerable. Provinces that had been the scene of successes in the career of the emperor were likely to be singled out for special favour. The first half of the fourth century in Britain was going to be an age of exceptional prosperity.

There could, of course, be problems from too much personal prosperity, not all of them obvious. For example, the new aristocracy of office, secular and ecclesiastical, gained not only wealth but also privileges, and these did not always work to the advantage of the state. Municipal gentry attaining senatorial rank, for example, or being appointed to certain positions in the imperial service, or becoming ordained in the Church, gained exemption from the extremely heavy financial burdens now being placed on *curiales* (the members of the class obliged to serve on the local *curia*, or council). The effects on taxation and regional administration became so serious that strict laws had to be enacted to avoid the worst financial consequences for the public purse of the privileges attached to a growing number of offices.

About the actual holders of the major offices in the reorganized structure of Roman Britain, we know very little. From Constantine's period as the western Augustus we have the name of L. Papius Pacatianus in the post of *vicarius* in the year 319. He later held the prestigious office of *consul ordinarius*, and was appointed to a praetorian prefecture. Under Constantius II, there is the case of the suicide of the *vicarius* Martinus, who tried to stop the excesses of retribution after the defeat of the usurper Magnentius in 353. In 357 or 358 the *vicarius* was the distinguished and civilized pagan Alypius, later sent by the Emperor Julian on a special mission to rebuild the Temple in Jerusalem, as part of that emperor's anti-Christian policy. Alypius' appointment in Britain probably lasted until 360. Ammianus, in his account of the reconstruction of the British provinces after the barbarian incursions of AD 367, mentions the appointment of one Civilis to what is surely the vicariate of the Britains. The poet Ausonius refers obliquely to at least one holder of the office from Gallia Belgica. Two other holders are known, one under either Theodosius the Great or Honorius, the second certainly in the latter reign. Chrysanthus was the son of a bishop in Constantinople, and had served at the imperial court. Before 395 he had been *consularis* of one of the provinces in Italy. Subsequent to the vicariate in Britain, he hoped for the office of city prefect at Constantinople, but he was compelled to accept the bishopric previously occupied by his father, gaining much credit for personal integrity and for generosity to the poor. The last known *vicarius* was Victorinus, a friend of the poet Rutilius Namatianus, who was a Gallic aristocrat with estates near Toulouse. He held the British office in the reign of Theodosius the Great or Honorius, almost certainly before 406, and Rutilius remarks on the popularity that he had gained among the provincials. He was certainly promoted after leaving Britain, which confirms the impression that we are given by what we know of the careers of the other *vicarii* mentioned, that they were men of education and high standing, both socially and in imperial circles. Rutilius dismisses the significance of the Britons themselves, but it is revealing that the emperors still felt it necessary to employ men of worth in the most senior administrative post in the island. It is also important to note that right to the end the empire continued to appoint to these very senior posts men who did not come from the provinces they were sent to govern. Though information on both third-century and fourth-century office-holders is fragmentary, one is left with the impression that the late Empire reverted to the practice of the Principate in sending men of wide experience and distinction to Britain.

Of the governors who presided over the individual provinces of the diocese, hardly anything is known. Constantine's reopening of provincial appointments to members of the senatorial order would lead one to expect the appearance of such people in British posts once more. The *Notitia* does record one of the provinces that was created in the Diocletianic reorganization as rating a *consularis*—the province of Maxima Caesariensis—but we do not know how early it received that designation. It is probable that such regrading within a particular diocese was applied first to the province that also contained the diocesan capital. If the British diocese was administered chiefly from London, then it seems very believable that London should house as governor of the local province a person with senatorial status, in addition to containing the superior establishment of the *vicarius* and the one, or possibly two, departments dealing with the money revenues of the

diocese, which were independent of the rest of the civil administration. The economic and social implications of such a concentration of the aristocracy of office in London are such as to
provoke interesting reflections on the nature of that city in the
fourth century that will be pursued later.

At least one governor of a British province in the mid-fourth
century possessed the attribute of good connections that became
more and more important as the emperor became ever more
remote and the bureaucracy of the court increasingly dense
around him. This was Flavius Sanctus, who married the sister-
in-law of the remarkable Gallo-Roman poet and professor
Ausonius, whose appointment as tutor to the young Gratian, subsequently an emperor, led to provincial governorships and eventually a consulship. Sanctus himself was almost certainly a member
of the Gallo-Roman aristocracy that played a prominent part
in the public life of the late Empire, and he may have been descended from a Sanctus who had held a consulship in the independent Gallic Empire. Flavius Sanctus' governorship was probably
around 350. Earlier in the fourth century—or possibly at the
end of the third—a Perpetuus, probably Hierocles Perpetuus, of
senatorial rank, is recorded in Rome as carrying out repairs on
the Sacred Way and as having held an equestrian governorship
in Britain. Finally, there is the problem of the equestrian L.
Septimius, recorded at Cirencester, who was formerly generally
accepted as a governor of the fourth-century province of Britannia Prima, and whose inscription consequently provided evidence for the location of the Diocletianic provinces. It is possible,
however, that he was in fact a third-century governor of Britannia
Superior, perhaps sometime after the collapse of the Gallic regime.

The sort of men we have seen in the vicariate or holding
provincial governorships came from varied backgrounds, but they
did have some traits in common. Some were Christian, many
were still pagan; most had been educated in the classical tradition, and some came from old families where paganism was
strong. Many of the latter held office, as we shall see later, primarily for social reasons and for the minimum period. Others,
often from backgrounds outside the old aristocracy, were career
administrators. However, taken as a whole, these holders of civil
office were increasingly separated in terms of career from the

professional soldiers. The latter were not necessarily unlettered, but they had different traditions and attitudes to life. The topmost level of Roman society was certainly tending to polarize into two groups, one based on senatorial families, often pagan and with an essentially civilian background, the other centred around the army, the emperor, and the court, largely Christian and military in its outlook. The professional civilian administrators, which many of the *vicarii* and governors now were, helped to bridge the cultural gap between the senatorial aristocracy and the court.

14

THE MIDDLE OF THE
FOURTH CENTURY

The immense personality and prestige of Constantine held the whole empire firm in his grip while he lived. His death in 337 started a chain of events that were to prove very serious for Britain. It began with an outbreak of murderous squabbling in the imperial family. Britain's early fourth-century age of peace and prosperity began to dissolve in the 340s, but for a brief moment the island seemed to have escaped the consequences of Constantine's death. They were momentous. For three months there was no Augustus at all: the instigators of a major army revolt in Constantinople refused to accept any of the proposed appointments to imperial rank other than the sons of Constantine themselves. The troops proceeded to dispose summarily of various other members of the imperial family and of a number of appointees left by the late emperor. His second son, Constantine II, had formally held the rank of Caesar since he was a month old, demonstrating how far imperial attitudes to the succession had reverted to former practices. Out of the chaos, this Constantine emerged as the senior Augustus, personally controlling Britain, Gaul, and Spain. Another brother, Constans, held Italy, Africa, and the Illyrian provinces, and a third, Constantius II, had Constantinople and most of the east. All three assumed the rank of Augustus.

The arrangement in the west did not work. Constantine II objected to the attitude of Constans and launched an invasion of Italy in 340. It was a disaster: he was defeated and killed at Aquileia. The shock must have been immense in Britain, which had not had a violent change of regime since the death of

Allectus, now forty-four years ago. Unlike much of the rest of the empire, for a generation or more leading civilians had not really been disturbed for political reasons other than those connected with the establishment of the Church—and that had been a more muted affair than elsewhere. The armies of the north-western part of the empire had not suffered any defeats. Indeed, Constantine the Great's own rise to power had been in the hands of these troops from the beginning, and he had finally achieved supremacy as a result of the massive victories they had won over his rivals. Now these north-western armies had been defeated in battle, and their emperor had been killed.

We have no knowledge of the immediate effects on the army in Britain. We do not have details of the military units that made up the army that Constantine II had with him in Italy in 340, or of what was lost at Aquileia. This means that we have no evidence to indicate which troops were drawn from Britain for this campaign. Constantine's single field army had been replaced after his death by three separate *comitatus*. This had given Constantine II a permanent field army of first-rate troops, and may have meant only relatively slight withdrawals from the garrisons in Britain, where few *comitatenses* are found at any period. Nevertheless, something happened, presumably late in 342, which brought Constans in person to Britain at the beginning of 343, in mid-winter—a very unusual time to cross the Channel. It has been conjectured that the refortification of cities in Britain was undertaken as the result of decisions taken by Constans during this visit, and that this may have been necessary because the army in Britain could not cope with barbarian attacks after being weakened by the postulated troop withdrawals by Constantine II two years earlier. This is a theory that should not be discounted, but it still rests on too many assumptions. We should be remembering the possibility of political and military unrest in a relatively inaccessible part of the defeated emperor's former domains as a reason for Constans' visit, particularly in winter, when conspirators might feel safe in Britain.

Turning for a moment to the broader military picture, two important developments appear in the Roman army at about this time that we need to note if we are to have a greater understanding of the military situation in Britain in the middle of the fourth century and later. Each emperor's military *comitatus* now proceeded to divide again, into field armies that operated separately from one another as required, though they were responsible to the same emperor. Each emperor kept a central field army with him, the commanders of which were entitled *magistri militum praesentales*, which marked them out from other *magistri militum*. Among the latter was the *magister equitum* who commanded a large force permanently stationed in Gaul. There were also smaller bodies of *comitatenses*, under the command of *comites rei militaris*, often created as temporary task forces for specific purposes.

There is a particularly interesting early example of the task force that relates to Britain. It is known that at some time before 350 the elder Gratian, father of the Emperor Valentinian I, held a command in Britain with the rank of *comes*. It seems quite likely that this was in some way connected with Constans' surprise visit of 343. Gratian had previously held the same rank in Africa, where the post subsequently became an established one. In Britain, however, since we find a *dux Britanniarum* in office later, we may presume that units of *comitatenses* had been posted in for a specific task and then probably withdrawn.

There are a few slight clues as to what Constans actually did during his winter visit. The part of Ammianus' text that deals with this period is lost, but later he speaks in passing of 'the *areani*, a category established by our forefathers, certain affairs relating to which I mentioned earlier in connection with the actions of Constans'. By 367 these men had the job of collecting information about tribes bordering on the Roman territories in Britain by moving about among them. This, or a similar patrol system, may go back to the withdrawal of the Antonine garrisons in Scotland or to Caracalla. Constans may have been reacting to events on the northern frontier, possibly reflected in signs of severe fire damage at three of the outpost forts of the Wall (Risingham, High Rochester, and Bewcastle), apparently occurring at some stage between the restoration at the beginning of the century and the barbarian war of 367, which will be described later. Of these three, the furthest forward, High Rochester, was not restored after the fire. Constans may have decided on a treaty arrangement, with the northern barbarians being monitored by *areani*.

Constans may also have strengthened the defences of the south. An increase in the number of coins from Richborough and Portchester suggests substantial activity at those sites in this part of the century. One theory would attribute the establishment of the post of *comes litoris Saxonici* itself to Constans, but there is certainly no reason to connect the elder Gratian's appointment with it. We have to be aware of what we are doing if we try to construct an archaeological picture of Constans' actions and then attach to it the brief literary references. We do *not* know that the reason for his journey was military, nor what business he had with the *areani*, nor for certain what the latter were. Even for 367 the evidence is only just enough to associate the *areani* positively with the northern frontier, but it does refer to 367 and not 343, and it does not prove that they acted in the north only. We cannot determine the exact dates of the damage to the three outpost forts. We do not even know the precise dates of the elder Gratian's service in Britain. The accumulation of possibilities does give some support to a general proposition. We should not go beyond this for the present.

The struggle between Constantine II and Constans had a further result of considerable importance for Britain. The military consequences of dividing the imperial *comitatus* have been discussed. But each of the three Augusti also had had his own praetorian prefect and the associated civil administration. Despite the defeat of Constantine II, the separate praetorian prefect for Britain, Gaul, and Spain continued to be appointed, even though there was now no locally based Augustus or Caesar. In other words, this north-western governmental structure was no longer seen as being attached to the person of the emperor. By continuing to make this appointment, Constans effectively recognized the need for a regional government for 'The Gauls' (Britain, France, Germany, and Spain), with a praetorian prefect not immediately attached to the retinue of the emperor, independent from the praetorian prefect of Italy and the rest of the west, and not affected by the way in which the empire as a whole was divided between emperors at any particular time.

Constans' sole rule in the west lasted ten years, with his brother Constantius II firmly established as his eastern colleague. We can therefore assume that the Gallic prefecture was well established before a new upheaval struck. In 350 Constans fell victim to a palace plot. The conspirators, gathered at Autun, proclaimed the elevation to the throne of Magnentius, a party to the plot and the commander of two units of the field army. Constans, who attempted flight, was overtaken and killed. Almost immediately two further Augusti were proclaimed by other groups—a nephew of Constantine in Rome, and Vetranio, *magister militum* to the late Constans, in Illyricum. The first of these was promptly put down by Magnentius. The second, though much more formidable, retired from the field and let Constantius II take over what may have been a substantial part of the main western field army.

Britain was now under the rule of Magnentius. It was to prove a disaster. We cannot estimate the amount of support for him in the island, but we have to remember that it was only ten years since Constans had defeated the north-western armies and killed his brother Constantine II. The savagery with which supporters of Magnentius were hunted down in Britain after his eventual fall suggests that sympathy for him was by no means negligible. The assertively Christian design of his coinage was doubtless intended to reassure the Christian lobby. Christianity had by now become closely identified with the imperial house, and its appearance on Magnentius' coins was probably also designed to emphasize his claimed legitimacy. It would seem that, though a pagan himself, he smiled upon Christians opposed on political or doctrinal grounds to Constantius. In Britain he probably attracted both Christians and pagans who had formerly supported Constantine II, or who had been repelled by the fratricidal struggle. He set about organizing his realm, appointing his brother Decentius as his Caesar in Gaul, and collecting forces for the war that was clearly coming. In the process he lost some support, for he offended members of the wealthier classes by the strictness of his taxation.

The personal background of Magnentius and Decentius is significant in the context of the age. Their family origin seems to have lain among the so-called *laeti* noted earlier, erstwhile Germanic barbarians who had been deliberately settled within the empire. The *laeti* were by now second- or third-generation Romans; much more recent German immigrants were to dominate Roman politics later in the century. Magnentius' own rule was not to last long. After a little over two years, he met Constantius II in battle near Mursa (Osijek) in Illyricum. We may guess that, with only part of the western *comitatenses* available to him, Magnentius reinforced his army for the campaign with frontier troops, possibly including detachments from Britain. The battle of Mursa was a tremendous one, and casualties were very high. Magnentius retreated, but in 353 he was confronted again in Gaul, where he was defeated and driven to suicide. After a long period of confident success, the Roman armies of the north-west had now been defeated three times, once under Constantine II in 340 and twice under Magnentius.

Britain had been part of Magnentius' dominions for three and a half years. The civil war had been a bitter one. Moreover, the fact that Magnentius had allowed pagan worship added a very nasty element to the situation, for both Constans and Constantius II were aggressive Christians. Magnentius' reign must have given a respite to pagans in Britain, and encouraged them to come out into the open. If so, it was probably disastrous for them, for Constantius' hatred of paganism was very real. He ordered the closing of all remaining temples, but he also went much further. He deeply shocked traditional Roman sentiment by removing the ancient Altar of Victory from the Senate House in Rome, which neither Constantine the Great nor his other sons had touched. This was coming close to what many felt lay at the heart of centuries of Roman success. He compounded this action by reaffirming the death penalty for individuals who offered pagan sacrifice or worshipped the images of the gods, acts that had been central to concepts of loyalty to state and home, which were strongest among the great aristocratic families.

It was, however, not only pagans who were in danger on account of their religion. In Constantine the Great's reign it had been clearly established that the emperor had both the authority and the duty to promote the unity of the Church and to suppress heresy. This was a development of major historical importance, the effects of which have not yet ceased to be felt. When Constantius defeated Magnentius and restored the empire to the rule of a single Augustus, the western and eastern churches were in a state of schism over the Creed. The bishops in the west (now men of importance) largely adhered to the Athanasian version (the Nicene Creed), believing the Father and the Son to be *of one substance*. The eastern bishops were mainly various shades of Arian, believing, in broad terms, that the Father and the Son were not the same, but *similar*. Constantius felt it necessary to call a series of Councils of the Church, and, unfortunately for the western bishops, to put them under irresistible pressure to accept the Arian view. By AD 360 this was universally imposed. It is ironic that Constantius managed both to make Christianity the only permitted religion throughout the whole empire and to force the Church to agree officially on fundamental doctrine, but that the Church itself was subsequently to declare Constantius' Councils irregular, and the Arian doctrine a major heresy. However, compulsory Christianity and the regulation of doctrine were now here to stay.

In the mean time, many people in Britain faced the prospect of serious trouble for recent acts or expressions of sympathy. Any such apprehension was well justified. Constantius sent to Britain one of his senior civil servants, the *notarius* or 'imperial notary' Paulus, to deal with disaffection. These notaries constituted a class of officials which became of considerable importance in the government of the empire. The head of the branch, the *primicerius notariorum*, controlled the *notitia* or establishment records of all official posts, both civil and military, and was responsible for the issue of their commissions to all the senior officers on both sides of the public service. They thus occupied a critical position in an imperial system in which patronage played a central part, and their detailed knowledge of individuals and their careers must have made them invaluable in the field of internal security. The branch is first attested at a fairly humdrum level in Constantine's day, but it later rose so far that, in the reign of Valentinian I (364–75), the *primicerius notariorum* is found with a higher status than the *vicarii* of dioceses, and subsequently all notaries became eligible for senatorial rank.

Paul's fearful reputation for ruthless cunning in the ensnaring of alleged opponents of the regime earned him the nickname of 'The Chain' (*Catena*). His brief in Britain was to arrest certain military men who had supported Magnentius. Meeting no resistance, he extended his operations without warning, trapping some who had been implicated, but also imprisoning many on trumped-up charges. Though it appears that he had exceeded his orders, the emperor subsequently approved of his actions and did nothing to prevent the conviction and punishment of those whom Paul had seized. The methods employed were so extreme, and the injustices so blatant that the *vicarius* of Britain, Martinus, himself a loyal supporter of the emperor, attempted to persuade Paul to release those who were not guilty. When he failed, he threatened to resign. This only resulted in false accusations against himself and other senior officers in Britain. As a final desperate act, Martinus was driven to attack Paul with a sword. Unsuccessful, he committed suicide. His name deserves to be remembered in Britain.

Ammianus' account suggests that the arrests and confiscations were most acute among the richer classes, as one might expect. Archaeologically, there is some evidence of abandonment or decline in a number of villas from about the middle of the century, which may have been associated with this purge. In this atmosphere it must have been difficult for anyone of any prominence not to be accused of treason, since political, military, or religious evidence could all provide grounds for condemnation. Even those who changed sides were not safe. Suspicion became endemic, and no one against whom an accusation was made escaped. It was a very unhappy time indeed. It may be in this context that we should place the strange appearance in Britain, at some time between 354 and 358, of local coins bearing the name of a 'Carausius', of whom we have no other evidence. In this miserable time, further pretenders are hardly unlikely; many people can have had nothing to lose. It is certainly reasonable to see the aftermath of Magnentius as the end of the brilliant period of prosperity that Britain had been enjoying. It is possible to argue that the island's society never properly recovered.

In 355 Constantius made a decision that took some heat out of the situation. He put his young cousin Julian in charge of Gaul and Britain, with the rank of Caesar. This was a remarkable appointment. Julian's father had been murdered by the troops during the debate about the succession to Constantine the Great, and his brother had been executed the previous year for incompetence. He had been brought up in deliberate obscurity in the east, partly in a remote fortress. This exclusion from public affairs (which probably saved his life) had the same effect on him as on the Emperor Claudius. He acquired a passionate interest in the past, in classical literature, Roman religion, and Roman tradition. He was to show originality, not to say eccentricity, and proved to be a man of great talents and integrity. Summoned out of obscurity by an unenthusiastic emperor, he won the allegiance of the troops in the west—if not the affection of his senior staff— by insisting on sharing their hardships in the field and by spectacular generalship. He fought a series of campaigns against the barbarians, who had taken the opportunities offered by the recent internal troubles in the empire to break into Gaul. Julian drove them out, and proceeded to campaign beyond the Rhine, inflicting considerable damage through speed and surprise. His tactics, as befitted someone devoted to reading Roman history, are reminiscent of those of Julius Caesar on the same ground four centuries earlier. They prove that, with inspired leadership, the Roman army could still perform feats equal to those of the past, feats of the type where training, organization, and discipline gave it superiority over the barbarians.

One of Julian's actions illustrates how Britain continued to be important to Roman power in the north-west of the empire as a diocese relatively undamaged by external attack. It was probably in connection with one of his operations against the barbarians, an expedition to the lower Rhine in 359, that in order to transport corn from Britain, Julian organized a fleet of 600 ships (400 of which were built specifically for the purpose, an act typical of him). Just as his grandfather Constantius I had drawn on Britain for skilled men to reconstruct the damaged cities of Gaul, so Julian used the abundance of British agriculture to supply the large quantities of stores needed to restore the effectiveness of the Rhine frontier. He rebuilt granaries on the Continent, and took military action to quell the tribes threatening the North Sea end of the Rhine, restoring a route on which traffic had been regular until it was interrupted, presumably through barbarian action. Along with the element of prestige associated with success in Britain that went back to the earliest Roman contacts, this matter of resources helps to explain the recurrent imperial concern for peace in Britain throughout the fourth century, when there were plenty of acute problems in areas much further away.

Physical prosperity, however, did not necessarily correspond with happiness in the period after the fall of Magnentius. Within a year of the campaign on the Rhine the morale of the British provinces was described as very low 'because of past calamities'.

Given a longer reign, Julian might have done much to raise the spirits of Britain by lightening the load that the government was increasingly piling on to the empire. Constantius had appointed one of his own men as the praetorian prefect to head Julian's civil administration. When this official provoked Julian by demanding a rise in taxes to meet government expenditure, the latter characteristically took over in person to demonstrate that an efficient and honest operation of the existing system could not only bring in sufficient revenue, but enough of a surplus to allow substantial reductions. On other occasions irritation at waste caused him to cut public spending on inessentials and to reduce the number of persons in state employment. To do this was to attempt to reverse the trend of three-quarters of a century or more. His interest in Britain is emphasized by the appointment of one of his most trusted associates, Alypius, as *vicarius*. Reform in the diocese can not have gone far, however, before fresh military problems fell upon the island.

At the beginning of 360 Julian was wintering in Paris, his favourite city, when he was informed that the Scots and the Picts had broken an agreement and were plundering lands close to the frontier in Britain. We do not know what this agreement was, but it may have been part of the arrangements made in 343 by Constans. Coming on top of the 'past calamities', this was spreading great alarm among the British provinces. Julian decided against emulating Constans' personal visit, considering that the problems facing him in his Continental provinces were too menacing. He therefore sent his *magister equitum*, Flavius Lupicinus, with four units of the field army—the *Heruli*, the *Batavi*, and two *numeri Moesiacorum*. This was an officer of higher rank than the *comes* Theodosius who was sent to Britain to tackle the great 'Barbarian Conspiracy' of 367. It suggests a very serious situation in 360. Julian, however, had immediate problems with his senior staff in Gaul, which may have affected his choice. There is no direct information on what Lupicinus managed to do in Britain, except that he halted at London, as it was now fully into winter. This, we are told, was so that he could move into battle more quickly once he had exact intelligence of how affairs stood. Major factors in this decision were probably that London was the centre of the road system and was almost certainly the home of the main departments of the civil administration, whose agents must constantly have been bringing in reports from all over the diocese. We may also guess that Lupicinus was able to bivouac or billet his four units of *comitatenses* within the walls of the city. In the event, there cannot have been much time before imperial politics again took a hand in changing the priorities.

During the same winter Constantius, uneasy at his cousin's successes and popularity, sent orders that Julian should detach four of his best units, the pick of the men in his two guards regiments, and a further 300 men from each of his other units for duty with the emperor. Two of the élite regiments specifically mentioned were the *Heruli* and *Batavi*, currently with Lupicinus in Britain. Perhaps Julian or his staff had received advance intelligence of Constantius' demands and had deliberately chosen them for service across the Channel. At any rate, the reaction of Julian's troops was unequivocal: they proclaimed him Augustus. Julian himself does not seem to have provoked this revolt or to have hurried to accept the elevation. His original inclination seems to have been not to resist Constantius' order. However, he did accede to his army's demand. There were some nasty moments: his relations with his senior officers were shaky. The future emperor Valentinian I, for example, son of that Gratian who had served in Britain as a *comes rei militaris*, was dismissed from Julian's staff in Gaul on what appears to have been no real evidence. Lupicinus was across the Channel, with some of the best units in the field army and the whole garrison of Britain, and Julian was not at all sure what his attitude would be when he heard the news of the proclamation. A further likely irritant was that Constantius had sent orders replacing Lupicinus as *magister equitum* by another officer. Like Domitian recalling Agricola, Julian resorted to an elaborate subterfuge to get Lupicinus back to Gaul, halting shipping across the Channel to prevent him from discovering the truth before he obeyed the order to return. This was successful, and Lupicinus was duly arrested. At the same time, Julian was still trying to come to an arrangement with Constantius. The latter refused any accommodation. In the end, Julian decided that he had to march east against his cousin, but before he reached Constantinople Constantius had died. The Roman world had been spared another great civil war. The empire was once again united under one government, and Julian was sole Augustus.

Julian was now able to come out in the open as a devoted pagan, set on restoring traditional Roman religious observances. These he not only permitted, but enthusiastically encouraged. The pagan cults had indeed survived, and between about 360 and 380 they enjoyed something of a revival, not by any means due to Julian alone, though it is worth noting that it was as early as 358 that Julian's pagan friend Alypius was *vicarius Britanniarum*. Not all Christian emperors made pagan observances impossible, and a Christian officer such as Lupicinus was recorded in his later career in the east as shielding the pagan writer Libanius from Christian attacks. This toleration continued for more than two decades after Julian had demonstrated that an official revival of paganism could actually happen, rather than remain a romantic traditionalist dream. Under Valentinian I, for example, we find a very distinguished prefect of the city of Rome restoring some of the most hallowed images of the gods in the ancient Forum itself. However, it is perhaps because Julian took his prejudice against the Church further than just favouring pagans and the old religion that he succeeded in producing little more than a temporary aberration in imperial policy. He not only abolished the penalties on pagan worship, but he also extended religious toleration to Christian heretics, abandoning the position established by Constantine that it was an imperial duty to promote unity in the Church. He seems to have enjoyed the spectacle of Christians in bitter disarray. He went even further, not only cancelling the extensive privileges that had been granted to churchmen, but also requiring the return of temple property. It is not perhaps surprising that his pagan revival did not generally outlive his early death, despite the survival of pagan practices in relatively unchristianized areas like Britain, and the strength of pagan sentiment among the senatorial class. The redistribution of wealth and the granting of privileges had by now been a fact for fifty years.

It was Julian's drawing of inspiration from the past that led to his death. His rule as sole emperor lasted only three years. His campaigns in Germany had demonstrated that it was still possible to beat back the barbarians by aggressive sorties beyond the frontier, rather than relying upon ever more elaborate static fortifications to resist attack. Arrived in the east and now in supreme power, Julian resolved on a great campaign to settle the problem of the Persians and other neighbours threatening the eastern frontier. He had the illustrious example of Trajan, if not Alexander, and conclusive victory in the east had been a recurrent dream of ambitious Roman generals for centuries. The dream had never been wholly fulfilled, the conquests never long-lasting, and the campaigns, if actually started, sometimes ended in terrible disasters. At the opposite end of the Roman world, we have seen how the conquest of Britain exercised the same sort of fascination over the Roman mind. Only Hadrian had applied the contrary policy at both extremes of the empire, but his views were not acceptable to subsequent imperial opinion. For Julian, as with so many of his predecessors, his eastern ambitions were cut short by his own death.

The fascination that the idea of conquest in the east held for Romans cannot be divorced from the facts that ever since the Republic the eastern part of the Roman world had been regarded as the largest source of revenue, and had a far greater density of the rich urban culture that was true civilization in Graeco-Roman eyes than the west. Like the west, however, it had suffered heavily from invasions in the third century, not only from the new Sassanian empire of Persia and from some dissident part-Roman regimes on the borders, but also from unhellenized barbarians such as the Goths, who raided not only the frontier provinces of the Danube, but also deep into Asia Minor and Greece. The eastern provinces still held a high position in Roman esteem, including the intellectual world, despite the fact that even Athens had been temporarily occupied by the barbarian Heruli in 267. The flourishing intellectual tradition of the Greek-speaking provinces is an essential element in the doctrinal debates in the Christian Church in the fourth century. These were at their most intense, bitter, and often violent in the eastern provinces, and occupied much of the attention of the emperors.

Rome's preoccupation with eastern affairs had become of greater importance to the balance of the empire when Constantine the Great founded Constantinople in 324 and lavished resources and attention on it. From the beginning it was different from previous imperial foundations, however large and splendid, because it was endowed with privileges parallel to those of the city of Rome. One of the more extraordinary of these was that Constantinople was provided with a free corn dole, in this case for 80,000 people. This ensured a rapid build-up of the urban population: it also created a second publicly subsidized metropolitan mob, which became of great political importance. It must have made senatorial families whom Constantine induced to emigrate from Rome feel quite at home.

There can be no doubt about what Constantine was doing, but in formal terms the status of the new city relied in his day on his personal *auctoritas* and the presence of the imperial court. It was not yet the undisputed hub of the empire. Indeed, the reappearance of multiple Augusti and imperial courts after Constantine's death ought to have checked its climb to pre-eminence. The seat of the senate and the ancient apparatus of the Roman state remained in Rome. However, in the mid-fourth-century period that we are now considering two crucial developments occurred in the status of Constantinople, both instituted by Constantius II. To understand them, we have to recall that the city of Rome, and in particular its senatorial element, was still substantially pagan. From the beginning Constantinople had been intended to be overwhelmingly Christian. In 340 Constantius formalized the establishment of a parallel senate at Constantinople, with the accompanying apparatus of traditional magistracies, and arranged that henceforth one of each pair of consuls should normally be inaugurated there. In 359 he introduced a prefect of the city for the eastern capital, with a full city administration. This is highly significant in its fourth-century context, for the office of *praefectus urbi* of the city of Rome was held in the greatest respect.

Besides being overwhelmingly Christian, there was a further important difference between Rome and Constantinople. The new senate and city prefecture, and the Roman nobility whose life they dominated, were located in the same city as the imperial court. The prerequisites for a permanent shift in the centre of gravity of the Roman empire from west to east were now complete. Further, the main structures for running two separate empires were now on a permanent footing, unlike the *ad hoc* arrangements made by imperial colleagues many times in the past. The differences between the eastern and western situations meant potentially very different political development; and the prestige of Constantine the Great and his Christian foundation provided an impetus for the eastern structure—at first sight so artificial as to be unlikely to survive—that gave it the probability of independent development and a good chance of survival whatever happened in the west. By the time Constantius II had died in 360, the view of the larger Roman world from Britain had fundamentally changed, though no one can have realized the full significance of this at the time.

There were changes of a more detailed kind that doubtless were noticed. New developments in the organization of the army mark further evolution. We have already noted how the military *comitatus*, originally comparatively small, had by now been converted into several separate field armies. Some of these no longer served in attendance on an emperor, but were becoming regional armies. This development was now marked by a formal distinction between those élite *comitatenses* who formed part of the force actually attendant on the emperor, and the rest. The former are first recorded with the new title of *palatini* in 365, two years after Julian's death, and it seems reasonably certain that their creation was part of the army reforms carried out by the new senior Augustus, Valentinian I. He had stationed himself in the west, and had sent his brother Valens to govern in the east. He seems quite deliberately to have made a more formal division between the western and eastern sections of the army by subdividing a large number of the units in the *comitatus*, naming those that he kept with him *seniores*, and those allocated to Valens *iuniores*. Extra regiments of *auxilia* were also raised, and were included in the 'palatine' forces. The *magistri militum* who commanded them were the *magistri praesentales* or *in praesenti* already noted.

Also from AD 365, we find another new title in the army: *pseudocomitatenses*, literally 'false' *comitatenses*. These seem to have been regular units drawn from the frontier garrisons (*limitanei*) that had been transferred to the field army but not upgraded. It had probably been noticed that the more the field army was increased by transfer from the static garrisons, the greater the total expenditure on military salaries and allowances—without any rise in the number of soldiers—if the units so transferred were given the higher pay and privileges accorded to *comitatenses*. In later sources one also finds *comitatenses* transferred from the regional to the palatine armies but retaining their former status. Conversely, in the course of time one comes across palatine units stationed in the regions but still called 'palatine': clearly, it was felt impossible to downgrade troops when military convenience dictated their redeployment away from the most prestigious postings. Whatever the actual job, the personal grade of a unit, and presumably of its individual soldiers, had to be maintained. There was doubtless no point in provoking a mutiny. One may suspect that soldiers could easily feel aggrieved by apparent demotion, but be mollified by the retention of status and by a formal, even if fictional, appearance of the situation being merely temporary.

In discussing the army reforms of Valentinian, we have moved a little ahead of our narrative. The orders that Lupicinus carried with him to Britain were not, one may suspect, just to do with a sudden crisis, but with the combined effects of fresh barbarian troubles and two decades of military and civil decline. Julian's intention, one may conjecture, was not merely to win a quick victory over the current batch of intruders, but to set in train a more thorough restoration of the diocese. In the event, of course, the exigencies of imperial politics forced the recall of Lupicinus. Julian's immediate survival was at stake, and considerations of a longer-term nature would have to wait. It is not, however, as certain as it once seemed that barbarian attacks on Britain resumed quickly. After relating details of the accession of Valentinian and his co-option of Valens, Ammianus paints a dramatic picture of the empire assaulted by barbarians from all sides: 'the most savage tribes being aroused, and each bursting through the frontier nearest to it'. Britain, we are told, was constantly being harassed by 'Picts, Saxons, Scots, and Attacotti'. Raids, it would seem, were coming from Scotland, Ireland, and across the North Sea from north Holland and Germany. In 360 itself the Scotti of Ireland had apparently been operating in the north of Roman Britain, perhaps attacking by sea from south-west Scotland. The origins of the Attacotti are unknown: they, like the Scotti, may have come from Ireland or the Western Isles. St Jerome observed this people's cannibalism in Gaul at this time. It has, in fact, been suggested that Ammianus' reference may be to the general period —including the well-attested combined raid of barbarians on Britain and elsewhere in 367, to which we shall come shortly— rather than to a separate attack occurring specifically in 364, which the point in Ammianus' text at which the reference occurs has generally been taken to imply.

If these attacks did occur in 364, the Roman response is likely to have been minimal, since considerable confusion had been caused by the death of Julian. This brought an abrupt end to the house of Constantine—and therefore to any obvious candidature for the succession—and reopened the religious question. The fact that there was not another vast internal upheaval can perhaps be explained by the perilous military situation. Julian's main army was in mid-campaign in the east, and barbarians were erupting on all sides. A young Christian officer from the Danube named Jovian was appointed Augustus, and managed to extricate the army in the field from its immediate predicament, ceding substantial Roman territories in the process, but he died in Constantinople in 364. A quite extraordinary conference of the holders of the senior military and civil posts then took place, and Valentinian, who had previously served in Gaul under Julian, was chosen. He had been, it will be recalled, one of the officers with whom Julian apparently could not get on. He was the son of the elder Gratian, and, despite his ability, had been retired by Julian, to be recalled by the short-lived Emperor Jovian. His strong Christian faith was probably an element in the antipathy he aroused in Julian, though we shall see that he, too, was to make unfortunate judgements in his appointments. It was perhaps his service in Gaul and his father's record that made him choose to base himself in the west, an interesting decision in view of the generally eastward trend of Roman preoccupations. He was a great practical soldier, possibly the last to make a major contribution to the strengthening of the whole western defence system. As an administrator he was able and efficient, but as a judge of subordinates he was bad. A devoted Christian, he had objected to taking part in pagan sacrifices under Julian. Most unfortunately, he accompanied this with antipathy towards the traditions of the old upper classes, even though he tried to help the less fortunate, who were certainly in need of imperial favour.

Valentinian's knowledge of Gaul under Julian must have made him keenly aware of problems and current priorities on the western frontiers. He spent most of the next ten years fighting the Alamanni on the Rhine, mainly based in Trier, which became once more a long-term imperial residence, as well as being the centre for the administration of the Gallic prefecture. There he must constantly have had the most up-to-date intelligence of affairs in Britain. One may assume, therefore, that Britain had as much military attention as was possible, but that this had to be seen in the greater context of the perennial struggle along the Rhine frontier, not to mention threats from elsewhere. For Valentinian's subjects, this conscientious attention may have been counterbalanced by his habit of promoting brutal and uncivilized men to high office, despite his own quick intelligence and literary tastes. For some members of the upper classes, already faced with sudden reversion to Christian rule, the outlook must have been unpleasing, not to say bleak.

We ought not to leave the mid-fourth century without touching on a theory that argues that by 350 the towns of Britain had declined to villages, and that they did not recover. The discovery of a farm-like complex inside the walls at Cirencester, and the presence on many urban sites of a substantial layer of 'dark earth' over earlier structures suggested widespread dereliction. To some extent, this was a false trail from the beginning, for agricultural buildings or other evidence of people who worked the soil are to be expected inside almost any ancient town. In some cases, farmers lived inside the town but farmed outside; in others, smallholdings within the urban area were cultivated. Even at Pompeii there is clear evidence of intramural market gardening. Another argument against the theory has only recently become apparent. It is now clear that the 'dark earth' itself dates from very different periods in different places. Certainly, it often appears in a late Roman context, but in London it has been observed in a second-century situation, and at Colchester it occurs after the Boudiccan fire, in one instance at least being superseded in the third century by renewed building. At Winchester, on the other hand, it can normally be dated to the very end of the Roman period, remaining unsealed until the earliest Saxon material was being deposited.

Much turns on how we view 'urban' life in the context of the fourth-century western provinces. There is a little evidence to suggest that Constantine appropriated city revenues as well as temple treasures and endowments. The sequestration of pagan religious funds will automatically have resulted in a very considerable reduction in a major element in the public life of the cities, since secular and religious ceremonial and the activities of the colleges of priests had been largely interlocked in the world of local government. We have already noted the sharp decline in private expenditure on public amenities by the end of the third century. But probably equally important in depressing the position of the cities as centres of a vigorous, locally initiated public life was the vast increase in imperial administration, when both public business and private interest must have been deflected away from the old institutions and towards the new centres of government and influence created by the multiplication of provinces and administrative departments. These new concentrations of power, too, are not likely to have been as stable as the old *civitas* capitals. Fourth-century governors, though they were no longer the great commanders-in-chief and viceroys of the early Empire, were often men of considerable standing. In the new, small civil provinces one may assume that the governors became a focus for the administrative and social world that must have detracted from the importance of the old city councils in the eyes of the local upper classes. One may assume, too, that these governors spent a proportion of their time travelling about their provinces with their staff, unlike the static councils of the old-style local government. All these factors will have militated against a revival of the earlier traditions of showy benefaction to the local city. Moreover, it was precisely the municipal aristocracy that was worst hit by the exactions of fourth-century government. Greater men, whether senators or imperial officers, were either in a better position to avoid the burdens or directly profited from the new order.

There does indeed seem to be much less archaeological evidence of expenditure on public buildings in the fourth century.

In London the basilica in the forum had actually been demolished in about 300 and was not replaced—at least, not on that site—and at Silchester it was turned over to industrial use. If the town council survived, it carried on its business in less grand premises. At Exeter, however, the basilica was modified in the middle of the fourth century, and a subsequent reflooring takes its occupation probably to the last quarter of the century. Then it, too, was demolished, and the site carefully cleared. Financial stringency is certainly suggested in some places by lowered standards in the municipal services, illustrated by the blocking of gutters or the accumulation of rubbish on such sites as the theatre at Verulamium. This by no means proves that the towns were less populous or active than before, only that their appearance, standards, and perhaps organization and functions were changing. We should not be surprised when we find large-scale residential development continuing in places as different as London and Carmarthen, since more and more property was falling into the hands of individuals and institutions exempt from municipal obligations—the state itself in various guises, the Church and its individual clergy, and members of the armed forces. All these classes were expanding as the curial class contracted—a situation that emperor after emperor deplored in the fourth century, but which was fostered by their own policies. Business in the towns may also have tended to fall into the same hands. There was certainly a decline in long-distance bulk trade under the late Empire, and we shall later observe how Britain became increasingly self-sufficient in many products. This is likely to have affected the prosperity of the great centres more than the small towns. There is some evidence in Britain that the differences between large and small towns became less significant in this period. Certainly, while there were factory-based industries and factory products to be distributed, trading centres were still required, and the towns provided them. Moreover, the landed estates still needed markets nearby so long as there were customers able to purchase their surpluses and manufactured goods to be bought. While there was a money economy, the economic necessity for urban centres remained. This is very different from the Mediterranean cultural and political role that may once have been envisaged for the towns of Britain, even if it was rarely achieved. One may certainly expect future research to show much more variation from town to town than in earlier periods, when illusions of civic independence and dignity were perhaps more universal. However, a pattern whereby the decay in civic centres was matched by the growth of relatively large houses (whose grounds may well account for some 'dark earth') would be consistent with the expansion in the number of officials requiring accommodation and the known fourth-century switch of expenditure from public benefaction to private display. But we have to be wary of arguing from the relatively small areas that have been excavated in many towns. Nor can we be sure that the same process applied everywhere. At Winchester there is some evidence of a denser, more industrialized occupation succeeding a spacious residential layout, the reverse of the more commonly encountered trend.

Whatever their primary function in fourth-century Britain, the continuing importance of the urban settlements is underlined by the extensive remodelling of the town walls that can be seen on many sites. The precise dating remains obscure and may not be the same throughout, but it seems to fall around, or a little after, the middle of the century. It has often been associated with the restoration of *civitates* (or *urbes*) and *castra* by the elder Theodosius after the barbarian invasion of 367 attested by Ammianus, but direct evidence is lacking. It may have been initiated rather earlier, perhaps by Constans, or under Magnentius, or during the expedition of Lupicinus in 360. There is certainly no evidence that the recall of Lupicinus had any disastrous effects in Britain, which may suggest that he achieved rather more than is generally supposed. The remodelling chiefly consisted of the adding of external towers to the existing curtain wall. In some, but not all, cases, their purpose probably included the use of fixed artillery, the mounted crossbows known as *ballistae*, which were also employed in wheeled versions by mobile troops. Addition of these towers usually necessitated the filling-in of earlier ditches that ran close to the walls, and replacement by a wider ditch, further out. Occasionally, the whole structure seems to be of one date, as at Caerwent, in south Wales. Most seem to have been constructed in the middle of the fourth century or a little later, though they follow the pattern already seen in Saxon Shore forts. By these means, the defences of large numbers of urban centres were

brought up to date. The overall purpose is likely at least partly
to have been associated with the military use of towns discussed
earlier; and at Gloucester, where the towers seem to have been
added fairly hastily at the end of the third century to a remodelling of the defences already under way, it has been suggested that
the town was specifically adapted for military use, a suggestion
that, as we have noted, has also been made for Canterbury. Both
these early examples should perhaps be associated with defensive
measures taken by Allectus but providing precedents to be followed in the troubles of the mid-fourth century. But we may
also assume that the defence of the civil town itself was in mind.
The design and execution of these improvements varies very considerably from place to place, and, as we saw in Godmanchester
in an earlier period, there is the likelihood that various owners
of land were responsible for sections of the defences. It is highly
significant that the long circuits of earlier centuries were retained:
the fourth-century modifications in Britain do not reflect the late
Roman tendency to establish small citadels in urban areas that is
found in many other parts of the empire. The implication is that
the larger area was worth defending, and that the capacity for
carrying out the work was on hand in the communities. All in
all, local responsibility for the execution of the work, with a minimum of central military supervision, seems highly likely. We have
to take into account, therefore, that it was thought worth refort-
ifying the towns in the middle of the century, and that resources,
almost certainly local, could be mobilized to carry it out. By the
360s the towns were, one may surmise, much poorer than they
had once been, politically inactive and socially weak, but by no
means dead.

15

THE RESTORATION
OF ORDER

Whether or not Valentinian had intended to turn to Britain as
part of his programme of strengthening the frontiers, his attention was forcibly drawn to the island by a spectacular and unforeseen climax in the harassment by barbarians. Struck by a serious
illness in 367, Valentinian discovered that names of possible successors to himself were being bandied about. His answer was to
appoint his 8-year-old son, Gratian, as co-emperor with himself
and Valens. The sequel suggests that some very shrewd and well-
informed minds were at work among the enemies of Rome. We
should not ignore the fact that in recent times a substantial number of Germans had been appointed alongside Romans at the
top levels in the military hierarchy. This continued to be the
practice. Thus, in the middle of the fourth century a profound
knowledge of Roman military affairs must have been built up
in professional Germanic military circles, amongst a class of men
not all of whom may have seen service under the empire. It is
not necessary to postulate treachery to account for the barbarians' capacity to assess accurately the effects on military readiness
for external attack of political events within the empire, though
this was indeed suspected in 354. As long ago as the first century, some of the most dangerous enemies of Rome had been
men like Arminius and Civilis, who had previously commanded
auxiliary units in the Roman army. The situation in the fourth
century, however, was of a different order of magnitude. Perhaps
a quarter of the army was of Germanic origin, and, though the
proportion does not seem to have climbed above this, a succession of Germans rose to appointments as *comes rei militaris* and

even *magister militum*. At army commander level, these men had an intimate knowledge of the Roman forces, handled the most confidential information on a routine basis, and in some cases served close to the emperor, observing how he dealt with the broad strategic issues and what affected his judgement. This adds up to a body of experience of tremendous potential importance to the enemies of Rome. This was not a matter of secret German patriotism, since the ancient Germans were so fragmented into hostile tribes that any general notion of that sort is unlikely to have been present. Moreover, such German officers normally became completely Romanized, a process that had been going on since the beginning of the empire. More importantly, German soldiers did sometimes visit their homes, and leakages of information must have occurred, whether inadvertently or through pressure on the men or their families. There can have been few remaining mysteries about how the empire and its armies worked. It is not therefore improbable that, whatever the means by which they received intelligence of the emperors' difficulties in the west in 367, the barbarians should have known of them and been able to assess their significance. What is remarkable is the way in which they exploited the opportunity.

Valentinian was on the road to Trier from Autun when news was brought to him of disaster in Britain. The various barbarian peoples that had been harassing both Britain and the Channel coast of Gaul had suddenly combined to organize a concerted attack, with the Picts (described as being divided into two main peoples, the Dicalydonae and the Verturiones), the Attacotti, and the Scots assaulting Britain, and the Franks and Saxons descending on the coasts of Gaul. Such a 'barbarian conspiracy' (*barbarica conspiratio*) was very rare. This was fortunate for the Romans, since it had always been extremely difficult for their defences to cope with simultaneous attacks. Diocletian's strengthening of the frontier garrisons, and the development and elaboration of mobile field armies were doubtless intended to mitigate this situation. In origin, the problem stemmed from Augustus' determination to keep the size of the armed forces to a minimum, stationing the bulk of the troops on the frontiers and relying on moving units from one frontier to another as pressures changed. But in the years since Diocletian's reforms there had been a number of civil

wars to weaken his dispositions, not to mention frequent fighting on a large scale against external enemies in many of the frontier areas. It is even possible that Valentinian's strengthening of
the frontier defences themselves had diverted resources away
from the field armies. Barbarians acting in concert created a very
alarming prospect. The events of 367 imply at least one very
capable and well-informed military mind on the barbarian side.
But they imply more: a leader with the personal reputation and
persuasiveness to weld such disparate peoples into a league to
take common action, if only for one operation, and—perhaps
even more remarkable—to keep news of such a plan secret from
the Romans. We are moving into an age when great personalities such as Alaric begin to appear on the barbarian side in the
west, men who treat with Roman emperors at their own level.
This had long been the case in the east, with such figures as the
Persian King of Kings. In the west, as we have noted, Germans
inside the empire were already appearing as generals in the
Roman armies, on equal terms with Romans. The day was not
far off when they would hold certain of the great offices of the
Roman state. Their position could indeed be equivocal: in the
next century figures such as Theodoric were to hold high rank
under the empire, while carving out for themselves vast kingdoms to be dominated by their barbarian followers.

In 367, however, although these elements were already present
in the Roman world, the attack was still unequivocally from without. Not that there had been no element of treason within the
Roman system: in Britain the *areani* had progressively abandoned
their duty (Ammianus tells us this in words that suggest a process that had been going on for some time). Seduced by offers
of booty to come, they had allied themselves in secret with the
barbarians. Just what they did, we do not know. It may well have
been passing information to the enemy, and giving misleading
intelligence to the Romans. This may lie behind one element of
the disaster that Valentinian now learnt about: his *dux* Fullofaudes
had been put out of action 'by the wiles of the enemy', either
killed or pinned down somewhere.

This was very serious. Fullofaudes probably held the post
later attested as *dux Britanniarum*, in command of the bulk of the
static garrison of Britain. We may guess that this defeat occurred

somewhere in the region of the northern frontier. None of the outpost forts in front of the Wall seems to have been held after this date, and though these may already have been abandoned, it may be that part of the treachery of the *areani* had been to betray any units that were beyond the Wall in 367. Signs of later reconstruction on the Wall itself may support the same hypothesis, possibly being repairs of damage caused by enemy action. Taken with the abolition of the *areani* by Valentinian's victorious general Theodosius, it suggests that the mid-fourth-century frontier arrangements had been disastrously inadequate.

However, before we turn to Theodosius' recovery and reconstruction of Britain, there are further details of 367. The elimination of the *dux* was only part of the calamity reported to Valentinian. Another of his generals had certainly been killed, this time an officer bearing the rank of *comes*. This commander, Nectaridus, is described as '*comes* of the maritime region (*comes maritimi tractus*)'. While it is likely that his command included the Saxon Shore forts of the south and east coast, later listed in the *Notitia* under the *comes litoris Saxonici*, it is perfectly possible that in 367 he also commanded forts on the west coast, notably Cardiff and Lancaster. The subsequent restoration of order included naval warfare against Saxons, reminding us that the primary role of the Saxons and Franks in this enterprise was to attack Gaul rather than Britain: the war was carried on by both sea and land. Nectaridus' authority in 367 may well have covered both sides of the Channel, and its overall scope may have been such as to require an officer of the rank of *comes*, as understood in Valentinian's day. It is possible that Nectaridus had been appointed to lead a task force specifically to clear out pirates, authorized either by Valentinian or even by Julian at some time after the hasty recall of Lupicinus. The loss of an officer of this rank would have been a serious blow to imperial prestige.

After their initial success, the barbarians expected no further serious resistance in Britain. They split up into small bands, collected booty as they went, and destroyed as much as they liked. Whatever central command existed among them could probably not have held them together beyond this point, even if it had wished to do so. Indeed, for the moment it was hardly necessary. Ammianus reports desertions from the Roman forces, and emphasizes that when Theodosius recovered Britain for Valentinian he had to repair forts and provide frontier garrisons. Given that he also had to restore at least some of the cities of Britain, we may assume that even town walls and any military forces within them had not always sufficed to keep the barbarians out. In the countryside Ammianus paints a picture of a dreadful mess, with bands of raiders wandering about unchecked, taking prisoners and looting where they fancied, and destroying and killing at will. In unprotected rural areas, and on the roads everywhere, it is likely that deserters from the Roman army were a real menace as well. The number of armed men on the loose was swelled by soldiers who, we are told, claimed to be on leave, a story that must have been difficult to check, even if anyone cared to enquire too closely. For the civil population, there was doubtless little to choose between them.

This episode is one of the very few instances in the history of Roman Britain where we can set against the archaeological record clear written evidence of destruction by enemies from without. Extensive traces of change have been noted in forts along the Wall and in the Pennine area to the south. The civil settlements outside the forts (except for Piercebridge, in the south of the frontier region and otherwise a special case) show little sign of reoccupation after this war. In the walled town of Corbridge there are signs of destruction at this time. Widespread chaos had certainly occurred, and substantial physical damage does seem to have accompanied it.

Valentinian reacted to the news from Britain in the same manner as Julian had in 360. He did not set sail for Britain himself, for, as we saw earlier, he already had a host of pressing problems on his hands before reports of the defeats in Britain arrived. Now the presence of the Saxons and Franks on the coast of Gaul will have tended to tie down the emperor and his *comitatus*, and may also have been designed deliberately to delay news crossing the Channel, thus doubly hindering the relief of Britain. Valentinian's first reaction was to send the commander of his guard, the *comes domesticorum* Severus, to see what could be done. Severus was almost immediately replaced by another officer, Jovinus. Finally, Valentinian took the decision to dispatch a task force very similar to the one that Julian had sent under Lupicinus. He selected four first-class units from the field army, the *Batavi, Heruli, Jovii*, and *Victores*. Of these, the first two had actually served in Lupicinus' expedition. In command Valentinian placed Flavius Theodosius, father of Theodosius the Great, who was to reign as emperor from 379 to 395 and may have served in this expedition. The elder Theodosius held the rank of *comes rei militaris*, lower than Lupicinus', but at the same level as Valentinian's own father when in Britain.

Theodosius established himself first at Richborough, once the main base for the Claudian invasion and now a major fortress in the coastal system. As soon as his four units were assembled, he advanced to London, eliminating bands of barbarians that he found scattered widely and laden down with captives, loot, and stolen herds. Ammianus tells us that he returned all but a small fraction of the booty to its rightful owners (in contrast to the alleged behaviour of Carausius), giving the balance to his troops as a reward. His unexpected arrival in London was greeted with great rejoicing by its inhabitants, who had been in despair. Theodosius entered the city like a general enjoying the honours of victory in Rome. He proceeded to take measures to restore the army of Britain as a fighting force, issuing a general pardon to those who had deserted, and recalling to the colours those who had claimed to be on leave. He put the administration back on its feet by arranging for an official named Civilis to take over as *vicarius*: it is not recorded what had happened to the previous *vicarius*, who had presumably been caught up in the events of 367. In the *Notitia* it is an interesting rarity that the *vicarius* of Britain is given unusual insignia, which may indicate command of troops, though we do not know on what scale this might have been. But Ammianus tells us that Civilis was a man of intelligence and rectitude. While the author is doubtless building up a portrait of Theodosius as a man of judgement in his appointments, nevertheless the times needed exceptional men.

Theodosius himself took the field. With energy, intelligence, and a fine army (as Ammianus tells us), he took every opportunity to trap what raiders he could, and to put to flight the varied barbarian peoples who had become confident and careless with success. In the context of the naval warfare against the Saxons that the poet Claudian claimed to have been part of the campaign, we may reasonably imagine Theodosius as directly exercising the command that had been in the hands of Nectaridus. It is interesting that no successor for Nectaridus is mentioned after the campaign was over (which is not the case with the land forces), reinforcing the notion that he had held a special commission, not the regular Saxon Shore appointment recorded later. The attack on the Saxons should have relieved the pressure on the northern coast of Gaul as well as on Britain. The harrying of Gaul was, as we have seen, a significant part of the total *barbarica conspiratio*, and perhaps came nearer to threatening imperial security at large than the assault on Britain, since it was not only closer to the administrative nerve-centre, but was occurring in a region where peasant revolt had historically been a problem.

There is some debate on how long an interval there was between the first news of the *barbarica conspiratio* reaching Valentinian, and Theodosius clearing the invaders out of the Roman part of Britain. However, in 368 or 369 Theodosius was able to embark upon his general programme of restoration, apparently on a large scale, to put the diocese back on its feet. Even discounting the powerful element of panegyric in the account, the military achievement was a great one. This was not just success in the field; it ranged from the initial and accurate analysis of the situation, through the rebuilding of a demoralized and disintegrating army into part of a force that went on to victory, to the replanning and physical reconstruction of the defensive system of Britain. To take command as *dux* when victory in the field had been achieved, Theodosius requested, and was granted, the appointment of a general named Dulcitius, whose reputation in his profession, like that of the new *vicarius*, was excellent.

We have already noted the signs of reconstruction in the forts in the north. Despite the listing of old-style auxiliary units as garrisons for the Wall forts in the *Notitia*, it is not certain that these were the actual forces in place after the war of 367. They may have remained on the list as the nominal or theoretical garrison, while more *ad hoc* bodies of troops actually held the forts. It has certainly been noted that the reconstruction work on the Wall in this period is of an inferior quality to that further south. On the other hand, a series of inscriptions mentioning civilian *civitates* from other parts of Britain may indicate that forced labour had been brought in to carry out a task that was regarded as urgent and important. In that case, the quality of the workmanship may reflect the skill of the workmen rather than the status of the troops in garrison. In one area of the north there is evidence of a brand-new series of constructions. The north-eastern coast of England was now provided with a set of well-fortified watch-towers, extending from Filey to Huntcliff, and possibly beyond. These may have been linked to the eastern end of the Wall system and provided this flank with the sort of warning system that had been available on the west in the second century. In the early days of the Wall the need for a coastal screen seems only to have been felt in the west, and was probably aimed at preventing the flank of the Wall being turned by enemies crossing the Solway Firth. That western system, despite some Antonine refurbishing, seems to have gone largely out of commission by the end of the second century. There is some evidence, however, that certain of the western forts and mile-fortlets were put back into operation in the fourth century, and that a military presence was maintained at some points on the coast for a great part of the century. In the east, especially after the extension of the Wall to Wallsend, attack by British tribes across the mouth of the Tyne had presumably not been anticipated, though one may presume that the river-entrance itself was closely watched, in view of its importance for military shipping. Now, however, deep-water sea-borne attack from outside Britain was a reality, and the need to provide the base at York and the other garrisons of the north with coastal warning systems had become apparent. Indeed, with raiders who were professional pirates, it may have been Roman shipping itself that was the most vulnerable target, with all that that implies in terms of disruption of military communications and supplies. These north-eastern signal stations may have come under a maritime command. They do not occur anywhere in the *Notitia*, and the only relevant inscription is extremely difficult to interpret. They may equally well, however, have been directly under the land forces that were probably still centred at York, or possibly were controlled from the fort at Malton.

The Theodosian reconstruction is a good point at which to consider some general features of the late Roman military scene in Britain, since they are of such wide-ranging significance that our view of them must colour our overall picture of Britain in the second half of the fourth century. This includes Roman relations with the tribes to the north of the Wall, the nature of the garrisoning of the Wall itself (touched on above), and—a matter that takes us away from the Wall to the island as a whole—the evidence for the widespread presence of Germanic 'mercenaries'.

It was long thought that the use of Roman names in the earliest generations of the well-known genealogies of the kings of the four kingdoms that were forming beyond the frontier in Scotland indicated that the northern tribes were now friendly to Rome. Indeed, the occurrence of the Celtic epithet *pesrut* (red cloak) had suggested a transfer of imperial authority, perhaps to client kings or semi-autonomous *praefecti*. This would accord with Theodosius' abolition of the *areani*, whom such new arrangements would make superfluous. Along with this, we were asked to see Hadrian's Wall as being occupied by a peasant militia, with the civil settlements (*vici*) in ruins, and the soldiers' families now living for safety inside the forts.

This picture did present some difficulties. It was hard to understand why, if the neighbouring barbarians were now friendly, the civilians should need to abandon the civil settlements. In fact, there is no unequivocal evidence for such a movement into the forts, nor is it absolutely certain that all the *vici* ceased occupation in 367. Peasant militia were primarily a feature of the fifth-century imperial system, after the end of official Roman rule in Britain. Such evidence as there is points to the Wall being garrisoned with regular troops until the end of imperial administration. With *areani* abolished, it will have been necessary to keep the frontier region in reliable hands: doubt has been thrown on the long-established view that there were now friendly relations with the northern British barbarians. It has been suggested that the adoption of Roman names by the northern tribes has nothing to do with political friendship, but with the spread of Christianity. It is also true that the genealogies of rulers of societies with few or no written records are extremely unreliable, as they frequently reveal more about the ancestors that the ruling house needs to claim to support its position in the present than its family history in the past. It is certainly telling that the east Yorkshire pottery characteristic of the period after the war of 367 does not appear north of the Wall. The most obvious explanation is that there were no further peaceful communications between the northern barbarians and the provincials once the invaders had been driven out by Theodosius. Traprain Law, the old hill-fort capital of the Votadini in southern Scotland, has produced extensive quantities of everyday Roman material from earlier periods. Now all it has to show is a great treasure of Roman plate, looted or perhaps received as a bribe.

Where do the 'German mercenaries' fit into the picture of fourth-century Britain? For a number of years it was thought that the presence of German mercenaries was indicated by the scattered occurrence in Britain of items of metalwork that appeared to be stylistically Germanic but that were identified as pieces of military uniform of late Roman date, particularly belt-buckles and other strap-fittings. These mercenaries, variously referred to by modern writers as *laeti* or *foederati*, were assumed to be in Roman pay, but essentially as irregulars. The finds have a further interest, in that they occur chiefly in the Midlands and the south, often in cities or rural contexts. Since these pieces were at first thought to be exclusively military, this led to the idea of barbarian troops being used to garrison the towns, and even to some being employed to guard individual estates. The discovery of coins from as early as 330–53 with this type of material in a city cemetery at Lankhills outside Winchester even encouraged the idea of barbarians being associated with a hypothetical reorganization of the British defences by Constans in 343. The interpretation of these Winchester burials, however, has come under intense debate, and, indeed, one alternative suggestion (linking them to the purge by Paulus after the fall of Magnentius) has already been mentioned. Another agrees that there is a distinctive group in the cemetery, but denies a Germanic identification. The mercenary theory was elaborated in three ways. German irregulars were associated with the adding of towers to town walls (requiring the availability of men who could handle catapults). Mercenaries were also seen as part of a field army, billeted in towns, or as allied troops who were given pieces of Roman estates as allotments. Indeed, we noted earlier that the substantial stationing of troops in cities could go back to Constantine the Great, and the practice of land-sharing certainly became established in the Germanic kingdoms that formed in the next two centuries in Gaul. This would all add up to a formidable picture, and, if true, would suggest major changes in the way of life of Roman Britain.

There are, nevertheless, serious weaknesses in the argument. In the first place, it is not certain that all these pieces of equipment were worn by soldiers. One is, of course, always uneasily aware of the dangers of assuming the presence of troops from the archaeological occurrence of stray items that may simply have been 'army surplus' or been mislaid. But in this case there are further difficulties. We have already noted the adoption of military systems of grading and insignia in the new civil administration. Another is the inherent danger of assuming nationality from style. Groups of finds from the late Roman Rhineland might justifiably suggest that Germanic styles of ornamentation were very much the 'ethnic' fashion of the period, often occurring on items manufactured in Roman provincial workshops. Moreover, it is also clear that some of the stylistic motifs commonly labelled as 'Germanic' were actually acquired by the barbarians from the Roman world, rather than vice versa.

A further consideration has now emerged. It has been shown that certain categories of equipment of the so-called Germanic type formed part of the official uniform issued to regular troops in the late Empire, and that some of it was probably made in the state ordnance factories of the Danubian provinces. This is not in the least inconsistent with the fact that there were many Germans serving in the regular army alongside Roman provincials, and indeed rising with them to the highest ranks, but it is most unlikely that such fourth-century regular soldiers wore different uniforms according to their national origins.

If mercenary irregulars cannot explain this material, do we have to accept the alternative theory, that there were regular troops in the cities and on the estates? Our general consideration of the role and appearance of late Roman towns has already suggested that there might be some intermittent presence of troops, on the move or billeted, and the probability that the heavily fortified towns played an important part in military strategy may also indicate some more permanent postings. It is true that the amount of military equipment is small. There is, for example, evidence of one (but perhaps only one) late Roman soldier in the city of Wroxeter. At Catterick, however, weapons and other military equipment have been found in association with town buildings that seem to have been altered in about ad 370 in a manner consistent with a change to military use. All in all, the presence of some bodies of troops in walled towns is likely—not, we may suppose, so much to defend the civil population as to watch it, while securing the defences for use in time of war as part of an overall strategy. It is very much less likely that soldiers were ever stationed on private estates; in general they are only likely to have been seen there officially when accompanying military or civil officers as escorts. It is perhaps reasonable to assume that *some* of the items of uniform were worn by soldiers, and that *some* of those from basically civil sites were (with rather less certainty) deposited where those soldiers were serving. Yet the use of individual soldiers—and small detachments—on official business that was not strictly military in character was a practice that went back to the earliest days of the Empire.

Theodosius' repair of the towns and forts, and the restoration of the civil and military hierarchies following his victories in the field, were not all that he did to return the island to the empire. There was another serious area of concern that affected the stability and security of the diocese. Ammianus gives an account of two matters that we have not touched on so far, in each of which he is able to give Theodosius credit for success, but where reading what he has to say suggests that all is not necessarily quite what it appears to be on the surface.

Of these two matters, one has given rise to great debate among Romano-British historians, but not necessarily for the most interesting reason. The problem lies in Ammianus' statement that Theodosius had regained a lost province, which seems to be regarded as a rather separate success from his recovery of Britain as a whole. We are told that he had 'recovered and restored to its former state a province that he had previously abandoned to enemy rule. This he did so that it had a properly appointed governor (*rectorem haberet legitimum*), and it was from that time onwards called "Valentia", by decision of the emperor.' There is general agreement that the new name was meant to refer both to Valentinian himself and to his brother Valens, but the location

of this province is disputed: indeed, this is the aspect of the affair
that has attracted particular attention. The *Notitia* has frequently
been scanned in this context. In it the list of units under the *dux
Britanniarum* is divided into two sections. The first records a group
of garrisons from Doncaster to the Tyne, all on the eastern side
of the country, except for a series along the Stainmore Pass route
to the west as far as Kirkby Thore. The second part is labelled
'per lineam valli', conventionally translated as 'along the Wall',
but in fact representing sites that run as far south as Ribchester on
the Ribble. The first half of this *per lineam valli* set is apparently
in geographical order, east to west, from Wallsend to Stanwix
(Carlisle). The second is not. There are differences between the
garrisons on the north-east list and those in the north-west. For
example, more changes of unit seem to have occurred in the
west than in the east; and there are forts inland in the west that,
archaeologically, seem to have been occupied after the war of 367
but are not listed under the *dux*. These differences have been
used to argue that the area now roughly represented by Cumbria
was more thoroughly devasted in 367. The argument then suggests that this region was reorganized and made into a fifth British
province by Theodosius, perhaps with its own separate military
command. Now it is perfectly possible to accept that this evidence does indicate that the north-west had been more disrupted
than the rest of the north and had had to be more thoroughly
reorganized, perhaps even with an independent military command, but none of that provides us with any evidence for locat-
ing the *civil* province of Valentia.

A more profitable line of enquiry may be to consider the political implication of Ammianus' words. He seems to say unequivocally that part of Britain was first abandoned by Theodosius,
and only later recovered and given 'a properly appointed governor'. This must indicate a change of circumstances or of policy
in the course of Theodosius' governance of Britain. Secondly,
Ammianus actually described the territory abandoned as 'a province'. Its designation as 'Valentia' ought therefore to be the renaming of an existing province, not the creation of a new one. Since
Valentia appears in the *Notitia* (with a *consularis* as governor) together with the other four known provinces of the British diocese,
it cannot be a renaming of one of the latter. It therefore looks

as if there were already five provinces in Britain *before* the expedition of Theodosius, and that he did not expect to secure one of them at first.

We have noted that Valentia seems to have received its new name as a compliment from Valentinian to himself and his brother. Yet Ammianus does make the slightly odd remark that the emperor named it 'as if celebrating a "minor triumph" (*velut ovans*)'. Such 'minor triumphs' ('ovations') were the formal honours that had traditionally been awarded in Republican times when the victory had been either unspectacular or over a slave revolt. The last actual ovation, with a full processional entry into Rome, to be recorded was that of Aulus Plautius, when he arrived back from Britain in AD 47. By that time even major victories only got an ovation if the general was not a member of the imperial family. After Aulus Plautius, generals no longer received a public ovation, but were granted them in title only. But there was one area in which full triumphs had always been avoided, even under the Republic. That was for victories over Romans, whether in civil war or otherwise. For true glory to be garnered, the enemy had to be foreign. The question that now occurs is: if Valentinian's general had recovered a Roman province from invading barbarians, why was the emperor's celebration so restrained? There was nothing new in an emperor taking the full glory for a victory that had been gained in his name rather than personally: anyhow, Ammianus is referring to Valentinian's action, not Theodosius'.

The use of the term *ovans* is not the only curious feature in Ammianus' account. The immediately preceding section records an extraordinary episode. A Pannonian named Valentinus had been sent into exile in Britain for a serious crime. He was the brother-in-law of Maximinus, one of the more sinister figures of the period. The latter had been put in charge of prosecuting members of the aristocracy in Rome for magical practices. Valentinian's own Christian rigour and his class prejudice against the Roman nobility are as well known as his misjudgements of men. Maximinus not surprisingly made himself thoroughly hated, before being appointed praetorian prefect of the Gauls in 371. For five years it was through him that the civil administration of Britain was accountable to the emperor. At this time, however, he was still harrying senators in Rome. Several of the members of his family fell foul of the emperor, but it is interesting to note that, though we are told Valentinus' crime was a very serious one, he was punished with exile rather than anything worse. This was a political mistake, due perhaps to some intercession with the emperor by Maximinus on behalf of his relative. Exile was, it is true, not uncommon as a punishment for upper-class offenders, particularly to islands; and there were other exiles in Britain at the time, emphasizing its remoteness in the Roman mind. However, on this occasion it was the presence of other exiles that made the error a dangerous one. Valentinus approached his fellow exiles, and offered enough prospect of booty to certain troops to persuade them to support him. He seems to have gathered together a substantial party. We are told, however, that Theodosius was too quick for him, and crushed the conspiracy. Valentinus and his closest associates were handed over to the *dux*, Dulcitius, for execution. The number condemned was deliberately kept small, and Theodosius forbade further investigations lest fear should spread and 'rouse again tempests lying dormant in the provinces', presumably the provinces of Britain.

With this affair in mind, it may be worth looking again at the matter of Valentia. The emperor was, as we have seen, remarkably restrained about regaining a province. Our source emphasizes that it was recovered after being initially abandoned by Theodosius to the rule of enemies (*in dicionem concesserat hostium*), and makes a special point of the fact that it now had 'a legitimate governor'. Is this necessarily a province recovered from the barbarians? So far our overall picture of the state of Britain on the arrival of Theodosius has, perhaps wrongly, been one of Roman organization in disarray and of a whole countryside roamed by barbarian war-parties. We have not seen Theodosius' operations as the reconquest of an island under foreign rule, but the sweeping-out of marauding bands. What, then, of this seemingly special case of a province regained for the legitimate government? 'Hostis' does not automatically mean a foreign enemy: it simply indicates an enemy of the state. Traditionally, Roman traitors had been formally declared *hostes*, including, under the Republic, the populist revolutionary Catiline, and even at one stage Julius Caesar himself. Had Valentia had an 'illegitimate' Roman regime? It is not possible to associate this specifically with the conspiracy of Valentinus, since Ammianus makes it clear that Theodosius' speed prevented that from developing into actual revolt. But that does not rule out the possibility that other dissident Romans had taken advantage of the confused situation in 367 to seize power in part of Britain. The conspiracy of Valentinus proves that there were men ready to try, and there must, as we have noted, have been malcontents of various political and religious factions. Valentinian I has been described in modern times as the last of the great Roman emperors in the west, and Theodosius' work of restoration in Britain was only part of the vast programme of reconstruction of the defences of the western provinces that was carried out under his direction. However, in some ways he may have worsened the instability of society in the west by further alienating the traditional upper classes from the emperors and the army. Theodosius' unwillingness to pursue the ramifications of Valentinus' conspiracy suggests that discontent was uncomfortably widespread, and there is that interesting reference to 'the tempests that lay dormant'. Was it in the newly named province of Valentia that a storm had been calmed? If a whole province that had successfully seceded was brought back without more ostentation than was necessary to underline the re-establishment of the emperor's authority, it would accord well with the remarkable blend of resolution and moderation that seems to mark the rest of Theodosius' restoration of Roman Britain.

This is an appropriate point at which to take a brief look at our impressions of Britain, and of the western part of the empire in general, before moving on to the narrative of the years that followed the completion of Theodosius' work in the island. One general historical observation is in place here. It is important that we should not fall into the common trap of equating 'late' with 'decadent', an aspect of the anthropomorphic idea that cultures always and inevitably rise, flourish, and decline, rather than change. In Romano-British archaeological circles this has been encouraged by two accidents. The first is that fourth- and fifth-century levels on sites normally lie closest to the surface, and are thus more easily damaged than the earlier deposits, or have been more readily missed by excavators prior to the development of current techniques. The second factor is that on Hadrian's Wall, where the 'Theodosian' reconstruction was first recognized, the workmanship attributed to him (without direct evidence) tends to be crude compared with earlier phases in construction. Such crudeness, as we have already noted, seems to be a phenomenon specific to the Wall and likely to have an explanation particular to it.

There are correctives to the picture of decay and disorder in the west that need to be registered. It is intriguing to note the terms in which Valentinian issued a directive in 369 to the praetorian prefects in the west concerning the duties of provincial governors. He instructed the prefects to remind their subordinate governors of the duty to reside at their official stations and to keep their official residences in good repair and properly furnished. So far this is consistent with a hopeless decline in morale in the face of overwhelming barbarian pressure and a breakdown in internal security. But what are we to make of the rest of the imperial instructions? The governor was not to go 'frequenting delightful retreats', nor to spend his time being entertained on the estates of local landowners. The latter practice was so common as to need the introduction of the drastic penalty of confiscation of the hosts' estates. It does, in fact, help to illuminate a very important feature of the political behaviour of the age, to which we shall shortly return, but it also says a lot about contemporary feelings with regard to security and the stability of life. Two years earlier, in the year 367 itself, the prefect of Egypt received an imperial letter ordering him to use his legal powers to prevent decurions, the members of town councils, from transferring their entire households from the cities to the countryside, 'an action which has repeatedly been forbidden by law'. It was clearly not an age when the well off, more likely than most to fear for the safety of themselves and their possessions and to be able to move house and home if they wished, felt an overwhelming need to shelter together in defended cities. It implies that serious barbarian attack was not considered likely, at least in some parts of the empire, and that a good level of internal order prevailed.

The fact that Roman civilians were in general forbidden to carry arms—except when on a dangerous journey—implies a great deal about life in the empire. Even under the late Empire there was no relaxation of this rule. Express permission was required before arms could be worn, and on those rare occasions when it was given, very unusual circumstances can be deduced. The chaos in Britain at the time of Theodosius' arrival has to be seen through Roman eyes. It was something extraordinary from which he rescued the diocese. Of course, in 367 itself there were doubtless very few Britons who contemplated moving to a new villa in the country, and during Theodosius' restoration one cannot imagine that the governors of the British provinces found that they could take many days off for hunting or house parties, but these were the norms of life.

There is another side to all this, for it recalls an important feature of upper-class life in the fourth century—a distaste, or at least an affectation of distaste, for *negotium*, public life, and in particular for the burden of office. By the middle of the fourth century it had become a polite commonplace to commiserate with someone on receiving an appointment, and to hope that he would soon be able to lay it down, though recognizing the honour bestowed. It was certainly still felt necessary for the family dignity to reach the most prestigious offices, but there are signs that these were often held for as short a time as possible, and sometimes avoided altogether. On the other hand, when the fourth-century aristocrats did occupy public posts, there is no sign that they did not carry out their duties conscientiously.

The death of Valentinian I in 375, caused characteristically by a fit of apoplexy at the behaviour of some barbarian envoys, ended an era of government that was competent, energetic, and tough, unpopular in influential circles, but, by succeeding standards, tolerant in the religious matters that were now so important. Valentinian's elder son Gratian, in control at Trier, accepted his young brother Valentinian II as nominal co-Augustus in the west, but proceeded to rid himself of his father's associates. For Britain, one happy result was the early fall of the dreadful Maximinus. The replacement of his influence, and that of his friends, at court by that of the cultivated Ausonius and his Gallic circle is of considerable importance, for it signifies the beginning of a drawing-together of the aristocratic classes and the imperial court. Though in public life they still had largely separate careers, there were increasing contacts and interchanges, and Christianity began to take a real hold in some of the principal aristocratic families.

The disgrace of the anti-aristocratic party may have been greeted with some pleasure, but in Britain another event must have caused sadness: news of the execution at Carthage of Theodosius, now risen to the rank of *magister equitum*, immediately after another victory over enemies of Rome. Nothing is known of the reason for this execution, but successful *magistri militum* could be felt as serious threats to new emperors. His family, however, did not remain in obscurity for long. In 378 the empire received a most dreadful blow, largely through its own fault. The brutal mishandling of the Goths on the Danube frontier by the eastern Augustus, Valentinian I's unstable brother Valens, ended in a tremendous defeat for the Roman army at the battle of Adrianople. A great part of the Roman forces, and the emperor himself, were lost. Gratian turned to Theodosius' son, also called Theodosius, for help, appointing him first to drive back the Goths, and in the following year proclaiming him Augustus, co-ruler with himself, to take Valens' place in the east.

This younger Theodosius, known to history as Theodosius the Great, is the central figure for the rest of the century, dominating the period until his death in 395. His Christian fervour matched that of Gratian. The history of the western part of the empire in the late fourth century in many ways reflects the fact that the prime concern of the senior Augustus was in the east. Seen from Britain, this meant a period of persistent instability in the proximate imperial government, in contrast to the relatively stable but distant authority in Constantinople. For Britain, this situation was not necessarily improved by occasional but powerful interventions from the east. The island itself was twice to move out of the control of the central imperial regime, for five years under Magnus Maximus (383–8), and for two years under Eugenius (392–4), which together represent nearly half of Theodosius' reign. Also running as a thread through the period is the growing political significance of the magnates of the Church, including such figures as Ambrosius, the great Catholic bishop of Milan. Elevated to episcopal office by popular acclaim after being governor of that part of Italy, Ambrose became a most powerful influence on Gratian, on Valentinian II, and on Theodosius the Great himself.

It was a mixture of religion and politics that weakened Gratian's reign. He fell out with the pagan aristocracy over religious matters even more decisively than his father, for he replaced tolerance with a policy of sweeping away what remained of Julian's pagan revival. He ordered the endowments of the Vestal Virgins and of other priestly colleges to be confiscated, and he went so far as to eject the Altar of Victory again from the Senate House in Rome. This was particularly resented by the senatorial party, now led by Ambrose's anti-Christian opponent Q. Aurelius Symmachus, one of the principal orators and public men of the age. Nevertheless, though Gratian may have struck at the political heart of the old religion, there is little evidence of repression in Britain, and paganism survived long after Julian, both in humble shrines and public places. We are most likely to find positive action against pagan religion in those places where troops were stationed and could be used to carry out imperial orders.

We do not know if pagan discontent actually weakened loyalty to Gratian in Britain. It is perhaps ironic that, though he was brought down by an army revolt that started in Britain in 383, the mutiny elevated to the throne an officer who proved quite as vigorous a Christian as Gratian himself. The latter's reign, in fact, was marked not only by action against pagans, but also by the sinister first use of the death penalty by the secular power against heresy. Magnus Maximus had served with the elder Theodosius in the British expedition, and, like him, came from Spain. He will have been acquainted with officers in the reconstituted army in Britain, and was perhaps well known to the younger Theodosius, now emperor in the east. There was some family connection between Maximus and the latter (we do not know what it was), and it is possible that the younger Theodosius' attested military service with his father had been alongside Maximus in the British campaign. It is quite likely, too, that Maximus was known at the western imperial court. We do not know what post he currently held in Britain. Our only evidence is a report of a victory by him over invading Picts and Scots, though this may have occurred after his elevation. It has been conjectured that he was *dux Britanniarum*, but the possibility that he held an appointment as a *comes*, like the elder Theodosius, cannot be ruled out.

The affair developed as a military usurpation in the traditional

style. Maximus himself was said to have been jealous of the promotion of the younger Theodosius, while the armies in the west
resented favours alleged to have been showered on certain barbarian Alans whom Gratian appointed to military posts. It was
the troops in Britain that offered the throne to Maximus. It may
be no more than a literary device that the historian Zosimus was
using in describing the British units as the most ill-tempered and
unruly, but something of their resistance to excessive discipline
and their involvement in coups over the centuries may have hung
around them. It is revealing that, in a panegyric delivered before
Theodosius only six years after this event, certain 'minders' (*satellites*) that Maximus sent to execute a leading supporter of Gratian
appear to be endowed with extra nastiness—and the death with
added humiliation—by their being described as British.

Maximus proceeded to invade Gaul from Britain, Gratian's
army began to desert, and the emperor himself was killed by
Maximus' *magister militum*. Maximus set up his court at Trier and
was baptized as a Catholic, securing his administration and the
Church at the same time. He now controlled the prefecture of
the Gauls, holding Britain, Gaul, and Spain. Maximus therefore
replaced Gratian *de facto* as Augustus, and was so recognized for
the time being by Theodosius, heavily committed in the east.
Meanwhile there were uneasy diplomatic relations with Gratian's
younger brother Valentinian II, resident in Italy. There were,
nevertheless, reasons why joint rule by Theodosius and Maximus
might have been a well-balanced arrangement. For the present,
it meant firm government from Trier by an emperor who had
been elevated by the army in Britain.

There is no evidence that the rule of Maximus had so far been
deleterious to the security of Britain. It is frequently conjectured
that Maximus' need for troops on the Continent depleted the
garrison of Britain so much that it never fully recovered. However, as with alleged withdrawals by earlier usurpers, the evidence
is extremely thin. The sixth-century British writer Gildas, the
reliability of whose sources is uncertain, lists three Pictish wars
before the middle of the fifth century, and states that the first of
these started after Maximus had invaded Gaul, continuing 'for
many years' (*multos per annos*). A study has suggested that it did
not come to an end until 389/90. If so, it does not seem to have

worried Maximus overmuch, perhaps because of the victory already mentioned, and because his army had not had to fight a war against Gratian. His main preoccupation must have been with Theodosius. Civil war was maybe inevitable, and there are signs that Theodosius at least was expecting it. However, it was not until Maximus decided to cross the Alps four years later to occupy the imperial city of Milan, from which Valentinian and his court fled ahead of him, that it became real. Maximus had obviously decided that the time had come to put an end to the rival western government in Italy, which was a permanent threat to his claim to equality with Theodosius. This does not look like the action of a leader with a serious war raging in his rear in Britain. On the contrary, it looks like the move of one who, having failed to secure his position absolutely by diplomacy, now felt strong enough militarily to risk the war with Theodosius that expelling Valentinian by force would certainly mean. Maximus' move failed, but he seems to have been defeated by superior generalship rather than by weakness caused by distractions behind. After careful preparations, Theodosius moved westwards in 388 with remarkable speed. His naval forces, bringing Valentinian back with them, slipped past Maximus' fleet, while his land armies first defeated Maximus' forces twice in Illyricum and finally caught and killed him at Aquileia.

It would certainly not be surprising if some of the troops from Britain were lost in Illyricum, or were deployed elsewhere in the course of the rearrangements that Theodosius must have had to make after his victory. However, we know so little about the disposition of troops in late fourth-century Britain that we cannot be sure that the evacuation of specific forts, where it can be demonstrated, represents a reduction in the total forces rather than a transfer elsewhere in the island. Theories that the Wall was abandoned since the northern barbarian tribes were now friendly have already been discarded, and a once strongly held notion that a northern chieftain named Cunedda, together with his people, was transferred to north Wales by Magnus Maximus no longer seems as convincing.

It does look as if some of the Pennine and Welsh forts were abandoned at this time, and the Twentieth legion was withdrawn from Chester. There is also the appearance of a unit called

Seguntienses among the *auxilia palatina* in Illyricum listed in the
Notitia, possibly garrison troops from Caernarvon promoted by
Maximus to the palatine army and not returned to Britain after
the victory of Theodosius. Military weakness in Wales may well
explain the Irish raids in remote coastal areas that by the end of
the century was developing into settlement. On the south coast,
Portchester may have lost what remained of its main garrison at
this time. But we should not think of the defence of Britain
solely in terms of troops stationed in the island. Maximus himself told Ambrose that he had large numbers of barbarians among
his fighting forces, and this may mean that he had avoided withdrawing too many regular units from their stations by recruiting
widely outside the empire for his campaigns. His military policy
was certainly very costly, and may have led him to enact unjust
confiscations of property as well as high taxation. But there were
those who praised his rule, and, as far as Britain is concerned,
the tenuous evidence for a dramatic and dangerous reduction in
garrison strength leaves the question very much open.

It does not look as if Britain fell into Theodosius' hands
straightaway, if Gildas' account of the end of the first of his Pictish
wars preserves an echo of the truth. He states that messages were
sent from Britain promising submission, and that when this had
been accepted, a *legio* was sent by sea and drove out the enemy.
This could indicate that the Pictish problem had become more
serious after the outbreak of civil war inside the empire—or perhaps in a period of confusion after Maximus had been killed—
and that the sending of a force from the Continent on the same
lines as the earlier expeditions of Lupicinus and Theodosius the
Elder was part of a bargain involving the surrender of Britain
that might not otherwise have been gained. The difficulties of
dislodging Carausius are not likely to have been forgotten. Gildas'
account, if true, indicates a successful operation, which may have
been accompanied by some overhauling of defences.

Important military changes were in progress across the empire.
Maximus' remark to Ambrose about the number of barbarians in
his forces was, of course, very much in line with the traditional concern to avoid Roman casualties, especially in civil war, but
it also reflects a momentous transformation that was taking place
during the reign of Theodosius the Great. This reign saw a much

greater employment of barbarian allies alongside regular troops. In the east Theodosius had had to cope with the massive loss of Roman soldiers at the battle of Adrianople in 378, the consequences of which brought him to the throne. In the west he was to fight two civil wars, the first against Maximus, the second six years later. The barbarians brought in now must not be confused with those barbarian allies recruited into the regular army, who, as we have seen, cannot be separated from their colleagues of Roman origin. The new allied barbarians (*foederati*) must also be differentiated from the communities of *laeti* noted earlier. The latter were settled under Roman officers, and in comparatively small numbers. The new 'federate' bodies of troops varied in size and composition, but the common characteristic that put them into a separate category was that they were independent barbarians, under their own rulers and following their own customs. The largest groups were nothing less than barbarian kingdoms on the move, and even when they were given land within the empire as payment for their services, they retained their position as free allies. We shall note later the fluctuating status of their commanders, the uneasy and sometimes bloody relationship between the regular army and these new allies, and the Roman reluctance to allow them into cities. But at this point it is important to note that a change had occurred under the pressure of expediency that was to assume immense significance in the future.

We should also observe another trend in some frontier provinces under the late Empire that ran counter to the policy that had been in force under Valentinian I, but incorporated elements that we have recognized before. The attempt to hold the whole frontier in great force was being replaced by a greater employment of the principle of defence in depth. Many forts were abandoned or lightly held; others, notably legionary fortresses, were given more powerful defences, but were occupied by units of relatively small size. Fortified granaries also make their appearance, presumably so that an invader could be prevented from seizing military supplies or living off the land. Towns were to act as impregnable strongholds during an invasion, and as springboards from which the main Roman striking forces could launch a counter-attack after an enemy thrust had exhausted itself.

We should not therefore, be surprised if reliable evidence one

day appears for the presence of organized barbarian allies in
Roman Britain at about the end of the fourth century, more
probably outside the cities than inside. We have already seen frontier garrisons being reduced but not eliminated, and we may suspect that the open spaces to be seen in towns earlier in the
century will have facilitated the regular stationing there of mobile
field units. We may, too, discover fortified stores, perhaps in old
forts. But it must be emphasized that, for Britain, this is as yet
no more than a theoretical model, and that it is very unlikely to
be encountered here before AD 380/90.

Having defeated Maximus in 388, Theodosius reinstated
Valentinian II, now sole Augustus in the west. However, he was
less than confident in the unfortunate young man's capacity to
rule, and made sure that a number of major offices, including
the praetorian prefecture of the Gauls, were held by men of his
own, many of whom he had brought with him from the east.
We have already mentioned Chrysanthus, the son of a bishop,
who had been governor of one of the 'consular' provinces of
Italy before being posted to Britain as *vicarius*. He was, it will be
recalled, a prospective candidate for the highest civil office in
Constantinople, the eastern prefecture of the city. Theodosius
clearly felt that he needed first-rate administrators to keep Britain
loyal once it had been recovered. Britain was still regarded as
important, even viewed from Constantinople.

This time the defeat of a north-western emperor in whose
charge Britain had lain did not mean a change in religious policy. Theodosius was as determined a Christian and a Catholic as
Maximus, and the growth in the power of the Church was
unchecked. There was a remarkable continuity in terms of the
personalities wielding influence at court, only incidentally affected
by violent changes in regime—and this applies to many secular
notables as well, both Christian and pagan—right through from
the reign of Gratian to the death of Theodosius and beyond.
Theodosius himself, not without signs of irritation, adopted as
one of his chief advisers the irrepressible bishop of Milan, and it
was probably under Ambrose's influence that the campaign against
paganism was eventually intensified, despite the emperor's own
considerable tolerance.

By 391 Ambrose had won, and Theodosius issued an order

making all sacrifices illegal, whether in public or private, and closing all temples. In addition, he imposed large fines on officials who did not enforce the law. This order was followed by a much more extreme one in 392 that prohibited the ancient domestic worship of the household gods, the *lares* and *penates*. No one was allowed to honour them in his own home with the traditional garlands, lamps, or incense, and the property in which their shrines were found was to be confiscated. The chilling atmosphere of extremism is unmistakable. However, there is evidence that enforcement was inefficient, and that it was pagan practices, not the mere expression of pagan beliefs, that were illegal.

The outlawing of pagan worship was intended to apply to the whole empire. However, the second decree was issued by Theodosius on his return to Constantinople, and in the meantime the west had again rebelled. The young emperor Valentinian had been left in the charge of Flavius Arbogastes, Theodosius' Frankish general, who had previously been employed to hunt down and kill the son of Maximus. The discovery of Valentinian's body hanging in his apartments put both Arbogast and Theodosius into impossible positions. Even if it was suicide—which is not improbable—the accusation of murder was inevitable. It was apparently with reluctance that Arbogast was forced into rebellion, declaring an administrator named Flavius Eugenius as emperor. Like Carausius a century earlier, Arbogast and Eugenius proclaimed the legitimacy of their own regime by continuing to recognize the imperial authority in the east, deliberately recording the titles of Theodosius and his elder son Arcadius as Augusti. There was, however, no joint rule of the empire. The west, including Britain, had for the present once again slipped from Theodosius' grasp. It was now in the hands of three men: Arbogast himself; Eugenius; and Virius Nicomachus Flavianus, praetorian prefect of Italy, who had had a distinguished career. The direct effects of their rule on Britain is unknown, but two features are worth noting. First, Arbogast conducted a successful campaign against the barbarians across the Rhine, and seems to have carried out restoration work at Cologne. Secondly, both he and Flavianus were enthusiastic pagans, while Eugenius was a Christian who could be persuaded that a pagan revival was inevitable. Temples could now be rebuilt, that great symbol, the Altar of Victory, was restored to the Senate

House, and the major public festivals were again celebrated. The Christian party was extremely worried, and though some leading aristocratic pagans, including Symmachus, kept fairly aloof, there is good reason to suppose the existence of real support.

This pagan regime did not last long. In 394 Theodosius invaded Italy for the second time to put down a rival emperor. In his army was a very large force of Goths. At the battle of the Frigidus, not far from where Maximus had been killed, the army of the west was defeated, Eugenius himself was executed, and Arbogast and Flavianus committed suicide. The empire was reunited under Theodosius.

By the end of the following January he, too, was dead. The triumph of the Church was now assured, and, whatever Theodosius' own motives, he had striven with considerable success to maintain or restore firm government and unity of policy throughout the whole empire. Partly by Theodosius' own efforts and partly under regimes hostile to him, the Roman army was still winning substantial victories against the pressure on the frontiers, however precarious the situation on some sectors of the imperial perimeter. It was, however, now an army with a risky dependence on large allied forces only loosely under its control. The death of Theodosius was in many ways the end of one age and the beginning of another.

IV

THE END OF
ROMAN BRITAIN

16

THE COLLAPSE OF IMPERIAL RULE IN BRITAIN

The death of Theodosius left the empire to his two sons Arcadius and Honorius, both already invested with the rank of Augustus. This is often taken as the point at which the division into eastern and western empires became final. To consider the division as absolute from this date is in fact a simplification that makes much subsequent history more difficult to comprehend than is necessary, but, in the context of the reign of Honorius and the story of the collapse of imperial control in the west, it has sufficient truth to be a vital factor in the events that concern this book. Honorius' reign, from 395 to 423, is a rare period in which the cumulative effect of changes that we have observed occurring over a long period combined with a series of crises to create a genuine turning-point in western history, nowhere more dramatically than in Britain. At the death of Theodosius the frontiers of the empire were still maintained, and within them the vast structure of Roman society and the Roman way of life stood largely intact. Both within and without the empire Rome's prestige and position in the world were not seriously doubted. By the time Honorius died, the western Roman world had been shattered into fragments, never to be restored. Though much of Rome's culture, way of life, and even prestige survived, the change is dramatic, and its effects on the north-western provinces are immense in scale and very varied in character. In 395 Britain was a stable and prosperous part of the prefecture of the Gauls. Its administration and its army were firmly answerable through

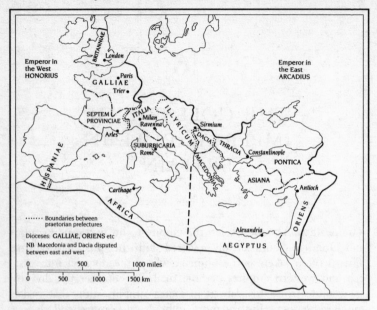

THE ROMAN EMPIRE *c.* AD 400. The five British provinces, making up the 'diocese of the Britains', were part of the 'praetorian prefecture of the Gauls', along with the dioceses of northern Gaul and Germany (*Galliae*), southern Gaul (*Septem Provinciae*), and Spain with the straits of Gibraltar (*Hispaniae*).

the established chains of command to the imperial government in Italy. Its culture, in common with its Gallic neighbours, was a mixture of local and cosmopolitan. Despite all the upheavals that had occurred in the previous two centuries, these were facts of life that no one would have had good reason to doubt were permanent. Yet by the time of Honorius' death, Britain had ceased forever to be part of the empire in any practical sense. The task of this chapter is to examine how this happened, and what it meant for Britain and her inhabitants.

The accession of Honorius and Arcadius was marked by a basic change in the role of the emperor. It affected east and west differently, and what happened is of major importance in comprehending subsequent events in the two halves of the empire. By and large, Roman emperors after Theodosius the Great were heads of state, but they no longer held effective power. This now fell into the hands of their chief ministers. The change was almost complete in the west, much less so in the east, where some emperors achieved absolute command of their realms. A crucial factor in this difference—not the only one, but perhaps the most important—was that whereas in the east these chief ministers generally held one of the civilian offices of state, in the west they were almost without exception the professional soldiers who commanded the army. A historical accident helped this process on its way. At the death of Theodosius, most of the field army of the entire empire was in the west, reunited after the defeat of Arbogast and Eugenius. In command was a figure whose name is well known to students of Roman Britain, a man whom this accident was to put into a position to dominate the history of the first part of Honorius' reign and fundamentally to affect the future of the west. This was the remarkable Flavius Stilicho, a Vandal by birth, but married to Theodosius the Great's formidable niece Serena. He had long been close to Theodosius, and in the later years of his reign he had become the emperor's chief lieutenant. The fact that Serena was also Theodosius' adopted daughter emphasized the connection, and since the real centre of authority normally lay at Constantinople while Theodosius was alive, Stilicho's claim to continued influence throughout the empire after the emperor's death is an understandable one. He was now *de facto* regent in the west, basing his authority on a claim that the dying emperor had secretly asked him to oversee both his sons. If this was indeed Theodosius' wish, his failure to make it public was calamitous. While Stilicho's rule was for a decade more or less unchallengeable in the west, where it had open support from Ambrose and powerful groups in both court and senate, it was never effective in the east. The dynastic connection of Stilicho and the imperial house was cemented by the marriage of Stilicho's daughter Maria to the young Honorius. The attention of the western government was dominated by attempts to assert authority in the east, and the west was chronically impoverished by being cut off from the sources of money, military supplies, and recruits that lay in the provinces under eastern control. The struggle for the Danubian provinces played a particularly crucial part in the story, and Rome's disastrous involvement with the Visigothic king Alaric, sometimes as an enemy and sometimes as an ally, was intimately connected with these issues.

Barbarian allies were becoming increasingly significant in Roman policy. We observed that the make-up of Roman armies had changed substantially during Theodosius' reign. We noted that Magnus Maximus claimed to have large numbers of barbarians in his pay (though that may have been an emergency measure), and in the war between Arbogast and Theodosius there were great contingents of Franks and Alamanni on the western side, and of Goths in the army of the east. It was now much more common for Roman generals to command forces that contained major contingents of barbarian troops under their own leaders, free *foederati*, and others. Some of the independent barbarian peoples co-operated with Rome on a strictly temporary, often purely cash, basis. They could amount to large armies on their own account, and getting them to combine for a campaign or to act on Rome's behalf was an important part of the imperial government's preoccupations. Diplomacy of this sort was at least in part forced on Rome by shortage of manpower in her own regular army, but it was very difficult to carry out successfully with the limited financial resources at the command of the western imperial government. It was made worse by the extreme reluctance of the Roman nobility to provide either cash or recruits from their own properties.

For the historian, the fact that the western *Notitia* gives no help in estimating the size and distribution of these purely barbarian troops in the Roman forces of the period makes it very much more difficult to assess the size of Roman armies. It is now, at the end of the fourth century and in the fifth, not earlier, that the likelihood of substantial groups of 'barbarian federates' needs to be taken into account in trying to understand Roman Britain, but our lack of knowledge about their location and numbers makes what we know about the movements of regular units, unlike earlier days, of comparatively little utility in calculating the total forces available to Roman commanders in Britain.

Whatever their numbers, the existence of these new barbarians within the empire was important socially and politically, as well as militarily. Various unpleasant incidents in this period make it clear that the barbarian soldiers themselves were felt to differ fundamentally from the regular army, and their families not to be part of the ordinary population. In 408, for example, we find Stilicho at one moment intending to use the barbarian part of his army to suppress a mutiny among his Roman units, at another warning the towns of northern Italy in which the barbarians' families were housed not to let these soldiers within the walls. Stilicho's own fall in the same year was followed by a terrible massacre by Roman troops of those families that did not escape to take refuge with Alaric, himself currently an ally of Rome.

The constraints on Stilicho's policy were thus crippling: indeed, by 408 we have the extraordinary sight of Stilicho and the Emperor Honorius attending the senate in person to try to persuade it to vote for diplomacy rather than war with Alaric. Not only does this reveal how the prestige of the imperial government had declined at home, and how the senate had once again, after centuries, become vitally involved in foreign policy, but also that Stilicho had a much clearer sight of changed realities than the senators. Both in the senate and at the imperial court old-fashioned Roman patriotism prevented a realistic appreciation of what was now possible, nor was this problem confined to the west. It was, of course, closely allied to the equally deep tradition that the highest glory for a Roman statesman was success in war. Roman opinion was largely wedded to attitudes it could no longer afford.

It is not therefore surprising that when the only contemporary source for Stilicho's policy towards Britain, the eulogizing court poet Claudian, mentions these provinces, it is in connection with claims of military success. It is not easy to deduce from his poetic language what actually happened. However, it looks as if the Roman forces were able to assert control over the sea approaches to the north-western provinces in 398, including the defeat of both Saxons and Irish Scots. It is not clear whether the Picts, also mentioned as beaten, are included among the sea-borne enemies or as a reference to a purely land campaign. With this remark of Claudian has been linked the second of Gildas' 'Pictish wars'. The latter reports an appeal for help from Britain, to which the Roman government again responded by sending an army against the enemy, this time 'against expectation'. If there is anything behind that phrase, it may suggest that the barbarians, as in 367, were taking advantage of the fact that the imperial government was distracted by other affairs. In the first half of 398 Stilicho had been involved in suppressing the potentially extremely damaging revolt, if that is the right word, led by Gildo, *comes Africae*, who had decided to assert allegiance to Arcadius and the eastern government on the issue of legitimacy. If anything was 'against expectation', it was the ease and speed with which Gildo was suppressed, leaving the western government free to turn to other problems, such as Britain.

We do not know whether Stilicho personally took charge in the British war. However, by the beginning of AD 400 the claims made in his honour are considerable. It is worth looking at Claudian's account in detail. After an introduction that depicts Britannia with the trappings of a Caledonian savage, she is made to declare:

When I too was about to succumb to the attack of neighbouring peoples —for the Scots had raised all Ireland against me, and the sea foamed under hostile oars—you, Stilicho, fortified me. This was to such effect that I no longer fear the weapons of the Scots, nor tremble at the Pict, nor along all my shore do I look for the approaching Saxon on each uncertain wind.

Earlier the previous year Claudian seems to have been expecting news of naval successes, waiting to hear of 'the Saxon conquered, the Ocean calmed, the Pict broken, and Britain secure'. Yet only a month after the detailed eulogy of January 400, the trumpeted claims of major success disappear, and they do not reappear. In mid-402 Claudian gives us news of troop withdrawals from Britain (to which we shall return), but this seems too late to explain the change of tone in 400. It is perhaps first worth noting that the eulogy of 400 does *not* confirm victory in battle, but concentrates on defence. Perhaps the answer is that there was no actual victory, and that it was becoming obvious that Stilicho was in fact having to run down the garrison of Britain. It has been suggested that Stilicho was already abandoning forts at an early stage of his regency. Gildas may help us to develop this idea. We have already seen that it would fit the general situation to have troops being withdrawn in 398. He goes on to state that just before the Romans left (after defeating the Picts in this second war), they helped the Britons to build the stone wall, constructed watch-towers on the south coast, and provided patterns of weapons for the Britons (*exemplaria armorum*). They then withdrew, and the Picts and Scots occupied British territory as far as the Wall (*muro tenus*).

If we really can put the accounts of Gildas and Claudian together, then perhaps we may conjecture the following course of events. The force sent out in 389 or 390 had become semipermanent (at this time there was a strong tendency for armies of *comitatenses* to become localized, each under a *comes* as before, but acquiring territorial titles). In 398 it was being recalled, perhaps with consequent adjustments in the stationing of the garrison units in Britain, including the evacuation of some less vital forts. The barbarians took the opportunity to attack, but were thrown off balance by the unexpected collapse of Gildo in Africa, and did not press home their attack. Finally, though the planned withdrawal was resumed, the warning was heeded, and measures were taken to strengthen the defences of Britain. We do not have to assume the large-scale removal of garrison *limitanei*: the fact that the barbarians stopped at the Wall suggests that the frontiers for the moment held. The provision of *exemplaria armorum*, and the instruction in the building of the stone wall are interesting: the first suggests that the central authorities supplied patterns so that equipment normally supplied by the state ordnance factories, especially in the disputed Danubian provinces, could be manufactured locally; the latter, while in itself probably an attempt to explain Hadrian's Wall when the truth about its construction had been lost, may preserve a tradition of deliberately instructing civilian builders in the techniques of military construction. We also ought to note the possibility that permission was given to disregard the *lex Julia de vi publica*, the ancient general prohibition on the carrying of arms by civilians. Yet we do not know how much of all this applies to the arming of civilians, and how much to the making of arrangements for the surviving garrisons of the regular army in Britain, whether in forts or in detachments in towns. Indeed, the withdrawal of *comitatenses*, whether from a previous task force or upgraded from among the regular units of the *limitanei*, may have led to the remaining regular units taking on new duties, including mobile ones with temporary billeting in towns. It is not irrelevant to note here that as early as AD 395 Stilicho's government had been attempting to divert municipal funds in the west to pay for local defence.

If what Gildas describes as the *legio* being withdrawn when the second Pictish war broke out was indeed the same force that had been sent by Theodosius the Great to deal with the first Pictish war in 389 or 390, it may have been in Britain much longer than was intended. If it was, then, a task force that had become almost a fixture, it provides one possible answer for the presence of a *comes Britanniarum* in the *Notitia Dignitatum*, over which much ink has been spilt. The *Notitia* army, nine units of *comitatenses*, looks just like such a task force. One cannot help suspecting that this might be the period when this post became a fixture in the army lists, even if (like others of its kind) it was from time to time held in abeyance.

If there was, therefore, a campaign in 398 against the barbarians threatening Britain, it is likely it was a sudden decision to seize an unforeseen opportunity. Yet Stilicho may have harboured long-term ambitions for a major offensive in Britain, though the times were generally inauspicious. The withdrawal of as many troops as possible in about 399, intended to be temporary, seems likely, coupled with a reorganization of the coastal command. Such a policy would seem particularly convincing if an unexpected success had sapped barbarian confidence. Even so, we shall see that Stilicho's withdrawals may not have been as drastic as has often been thought. But for the moment he needed all the troops he could obtain. We ourselves do not know precisely what Alaric had been doing since he retreated into Epirus with his Visigoths in 397, but there is no reason to think that the western Romans were so ignorant. However, there was one factor that must have been quite enough to worry Stilicho. In 397 the eastern government had forbidden him to pursue Alaric—they were very unwilling to see his power increase to the extent that victory over the Visigoths would mean—but now they had gone much further by granting Alaric the rank of *magister militum per Illyricum*, which gave him the opportunity to draw on the Roman military ordnance factories in the Balkan provinces to equip his men. It would make sense if Stilicho still saw Alaric as the principal

threat, and decided to collect such forces as he could before tackling him again. Nor, for that matter, had Stilicho given up his
claims on Constantinople. The appointment of Alaric in Illyricum
by the government of Arcadius was especially pointed, since the
provinces of eastern Illyricum were themselves a matter of dispute between east and west. There was a double reason, therefore, for dealing with Alaric, one way or another.

Towards the end of the summer of 401 the Visigothic threat
to the west became acute once more. Alaric came down through
the Alps and wintered in northern Italy. Stilicho spent that winter raising recruits on the Danube; he also had the walls of Rome
itself put into order (it was not just the provincials that were
being urged into repairing their defences). Among the troops
collected by Stilicho, Claudian describes a *legio* (the same word),
'protector of the furthest Britons, which curbs the ferocious Scot
and has watched the tattooed life draining from the dying Picts'.
If Claudian could be trusted not to be using literary convention
—which we may legitimately doubt—this ought to mean part
of the static garrison of northern Britain, but it is just as likely
that this is the same force that was being withdrawn at the time
of Gildas' second Pictish war. One may perhaps guess that if this
meant leaving the post of *comes Britanniarum* without a substantial body of troops, then there was occasion for a reorganization
of the coastal defences of Britain that fixed the Saxon Shore in
the form in which it stands in the *Notitia*. It is not impossible
that the very title 'comes litoris Saxonici' (which does not appear
anywhere earlier) owes its existence to Stilicho.

The fact that the *Notitia* lists a number of British units as serving elsewhere in the empire might be evidence that Stilicho's
withdrawal of troops from Britain was substantial, and that they
did not come back. On the other hand, we do not know that
these units were not transferred in some previous phase. Indeed,
for earlier periods, when we have more details about the recruiting of troops, it seems that very few units raised in Britain were
actually stationed there. The fact that these particular troops are
found in the eastern as well as the western sections of the *Notitia*
makes a date for transfer substantially after 395 difficult to accept.
Moreover, we have already noted that our lack of knowledge
about the barbarians in the western Roman service at the end

of the fourth century makes it unsafe to assume that any removal of regular units necessarily reduced the total garrison of Britain. On the other hand, there is another piece of evidence that *could* support the idea that Stilicho's withdrawal of troops at this time was on a large scale. The issue of coinage by emperors was always primarily for the purposes of government expenditure, pre-eminently for the payment of troops, not for the general purposes of the economy. There had been no mint in Britain since the time of Magnus Maximus, and the last Roman coins to occur in large numbers are those issues that Arcadius and Honorius struck down to AD 402. Coins were normally shipped in bulk to the provinces. The reduction in Britain from 402 may imply that there were no longer enough Roman troops in Britain to be reflected by significant finds of coins. This would certainly support the common view that Stilicho stripped Britain of most of what remained of its garrison. Yet it could reflect a replacement of regular troops by barbarians, who received grants of provincial land in return for military obligations. Equally—and perhaps more probable—it may mean that Honorius' government, desperately short of cash and having extreme difficulty in raising the money for war and diplomacy with the Goths in Italy, simply stopped paying the garrison and the civil service in Britain. Nor is it impossible that disorder in Italy and Gaul made the job of ensuring the trans-shipment of cash to Britain extremely difficult. Any or all of these explanations would have the same effect in Britain, and might well help to explain the extreme mood of discontent there that was to lead to three successive revolts in 406–7.

However, on the larger imperial scene, Stilicho's moves were rewarded with limited but, for the moment, effective military success. Alaric suffered sufficient losses in battle in 402 for him to accept an agreement with Stilicho that he should withdraw from Italy. The immediate threat was thus removed, but there were important long-term political consequences in the permanent retreat of Honorius and the imperial court from Milan to the remote Adriatic city of Ravenna. This change established the centre of government close to the great naval base that looked to the Mediterranean and the eastern empire. The 'Milan–Trier axis' from which the north-western provinces had been governed was now broken.

It is difficult to blame Honorius. Nor was it any time to be moving troops back to the outlying provinces. In 404 another Gothic army followed Alaric, and it was not until 405 that Stilicho was able to bring their king, Radagaisus, to battle and defeat him at Fiesole near Florence in old Roman style, subsequently enrolling a large number of his men in the Roman army. For the moment, western military prestige was restored, but the success was short-lived. On the very last day of 406 a horde of Suebi, Vandals, and Alans crossed the Rhine, defeated the Frankish federate forces opposed to them, and pressed on into Gaul. Major invasions of this kind had, of course, happened before, but this time the consequences were irreversible. At just about the same moment (the exact chronology is uncertain) a mutiny against Stilicho detached the British diocese from the western imperial government. The outcome of these two events was to prove fatal for Britain as part of the Roman world—but not immediately.

There is some sign that the situation in Britain was already tense. Reports from Irish sources of attacks on the south coast of Britain by the 'high king' of Ireland, Niall of the Nine Hostages, are perhaps to be associated with the year 405. It looks as if Stilicho's work on the coastal system in 399, conjectured above, was based on an accurate assessment of returning danger. Barbarian confidence was coming back. Moreover, the Gothic wars of 402–3 and 404–5 meant the concentration of western troops and of Stilicho's personal attention on Italy, not to mention the eastern empire. There is argument about whether the first of the German invaders were already penetrating the Rhine frontier when elements in Britain seized the opportunity for military revolt. The army first elevated a soldier named Marcus, but very soon murdered him, as was the wont of mutinous troops who did not get quite what they had expected. He was replaced by a Briton named Gratian, who appears to have been a civilian and was probably a member of the local Romano-British upper class. By this time—Gratian was proclaimed in 407—the barbarians were certainly across the Rhine. Gratian's reign was brief: he was deposed and murdered after four months. It is possible that the barbarians' move across northern Gaul was enough to provoke the forces in Britain into replacing their emperor.

Zosimus certainly alleges that the British army feared a barbarian crossing of the Channel, and they may well have believed that they would receive little help from the imperial government. Indeed, before the German invasion, and while basking in the success of defeating Radagaisus in Italy in 405, Stilicho had revived a project that may seem extraordinarily dubious to us, but underlines the way in which Roman foreign policy now worked. His scheme was to co-operate with Alaric in detaching the provinces of eastern Illyricum from the government of Arcadius in Constantinople. There were thus not likely to be many Roman troops available for strengthening remote western provinces: in 406 we find Honorius urging the *provinciales* of the west to take up arms in their own defence, and offering freedom to slaves who volunteered to join them. Nor were deals with the Goths likely to be cheap—at one stage Alaric asked for the whole province of Noricum as land for his followers.

The army of Britain may have believed that the island should not stand alone, for, having deposed Gratian, they elevated a soldier with wide ambitions. The fact that a traditional attempt from Britain on the empire was even contemplated—the sort of action undertaken by Clodius Albinus, Constantine, and Magnus Maximus—suggests that the army in Britain felt that it was still sufficiently strong to overawe and win the support of the surviving Roman and allied forces in Gaul and Germany, or to defeat them if they remained loyal to the government at Ravenna, and sufficient, too, to risk a major war against the German invaders. This does not really support the view that Stilicho had drained Britain of troops in 401 (or, if so, that they had not been replaced). Indeed, the initiative is assumed to have come from the army itself. It is just possible that there were still Continental *comitatenses* in Britain who did not want to see their home provinces devastated, or to be stationed permanently across the dreaded Ocean. Moreover, for troops with homes in Britain or the neighbouring provinces, it was probably preferable to be part of a stable north-western army than under threat of an eastern campaign, with a doubtful ally, against the power and prestige of the senior Augustus. In addition, there were the old attractions of booty and rapid promotion as the rewards of successful civil war, for which the confused situation in Gaul may have looked most promising. Certainly, one ancient source thought that the British army had probably elevated all three of their pretenders in order to gain the empire, and he believed that Constantine III was chosen because the great name he bore suggested that he would succeed in grasping the imperial throne.

Whatever the army's motives, Constantine moved swiftly from Britain into Gaul before the Germans could occupy the Channel coast, sending his own officers ahead to take command of the surviving Roman units where they could. In the event, the barbarians turned southwards. By the end of 407, but only after stiff fighting, apparently against loyalist forces, Constantine had taken over the administration of Gaul and was repairing the defences of the Rhine and closing the Alpine passes into Italy. He did not manage to bring under control all the barbarian invaders who still moved about Gaul; but in the following year his son Constans and his British general Gerontius took Spain in a swift campaign, rooting out opposition by relatives of the Theodosian imperial family. In 408 Stilicho seems to have incited some unspecified barbarian tribes to spread further havoc in Gaul, presumably in an attempt to dislodge Constantine. However, in 409 the successes won by the rival regime forced Honorius to recognize Constantine as Augustus and to hold the consulship jointly with him.

It looked for the moment as if the army of Britain had made the right decision. Apart from the bands of barbarians still loose in Gaul (and from the purely British point of view, they were at least heading for Spain), Britain was once again part of a united Gallic prefecture under firm Roman control. In Constantine III they had a properly legitimized emperor who owed his elevation to them, and whose Continental forces contained senior officers from their own number. He was resident in the prefecture, and one of his major concerns was to be the security of the northern frontiers.

For Britain, however, there was a disquieting feature in the situation of quite a different kind. We have already noted the retreat of the western government from Milan to Ravenna, and we have mentioned how this weakened the traditional axis of administration. We have also observed how Trier had been the effective centre of government, as far as Britain and the neighbouring provinces were concerned, for more than a century. Now Constantine found that the capital of the prefecture had been moved very far south, to Arles, a transfer that had very probably only just happened as a direct consequence of the barbarian invasion of 406. Indeed, one might perhaps hazard a guess that a partial flight of the administration from Trier was a contributory cause of the moves in Britain. The change was a permanent one, and the hub of Constantine III's government was in consequence much more distant from the affairs of Britain than it would otherwise have been. The centre of gravity of the Gallic prefecture was now inevitably Mediterranean rather than northern.

In the mean time, however, the actions of the army of Britain had had much greater consequences for the history of the Roman world as a whole than anyone had anticipated. Constantine's neutralization of the remaining loyalist forces in Gaul by the end of 407 put an end to Stilicho's plan for a joint operation with Alaric against the eastern government, but it was too late to prevent Alaric from marching into Italy on his way to join forces with the Romans. Unfortunately, Alaric considered—with reason— that he had the right to be paid for his march into Italy, and a series of immensely complicated and extraordinary events followed, disastrous for the empire.

The year 409 soon demonstrated the fragility of the alliance between Stilicho, Honorius, and the senate. This had depended on success. The same year witnessed a temporary alliance between Alaric and the senate against Honorius, including the elevation of a puppet emperor by the Visigothic king. It also saw the death of the eastern emperor Arcadius, followed by a plan by Stilicho and Honorius to take control of the government at Constantinople, reuniting the empire. This foundered when Stilicho discovered that Honorius had changed sides under the domination of a rival court party that favoured peace with the east. He was too late. His enemies at court outmanœuvred him, and swiftly engineered his arrest and death. Stilicho had attempted to continue the tradition of a Roman world dominated by a single strong man, but the unforeseen consequences of his actions contributed substantially to the approaching break-up of the empire in the west. In the short run, his overthrow simply added to the confusion reigning in Ravenna and Rome.

The following year, 410, was the most traumatic of all, for the breakdown of relations between the senate and Alaric led to a devastating sack of Rome itself by the latter's Gothic troops. The effect of this almost accidental incident, largely brought about by Roman diplomatic incompetence, factional strife, and the unwillingness of the upper classes to dip into their own pockets for the public good, has to be seen in the context of the eight centuries of security from foreign enemies since northern barbarians had last sacked the city, and the belief of both Romans and probably most contemporary barbarians as well that the empire could not be defeated.

This is perhaps one reason why senators who could quite easily have paid what Alaric at one stage requested for services rendered would not co-operate. But the imperial government, too, cannot be absolved of being bemused by the legendary invincibility of Roman arms. Alaric's sack of Rome has left him with the reputation of a monster, but the behaviour of both Romans and other barbarians towards him and his people was certainly no better than his towards them, and sometimes worse. That, too, was consistent with Roman tradition, since their attitude towards peoples outside the empire had almost always been strictly pragmatic, untouched by feelings of moral obligation of any kind.

The sack was to be Alaric's last major act before his death in the same year. However, a new Gothic figure had entered the scene, Alaric's brother Athaulf, whose career was to accelerate the fusing of Roman and barbarian worlds. In 409 he had brought another Gothic army to reinforce Alaric's in Italy. Honorius was in a desperate state. He had sought, as we have seen, to neutralize the rival Roman empire to the north by recognizing Constantine III. The cities of north Italy were ordered to raise their own troops, and the court at Ravenna was in a state of chaos after the execution of Stilicho. This was not really resolved until a string of *coups d'état* ended with the establishment of another general, Flavius Constantius, in a position similar to that formerly held by Stilicho. With some stability restored to the western government at Ravenna, there was now a prospect of being able to deal with Constantine. Honorius' hand was further strengthened by the changed situation brought about by the restoration of good relations between Ravenna and Constantinople.

Circumstances were changing in the north-west, too. Constantine III's empire was disintegrating, partly no doubt due to external pressures, but also to a great extent to internal causes. Gerontius and Constans, having taken Spain, seem to have made a serious mistake by handing over the defence of the Pyrenean passes to barbarian federate troops. In 409 these failed to resist the Germans who had crossed Gaul, taking all they could, and were now intent on starting on a similar process in Spain. Constans sent orders dismissing Gerontius from his post as *magister militum*, but it was no moment for heeding such a command. Gerontius proclaimed a rival emperor instead, one Maximus. The Spanish part of Constantine's empire and the army under Gerontius' command were now out of his control, and about to become dangerously hostile. Gerontius and Maximus were shortly to invade Gaul, bringing barbarian allies with them. Yet in the same year Constantine himself was attempting to take advantage of the chaos in Italy by advancing into the northern part of the country. There is a possibility that he had ideas of rounding off his conquests by expelling Honorius from the western throne, or it may have been that he intended to cement his nominal alliance by supporting Honorius against Alaric. Whatever his precise intention, it was not to work. Despite Honorius' desperate plight, Constantine's own realm was disintegrating. Gerontius and Maximus defeated Constans in battle, and slew him. Constantine, having withdrawn from Italy, was himself besieged in the city of Arles. The empire set up by the British army was now in a very serious state of civil war. In addition, a substantial part of the Burgundian nation took this chance to settle inside the Roman frontier on the Rhine. Constantine III had proved unable to control his own armies. Gaul—which he might have been expected to clear of the German invaders—had been looted from one end to the other, and now Spain was laid open to the same treatment. The Burgundians looked like setting up a permanent kingdom inside the Rhine frontier that he had been trying to repair. He was now besieged in his capital, which implies not only that he could not enforce his will elsewhere in his empire, but that normal administrative communications (including the collection of taxes and the payment of troops) were abruptly severed between Arles and his provinces, including the diocese of Britain.

In the mean time, probably in 408, while the Germans were still ravaging Gaul and while the attention of Constantine's government had been on its campaign in Spain, barbarians had launched a serious and destructive attack on Britain. Constantine probably did not have the troops to spare to deal with this emergency. In 409 his situation became much worse. Zosimus describes the dramatic consequences:

Gerontius . . . gaining the support of the troops [in Spain], caused the barbarians in Gaul to make war on Constantine. Since Constantine failed to resist this attack (the larger part of his army being in Spain), the barbarians across the Rhine attacked everywhere with all their strength, and brought the people of Britain and some of the nations of Gaul to the point where they revolted from Roman rule and lived by themselves, no longer obeying Roman laws. The Britons took up arms and, fighting for themselves, freed the cities from the barbarian pressure; and all of Armorica and other provinces of Gaul, in imitation of the Britons, freed themselves in the same manner, expelling the Roman officials and setting up their own administration as well as they could.

The year 409, therefore, had started with Constantine III as Augustus, but with his British provinces already hard pressed by a barbarian attack that had been launched the previous year. By 410 he had lost Britain as well as Spain.

In Britain the revolt implies that those of his administration who had remained loyal were now ejected. It is worth looking at the civil and military aspects separately. And it is also worth considering for a moment the sort of men who staffed the senior posts in the imperial administration in the early fifth century, because it helps us to see the context of the expulsion. In ordinary times, when there was no rival regime to prevent the central government from acting normally, the *vicarius* of the diocese and the governors of his provinces would still have been appointed by the government in Italy, and probably, but not always, they would have come from one of the western provinces of the empire. We have noted at least one *vicarius* from the city of Constantinople itself, though after 395 the jobs are more likely to have gone to loyal adherents to the western court. Indeed, in the west, unlike the east, the great land-owning families once again dominated the civil offices in the fifth century. In 417 we find the distinguished Gallic landowner Rutilius Namatianus stopping off on a journey home to visit another Gaul, Victorinus, an Aquitanian who had served at court, like so many of his compatriots since the days of Ausonius' friendship with Gratian. Before his time at court this Victorinus had been *vicarius* of Britain. It is reasonably certain that he headed the British diocese before the usurpation of Marcus in 406. He had retired to Aquitania after serving in Britain and Italy, but had retreated before the barbarian disruption of his Gallic homeland in 409 or 414 to other property belonging to him in Italy, which promised more security. The world was shrinking for the western provincial aristocrats, but they were to display an astonishing capacity for survival. Victorinus had sought a tranquil retirement. Others were to retain considerable property and influence in their home provinces in spite of the profound changes in their world.

One notes that Victorinus was a provincial, but not a Romano-Briton. There had been a convention that governors should not head their home provinces. Army officers, as we have seen, might be German rather than Roman by descent, but that does not say anything about their personal place of origin, and they too would receive their commands from Italy and would have a varied career. Even if we assume that some of the men appointed to Britain by Stilicho changed sides in 406, the usurpers will still have had to fill vacant posts. Constantine III almost immediately had the whole of the Gallic prefecture to draw upon. Yet it is not surprising to find a Briton, Gerontius, in his most senior military post. The British army had put Constantine into power and needed to be rewarded: moreover, Britain had had a much larger garrison than Spain and Gaul, and the Rhine army had just been involved in defeat. On the other hand, we find the civil office of praetorian prefect being occupied first by a Gallo-Roman noble, Apollinaris. He was the grandfather of the famous statesman and author Sidonius Apollinaris, and is typical of that group of Gallo-Romans which had been supplying many of the leading personalities of the central imperial court and administration. He was followed by another such man, Decimius Rusticus, and it is very significant that the political traditions of their families were not seriously interrupted even when Constantine's empire fell. The sons of both had distinguished careers in the imperial service, and Apollinaris' son actually came back from Italy to hold the praetorian prefecture in Gaul under the restored legit-imist regime.

Romano-British nobles do not seem to have been playing the same sort of part in the imperial government, and it is therefore perhaps unlikely that Constantine could draw on a similar pool of experience from among them to fill his senior civilian posts, either in Gaul and Spain or in Britain itself. Doubtless some of the men who did hold the posts under him owned property in the island, even if they were not resident, but their local involve-ment was probably minimal. It is also worth remembering that the tenure of senior posts was tending to be comparatively short. All this adds up to the likelihood that the Constantinian civil administration ejected by the Britons was largely staffed, at least at the senior levels, by strangers. These are the 'Romans' who were expelled. That it could be done at all perhaps supports the notion that only relatively few regular military units were left— or at least, only a few that bothered to remain loyal.

It is impossible to believe, whatever the troop withdrawals made by Constantine, that the whole military apparatus had been dismantled by him. The skeleton, at least of a command and main-tenance structure, must have remained. We may reasonably ask both what happened to it during the ejection of the Constan-tinian officers, and how the remaining troops had been reacting to events on the Continent. One cannot help suspecting that the period between the revolt of Gerontius in Spain and the expul-sion of the officials from Britain was the actual moment when large bodies of troops had left Britain, whether in response to orders, or of their own volition to seek their fortunes in the re-newed troubles on the Continent. Many of the troops who were still in Britain at this point may have felt that their sympathies lay with their colleagues supporting Gerontius in Spain rather than with Constantine at Arles; others may well have been bar-barian allies who had no particular reason to stay loyal to any-one—unless he paid, and paid well. However, none of this carries with it the implication that anyone thought that the whole elab-orate structure of the army in Britain had come to an end for ever. Certainly, until the expulsion of Constantine's men by the Britons, we may reasonably assume that at least a core of officers and men remained at their posts in the island. Indeed, the army was so central to Roman administration that it is difficult to see what the expulsion could mean if it did not involve the holders of military as well as civil office.

We are greatly hampered by a total lack of direct information on what happened to any troops remaining in Britain after 409. We have very largely to rely on analogy drawn from the collapse of better-documented provinces and the general dissolution of the Roman forces in the west. However, it is worth looking briefly here at what may have happened, with the warning that much of the argument is based on similar situations that occurred in other parts of the west much later in the century.

If the *Notitia* reflects the state of the official records around AD 420/5, as some students of the document think, then the lists for Britain can hardly have been other than a paper establishment. There is no evidence for an imperial reoccupation after the break with Rome that will stand up to serious scrutiny. It is, of course, perfectly possible that the old British establishment remained in the files from nothing more than administrative inertia. On the other hand, there is no cause to think that the Roman author-ities would have assumed Britain to be permanently lost. Provinces, including those of Britain, had been lost and regained many times before. There was probably no reason to delete the British section, and a positive advantage in having a reference list that would act as a contingency plan for the day when the restora-tion of Britain to its normal form of government became a real-ity. Nevertheless, the military establishment described in the *Notitia* cannot reflect even in part anything that was actually in being in Britain after the break with Roman rule. If the British rejection of Roman government—first that of Constantine III and thereafter, in all probability, that of the restored legitimist regime in Gaul—was substantially fuelled by a desire to rid them-selves once and for all of the burden of the imperial establish-ment, the likelihood of their being able or wanting to maintain the very expensive late Roman military system seems extremely slim. We are, after all, told that the Britons successfully organized their own defence at that time.

We have a little guidance as to what could happen to regular units when the link with the central command was broken. One of the most quoted and graphic sources is Eugippius' *Life of St*

Severinus, which describes the situation in Noricum in the 470s, half a century or so later. There were still many regular units stationed at various cities in that province, but when their pay ceased to arrive, they were disbanded, and the frontier was abandoned with them. One last unit dispatched a deputation to Italy to collect what was due: when this failed to return, this unit, too, disbanded itself. That enabled the neighbouring barbarian king to cross the Danube and take over military control of the Roman towns and their populations. This is, of course, long after Britain became separated from the empire, but, in the absence of contrary evidence, it is perhaps fair to guess that something similar may have happened to any regular troops that had not left Britain in 409. While we may be certain that Constantine III would have had to pay his troops generously when they elevated him, as was the invariable custom, it is extremely unlikely that any cash would have come through for troops remaining in Britain after the revolt, even if, as is improbable, Constantine had been able to keep up payments once Gerontius had intervened in Gaul. A rapid dissolution of those regular units in Britain at this point is therefore indicated. A hint of what this process might have involved at its most orderly is given by a reference to the inclusion in the Roman forces at the battle of the Catalaunian Plains, which took place in Gaul in 451, of the Olibriones, 'who had once been Roman soldiers'. This description suggests a regular unit that had been settled on the land like *laeti*, with an obligation to military service when required, kept together, but presumably not paid. Even this degree of organization was probably a rare exception, but it is a great deal more likely than that local initiative took over responsibility in Britain for regular wages and provision in kind.

The latter, as we have noted, had reached a high level in the fourth century, and involved state factories on a large scale. To control it required the intricate bureaucracy of praetorian prefects, *vicarii*, and provincial governors, the very officialdom that we assume the Britons expelled. It would, moreover, have required the active support of the Romano-British landowners to maintain the regular army. Yet that system was extremely unpopular with the Roman land-owning class elsewhere. Not only was it very expensive in cash terms, it also imposed what was felt to be an intolerable burden on the manpower required for agricultural estates—conscription. The late Empire is marked by a continuous struggle between the propertied class and the imperial government over recruiting, and in the fifth century this land-owning aristocracy was in control of the civilian offices within whose remit recruiting lay. One must, indeed, wonder with what enthusiasm the civil service now responded to the demands of the emperor and his generals. It was not as if the regular army had proved politically reliable. For centuries it had been tolerated at best, and was often hated by the civilian population at large, bringing disaster on more than one noble family by its emperor-making and civil wars. It was not even popular under the late Empire with those actually compelled to serve in the ranks, if the savage penalties for evasion are a guide. Settlement on the land would have avoided the probability of another coup by unpaid and disaffected troops, would have been a much cheaper method of retaining a reserve than by keeping them as a standing army, and would have added to the agricultural labour force. Indeed, the last advantage could probably have been gained very simply and with little risk by allowing the last units to dissolve of their own accord, if they were by now very few. Some such move to the land, organized, disorganized, or a mixture of the two, may indeed explain some of the finds of late Roman military equipment on villa sites, and helps to fill in our picture of society immediately after the break with Rome.

By 409 the practice of relying upon barbarian soldiers employed on contract was becoming common in other parts of the Roman world. The inherent dangers in Britain becoming totally dependent upon them are therefore not likely to have been widely appreciated—or, if appreciated, not strong enough to overcome the realities of contemporary practice. In the face of the widespread resistance in the western world to the burdens of the army, it would hardly have been practical politics for British rulers after 409 to win the necessary support among the civilian population to maintain regular units, even if they wished to do so. This was not just a matter of a central authority with the will to issue the orders and command the loyalty of troops: it was also a question of paying for a network of officials physically to collect and account for both taxes and actual recruits. That network formed a major part of the system that the Britons had just rejected; and while there is no positive evidence that the Britons did not replace these officials with their own nominees, there is no reason why they should have done so, unless a new usurper commanded the overwhelming military support necessary to force it upon them. In this general context, the eventual British employment of barbarian federates wholesale takes on a certain inevitability.

We do not know what form of administration emerged after the break from Roman rule, but we can set one very important limit to the possibilities. We have noted that the Romano-British upper classes had not shared in that burst of activity in the latter part of the fourth century and the early fifth that had put their Gallo-Roman counterparts into leading positions in the imperial hierarchy. This must have meant that, apart from any senior officials previously posted to Britain who had changed sides rather than be ejected or murdered, Britain was now very short of men with experience of high office. It would therefore have been extremely difficult—even if they had wished to do so—to organize the sort of centralized system that Constantine III and his many predecessors had been able to achieve in their northwestern empires, able to draw on a wide area of the west for the men to run the machinery of government. There is no reason to suppose that the traditions and attitudes of the Romano-British were any different from those of the Gallo-Romans, but the fortunes of recent politics had not given them the same opportunities. The purge of Constantine's administrators seems to have been thorough: the gap to be filled was large. A Christian tract known as the *De Vita Christiana* dates from about AD 411. This may very likely have emanated from Britain, and while there is no direct evidence for the context, it is not improbable that it refers to the overthrow of Constantine III's men in Britain.

We see before us plenty of examples of wicked men, the sum of their sins complete, who are at this present moment being judged, and denied this present life no less than the life to come . . . Those who have freely shed the blood of others are now being forced to spill their own . . . Some lie unburied, food for the beasts and birds of the air. Others . . . have been individually torn limb from limb . . . Their judgements killed many husbands, widowed many women, orphaned many children. They made them beggars and left them bare . . . for they plundered the children of the men they killed. Now it is their wives who are widows, their sons who are orphans, begging their daily bread from others.

It is, of course, likely that there were some people at all levels in Constantine's service who did in fact manage to change sides when they saw how the wind was blowing: such changes of regime were too common an occurrence to cause a wholesale flight from Britain of the entire corps of military and civil office-holders, faithful to the last. But even they, strengthened by local appointments, could hardly have kept the whole administrative machine working, including any surviving sections of the regular army, when cash remittances from central funds to the diocesan treasuries stopped. Salaries and running costs were enormous, and we have to reckon with an extreme lack of enthusiasm on the part of the provincial aristocracy to take office in a new diocesan administration—besides being unwilling to pay the necessary central taxes or to supply recruits from their estates once imperial pressure could no longer be applied, either from Arles or Ravenna. When Zosimus tells us that the Britons were living on their own, no longer obedient to Roman laws, and that other provinces copied their example, establishing their own administration as best they could, we have to expect not a new central administration in London, or even in the separate provinces that made up the British diocese, but a whole series of local arrangements, probably differing greatly from place to place.

Much has been made of a 'rescript' from Honorius in 410, alleged to have been addressed to the cities of Britain, instructing them to organize their own defence. This has been interpreted as an answer to a loyalist appeal to Ravenna. Rescripts were one of the ways in which the emperors laid down laws and issued instructions, and they took the form of answers to queries addressed to them. It would imply an appeal for help, or at least a request for instruction. However, it is not possible to build a picture of a loyalist party in Britain on this basis. It may at most have been no more than a readiness to barter submission to imperial authority in return for assistance (as in 389). But even if we could be certain that it was a formal rescript, which we cannot, it is not even possible to be entirely sure that Britain was the province concerned—it has been suggested that the text may refer to Brettia (Bruttium, in Italy).

A case has been made for a struggle in the early fifth century between Pelagian heretics and a loyalist Catholic party in Britain (Pelagius himself had originally come from Britain), and this would imply that the prime issue now was heresy rather than paganism (despite a short-lived pagan revival in Alaric's time in the western senate itself). But though religion remained extremely important in politics, it is not necessary to invoke it as a major reason for the actions of the British. Weight has been put on the fact that the letter is addressed to the cities, not to a *vicarius* of Britain (nor, for that matter, to a *comes* or *dux*). Yet Honorius could hardly have done otherwise. Constantine's officers were out —and anyhow, Honorius is unlikely to have wished to recognize them even if they had not been. We have just seen that there is every reason to doubt that the Britons had restaffed the central administration. With Constantine III himself still at Arles, and barbarians in Gaul and Italy, Honorius could have had no chance of getting men from Italy to take over the British diocese in the normal way, even if there was a loyalist party asking for it. In fact, if it really was Britain that was addressed, he was simply giving the same instructions in a time of emergency that he had already given to cities much closer to home, where there was every chance of restoring normal conditions in due course. There is no cause to assume that Honorius was deliberately abandoning Britain for ever. This may indeed be the point at which the Romano-Britons lost confidence in their last candidate for the imperial throne and decided to try doing without another, not to mention all the expensive trappings that went with imperial administration, but that does not mean that they no longer believed in the credibility of the western imperial government itself, even if some of them hoped to keep out of its clutches.

17

POSTSCRIPT TO
ROMAN BRITAIN

If we do not take the revolt of Britain from the rule of Constantine III as marking the end of Roman Britain, then we shall have to admit that there is insufficient evidence to determine conclusively when the phenomenon that we have been studying as 'Roman Britain' came to a close. The literary evidence for specific events and for the actions—even the existence—of individual people in Britain after 410 is exceedingly scrappy and difficult to interpret, while the archaeology is subject to widely differing interpretations. However, there is just enough material that can safely be put together to indicate that by the middle of the fifth century Britain had changed beyond recognition. It is also clear that it had evolved on very different lines from most of Roman Gaul. By the 440s—at the latest—a distinctively 'post-Roman' society had emerged in Britain. Recent research strongly suggests that the society we have been studying disintegrated fairly rapidly after the revolt, to such an extent that it is, in fact, right to take 409 or 410 as marking the end of Roman Britain. That being so, it is not the task of this book to pursue the narrative of Britain far into the fifth century—that is a matter for the historians of post-Roman, Celtic, and Anglo-Saxon Britain—but to see what the nature of this disintegration can tell us about the late Roman society that had just collapsed.

The first question that springs to mind is why there was no reconquest of Britain by Roman forces from the Continent. As early as 411 the government of Honorius was regaining the initiative over its enemies. Honorius' generals Flavius Constantius

WESTERN EUROPE *c.* AD 420.

and Ulphilas marched on Arles, where Constantine III was being besieged by Gerontius. The latter fled at the approach of the imperial army, and shortly afterwards committed suicide. Honorius' army went on to defeat Frankish and Alamannic reinforcements who had been marching to join Constantine, and was rewarded by the surrender of Constantine himself, who was soon executed. There must have been many in Britain who now expected the immediate return of imperial officials.

There was, however, one further act of rebellion before the rival western empire that had been set up by the army of Britain finally collapsed. The former Constantinian praetorian prefect Decimius Rusticus assisted in the proclamation of yet another emperor, Jovinus, on the Rhine. He was supported by Burgundians, Alans, and others, who were now settled within the frontier and had perhaps been accepted by Constantine as its defenders. However, the main Visigothic force was now in Gaul, and, after briefly flirting with this new usurpation, its leader, Athaulf, took the opportunity to negotiate peace with Honorius, promising the heads of Jovinus and his brother, an offer that was readily accepted. Jovinus was executed by Honorius' praetorian prefect of Gaul, and the empire formed by Constantine III finally came to an end. The mistake, as far as recovering Britain and other parts of the empire currently out of control was concerned, was to follow the execution of Jovinus with a ruthless purge of the officers who had served Constantine or Jovinus and of many aristocrats (*multique nobiles*), presumably notables from the various provinces of the Constantinian realm.

Against the background of this purge, it is not surprising that now, in 413, Britain seems to have made no move to bring itself back under Honorius' control, even if some Romano-Britons might earlier have been prepared to accept the financial burden of Roman rule again. Procopius, the sixth-century historian who became prefect of the city of Constantinople under Justinian and who had some direct knowledge of the west, having served with Belisarius in the reconquest of Italy, describes how, though Constantine had been defeated, 'the Romans were never able to recover Britain, but from that time it remained on its own under "tyrants" (local usurpers).'

Why did Honorius' generals not attempt to recapture Britain by force of arms? In theory, the rule of Honorius had now been re-established throughout Gaul and Spain. In fact, he was still in a very weak position. One reason why nothing decisive was done about the Goths—and without that, Gaul could not be properly brought under control—was that they still held Honorius' half-sister Galla Placidia, whom Alaric had captured during the sack of Rome in 410. The Visigothic army that had suppressed Jovinus was now moving southwards from the Rhineland, accompanied by an important group of Alans. It was to have a very chequered history in the next year or two, and several times tried to make deals with the Romans. Athaulf went so far as to marry Galla Placidia, and seems to have had a genuine desire to unite the Roman and Gothic nations. It was not until after his death and the return of Galla Placidia to Honorius that the Visigoths were turned out of Spain and, in return for a pledge of military support for Rome, were settled in a permanent kingdom in 418 by Flavius Constantius. This new kingdom embraced the lands of Aquitania, a large and rich region stretching from the lower Loire to the Garonne, the homeland of many of the most distinguished men that Roman Gaul had produced, particularly in the past half-century.

Unquestionably, AD 418 marks a new era in the history of the west. The Rhineland was partly Burgundian, the Suebi and the Franks had much of north-eastern Gaul, and even in the parts of north-western and central Gaul that were still Roman the writ of the prefecture based at Arles could only be enforced spasmodically. There are signs that central Gaul was taxed, but Armorica was persistently the seat of peasant revolts. In the region of the Loire disorder was felt to reign, judged by the standards of southern Gaul. Roman intervention tended to be in terms of punitive expeditions. In 417, for example, the first time that we hear of Romans using force in northern Gaul since the fall of Constantine's empire, Rutilius Namatianus' relation Exuperantius put down a slave revolt, 'restoring law and liberty', in other words bringing back the normal order of things. This restoration, how-ever, does not seem to have been permanent. Later interventions were necessary, but more and more through the agency of bar-barian federates rather than the direct use of Roman troops.

It is clear that, both in the territories of the south still regu-larly controlled by the Arles prefecture and in the regions of settled barbarian rule, the structure of Roman administration remained largely in place. Most of the peoples involved had been in contact with the empire for a very long time, and we have noted how some individuals had risen to high positions within the empire over the previous century. It has even been sug-gested that in some cases where formal settlements were made between barbarians and Romans, the former received grants of taxation rights rather than land. It was certainly important to the barbarians that the everyday working of society should continue. Many Gallo-Roman nobles came to a reasonable accommoda-tion with the new, generally friendly, and often Christian (if Arian) barbarian kingdoms, which allowed them to maintain a fairly high standard of living, the greatest of them continuing to style themselves senators and to live a country life still essentially that of the great Roman villa-owner.

In the Roman-controlled territories of the Arles prefecture the private style of life of the rich was not dissimilar: indeed, they were in close personal contact with their peers in the allied Visigothic kingdom. In political terms, things were very different from the days before Constantine III. Before the barbarian invasions of 406 and Constantine's seizure of power, the praetorian prefects of Gaul had been sent out in the traditional way from Italy, usually after a career including posts in other parts of the empire. There had been much movement the other way, too, with Aquitanians in particular dominating the imperial court and penetrating the senatorial aristocracy. Now Aquitania itself was Gothic, and from now on not one of Gaul's praetorian prefects can be shown to have been other than a Gallo-Roman noble. This new regime in Arles, while not in rebellion from Ravenna, did not necessarily always share common interests with it. Moreover, its authority does not seem to have extended to northern Gaul: in the same year as the Visigoths were settled in Aquitania, the praetorian prefect revived the provincial council of the Gauls at Arles, but, significantly, no northern *civitates* sent representatives.

Militarily, the Roman position continued to be weakened by internal dissension. Right at the centre of the problem was the ancient tradition of unbounded ambition and vicious competition between the leading Romans of the day. Even though the western empire was falling apart around them, the struggles continued with the old vigour. Flavius Constantius very briefly followed Honorius on the throne, having married Galla Placidia, but within a year he was dead. The thirty-year reign of their son Valentinian III was a catalogue of disasters, including the loss of Africa to the Vandals in 428. This very seriously weakened the resources of the western imperial government. The earlier part of the reign was also marked by a bitter struggle between Galla Placidia as regent and the leading military man of the age, Flavius Aetius. The latter, often portrayed as the last Roman hero because of his defeat of Attila, owed his own initial position to his appointment as *magister militum* by yet another usurper, and he only retained it in the face of Placidia's hostility because a large army of Huns was backing him. In later years he was to be in virtual control of the western government. Attention had also to be concentrated on new barbarian threats, including the growing power of the Huns themselves. There is no clear evidence that the Romans were sufficiently strong in north-western Gaul to tackle a reconquest of Britain before the archaeology suggests that there had been a general collapse in the island, though there are slight hints in the literature that some military move might have been expected. Nevertheless, it is probable that the only period when Aetius might have turned his attention to Britain was between 425 and 429. There is no sign that anything was in fact attempted. On the contrary, we shall see shortly that the one attested intervention by authority from the Continent was through the medium of the Church, not the army, and came right at the end of this possible window of opportunity. Thereafter Aetius was occupied with the internal politics of the central government, civil war, and campaigns against barbarian enemies. The sixth-century British writer Gildas reports an appeal from Britain for assistance against barbarian attack in or after his third consulship (446), and records that no help came. The last great Roman military success in the west was the halting of Attila by Aetius in 451. His army at the battle of the Catalaunian Plains was a combination of Roman troops, Visigoths, and other allies. In 454 Valentinian committed the ultimate folly of murdering Aetius. Thereafter the remaining western regular army was allowed to run down. The government no longer enforced conscription, which had been so unpopular with landowners, and imperial military initiatives increasingly relied on barbarian manpower. However, neither the emergent barbarian strongmen, nor the emperors they nominally served, were ever again able to secure any general control in the western part of the empire. In 476 the barbarian *condottiere* Odoacer deposed the last emperor resident in Italy—Romulus Augustulus—and was recognized as king of Italy by the emperor's eastern colleague Zeno. An embassy that, at Odoacer's instance, the senate in Rome sent to Constantinople argued that a western emperor was no longer necessary. Zeno indicated that a rival Augustus, Julius Nepos, who had been driven out of Italy in 475 but still controlled Dalmatia, should be recognized. Zeno seems, however, to have been content to see this as a nominal arrangement, since he declined to assist Nepos in regaining power. The latter's murder in 480 finally ended the sequence of western emperors. Henceforth there was only one imperial throne, and the fragments of the empire in the west, while in some cases recognizing a nominal allegiance to Constantinople, went their own ways.

Gildas' report of an appeal to Aetius is one of three literary references that have suggested to scholars that the decisive stage in the take-over of England by Anglo-Saxons occurred in the 440s. Of the others, the best known to English readers is the assertion of the great eighth-century Anglian historian Bede that dates the 'coming of the Saxons' (*adventus Saxonum*) to AD 449. The general period, if not the precise date, has seemed to be confirmed by a document known as the *Gallic Chronicle of 452* and composed in that year, stating that Britain fell under Saxon control in 441. Much ingenuity has been expended on these references and on other, less solid, sources, but the overall difficulty is that it is extraordinarily difficult to match the idea of a major Saxon take-over in the 440s either with the archaeology or with other literary evidence that indicates a slow and often halted or reversed spread of Anglo-Saxon occupation, which did not really extend over most of England until the sixth century. It is only possible to speculate that there were indeed events in the 440s that gave rise to reports of Saxon successes in Britain that were sufficiently impressive to be recorded by an author in Gaul and to surface long after in the works of Gildas and Bede. We cannot, however, assume that the chronicler of 452, writing in southern Gaul, had access to reliable information on the *extent* of such Saxon successes. Indeed, we shall see shortly that Britain was in such a fragmented condition by this time that it is extremely unlikely that anyone could have come to a reliable general conclusion. It is much more probable that the reports concerned events that, however spectacular, affected a restricted area or areas of Britain, and may not even represent more than a temporary condition.

We must now turn to what archaeology suggests had been happening among the Britons since the break with Roman rule. The feature that startles anyone used to Roman sites in Britain is the almost total absence of coins or pottery. In fact, it is now clear that by about 420 or 430 society in Britain had effectively stopped using coins and had no source of factory-manufactured pottery other than the very occasional import. These two facts are in themselves extremely significant. But they also pose a great problem for the archaeologist: without these familiar dating materials, it becomes very difficult to determine how long a span of time is indicated by the stratigraphic layers occurring above deposits dated to the late fourth or early fifth century.

There are, however, places where such layers exist. At Verulamium a truly remarkable sequence of late occupation was found on one site. First of all, two large town houses with good mosaics were built towards the end of the fourth century. On top of one of these mosaics a corn-drying plant was subsequently constructed: the excavator suggested that the absence of coins or pottery in this phase indicated a date after about 430, though that may be a little late. This drying plant was in use long enough for it to need repair, before the whole structure was demolished to make way for a large stone barn or hall. This building had itself come down before a brand-new water-main was laid across the site, constructed in normal Roman fashion. A substantial population seems to be implied, along with some form of organization with control of the source of the water-supply and enough confidence in the future to make the work seem worth while. A date in the middle of the century for the water-main might not be too late. In London a large house that had first been built at the end of the second century or the beginning of the third was reconstructed several times before the early fifth century. The stoke-hole for the residential part of the house still contained ash when it was excavated, and in it was found the handle of a large amphora of east-Mediterranean manufacture that was probably imported in the fifth century rather than the fourth. At this stage the house was still in normal use. A hoard of coins from not earlier than 395 seems to have fallen from its hiding-place into the debris of this part of the house after it had collapsed. This supports the idea that the house was still inhabited in the early fifth century. In the separate bath-block a Saxon brooch of a type thought to have been made around AD 450 was found on top of the fallen remains of the roof, but the furnace for these baths was not in use in the final phase of occupation of the main house, and the length of time that an object of personal adornment of this kind might remain in someone's possession must be quite uncertain. Overall, it looks as if the Roman building may

URBAN CENTRES at which fifth-century activity of any sort has been tentatively detected.

have become derelict at some point in the fifth century, but not necessarily very early. At Cirencester life went on after coinage ceased to circulate: the forum was maintained after that stage. In Bath a sequence of layers in the temple precinct almost certainly runs into the fifth century before being sealed by collapsed masonry, and may well end at around 430, with the final deposit containing significantly less pottery than those before.

At Canterbury, Lincoln, Exeter, and Wroxeter there is also activity that can be dated later than the beginning of the fifth century. It is, however, extremely difficult to point to any convincing examples of unbroken urban life in Britain from the Roman period to the revival of towns in mid-Saxon times. The length of continuing activity into the fifth century seems to vary from town to town, but in each case the evidence does seem at present to peter out. It is particularly telling that city cemeteries seem to have been dispensed with. At Winchester and Dorchester (Dorset) large cemeteries seem to terminate in about 420, and in the Bath Gate cemetery of Cirencester the latest dated burial was marked by a coin of Honorius. This suggests either that there were no longer substantial populations within these towns, or that burials were now taking place inside them. The latter would in itself indicate a breakdown in normal Roman controls. It is possible that such a disregard of Roman law was part of the picture that Zosimus had in mind when he referred to Britain's conduct after the revolt of 409.

It is perhaps not a coincidence that literature gives us a rare and vivid glimpse of life in this period in Britain that is almost certainly to be located at Verulamium. It involves the remarkable St Germanus, bishop of Auxerre. Already, possibly in 403, Victricius, bishop of Rouen, had visited Britain at the request of his fellow bishops in Gaul to restore peace among the clergy in Britain. By 429 the Pelagian heresy, possibly the problem previously addressed by Victricius, was a serious issue in Britain. Following an appeal from Britain to the Church in Gaul, and at the instance of a deacon named Palladius, Pope Celestine I appointed Germanus to combat the heresy. Germanus was accompanied on this mission by another bishop, Lupus of Troyes. This ought to mean that at Rome and in Gaul Britain was still regarded as part of the empire, since the Catholic Church had no general interest in evangelizing barbarians outside the empire. A slight uncertainty exists in this case because in 431 Celestine consecrated a bishop for Ireland. However, the fact that this bishop was also named Palladius has led to the speculation that this was the deacon who had influenced the pope to authorize the visit of Germanus. This might suggest some unusual personal interest in the region. More powerfully, it has also been argued that Palladius was being sent specifically to take care of existing Christian communities of Romans outside the imperial frontiers, rather than to evangelize the Irish. The Christian author Prosper of Aquitaine, writing within a couple of years of the event, balanced the dispatch of Palladius to Ireland with that of Germanus to Britain, citing the keeping of the 'Roman island' (Britain) Catholic alongside the making of the 'barbarian' one Christian. This, however, was a literary device, and cannot safely be used to prove that Palladius was converting barbarians. What is certain is that the device would have fallen completely flat if Britain were not still considered to be Roman in the early 430s.

In Britain the chief opponent of the visitors was a leading Pelagian named Agricola, himself the son of a Pelagian bishop. The confrontation between the Catholic envoys and the Pelagians took place at a public meeting. The religious and political importance that was clearly attached locally to the issue is underlined by the huge crowd (*immensa multitudo*) that came to hear the episcopal visitors. The Pelagian party was 'conspicuous for riches, brilliant in dress, and surrounded by a fawning multitude'. Such conspicuous wealth is characteristic of the Roman world, particularly in the fourth and fifth centuries; the fawning multitude reminds us of the ancient aristocratic tradition of the *clientela*; and the brilliant costume reflects the period's taste for splendid multicoloured dress, seen, for example, in the wall-paintings of the Lullingstone villa. There is more than a little echo of the rescript of Honorius that made the Pelagian heresy illegal in 418, in which the emperor accused the Pelagians of 'considering it a mark of common vulgarity to agree with opinions everyone else holds'.

The success of Germanus and Lupus in bringing the crowd over to the official doctrine in the face of such opposition is a testimony to the still effective powers of public debate, employing the art of rhetoric in which a Roman gentleman was trained.

It also displays the diplomatic powers that Germanus showed else-where in his career, and that were becoming of prime impor-tance in this new world, where the final sanction of Roman military power was no longer easily available. It may have owed more than a little, too, to the surviving prestige of Rome itself, since the mission from Gaul represented both the official Catholic faith of the western imperial court and the full weight of imper-ial law, while the choice of spokesmen had the backing of the pope himself.

What happened after the meeting is very interesting. The Gallic bishops paid a visit to the shrine of St Alban. This is what almost certainly places the debate at Verulamium. Excavation at St Albans cathedral has revealed an open space that was in use in the fifth century, very probably for pilgrimages and just such visits as these. It is significant that Pelagian doctrine disapproved of veneration of this sort, and the Catholic bishops' action may represent a deliberate intervention to encourage the survival of a cult that had official approval. We are also told of the miracu-lous healing of the child of 'a man with tribunician power' (*vir tribuniciae potestatis*). At first sight it looks as if what we have here is proof that a city garrison of Roman type was still in being. Since Germanus had once been a lawyer and a provincial gov-ernor, he would certainly know a legitimate officer when he met one, and if he came back from Britain saying that he had met such a person, we ought, if his biographer has not distorted his account, to be able to believe him. However, it is perfectly pos-sible that the man had commanded a unit that had disbanded after the break with Rome. Moreover, we also find the rank of military tribune being granted to a category of civil servant not long after this date. It is therefore clear that we cannot use this man's existence to assume the presence of regular troops. It does, however, add to the impression already gained from the archae-ology and from the nature of the meeting between the prelates and the heretics that Verulamium retained something of a life-style significantly above the subsistence level.

The final act in Germanus' mission has its own interest for us, since it underlines the *ad hoc* nature of society in this age. He now proceeded to organize and lead the Britons in a war against a combined army of Picts and Saxons. The tale is that he baptized his men and taught them to shout 'Alleluia' as their battle-cry, causing the enemy to flee in dismay. We do not know where this battle was fought, though the description of the ground, as lying in mountainous country near a large river, is circumstantial enough to suggest that it was a good march away from Verulamium. That Germanus had to take the lead at all may suggest either that the bulk of the local notables were among the discredited Pelagians, or that the latter, worsted in argument, were enlisting the help of barbarian allies, the very Picts and Saxons whom Germanus now defeated in battle. Such alliances were, of course, the common currency of the age on the Continent. The mass baptism sounds suspiciously like conventional colouring written into the saint's *Life* by the hagiographer, but, if it happened, it would suggest the persistence of a substantial pagan element among the Britons, perhaps among those of the rural poor whose origins were not on the estates of Christian landowners.

Despite this evidence for paganism, the survival of Christianity on a considerable scale is not in doubt. On the contrary, it was more than survival, for the Celtic Church that featured so significantly in the life of sixth-century Britain was in a direct line of descent from the Church in Roman Britain. This Celtic Church had a substantial period of separate development before the arrival of the mission of St Augustine of Canterbury in Britain in 597, and the differences in liturgical practice between the British and contemporary Roman Churches were sufficiently great to keep the two apart until the process of submission of the insular Church to Rome that started at the Synod of Whitby in 664. It is particularly interesting that Augustine criticized the British Church for not following the contemporary Roman calculation of the date of Easter, for it is clear that the Britons were using the tables that Pope Leo I had announced in 454 as being computed, which by then had been superseded. That must mean that they had still been in contact with the Continental Churches at that time or at some subsequent date. They seem to have lost contact later, and it is probable that other features of the Celtic Church that were to cause problems with the Roman Church at the end of the sixth century developed after the middle of the fifth. It is unsafe to reflect back on to the period immediately after the break with Rome specific features of the Celtic Church that became apparent later, such as the domination of that Church by monasticism. It is, however, reasonable to infer that the Celtic Church could not have become so powerful if it had not survived the political break with Rome and maintained considerable strength during the disintegration of Roman Britain. We have already noted that in 429 the Roman Church authorities still considered it important to deal with heresy in Britain. The *Life of St Germanus* claims a second visit by Germanus to deal with the remnants of Pelagianism. This is undated, but, if it took place, it has to have been before about 448, the probable date of his death. The author of the *Life* asserts that in his own time, the second half of the fifth century, there were no heresies extant in Britain. It is entirely uncertain whether he could have had reliable information on the latter score, but it does help to underline the point that in the middle of the century the Christian community in Britain was still in full contact with the main stream of the Church.

It is significant that the Christians in Ireland also adopted the computation for Easter announced in 454. It is possible that their contacts were directly with Gaul, though it seems more likely that they were via Britain. It is unfortunate that the dates of St Patrick's life and of the various events in it are subject to major controversy. It is clear that his forebears were Romano-British Christian gentry, and his description of his kidnapping by Irish pirates, together with his parents' male and female slaves, when he was just under 16 seems to indicate a modest but operational villa estate, and a continuing social milieu in which his father had been a member of a local council and was a deacon of the Church. The dates for Patrick's life proposed by scholars, however, vary so much that the whole of this boyhood might have taken place before 410. All we can usefully extract is that his escape from slavery after six years, his eventual arrival home, and his period of sojourn there before his return as bishop to Ireland cannot have occurred *earlier* than about 410. We can, presumably, assume that life in his parents' society had not been totally turned upside down by this time, and that it remained tolerable until the end of this phase in his life. A late date would thus be interesting. It is certainly not seriously suggested that he went to Ireland as bishop before Palladius did (i.e. before 431), but the truth is that it might not have been very much later. His stay at home could therefore have fallen within the archaeologically determined period of post-Roman disintegration in Britain, but it need not have outlasted it. The (unreliable) traditional date for the beginning of his episcopate is 432, but, even if correct, it is of no help in extending the period beyond the dates that we have been considering.

Much more shadowy than Patrick—and perhaps occupying a larger niche in modern writing of the period than is justified— is the figure of Vortigern. Gildas, whose principal aim was to castigate the leaders of his own day, alleges that an unnamed *superbus tyrannus* imported Saxons to fight against attacks by northern peoples. The Saxons subsequently rebelled, and were the chief cause of the downfall of Britain and its being overrun by barbarians. Whether or not this was the same Vortigern whose name occurs elsewhere, and whether or not he was an actual historical figure, are both quite uncertain. It is safe only to note that he could fit in among the 'tyrants' mentioned by Procopius, and to speculate with some confidence that such usurpers are more likely to have achieved local or regional rule than to have held the whole of Britain. Whatever the ambitions of these men, Constantine III was probably the last person elevated in Britain to have controlled the whole of the British diocese, since, unlike them, he had the Roman administrative machine still in place and a garrison under regular command. It is possible that in one former Roman city we have archaeological evidence for the presence of a post-Roman local ruler. At Wroxeter the disused basilican hall of the public baths was finally demolished, and a number of timber buildings were constructed. One of these structures was a large residential building of Roman type. The latest-dating evidence was a coin of 395/402. It is therefore possible that these developments occurred before the break with Rome, but the excavator thought, quite reasonably, that what we are seeing here is a centre of power occupied by one of the leaders of the immediate post-Roman period. Certainly, the reversion to timber for the construction of a substantial building might suggest a period in which skilled manpower was still available, but the sort of organization of transport and industry required for masonry structures had disappeared. It could also suggest, too, that the person commissioning the building controlled only a limited district.

Proving the occupation of Roman military sites after the break with Rome is even more problematic than for the towns. Indeed, on general grounds one may expect that any continued military activity is more likely to have been associated with urban centres than with the old forts and fortresses. However, on one site on Hadrian's Wall excavation was thought to indicate the sort of evidence that might also exist elsewhere. This is ironic, since until relatively recently it was thought that the Wall was abandoned early. It is now considered that activity lasted to the end of Roman rule, though the exact nature of the occupation within the forts is uncertain. At Birdoswald fort one of the stone granaries was converted to an open hall with a hearth; another, which had collapsed, was at least partially rebuilt in timber; and a third timber hall was constructed from new. Re-examination of the evidence has suggested that the use of timber was to solve a structural problem on the site that had rendered the existing stone buildings unstable. It is therefore not necessary to assume a post-Roman date. On the other hand, it does indicate the presence in later-Roman Britain of a technological understanding of large timber buildings that could be adapted to post-Roman conditions. One cannot help wondering whether the barn-like building that preceded the water-main at Verulamium falls into this same category. Whether it looks forward to the aristocratic halls of Anglo-Saxon England, back to the simple 'basilican villas' of Roman Britain, or to the official storage facilities for grain and military equipment under Roman government, is unclear. The likelihood is that usages varied from place to place and over time. A characteristic architectural form for the period does, however, seem to be emerging.

In the countryside the archaeological evidence is even more difficult to interpret than in the urban areas or on the former military sites. In the case of villas, it is not uncommon to find excavators reporting 'squatter occupation' as the last phase of activity. Datable finds tend to be absent or very scarce, and in the latter case they are almost always restricted to the latest sorts of Roman material. Depending on whether the excavators are inclined to believe in continuing occupation after the break with Rome or to see Roman Britain as in a state of severe decline before the end of the fourth century, such material is taken either

as indicating a collapse by 410, or as residual, or as suggesting
use well into the fifth century. The structural evidence for such
occupation usually takes the form of hearths on top of mosaics,
sometimes accompanied by domestic rubbish, and is often in the
context of an apparent reduction in the number of rooms in use.
An alternative—and more convincing—interpretation is suggested
by the villa at Redlands Farm, at Stanwick in Northamptonshire,
where this sort of activity seems to represent the last phase in
the continuous evolution of the house, rather than casual use by
squatters of abandoned buildings. At Redlands Farm the two
wings of the villa were demolished (one had become dangerous),
but the central section continued to be occupied. The finds
associated with this occupation indicated a sharp drop in the standard of living. Overall, the picture is one of impoverished inhabitants, unable or unwilling to keep up the whole of a large house.
A similar view may be taken of fifth-century changes revealed
by excavation at the Gloucestershire villa of Frocester Court.
There one half of the main building was destroyed by fire, and
was not repaired, but the other remained in use. The occurrence
of a particular sort of crude pottery known as 'grass-tempered
ware', which occurs only in post-Roman contexts, puts this continued occupation into the period that we are considering. In
the fourth century the courtyard in front of the house had been
laid out as a garden, but in the fifth this was largely destroyed
by agricultural activity.

If such villas were still owned by the same family or class of
people as they had been in the fourth century, it is possible that
the social need to maintain all their facilities—for example, for
entertaining—no longer applied. Equally, one can readily imagine that it was not easy to retain the slave or tied labour that
was required to keep up a large house. If the family had departed,
or if the estate was owned by more important landlords who
no longer visited, then the main house may well have been taken
over by a foreman or estate workers who had no need of the
whole complex, and no interest—or perhaps resources—for the
upkeep of all its amenities. What is absent is convincing evidence
for the arrival and occupation of villas by invading barbarians,
Saxons or otherwise. At one time this absence was thought to
indicate a shunning of abandoned Roman sites by superstitious

Saxons. It later became apparent that the earliest evidence of Saxon settlement tended to come from near, but not in, Roman sites. Some opinion favoured the notion of barbarian mercenaries being hired to protect villas towards the end of, and after, the Roman period. This was mostly based not on settlement evidence, but on the occurrence of 'Germanic' military equipment in villas. While such hiring is not in the least improbable, we have noted earlier that this material is no longer seen as evidence for the presence of barbarians or even necessarily as military. In fact, if an explanation is required for a negative, then it is much more likely that when Saxons did eventually arrive in numbers, the villas were so ruinous and overgrown that it was easier to settle on new sites, even if the incomers were farming the same land. In much of Britain, indeed, it is difficult to find any evidence of Saxons at all within the period in which villas retained anything that can reasonably be interpreted as signs of activity, and this includes some of the areas where villas had been at their densest and richest.

It is even more difficult to discover what was happening on the more basic rural settlements. Many of these produce few finds other than pottery (and there is less of that than on other categories of site), even within the Roman period proper. The cessation of Roman pottery production leaves us with little information as to their continued existence. It seems likely—especially in the more remote areas of Britain—that the everyday way of life carried on much as before, though the inhabitants must have been affected by the disruption to long-established patterns of agricultural economics and of control at the local level. At Cannington in Somerset a large rural cemetery was in use, presumably without a break, from the second century right through to the seventh or eighth. It is extremely difficult to demonstrate continuous use of settlements themselves, even of the humblest sort, though excavation at places such as Yarnton near Oxford, from which Iron Age, Roman, and Anglo-Saxon material has come, may produce just such a sequence. In general, evidence from such sites points to a shifting of the actual habitation, often within quite a small area, while the same land was farmed. Very occasionally, there are signs of new settlements being established in the fifth century that cannot, by any stretch of the imagination, archaeologically

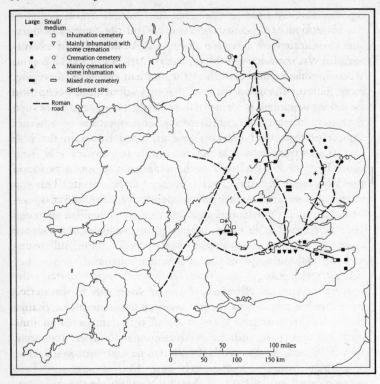

ANGLO-SAXON CEMETERIES AND SETTLEMENTS of relatively early fifth-century date continue to be identified, though the criteria are debatable and the ethnic identification of specific populations—as distinct from their tastes in goods and dwellings—is uncertain.

be assigned to Saxon immigration. One such instance followed the disuse of the Roman cemetery at Poundbury, in Dorset. Here we may assume a substantial gap in time after the end of the cemetery and the arrival of settlers who probably were not local, for it is otherwise difficult to imagine people choosing to live and farm on such a site. It is therefore likely that this occurred towards the end of the period we are considering, no earlier than the middle of the century.

There is one exceptional category of rural site that may indicate the response of at least a few of the villa-owning class to the insecurities of the period. The hill-fort of South Cadbury was refortified late in the fifth century, and the type of occupation is indicated by a large timber hall. At the time of excavation this was considered to be typically 'Dark Age', and analogous to later royal settlements such as the Anglian centre at Yeavering. Nevertheless, it was put forward that at Cadbury the occupation should be regarded as British (it certainly pre-dates the known Saxon conquest of the south-west). The question of whether such reoccupation of hill-forts also occurred earlier in the fifth century has been answered by excavation at Crickley Hill, near Gloucester. Domestic occupation of a superior sort was found inside the rampart, and a contemporary village outside. This was an area that had had an exceptional density of villas, and it is reasonable to suppose that a family from one of them had migrated to a safer site. Unlike fifth-century Gaul, we have no evidence of British landowners possessing hill-fortresses while still maintaining their villas, though the possibility remains.

Returning now to the point from which we started—the almost total absence of coins and pottery from sites of this period —we can just about begin to put together a picture of the change in society. New bronze coins stopped being imported in bulk after 402; few issues in gold or silver later than about 406 occur in Britain, and none struck after the fall of Constantine III. The cessation of bronze from 402 may have been accompanied by a slowing-down of everyday commercial activity, but it is inconclusive in itself, as major fluctuations in minting are a notable feature of the history of the currency in the fourth century. It is more interesting that no later bronze appears. Coin specialists suggest that it had ceased to be used in everyday transactions in Britain by about 420. It is highly significant that new gold and silver coins issued after the first decade of the fifth century are not found, for these were used by the state for major payments such as salaries to troops and officials, and large purchases of supplies for government purposes. Normally, as much as possible of the gold and silver was recovered by the central government by means of direct taxation and by requiring authorized money-changers—and perhaps others—to surrender coins in precious metals in exchange for bronze. The remarkable number of hoards of existing coin in precious metals from this period in Britain is not paralleled in Gaul, and strongly suggests that the system of taxation had broken down. This is supported by the presence in these hoards of a practice very rare previously: the dishonest clipping of coins for personal gain. This had been forbidden in the fourth century under the most stringent penalties, and would have been immediately detected by the tax-collectors, had they still been operating. An indication that tax-collection did stop abruptly is suggested by the extraordinary coin finds at Richborough. Out of more than 50,000 coins of all periods from the site, 20,000 were bronze coins of the latest period of importation, ending with issues of 402. It looks as if these were stock, intended for the process of exchange with gold and silver, but off-loaded at the port by finance officials expelled in 409, maybe expecting to return.

The demise of the pottery industry adds further material to our picture of the condition of Britain after the break with Rome. No pottery-manufacturing centres have yet been proved to have been in production after 410, and the layers of sites such as Wroxeter and Verulamium that show extended fifth-century occupation have not produced late Roman pottery in the sort of quantity that would indicate that it could still be obtained as an everyday commodity in the market. The causes of the apparent collapse were probably various. The large producers had traditionally sold principally through the towns and to the government. The disappearance of the military market, and the decline of the towns must have removed the economic basis of their operations, and one of the means by which their goods had been retailed. It also seems very unlikely that the long-distance transport on which the large factories relied remained safe and economical, a factor that we have already mentioned in the context of the revival of timber construction for major buildings. But these cannot have been the only factors, since the small local potteries also seem to have ceased production. The only ware still found—in very small quantities—is the extremely crude, so-called 'grass-tempered' pottery, noted above in connection with the Frocester Court villa, which shows no indication of having been made commercially.

Is it possible to suggest a common factor? It is indeed—and in doing so, we begin to approach one of the central agents in the overall collapse. It is self-evident that the mass-production potteries could not have operated without a money economy, unless their production had been solely for a customer who owned them outright (for which there is no evidence). Even the small producers would have found it almost impossible to trade on a barter system, unless their operation was at the village level. But what actually energized the money economy of the late Roman empire was the vast flow of transactions caused, directly and indirectly, by the operation of government expenditure and the tax system. We have already noted how money expended on pay and procurement was recovered through taxation: it had, of course, flowed through the economy before it returned to the treasury. In doing so, it stimulated money-based activity in every direction, multiplying the size of the money economy as it did so. Moreover, even where activities and relationships might otherwise have been on the basis of barter or service, the use of money was naturally stimulated by the fact that the tax-paying populace needed to obtain coin or bullion to render up to the collectors.

It is obvious that the expulsion of Constantine III's officials must have meant the end of imperial expenditure and taxation in Britain, and we have seen that there is no evidence that any such imperially controlled financial structure ever returned. All the evidence that we have been considering also points to the absence of any British-based replacement. The picture of Britain in the first twenty years or so after the break with Roman rule begins to take shape, if dimly. It is improbable that there was any central authority. Constantine's officials had been expelled, and the state financial system had been dismantled. The provincial council, even if it was still in being in 409, is unlikely to have supplied an alternative government, since the principal purpose of its proceedings had been the expression of loyalty to the emperor. Indeed, unlike the position in the southern dioceses of the prefecture of which Britain had formed a part, there was no longer any way in which a praetorian prefect of the period (or his *vicarius*) could have secured attendance at a council in Britain, even if he had summoned it. It is perhaps also unlikely that the councils of the *civitates* played any significant role, since in the late Roman world they had become largely a means for the local administration of the demands of central government, particularly taxation, and the burdens of membership had been something to avoid. Nor is there any sign that the underlying British tribal divisions, on which the Roman *civitates* had been at least partly based, survived, or revived. Even in those areas that did not subsequently fall to the Saxons, and in which the post-Roman language was Celtic, there is no sign of pre-Roman tribal survival. In so far as there had been instances of institutional continuity from pre-Roman times, they probably met their end in this period. We are left with the likelihood of a large number of centres of power, set up wherever someone could seize or maintain authority, and varying greatly both in location and the area over which they could exercise control. Some may have been centred on fortified towns such as Wroxeter, or forts such as Birdoswald, or hill-forts like Crickley Hill. It is not impossible to envisage certain villas continuing for a while in reduced circumstances but on a basis of self-sufficiency, some doubtless under the protection of a local *tyrannus*. It has been suggested that the later Anglo-Saxon kingdoms emerged slowly from an early stage in the Saxon settlement of England, between about AD 450 and 600, that consisted of hundreds of tiny 'statelets' or local centres of power. This is much easier to understand if, of its own accord, Britain had already fragmented into similar units in the first half of the fifth century. In the case of the Roman town of Great Chesterford in Essex, such a post-Roman statelet may have passed directly into Saxon control. Elsewhere we may imagine a frequently changing pattern of merging, splitting, and superimposition. Unlike the Germanic masters of Gaul, the Saxons who gradually took over what had been the most Romanized parts of Britain had no unitary political or economic structure to acquire and adapt. The consequences of the revolt against Constantine III had been a form of implosion, whereby the excision of the central institutions of the state had caused society to collapse in on itself. By the middle of the fifth century Britain was materially more impoverished and institutionally more primitive than it had been when Claudius' army landed in AD 43.

The implications for our assessment of Roman Britain of the condition to which Britain had now fallen, and the reasons for it, are profound. It becomes clear that Britain had become so fundamentally integrated into the late Roman state that separation was fatal. The once-popular view that Romanization was a veneer on a Celtic society that reverted to its 'natural' condition as soon as Roman government was removed is untenable. It is also difficult to maintain that the events of 409 or 410 are hardly significant, against an allegedly largely unbroken process by which an essentially rural late Roman Britain became Anglo-Saxon and early medieval England. If the island had not revolted in the way that it did, the barbarian incomers might have had a working structure of institutions to take over. This is what happened in Gaul. The extent and success of that take-over was, admittedly, very varied, depending on the sophistication of the new masters and the length of time they had been involved with Rome. However, vastly more barbarians than the few Germans who reached very high positions within the empire must have had significant experience of the everyday systems of Roman life. While it is true that the contacts between the relatively remote Anglo-Saxons and Rome had not been as close as they had been with most of the other northern barbarian peoples coming into the empire, nevertheless, in Gaul all the incomers were profoundly affected by what they took over, in a manner that did not happen in Britain. Roman Britain could not survive without the institutions of the Roman state, and it would probably have displayed the same disintegration even if control had eventually passed to some other incomers than the Saxons or to no incomer at all. It collapsed because of its revolt against the late Roman form of state. Its degree of Romanization had been too great, not too little.

V

BRITAIN UNDER
ROMAN RULE

18

THE ASSIMILATION
OF BRITAIN

To understand how the provinces came to be Romanized, we
have to abandon some of our common conceptions. There is
little evidence that the Romans had any general racial prejudice
in the modern sense. Hence they assumed that anyone, or almost
anyone, could absorb Roman culture and manners, even as they
themselves (despite the protests of moralists and conservatives)
borrowed extensively from other cultures, especially in the fields
of art and religion. They had a keen sense of class and an enormous pride in their family histories, but on the whole they
treated a man on the basis of what he was now rather than on
the background from which he had come, though they were not
above making fun of the *nouveaux riches*. Moreover, while there
were privileges attached to class and legal status—slave, freedman,
citizen or non-citizen, equestrian, senator—there was nothing
immutable about a man's position. This is a real difference between Rome and the classical Greek world before it, and, in
many senses, the medieval to come. In the letters of that Italian
aristocrat Pliny the Younger we have the cautionary tale of the
senator Macedo. Macedo was an ex-praetor, and therefore only
one stage from the highest of all social levels, those who had
held the consulship. He was murdered by his slaves, and Pliny
draws the lesson that no master can feel secure because he is kind
to his slaves: slaves are naturally savage and, given the chance,
will murder out of sheer love of violence, not because they have
thought out the advantages by use of reason (indeed, the penalties were so awful that it is difficult to see how they could have
reasoned thus). But Pliny goes on to say that of course Macedo

was a pretty unpleasant master, only too inclined to forget that his own father had been a slave—or perhaps because of it.

It is highly significant that, in his account of how Agricola fostered Roman culture among the Britons, Tacitus singles out the teaching of liberal arts to the children of their leading men. 'The result was that those who had once shunned the Latin language now sought fluency in it.' The key to participation in the Roman way of life was Latin. A gentleman with pretensions to culture was expected to read Greek, but the language of law and public administration was Latin, and it was essential to speak it to get on in the complex world of the empire. There is some evidence that in Britain it remained a second language, but, like English in India, it was not only indispensable for public affairs, but the only practical *lingua franca* in what was becoming a very mixed population. We should have quite the wrong impression if we thought of Roman Britain as comprising Romans from Italy or long-Romanized Mediterranean provinces on the one side facing native Britons on the other. The satirist Juvenal complained bitterly that the city of Rome was being polluted by the influx of easterners. Britain was remote and peripheral, but inscriptions here record a fair sprinkling of Greeks, even of Syrians, numbers of Gauls, and above all Germans. In the eastern provinces of the empire they eventually used Greek as their means of overcoming the innumerable problems of language: in the west it had to be Latin.

The rather archaic type of spoken Latin that appears to have been more common in Britain than in other western provinces has suggested that it was—at least in the early days—largely learnt at school, and maintained in this form by the educated speech of the island. This underlines the rather isolated nature of the Romano-British upper classes, who seem to play little part in the empire as a whole. Celtic certainly survived, as is obvious not only from the existence of Welsh and Cornish, which are linguistically separate from the Irish languages and were therefore not reimported after the Roman period, but also in the incorporation into Celtic of many words from Latin to describe concepts and articles not previously available. These are essentially the kind of terms that would be needed in urban or villa society, and correspond with the distribution of graffiti in Latin, which occur on military, town, and villa sites, but very rarely in the 'native' farms and villages. At the bottom end of the scale, the industrial worker could clearly use Latin. From London comes a tile inscribed thus before firing: 'Austalis has been wandering off on his own every day for a fortnight', the relic of a shop-floor grievance; and there is one from Silchester with a couple of words echoing the opening of the second book of the *Aeneid*. It has been argued that this should cause no surprise: if one wanted to write, one had to write in Latin, as Celtic had no script. This is not entirely true, but any written Celtic in Britain was probably confined to the priestly and possibly princely classes. It is maybe reasonable to suppose that in remote settlements little Latin was spoken and relatively little understood (though we shall look at the role of army service in the spread of the Latin tongue). Villa-owners, traders, and officials had to communicate with native peasants, whatever their own origins. But one may suspect that such contact was often through the slave bailiff or clerk, and it was the latter, who as slaves and freedmen often rose into the lower middle class and beyond, who are most likely to have been bilingual. Once the local aristocracy had adopted Latin with enthusiasm, they will certainly have demanded good spoken and written Latin from their upper servants, secretaries, and the tutors they provided for their children, if, as Tacitus says, they were swept with the fashion for all things Roman. They could hardly let themselves down in front of their neighbours or the Roman upper classes with whom they mixed by having half-barbarian homes.

Despite the deliberate education of young British aristocrats, by far the greatest reason for the spread of practical Latin was the army. Not only did a soldier need to speak Latin, he also needed to be able to read it. He might enter the auxilia of the early Empire as a raw barbarian provincial: he left it with two decades' experience of literacy and numeracy in Latin, an extensive knowledge of Roman skills in a very wide range of trades, and, perhaps most valued of all, Roman citizenship. It is true that only in times of extreme emergency were the legions themselves recruited from men who were not already Roman citizens, though grants of citizenship for this purpose to individuals were apparently fairly freely made. Except for the raising of entirely new legions, recruitment in the second and third centuries seems to have been in the hands of the governors of the provinces in which they were stationed. Indeed, as early as the beginning of the second century Italians were no longer entering the legions as individual volunteers, but preferred to serve in the more prestigious and much more lucrative praetorian guard and other special units. Henceforth, legionary recruits tended to come from wherever citizens were found, particularly the civil settlements around the legionary bases, where sons frequently followed family tradition. Before the civil wars of 68–9 auxiliary units were normally stationed in or near the areas from which they were raised: after that upheaval they were usually posted elsewhere, and rarely continued to draw recruits from their original provinces, except for certain units with highly specialized equipment. In the second century, therefore, both legions and auxilia were eventually largely made up of local recruits. As the number of provincials with Roman citizenship grew, the type of recruit that each category attracted varied less and less, though there were still important differences in the entry standards required and in the pay and status during service. Again, except in times of emergency or in the special case of auxiliary units compulsorily raised from newly conquered regions or exacted from enemies as part of a peace settlement, conscription was largely avoided until the fourth century. Its unpopularity with landowners, who saw their workers being drained away when it had to be brought in, perhaps best explains the unwillingness of earlier emperors to impose it. It may also have been considered that much better material could be obtained by offering a secure and attractive career to volunteers. Hence the importance of the gradual build-up in provincial families of the tradition of joining the army. Ironically, this probably facilitated the imposition of a hereditary obligation to military service on such families in the fourth century, which must have lightened the total burden that the forced levy of men imposed on the rural estates. In Britain, where the establishment changed comparatively little, things probably went on much as before. The growth of field armies required different methods, and this is where we should chiefly seek the newer types of recruit: barbarians recently settled and Romanized within the empire with an obligation to service, free barbarians from outside the frontiers as volunteers, and conscripts from Roman estates.

Until the reign of Septimius Severus, soldiers, other than officers, were not permitted to marry, but there is a large body of evidence that many had wives, though they were not legally recognized as such. Under Roman law, illegitimate children followed the condition of their mother, so before Severus' reign the children of serving soldiers were citizens or non-citizens according to their mother's status. However, there is the extremely important qualification that the grant of citizenship to time-expired auxiliaries also included the right to full legal marriage with wives that they had at the time of their discharge from the army or that they took thereafter. There is no evidence that the wives themselves became citizens, but the children, now being legitimate sons of Roman fathers, were Romans. This latter right was partially abrogated in the second century, when, in order to encourage recruiting, the sons had to wait for their own citizenship until they themselves enrolled in the army. Even this became largely a dead letter by the late Antonine period, as by then most recruits were already Roman citizens on entry, since both their parents had achieved the citizenship by one means or another. The total effect was to set up a machine that passed large numbers of provincials through a long training process that turned them into complete Romans.

We have seen how—for example, under Claudius at Colchester —legionary veterans were viewed as forming some kind of military reserve. But veterans were also important in provincial society, particularly where there was a large garrison. This was not confined to the deliberately founded *coloniae*, nor to ex-legionaries alone. Compulsory savings schemes (and grants of land in some cases) made them men of substance in their communities. If one takes as an example T. Flavius Longinus, who had held commissioned rank in the auxiliary cavalry unit *ala* II *Pannoniorum*, we find him elected to the councils of a colony, a *municipium*, and the *canabae* or civil settlement surrounding a legionary fortress. Even during his service a soldier might have a slave or two of his own, or a freedman, like the young Moor Victor who worked for Numerianus, a trooper of *ala* I *Asturum*, which was stationed at the military port at the mouth of the Tyne. Soldiers could engage in business (other than farming) in the provinces in which they were stationed, and it is likely that such slaves and freed-men often acted as their agents in such matters, since their masters were not granted leave by the army for personal affairs (*negotia privata*). It is clear that as early as the first century soldiers in some provinces had their *familiae* resident near them. We have seen that the extramural settlements in which we may suppose many of them to have lived grew into active centres of trade, and one may suspect that soldiers and their establishments played a very considerable part in this, and greatly accelerated the merging of Roman and native. As we have noted, in the early third century soldiers were granted the legal right to set up a home (*domum comparare*), including without doubt not only a wife and children, but also the slaves and freedmen that made up a Roman household. The third-century emperors were very ready to follow Severus' precept in favouring the soldiers above all else, but here the state was probably doing no more than recognizing fact while making it appear a favour. The fact that the civil settlements were now allowed to cross the Vallum on Hadrian's Wall and crowd up to the walls of the forts is a different matter. This was a real concession to the troops and their families. Soldiers' sons—and, indeed, the whole of these communities—must have been very well acquainted with the ways of the Roman army, so that by the time young men from these settlements came to enter the local unit they were already well prepared for service. Moreover, we may reasonably assume that such communities became thoroughly imbued not only with the Roman way of doing things, but also with the mood of the army of the time. This cannot have been without considerable social and political importance. In the final event, it was the support of the troops that so often made or unmade emperors, and these settlements must have comprised one of the main seed-beds in which the attitudes of ordinary soldiers were formed. The third century provides us with a particularly clear indication of the status of the Roman soldier in his world. By that time, as we have observed, the old distinction between citizens and non-citizens was disappearing and was very soon to be almost entirely abolished by law. In its place a new legal concept had appeared, a distinction between the upper category of society (*honestiores*) and the lower (*humiliores*). Both were free, not slaves, but in many respects they were now treated differently before the law. In particular, the punishments for criminal offences were much more physically degrading for *humiliores* than for *honestiores*. The former might, for example, be sent to forced labour in the mines for a crime for which the latter would be banished to an island. The cruellest forms of execution—such as being thrown to the beasts in the amphitheatre—were also mostly reserved for the lower class. The line between them was not strictly defined, but in general it appears that military veterans were accepted as *honestiores*. It is not therefore surprising to find them rising to positions of eminence in civic life, and their progeny climbing to greater heights. It has been observed that relatively few veterans are recorded on the inscriptions of the northern frontier of Britain, and it has been surmised that either the climate drove them south on retirement, or that few lived that long. But it may have been the much greater density of cities further south, and the attractions of villa properties, of which there were very few in the north, that led them to retire away from their stations. Veterans do appear in greater numbers outside the legionary fortresses, and the fact that these settlements were much larger, and more urban, and situated in pleasanter places than many of the *vici* of the smaller forts perhaps supports a preference for civic amenities and prospects, but it may only reflect the general thinness of our knowledge about the recruiting and subsequent lives of soldiers in the army in Britain. We are sure, however, that Roman troops often developed strong affinities with the peoples and localities where they served. This process could go so far as to include legionaries, even in the early days of the Empire, when they were likely to have been recruited far away. In the Year of the Four Emperors, Tacitus tells us, this intermingling was one of the main reasons that caused the legions stationed in Syria to declare for Vespasian:

What most of all inflamed opinion in the province and army alike was that Mucianus declared that Vitellius intended to transfer the legions on the German frontier to the quiet and lucrative life of service in Syria, and send the Syrian garrison to the fortresses in Germany, where they would endure hard work and a bitter climate. It was also a matter of the provincials preferring to deal with soldiers with whom they had long been on terms of familiarity (indeed, there were ties of marriage and property in many cases), as much as the fact that the troops had served so long in those bases that they had grown fond of them, as if they were their own family homes.

Sometimes retired soldiers returned to a province in which they had previously been stationed. There is the third-century example of Tiberius Flavius Virilis, who had held four jobs in the centurionate in legions in Britain, and had acquired a wife who was almost certainly a Briton. He had other postings, including one in Algeria, and on retirement he seems to have gone back to settle alongside the station of his former unit there. Intermarriage and movement of this sort around the empire helped considerably to make the provinces what they were.

Veterans occasionally engaged in commerce, and are recorded in one case as living in a settlement together with traders. However, the fact that the army attracted merchants from other parts of the empire is probably much more important. One of the best-known British examples is Barates of Palmyra, who appears to have been a dealer in military standards or banners. He himself was commemorated at Corbridge with a comparatively humble tombstone. His wife, however, has a much more remarkable monument at South Shields. It has many noteworthy features, not least the facts that it seems to have been carved by an eastern craftsman and that the inscription is bilingual, in Latin and Palmyrene. From it we learn that Regina had been Barates' slave before he freed her and married her, and that she was Catuvellaunian, a member of what had once been the proudest nation in Britain. These personal changes of fortune and the mixture of races in this marriage demonstrate how varied and colourful society could be, even in so remote a province as Britain. It underlines our earlier points, as to why the working language had to be Latin, and how the common culture, however peculiarly it might sometimes be interpreted, was Roman.

Nearly all the people that we have been considering so far were long-term residents in the particular province. We should not, however, forget the impact of the large number of Romans —from many parts of the empire, but predominantly from Italy and the most Romanized regions of the west—who came on short-term appointments at every level of military and civil government. These included the governor and the procurator, legionary legates, military tribunes, centurions, commanders of auxiliary units, and a host of lesser men in other public posts. Most could bring their households with them, and many had official accommodation provided with the job. This meant an ever-changing social scene, and secured employment in all the service industries that provided them with the standard of life they expected. It is not surprising that, to take just one example of such a creation of employment, we find a mason from the region of Chartres working at the Roman spa of Bath.

Romans were used to public bathing establishments, often on a huge scale, as major focuses for relaxation and social intercourse. Any substantial Romano-British town—and many small ones—would expect to build one as a matter of course. Bath is, of course, exceptional, in that it was the centre of a major healing cult, as were many of the great shrines of the Middle Ages, but its social function should not be overlooked. Romans seem to have gone there in substantial numbers, mostly, to judge from the inscriptions found there, from the middle ranks of official society including many army officers—with whom the local gentry might easily mix. Later in this book we shall look in some detail at the extraordinary variety of race and culture in the religions of Roman Britain, but in the context raised by the subject of Romanization and the function of such centres as Bath, it is worth making briefly one or two points. It helped the process of Romanization greatly that the Romans were deeply devoted to the notion that every place had its guardian spirit, for it was therefore relatively easy for them to respect local deities, such as Sulis at Bath, and to identify them with their own, as, for example, 'Sulis Minerva'. The grandest manifestations of Roman religion were, of course, the great festivals of the 'Capitoline triad'—Jupiter, Juno, and Minerva—and the cult of Rome and the imperial house, in which the highest Roman officials and the leading provincials took part. The latter had had a disastrous start at Colchester, but the gradual social and political fusing of the varied elements in the society of the province, permanent and temporary, made religion more and more of a bond. Like the military ceremonies and sacrifices to the Imperial Cult carried out by every unit of the Roman army, these civil observances were essentially about loyalty to the state. Indeed, the very fact that more and more provincials had served in the Roman army meant that the local element in the public observances of the state religion was increasingly one that had been exposed for years to the daily ritual of Rome and the public expression of allegiance. For the first three centuries of the Christian era the Roman authorities had extreme difficulty in understanding that Christian refusal to take part in such worship was not a sign of disloyalty. When the situation was reversed and Christianity became the state religion, emperors considered its rejection—indeed, the rejection of the particular brand of orthodoxy they happened to support at the time—to be equally treasonable. State religion was an essential part of government, and government in the Roman empire was as much a matter of ensuring loyalty to the emperor as it was of administration. The Roman genius for organization was essentially employed by government in the interests of power and security. Government in practice often failed to secure those ends, but, as we have noted, the side-effect of their efforts was long periods of peace and internal order in which vast numbers of ordinary people were able to go about their everyday business relatively undisturbed.

In the earlier chapters of this book we have seen the Roman government of Britain proceed from the *ad hoc* arrangements of the conquest period to its regular form under the early Empire, whereby the *legatus Augusti* and *procurator provinciae*, each with their administrative substructures, controlled the whole of the conquered territories. In the third century the island is divided into two provinces, with a slowly changing but essentially unmodified framework, now in duplicate. In the fourth the changes are much more drastic: two provinces become four and then five, but, much more importantly, the division is no longer between general administration (including command of the army in Britain) and finance, but between military and civil. In his civil role, the old *legatus Augusti* of the undivided province reappears in the person of the *vicarius*, to whom the governors of the individual fourth-century provinces are responsible. However, unlike the *legatus Augusti*, he does not have a direct relationship with the emperor, but is himself accountable to the praetorian prefect of the Gauls, under whose control Britain is included. The praetorian prefect becomes a civil official, who from time to time is responsible to one of two or more Augusti rather than to a sole emperor. The army now has its own separate organization, independent of provincial boundaries, and with *comites* and *duces* responsible to a *magister militum* in Gaul or elsewhere.

These changes had important consequences for the location of the centres of power, as they affected people in Britain in practical terms. Apart from occasional incidents such as imperial visits —for example, by Hadrian or Septimius Severus—or when the island became involved in a claim to the throne—as with Clodius Albinus or Constantine the Great—the patterns remained constant for long periods. After an initial period at Colchester, from Flavian times to the early third century a single *legatus Augusti* was based at London, with direct access to the emperor. In the first half of the third century there were two such centres, London and York, but soon after the middle of the century, though this remained the formal position, the real centre of power shifted to northern Gaul, most frequently to Cologne or Trier. At the end of the century this became formalized under the Tetrarchy, followed in the fourth century by the establishment of the prefecture of the Gauls. The multiplication of layers in the governmental structure, and the deliberate withdrawal of emperors from ready accessibility meant that individual provincial governors were now relatively removed from the fount of authority. Nevertheless, the establishment of the provinces of Britain as a complete diocese within the prefecture meant that the *vicarius* himself was only one step away from the proximate emperor, at least on paper, through the praetorian prefect. London thus regained its position as the centre of government. But it was now more limited, not only because the praetorian prefect himself became more distant from the court as his post in Gaul became a fixed one and another praetorian prefect accompanied the emperor, but also because the greatest influence on the emperors in the west was coming to be the *magistri militum*, to whom the military commanders in Britain were largely responsible. Access to anyone who could speak with imperial authority was becoming more and more remote. This was compounded in the long periods when the senior Augustus was resident in Constantinople. It is hardly surprising that there was a rash of usurpers in Britain at the beginning of the fifth century, or that the case seemed hopeless when the last of them, Constantine III, was forced to set up his court not in London or Trier, but far away in Arles, with barbarians at large in between.

If we have seemed to harp on this matter of accessibility, it is with good reason. Pliny's correspondence with Trajan shows that the emperor was closely involved in what we might think of as minor details of provincial administration. Though Pliny himself was rather a timid administrator, even the most independent-minded governor is likely to have hesitated before taking decisions of importance without referring back to the emperor. Thus a negligent emperor or slow communications could paralyse the system. Moreover, all important appointments were made by the emperor, and a conscientious ruler could take a great deal of interest in the career and performance of individuals at every level. This sort of 'performance appraisal' from the top doubtless kept officials up to the mark, but Pliny's letters also show the other side—that since everyone's job (and sometimes his fortune and even his life) depended on the emperor, it was extremely important to have his ear, both for one's own advancement and that of one's friends and clients. Under the early Empire, when the provincial governors came from the same class as the emperor and were well known to him socially, in action in the senate and lawcourts, and as his generals in war, their personal status in the province was enormous, and their own accessibility was crucial to the provincials. They, too, had important patronage at their command, and we find Pliny writing to his friends asking them to take protégés of his own on to their staffs, though the emperor usually reserved entirely to himself the choice of men for such senior positions as the command of legions.

This situation inevitably led to great uncertainty. It is easy to become so absorbed in the careers of the hundreds of individuals whose appointments are known in great detail from the thousands of inscriptions surviving throughout the empire that we assume the existence of 'standard careers' and forget that there was little to stop a capricious emperor from interfering with the system. In some ways, the death or fall of an emperor or his favourite adviser was not unlike a change of president in the United

States, where vastly more appointments are a matter of party—indeed, of one man and his personal advisers—than is the case in Britain today. Similarly, the disgrace of an individual Roman senator could bring the ruin of the many careers that depended on his influence. Patronage ran through the Roman system from top to bottom, and Rome cannot be understood without grasping that fact. Nor was it felt to be dishonourable, rather it was a matter of pride and obligation, to do the best for those who depended upon it. And a good emperor was expected to be the greatest and best patron of all.

The third-century trend towards excluding senators from military commands and provincial governorships and replacing them with equestrians—including many who had risen from the ranks—changed the personnel and, doubtless, the social character of the relationships, but it remained just as important for provincials to have the ear of the governor. But with the great changes that came under the Tetrarchy, there was no longer to be a governor with both military and civil power, or one who was likely to be well known personally to the emperor. It was now extremely difficult to approach the emperor at all; his associates were likely to be the professional soldiers who commanded the field armies—not even the frontier garrisons—and he was surrounded by a massive screen of protocol operated by an elaborate hierarchy of court functionaries, notably the notorious, if unfortunate, eunuch chamberlains. It is ironic that, to a great extent, an emperor's job had been an impossible one in the first and second centuries because he was too accessible, and in the fourth and fifth because he was too out of touch. In the third he was too busy trying to keep alive to be much bothered about provincial administration.

The growing evidence for London's role as the capital of Roman Britain gives us some interesting insights into life at the centre of a Roman province. The early second-century statue of a military clerk, now in the Museum of London, is particularly telling. It depicts him in uniform, with his writing materials in one hand, making his function clear, but his military cloak is deliberately arranged to reveal the short sword worn on his right side, which proclaims his status as a soldier and one of which he is obviously proud. There survives the text of a letter that we know came from the secretariat of a British governor, and it displays a remarkably high standard of Latin. It is an interesting fact that of the twenty or so Londoners from the Roman period whose names we know, eight are soldiers, including representatives of the Sixth, the Twentieth, and the Second *Augusta* legions. One member of the last records his legion with the additional title of 'Antoniniana', which probably puts him in the reign of Caracalla. This has an additional interest for us, for it was in the third century that there was an important change in military careers. Up to then, soldiers had normally carried out the full range of duties in the course of their service. Now there was a strong tendency for some to spend their whole careers as fighting soldiers, and for others to be kept permanently in administrative postings. This in a curious way foreshadows the late Empire, when civil officials were nominally enrolled in military units and adopted the trappings of the army, but continued to perform purely civilian tasks. A governor's headquarters had always been run by a staff of officers drawn from the army. His chief administrative officer was a centurion of senior rank, the *princeps praetorii*, who had six heads of department beneath him, three *commentarienses* on the legal side, and three *cornicularii* or adjutants. Each of these had their own assistants. It is interesting to speculate whether any noticeable change came over the character of the headquarters when it became more common for some soldiers to spend their entire careers in administration.

There is no particular reason to doubt that most, probably all, of the soldiers mentioned at London were men detached from their units for service on the governor's staff. Covering an area of 5 hectares (12.5 acres), the Cripplegate fort is quite large enough to have accommodated men employed on a wide number of duties, and it may have functioned as a military headquarters for the whole province. But a governor also had two other major bodies of troops attached directly to him, his personal guard, generally assumed to be made up of 500 cavalry and 500 infantry (the *numeri* of *singulares consularis*), and the *beneficiarii consularis* who acted as police and administrative officers. It is very unlikely that Cripplegate also accommodated an urban cohort. Trajan is on record as refusing a request to send even a single centurion to aid the magistrates of an eastern city. He explains that he has decided to follow the practice of his predecessors in supplying Byzantium with a garrison commanded by a legionary centurion to support the city authorities only because it is exceptional in being a focal point for large numbers of travellers from all directions. That case therefore does not set a precedent, and to agree to the present request would open the floodgates. London was certainly also a great centre of traffic, but hardly on the scale of Byzantium. Moreover, as the capital, it will often have had the governor and his troops on hand to suppress any trouble. Yet even the troops that we can be reasonably certain were at the governor's immediate disposal might be thought a tight fit at Cripplegate, if we did not know that individuals were often stationed elsewhere for specific purposes. For the third century it has been assumed that there was a second guard unit when the island was divided between two governors, and it is even more difficult to see where they could have been accommodated in York if it were not for out-stationing. All five *singulares* recorded in Britain appear at forts in the north, and there is also evidence that the *singulares* as a whole were regarded as a mobile reserve that could be moved to other provinces when the need arose. We thus have a picture of a body of troops who might be expected to move about a good deal more than most (which is rather what one might expect of a governor's own guard, since he must have travelled a good deal in his own province), and who were often separated from their families. The British evidence suggests that men of the guard were often scattered on individual assignments about the Lower province. At Catterick, and perhaps at Vindolanda (Chesterholm) as well, they are associated with *beneficiarii*. Since the latter do not seem to have been provided with staff of their own, it has been suggested that some *singulares* were responsible for operating communications between the governor and such agents in the field. We may perhaps imagine them as travelling fairly frequently between the headquarters and the stations of the *beneficiarii* with orders and reports, and doubtless they had to catch up with the governor if he was on campaign or on a progress round his province.

The governor's *beneficiarii* were also normally based at headquarters, but, like the *singulares*, they are found from time to time stationed by themselves at distant points, for example, at Vindolanda, as just mentioned, Greta Bridge, Binchester, Risingham, and Dorchester-on-Thames. They seem from the inscriptions to have proliferated in the north in the third century, and it has been suggested that one of their functions was to provide surveillance for the civil settlements that burgeoned outside the forts in that period. The fact that the Severan emperors deliberately increased the privileges of the troops did not mean that they were unmindful of the need for discipline and political security. By such means the governor could keep a sharp eye on areas that were nominally the responsibility of the local authorities, and also on key points in the road system. The first two of the inscriptions mentioned above also bring another very interesting feature of third-century organization in Britain to our attention. Both of them specifically state that the officers serve the governor of *Upper* Britain—and the others imply the same—though all except the last were found at sites in *Lower* Britain. In other words, the consular governor in London was not only superior in status to his praetorian colleague in York, he also maintained some officers in the northern province who were directly responsible to himself. This may have a straightforward administrative explanation, though one may suspect that, like the dividing of large provinces under the Severan emperors, it was another manifestation of the desire to tighten internal security.

These examples of the intervention of the governor of one province in the affairs of another should alert us to the danger of assuming too readily that modern ideas of boundaries and frontiers can be transferred to Roman times. It is, of course, true that the Romans were careful to define the limits of authority. The basic meaning of the word *territorium* is lands or territory under a particular authority, and a specific officer was left in no doubt of the boundaries within which his writ ran. Even in Republican times a proconsul could act only within his province, and he automatically forfeited his commission when he crossed the city limits of Rome itself. Yet there are two points that complicate the issue. The first is that different officers and bodies had different powers and different limits. These limits might be geographical or of some other kind. For example, magistrates of a local *civitas*, depending on their status and detailed local powers, might have the jurisdiction to try cases that occurred within their geographical boundaries, but only certain types of case and certain types of person. A governor could try a much wider range of cases, had greater powers of sentencing, and his limits were those of the whole province. Secondly, when it came to the frontiers of the empire itself, these principles were modified. The long dominance of Roman frontier studies over the study of Roman Britain gave rise to a widespread assumption that a fortified line was the 'frontier of the empire'. It is, of course, clear that a governor of a frontier province must have known how far he could go geographically, since he was forbidden to make war outside his province without authority from Rome. Yet that may not mean that he could not take other action, and it certainly does not mean that his forward line of posts was necessarily the limit of the empire. Since the imperial estate in Upper Germany extended on both sides of the *limes*, then the procurator at any rate must have been able to issue valid orders beyond the military *limes*, and it is difficult to believe that the governor could not do the same.

The emperor himself was the proconsul of all the frontier provinces—indeed, from fairly early in the Principate, of all provinces with any substantial army and of many others. The executive governor of such a province was the *legatus Augusti*, a deputy who carried out within defined geographical and functional limits the duties and powers of the emperor as proconsul. Thus the governor was limited by whatever restrictions the emperor chose; but the emperor himself, as the proconsular representative or the embodiment of Rome, had no such limits, and to him and to Rome the 'frontier' had no reality except as the limit beyond which the practical constraints of the moment prevented power or influence being exercised. Rome might indeed voluntarily bind herself to agreements with neighbouring states, but these were matters of temporary expediency, and did not abrogate her right in her own eyes to act arbitrarily and unilaterally if she felt it desirable. By the early second century the concept had shifted slightly, and we find the historian Appian explaining that Rome did not choose to incorporate certain areas within her realm, even when begged to do so by the inhabitants, because they would bring her no benefit. Other poor regions Rome was good-hearted enough to subsidize. But there is still no sign that she doubted her right to make the decisions: she appoints kings of her own choosing to foreign states if there is no current advantage in conquest. Thus the absolute concept of Roman right to rule is still paramount. Whether it is Trajan choosing expansion, or Hadrian electing for consolidation and defence, the basic assumption remains unaltered.

At the level of the local community or the individual, Rome similarly reserved to herself the right to make the rules. There were elaborate provisions in Roman law that regulated the private legal relationships between citizens and non-citizens (*peregrini*), for example, in marriage and litigation, and between *peregrini* themselves when they made use of the Roman courts. The position of communities and individuals with full or partial citizenship ('Latin' cities, for example, or freedmen) in relation to Roman and non-Roman authorities was laid down, but this did not reduce the final authority of the Senate and People of Rome —in practical terms, generally the emperor—inside or outside the current boundaries of Roman occupation. It is not, therefore, surprising that a Roman governor needed to have a keen understanding of both the theoretical and actual limits of his power, and a thorough grounding in law and practical politics was as important as military aptitude and experience.

The governor was the chief justice of his province and he had the *ius gladii*, the power to sentence to death, though Roman citizens could demand to be tried at Rome. His duties included not only heading the judicial service, but also hearing petitions and presiding at trials in his capital and at assizes around his province. From time to time, as we have noted previously, his other commitments, military and civil, or the sheer volume of legal work were such that a special judicial officer was appointed to act as the governor's deputy in the administration of justice, the *legatus iuridicus* who had praetorian rank. This post was introduced by Vespasian. We have noted already three by name in Britain—C. Salvius Liberalis and Javolenus Priscus, who served during or just after the governorship of Agricola, when the load on the governor must have been extreme, and M. Antius Crescens Calpurnianus, who was acting governor for a short while under Commodus or Septimius Severus. We also know of C. Sabucius Maior Caecilianus, who served in the reign of Marcus Aurelius, and of M. Vettius Valens, to whom we shall return shortly. A handsome fragmentary inscription on green slate was found in

London, celebrating one of Trajan's Dacian victories, either in 102 or 106, and apparently set up by a *legatus iuridicus provinciae Britanniae*. The *commentarienses*, who included the heads of the legal departments who worked in the governor's headquarters under his chief administrator, have already been mentioned. Also attached to the staff was the corps of *speculatores*, consisting of ten men from each of the legions in the province, whose main functions were concerned with the law, including the holding of prisoners and the carrying-out of executions. The tombstone of one of these men was found in Blackfriars, and was erected by two of his fellow *speculatores* from the same legion.

We have heard much of corruption, injustice, disorder, and civil war in the empire, but the fact remains that the imposition of Roman rule meant the substitution of a world based on recognized, written civil and criminal law for one in which tribal custom and the ever-present threat of local warfare dominated relationships between individuals and between communities. It is a fact of the highest significance that throughout the period of imperial rule it was forbidden for civilians to carry arms, except in certain carefully defined circumstances. While this had the primary purpose of preventing internal disorder, nevertheless the mere fact that it was possible to retain it as a general law for so long implies that everyday life enjoyed a state of peace and stability that, seen in the perspective of history, is quite exceptional. Similarly, while individual instances of maladministration and uneven application of the law abound in the records, it is likely that the exceptional and the sensational were the most reported. It is not unreasonable to assume that in his everyday affairs the ordinary inhabitant of the empire enjoyed such protection as the law afforded his particular class and circumstance, and, perhaps of more importance in day-to-day matters, that his transactions with his neighbours were governed by rules that had the backing of a developed legal system. The very existence of such a system must of itself have transformed the relationships between individuals and have often made the settlement of business, even disputes, a matter of discussion and agreed settlement where it might once have led to armed conflict. But it also, particularly if the individual had a patron, meant access to legal arbitration. The more Romanized a province became, the more this must have improved internal stability as provincials became used to legal redress as the normal means for settling disagreements. On the other hand, it must also have meant an enormous increase in routine cases, either for hearing in the courts, for arbitration, or for presentation as petitions for decision by the governor. What the governor gained in time previously taken up by problems of public order and security within the province as the rule of law became generally accepted, he must have lost by the increase in volume of legal business falling on the system for which he held responsibility.

When we reflect on what opportunities afforded by his job must most have appealed to an ambitious Roman governor, we still have to remember what Cicero told us, that, despite the immense importance that the conduct of legal business had in Roman public life, military affairs commanded the higher prestige. The command of the army of Britain must have remained uppermost in the minds of the governors under the early Empire. Responsible directly to them were the legionary commanding officers, each an ex-praetor with the title *legatus Augusti*, but without the suffix *pro praetore* which was reserved for the governor himself. They took their orders from the governor, whether he was an ex-consul, which was the case for the whole of Britain in the first and second centuries and for the Upper province in the early third; or an ex-praetor, which was the case for the Lower province. The latter officer seemingly also commanded the Sixth legion, and we may assume that there was a combined headquarters at York. It is likely, though not proven, that each legionary commander controlled the auxiliary forces in his area. Similarly, it is sometimes argued that the senior auxiliary commander—in other words, the commander of the auxiliary unit with the highest status—might exercise delegated command over other auxiliary units in a particular district. Thus it is possible that the commander of the *ala Petriana*, one of the rare 1,000-strong units of auxiliary cavalry, which was stationed fairly certainly at Stanwix from the 160s, exercised immediate command of the Wall garrisons. Through him, the other auxiliary commanders would then be responsible to York. Nevertheless, the way in which the structure worked both in theory and practice remains subject to debate.

The fleet under the early Empire, the *classis Britannica*, presents greater problems. Its everyday function was as a support arm, transporting troops and supplies, though it was on occasion used during a campaign, in a raiding and scouting role closely integrated with the land forces. In at least the first and second centuries its bases all seem to be in the south, first at Richborough and then at Dover from about 130 or 140, after a move perhaps initially mooted under Trajan. The fleet commander, unlike the legionary legates, was an equestrian. The post was one of those that featured in careers that included provincial procuratorships. It ranked high as such, with only the command of the *classis Germanica* equalling it amongst the provincial fleets. The most interesting known occupant of the post was M. Maenius Agrippa, who held the positions of *praefectus classis Britannicae* and *procurator provinciae Britanniae*. He was a man of some note, among whose distinctions were having acted as host to Hadrian himself, and being the father of a senator. The relationship of the fleet to the governor of Britain is unclear, since it also had a major fort in Boulogne. The fleet had occupied a base there from the middle of the first century, and was provided with a stone fort in the Trajanic period. We do not know whether the prefect of the fleet was responsible both to the governor of Britain and the governor of Gallia Belgica (which seems improbable), or to the former (since he was of higher rank, an ex-consul as opposed to an ex-praetor), or to the latter (since the fort at Boulogne was much larger than that at Dover), or direct to the emperor. The last possibility might best have suited an ever-suspicious imperial government, removing control of the Channel crossing from both legates, and providing a means of isolating the exceptionally large army of Britain in times of political uncertainty.

Radical alterations to the dispositions of the fleet occurred in the third century. The fort at Dover was dismantled around 210, the iron-making establishments that it had operated inland were closed down, and the last reference to it as *classis Britannica* occurs in an inscription from the reign of Philip (244–9). Parts of the fort at Boulogne fell into disuse in the same period, and it was finally abandoned not long after 270. It was superseded by an entirely new fortification on almost the same site, which may have served both civil administration and naval purposes. In the same period a fort of late Roman type was constructed at Dover, partly over the site of the former *classis Britannica* fort. This subsequently appears in the list of garrisons of the Saxon Shore.

It is possible that the financial administration of Britain, under the *procurator provinciae* himself, had already moved to London before the governor's headquarters left Colchester. It was almost certainly in London when Classicianus' wife erected the great monument to her husband very shortly after the Boudiccan revolt had been put down. The evidence for this includes the discovery of gold-smelting activity on the site of the later Flavian governor's palace, which can therefore be dated to early Flavian times or before, and the find of an official iron punch, which was probably used for marking gold. Taxes paid in gold were regularly melted down into bars and impressed with the official stamp. The provincial procurators also moved about the province from time to time, and we have noted a number of instances when they are recorded elsewhere. They were responsible for public enterprises of various kinds, including crown estates, and it is likely that those imperial freedmen of whom we have records were in their service, or assisted the local procurators or agents who operated enterprises themselves or who supervised the letting-out of crown property to tenants. One such *libertus Augusti*, in collaboration with three men whose status is unknown, restored the temple of Jupiter Optimus Maximus in London—the stone was later reused in the river wall. Another erected a statue to the personified goddess Britannia at York, and a further imperial freedman is found at Combe Down in Somerset in the reign of Caracalla or Elagabalus reconstructing the *principia* or headquarters building. Taken with a lead seal from the same building, it seems highly likely that this was a district office from which local imperial lands or industries were run. We have to remember that imperial property was increasing more or less all the time. Certain industries (probably salt production, for example) had always been state monopolies, but the personal property of each emperor was absorbed into the crown estates. Huge wealth was acquired by confiscations, particularly after civil wars and during deliberate campaigns against opposition to the throne, as under Domitian. Other acquisitions came from legacies to the emperor (particularly as a result of the very common practice of leaving the emperor a share in one's will), and by the provision in Roman law that, in the case of intestacy, the deceased's estate went to the state. Hence the administration of the personal property of the reigning emperor and the general crown property (in practice hardly distinguishable) became a larger and larger operation, and its manipulation an important part of financial and political control.

The workings of the government departments in London were brought vividly to life by the discovery of a writing-tablet branded with the mark of the provincial procurator, and perhaps even more by three small seal-boxes bearing the eagle and the portraits of Vespasian and Domitian, the first in Aldgate, and the two of Domitian in the Walbrook stream, close to the governor's palace. It is unlikely that such seals could be used without the authority of the most senior officers in the province.

The financial administration was still based in London in the fourth century, as the *Notitia* records the *praepositus thesaurorum Augustensium* (after the city's fourth-century title 'Augusta') there. The safe keeping and administration of large sums of money for the payment of troops and officials was always important. It became particularly so under the late Empire, when the practice of regular 'donatives' developed. These were bonuses that were paid at an emperor's accession, on his birthday, and at the five-yearly renewal of the imperial vows. As well as coins, ingots of silver figured in these payments. Senior officers also received gifts of silver plate on certain occasions. These distributions came to be expected, and were an important element in the struggle to retain loyalty. It is interesting that one of the best-known of the silver ingots bears the stamp of Magnentius, and was part of one of the largest late Roman hoards found to date. It came from the fourth-century fort at Kaiseraugst, on the Rhine in Switzerland, and it is likely that it had been in the hands of the emperor's staff or in the personal baggage of one of his most senior supporters. It was probably buried between Magnentius' defeat at Mursa in 351 and his suicide in 353. This was followed, it will be remembered, by the purging from Britain of alleged dissidents by Paul the Chain. Treasures of this sort were doubtless one of his prime targets.

There is just enough evidence to confirm the existence of a

provincial council in Britain. This was a formal assembly that brought together the leading members of the provincial community, and its official function was chiefly to display loyalty to Rome and the emperor. However, failure to pass the customary vote of thanks to an outgoing governor could provoke an imperial investigation into that officer's conduct, potentially a check of considerable importance. The British council may originally have met at Colchester, but such evidence as we have is associated with London. In 1806 an impressive hexagonal statue-base was discovered in London on Ludgate Hill, bearing an inscription erected by Anencletus, a slave in the service of the province (*provincialis*), to the memory of his 19-year-old wife Claudia Martina. It is probably of late first-century date, and suggests that there was an office in London to arrange the business and meetings of the council at that time. Another inscription, found near Cannon Street, is a dedication to the *numen* of the emperor by the province of Britain (*provincia Britannia*), and it seems likely that this was put up by the provincial council, probably voted for at a meeting in London.

We mentioned earlier M. Vettius Valens, *iuridicus Britanniae*, who had been in office in about the middle of the second century. He seems to have been both trusted by the provincials and thought to have influence at Rome, for he was invited to become patron of the province. This type of association was common, and went back to the Republic. With friends at Rome, it was possible to bypass the governor or procurator and appeal for help against maladministration. The power that aggrieved provincial communities could sometimes exercise is illustrated by a case in which both Pliny and Tacitus were involved as advocates. Early in the reign of Trajan the provinces of Africa and of Baetica in Spain suffered successively from the same two disreputable governors. In the case of Priscus, governor of Africa, the charge against him was brought by a single city, but Classicus, governor of Baetica, was accused by the whole province, presumably acting through the provincial council. In AD 93 the senate had appointed Pliny to act for Baetica in another case; now the provincials asked the senate to appoint Pliny again, as they had been very satisfied with his previous conduct on their behalf. He claims to have been persuaded into it against his will, but he is clearly proud of the affair. The case was obviously taken very seriously, since it was heard in the senate, with both Pliny and Tacitus appearing for the prosecution, and in the presence of Trajan himself. Classicus had in fact committed suicide, but the action continued, a right that the provincials were entitled to insist upon. They won their case, and all the possessions in Classicus' estate that had been acquired since his appointment to Baetica were confiscated and divided among the people he had defrauded; a number of lesser officials and accomplices were also found guilty at the same time. The case illustrates how, though a governor had virtually unlimited power while within his province, it was possible for him subsequently to be brought very effectively to account. This might be done by direct appeal to Rome, but there is no doubt that it helped a great deal to have influential friends in the capital. To emulate what a whole province might do was much more difficult for a small community or a single individual, and to them the possession of a patron was of even greater importance. We noted earlier how the decurions of the *respublica Silurum* had marked their respect for just such a man by a notable inscription in their city at Caerwent, though we do not know whether he had actually accepted an invitation to be their patron.

The Silures had once been so savage that, as we have seen, Ostorius Scapula had intended to exterminate them. Fortunately, they had survived, to become one of those essential bastions of Roman stability, a Romanized community that organized and ran itself on Roman lines derived eventually from the formal structure of Rome itself. The various forms that these local authorities might take have been mentioned from time to time—from deliberately planted citizen *coloniae* (in later times the title was sometimes bestowed on existing communities as an honour), through grades of *municipia* (in certain types of which in early times only those who had been elected to principal office received the Roman citizenship if they did not already possess it), down to peregrine *civitates*. Within any of these authorities there might be subdivisions, generally called *vici*, wards or villages, with their own minor officers or *magistri*. In some areas it seems likely that the Gallic *pagus* or rural district survived as part of the subordinate system.

The Roman objective, of course, was not to confer local

autonomy as a political principle, but to transfer as much as possible of the burden of government, the administration of justice, and the collection of taxes on to the locals as soon as possible. Without such delegation, the imperial machine either became so stretched that it could not be run efficiently, or it needed endless resources. The abandonment of client kingdoms as a normal method of indirect government in the course of the first century was largely due to their unreliability. Replacing them with communities organized on Roman lines, administering their districts within clear terms of reference, was obviously preferable. It relieved the pressure on the Roman provincial government to a very significant extent. One detects a distinct note of irritation when Trajan and subsequent emperors were forced to introduce imperial commissioners to regulate the affairs of communities which had proved incapable of sound self-management. The trend towards ever-increasing centralization and growing imperial bureaucracy cannot be blamed solely on emperors bent on consolidating their power and increasing their control of the wealth of the empire. The responsibility has to be shared by provincials who could not, or would not, order their own affairs sensibly. Yet centralization was a very slow, never-ending process, and for centuries the contribution of local effort, fuelled by the ambition of local families and urged on by government pressure, was crucial in running the empire.

There were areas where the governor and procurator were not so fortunate in having much of the routine administration taken off their hands by unpaid local worthies. There is, of course, the special case of land specifically needed for army purposes, but there were also civil districts where the imposition of direct rule was felt necessary. Elsewhere in the empire it is not unusual to find centurions acting as district commissioners in charge of such areas. So far we do not have any examples of the *praefectus civitatis* in Britain, but it is likely that they occurred, especially in the early days when proper local authorities were first being formed out of the old tribal organization, and one might expect them—or their equivalents—at a later date in some of the most difficult areas. One special case is the appointment of a legionary centurion as commander of the Sarmatian cavalry unit at Ribchester who also had the title *praepositus regionis*. Two holders of this post are known, one at some point between 222 and 235, the other in 238 or later. It has been argued that, on discharge, those of the Sarmatians who had been compulsorily enrolled and sent to Britain by Marcus Aurelius in 175, and had not subsequently been posted elsewhere, were settled together on land in the neighbourhood of Ribchester. However, these appointments were made a quarter of a century or more after the last of the original Sarmatians is likely to have left the army, and it is difficult to believe that they still needed special surveillance. Unless the post (or title alone) remained out of administrative inertia, it is likely that this district required direct control for some other reason than a need to supervise an unusual group of veteran settlements. One suggestion has been that, as a consequence of the Sarmatian settlement, the area had developed into an important breeding-centre for cavalry horses. However, it is difficult to see why the commander of the local unit had a special title, since other auxiliary forts are known to have had *territoria*, and the district could have formed part of the *prata legionis* if it was felt desirable to have it directly under legionary control. The instance has not yet been completely explained, and others may well be found.

There is little doubt that most of the land that was not imperial estate or directly in army possession came to be administered by the normal civil local authorities. Moreover, whether it is lack of evidence, or a compliment to the integrity of the British, there are no known instances of the appointment of *correctores* and other officials who were put in by emperors in other, more sophisticated, provinces to disentangle the finances and administration of cities. Britain seems in general to have been peacefully and quietly governed under her local gentry. And if at times it was not, then ordinary *civitates* could be overruled immediately by a Roman officer with delegated *imperium*: the powers of the local authorities were limited and were granted for the convenience of the Roman administration, not to stand in its way.

19

THE HISTORICAL
GEOGRAPHY OF
ROMAN BRITAIN

Writing under Trajan, Tacitus displays sublime confidence in his geographical knowledge:

Many previous writers have spoken of the situation and peoples of Britain. I am proposing to do so again, not to compete with them in ingenuity and diligence of research, but because the conquest was only completed at the time of which I am writing. My predecessors had to fill out their lack of information with tricks of style: I can offer facts. Britain is the largest island known to us Romans. Its shape and location cause it to face Germany to the east, Spain to the west, and its southern shore is in sight of Gaul. The northern coasts are pounded by the vastness of the open sea, for no land faces them. Livy and Fabius Rusticus, the best of the older and more recent writers, have compared the shape of the island to an elongated triangle or an axe. This is indeed the shape as far as Caledonia, hence the usual description. But, going further, one finds a very large tract of country extending to the furthest point of land and tapering into a wedge-shape. The coastline of that remote sea was explored then [under Agricola], and Britain proved by circumnavigation to be an island. At the same time the Orkneys were discovered and taken. Shetland was seen in the distance, but orders and the onset of winter prevented the fleet from approaching nearer . . .

Tacitus then goes on to look at the composition of the population:

Who the original inhabitants of Britain were is impossible to be certain, as is common with barbarians: we do not know whether they were aboriginal or immigrant. Nevertheless, their physical characteristics vary a good deal, and that in itself is evidence. The people of Caledonia have large limbs and reddish hair, which indicates a Germanic origin; the Silures have darker skins and tend to have curly hair, and the fact that their land lies opposite Spain makes it probable that they originated from the Iberian peninsula. Those closest to the Gauls resemble them, whether because original characteristics of race persist, or because lands that come close together have similar climates. On the whole, however, we may assume that it was Gauls who occupied the island opposite them . . .

After a consideration of the language of Britain—and some pointed comparisons of the manners and virtues of the Britons and Gauls, which remind us that his primary purpose is edification, not geography or history—he gives us some notes on the environment:

The climate is unpleasant, with frequent rain and mist, but it does not suffer from extreme cold. The day is longer than elsewhere in the empire, and the night is clear and in the north short, with only a brief interval between nightfall and first light. If there is no cloud, it is said you can see the glow of the sun all night . . . The soil is fertile and is suitable for all crops except the vine, olive, and other plants requiring warmer climates. Crops grow quickly but ripen slowly. This is due to the high rainfall and dampness of the soil. Britain contains deposits of gold, silver, and other metals, wages of victory. There are also pearls in the surrounding seas, though they are dark and uneven in colour. Some think the locals unskilled at finding them . . . I prefer to believe that the quality is too low to make them worth while than that we are not sufficiently avaricious to insist on it.

What Tacitus does not give us—and there is no reason why he should—is figures, and without figures it is extremely difficult to employ the approaches of a modern geographer or economist. Yet much modern work on Roman Britain has been written as if we had such figures, and what in another field would be dismissed as merely anecdotal evidence is taken as highly significant. However, there is one area in which we can begin to indicate figures. It is the size of the population. This is of central importance, for until we have some idea of whether there was one person or a hundred to the square mile, we can form no sensible picture, for the whole balance of man and nature (and man and fellow man) is quite different depending on scale.

For medieval England, historians have expended a great deal of effort on estimating the size of the population at different periods. Their conclusions are very varied, since the evidence is subject to different interpretations, but they are right to place so much importance on the subject. It is extremely difficult to approach many aspects of life in the past without an idea not only of the size, but also of the density and distribution of its people. In 1929 R. G. Collingwood doubted that it was possible to conceive of figures that 'could allow to Britain more than half a million or at most a million inhabitants'. In 1930 Sir Mortimer Wheeler calculated 1.5 million, and in 1976 W. G. Hoskins, writing a new introduction to a reprint of his 1955 classic *The Making of the English Landscape* commented: 'All our previous estimates of population in Romano-British times, and possibly even in the prehistoric period, have been far too low.' S. S. Frere's estimate in 1967 of almost 2 million for the end of the second century had risen to almost 3 million by 1987. His numbers were obtained by considering—among other factors—the size of city amphitheatres, Tacitus' figures for losses during the Boudiccan rebellion, the medieval populations of towns that remained within the circuit of their Roman walls, the calculable size of the army, and approximations for the dependants of soldiers.

Regional studies consistently indicate that we tend to underestimate the number of Roman sites. A study of the Tame and Middle Trent rivers that was published in 1977 produced so many new sites that it was suggested that 'if these increases reflect a national trend it may be necessary to revise the estimate of the Romano-British population to 5 or 6 millions'. If further local studies were to confirm these calculations, we should not be comparing Roman Britain with England at the time of Domesday Book (work on the population in 1086 has suggested figures of 1.75–2.25 million), but with the island in the middle of the fourteenth century, shortly before the Black Death, for which a figure towards the upper end of the range 4.5–6 million is thought likely. Of recent estimates for Roman Britain, T. W. Potter and C. M. Johns's 2.5 million is at the bottom of the plausible range, while M. J. Millett's 3.7 million is perhaps somewhat below the top. Allowing for the fact that Roman Britain covered a rather larger area than England alone, and that the medieval peak may have been a little earlier (a rather larger figure has been hazarded for about 1300), nevertheless it is clear that we are facing a very different density from Collingwood's. Indeed, some historians have conjectured that the fourteenth-century population was about as large as the country could support agriculturally before the technical improvements of the early modern period. We may reflect with interest, too, on the comparison between the proposed figures for Roman Britain and those suggested for the middle of the reign of Henry VIII, somewhere in the region of 2.25–2.75 million. But, such musings apart, the Romano-British estimate does pose very acute problems for the student of the centuries between Roman Britain and the Norman Conquest, for it is necessary to take into account a fall in population to around 2 million—indeed, to presumably something well below that figure, since it is very unlikely that there was no growth in the relatively settled conditions of late Saxon England. Our immediate concern, however, is to enquire whether any changes can be detected within the Roman period itself, and in particular after AD 200.

It should be said straightaway that the direct evidence for Britain is so thin as to be practically non-existent. All we have is a few pieces of information to interpret by analogy from elsewhere, and the interpretation itself largely depends on general theories similarly derived. It has often been held that the population of the empire declined from about 200 onwards. Very briefly, the usual argument for decline depends on two main elements: evidence for abandoned land (*agri deserti*) and for a severe shortage of labour. Laws about *agri deserti* confirm that emperors were attempting to deal with the problem from the third century to the sixth. It is argued that the total amount of food produced must have declined, and that since there is no evidence for the empire exporting or importing food, the population must have been smaller. Furthermore, any increase in the inequalities of distribution of resources under the late Empire in favour of the army, civil service, and most of the clergy are likely to have hit the bulk of the population hard. Signs of a shortage of manpower are reflected in imperial prohibitions on workers in the mines, in the state factories, and on the land leaving their jobs. They are also seen in the measures that landowners took to retain workers on the land—paying to avoid their conscription, accepting prisoners of war, pursuing fugitives, and taking in those who had fled from elsewhere.

Acceptance of this general theory has led to a search for causes, many of them medical or socio-medical—malnutrition, infant mortality (from natural causes and from infanticide), low adult life expectancy, plague, an alleged unwillingness of the upper classes to have children, and even lead-poisoning from the water-system. Yet at bottom the theory itself depends on such thin evidence that there is no need to produce an explanation for it. We simply do not know whether there was a substantial overall change in the size of the population or not. Just how thin that evidence is, we ought briefly to note, if only to avoid wasting more time on impossible calculations.

The actual figures for *agri deserti* are extremely few. It is true that there were some areas of the empire where conditions were particularly difficult and where the loss, as in Africa, was up to 50 per cent by the fifth century, and 10 or 15 per cent in others. Yet the latter is in itself a small figure, and would only be of great importance if all the cultivable land in the empire had once been farmed. But any estimates of the entire population of the empire at its peak show so small a number of people spread over so vast an area that it is difficult to believe that this proposition can ever have been true, even if, at least for Britain, the older population figures ought to be increased several-fold. Nor do we know enough about the other side of the picture—new land brought into cultivation. In fact, if agricultural land was becoming less and less attractive, then it ought to have been reflected in the value put upon it. Yet the price of good land remained high, and the yield of rents and taxes substantial. Why, then, the imperial concern about abandoned land? We have already noted Hadrian's interest in the problem—which puts it well before the generally accepted beginning of decline—in connection with the Fens. The story of the Fens is instructive. The large-scale exploitation seems to be Hadrianic, and a great deal of it was short-lived—partly due to the deterioration of drainage probably caused by changes in the relative land- and sea-level, and partly to errors by Roman engineers. In Britain, at any rate, we have to take into account the possibilities of ill-judged expansion on to land that was easy to work initially (and, being previously uncultivated, was simple to take over), but presented long-term difficulties; and we also have to consider the changes in climate and other environmental factors, which we shall examine later. We have to allow for the possibility that the *location* and perhaps the *type* of agriculture changed, rather than its total output of food, even if methods and yields altered little. Is there, then, another reason, other than the food supply, why emperors should have been so concerned? If more and more land fell into the hands of the emperor, of great senatorial families whom the later emperors proved increasingly unable to tax effectively, and, from the fourth century onwards, of the privileged Church and individual churchmen, then less and less good land is likely to have been held by the smaller gentry who were either the *curiales* of the provincial cities or free farmers, whether owners or tenants. This would have left much less land and people to tax when the need to raise money was increasingly pressing. Thus, any abandonment of land would become a more and more serious matter for the imperial government, even if the total amount uncultivated remained the same.

The same sort of reasoning can be applied to the manpower shortage. The Tetrarchy, by restoring the army and very substantially increasing the administration, must have created a vast magnet to draw men away from increasingly grim prospects on the land into secure and regularly paid employment and a privileged position in society by joining the government service. In the course of the fourth century these advantages were also offered by the Church, where salaried posts and opportunities for advancement multiplied, despite the honourable, if eccentric, exception of the ascetics. It is not surprising that the labour problem was worst in agriculture, nor that many of the disputes were about conscription—in other words, about forcing landowners to give up their men. Nor is it surprising to find that miners and workers in the state factories in the fourth century were among those compelled to stay at their jobs, for these were essential to the contemporary system of military supply.

It is the barbarians within the frontiers who make up the element that we have so far left out of the calculation. As early as the reign of Marcus Aurelius we have seen them being deliberately settled inside the empire, most notably in the Danube region on abandoned land, but even, in the case of the Sarmatians, in Britain. Under Probus there were Burgundians, too, in Britain, and towards the end of the third century we see German *laeti* being brought into northern Gaul to re-establish cultivation on estates that had been devastated by recent invasions. People such as these became settled inhabitants of the empire, and in the fourth century—even more in the fifth—the presence of families with such origins must have become a regular feature of daily life in many parts of the Roman world. Where they came in as prisoners of war and were not drafted straight into the army, they can probably be included in the category of agricultural *coloni* on large estates, whom we are told were in short supply; but those who arrived as free settlers cannot be thus treated, and we have no way of estimating their numbers. We have already seen how our lack of knowledge about the size of the barbarian allied contingents in the late army makes estimates of military manpower difficult. It is now obvious that the barbarian element makes calculation of the *total* population of the empire hazardous. We can reasonably argue for a redistribution of wealth away from the indigenous peasants and smaller landowners, which may have led to an actual decline in their numbers; but we certainly have woefully insufficient evidence to say whether there was a net decrease or increase in the population of the empire at large after AD 200, let alone that of Britain.

Turning now from the size of the ancient population to its physical condition, it is symptomatic once again of our reliance on shaky and anecdotal evidence that, when we try to look at the population at large, we find that Galen's much-quoted study of malnutrition in countryfolk comes from the middle of the second century, when general theory would put the prosperity of the empire at its highest. Yet there are some things that we can say about the medical condition of people in the Roman world that are worth noting, as they add greatly to our understanding of their lives and the atmosphere in which they lived. One source of information is the enormous number of tombstones with detailed inscriptions. These indicate a high rate of mortality among infants and small children, and that men as a whole lived rather longer than women. We are accustomed to thinking of a high incidence of death in childbirth as a major feature of all periods up to living memory, but it has been pointed out that we are conditioned by the Victorian period, the maternal death-rate being exceptionally high in the nineteenth century. Of those who survived childhood in the Roman world, inscriptions in some areas suggest a life expectancy of around thirty years for women and forty-five for men: more detailed figures for Africa give only 28 per cent of women and 38 per cent of men as reaching the age of 62. The overall expectation of life under the Empire is a subject of some controversy, but since the very poorest people (particularly in the countryside, where there were not the same opportunities of belonging to a burial club that would record their deaths) could probably rarely afford a regular tomb-stone, the general impression is unlikely to be optimistic. For the frontier areas, the higher expectation for men is perhaps explained by better hygiene, diet, and medical care among the troops than among the civilian population. If he was not actually killed or wounded in action, a soldier doubtless had a much healthier life, and for very long periods many units probably saw no fighting. Even men whose role was officially a front-line one may have gone through their entire army careers without ever being involved in action.

Most of this information is derived from inscriptions. It is extremely patchy and the coverage is suspect, even though there are many examples. More recently, archaeologists have begun to build up a fund of more reliable information from the large-scale excavation of Roman cemeteries. For the early Empire, the study of skeletal remains is made very difficult by the fact that the prevalent burial rite was cremation, though this was by no means universal. However, as inhumation became more common and eventually normal, it becomes much easier. One of the earliest publications to describe the excavation of such a cemetery under modern conditions was that of the Trentholme Drive cemetery at York. This had particularly interesting possibilities, as it was thought to have been used mainly by the lower classes. Comparison of bones from this sort of cemetery with those associated with funerary inscriptions may eventually, when enough of them have been studied, provide fresh insight into the physical condition of the poorest people, at least in urban society. Other important reports describe the work on, for example, the great Poundbury cemetery at Dorchester in Dorset, and the fourth-century Lank-hills burials at Winchester. It is too early yet to make generalizations, but there is no doubt that there is a real chance of building up significant medical statistics. We are beginning to form some idea of the wide mixture of physical type, of diet, of disease, and of expectation of life. We still need a wider range of sites, and we are particularly hampered by the fact that rural cemeteries, when they occur at all, tend to be small. A parallel line of enquiry is human parasitology, the study of vermin, and possibly bacteriology. York again gives us information from the sewers about parasites, and from a granary about problems of infestation in grain and how the Romans dealt with it. At Vindolanda the excavator recovered living bacteriological material from a Roman deposit. At the same time, new methods of analysis of human bone are providing genetic information of great importance on the composition of communities and the movement of populations. If we can resist the temptation to draw sensational general conclusions from a few samples, and allow the evidence to accumulate gradually, we have at our disposal fresh sources of evidence on the Roman past, complementing, but not superseding, other means of enquiry.

It now seems possible that we shall be able to identify at least some of the prevalent diseases and causes of death in Roman Britain, but, since some of them leave no trace, we are unlikely ever to have a comprehensive picture. One of the most difficult problems is that of epidemics or plagues. It is rarely possible to identify those described by ancient writers in modern terms. This is partly because the organisms causing them tend to mutate, and partly because resistance and the build-up of natural immunization are so variable in different populations at different times that the symptoms described are not sufficiently clear. But the literary references cannot be ignored. For example, the plague that went through Europe in 166–7, brought back by Lucius Verus' troops from his eastern campaign, is unlikely to have missed Britain. One of the penalties of the immense network of communications, and of the constant movement of soldiers, officials, and merchants about the Roman world and beyond must have been a much greater exposure of Britain to epidemics; and one may reasonably assume that—at least in the earlier days—there were serious consequences even from otherwise mild infections that were new to the island. A case has been made for thinking that the incidence of plague in the fifth century was one major reason for the abandonment of towns in Britain. We may hesitate to follow the identification of particular cities in Britain probably affected by plague, but we may consider it reasonable to suppose that any town that had survived to the middle of the fifth century but then was severely hit by disease is much less likely to have recovered or to have been reoccupied than when there was still a Roman government in control of the island.

In the first chapter we saw how the broad division of Britain into highland and lowland zones had dominated thinking about the later prehistoric and Roman periods; how it partially held good, but needed to be extensively qualified; and how we have to take into account the fact that man's capacity for tackling and intentionally or unintentionally altering his environment has varied greatly at different periods in the past. Unfortunately, Romano-British archaeologists adopted the geographical 'zone' concept from the prehistorians and geographers at a time when Roman Britain was seen very clearly as being divided, politically and socially, into a civil zone in the south and east of the island, and a military zone in Wales and the north. Hence the two concepts had become conflated, and there was a strong tendency to assume that the character of the Roman occupation was determined by the terrain, and was both inevitable and permanent. We have seen this approach breaking down. Today, we have to be much more cautious, and in particular we need to take care in defining periods within Roman times, since we now recognize extensive change in the five centuries that are our chief concern.

Few would now accept Sir Cyril Fox's poetic vision of the ancient condition of southern Britain as being dominated by 'an illimitable forest of "damp" oakwood, ash and thorn and bramble, largely untrodden. This forest was in a sense unbroken, for without emerging from its canopy a squirrel could traverse the country from end to end . . .' Even for the beginning of the Iron Age, the period about which he was writing, this picture no longer holds good, and by the time of the Roman conquest the land was more open and settled than was previously thought. The question to which we have to address ourselves is whether a further transformation occurred in Roman times. Prehistorians often take a negative view, arguing that agriculture was already of the same general character and occupied much the same area of land when the Romans arrived as it was to do throughout the period of Roman rule itself. In its turn, that forces us back to population size, for it raises the question of whether the Iron Age population was already approaching the size that we have tentatively postulated for Roman Britain. In making such a hypothetical calculation, we might reasonably subtract the Roman army and administration, though we may perhaps allow for a few British aristocrats who spent more time on war and hunting than speeding the plough. The hypothesis we can then put to the prehistorians is a pre-Roman Iron Age population substantially larger than at the time of Domesday Book.

Experimental work carried out at the reconstruction of an Iron Age farm at Butser in Hampshire produced figures for the amount of farmland required to fill a single grain-storage pit of the type present in very large number on Iron Age sites. The area is so large—in round figures something between a half and three-quarters of a hectare—that it led the director of the Butser project to observe that 'the major implication is that in the Iron Age there was virtually total domination of the landscape and a proportionally large population.' This, as he observed, was supported by analysis of aerial photographs, suggesting that 'our problem in the future will be to isolate the areas where prehistoric man was not active.' Prehistorians who do not accept such a large Iron Age density of settlement would have to postulate a very substantial population growth during the Roman period, say in the first and second centuries, with either more agricultural land cleared or higher productivity. The truth probably lies in a moderate increase in population under Roman rule, and a sharp decline sometime after the end of it. We do know of land that the Romans opened up (which we shall consider later in this chapter), and can reasonably conjecture an increase in productivity (which we shall examine in the next).

It is difficult to believe that Roman activity had no real effect on the ecology of Britain. In relation to military activity alone, one cannot help recalling Sir Ian Richmond's comment that the stripping of a wide belt of land to provide the materials for the original Turf Wall phase of the western end of Hadrian's Wall must have devastated the landscape through which it passed. Nor can one forget a demonstration from the appearance of pollen in lake deposits in Italy that the driving of a Roman highway through the Ciminian Forest extensively altered the ecology of the area. We have a great deal to learn about how the creation of cities and of new types of rural centre, and deliberate Roman interference with the natural pattern of things (for example, the digging of canals and diverting watercourses) affected the environment. We have previously noted how it became clear in the Fens that there had been much less Iron Age occupation than Roman, and that it looked as if the Romans took advantage of a natural change in the balance of sea and land, but that in the course of the second century the water-level began to rise again. Such changes in relative sea-level, however, do not seem to have been the same all round the coast. In London, for example, the waterfront wharves were moved forward in successive rebuildings, apparently to compensate for a river-level that continued to fall in response to a lower sea-level and reduced tidal reach, at least until the mid-third century. It was still relatively low when the riverside city wall was built in the later third century, but there is evidence for rising levels in the fourth. On the west coasts of Britain there are points where the fall seems to have occurred much earlier, with water-levels rising again by the beginning of the second century and remaining high in the third. While such variations make it unsafe to speculate about any particular location without local evidence, it is at least clear that there were many places where the coastline and coastal conditions were different from the present. It would now appear, for example, that much of the intense Roman occupation in the northern Fens was probably on large offshore islands. There is, however, no guarantee that the situation was static throughout the Roman period, and the effect on the coast of the radical changes in the courses of rivers observed further south in the Fenland basin is likely to have been considerable.

It is clear that in the Wash area, subsequent to the Roman period, the land has actually been *encroaching* on the sea, despite a higher relative sea-level, at least partly due to the intervention of man since early medieval times. The construction of successive seaward dykes has led to the natural creation of silt marshland in front of each of them, so that the land has advanced in stages. Elsewhere severe erosion has meant a *loss* of land—for example, at some of the Saxon Shore sites. There is no simple equation between sea-level and coastline. It is therefore exceptionally difficult to envisage the actual coastal appearance of Britain in Roman times, or how much it altered between the first century BC and the fifth century AD. Like the population problem, it can only be solved by the testing of general hypotheses by means of a very large number of very detailed local studies, and by a readiness to accept that local conditions almost certainly often ran quite contrary to general trends. What we need to appreciate most of all is that we cannot rely on modern or medieval coastal conditions as an indication of Roman ones, and to recognize the magnitude of the changes that have clearly taken place in many places.

What happened to the landscape of Britain in the fifth century, in the years after the end of Roman rule, is even more difficult to determine. One may assume that these problems connected with, or worsened by, administrative failures under Roman rule are likely to have been even greater then. On a more local scale, man's effects on the environment are likely to have been much more varied as central government broke down. It is important for the study of the landscape that very early Saxon settlement has been observed on or near Roman sites, while mid-Saxons seem to have founded new settlements on different sites. This suggests that the physical conditions were broadly the same in the fifth century as in the fourth. It also implies that no large-scale dereliction of agricultural land had taken place, at least not of such an order as to require more work to restore it than to open up fresh lands. While the early Saxons were settling alongside, and perhaps intermingling with, the Romano-British population (still under Roman rule or its immediate 'sub-Roman' successors), or taking over Roman lands just vacated, the late Roman landscape pattern is likely to have persisted.

Much has been made in the past of the notion that the Saxons were forced into cultivating virgin land because it was impossible to reclaim Romano-British fields that had been abandoned and run to ruin. It has, however, been from observation of land near Monmouth in the Welsh border country that the process is

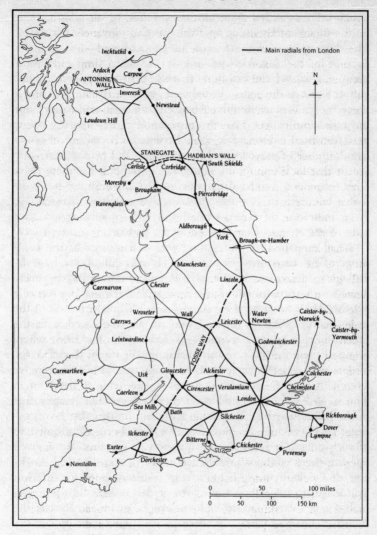

Main radials from London

N

Inchtuthil

Ardoch • Carpow
ANTONINE
WALL
Inveresk
• Newstead

Loudoun Hill

STANEGATE HADRIAN'S WALL
Carlisle Corbridge ⊢ South Shields
Moresby
Brougham
Ravenglass ⊢ Piercebridge

Aldborough

York
Brough-on-Humber

Manchester

Lincoln

Caernarvon
Chester

Wroxeter Wall
Caersws Leicester Water Caistor-by-
Newton Norwich
Leintwardine
Godmanchester Caister-by-
Yarmouth

FOSSE WAY

Carmarthen Gloucester Alchester Colchester
Usk Cirencester Verulamium Chelmsford
Caerleon London
Sea Mills Bath Silchester Richborough
Ilchester Bitterne Dover
Exeter Chichester Lympne
Nanstallon Dorchester Pevensey

0   50   100 miles
0   50   100   150 km

THE ROAD SYSTEM OF ROMAN BRITAIN. Some of the lesser roads have been omitted for the sake of clarity. Water transport—inland and by sea—complemented road transport, but knowledge of the routes is too fragmentary to permit reliable mapping.

much more complex. Agricultural land that was abandoned there in the nineteenth century became a tangled jungle for fifty years, but thereafter, as trees matured, the undergrowth died back for lack of light, the sodden ground was naturally dried out by the trees, and the whole area became easily penetrable again. At that point forest husbandry or clearance becomes relatively simple once more. Where there has been a real gap in occupation, one may therefore expect it to be something like half a century before resettlement is likely, and in these circumstances changes of settlement site and land division are probable. But where there was no substantial break, then a continuity of pattern is perhaps more likely than not (provided that methods of farming are not radically different), *even if the population has completely changed*. We have, therefore, to reckon with the survival of some agricultural units from Roman times to the recent past or even the present.

In all probability we are faced with real change in the landscape of Britain, caused by changing climatic conditions, by technological innovation in the later Roman period, and by man's behaviour during the often disorderly replacement of Roman rule by the sub-Roman kingdoms and the full Saxon conquest of the sixth century. On the other hand, we are also faced with the strong likelihood of continuity of activity on the land, where none of these factors was overwhelming. We might therefore appropriately end this review of the landscape with one tentative comment on the effects of political change between the Roman period and the Saxon and early medieval periods, namely that such change may have had much less effect on the ways of organizing and working the land than we have been accustomed to think. Indeed, it provokes the question of whether, for a given locality, there was much difference in practice, as far as the working of the land went, between the relationship of the Roman gentleman to his agricultural slaves or tied *coloni*, and the Saxon noble to his slaves and dependent farmers, or for that matter the Norman knight to his serfs. Perhaps we might even project the pattern back, and suggest that some of the Iron Age aristocrats who were to become the *curiales* of Roman Britain already had a very similar relationship to the people who worked the same land in their time. If the population really was of much the same order of magnitude before the Roman conquest as shortly after the Norman, then suspicions of substantial continuity in land-use may well be right. This would lead us to two conclusions. One is that it was often the people who changed rather than the man-made landscape—perhaps only the actual land-owning class. Secondly, this approach implies that the residence of the owner of the land, or even the settlement from which it was worked, is of less importance than the unit of land itself. This in its turn strongly suggests that it is worth extending the practice of trying to isolate such traditional units as still exist, or have done so in the recent past, and of tracing them back as far as possible, alongside the study of the distribution of settlements of different periods, which is now so well and successfully established.

Where Roman Britain differs most sharply in its historical geography from the periods immediately before and after it is in its provision of communications by land and water. It is true that the ease with which heavy loads could be transported by water as opposed to land was of cardinal importance in the ancient world, conferring great advantages on those settlements on coasts with good havens or on navigable waterways. It is also, conversely, true that the risks of shipwreck and sometimes of piracy were high. Transport by road was generally safer—though bandits were not unknown in Roman times—but, with ox-power for heavy loads, it was slow and laborious. This is not to say that the Romans did not have the technology to handle large cargoes over long distances. Where imperial prestige was concerned, they could perform enormous feats of transportation. Granite columns for public buildings in Rome, for example, were brought by road from the quarries in the Red Sea mountains of Egypt to the Nile, and thence by river and sea to Italy. Nor was this confined to rare special projects. For centuries huge quantities of grain were shipped to supply the free corn distribution to the city populace of Rome. Some historians who overlook the archaeology argue that such feats are irrelevant to consideration of the everyday place of transport in the Roman world. They rightly point to the fact that the primary motives here were not commercial, but political and—in the case of the construction of temples—religious. As with the Pyramids, rulers of great states can always ignore the ordinary constraints of economics in such instances. It is not, however, sound to go on to affirm that the costs of transport meant that long-distance trade for commercial profit was confined to luxury goods, where high unit values justified the cost of carriage. To argue thus flies in the face of the evidence on the ground. An enormous amount of archaeological material from Roman sites throughout the empire, including Britain, proves the mass distribution of goods over long distances, and a high proportion must have gone to private individuals. Pottery is the most obvious category, and the one that has been subjected to the most sophisticated and detailed analysis. Samian from Gaul, for example, or the British Nene Valley wares appear all over the country, in towns and in the villas of the well-to-do, but also in the humblest 'native' sites, not always in large quantities, but still present and clearly available to ordinary people. Another example is oysters. Their shells appear on almost every Romano-British site. They imply an efficient and fairly rapid use of road transport: if they were carried in tanks of water, they were very heavy; if without water, then they required speedy delivery before they were dead and dangerous. These are only two out of many items that are so common as to be almost an embarrassment to excavators of Romano-British sites. They cannot be ignored as occasional finds—on the contrary, it is their sheer quantity and ubiquity that hinder quantification and analysis.

For shipping cargoes in and out of Britain, it is clear that Dover and Richborough served as the principal ports for the short Channel crossing to Boulogne, and it is possible that the Tyne communicated directly with the Rhine. Exeter and the ports of Southampton Water were almost certainly heavily used, and it is probable that the Wash and the East Anglian estuaries further south were also busy. Until the middle of the third century, however, the greatest traffic was generally through London, the hub of the road system and the centre of government. Considerable remains of the Roman waterfront have been explored, and the wrecks of river-craft and coastal ships have been found in the Thames, the most notable being that found at Blackfriars; the date of its launching or refit is established by a coin of Domitian that was deliberately placed in the socket into which the mast was stepped. The importance of canals in Roman Britain is more problematic. It is reasonably certain that the Foss Dyke between the Trent and Lincoln was a canal, probably associated with military supplies to York. However, it is now very doubtful whether the Lincolnshire Car Dyke (or even the Cambridgeshire watercourse of the same name) was used for transport. The former, with a parallel artificial cut in front of it, was almost certainly a Roman catch-water drain between the high ground of the Fen Edge and the new lands beyond. Other cuts, particularly those of the south-eastern Fens, may have had a dual function, serving both for water control and as routes for barges, particularly where they linked navigable rivers. In the transport field, the most important function of waterways must always have been the provision of access to the sea for inland areas.

We have so far concentrated on communications as they related to the commercial distribution of goods. Yet the primary purposes of the system were military and political. Indeed, since it permitted the rapid conveyance of people and messages, it was vital to the running of the empire. That is not, of course, to overlook the commercial importance of that factor, even if incidental. We have writing-tablets from Roman Britain bearing business messages that indicate the sort of purely civil information that was carried. There is, for example, a letter found in London between an owner and his steward about the sale of a slave-girl and other business matters. Substantial correspondence about private business has come from the Vindolanda excavations, and one letter in particular illustrates how many of the goods that have been found as archaeological objects on sites reached their users. Written by an entrepreneur named Octavius—it is not clear whether he was a civilian or a soldier in business on the side—it opens a window on a world in which deals are struck and money is exchanged. In this case it looks as if the writer is supplying the military quartermaster with grain, hides, and animal sinew, as the quantities of goods and sums of money are quite large. Whether or not the transactions are in fact semi-official or private, it appears that he has laid out money in advance on a grain delivery, and is seriously worried about cash flow and the impending loss of his deposit, unless more money is sent. He has already been let down by a customer for hides, who has failed to turn up, having bought what he wanted elsewhere. What is perhaps most significant, he asks his addressee, Candidus, to check up on a sum of money that should have been credited to his account with a third party, one Tertius; a fourth person, named Fatalis, has paid this money over to Tertius (it had presumably been a debt owed to Octavius, or was being paid on his behalf in some deal). We catch a glimpse of a sophisticated money economy at work, one that renders credible the existence of sufficient underlying mechanisms of finance and information to support the vast distribution of everyday goods over the Roman world. The physical problems of that distribution do not go unnoticed in this letter, for we learn that the hides and a wagon are at Catterick, but that Octavius has hesitated to collect them while the roads are bad (presumably in winter), lest the animals are injured. The importance of the written message in all this is underlined by Octavius' request that Candidus send a letter of authorization to Catterick, so that the goods can be released.

The prime reasons why the Roman state took such an interest in promoting and protecting the flow of information were, of course, political and administrative. The roads and ports served not only to facilitate the passage of troops and their supplies, but also to carry imperial messengers and duly authorized officials. Speed was a vitally important feature of the *cursus publicus* or Imperial Post: without it the extreme difficulties that the emperors had in knowing what was going on in the empire and maintaining control over it would have become overwhelming. A normal rate of travel by the Post was in the region of fifty miles a day, but faster journeys were made: Tiberius once managed the feat of two hundred miles in the space of twenty-four hours. Governors were responsible for seeing that the main highways required for official purposes were maintained, and that the system of stations for changing horses (*mutationes*) and posting-houses (*mansiones*) was kept up and strictly regulated. Individuals could only travel by the Imperial Post if they were issued with a permit, and these permits were sent out to governors by the emperor. The seriousness with which this was regarded is illustrated by an exchange of letters between Trajan and Pliny. Pliny wrote from Bithynia enquiring if out-of-date permits could be used, as he was anxious not to hold up important dispatches. Trajan was short and sharp in reply: 'Permits must not be used after they are out of date. It is my invariable rule to have fresh permits sent to each province before the dates they can be required.' Trajan himself could be generous, for when Pliny later wrote to apologize profusely for having given his wife a permit to travel in connection with a family bereavement, the emperor replied kindly and excused him. There is implied in this latter correspondence that governors or equivalent officers were sometimes in the habit of issuing permits for private travel, but an inscription from Burdur in Turkey suggests that Pliny is emphasizing his own otherwise impeccable adherence to regulations, rather than nervousness about the use of a discretion that he officially possessed. This inscription, dated to the time of Tiberius, shows that the official system was in being as early as Augustus' reign, and was already abused.

The methods of funding and operational arrangements changed over time, but in general the financial responsibility for providing this transport was laid on the local communities, and bitter complaints about cost and misuse recur throughout the Roman period. The Burdur inscription defines who was then entitled to use the service—broadly speaking, only people on official business who carried a permit issued by the provincial governor or the governor of another province—how much transport each grade could command, and with what priority. Theoretically, many of these travellers had to pay for what they used and could not demand extra services, but this was where the complaints chiefly originated. The inscription lays down that goods for sale must not be carried by such transport (which suggests that they often were). It also restricts those persons entitled to free transport and free lodging. These included the members of the governor's staff, persons on military business from other provinces, imperial freedmen, and imperial slaves and their beasts. The cost fell on the local authorities, but by the third century the actual provision was regularly organized by the provincial administration. In the third and fourth centuries the word *mansio* regularly describes the actual station, but in the Tiberian inscription it seems to be used in the abstract sense of the service itself. The actual system of stations may not yet have been generally set up in the first century, only the obligation to provide the service laid on the local communities. Buildings for this purpose appear in Britain as early, for example, as that reasonably identified at Chelmsford, which was put up in the late first century and, with some alterations in the middle of the second, continued substantially unaltered until the end of the Roman period. This is perhaps an early example of official provision, or it may originally have been erected by the local authority on its own initiative, as a less troublesome way of meeting its obligations than an *ad hoc* search for accommodation and transport every time someone arrived with a permit. Some may even have originated as privately owned inns. Varro, writing in the late first century BC, before the establishment of the Principate, suggested that owning an inn was a profitable sideline for a villa estate that lay near a road. Eventually the state may have reorganized and extended the provision of staff and buildings, particularly where the services that the law prescribed in imperial times were not being efficiently provided. The detailed entitlements to services continued to be regulated by the grade of the traveller, and we find that a late Roman *vicarius* could claim a set provision, just as his predecessors had been able to do for three hundred years or more.

It is likely that many of the small towns that grew up on the main routes of Britain, for example, those spaced along Watling Street, either originated as post-houses or were kept going as settlements in the period immediately after the army had moved on by the presence of such an establishment. The Post system was kept up conscientiously, as the history of the *mansio* at Chelmsford would illustrate. Another of these urban examples excavated in recent years is to be found in the small walled town of Godmanchester. Continuing excavation on the site at Wall in Staffordshire will, it may be hoped, give us more detail for one of the great highways of the province. It is likely, too, that the buildings identified as *mansiones* outside such forts as Benwell or Vindolanda in the frontier region were used by people travelling officially. At forts they were usually the only reasonably spacious and comfortable residential accommodation, other than the commandant's house, that was capable of housing a person of consequence and a few servants, and they were sharply differentiated from the ordinary run of private houses and shops outside the fort. They must have been particularly welcome to those persons obliged to travel in outlandish parts of the empire who, in more civilized regions, would have scorned public inns and moved from hospitality at one friend's villa to another, by far the preferred method of travel among the aristocracy.

We need have little doubt that the imperial government attached great importance to the maintenance of administrative and military communications throughout the whole period of the Empire. Inscribed milestones certainly record road mainten- ance until the middle of the fourth century, and though the British series (which anyhow is not large) gives out then, the survival of the roads as important features in subsequent periods is circumstantial evidence that upkeep continued on a substantial scale in the open country, just as more direct evidence from towns shows us that streets were resurfaced into the fifth century. The fact that Rutilius Namatianus noted it as worthy of special com- ment that the bridges were still down and the posting-inns were deserted in Italy after the sack of Rome by Alaric suggests that, to his Gallic correspondent, such a failure in the system would still have seemed unusual in 417. We may perhaps assume that the regular maintenance of main roads in Britain continued at least until 409, and that lesser roads, which were the respons- ibility of the local authorities, were perhaps kept up longer still, but with wide variations in standard and persistence.

Rutilius clearly also felt that to travel by sea required an expla- nation; we know how it was feared, and that the normal season was limited by the design of ships and navigational aids. Yet the case should not be overstated. All travel to Britain had to be by sea, many private individuals made the journey, and in our con- sideration of official travel the importance of the sea routes must not be overlooked. Indeed, even when there was the alternative of travel by land, official journeys were not automatically made thus. Pliny the Younger, travelling with his entire staff to his ap- pointment in Bithynia, writes to Trajan that he decided to travel partly by carriage and partly by coastal boat, 'for the great heat makes it too difficult to go all the way by road and the prevail- ing wind prevents me from travelling entirely by sea'. He had originally intended to go the whole way by ship—but, it will be noted, that was in summer. All the remains of ships of the Roman period so far discovered in Britain have been merchant in char- acter, and there is no reason to think that official passengers may not have travelled by civilian transport. However, it may also be assumed that the fleet played an important part in the carrying of official travellers, especially when there were security problems to be considered.

We have so far considered imperial communications largely in terms of official travellers. However, there were two other aspects of major importance. One was the carriage of official goods, whether a small package, or a shipment of military stores, or the output of publicly controlled industries such as the iron-working of the Weald in which the British fleet was involved. An important source of information on such traffic is provided by official sealings and labels; the examples found in Britain were mostly made of lead. Some were issued by the emperor, others came from the administration of the province, and yet others from tax officers. Only a few originated with civic authorities, but a large number came from military units. Labels of the Neronian period, giving the weight and value of packages, have been found at Usk in Wales, and a second-century sealing has come from Wallsend on Hadrian's Wall. A large batch of seal-ings dated to the third century has come from the stores base at South Shields, probably to be associated with Severus' war in Scotland. Those from the Pennines that probably indicate official control of the lead-workings around Alston are well known. Others, from the fort at Brough-under-Stainmore, have suggest-ed that this was a collecting-point for traffic from other military stations. Where private sealings occur along with those of mili-tary units, they may well have been attached to packets dispatched by duly authorized officers via the official system. Procedures doubtless changed, but the traffic was clearly frequent and long-standing.

The other form of official traffic was of equal or even greater importance—the passing of official messages. Frequent use was, of course, made of messengers travelling by the Imperial Post, and we may recall how Domitian's courier met Agricola's ship in the Channel as the latter was on his way home from his pro-vince. But use could also be made of signal stations, though we do not know how sophisticated the messages sent by them could be. The reliefs on Trajan's Column in Rome show towers with flares and piles of bonfire material that could be used for beacons, though these may have been no more than a way of providing a form of security lighting. Platforms have been found on the Stainmore Pass, and first-century towers on the Gask Ridge in Scotland. Some other British examples are a tower at Pike Hill, incorporated into the structure of Hadrian's Wall but apparently of earlier origin, and others on the Roman road from Annandale into Clydesdale. These could largely be explained as having a fairly local tactical purpose. A late tower found at Wapping, just to the east of the Roman city of London, which was perhaps part of a system for passing messages to the capital, may have had no more than a purely defensive role in providing an early warning of danger to the city, but on the other hand it raises interesting but unanswered questions of a possible function in transmitting urgent signals to and from the military and civil government. In the final analysis, information was the most vital commodity to pass along all these routes, because intelligence meant power, and without it the whole apparatus by which the empire was controlled could not have worked. In this context, the unique position of Britain among the heavily garrisoned areas of the empire —an island separated from the Continent by the often-difficult waters of the Channel—takes on a new significance. This, we need not doubt, was well appreciated on those not inconsiderable occasions when Britain took a leading role in proclaiming emperors or arousing suspicions of conspiracy in the minds of the imperial government of the day.

20

TOWN AND
COUNTRY

The relationship between town and country in Roman Britain
is a subject on which opinion has veered between R. G. Collingwood's view that the towns were mere parasites on the country,
and J. S. Wacher's opinion that they were the vital catalyst
between new ideas from the classical world and those of Celtic
society that transformed Iron Age Britain into a land fully integrated into the empire. Some have seen the Roman towns as a
largely superficial imposition on a way of life that was hardly
changed by the Roman conquest, and in many areas lasted long
after the end of Roman rule and the decay of the cities themselves. Others have argued that towns survived well into the fifth
century because of their own strength, while the characteristic
society of the Romano-British countryside broke down. One
question we must ask is whether, behind the discussion, there is
not an assumption in many people's minds that the two modes
of settlement, urban and rural, were totally distinct, even opposed,
forms of existence.

The modern reader needs first and foremost to understand that,
to the Roman—indeed, to the classical world as a whole—the
proper mode of life was that of the city-state. In one sense the
empire was the city of Rome and its conquered territories, in
another it was a vast patchwork of *civitates*, city-states of varying
status, but all striving towards the character and condition of
assemblies of Romans, with their own local constitutions and
customs based more or less closely on that of Rome itself, and
subject to the overriding control of Roman magistrates. Since
the emperor held an overwhelming and unique combination of

those magistracies, allowing him to speak for Senate and People, every *civitas* naturally recognized his supreme power, both *imperium* and *auctoritas*.

For the same reason they were also subject to his deputies: the provincial governors and others who derived their authority from him. But as city-states they had their own functions and duties, and cannot be written off as formal luxuries. They were part of a sophisticated system, and had been deliberately created. To recapitulate what has been said before about the local authorities: they were broadly divided into *coloniae*, *municipia*, and ordinary *civitates*. There are four known examples of *coloniae* in Britain: three deliberately founded as veteran settlements—Colchester, Lincoln, and Gloucester—and one, York, that was raised to that status from humble origins, probably at the time of the residence there of Severus and the other members of the imperial family. The large settlements, or *canabae*, that grew outside the other permanent legionary bases at Caerleon and Chester may not have received the same rank, but London, as the metropolis of Britain, ought to have received a title. Certainly, its fourth-century name, Augusta, indicates a high status. Verulamium is the only reasonably certain example of a *municipium*, but there is some evidence pointing in that direction elsewhere, for example, for Leicester. It is highly likely, too, that other major cities that had grown from native settlements, or had been formed as urban centres for the new local authorities based on the native aristocracy and had flourished as such, were granted this status. The main difference between these and the other *civitates* was that they were chartered Roman cities and that all, or most, of their governing class were Roman citizens. This distinction faded with the rapid growth of the citizenship in the second century, and disappeared with the *Constitutio Antoniniana* in the third, but the titles were still sought. The core of the organization was the *ordo* of decurions or members of the council (more commonly known under the late Empire as *curiales*, after the *curia* or council-chamber). The minimum age-limit for membership was normally 30, and its character is immediately recognizable by the facts that, from the second century at least, popular election was replaced by co-option, and that members were required to have a certain level of property (an almost universal feature of qualification for rank or office throughout the empire at both national and local level). The membership of the *ordo* was commonly set at one hundred. A councillor's availability for duty and his stake in the well-being of the community were assured, at least in law, by a rule requiring him to maintain a house of a specific minimum size within it. In this respect, as in most others, the constitutions of the local authorities copied, in an appropriately scaled-down form, the pattern of Rome itself: senators were expected to own property in Italy, whatever their origin. In formal terms, the local councillor's house was to be in the relevant city or within a mile of it, but some of the places in Britain that were certainly the centres of their *civitates*—for example, Silchester—were too small for this to have been enforced. It is therefore probable that, particularly in the earlier days of a province, the requirement was interpreted as residence within the boundaries of the *civitas*, an interpretation that would have caused little legal difficulty. Under the late Empire, this theoretical problem was overtaken by more serious ones, as the *ordo* can rarely have been up to strength in that period, due to deliberate avoidance of office. In the heyday of the local administrations, however, there must have been a total of around 2,000 decurions in Britain at any one time. It is an interesting corrective to the notion that they were a tiny oligarchy that, if our population figures are roughly right, then something around one person in every two thousand was a decurion. When one subtracts women, children, slaves, freedmen, most soldiers, and an increasing number of people who were exempt from service on the councils (such as senators and, in the fourth century, Christian priests), the proportion is quite impressive.

The cities were run by two senior and two junior magistrates, elected by the councils, who had responsibility for a wide range of local services, including such matters as water-supplies, and presided in the local courts. Gradually, the attractions of office became less. It could be very expensive. Many municipal dues were levied in the form of services to be provided free by the wealthier citizens, and a newly elected magistrate, as at Rome, was expected to become a local benefactor as well. New decurions paid an entrance fee, and the expenses of holding a local magistracy were likely to be heavy. Perhaps the most crucial function of the councils in the eyes of government was their responsibility for the collection of taxes. This was not just the levying of local taxes for local purposes, but national taxes as well. Diocletian made the individual councillors personally responsible for this. This must have been highly unpopular, though it probably codified a practice that imperial officials had already been carrying out. The councils' actual freedom of action had also been severely curtailed. The reader will recall that Trajan introduced commissioners in many cities to prevent the mishandling of municipal funds and needless extravagance. We find the emperor allowing the city of Sinope, in Bithynia, an aqueduct, provided that Pliny is satisfied that his own engineers approve the line and that the town bears the whole cost. Prusa, in the same province, has to ask for permission to rebuild its public baths, which are old and in poor repair, and is told that it can use its own money to do so, provided that essential services are not starved of funds as a result. Bithynia had certainly come under special scrutiny, and so may be rather exceptional for the beginning of the second century, but commissioners gradually became common and turned into permanent paid officials. It is not surprising that we find so many fourth-century imperial laws to prevent those qualified for service as *curiales* from avoiding it.

The burdens on the *curiales* were vastly increased by direct acts of government in the first half of the fourth century, and they were only partially alleviated thereafter. Constantine, as we have seen, confiscated the treasures and endowments of the pagan temples. This immediately affected the finances of the cities, since they had managed the funds of many of them, and was only partly eased later in the century when the public religious observances for which they had been responsible were formally prohibited. Moreover, Constantine had not stopped at the temples. He also deprived the local authorities of the revenue raised from local taxes, which henceforth was paid into central funds. This was compounded by a further massive blow, probably under Constantius II, when the cities suffered the transfer to the emperor of the lands and endowments that, as corporations, they had acquired over the centuries. By the middle of the century, therefore, all the expense on public works, which had formerly been defrayed at least partly from municipal funds, now had to come out of the pockets of the *curiales*. This reason alone would be sufficient to explain the sharp decline in civic standards. The Emperor Julian returned some financial independence to the cities, but this was rapidly reversed by his successors. The situation had become so serious by 374 that the cities were allowed to keep one-third of the income from the properties they had once owned, as well as the same proportion of the local taxes. By the beginning of the fifth century there are signs in parts of the empire that they were building up some accumulation of capital again, from bequests and other sources, and that they had regained certain powers of local taxation. There is reason to believe, therefore, that the cities of Britain are likely to have been in a better financial state under Honorius than that to which they must have sunk in the middle of the fourth century.

The public services provided were on the whole worth while. Many towns had an engineered water-supply, even if the provision was rather less in Britain than to military establishments. It went to public installations, such as the town baths and—for example, at Lincoln—to fountains in the streets. Private individuals could be connected to the supply on payment of charges. The surplus flushed the sewers, and waste water was normally channelled into a proper system of drains. Not all of these features have been proved at every town, but where a supply has been discovered, an outfall must be implied, and vice versa. But things could go wrong with municipal engineering, sometimes through ambition outstripping financial resources, and sometimes through incompetent architects. At Cirencester the forum subsided into an old military ditch, and we find Pliny writing to Trajan to say that the city of Nicaea has spent an enormous amount of money on a theatre that it cannot finish because the foundations have been badly designed and the building is sinking. In another city a huge set of public baths had been started on an unsuitable site. In both cases the question is whether to make the best of a bad job and finish the building as well as may be, or to start afresh on a new site. Pliny asks the emperor to send out an architect to investigate and advise. Trajan replies that *every province* has architects that can tackle such enquiries, and that it is a problem for Pliny to settle on the spot.

As well as baths and theatres, the cities also provided the highly popular entertainment of the 'games'. There is no unequivocal evidence in Britain so far either of the aristocratic and, at least theoretically, amateur athletics known elsewhere in the empire, or of the construction of 'circuses' for horse- and chariot-racing, though Procopius tells us that by the sixth century every part of the empire suffered from the polarization of the population, even in individual families and between husband and wife, into fanatical and often violent supporters of the two teams or 'factions', the Blues and the Greens. However, the existence of civil amphitheatres is certain at a number of Romano-British towns, and probable at several others. Beast-shows were always popular, and gladiators were not finally banned in the west by the Christian emperors until the reign of Honorius. Both were extremely expensive forms of entertainment, sometimes provided by the council or other official bodies, often by rich private individuals. Entry was usually free, and under the Republic these games had been a popular means of winning votes. Even during the Empire they were felt to be politically sensitive, for they drew spectacular attention to the wealth and influence of an individual. Gladiatorial shows, in particular, always required official permission, and in Italy their presentation was restricted to the imperial family from Domitian's time. In the provinces this absolute restriction did not apply, and it was possible for immense sums to be expended on this side of provincial life. Unattractive though it is to us today, it nevertheless must have fulfilled an important function in providing mass relaxation for all classes of the population, and in establishing the city as a regional centre of amusement and pleasure as well as of commerce and administration. On the other hand, the violence associated with the Blues and the Greens is unlikely to have been the only disorder caused by supporters at public events. Indeed, we know that riots were not uncommon under the late Empire in connection with the election of bishops, and this aspect of urban life suggests that cities may often have been more attractive to visit than to live in.

The cities were responsible for the upkeep of public temples and the provision of official religious ceremonial. This was supervised by city priests, of which there were several grades, the best known being the *seviri Augustales*. Their function in the celebration of the Imperial Cult was important, and the group had a special social role in that its members, unlike the decurions and magistrates, did not have to be of free birth. This provided a route by which well-to-do freedmen could enter the higher ranks of local society, and their own sons could aspire to municipal office and beyond. Since many of these families were of foreign origin or had originally been taken prisoner in the wars of conquest, the local upper classes were thus enriched by fresh blood. M. Aurelius Lunaris describes himself as *sevir Augustalis* of the colonies of Lincoln and of York, 'in the Province of Lower Britain', on a dedication that he erected in 237 in Bordeaux. His family's free status was, judging from his name, relatively recent, and he is presumed to have been shipping wine from the Gironde to Britain. Another *sevir Augustalis* of York was M. Verecundius Diogenes, whose Greek name may originate from slave ancestry. He himself came from the *civitas* centred on Bourges in the Loire region, where his family had clearly been absorbed into the Gallo-Roman community, and his wife was Sardinian. Lesser colleges of priests widened even further the net that drew people into public or semi-public affairs.

In theory at least, there was a distinction between the chartered towns, the *coloniae* and *municipia*, and the urban centres of the other *civitates* in terms of their relationship to the lands that surrounded them. The actual relationship in each case was detailed in the charter of the particular authority. Broadly speaking, a chartered town was itself an official Roman unit of government, the land around it was its *territorium* and subject to it, and citizens born there gave the city as their official place of birth, their *origo*, where they had civic rights and duties. In the other cases the *civitas* or tribal area was the unit, and the city had no separate formal existence, though in both groups the concept is the same, the city-state. There are occasional variations, even cases such as Avenches in Switzerland, where the *civitas* of the people from the surrounding countryside seems to have had a separate formal existence alongside the city itself.

Before the spread of the citizenship that culminated in the *Constitutio Antoniniana*, a citizen's *origo* mattered a good deal, and this is one reason why auxiliary veterans might carry with them a diploma that recorded their grant of Roman citizenship. Legionary soldiers' children, being sons of citizens, required an *origo*, but they were often born in the *canabae* outside the fortress.

They were given the origin 'at the camp' (*castris*). This was not wholly a legal fiction, since a legion was a citizen body, commanded by a Roman magistrate—or rather by the deputy (*legatus*) of the most powerful of magistrates, the emperor. It could therefore possess a *territorium* of its own, and could be regarded as the equivalent of a chartered town. But all these distinctions became blurred, and it is likely that even while they still retained practical importance, many people did not understand their niceties. Hence we can place little reliance on the phrases used on private inscriptions, such as tombstones, to prove the constitutional position of cities, unless the inscription is very clearly giving a precise definition of legal status. Of more immediate importance to the individual—unless he became seriously entangled with the criminal law and needed to prove his citizenship— was the distinction between a *civis* of the local authority within whose boundaries a person was living, usually someone who was born there and who could not escape certain local obligations, and an *incola*, or resident incomer from elsewhere, for whom there were different rules.

The two third-century provincial capitals, London and York, provide illuminating examples of how such cities could reach the same point in quite different ways. In neither case is the evidence absolutely firm, but the details hang together reasonably well and, for this purpose, they can be filled out with analogy from elsewhere. Tacitus tells us that at the time of the Boudiccan rebellion London was 'not indeed graced with the title of *colonia* but thronged with merchants and a famous centre of commerce'. We know that groups of Roman citizens, often merchants, resident abroad sometimes formed an expatriate organization (*conventus*). An interesting Danubian example is provided by the 'Roman citizens from Italy and other provinces residing in Raetia' (*cives Romani ex Italia et aliis provinciis in Raetia consistentes*), which illustrates that such people were not necessarily all from the same part of the empire. Another inscription gives us 'retired soldiers and local people (*pagani*) living together within the same walls', and we have already seen how the German and Roman inhabitants of Cologne felt themselves as one people in time of crisis. However, in the case of London, it is possible that the large number of *incolae* from other places may at first have stunted the

growth of a local *ordo* at the same time as it boosted the size of
the city.

At York we have a different form of growth. Prior to the early
third century there was no provincial capital here, but a major
legionary fortress, the hub of the army in the north. *Canabae* developed outside its walls in the usual way, and a further civil settlement grew up just across the river to the south. Again we have
a Danubian inscription to help. We find the *cives Agrippinenses
Transalpini* from the great colony of Cologne on the Rhine settled
far away in the legionary *canabae* of Aquincum. This inscription
shows us how such expatriates mingled with the local population, since they joined with a Roman citizen who was born in
the *canabae* there in erecting a memorial to his wife. Gradually
a new community could form out of such a society, and hope
for elevation to chartered status.

It is, however, notable that in most of the known cases it was
not the *canabae* themselves that were made into cities, but a new
foundation created a short distance away, or a pre-existing adjacent settlement. This may have been to avoid any problems that
would arise if an independent *colonia* existed right up to the walls
of the legionary fortress, particularly as there were often military
installations, such as bath-houses, outside the perimeter itself.
At York it is virtually certain that the *colonia* consisted of the
settlement across the river, raised to that status certainly by 237, and
probably either at the time of Severus' residence there (we have
a reference to a *domus palatina*) or when York became the capital of the new province of Britannia Inferior. It has been noted
that the fourth-century description of Severus' death at York in
211 describes it as a *municipium*. If there is any chance of this
being accurate, it suggests an intermediate stage. Either or both
grants may well have been a reward for loyalty to the Severan
house.

As to the ordinary *civitates*, the rate of development is likely
to have been very variable between one and another. At Silchester there is an intriguing fragment of an inscription that seems
to record a *collegium peregrinorum*, suggesting that, in what one
assumes was still a non-citizen ('peregrine') *civitas* in formal terms,
the non-citizens were now in such a minority that they had
formed their own association. In the case of a *civitas* like the

Atrebates, with Silchester in the centre of a peaceful and well-Romanized countryside, one may guess that there was comparatively little difference in the level of Romanization and the spread of citizenship between the town-dwellers and the country people. The distinction, anyhow, would have been an unreal one to the upper classes, particularly where the countryside, with its villas, was well developed and the town was relatively unsophisticated. A rather different situation may have obtained in the *civitas Cornoviorum*, with its centre at Wroxeter (Viroconium). The origin of the town may have lain in the *canabae* of the early legionary base, but they had only a relatively short time to develop before the army moved on, and we have seen the *civitas* capital suffering a distinctly shaky start in the Flavian period. It looks as if they needed a determined push from Hadrian to sort out their affairs and build themselves a proper civic centre. Their hinterland to the west had still been close to the scene of serious fighting as late as Agricola's war with the Ordovices. Forts were retained throughout their district for much of the first century, and for far longer they lay under the shadow of the tribes of the Welsh hills, which continued to need some military supervision. This is perhaps the reason for the comparatively small number of villas in the surrounding countryside, and for the exceptionally large and numerous private houses in the city itself. There is nothing that indicates a difference of status here between town and country, but in practice the contrast must have been marked.

Cirencester and Gloucester are neighbouring cities whose development, and that of their countryside, is worth comparing. Cirencester, Corinium Dobunnorum, also probably started as a civil settlement outside the early fort, though here as usual it is very difficult to demonstrate actual continuity between such a *vicus* and the subsequent town. Nevertheless, its extremely favourable position in the highway system may well have encouraged traders to stay who would otherwise have followed the troops. It is very likely that a general market had grown up, even if unofficially, and one would expect a posting-station to have been retained after the army had gone. Indeed, the importance of the site as a centre of commerce is underlined by the fact that in the Hadrianic period it became one of the towns to build a regular market-hall (*macellum*). But there were other reasons for its prosperity as well. In the fourth century it was probably the seat of the governor of a province, and this will have given an additional fillip to the second largest city in Britain. Here not only were the town and its private houses of a high standard, but it became the centre of the richest area of villa estates, for which the terrain was particularly attractive. We have, though, no evidence for Cirencester itself having any special status, but one might expect the whole community to have acquired at least an honorific title. In apparent contrast, Gloucester started as a full Roman colony, Glevum, *colonia Glevensis*, founded as a settlement of legionary veterans at the end of the first century, when it should have been able to take advantage of the Flavian impetus to Romanization in Britain. It ought, too, to have benefited from its position on the Severn, though navigation is not easy, and a port seems eventually to have developed, as did the later one, on the Avon near Bristol. Whatever the exact reason, Gloucester does not seem to have attracted the merchants and other foreigners that one might have expected. Nor does it seem to have the same rich hinterland as Cirencester, even though we do not know where the boundary ran between the colony and the *civitas Dobunnorum* to the east. To the west were the Silures, who had had such a savage reputation in the fairly recent past, and the lesson of Colchester had perhaps taught Roman colonists to tread warily where their British neighbours were concerned. It has been suggested that both Lincoln and Gloucester were, unlike Colchester, settled in previously sparsely inhabited territory for just that reason. The riverside lands, too, may have been unattractive to the ex-legionaries as sites for villas, and they may have preferred the comfort and security of the city, farming their lands at a distance or through tenants. Though they had a flourishing municipal organization, their housing closely followed the lines of the preceding legionary phase; here on the fringe of the Roman world they may have felt little inclination at first to move out into the countryside and set themselves up as an essentially villa–dwelling gentry, unlike their British counterparts—or, indeed, their Roman ones in more settled parts of the island. Later, as the area became more peaceful, the colony faced competition from the now-flourishing *civitas Silurum*, centred on Caerwent, and just possibly from a *municipium* or *colonia* at Caerleon, as well as from Cirencester itself. Whatever the reason, it never regained the supremacy among the cities of the south-west that it ought to have had, nor did it raise the standard of its *territorium* to equal its splendid neighbour. It is not therefore surprising that the fourth-century government brushed aside old distinctions and acknowledged reality if it settled on Cirencester and its region as the centre of a new province.

However, we are justified in enquiring whether the ways of life in Cirencester and Gloucester were really so different. Was the former solely the residence of the rich and the place of business of officials, merchants, and master craftsmen? Was the latter in contrast purely a close-knit community of veterans and their descendants, owning allocations of land outside the city? The excavation of what appears to be a very comfortable and prosperous fourth-century farmhouse and associated buildings *inside* the walls of Cirencester ought to make us think twice about our conception of Romano-British cities. A purely 'urban' concept is anachronistic. It is also insular, as a cursory exploration of the back streets of many a modern French or German town of moderate size will reveal. We have to expect a proportion of the inhabitants of most ancient cities to be farming land outside the town or to be closely involved with agriculture. Similarly, we may expect to find farms or 'suburban' villas directly adjacent to the town, as at Kenchester, where many of the advantages of both worlds might be obtained. With the cost of transport high, land for horticulture and pasture was a valuable asset for a city to have in its immediate neighbourhood, to supply it with vegetables, fruit, and other produce for the table. Nor should the presence of farm buildings or even cultivated ground within city walls be taken as proof of the decline or abandonment of urban life. Surviving records of medieval walled towns show many examples of orchards, kitchen gardens, and closes for animals.

There were hardly any cities in the ancient world that were sharply divided from the country as are the industrial centres of today. Rome, Constantinople, Alexandria, and perhaps one or two others were large enough to have had a life largely divorced from the country, and the first two of these had a state-organized, free, or heavily subsidized food supply that allowed their urban proletariat to exist without being supported either by work on the land or by the employment now provided in cities by modern industry. Virgil's awe-struck peasant exclaims:

I was ignorant enough to think that the city they call Rome . . . would be like our local town, where we often drive our young lambs. I assumed that one could imagine the large from the small, as the dog is to the puppy, or the kid to the goat. But Rome stands out from all other cities as the cypress towers above the lowly shrubs.

The rest of the free town-dwelling world, if it was not of private means or in public employ, either had to work in trade or in the craft and service industries of the city, or was employed in the suburbs and surrounding countryside in agriculture or rurally based industry.

We can now turn to look at the network of country towns, villages, villas, and farms of rural Britain. Two aspects that were of great importance to the countryman, religion and industry, will be touched upon only briefly, as each needs also to be seen in the context of Roman Britain as a whole, and taken a little later. For the moment, let us continue to hunt down the mistaken notions that have grown up about the contrast between 'town' on the one hand and 'country' on the other. Two further misconceptions were generally prevalent on this subject until quite recently. One is that there were no villages in Roman Britain, only isolated farms and villas, or at the most a hamlet of two or three homesteads—and even these were on occasion explained away as the product of the 'extended family', or of the practice (known from Welsh law) of subdividing the property among all the sons instead of following inheritance by primogeniture. This was believed to be the Celtic pattern, and to have persisted unchanged throughout the Roman period and beyond. The second is that a 'town' in Roman Britain can only be called such if it is demonstrated by written evidence to have been a *colonia, municipium*, or the centre of an ordinary *civitas*, or if it can be shown archaeologically to possess the main public buildings of a local authority (forum and basilica)—with a strong inclination towards such an assumption in those cases where these buildings have not yet been found, but other suggestive features exist, such as exceptional size or the possession of a regular grid of streets.

The assumption that there were no villages had been viewed with growing mistrust by many, and was finally dissolved in the 1960s by demonstrations that there were large numbers of 'nucleated settlements' in Britain, ranging from tiny hamlets to large villages or small towns, depending on one's preference for the English term to describe them. Since then the idea has been widely accepted. It is much strengthened by the work of Iron Age specialists, for example at Danebury hill-fort in Hampshire, which has shown that permanent settlements on a very substantial scale were well established in the pre-Roman period. Furthermore, we no longer have to treat the centres of the Catuvellauni and others, *oppida* such as Cunobelinus' seat at Colchester, as rarities imported from the Continent at the last moment before the Roman occupation and essentially un-British. Nor do we have to find convoluted reasons to explain the Roman 'nucleated' settlements of the north, especially those long known on the fells of Cumbria, or the 'minor settlements' that occur on many of the roads in the south.

However, the idea that a 'town' has to be the centre of a local authority still gives trouble. Given that the problem derives from difficulties in understanding the Roman structure, it can best be dispelled by adding briefly to what has already been said about the organization of local government. The Romans themselves seem in practice often not to have been very precise in their use of terms, and it is clear that in ordinary parlance the city frequently became identified with the *civitas* itself. This is particularly clear from the place-names of Gaul, where, for example, Lutetia Parisiorum has survived as Paris, and Augusta Treverorum as Trier, the name of the people, not the city, having predominated in the later Roman period. This process is much less pronounced in Britain, but Durovernum Cantiacorum has become Canterbury, and the process was under way within the Roman period elsewhere in the province. But there were occasions when the Romans had to be precise, chiefly in matters to do with a man's official birthplace and the law. Fortunately, there is an admirable authority, the jurist Ulpian, who wrote under Caracalla and was held in high regard for his knowledge and handling of earlier legal writings and precedents. Roman law was a practical subject, and the jurists wrote for the men who were responsible for applying it. Ulpian clearly felt it was necessary to define the position of a man born in a *vicus*, any *vicus*. The problem was therefore, we may presume, one that faced magistrates and on which they needed guidance. 'The man who was born in a *vicus*', he says 'is considered a citizen of that authority (*res publica*) to which his *vicus* answers.' In Roman eyes, then, there was a *res publica* and a *vicus*. We know that the *res publica* was a unit of government that could be a civil organization, such as a *colonia*, or a *municipium*, or an ordinary *civitas*. We have the example of the Silures using the term to refer to their *civitas* on an inscription contemporary with Ulpian himself. The unit could also be a military one, like a legion; and there were *vici* on imperial estates (*saltus*), where the immediate authority was the *procurator saltus*, responsible to the procurator of the province. In legal terms, therefore, the *res publica* is not a place, but something in which authority resides.

Once we realize that, for this purpose, a *colonia* or *municipium* is the *ordo* and citizens (like the 'Senate and People of Rome'), not the physical city, we should have no difficulty in seeing how, in an ordinary *civitas*, it is the *ordo* and *cives* that are relevant, not the city in which the administrative functions may chiefly be carried out. Conversely, the absence of a forum and basilica does not tell us anything about the status of a town, just that the *res publica* did not use it to carry out certain administrative functions. This is why *vicus* can be used indiscriminately of a village, a settlement outside a fort, a ward of a city, even a subdivision of the *canabae* of a legion. Ulpian was dealing with a universal problem. An individual or an administrator needed to know how people were to be classified. The case of someone who was born inside the walls of a colony was the easiest, and the problems became increasingly more difficult as one came to the man whose birthplace was, say, the *canabae* of a legion or an imperial estate. Ulpian is saying: find the *res publica* and you will classify the man. This is advice of immediate value to the harassed official trying to determine who has jurisdiction in a particular case or to assess liability for taxation or public service. In common usage, the *civitas* did often come to be identified with the city at its centre. We have noted how the classical world thought in terms of the city-state, of which the clearest symbol was the actual city. But armed with his Ulpian, the local magistrate or administrator could determine the situation of someone born in the neighbouring countryside. The normal presumption would be that there was no difficulty: he was in exactly the same position as someone whose place of birth was one of the *vici* of the city itself. But suppose the man claimed that he was not subject to the jurisdiction of the *civitas*. Then the simple rule was to find whether his *vicus* was in fact subject to some other *res publica*. What matters is not the physical location of the *res publica*, but of the *vicus*. Does it lie within or without the boundaries of the magistrate's authority? If within, there is no problem. The crucial matter is not a difference in status between the city and other towns or villages within the boundaries of the *civitas*, but determining the limits of jurisdiction.

As to the *res publica* itself, if the *ordo* chose to meet in the middle of nowhere within its own boundaries, that is where the embodiment of the *res publica*, in other words, its magistrates and *ordo*, would for that moment reside. It follows, therefore, that the possession of a forum and basilica does not in itself prove that a town had a special status apart from other settlements within the *civitas*, only that it was found convenient for the *ordo* to meet there. The provision of buildings for the *ordo* and magistrates, and the usual accretion of permanent staff and records would follow naturally from such a decision, but it also follows that the absence of these buildings from a particular Romano-British urban site cannot be used to prove that it had a lower *legal* status. The country town might have less prestige than the '*civitas* capital' (though, as we shall see, it might be no smaller), but it could still be a town in the common sense of the word. Indeed, the archaeologist's term '*civitas* capital' may itself be confusing us, since it is perfectly possible to conceive of a *civitas* that had no one principal town, yet functioned normally through a rural network of small towns and villages.

We have also to remember that the government of the *civitas* by its *ordo* and magistrates was only one of the activities that a town could house, and even in the case of a fairly extensive town, there is no need to assume that local government was its chief function—or even that it was one of its functions at all. If we can accept that there was a continuous spectrum from hamlet to city, we can turn—without being bothered further by definitions of status—to the very significant part that the country towns played in the landscape of Roman Britain. We noted earlier the importance of the substantial *vici* outside the forts, and their relationship to their hinterland. In the parts of the province where no or very few garrisons remained, the 'small town' was equally important.

A primary question is the matter of size. It has been pointed out that to calculate the area enclosed by walls can be misleading, as the extent of extramural occupation—or of occupation before the walls were built—is not thereby taken into account. Moreover, it does not tell one anything about the *density* of occupation. In addition, some small towns seem to have remained unwalled. Nevertheless, their size *relative* to the large towns, and the range within their own group are determinable in general terms by looking at walled areas. The administrative capitals, for want of a better term, range from Caistor-by-Norwich (Venta Icenorum) at 35 acres (14 hectares) within the walls, to Cirencester at 240 acres (97), with London far outstripping all at 330 (134). The walled small towns run from Ancaster at 10 acres (4), to Chesterton (Water Newton) with 45 acres (18), though the last is about 10 acres bigger than any of the others. Yet Hockwold on the edge of the Norfolk Fens, which is unwalled and whose edges are very difficult to define, is at least as large as Chesterton and probably larger. The large towns themselves average around 100 acres (40), while Gloucester (46 acres, 19 hectares) and the first stage of Lincoln (41 acres, 17 hectares) are misleading, because they represent densely packed veteran settlements inside old legionary sites. Nevertheless, in size the small towns do overlap the undoubted administrative capitals, and as a group they represent the lower end of a continuous scale.

Where the small towns do, however, seem to show a real difference from the large is in their lack of planning, given that our knowledge of their interior layouts is still very sketchy. In certain cases, for example Catterick or Alchester, there is something approaching a grid of streets, but it seems incomplete, and blocks (*insulae*) are irregularly subdivided by lanes. In others, the main street is the only dominant feature, as at Kenchester. The same variety characterizes the civil settlements outside the forts of the northern frontier and the *vicus* recently discovered alongside the fort at Brancaster. The area of crop-marks so far noted at this latter site is 57 acres (23 hectares), and finds have been noted on the ground even further afield. Looking at the published aerial photographs, one cannot help being struck by the resemblance both to Hockwold (and a number of lesser Fenland sites) and to the internal appearance of the small walled towns. At Brancaster there is some attempt at overall rectilinear planning, with a main crossroads visible east of the fort and another to the west, but there is much irregular subdivision, and the ends of the principal thoroughfares divide and wander off. Returning to the north, much the same pattern can be seen at Corbridge, where a walled town developed around the military base. The overall pattern, therefore, is very similar, whether in the south or the north, whether walled or unwalled, and whether the civilian settlement is associated with active military stations or is without any known military connection. In summary, what we are saying is that there is a very substantial number of nucleated civil settlements with broadly similar characteristics that cannot be clearly distinguished on archaeological or historical grounds from the administrative capitals at one end of the scale, or the smaller villages and hamlets at the other. This means that quite a lot of civilians in Roman Britain were living in settlements that were neither large towns nor single farms. Allowing for differences of a regional nature and in the circumstances in which individual settlements originated and developed, there is a broad similarity that not only makes us further revise our older notions of the division between town and country, but has important implications both for the transmission of ideas and the general way of life in Roman Britain.

If we look at some of the activities that have been detected in these small towns and their environs, we should get a better idea of how they relate to the countryside. For this purpose, it is fair to exclude the settlements outside the forts, since it is clear that so many of their inhabitants were soldiers' families or civilians otherwise dependent on the army for a living, though their probable function as a market and point of contact with the local farming population is not doubted. For the other small towns, their connections seem to be predominantly agricultural, though there are important signs of industry, for example, at Camerton in Somerset, which has produced a range of pewter moulds, doubtless connected with the lead production of the nearby Mendip mines and the tin deposits of the south-west. Inside the small towns the ubiquitous 'strip-house' appears, well known in both the settlements outside the forts and in cities such as Verulamium. This type of building is in fact almost inevitable where street-frontage is limited, and while, as at Housesteads, it is clear it was sometimes an open-fronted shop or workshop, with storage and living accommodation behind or above, it is probable that it was also used for other purposes, frequently as a dwelling without commercial activity. The presence of the 'aisled building' in one or two small towns has been noted. This is common in the countryside as a farmhouse or barn, often as part of a larger villa complex, where it may have been used to house workers as well as animals and farm equipment, but it does not seem to be a regular city type. Temples seem to be relatively common, which was normal both in ancient cities and the country-side, and we ought not to forget their effect on the economic life of a town, or their role in bringing people together, with results that were not all connected with religion. A place like Springhead, in Kent, which had a large group of religious build-ings reminiscent of the 'temple region' of the city of Trier, may well have become prosperous as a pagan pilgrimage centre. But in the end we have to come back to agriculture.

The grouping of the villas themselves is also worth further exploration in this context. It has been observed that hardly any villas were more than half a day's ride from a town, yet it is often the smaller towns of which this is true, not the main cities. This suggests villas that had a good deal of day-to-day business with the country towns, and only on infrequent occasions with the cities. It is not difficult to imagine why. It must surely be that the lesser towns provided the essential services, shops, and mar-keting facilities, but had nothing that would encourage the upper classes to move into them, a point supported by the apparently sparse provision of such amenities as public baths. The cities did have the facilities for civilized living, and also an active public life. Thus we may imagine the upper-class Romano-Briton either moving into a city, or living part of his time on his country property and part in the city. Indeed, he might even prefer the provincial capital itself to his own local city, when public duties did not compel him to spend his time in the local courts and council-chamber.

The small town, therefore, is essentially dependent on the countryside, either because it houses people who work the land, or because it serves the daily needs of the estates and peasant farmers of the district, probably both. Even where there is industry on any scale, this is still true, since in Roman times industry was by and large located in the country, not the big cities. The distribution of villas, however, points to one other function that the country town may commonly have had. We have already noted the development of small towns on the main highways, particularly in connection with the Imperial Post, and have cited some examples of *mansiones*, as at Godmanchester. Various modern writers have pointed out an interesting phenomenon: that towns in Roman Britain, especially small towns, often have just one villa close to them, for example, Great Casterton. These have been named 'satellite villas', and may in some cases in fact have been *mansiones*. But if these satellites do have an official purpose, there may well have been various services that used them. One thinks of the *beneficiarius consularis* at Dorchester-on-Thames, for example, or the imperial freedman Naevius in the employ of the procurator's department, whose reused inscription was found near the villa at Combe Down just outside Bath. Where the occasional villa occurs just outside a city, as at Cirencester, one is tempted to think of more exalted officials, such as the *correctores*, who, as we have noted, are known to have been appointed in other provinces to supervise the running of local government on behalf of the emperor.

In the case of a major city such as Cirencester, one may expect sometimes to find the sort of luxurious villa (for example, Woodchester) further out, a place to which a prominent gentleman might ride out for the night after a day's work in public affairs, as Pliny liked to do from Rome to his place at Laurentum. In the fourth century, the period to which Woodchester and its like in Britain chiefly belong, Ausonius describes his country house as being not far from the city, yet not close to it either, so that he can exchange one for the other, as the fancy takes

him. It is not clear to what extent this was considered acceptable behaviour by the authorities. Probably people of the highest senatorial rank could do much as they pleased, in Ausonius'
day as much as in Pliny's. However, in the fourth century emperors seem to have made strenuous efforts to prevent members
of the local *ordo* from moving completely into the countryside.
Laws of 367 and of 396/7 specifically prohibit the practice, with
the latter laying down confiscation of the country property
as the penalty for so 'impiously abandoning one's native town',
and the former emphasizing that there had been many previous
edicts on the subject. The laws can hardly have been to prevent
tax evasion, since *curiales* who moved house would still have remained responsible for their public duties and taxes. A more likely
motive on the part of the councillors was avoidance of the unofficial burdens placed upon them by custom rather than by law.
What this could mean to a Roman gentleman is illustrated by
the case of the writer Apuleius in the second century. His marriage took place at the suburban villa that belonged to the widow
who was to be his bride in order to avoid the distribution of
largesse to the urban populace that had taken place at the marriage of her son. The emperors seem to have been particularly
troubled by a threatened decay of the cities, perhaps motivated
by the greater difficulty of political surveillance in the countryside. It is ironic that the moralists of the Republic had deplored
the opposite movement. Varro laments the fact that in the good
old days people only attended to business in town one day in
eight, while in his day, the late first century BC, practically all
heads of families have moved into the city. But we have to remember that he is speaking from the traditionalist standpoint that
believed that country life and country people were infinitely
preferable to the city. Moreover, when he was writing there was
no threat to urban prosperity or to the political organization that
depended on it, and his preoccupations were quite different from
those of the late Roman emperors, though his ideals were the
same as many fourth- and fifth-century Romans. But emperors
had to deal with the immediate problems facing them, and their
edicts reflect what was actually happening. The frequency with
which these had apparently been issued indicates that little headway was made. Whatever the full reasons for the legislation, the

practice was clearly common, and in Britain it fits with the evidence for the construction and refurbishing of villas late in the fourth century to confirm that the Roman pleasure in the countryside was still unabated. There is no sign here of a wealthy class taking shelter behind the city walls, retreating from a countryside no longer safe.

So far in this chapter we have assumed that the inhabitants of the Romano-British villas were local gentry, apart from the few officials about whom we have speculated. However, it is evident that even in Britain the pattern was much more complicated. Some of the grandest villas, such as Fishbourne or Folkestone, were indeed probably official residences, yet many, both large and small, must have belonged to private individuals other than the *curiales* of the cities of Britain. We have mentioned the possibility that much land was owned by rich men who lived elsewhere in the empire. Even British landowners need not have been local individuals, and in some cases they may have been institutions; much land is also likely to have been owned by landowners overseas. One of the great private benefactors of the Christian Church was the lady Melania, who, in order to give to the Church, sold off lands in Italy, Sicily, and several provinces in North Africa. She also had property in Spain and in Britain. Even small landowners relatively rarely held a single, compact block of land, and estates normally consisted of holdings in various places. Pliny the Younger, indeed, discussed the advantages and disadvantages of this system. Though the accumulation of such scattered holdings might be accidental or deliberate, the advantage was the spreading of risk against natural or man-made disaster.

Land was not only attractive because it was the basis of high social respectability: it was also extremely profitable to be the owner of landed property on a large scale. Melania drew a huge income, yet financially she was only in the middle rank of the fourth-century senatorial class in the west. This, of course, was also the century of the greatest development of the villa in Britain, and we noted earlier the suspicion that some owners may have transferred themselves, or at least their investments, from Gaul to Britain. We have no way of knowing how often a particular villa might see its owner, if ever. We must very often be dealing with tenants or bailiffs, and the latter, the *vilicus*, was frequently a freedman or a trusted slave. Yet some great owners did care about their property and travelled to visit it. Pliny complains frequently about the labour of looking after his own and his mother's estates, yet conveys the impression that he rather enjoyed it. The relationship between such a landlord and the country people, both his own tenants and the people of the local town, is brought out in a letter he wrote to the emperor:

Your late adoptive father, Sir, the deified emperor Nerva, encouraged public benefactions both in his speeches and by his example. I asked him if I might transfer to the town of Tifernum statues of earlier emperors that I had acquired as the result of legacies, and which, as they came, I had housed on my estate some way from the town. I further asked if I might add one of himself. He gave his permission, and I wrote immediately to the town council asking them to designate a site on which I could erect a temple at my own cost. Their answer did me the honour of allowing me to choose the site myself . . . I should therefore be very grateful if you would let me add a statue of yourself to the others that will be housed at the temple I am intending to build, and also give me leave of absence from my duties so that I can have the work done as soon as possible. However, I should be lacking in candour if I exploited your kindness by not mentioning the benefit to my own private affairs. The farms I possess in that area produce an income of over 400,000 sesterces, and I cannot put off letting them, particularly as the new tenants should be in to take care of the pruning of the vines, and this has to be carried out more or less immediately. Also, a series of bad harvests have made me think that I must consider reducing the rents, and to estimate the amounts I must be there myself. If you will allow me thirty days leave, I shall be most grateful at being able to complete my demonstration of loyalty to you and settle my own affairs there. I am afraid I cannot manage in less time, as the town and the farms are more than 150 miles from Rome.

It will readily be appreciated from this that it is generally impossible to know from archaeological evidence alone whether, on a particular villa site, we are dealing with a resident owner or someone who rarely appeared in person, if ever. Cato urged owners to build a *villa urbana* on their properties, for it would give them an incentive to visit them, for a farm that was frequently seen by its proprietor was one that flourished. This wise advice, however, should not lead us to assume (as is often the case) that a Roman villa was always a farm. A villa was a Roman house in the country. A *villa urbana* was a country house with pretensions to dignified living; a *villa rustica* was purely functional. Both might exist on one estate, or even in the same complex. Varro makes it perfectly clear that the term 'villa' is properly applied to both categories. He thought that it ought to be associated with husbandry, but he was writing against the background of a traditional belief in the moral worth of country life and labour, and as a hard-headed Roman. Property ought to pay. We do not have to take his definition too seriously: he was prepared to allow chickens, bees, an aviary, a fish-pond, a warren, or even the rearing of dormice for the table, to qualify. Pliny, discussing a small country property in which Suetonius was interested, remarks that a literary man needs only a modest house and enough land to go with it to provide pleasure. Under the umbrella term 'villa', the range was enormous, from the seaside establishments of the very rich outside Rome, to the smallholder's farmhouse. It is equally clear that, between one owner and another, the importance of the 'economic' activity varied very greatly.

An occasional Romano-British villa, such as Lullingstone, in Kent, allows one to guess at the sort of owner. A pair of Antonine portrait busts were carefully preserved there, of a kind that suggests that the family included holders of public office. It is equally rare to have sufficient evidence to postulate imperial estate or, in the late period, Church property. The ninety-seven infant burials found at the Hambleden villa near Marlow raised the possibility of a rural industry employing female slaves. The fact that the villa was a modest one, facing away from the compound, has suggested that the enterprise was an imperial weaving-mill or a similar state concern supervised by an official, though it could equally well have been under the resident agent of a great property owner. In the case of the very simple villas, we cannot know whether they were in the hands of free owners of modest means, or tenants (in the fourth century probably tied to the land), or bailiffs.

Proceeding down the scale from these simple villas, there is a gradual progression to the more or less untouched native farm, and no clear line can be drawn between them. Differences in prosperity, in the availability and price of materials, and in local taste make it extremely likely that what was acceptable in one part of the country was not acceptable in another, even at the same level in society, and that these standards changed with time within a locality. In the Fens, for example, there is very little large timber and no stone to be had locally: the building materials to hand are clay and reeds. Yet comfortable and long-lasting houses are still made of these materials in East Anglia, and both the size of the house-plots and the amount of Roman portable objects, including plate and coin hoards, that have been found in the region suggest a good standard of life. Future research has to concentrate on defining the standards within a particular area at a particular time, comparing sites with their neighbours and establishing local definitions, before it will be possible to label any one example with confidence. We have to recognize that when we use 'villa' as a technical term in Romano-British studies, we have to use it with different emphases and degrees of precision depending on circumstances. We also have to recognize that when we use it thus, we may not be employing it in quite the way that a Roman would have done. It is quite obvious that we should follow Roman practice and confine it to houses in the country. But our problem is a special one: we need some criteria by which to distinguish the *archaeological* remains of villas. Thus, for our purposes, we may need to be more exclusive in our use of the word than they were. Just where a Roman would have drawn the line between a 'native' house and a villa at the lower end of the scale, we do not know, and the probability is that he would not have needed to worry about it. Even remembering the proviso about establishing standards for particular times and places, it is, for example, impossible to know whether the large farmhouses of the fourth-century northern Fenlands would have been villas or not to a Roman observer. But, without being too pedantic, we need both local definitions and a broader definition, one that is not too far from the concept of a 'Roman villa', which has an accepted, if in detail inaccurate, meaning to the informed layman. Probably the nearest we can get to such a description is to apply the word to any house in the countryside that shows clear signs of the inhabitants having both accepted the Roman style of life to a significant degree, and of having achieved the prosperity to put this into practice in more than a very minor way. Archaeologically, this is likely to require signs of Roman forms of building construction and decoration to a certain level—for example, tiles, dressed stone, painted plaster, hypocausts, or mosaics. An abundance of pottery or small finds of little intrinsic value will not do for this purpose, as there is ample evidence of these being acquired by communities that otherwise changed their style of life very little. On the other hand, we shall certainly miss some villas by using these criteria, since there must have been examples (particularly where building materials were expensive or relatively impermanent) that do not show up archaeologically, but whose inhabitants had adopted personal fashions and a Roman outlook on life to a considerable degree. Such are the limitations of archaeology.

Having admitted the uncertainties inherent in the nature of the evidence, it is nevertheless worth looking at the distribution of Romano-British villas in one or two stretches of countryside, for something of social significance may emerge. We may start by taking the very example of the Fenland, for there is a major difference between the seaward and inland parts of it. There are no unmistakably Romanized houses on the silt lands towards the Wash (if we can omit the large fourth-century farms, whose status is uncertain). It appears that, once the district to be occupied was defined by higher authority, a large number of peasant cultivators were allowed to develop the land in the early second century as best they could, probably, but not certainly, as tenants of imperial property. Thus the overall pattern is built up of hundreds of small single farms and nucleated settlements, surrounded by their stockyards and other small enclosures, some of which were probably tilled, and tending to cluster in groups with large open areas between, not unlike much of the medieval English landscape. But of the Fen Edge inland, it was noted in 1970:

The skirtlands present a rather different pattern of settlement. The small single farms or minor village settlements still appear, but there is a fair sprinkling of sites on which there are known or probable villas (e.g. at Exning, Swaffham Prior and Feltwell). These occur even as near the silts as the island of Stonea and Denver. It might be thought that some of these represent the estates of private persons, perhaps the *conductores* who farmed the rents of the imperial properties. At any rate it is impossible to argue for an imperial estate in the peat fens and their skirtlands as a whole on the grounds of a uniform lack of villas, though of course this cannot rule out the possibility that the emperors acquired these villa properties piecemeal . . . Indeed there is a little evidence for the presence of one of the Severan political party on one of the sites at Mildenhall, which suggests that the process of confiscation which was so drastic in Spain was being carried out also in the province which had produced Severus' most formidable rival. It also does not rule out the presence of substantial blocks of imperial domain land in between these private estates—part . . . has this appearance and significantly seems to have traces of planned layout. Nevertheless, remains in the skirtland seem to suggest the individual *fundus* (farm or estate) as the unit rather than vast tracts of imperial *saltus* let out to small tenants. This is, indeed, likely, since most of it was not virgin land, unlike the silts, but had had Iron Age occupation even if this was sometimes sparse. Similarly in the area immediately adjoining the fen edge proper, around Maxey and Tallington, pre-Roman boundaries were retained in use. It seems very likely that some properties passed into Roman hands intact, or remained in those of Romanized descendants of the pre-Roman owners. Such people, moreover, are the most likely to have become decurions and *conductores*.

Other types of evidence from different parts of the country point in the same direction. It may well have been Romanized gentry of this sort who erected the great barrows or burial mounds known as the Bartlow Hills, on the Essex border not many miles south of the Fen Edge. There is a little evidence for a modest villa alongside these striking family monuments, one of which produced, among the rich collection of grave-goods of Roman manufacture, an iron folding-stool such as a slave would carry for his master's use. As Agricola realized, it was not too difficult for tribal aristocrats to adopt Roman ways. The villa at Park Street in Hertfordshire was preceded by a native farm, and it was the earlier phase that produced a slave chain and a manacle. Similarly, the great Iron Age hoard of metalwork found in the ancient lake of Llyn Cerrig on Anglesey represents a collection of objects from many parts of Britain, and seems to have been thrown in as votive deposits. It includes a gang chain, which must have been made for slaves or prisoners well before the Roman conquest. There is no direct evidence in Roman Britain for the great slave-run estates or *latifundia* of Republican Italy, with their barracks reminiscent of the American south. By imperial times Roman writers were doubting their economic efficiency and rating tenant farmers more highly. Indeed, Varro, writing in the late first century BC, was already preferring free labourers to slaves, as bringing a better return. Cato, a century earlier, had noted the rations to be allowed for chain-gangs, but was talking at that early date about the rules for tenancies in which free men worked the land in exchange for a small portion of the crop. Under the Empire, as conquests became less frequent and the demands of the army for recruits from captured barbarians rose, the availability of new slaves must have decreased. Home-bred slaves were, indeed, barred from joining the army under severe penalties—an enactment much in the interest of the slave-owners —but prisoners of war were a different case if the state decided to enrol them. By the second century AD there was a move towards the system of rents being paid as a percentage of the crop rather than as a fixed annual sum, as being more flexible in terms of good years and bad, and overcoming the sort of management problem that we have seen worrying Pliny. Two seasons of excavation on the large second-century village or small town at Hockwold produced vast quantities of coarse pottery (though very little fine) but not a single coin, and there is a suspicion that the settlement had been attached to a villa. It looked like a settlement where money was hardly used, and suggested either slaves or tenants paying in kind.

Security for the tenant on a Roman estate was theoretically very poor: tenancies were relet at regular intervals, normally every five years or less, and the system is reminiscent of the 'hiring-fairs' for servants that existed in rural England until recent times. Nevertheless, in practice a good tenant was a great asset, and one may imagine that the reletting of the tenancies on an estate was often more like the stages in a modern lease when the rent may be revised. Moreover, emperors anxious to encourage the cultivation of marginal lands improved security of tenure, sometimes making it hereditary, and granting remission of rent for those prepared to take on poor land. In some cases, those who wanted good land had also to take a proportion of bad. The movement over the centuries was away from slave-worked, direct-labour estates towards a system of long-term tenancies, passing from generation to generation. Diocletian's act in making these *coloni* into a tied occupation, like so many of his reforms, took an existing

trend, enlarged upon it, and gave it the force of law. In the fourth
century the villa system was indeed beginning to look very like
the medieval relationship of lord and peasant.

Returning to the southern Fenlands, we find that the occupation clustered thickly in a band along the slopes leading down
towards the peat fen proper, with practically no finds actually
from the peat itself, yet soon becoming scarce as one proceeds
uphill further away from the fen. There was intense utilization
of the gravel terraces by farms of simple native type, and such
villas as there were had pleasant sites on the slopes. It seems clear
that the fen was being intensively exploited, and that Roman
settlement and field systems came as close as possible to (and
clearly occasionally below) the flood-line. As far as can be judged,
the villas themselves were comparatively modest, probably in the
main representing the homes of native farmers who had managed to achieve a reasonable degree of Roman comfort. But there
were a few rather grander establishments (for example, the probable villa at Fenhouse Farm, Brandon). Indeed the south-eastern
corner of the Fenland does seem to have been a sector where
there was some concentration of larger villas, and perhaps rather
fewer native farms. Nevertheless, we may be reasonably certain
that all these villas were making the maximum possible use of
the fen, without being uncomfortably close to it.

A very similar pattern, with villa settlement relatively high on
the slope and native farms further down, is emerging on the
northern edge of the Somerset levels. A more extreme example of
this tendency of villa and native types of establishment to occupy
separate but adjacent areas appears in yet another part of the
country. The upper Thames gravel terraces were intensively
settled and farmed in Iron Age and Roman times. The general
appearance of the native settlements is very similar to those in
the Fens. Here, however, an important extra dimension has been
added to our knowledge. In the Fenland the waterlogged nature
of the land in the immediate pre-Roman period had prevented
late Iron Age occupation. In the upper Thames Valley, on the
other hand, Iron Age farmers had been active, and it is clear that
the decisive change to a settled form of agriculture with regular
boundaries had already taken place before the area fell into
Roman hands. Yet there is very little trace of villas on the river-

plain itself—a marginal site being the probable villa at Red Lodge, Ducklington, near Witney. Yet once the slopes of the Cotswolds are reached, the valleys of the tributaries of the Thames, particularly the Windrush, Evenlode, and Glyme, are thick with villas. They were presumably served by side-roads (*deverticula*) off Akeman Street, which crosses these valleys on its way from Alchester to Cirencester. Today this is still a district of large country houses, and, like theirs, the home-farm boundaries of the villas must often have come close to one another or marched together, making a continuous landscape. These villas fall into the eastern sector of the great spread of villas around Cirencester, and number amongst them such celebrated examples as North Leigh, Stonesfield, and Ditchley. One may hazard a guess that the villas belonged to landowners who deliberately chose to site their country houses and parks in these very pleasing upland valleys, each close to the congenial company of his neighbours, in good sporting country, and conveniently sited adjacent to the fast road to the small town of Alchester, which was ten miles or so in one direction, and the city of Cirencester, around twenty-five in the other. At the same time, we may surmise, their tenants were farming other properties belonging to them on the less picturesque, but easily worked, flat lands along the Thames itself. There, with some boundaries already fixed and a settled pattern of agriculture already in operation, the landowners (Roman or Romano-Briton) will have been obliged to make few changes in the physical layout of the landscape or in methods of working, but, one suspects, many in organization and management.

We are still hampered in any attempt to reconstruct life in a villa by the strange fact that, even after two centuries of digging on villa sites, there are relatively few in which both the main house and the subsidiary buildings have been excavated. The second problem is the impossibility of being sure to what use many of the rooms in any particular villa were put. Nevertheless, we can say that the diversity of plan is wide. At one end there is the simple single range, often quite small, only differentiated in our definition from the native house by the use of some Roman materials—tiles, perhaps, or cut stone, or wall-plaster, or concrete floors—and a rectangular plan (though rectangular, rather than round, houses are not entirely unknown in Iron Age

Britain). To this was sometimes added a corridor, and then short wings, between which the corridor might make a veranda. In some instances a second corridor is found at the back. A similar structure tends to form the core of the larger villas. Here it is not unusual to find much longer wings, which are then joined at their ends by a wall and gate, making an enclosed front yard or garden. It is relatively rare to find a court completely enclosed on all sides by buildings, though Fishbourne does display this feature and has minor courts of the same type also incorporated in the wings. Beyond the gate is sometimes a second courtyard and a second wall and gate or gatehouse, this lower court seeming to contain more humble buildings. It is not uncommon for one of the wings or lesser buildings to be in the form of the aisled building, which also occurs by itself as a small villa. The main house is generally supplied with at least one bath-suite, usually in a wing and sometimes more or less self-contained. The centre is frequently occupied by a large room, often with a substantial alcove at the back and small passage-like rooms at the side. This room may possess the best mosaics in the house and be one of those heated by means of underfloor and wall ducts, the latter also serving as flues to draw off the smoke from the furnace that supplies heat to the hypocaust below the floor. It is reasonable to assume that this main room is the principal reception room, often serving as the *triclinium* or main dining-room, the top table being placed in the alcove. The side-rooms may well be pantries and serveries. Kitchens are found in the wings; a water-supply by well, spring, or pipe is to be expected, and drains were provided for baths, kitchen, and latrines.

The outer court is most likely to show signs of use for service and agricultural purposes, but this is where our knowledge from excavations fails us most, since primary concentration has until very recently been on the mosaics, wall-plaster, and more elaborate architecture of the principal blocks. We should, however, expect at the least to find stables, coach-house, accommodation for domestic and perhaps farm staff, and storage of every kind, including barns and granaries. We are also likely to find evidence of crafts, such as metalworking. It is important not to magnify all such signs with the misleading term 'industry'. The needs of a large house and estate have, until recent times, always made it economical and sensible to employ a number of crafts-men to make and repair items required by the establishment, and to carry out quite elaborate processes, such as brewing or smithing.

One observation made in the southern Fenland has been par-alleled elsewhere in Britain, notably at Stanwick in Northampton-shire. This is the apparent association of a villa with a village—for example, at Denver, Brandon, and Somersham/Colne. This con-junction of manor-house with village is common in Gaul, where it has been suggested that the village could often outlive the villa, and we should perhaps be more on the look-out in Britain for the remains of villas close to Saxon settlements or to medieval villages. Deserted medieval villages and excavations in churches and churchyards may be particularly rewarding in this context. The observations that the barn at Rivenhall became a ready-made Saxon hall in the fifth century, and that finds from the churchyard point to continued occupation of the site through-out Anglo-Saxon times suggest at the least that suitable parts of villa outbuildings could be used in apparently peaceful continu-ity. The same is perhaps much more likely to have been true on a wide scale of the associated villages, where Germanic people may already have been settled, or where a purely British peasant population simply passed from one master to another.

We can study peasant settlement in the Roman period in two ways. The Fenland survey allowed us to look at a large area where there had been much less Iron Age occupation, so that it was possible to study a pattern of peasant occupation without it hav-ing been predetermined by existing settlement. Other projects in the south seek to look at the problem the other way round—from the total history of a landscape where there has been more or less continuous farming before, during, and after the Roman period and on to the present day. In the permanently garrisoned areas of Britain the impact of Rome is likely to have been different from those where an almost totally civilian way of life developed, but it was not necessarily any the less. The commu-nities perhaps least likely to have been culturally affected are those that dwelt beyond Hadrian's Wall. It is outside the present brief to deal with the peoples of the Highlands of Scotland and the northern isles, who were never thoroughly conquered and only momentarily even in name within the empire. But for the sites between the Antonine and Hadrianic Walls we are fortunate that many years of field-work and excavation have given us a considerable amount of detailed information.

This work on the Roman 'intramural zone' is being joined by much needed reappraisal of the native communities of the north-west, *behind* Hadrian's Wall. These sites are perhaps the most likely of the rural settlements of the north to show signs of close contact with the Roman military and with the mixed civilian population settled outside the forts, and probably formed the core of the farming population of the *civitas Carvetiorum* that was eventually organized. Long-term survey work on the more remote and often wilder western fells in Cumbria and Lancashire tackled an intermediate situation. There the communities were continuously ringed by Roman garrisons for over three hundred years. It is true that many of the settlements lay in the kind of countryside that was extremely difficult to police, and, as in the early days, the network of forts doubtless continued to perform the essential function of control. Nevertheless, ecological research suggested that the environment was not as harsh as would appear from the modern landscape, since the woodland cover was apparently greater. There is evidence for forest and grassland pastoralism and some arable cultivation, raising the possibility that troops continued to be stationed here in large numbers because they could be fed easily from a population less able to complain effectively than the villa-owners of the south. Either way, any economic or cultural advantages that the locals in these frontier districts gained from Roman rule are likely to have been won against decidedly adverse circumstances.

21

THE ECONOMY

The 'economics' of the ancient world is an area in which we are more in danger of anachronism than perhaps any other. Though emperors intervened from time to time in one 'economic' field or another—debasing or reforming currency, trying to control prices or the movement of labour, imposing or altering taxes—few, if any, of their measures had an economic motive in the sense employed in modern government. It was in terms of revenue and politics that emperors considered the economy of provinces, not in the context of any general economic theory aimed at a common good. No one attempted to co-ordinate the economic life of the Roman world. If we are to avoid being unhistorical, ancient economics can only be viewed as the separate activities of enormous numbers of individuals pursuing their own activities, some of their own free will, some under compulsion. This chapter might, indeed, have been better entitled 'Wealth and Work' than 'The Economy', though nowadays a section on economics is expected from historians of any culture. The sum of all this activity does add up to a whole, however incoherent and constantly changing, but that whole must be recognized as the undirected and largely accidental thing that it was.

Archaeologists under pressure to account for the distribution of particular categories of artefacts are peculiarly prone to fall into the temptation of employing whatever fashionable economic theory seems to fit their observations, however distant in place or time the society on which it was originally erected. We are not considering here those mathematical hypotheses or 'models' constructed by observing patterns apparently discernible in material from the same period of history, though those may individually be subject to objections of their own. The question is one of analogies taken from primitive or early peoples irrespective of date or location, which are particularly dangerous where there is little or no written evidence against which they can be tested. In general, they can be dismissed. However, there is one theory derived from economic anthropology that cannot be ignored, since its influence is strong on modern archaeological thought. It divides 'trade' or the exchange of material objects into two. In primitive societies the objects exchanged, the value set upon them, and the methods of exchange are largely determined by social factors. In sophisticated economies trade is, on the contrary, an activity in itself, with the objective of making profits for the trader or entrepreneur. The theory as applied to Britain sees the Iron Age down to the Roman conquest as almost entirely in the former condition. Valued objects are exchanged as gifts, often as part of an elaborate ritual relating to kinship or political relationships, and chiefly among the élite. The Roman empire appears in contrast as an advanced commercial society. The conquest is seen in economic terms as the imposition of a fundamentally alien system, rooted in completely different attitudes to society and exchange. Further elaboration of the theory seeks to explain features of coin-usage before and in the first few years after the conquest, and to attribute the relative slowness of urbanization to difficulties on the part of the Britons in assimilating the new ways. Only comparatively late does Britain accept the commercial approach to life sufficiently to become wholly integrated into a system of long-distance trade between centres of manufacture based on a fully monetary system.

The original theory, however, has a fundamental flaw. In the simplistic form in which it is applied to Roman Britain, it assumes an almost complete antithesis between one system and the other. This is false. Both can exist within a single society. In modern Japan a highly developed ritual of giving is embedded in social relationships, where favours must be balanced in honour by gifts, and gift by gift. Yet we can hardly ignore the fact that Japan today demonstrates an exceptionally high level of aggressive commercial enterprise. But we do not have to look for modern analogies to illustrate the point. The Roman world itself, through the all-pervasive institution of the *clientela* and the mutual obligations of patronage as practised at many levels of society, displayed immensely strong bonds of social duty, marked by exchanges of favours and gifts, by the public recognition of indebtedness, and by the honour that was obtained from acquiring, through the use of influence, advantages for others where social ties dictated. At the same time, the Romans were exploiting every means of making money through industry and commerce, with the senatorial class making the gesture of recognizing ancient taboos against such traditionally degrading activity by putting up the thin pretence of working through nominees. Commercial activity was, we may confidently assert, much more important in Roman society than it had been in Iron Age Britain, but whatever the truth about individual artefacts found here, we cannot use a supposed antithesis between the attitudes of the British élites towards money and exchange and those of the Roman invaders either to explain political tensions after the conquest or to invent economic ones.

As with the population—a subject with which it is, of course, linked—the Romano-British economy has left us almost totally deficient in reliable statistics. That alone would make most modern methods of studying economic life inapplicable. We are, moreover, dealing with a world that, though highly sophisticated, worked in such a different way from our own that many of the commonplaces of modern economics are largely irrelevant. Take, for example, the concept of the balance of trade. In terms of the financial relationship of the Roman empire with the outside world, this may make some limited sense, since many of the most expensive imports had to be paid for in the only acceptable way, in precious metals (whether in the form of coin, when not debased, or bullion), and the Roman state could only lay its hands on a certain amount of those metals. Whether the imports were paid for by the state or individuals, there was probably a net outflow of wealth in that sense. But one may suspect that since this was largely a matter of the luxury trades, the effect was small. On some frontiers the empire was exporting manufactured goods, and may well have gained more than it lost. But figures for volume—indeed, even order of magnitude—are so lacking as to make estimates entirely vain.

If one attempts to consider the balance of trade of a single province, such as Britain, the concept is almost meaningless, since the empire had a single currency and no internal tariff barriers. There were, certainly, frontier duties of a sort (*portoria*), but these were a form of tax and not intended to manipulate trade for economic purposes. It is revealing that the writer Strabo, working in the last days of the Roman Republic and the early years of the Principate, remarked that if Britain were to be conquered, there would be an actual loss of revenue to Rome. It is known that provinces were grouped together for the purposes of the *portoria*, and it is quite likely that a higher rate was levied on trade at the frontiers of the empire itself. This therefore implies either that, if conquered, Britain would be included with Gaul and no border taxes would be collected, or that the rate would be much reduced. The actual percentage at which this border tax was levied, however, never seems to have been high, and the change can have had little effect on the flow of trade or on prices when Britain was incorporated in the empire. Strabo was thinking purely in fiscal terms.

While it is probably fruitless to seek to understand the underlying working of the ancient economy, we can look at the surface and gain some idea of how ordinary people were affected by economic activity. In terms of employment, at least three-quarters of the people in Roman Britain, probably more, were in agriculture. By the fourth century the country was apparently more than self-sufficient in grain, since in an emergency Julian was able to increase regular shipments to the Rhine. In the first century Agricola had dealt with abuses in the levying of corn supplies from the provincials for the army, but there is no hint that grain was in short supply even at that early date, merely that the system was being deliberately mishandled for dishonest purposes by Roman officials. Corn was supposed to be delivered to a convenient point and paid for by the authorities: under proper management, this ought to have meant a guaranteed market and a cash income for the producers, something they can never have had on any scale before. This by itself represents a revolution in agricultural economics, even if the price offered by the army was not generous. The Roman army consumed enormous quantities of grain. One modern estimate put the need of a legion at 500 bushels a week. In addition, we now have ample evidence that

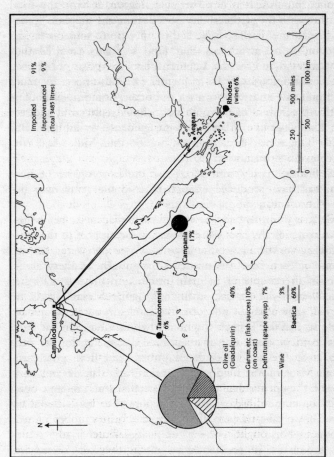

IMPORTS TO THE EARLY CAPITAL. Analysis of amphora contents on a site at Colchester reveals that before the Boudiccan war southern Spain was by far the largest supplier, and that Spanish olive oil made up 40 per cent of the total by volume.

Imported 91%
Unprovenanced 9%
(Total 3485 litres)

Rhodes (wine) 6%

Aegean 2%

Campania 17%

Tarraconensis 6%

Camulodunum

Olive oil (Guadalquivir) 40%

Garum, etc (fish sauces) 10% (on coast)

Defrutum (grape syrup) 7%

Wine 3%

Baetica 60%

N

0   250   500
0   500   1000 km
0   250   500 miles

the army had a much more mixed diet than was once believed. Substantial quantities of meat, vegetables, and fruit had to be found for the troops as well as cereals. The supply operation was enormous. The government set a fixed price and decided how much was to be purchased in any particular region, leaving the local authorities with the responsibility of collecting the supplies. Sometimes the army itself handled the operation, sometimes the procurator or other officials, and food was also acquired thus for civilian staff and for the Imperial Post. There was, of course, ample opportunity under lax emperors or local officers for fraud on the one side and extortion on the other. Some scholars consider that the system of purchase was wholly replaced by a direct tax in kind (*annona militaris*), but the evidence is disputed. But whether bought or collected direct, the food still had to be forthcoming in huge quantities.

This brings sharply into focus the crucial problem of how Britain can have produced enough to feed the army over and above the civilian population unless overall production was increased very substantially beyond what it had been before the Roman conquest. Without any allowance for supplies to the cities or exports, something in the region of 100,000 acres (40,000 hectares) of corn land was needed to supply the military alone. Moreover, in this matter of grain production there is a further puzzle. Where the typical, small, rectangular 'Celtic' fields are preserved, they often do not look like arable on a scale to achieve this result. For the Fenlands, where a whole landscape has been revealed (and where it was once assumed that the enclosures were largely arable fields), the evidence points away from grain production. Most of the field-enclosures are quite small, and huddle round the settlements. Between the settlements are large open spaces, sometimes divided by watercourses or long boundary ditches. If we take this together with the large number of animal bones—horse, cattle, sheep, or goats—found in the settlements, the picture is consistent with animal husbandry on ranches or common land. These animals were of great military importance: wool was required for military uniforms; hide was used for tents, shields, protective clothing, straps, and belts; gut was probably required for the torsion parts of artillery. Horses became more and more important, as the cavalry arm increased. And there was, of course, also the matter of food. Analysis of bones at Hockwold indicated that all the types of animal represented there were eaten locally, but suggested that there was little slaughtering of young animals—there was certainly no evidence of a need to reduce herds in winter. It is known that the transhipment of beasts on the hoof and as salted meat was part of the officially organized system of supply in the Roman world. With this, may have been associated the large number of sites in the region that have produced vessels used in the salt industry. This would, of course, affect the bone statistics at the farms where the animals were raised but not consumed. On the other hand, the large numbers of bones from older animals indicated substantial dairy and wool-farming.

The Fenland, then, is eliminated as a major cereal producer. The small enclosures that clustered around the settlements probably represent yards, paddocks, and gardens. Some of them may well have grown produce for the use of the farmers and their families, and, as in the upper Thames Valley, there may have been hay meadows, but the chief output depended primarily on open pasture. This warns us to be cautious elsewhere of assuming, without closer examination, that relatively small areas of 'Celtic fields' associated with settlements represent arable on any scale. It is, of course, true that there are places where there are really substantial areas covered with rectangular fields, for example, Bathampton Down in the south-west, or Grassington in Yorkshire. There is, in fact, good reason to think that arable agriculture was practised quite extensively in the highland zone of Britain as well as the lowland. Roman organization was certainly capable, as we have just mentioned, of transportation over long distances, but it is also known that efforts were made to supply the army as much as possible from nearby sources. We may thus assume that while the bulk of the army was in the north and Wales, the army drew the maximum quantities of corn from neighbouring upland farms, before searching for sources further afield.

This still leaves us with questions as to how the increased production was achieved, a problem the more acute if the garrisons were entirely supplied by the highlands rather than the villas of the lowlands, though it is unnecessary to press the argument that far. The question of improved agricultural technology under the

Romans has from time to time been raised and often dismissed. At one time it was thought that the 'Belgic' people introduced a wheeled plough, enabling them to farm heavier soils previously unworkable, but that theory is currently out of fashion. However, recent re-examination of the famous Piercebridge bronze model of a Roman ploughman and his team has suggested an advanced version of the prehistoric 'ard', which has had a flange added to the share, earth-boards, and a coulter or cutting tool, which would be capable of working fairly heavy soils behind a pair of oxen or cows. Indeed, experiments at Butser have indicated that even the simple ard (provided that the tip of the wooden spike is protected with metal to prevent rapid wear) can cope effectively with heavy soils. It is very important that we should not imagine the Roman farmer as being restricted by his tools to cultivating only the easiest land and excluded from soils worked extensively in later ages. In some respects, in fact, the Roman may have had more advanced technology at his command than his Iron Age predecessor. The multiple reaping-machine, known from the Buzenol relief sculpture in Belgium, has not yet been found in Britain, but some of the enormous scythes or reed-cutting blades found on the Fen Edge prove the capacity for producing large hand- or semi-mechanical tools. But, overall, the farming techniques required for large-scale production were probably already here before the conquest.

It is quite possible that the existing Iron Age agricultural system could have produced more than it did if the incentives had been there. With the arrival of the Romans, came a ready availability of consumer goods to encourage the farmer to produce a surplus that could be sold (not to mention a taxation system that imposed a need to raise cash), and officials to back this up with compulsion if need be. It is also likely that the widespread adoption of more efficient methods of processing and storage of food in bulk in the Roman period also encouraged the farmer to produce more. Modern experiments have shown that Iron Age grain-storage pits worked well if properly made, but it is difficult to see why a farmer should store more than he—and perhaps his lord—required for immediate use and a modest reserve, except in areas where grain was being produced for export. But with military and civil granaries ready to take what he could grow, an entirely new dimension entered the economics of farming.

Despite the potential of the native farm, however, it was probably the advent of the Roman or Romanized estate-owner that actually changed the scale of agricultural output, taken over the whole country. This new system we can broadly call the villa economy, remembering, however, that it is highly likely that many of the old native farms became part of the organization without necessarily being adjacent to a villa or being directly run from a villa. The agricultural surplus to feed the urban population had to come from somewhere, and if we can now see the army as being largely supplied from its highland hinterland, then the main production of the lowland farms can have gone to the cities. In that market, prices could not be fixed by the private consumer to the extent that the army could achieve, and a much better return to the producer can be imagined. A small proportion of the surplus from the farms was doubtless earmarked for the governor and other official purposes—and this must have increased in the south with the re-establishment of garrisons in the third and fourth centuries—but most of it was presumably available on the open market for the highest price it could fetch. Nor should we assume that imperial estates were outside this system, for in areas where the immediate priority was not keeping the army supplied, the emperor will surely have expected his lands to produce the maximum profit. In organizational terms, no clear line can be drawn between estates belonging to the emperor and to private owners; the economics were broadly the same for both categories, except in so far as the private owner may often have consumed a larger proportion of the products of the estate himself, and have spent more of the profits on non-utilitarian projects, such as villas and other beautification, than on the actual estate itself. The real change in the system from prehistoric to Roman times is a matter of character of ownership, direction, and philosophy. The direction may come from a private owner working his estate himself or through tenants, or it may be an imperial procurator letting the land out to small farmers or large. But the essential concept common to all is the landed estate *existing in a world with money economy, urban markets,*

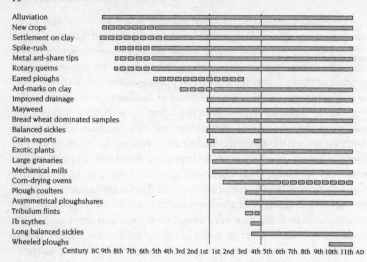

Century BC 9th 8th 7th 6th 5th 4th 3rd 2nd 1st 1st 2nd 3rd 4th 5th 6th 7th 8th 9th 10th 11th AD

AGRICULTURAL INNOVATION in Britain under Roman rule was considerable, as this chart illustrates. Much of it occurred in the late Roman period, possibly triggered by shortage of labour but almost certainly also associated with richer estates, demonstrating that this was not an era of stagnation in the countryside.

and the availability of organized transport. Someone now not only had to think about making the crops grow, but also had to keep accounts, calculate profit and loss, and take heed of the requirements of officialdom. We have passed from a comparatively primitive world to one in which conscious estate management is not only practised, but also it must be remembered, studied, and written about. Some owners were doubtless willing simply to allow their stewards to collect rent from the peasants or to drive the slaves, but many must have read their Columella or Varro. Though the detailed precepts of those authors might be more applicable to Mediterranean agriculture, the reader must have been fully aware that the management of country estates was a proper subject for a Roman gentleman, and been prepared to think about ways of extracting more profit from the land. They were often now in the position of having bigger and much more varied overall holdings of land, with parcels and whole farms in different districts or even different provinces. Large landowners will have had wider information and substantial resources at their command. In estate management this means the ability to take decisions (including investment and the buying and selling of land, as well as how to farm particular properties) within a broader context—though doubtless often with results not much to the liking of individual tenants or other local people.

For a long time it was thought that in the fourth century there was a widespread change from arable cultivation to grazing, representing large-scale ranching on the part of selfish villa-owners in place of labour-intensive arable farming. This was seen as depressing the lot of the peasant farmer—even dispossessing him. Indeed, long ago Varro had deplored the turning-over of arable to pasture. Yet we have to remember that Roman writers of the first century BC were living in the recent shadow of the social and political upheavals associated in their minds with the drift of the Italian small farmer to Rome; and we ourselves are conditioned by tales of the complaints of late medieval peasants against sheep and by the historical legacy of the Highland clearances. We have to dismiss these influences, and see Romano–British villa agriculture in terms of a much more mixed production at all periods than previously imagined. Against an increasing pressure on agricultural labour in the later Empire, any movement towards increased animal husbandry that might be detected in particular districts must be recognized as a sign of prudent management of the land.

The picture of a farming system that could both support the larger non-agricultural population of the Roman period and bring a handsome return to its owners begins to build up. On the scale and character of estates, we have already noted that historians have tended to assume too readily what we might call a 'unitary' estate. Few large country landowners today are lucky enough to possess all their land in one piece, even on a single estate, and great efforts are frequently made to tidy up the holding and increase efficiency by purchase of adjacent fields or whole farms. Pliny the Younger, as we noted earlier, rehearsed the arguments for and against this practice. On the one hand, he pointed out, there were the obvious economies: only one house had to be kept and furnished (including single sets of hunting-gear and the like); one bailiff could supervise the whole property, and the owner would need no more than a single foreman. On the other hand there was the risk of putting all one's eggs in one basket. It might be better to spread the risk from weather and the other hazards of farming by having land in different places. But in the end the choice came down to the quality of the land and buildings, how much money would need to be put into the property, and whether the purchase price was right.

Other factors also affected the size and character of estates. Losses occurred through forced sale of parcels of land in times of hardship. On the other hand there were accretions through inheritance or marriage, not necessarily resulting in a tidy overall holding. It may perhaps have been comparatively easy to establish a neat estate at the time of the conquest, but three hundred years later it is extremely unlikely that this was still the case. We suggested earlier that villa-owners were leasing out land away from the villa and its immediate surroundings to peasant farmers. This means that a single villa might have as part of its economy not only the home farm and tenants adjacent to it, but other tenants well away from its boundaries. This would considerably increase the size of the financial and management unit that a single villa represented; and we have to remember that we are talking in terms of upwards of 1,000 villas. If we add to that the probability that many were backed by the resources of very large landowners, including the emperor himself, then the hypothesis of a large overall rise in production from the land under Roman rule becomes feasible. This could be true with minimal change in technology, and perhaps without any substantial increase in the rural population.

Anyone who has excavated on Romano-British sites will know that, by and large, they indicate a population that was a heavy consumer of manufactured goods; and in the south at least, this extends even to the humblest peasant settlements. The finds imply a large volume of trade, both of items produced in Britain and of imports from other provinces. This in its turn implies industry, and we shall see that Britain was not only a manufacturing province, but a primary producer of raw materials as well. We also have to take account of important commercial activities that do not fall under any of these heads, notably the building industry and all its associated trades, which in itself was an importer of materials and a major stimulus to home production.

There is no doubt that the Romans regarded Britain as a valuable producer. Before the conquest Strabo listed agricultural exports (cattle, hides, and corn), hunting-dogs, slaves, and metals —gold, silver, and iron. Tacitus confirmed the richness of the crops and the importance of the mineral deposits of the island. At the end of the third century the author of the panegyric to Constantius as Caesar still saw Britain in the same terms: the abundance of the crops, the great amount of pasture, and the large quantities of metal ores. But the panegyrist also went on to talk not only of Britain 'with ports on every side', but also of its enormous profitability in terms of financial revenue. Throughout its contact with Britain, the Roman view had little reference to any idyllic vision of bountiful plenty, and a great deal to do with profit, the prize of victory.

We have seen that the Romans set a high store on the prospects of a good return from the extractive industries, principally metals. Britain was to supply gold, silver, lead, iron, copper, and tin. Both Caesar and Tacitus also clearly put pearls under the extractive heading, though the output is likely to have been tiny. Not so, as we have seen, the oysters themselves! Stone was very extensively quarried, and only in a small number of cases, as at Fishbourne, do we have evidence for the import of special stone from far away, except in relatively small pieces, such as are from time to time found in mosaics and cladding. The wholesale importing of large blocks or part-finished architectural sections, as the ancients were accustomed to do in the Mediterranean, does not seem to have been a feature of importance. Nevertheless, the transporting of stone around Britain was often undertaken. The great slabs of the monument of Classicianus, for example, were brought from one of the limestone areas to London. This emphasizes the mechanical efficiency of Roman transport, whatever its financial cost. Timber was perhaps the largest of the industries supplying the building trade, particularly in the first and early second centuries, when most military as well as private buildings were in timber or half-timber. It must always have been in great demand, not only for the minor trades, such as door- and furniture-making, but to supply major items such as

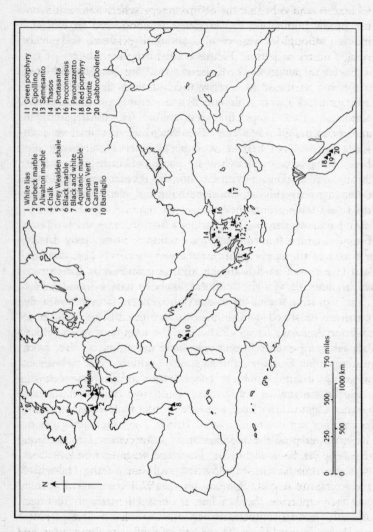

1 White lias
2 Purbeck marble
3 Alwalton marble
4 Chalk
5 Grey Wealden shale
6 Black marble
7 Black and white
   Aquitanic marble
8 Campan Vert
9 Carrara
10 Bardiglio

11 Green porphyry
12 Cipollino
13 Semesanto
14 Thasos
15 Portasanta
16 Proconnesus
17 Pavonazzetto
18 Red porphyry
19 Diorite
20 Gabbro/Dolerite

A LUXURY IMPORT TRADE: sources of ornamental building-stone for London.

beams and joists for roofs and floors. Moreover, it was widely used for many heavy constructions like bridges and wharves, even for cranes and other pieces of machinery where we would now use metal. Lumbering can properly be considered an extractive industry, though there seems to be some evidence for replacement forestry as part of Romano-British agriculture.

Fuel and power in the ancient world are subjects on which much has been said and still relatively little is known, as figures are again lacking. It is reasonably clear that the main source of fuel was timber. The charcoal-burner is a traditional part of the ancient scene, gaining literary immortality in Aristophanes' political comedy *The Acharnians*. Since the charcoal industry must have added greatly to the ancient consumption of natural forest, its impact on the environment needs reinvestigation. In Britain open-cast coal-mining also provided what may have been more than a minor percentage of the energy requirements both for industry and domestic use. Coal appears, for example, at Heronbridge, where a Roman dock was excavated, from a level dated to the end of the first century or the early second. This dock was within easy reach of both the legionary fortress at Chester and the military tile-factory at Holt. Similarly, coal is found in substantial quantities in forts in the north. There is little doubt that the army made considerable use of it in metal-working, and probably for domestic purposes as well. It appears, too, in the Clwyd lead-processing works, and was used by villas in the south-west for operating their central heating systems. The wonder expressed by the geographical writer Solinus at the strange glowing coals on the altar of Sulis at Bath must have caused considerable amusement to those local gentry who had it shovelled into their hypocausts.

For water-power, there is perhaps more evidence to be found than has yet been identified. Leats and fragments of the works of water-mills at Chesters, Willowford, and on the Haltwhistle Burn indicate that the garrison of the Wall was operating mills, and there are traces in the south at Great Chesterford, Silchester, and Redlands Farm, Stanwick. On the other hand, donkey-power has been implied from fragments of mills at Cirencester and London, and this seems very likely. The ubiquity and efficiency, even to this day, of donkey- and other animal power in the

Mediterranean for grinding and water-lifting suggests that this source of energy was common in the Roman provinces. However, the Romans were capable of constructing extremely elaborate systems to exploit the power of water. In the great complex of mills at Barbegal, near Arles, the designers made the maximum use of the energy available by arranging the sixteen wheels in two series down a hillside. Moreover, water-mills could apparently be built quite quickly. As late as the sixth century we find Justinian's general Belisarius building mills on the Tiber during the siege of Rome to provide emergency food supplies for the city, which suggests not only that experienced designers, craftsmen, and the necessary materials were still to hand, but also that the machinery could be built and installed in a reasonably short time.

The series principle is also seen in the enormous water-wheels that drained the different levels of galleries, one above the other, in the mines of Roman Spain. Similar wheels operated in the Roman gold-mines at Dolaucothi in Wales. The availability of this new mining technology must have given Roman miners an advantage over their Iron Age predecessors not unlike the revolution in the Cornish mining industry made possible by the beam-engine. But it is noticeable that where we have such evidence in Roman Britain, it is in an industry where the product is exceptionally valuable, and where the imperial government was directly interested. The implication is that such installations needed very substantial resources: the ancient world's real lack was not knowledge of how to build some types of large machinery or to carry out complex civil engineering works associated with them, but methods of harnessing and applying energy that were relatively cheap to install and maintain, and whose profitability, once running, was much higher than the use of human and animal power. It is often alleged that the availability of slaves inhibited the technological development of the ancient world, yet Roman authors compare the productivity of slaves unfavourably to that of free workers. We have already noted the decline in the supply of slaves during the Roman period, and although criminals were often condemned to the mines, surviving legislation indicates that mining in particular was frequently in the hands of concessionaires.

Exploitation of the main metal deposits in Britain seems to

have started as soon as the army had won control of each district. This underlines the acute Roman appreciation of the profits of victory. The clearest example of the way in which the organization then developed is the lead-mining industry. The attraction of this product, of course, was not only the lead itself, but also the prospect of extracting silver from it. Gold and silver were obviously vitally important to the imperial government, both for coinage and, under the late Empire, for official payments in plate and ingots. Wherever there is a lead-mining district in Britain, there we should be looking for a military presence, however small. The fort at Whitley Castle near Alston surely supervised the Northumberland lead-mines, but so far evidence is lacking elsewhere on the ground. However, for the Welsh gold-mine at Dolaucothi we do have the fort situated alongside at Pumpsaint. In the course of its life this fort was halved in size, suggesting that though the district in general was pacified, the mines still needed guarding, partly perhaps due to the intrinsic value of the product, but possibly also because of convict labour. For the relatively much larger lead and silver industry, we have better evidence from the discovery of stamped ingots or 'pigs' of lead. It seems reasonably certain that the earliest area to be exploited was the Mendips, since two pigs that were lost in transit towards the south coast bear inscriptions that show that they were cast in AD 49. Another was found on the Somme, stamped by the Second legion under Nero. It may be assumed that a primary task of Vespasian's force in the invasion was to secure the rich metal-bearing areas of the west, and while the Second was consolidating its hold on the population, it clearly supervised the development of the mines.

The army may well have continued to provide security and transport, but at an early stage the government followed its usual course in handing out the immediate administration of the workings to concessionaires (*conductores*). Claims were probably let out by a procurator of mines, and we find both individuals and companies. C. Nipius Ascanius was acting as an imperial agent in AD 60, when his name was stamped on a pig of lead found at Bossington, in Hampshire. Another stamped pig, however, from Carmel (Clwyd), suggests that he later went into business for himself.

By Flavian times the much greater ease with which the surface deposits of Britain could be worked than the mines of Spain and Gaul had proved a serious embarrassment to the imperial government, and production was limited by law, presumably for political reasons such as the protection of interests in the other provinces. But there was clearly still an important local demand for lead for official purposes, as is indicated by the water-pipe from Chester, stamped with the name of Julius Agricola as governor, and the plates of lead with which the Great Bath was lined at Aquae Sulis. This official interest probably explains an apparent change of policy under Hadrian, when the appearance of the emperor's name on pigs from the Derbyshire field, and the absence of private stamps elsewhere suggest closer control of the industry. This may well have been due to the requirements of the vast new military works initiated by Hadrian.

It is not unreasonable to suspect that at this point the limit on production was lifted, and exploitation under imperial management probably continued at a fairly high level throughout the construction and modification of the Hadrianic and Antonine Walls. It is perhaps no coincidence that the last dated pigs are from the reign of Septimius Severus, suggesting that when the Severan reconstruction of Hadrian's Wall had been completed, then demand dropped sharply, and it was no longer necessary to keep the direct administration in being. Without a large requirement for lead as construction material, the relatively low yield of silver from the British ore, particularly the Derby, Shropshire, and Yorkshire deposits, may well have rendered the system unprofitable. However, mining continued, but in the south it was probably in private hands. Nevertheless, since mine-owners had to surrender half their production to the state for the use of the mints, the industry remained of interest to the Roman government while costing it nothing to run.

In the third and fourth centuries there was fresh demand for lead from the British pewter manufacturers, as they filled the gap in the domestic market caused by the decline that we shall observe in the import of fine pottery, and from undertakers, as a fashion for lead coffins spread. Connected with the rise of pewter must have been the increased production that has been noted in the British tin-mines. These indeed seem to have been under some

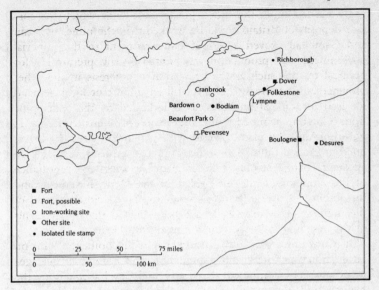

AN INDUSTRY UNDER IMPERIAL CONTROL: the Wealden iron industry. Map of sites at which tiles with the stamp of the Channel fleet (*classis Britannica*) have been found.

degree of state control under the late Empire, as a stamped ingot from Cornwall attests. Both the Spanish tin-mines and the Gallic pottery industries were in decline in this age of barbarian invasions and civil war, and British industry clearly benefited by the opportunity to exploit the market for good quality tableware. There are special difficulties in dating the usage of pewter, since individual pieces not only had a long working life, but could, unlike pottery, be reused as raw material in the factories. It is certain that fine pottery was often treasured, and therefore can appear apparently out of context alongside later coarse wares in the same excavation level, and much samian has been repaired by riveting. Pewter could be even longer-lived, and is also much more easily mended. Nevertheless, the Camerton pewter-works in the Mendips have not been shown to be in operation before the middle of the third century, and most British pewter seems to date from the late third century or the fourth.

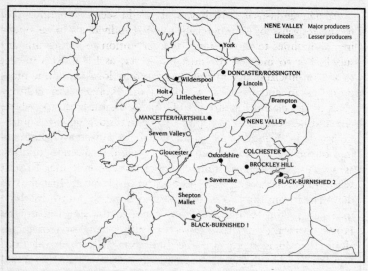

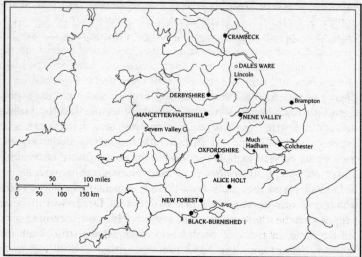

CHANGE IN AN INDUSTRY. *Above*: pottery production in Britain in the late first and second centuries: main groups of kilns. Military purchasers were particularly important. Some pottery was made directly by the army, and some civilian production moved closer to the market. *Below*: pottery production in Britain in the third and fourth centuries: main groups of kilns. There is a marked change towards large producers based in the countryside, such as in the New Forest (Alice Holt) and Oxfordshire.

Ancient industrial growth was, it would seem, sometimes due to the response of commercially minded individuals to an opening, sometimes to direct imperial intervention to secure military supplies or to increase revenue, but never, as far as we can see, to acts of official policy intended to promote local economic prosperity as an end in itself. Work on the Roman iron industry gives us the clearest picture yet of a major British industry whose rise and fall seems directly linked to central government requirements. It is an industry, too, for which we now have glimmerings of those real statistics whose overwhelming absence stultifies, as we have noted, most studies of ancient economic life. To start with the distribution, iron production in Roman Britain was dominated from the late first century to the early fourth by three main areas—the Weald, stretching down to the south coast, the Forest of Dean, and, to a lesser extent, a string of settlements along the 'Jurassic Ridge', the limestone hills that run from Somerset to Northamptonshire and Lincoln. Both in the Weald and the Forest of Dean there is reason to suspect imperial estates, but the Weald discloses an important subtlety. While the western part appears to have been worked by free miners, the east can convincingly be associated with direct involvement of the Roman fleet in Britain, the *classis Britannica*. State involvement on a substantial scale may have started there under Agricola, when major new requirements for iron were created by the large programme of public and private works initiated by him. It seems very likely that a notable role of the fleet was the provision of supplies and technical expertise to the industry, and the exporting of its products. There can be little doubt that the Wealden iron industry was considered of major strategic importance.

Expansion of this south-coast industry seems to have coincided with a similar development in the Forest of Dean, and the date appears to be the early second century. It is very tempting to link this, as in the case of the lead industry, with the Wall and the Hadrianic/Antonine impetus in the cities. This brings us to the figures that have been extracted from the large quantity of data available in the form of slag-heaps. Very briefly, the method of analysis is based on the total amount of slag produced by a site during its life (the length of time and historical period of its operation being dated by the usual archaeological methods), and the probable consumption of iron by Britain under various main headings such as buildings, weapons, tools, and—least easy of all to estimate—ships and boats. By the end of the first century Britain was self-sufficient in iron production. If the true figure for population was in the region of 4 million, then most or all of the production from the civilian works could have been used in Britain, but a substantial surplus may still have remained from the official factories.

There seems, then, a case for supposing that a considerable volume of iron was exported. Where might it go? There is no positive confirmation yet, but the army of the Rhine and the flourishing civil markets of Gaul seem very strong possibilities on general grounds. That this may indeed have been so is supported by an important piece of negative evidence. Around the middle of the third century the official ironworks in the eastern Weald closed down—when the fort at Dover has been demolished, the main base of the *classis Britannica* at Boulogne is reduced, and that fleet itself eventually disappears from the record. One cannot help guessing that this may have had something to do with the barbarian invasions of Gaul, the Gallic Empire, and all the associated political and military upheavals of the second half of the third century on the Continent, though the process seems to have begun in the Severan period. The adverse conditions in Gallic cities, and the impoverishment of the countryside of northern Gaul, marked by abandoned villas, may indicate a collapse of the civil market for British iron abroad. The usurpation of Carausius may well then have cut Britain off at a critical moment from the opportunities presented by the great reconstruction under the Tetrarchy. Another possibility is that the south coast was becoming too vulnerable to pirates, and it is perhaps not pressing speculation too far to suggest that the final closing-down of the eastern Wealden enterprises may be intimately connected with the development of the coastal forts. Naval resources could, on this view, no longer be spared for their old supply and transport function, supporting the Weald industry; instead, they were needed in patrol and attack roles. Moreover, a legacy of Clodius Albinus' challenge for the throne may have been the feeling that it was dangerous to leave the major source of a vital strategic material for the Continent in Britain. Exploitation of Gallic deposits of iron, even if more difficult to work, would be deemed safer in those suspicious times. The British sources of iron could be left to supply Britain alone.

After the loss of the eastern Weald, the general level of production in Britain declined slowly from the middle of the third century. One may reasonably assume that military requirements within Britain (now that their eastern Weald works were shut), and the revival in the building industry from the last quarter of the third century together provided a market for the rest, and it is possible exports revived under the Tetrarchy. Around the middle of the fourth century the output from the surviving main producers seems to have dropped substantially, and it is reasonable to associate this with the troubles that hit Britain at that time. However, that this affected producers more than consumers is suggested by a notable increase in smaller-scale iron-working in towns and villas. We cannot, therefore, argue a collapse in demand. Moreover, the main iron-producing areas seem to have remained active to the end of the century, even if at a much reduced level. In the last quarter of the century there was much domestic activity, as most of the main works closed down. This process, and the point at which it became critical, remains to be charted in detail, and much closer dating is required. It must be connected intimately with the breakdown of central administration and communications, and perhaps most of all with the disintegration of the army and its procurement service. If in the future we can place this more accurately, we shall have a sharper insight into the critical periods AD 369 to 409 and the years immediately after the break with Roman rule.

We should now turn to the best-known class of artefact from Roman Britain: pottery. Here we have a different archaeological situation to consider. Unlike the iron industry, the evidence comes chiefly from the product itself rather than from the factory (though a growing amount of knowledge is being gained about the production sites). This allows us to look at a different aspect of the ancient world: the distribution of some of the most common articles of daily life—and therefore, by implication, the shopping habits of the population—and the success or failure of different commercial concerns competing for a mass market. Pottery, in fact, has survived in such enormous quantities, and has such distinct forms and fabrics, that it is possible to study the location and chronology of its manufacture and changes in style and taste with some hope of arriving at reliable answers to some of the questions that one would ask in investigating a modern trade from manufacture to customer. A less satisfactory aspect is that so many scholars have specialized in the subject that there is much disagreement in detail, not untouched by *odium academicum*. However, some general points can be made with more confidence than on any other ancient product. It is clear that there were two main markets: direct supply to the army, and sale to the general public. There had already been a flourishing trade in home-produced and imported wares in the south-east before the conquest, and this included products from the empire. The army seems to have started off with the stock that it brought with it. Some potters obviously accompanied the invading troops or came soon after, but local skill was soon utilized. Apart from a relatively small amount of production by the Roman army itself, which hardly went beyond the early second century, we have to reckon with two major categories of pottery in use in Britain—items that were imported from factories abroad, and those that were made in similar potteries in Britain. Both were in civilian hands. In addition, there are certain special types of pot—notably the earthenware amphorae that were filled with oil, wine, or other products—that came in chiefly as containers. Their origin therefore reflects the trade in the commodity carried in them, not in pottery itself, and they were often reused for other purposes, as oil drums or plastic containers are today.

For pottery made in Britain, a distinction is drawn between the major producers and the large number of smaller concerns. The latter made the bulk of the pottery used, and mostly sold only to a very local market. The major producers, on the other hand, chiefly supplied the army, and may (though it is much argued about) have had contracts to do so. Their production often concentrated on particular sorts of pot. It was the finer wares that continued to be imported for longest. The two outstanding groups were the glossy red ware known generally as samian or *terra sigillata*, and the black or dark brown pots from the Rhineland and central Gaul. In the earliest days the red pottery came from the Arretine works in Italy, but the market was soon captured by the great factories of southern Gaul. These sent huge quantities of their pottery to Britain until, towards the end of the first century, they were challenged by new factories producing a similar product in central Gaul. For most of the second century this new group supplied nearly all the samian for Britain, though yet another offshoot of the industry set itself up in eastern Gaul and was able to achieve some penetration of the British market. The central Gaulish industry subsequently contracted severely, at the end of the second century or some time in the early third, and hardly any pottery from there appears in Britain thereafter. Since the dating for the cessation of production of central Gaulish samian formerly depended on the assumption of a destruction of Hadrian's Wall in 197—and we have seen how thin the evidence for that is—we can no longer presume that the cause was destruction of factories in Gaul during the war between Septimius Severus and Clodius Albinus. It is perfectly possible that the end came as the result of political or commercial pressures, and at a rather later date. The eastern Gaulish manufacturers managed to hold on to some of their gains overall, but relatively little of their production is found in Britain. In the latter part of the second century the dark-finished fine pottery of the Rhineland and Gaul began to appear in Britain in considerable quantities. This seems to have managed to retain a substantial market here in the third century. However, in the second half of the second century a flourishing British pottery industry had emerged that was producing not only coarse wares, but also some fine pottery ('Castor ware') that is remarkably like Rhenish. Thus, by the end of the second century the British consumer of fine pottery had a choice of central or eastern Gaulish samian, Rhenish, Gaulish or British dark wares, and a number of lesser but good-quality makes. The failure of the central Gaulish industry may indeed have been due to competition, with British taste having been caught by the newer dark wares even though other provinces continued to take the red pottery of east Gaul. There is no doubt that the British potters were not slow to take advantage of the collapse of the import trade in samian, though the difficulty in distinguishing Castor ware from the Continental types makes it impossible to know what proportion of the market they captured with any certainty.

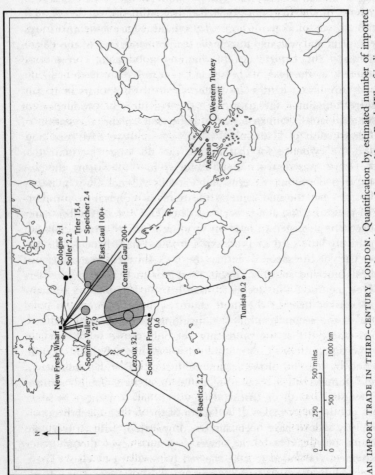

AN IMPORT TRADE IN THIRD-CENTURY LONDON. Quantification by estimated number of imported pottery vessels of the period around 225/245 from the waterfront at New Fresh Wharf indicates central Gaul as the biggest supplier at that time, twice the size of eastern Gaul, the only other large source.

Of the British groups of potteries producing both coarse and fine wares, the most notable was that in the Nene Valley around Peterborough. The area had great advantages—not only suitable raw materials, but an excellent position in the communications system. In the first century it had been the site of the vexillation fortress of Longthorpe. It lay on the edge of the enormous second-century development of the Fenland, with immediate access to the Fenland waterways, and good river connections inland to carry away its products in bulk. It may have had one other advantage as well. Between the Roman town of Chesterton and the medieval village of Castor, aerial photography shows an extraordinarily densely packed suburb that has every appearance of representing intensive industrial development. Overlooking that development was a very large villa, the fragments of which have been apparent for a long time in and around Castor churchyard. One cannot help suspecting that here lay the headquarters of a *procurator saltus* who oversaw the Fenland development. The advantages to the new industry of being at the centre of communications to a very large local market on which to build its initial prosperity are obvious. One may perhaps speculate a little further that the early failure of part of the Hadrianic agricultural and salt-producing colonization of the Fenlands may have turned the attention of the procurator and his masters to new ways of exploiting the region. The encouragement of the pottery industry might have been one of those ways, particularly if the salt industry of the Fens proper had not grown quite as much as had been hoped. Around Chesterton we have the typical Romano-British industrial picture. Even the largest industries, like salt and pottery, were located in the countryside. The settlement itself has the characteristics of a small town, not a large one, and it appears to be an appendage of the industries, not they of it. It was the raw materials, the fuel, and the communications that these industries needed to flourish, not a large urban work-force; and apart from the one great villa—which we have guessed was an official residence—they did not attract the sort of wealthy benefactors or inhabitants who could transform a small town into a city.

By the Severan period the Nene Valley potteries were in full production, and other smaller centres of fine-ware manufacture entered the market now being vacated by samian. Later on in the century an important fine-pottery centre emerged, or rather re-emerged, in the Oxford region, some of whose kilns were excavated on the Churchill Hospital site in Headington. These Oxford potters took a major share of the market in the fourth century, and we shall shortly look a little closer at the distribution pattern. This pottery belongs to the group known as 'colour-coated', as do the wares made in the fourth century in Hampshire in the New Forest. Yet another good-quality southern producer in the fourth century was the Farnham group of potters, to whom we shall also return.

In the troubles that struck Britain in the third quarter of the fourth century very serious damage seems to have been done to the general prosperity of the home pottery industry, and this extended to the great producers of coarse ware for the army as well as the fine-ware producers. For a long time the origin of the so-called 'black-burnished ware' was entirely unknown. It is now thought there were two main centres, one in Dorset, the other somewhere in eastern England. From about AD 120 until the war of 367 the Dorset potters were major suppliers to the army and the north in general, and between about 140 and 250 they were joined by the eastern factories. There is a similar pattern for the large-scale production of *mortaria* or mixing-bowls in factories operating near Nuneaton at Mancetter and Hartshill. These supplied the army in the north from around the beginning of the second century, but this also stopped with the war of 367. After the restoration of Britain by Theodosius, a decision seems to have been taken to switch northern military orders to a pottery near Malton that had been operating since some time before the middle of the century. This 'Crambeck ware' factory expanded its production to take the large part of this market until it finally disappeared. The same market was also entered in quantity at about the same time by the manufacturer of the 'Huntcliff' cooking-pot in the east Yorkshire area. It is not known whether the war had largely destroyed the former main factories or whether costs were now being cut by reducing transport distances. It may indeed be that long-distance transport, especially by sea, was now much more risky, or that the opportunity was taken to change an arrangement that had gone unchallenged for nearly three centuries even though there were now much more convenient sources of supply.

It has been worth outlining some of the main trends in Roman pottery in Britain because of the great quantity in which it has survived and the detail in which it has been studied. For these reasons, it is useful to look at certain studies of parts of the pottery industry, for they tell us much about what can and what cannot be extracted from the evidence.

We noted earlier the Farnham group of potters who were active in the fourth century. They were only part of a much larger industry that had been in operation for a long time. The whole complex centres on the medieval royal forest of Alice Holt, which helps to explain why the remains were undisturbed for so long after the Roman period. The discovery of more than eighty dumps of 'wasters' or rejects has permitted a type of study hardly conceivable elsewhere in Britain. It has been possible to construct a complete sequence of pot types from the first century to the fifth, obtaining their relative chronology from the dumps, and their dating by comparison with finds from excavations where other forms of evidence are available. The fortunate circumstances —that there were so many dumps, and that many of them have been hardly disturbed since first deposited—have established a sound basis for charting the development of an industry and its reactions to changing conditions. By relating examination of the factory area to discoveries of the finished product in the places where it actually ended up, historical dates have been assigned to the changes observable at the point of manufacture, and the market distribution of the wares in different periods has been assessed. The results show a successful but comparatively local sale of the output in the second half of the first century, with the pot types being adapted from native British forms. In the second century the makers continued these types in production, but they seem to have been obliged to manufacture black-burnished ware alongside them in order to compete with the newly emerged Dorset industry. This enabled the Alice Holt potters to avoid commercial extinction, and to survive to take advantage of the changes in the market in the middle of the third century that we have already observed in connection with other products. At that stage they came to the fore as a major producer. The turning-point in their career, in fact, seems to have been the winning of the London market for coarse pottery, which they dominated for much of the fourth century. In the late fourth century they once again took advantage of changes in the country-wide situation, and with new forms and fabrics they maintained their success. Their market sensitivity is well illustrated by the way in which they picked up a general change in fashion towards pottery in buff fabric, evident in Britain south of the Thames from around AD 330; and even their very latest wares reflect the tastes of the close of the fourth century and the beginning of the fifth. They retained this flexibility to the end.

The study of the Alice Holt industry was conducted on classic archaeological lines. It is worth comparing with certain other recent Romano-British pottery studies based on contemporary marketing theory and mathematical models. Here, too, the results seem promising, though at times more controversial. One study suggested that, broadly speaking, there were four categories of coarse-pottery production, each of which displayed a different pattern of distribution. The first was the medium-scale producer, whose sales depended on easy access to a town as the focus for distribution. The area reached in quantity was not regular around the town, but elongated along any main roads radiating from it. These producers seem to have been able to sell around the factory, around a nearby town, and along the main roads. This emphasizes the function of the town as a market, and its link to the countryside—and it ought to be added that the pattern seemed to hold good for the more substantial small towns as well as for the cities. It was right not to try to push the theory as far as to claim that the potters were sending their wares out by means of itinerant traders along the roads to minor markets, since the pattern may equally reflect the ease with which country shoppers could come into the town. Indeed, examination of Hampshire pottery apparently made adjacent to Chichester shows that the distribution extended markedly to the east and along Stane Street to the north-east, but fell off rapidly in the direction of Winchester. This is what one would expect with competing centres of retailing; and it is a pattern more easily detected from artefacts in the ancient world, where different sources of supply are more likely to have been used by different towns, than in the modern, where products tend to be manufactured and distributed nationally. The same sort of distribution pattern was also discernible in certain other products, such as roofing and flue-tiles, and other items that could normally be obtained locally only through a town. It also appeared in the more expensive types of pottery, such as samian, *mortaria*, and to some extent the fine wares from the Oxford and New Forest factories.

The second category was the very large producer of coarse pottery, such as Alice Holt or the coarse-ware potters of Oxford. The distribution of these pots does not seem to be markedly affected by either towns or main roads, and the suggestion is that the initial cost of the product was kept so low by economy of scale that the amount added by transport was not sufficient to make the price prohibitive. It is therefore reasonable to assume that where the buyer was within easy reach of a town, he had a choice of products, but where he was relatively remote, only the coarse wares were available to him. There was, however, one particular exception: the fine ware of the Oxford kilns, which seems not only to have overcome this disadvantage and to have been sold throughout the region, irrespective of urban centres or roads, but also to have competed successfully with the fine wares from the New Forest. Thus, Oxford wares were sold much nearer to the New Forest than vice versa. One reason for this is perhaps that the much larger production of fine wares from Oxford may have put them on a closer footing with coarse pottery in terms of price. The Oxford producers would therefore have had a big advantage over the New Forest ware even on its own ground, though obviously this diminished in the districts very near to the New Forest factories and their main retailing points.

The third category of pottery producer was the very small business, which often does not seem to have been near a convenient market town, and whose wares apparently had a very localized distribution. Nevertheless, they have to be taken into account when studying apparent anomalies in the distribution of the larger factories, and it may well be that in many places they could offer the local buyer a very competitive service, with a lower price for the same type of product or a better-quality pot at the same price. This is the point at which the medium-sized factory was probably least able to compete in the more remote districts, which is indeed reflected in the observed patterns of distribution that we have been considering.

So far we have largely been considering the private sector of the buying public, where we have implicitly assumed a modicum of free play of market forces. The final category was perhaps the most important: meeting the requirements of the army and other parts of the government service, for which official arrangements may have existed. It is indeed doubtful if some of the major producers would have survived or operated on anything more than a local scale without it; and we have already seen that this is an area where conscious decisions of officialdom, possibly (but by no means certainly) including issuing large-scale contracts, affected the pattern drastically. Ordinary 'commercial' considerations are not necessarily the controlling factor here, any more than in modern deals in military supplies. We saw Dorset as a major supplier for the Roman army in the north. If formal contracts did not exist, the manufacturer who transported his pots to the north and offered them to the military purchasers may have been able to overcome the cost of moving them simply by saturating the market and obtaining a virtual monopoly. On the other hand, if there were contracts, very large orders (with the assurance that everything produced would be bought) may have allowed the factories to offer exceptionally low prices that were both attractive to the army and allowed the manufacturer to offset the other advantages against his transport costs. Again, the army may have costed transport quite separately in its accounts or not at all, so that it did not have to appear in the price offered by the manufacturer. Nor can we rule out politics and personal influence as probable factors; in a Roman context, it would be abnormal for them to be absent. It is therefore probably futile to expect ordinary market considerations to have been dominant in the choice of supplier. Yet, by allowing the growth of particular producers, these official decisions must have immensely affected the rest of the industry. Thus we have to be very wary of models that attempt to explain pottery distribution on the assumption that an essentially free market was in operation. Equally, we may be sure that the Romans would not have comprehended the concepts of 'fair' and 'unfair' competition in use today.

In order to round off the picture of the character of industry and trade in Roman Britain, we should look briefly at three other areas of commercial activity. They are the wine trade, the textile industry, and the workshops of the urban craftsmen. None of them escaped the effects of the course of political events, and in the first two at least, we shall see evidence of government intervention, direct or indirect.

The import trade in wine was already well established before the Roman conquest, indeed even before Caesar. South Italian wine was coming in through the south coast of England in amphorae in the first half of the first century BC and possibly even earlier. One may perhaps imagine that among the agents from whom the Romans received intelligence of Britain were these wine-merchants. It may have been unfriendly relations between Caesar and the southern Britons that caused an apparent shift in this trade eastwards to the Trinovantes around Colchester, but it is reasonable to assume that Cunobelinus, his nobles, and his feuding sons, once the Catuvellauni had absorbed the Trinovantes, kept up the consumption of wine with the same fine disregard for nationalism in trade that is reflected in their conspicuous consumption of other luxury articles from the empire, whatever their individual political adherences.

One problem in studying the wine trade is that amphorae were also used as containers for olive oil, fruit, and the fish sauce that was very popular with Roman cooks. A study of the Roman amphorae from Spain has suggested that certain types were particularly used for the last commodity, though, to quote a scholarly comment on one of the best-known Iron Age warrior burials, 'not everyone may believe that the Snailwell chieftain went to the next world with jars of fish sauce'. However, the former contents of amphorae can sometimes be identified by laboratory analysis, and it may be possible to eliminate these. Spanish oil and sauce were certainly entering the country in this period, but it is possible that the Spanish amphorae of the first and second centuries found in Britain represent an extensive wine trade that was already taking over from the principal Italian shippers before the conquest, and expanded greatly under Roman rule. Imperial concern about competition outside Italy is indeed reflected in Domitian's edict ordering the destruction of vineyards beyond the Alps, but it seems to have had no practical effect. In Gaul, in particular, the second century seems to be marked by more and more vine-growing. By the end of the century wine was certainly being transported on the Moselle, if not yet grown there.

The civil war between Septimius Severus and Clodius Albinus seems to have disrupted the wine trade very severely. After the Severan victory, punitive action and confiscations in Spain resulted in Spanish wine no longer reaching Britain in anything but the tiniest quantities. Indeed, the presence of one of the very few Spanish amphora-stamps of the period on a Fen Edge site near Mildenhall has suggested that one of the Severan party was present there, possibly carrying out the confiscation of properties and their incorporation in the imperial estates. Nevertheless, this set-back to one supplier was, as in other industries, apparently taken as an opportunity by others. The two main foreign suppliers were probably now Germany and the Gironde, and there is one clue that the two trades were linked. Rhenish amphorae furnish evidence of wine from German vineyards, and we have two inscriptions relating to Bordeaux, one the stone of M. Aurelius Lunaris, whom we have already met as a *sevir Augustalis* of both York and Lincoln, and the other recording L. Solimarius Secundinus of Bordeaux, who is described as a merchant in the British trade (*negotiator Britannicianus*). The particularly interesting point about the latter man is that he originated from the Rhineland, suggesting either that he learnt his business there and then moved to Bordeaux, or that like many present-day wine merchants, he dealt in the products of more than one region. Oddly enough, we do not have any indisputable evidence that the trade with the Gironde was in fact in wine. There are something like fifty examples of wine-barrels known from the north-western provinces, made from more than one type of wood, and it has been suggested that barrels of silver fir found at Silchester (barrels and tubs were reusable as well-linings) represent the Bordeaux trade, since that particular tree is not found closer than the southern part of France. One barrel from London, and many in Belgium are made of Alpine wood, suggesting shipment along the Rhine, which would indeed be an easier route, with much less mileage by sea. Less, in fact, is known about the *vignoble Bordelais* in the Roman period than one would wish. Certainly, vines seem to have been grown in districts that are no longer producers today, as the extensive *cave* discovered at Allas-les-Mines, in the deep valley of the upper reaches of the River Dordogne, indicates. This may be due to climatic and landscape change; but if these upland vineyards were contributing to the export trade, prices must have been high, since the river is difficult. Indeed, in more recent times it was customary to break up the river-craft when they reached Bordeaux, as the return journey against the current was too difficult. There is one possible line of research on contact with Britain suggested by medieval Saint-Émilion, where the streets are cobbled with stone alleged to have been brought as ballast in the empty wine-ships from Britain. Similar petrological examination on Roman sites in the region might well yield significant results.

It is difficult to know what effect further government intervention later on in the third century had on the trade. In 277, shortly after the collapse of the Gallic Empire and immediately following the devastation of the economy of Gaul by the barbarian invasion of 276, the Emperor Probus lifted the legal restrictions on the production of wine in Britain and Gaul. It ought to have invigorated the Gallic producers, and one might expect the encouragement of new developments further north, where the impact of the German onslaught had first been felt. In the fourth century Ausonius praised the wine of the Moselle, where local production was very probably stimulated by the presence of the imperial capital at Trier. The Loire would have been well placed to serve the British market, and the Emperor Julian's reference to vineyards in the neighbourhood of Paris may reflect an outlier of this region or of Champagne. The evidence for British vine-growing is so far exceedingly thin, though there is some reason to think that this may partly be due to inadequate recording in past excavations. If there were British vineyards, we do not know if their production went beyond the small-scale operation that has revived in this country in recent years, nor whether it extended beyond domestic consumption to the commercial market. As today, it had severe competition from British beer, a commodity important enough to be noted in Diocletian's Price Edict, where its price was fixed at twice that of Egyptian.

Another British industry specifically noted in the Price Edict is textiles. This included the British duffel coat (*byrrus Britannicus*) and a woollen rug (*tapete Britannicum*), indicating that by the beginning of the fourth century made-up garments from Britain were common enough to be worth regulating. It is possible that some British products had the exclusivity of Harris Tweed or Otterburn cloth, for in the early third century a garment called a *tossia Britannica* is recorded on an inscription as a present that the governor Claudius Paulinus sent to someone in Gaul. It was at one time thought that the great fourth-century villas were accompanied by a widespread replacement of labour-intensive arable farming by sheep ranches, partly influenced by the extreme shortage of manpower then envisaged for the period. Yet the bone analysis from the Fenland argued strongly for the keeping of beasts for wool in an area where the population seems to have been relatively dense on the land. Nor is it at all certain that all the wool used was produced inside the provinces of Britain. A Roman model of a bale of wool found in Skye suggests that raw material was being imported into Roman territory for processing. It could, too, explain other Roman objects found in Scotland, even in the far north, which may have been bartered for wool.

Finished woollen products like those in the Price Edict were presumably regularly exported to other parts of the Roman world as well as sold in Britain. It is interesting that two of the largest pieces of wool-processing equipment known in Britain do not come, as one might expect, from the countryside, but from towns, Great Chesterford and Caistor-by-Norwich. Similarly, when the *Notitia* mentions one of the state weaving-mills that supplied the fourth-century army with uniforms as being situated in Britain, it is at a town, for it lists the *procurator gynaecii in Britannis Ventensis*. This mill may have been at Venta Belgarum (Winchester), or Venta Icenorum (Caistor-by-Norwich), or even Venta Silurum (Caerwent), but it does indicate a site in or near a town, and a relatively important one. Similarly, on the Continent there were such official mills at Trier, Rheims, and Tournai. Unlike the other industries so far considered, this seems to have been an urban one.

Another trade centred on certain Romano-British towns, but carrying out much of its actual work in the villas, was the mosaic industry. It can be fairly described as industrial, because it is clear that there were at least four, possibly five, identifiable schools of mosaicists—whether large firms or groups of craftsmen working in a common style and using common pattern-books we do not know—centred on Cirencester, Chesterton (Water Newton), Dorchester (Dorset), Brough-on-Humber, and somewhere in the centre of the south. All were at their peak in the fourth century, laying pavements chiefly in the villas, and clearly responding to the flowering of villa life in the first half of the century. There is some sign that the areas in which they operated were not mutually exclusive—in other words, that there was an element of competition. Nevertheless, the Cirencester school, at the centre of the richest villa area of the period, is among the greatest, and we may assume that it earned a good deal of money for its proprietors. There is no direct evidence that the schools were urban. It is true that the more complicated sections of mosaic—especially pictorial roundels and the like—seem to have been prefabricated by the leading craftsmen before being laid, but this may have been done on site. However, between jobs it seems possible that stores and tools were held in mosaic firms' yards, and one may assume that there was a drawing-office or library of designs and accommodation for the clerks who handled the accounts and other records. Though it is not possible yet to identify similar schools for earlier periods, there is no reason to doubt that, at least from the second century, similar British firms were established, even if in the early years after the conquest much work was carried out under the supervision of Continental master craftsmen. In terms of individual products, the output of the mosaic firms was, of course, infinitesimal compared with the other industries we have so far considered, but it has to be remembered that each piece was a large-scale luxury item, and one may fairly guess that the financial turnover of one of these businesses would bear comparison with the mass-producing manufacturers of more everyday goods. The impact of the mosaicists on their local towns, in terms of wealth generated, ought not to be underrated therefore, and we should remember that they were only one among a number of crafts in probably the same financial league that are implied by the prosperity of the building industry—for example, the makers of decorative and architectural sculpture and the painters of murals, all of whom must, to a

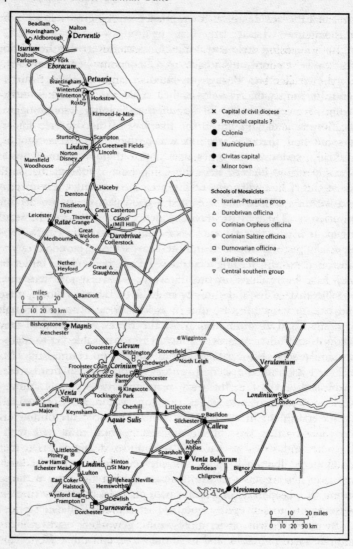

IDENTIFICATION OF FIRMS WITHIN AN INDUSTRY. For mosaics this has had some success, though much is debated. These maps show one attempt, identifying the work of studios (*officinae*) based on Cirencester (*Corinium*), Dorchester, Dorset (*Durnovaria*), Ilchester (*Lindinis*), Aldborough (*Isurium*), Brough-on-Humber (*Petuaria*), and Chesterton/Water Newton (*Durobrivae*), plus a central southern group.

greater or lesser degree, have needed a working base in or near the cities.

Before closing this survey of trade and industry, we should not pass over the contribution made to the economy of Roman towns by the smaller businesses represented in large numbers by individual urban craftsmen and shops. Detailed remains of their establishments are, of course, well known from Pompeii, Herculaneum, and Ostia, and range from the purely retail and service trades, like butchers, greengrocers, bars, and brothels, to jewellers, smiths, and bronze-workers, who made and sold goods direct. Some establishments, such as bakeries, could be on a substantial scale while still contained in city blocks or *insulae*; and Ostia in particular has a number of examples of warehouses and safe-deposit buildings that must have served many trades. In Britain the retail trade is well illustrated by a shop selling fine pottery that was destroyed by fire in the forum at Wroxeter in the middle of the second century, its stock preserved in the debris in the order in which it had fallen from the shelves. At Verulamium extensive ranges of small shops, apparently leased from larger landlords, were flourishing before the Boudiccan sack of the town, and though it seems to have been something like fifteen years before they revived, they then went on reconstructing themselves on the same lines, more or less unchanged, for another three-quarters of a century. Around AD 150 these shopkeepers seem to have bought up their leases, for they were then rebuilding separately. Nevertheless, they retained what must have been a pleasant covered arcade along the front. Shortly afterwards the whole area was destroyed by fire, and subsequently much of the town was occupied by large town houses. This, of course, does not mean that retail trade dwindled. In fact, it probably increased as a direct consequence of the arrival of the gentry, but one may imagine astute shopkeepers who had acquired their leases now seeing an opportunity to sell these prime sites at a much enhanced price.

As in the Italian cities, smiths, bronze-workers, and jewellers are all attested in the shops at Verulamium, and the evidence for gold-smelting under the governor's palace in London, though probably official, could have come from a private jeweller. A particularly interesting luxury trade was the making of decorative pieces from Whitby jet. Evidence for such manufacture is recorded at

York, and the objects themselves are also surprisingly common in the Rhineland, but without any sign of waste material. It is therefore almost certain that the jet ornaments were exported as finished articles, probably from York itself. In the larger towns one may expect a municipal market-building or *macellum*: such buildings are already known at Cirencester, Leicester, and Verulamium. We may have a suspicion that the much disputed Site XI at Corbridge is neither an unfinished military headquarters building nor a projected forum for the civil town, but a public market. It might even have been, like the Piazzale delle Corporazioni at Ostia, a building providing guild-rooms for associations of merchants, in this case supplying the army and trading beyond the Wall. Barates of Palmyra, a supplier of flags or standards, is buried at Corbridge, and one can reasonably imagine that the purveyors of black-burnished ware, for example, had accommodation somewhere in the north. We know of *collegia* or associations in Britain that may have been comprised of merchants or craftsmen, but the actual trade is only specified in one case, the 'Cogidubnus' inscription at Chichester, where the donors specify themselves as 'the guild of smiths (*collegium fabrorum*) and its individual members'.

The Chichester guild was prudently honouring the imperial house, and had sought the permission of Cogidubnus. The dedication to Neptune and Minerva, deities of the sea and of skill, perhaps suggests they were primarily engaged in metalwork for ships, and the probability that there was a military stores depot at Chichester in the first century implies an official market for their craft. Prudence of another sort is demonstrated by the dedication to an unknown deity by a trader at Bowness-on-Solway, apparently as he was about to set out upon some commercial enterprise: 'And if my venture should prosper, then I promise to gild every letter of the verse inscribed on this stone.' To succeed in business in the ancient world, one needed friends, the favour of officialdom, a record of loyalty to the state, and the good offices of the gods.

People also needed one other commodity—money. Senators were theoretically barred from engaging in commerce, hence both the emergence of the equestrian class as the greatest power in the world of finance and business, and the extensive use of freedmen as agents to run concerns. Nevertheless, the involvement of the richest men in Rome in provincial business was often, as we have noted, hardly concealed, and Dio's statement that Seneca had ten million sesterces out on loan in Britain before the Boudiccan rebellion shows how large the investment could be. However, despite the large sums of money from private sources such as this in the first century, there is real doubt as to the extent to which Britain had a monetary economy at that time. Though the evidence is unclear, it does appear that the total number of coins in circulation was relatively smaller in Britain than in southern Gaul or Italy, and they tend to be found more often in towns than in the countryside. The relative rarity of early coins of small denominations in Britain may also support the notion of the slow development of a fully money-based system, since army pay, the chief reason why coinage was imported in bulk, seems to have been issued in fairly large denominations. However, in the second century the quantity of coins in circulation rises to equal the other western provinces, which would be consistent with the Flavian impetus to urban life, and the subsequent strengthening of the towns in the first half of the second century. There is considerable evidence in Britain, too, for widespread copying of coins. This may not always be a matter of forgery, since there are signs that it was sometimes permitted because of a shortage of coinage.

The progressive debasement of the coinage was a method that many emperors adopted to alleviate their financial difficulties, though there is no simple answer to the effect that this may have had on real prices or ease of trade. Usurpers needed coinage to pay their troops and officials, and, being cut off from central supplies, they often set up their own mints. These coins passed into general circulation. Such usurpers often sought popularity by increasing pay for the troops and, at least at first, improving the quality of the coins themselves. Thus the proclamation of a would-be emperor, and an immediate payment of a donative to the troops, with the promise of more to come, might stimulate trade. The earliest known Roman mint in Britain is of this kind. Carausius struck coins at London and at another site, possibly Colchester. His successor Allectus continued the practice. The London mint was in fact kept working until around 326, and was for a short time revived by Magnus Maximus. Apart from these relatively brief periods, Britain relied for its supply of actual cash on Continental mints and to some extent on copying.

Though it has generally been considered that, under the late Empire, the importance of the money economy declined overall, there is some reason to think that the money-based economy did not develop to its fullest extent in Britain until the third century. It is also necessary to recall that without the presence of the machinery of the Roman state—particularly of the army—there would have been no general money economy in Britain at all, since the actual supply of coin was intimately connected with it. We have already seen how the cessation of the cycle of payment and taxation at the point of break from Roman rule must have struck at the centre of the entire society. From this point on, too, there can have been no resumption of bulk importation of the coinage itself, and whatever residual use of coins occurred internally must have been in old pieces, as the use of 'clipped *siliquae*' noted earlier demonstrates.

It is difficult to estimate from the amount of wear on the latest Roman coins found in Britain how long they were in general circulation, but by 420 or 430 coinage seems no longer to have been a normal means of exchange. As we noted earlier, it does not seem fanciful to link the collapse of mass-production industry with this phenomenon. The withdrawal or dissolution of the regular army must have dealt it a tremendous blow, as contracts ceased to be honoured or large purchases made. It seems likely that it was finished off because the distribution system on which the factories that supplied the civilian market depended could not survive, for, except in the case of the smallest local concern, it is impossible to see how it could have worked without coinage circulating on an everyday basis.

To summarize the monetary history of early Britain is to pass the story of Roman Britain in review. There is real doubt as to whether coins were used as currency to any significant degree before the Roman conquest: it is more than likely that the Celtic pieces and the occasional Roman coins found in Iron Age contexts represent gifts or symbolic offerings, perhaps between potentates, rather than trade. It was the arrival of large numbers of soldiers and officials who were paid in cash that started to create the money economy. Thus the introduction of the vast superstructure of a Roman province, in theory a massive burden on a country that had managed to do without it, brought with it the money that established a very substantial network of industry and commerce, some of it on a considerable scale by any standard, both possible and profitable, and transformed the prospects of British agriculture. In Boudicca's time the advantages were certainly not apparent to the Britons, at least among their leaders. Cash tended to flow into the pockets of the small trader or producer and the humble provincial who was recruited into the Roman army or other branches of the government service. Wealth drained out of the estates of the British nobility, who were expected to bear the expense of civic and provincial display and suffered the depredations of corrupt Roman officials. It took the patient work of Flavian and subsequent administrations to bring them round. But by the late fourth century the army had once more become unpopular throughout the empire, and its run-down in Britain may well not have been lamented, as we have seen, among leading Romano-British provincials. Central funds had probably already ceased to come in before the break with Roman rule, but the expulsion of Constantine III's officials finally demolished the edifice of provincial government. The Britons had thus knocked out the corner-stone of their own economy. To many of the British landowners, this may have mattered comparatively little at first compared with the relief from imperial taxation, whether imposed by Arles or Ravenna, and the constant demand for recruits. The collapse of large-scale trade and industry probably hit some of those who had money invested in business. On the other hand, by the fifth century it was the state rather than private individuals that controlled much of industry in the empire, and many wealthy provincials probably welcomed the availability of cheap labour to serve on the land as men were thrown out of work. In Gaul the rich retired, not uncomfortably, to their estates, and in Italy the senate became more and more disenchanted with the imperial structure. In the first century the British aristocracy eventually accepted that the empire was in their interest. In the fifth century this was no longer axiomatic, and at least some of them were prepared to seize the opportunity to cut themselves free.

Economic power in the west had become increasingly polarized, between the emperor and the state on one side, and the greater land-owning aristocracy on the other. First the pagan religious institutions and then the cities had lost their wealth. Spending by impoverished individual *curiales* and by the municipalities themselves was sharply reduced, with all that that meant for the many trades that had flourished on it. In Britain the effect was not balanced by a rich Church, nor by the presence of large bodies of the best-paid troops and officials. It was not even softened, as it was on the Continent, by the establishment of barbarian kingdoms that continued to demand the output of long-established Roman factories. The fifth-century revolt from Roman rule must have completed the process. It was the middle classes and the artisans whose occupations and prosperity were swept away as the basis of their commercial world dissolved.

The prospects for the Romano-British upper class may have appeared bright in 409, and it is not surprising that literary sources allege that there was a period of great prosperity following the break. The rich might well have continued to live as well as before in many respects—if not better—had the relations between Roman and barbarian in fifth-century Gaul been paralleled in Britain. But the political gamble failed, and the economic pattern of Britain had been destroyed, with very little advantage to anyone, even the barbarians, for a very long time to come.

22

RELIGION AND
SOCIETY

Religion, in all its many aspects, was so embedded in the culture of the ancient world that it is impossible to consider one without the other. Already in the second century BC the Greek politician and historian Polybius had assessed the position of religion in Roman society as the cement of the Roman state. But religion was much more than just a matter of public observance and political loyalty. It permeated every side of life, and took many different forms. Our period saw the defeat of the old public religion of the Olympian gods, and the emergence of new religions demanding personal commitment. Some were based on private devotion; others evolved into highly organized societies of their own. At the same time, the equally personal and very ancient belief in the local deities of family, home, and place retained an immense hold over the mind.

One of the reasons why religion in Roman Britain is both so confusing and often so difficult to interpret is the tendency in the Roman world to 'conflate' with classical gods the deities of the peoples that the Romans conquered or that were imported into the empire. This process greatly helped the integration of Roman and conquered, for the Romans were extremely tolerant of foreign religions, provided that there was no suspicion of political conspiracy (they strongly disliked closed groups and societies) and that the rites were not so repugnant as to be intolerable (such as human sacrifice). The fact that the native deities were often much less clearly defined or differentiated from one another than the Graeco-Roman gods meant that the identification could vary from place to place, and it is often difficult for us to determine precisely which deity is involved. There was a further reason for the distortion that often occurred in presenting native gods in Roman guise. Representational sculpture was more or less unknown in pre-Roman Britain, and, as far as we know, written dedications were foreign to it. Thus, when people came to imitate Roman ways by erecting statues and inscribed altars to local gods, this could only be done by means of classical forms of expression, even though the deities and the ideas they represented might be quite alien.

It is possible to erect a framework to classify the cults found in Roman Britain, but it has to be understood that it is no more than a rough one and cannot be made more precise. The first main group are the native cults, those already in Britain before the conquest. They themselves were very mixed, having grown up locally or been imported in the pre-Roman period. Indeed, it is highly probable that we unwittingly include in this native or 'Celtic' group many cults that came in from other Celtic provinces *after* the Roman invasion but are more or less impossible to distinguish from those already here. One of the best examples of a goddess likely to have been purely native and local is Coventina, the water-goddess of Carrawburgh on Hadrian's Wall, to whom we shall return. As an instance of a Celtic import, we may take the 'Mars Lenus or Ocelus Vellaunus' who is found on one dedication at Caerwent, with the 'Mars Ocelus' on another Caerwent stone, and look at them in the light of the great sanctuary of Lenus Mars at Trier, itself the site of a dedication by a man from Britain. Here we have the identification of the Roman Mars with a Celtic deity under more than one name, or possibly with more than one deity, and there is a strong probability that at Caerwent he was an import from the Rhineland.

The second main group is comprised of the purely classical gods of the Graeco-Roman world, such as appear on the Minerva and Neptune inscription at Chichester. These are the deities of the Olympian pantheon. We have another normal form of Roman deity in dedications like those to Fortuna and Bonus Eventus, honoured by a husband and wife at Caerleon. Other 'personifications'—of Rome herself, of provinces, cities, or regions—were also a regular Roman form of expression. In the case of the goddesses of some of the British tribes—for example Dea Brigantia

—one might suspect a pre-Roman tribal deity in Roman dress, but one could easily be wrong. Also Graeco-Roman, but of more recent origin, was the Imperial Cult. Some of its roots lay in the 'ruler-cults' of non-Roman states, particularly Egypt and the east, but it was undoubtedly Mediterranean rather than north-western.

The third main group is made up of non-Roman cults that were pure imports and had no native counterparts. From the west, from inside other western provinces and beyond, came some striking Germanic cults, probably chiefly through soldiers of German origin. An example is recorded on the altar to the Imperial Cult and to 'the goddesses the Alaisiagae, Baudihillia and Friagabis' set up at Housesteads by the *numerus* of Hnaudifridus. From the east came deities that had long been accepted by Rome, such as Isis (to whom there was a temple at London), or Jupiter Dolichenus from Syria, or Sol Invictus, the Unconquered Sun, both of the latter apparently introduced into Britain in the second century and popular in the third, and both at one time or another patronized by the imperial family. Less common eastern deities, such as Astarte, were probably the object of devotions by a small group of people or a single individual. In the long run, much more important were the 'mystery-religions' imported from the east, in which initiation and membership of a congregation promised the worshipper a religious experience particular to that religion and often associated with sacraments and beliefs in eternity or salvation. Among the most famous had been the mysteries of Eleusis in Attica, which were highly respectable and supported by Graecophile emperors, and the less publicly approved 'enthusiastic' cults that involved forms of religious hysteria, for example, that of Cybele. But the greatest were Mithraism and Christianity. The religion of Mithras was a version of the Persian creed of Zoroaster. It became popular in the west among army officers and men of business, since it insisted on strict principles of discipline and integrity. It was exclusive in its membership, in direct contrast to Christianity, which in some other ways it resembled.

We have noted the vast variety of ancient religion, and the difficulty that the classical world itself had in equating Celtic religions neatly with its own cults. The 'Mars' we met at Caerwent and Trier, for example, was probably not simply the Roman god of war, but embodied a much wider Celtic concept of a 'high god'. The difficulty partly sprang from that fact that the native gods had less pronounced individual characteristics. Consequently, a Celtic god may be identified as Mars in one place or at one time, and as Mercury in another. Nevertheless, it does appear that there was a Celtic concept of a supreme or high god and a multitude of lesser deities, some widely worshipped, others very local indeed. Notable features are 'triads' or groups of three, some animal, others human, such as the very popular *matres* or mother-goddesses particularly common in the Rhineland. Also widely found are a horned god, sometimes named as Cernunnos, and a god with a wheel. There is also a rider-god, at times associated with Jupiter and appearing in the Rhineland on the so-called 'Jupiter Columns', of which the re-dedication of a column by a provincial governor at Cirencester may be one British example. Popular among the Celtic peoples was the equestrian goddess Epona, a cult apparently spreading out from the centre of Gallic resistance at Alesia, the scene of Caesar's final victory and capture of Vercingetorix. Her cult spread widely under Rome, and on occasion she appears to merge with the *matres* as a goddess of plenty.

Many of the native deities are associated with water, and in particular with springs (as Sulis Minerva at Bath) or sources of rivers (for example, the Seine). Ritual pits and shafts also occur quite frequently, and there may have been a close association with the water-cult, as they often appear to have started life as wells. Indeed, it is frequently difficult to be clear whether a shaft that has been filled and contains large quantities of artefacts was originally dug as a well or as a ritual shaft. Such shafts sometimes show signs of sacrifice. There was also, particularly in southern Gaul before the Roman conquest, a Celtic cult of the severed head.

Burial rites in the Celtic world were varied, including both cremation and various forms of inhumation, and, as in pre-Iron Age Britain, the barrow or burial-mound still persisted in late pre-Roman times, though less commonly. Burial with weapons or other possessions also continued, though it has often been noted that the number of rich Iron Age 'warrior graves' found in Britain is very small. It is also true that the overall number of

Iron Age burials of any type recorded in Britain is small in comparison with other periods, and it has been conjectured that disposal of the dead by means of exposure of the body or by deposition in rivers may have been practised. Very common on the Continent are cemeteries in rectangular enclosures. There are several of these in Britain, and this is a function that needs to be kept in mind when considering the rectangular and 'sub-rectangular' enclosures that are quite frequently discovered in Iron Age and Roman contexts in Britain.

The form of the Celtic shrine is a contentious subject. A notable feature of the north-western Roman provinces is the so-called 'Romano-Celtic' temple. These range in size, but are generally fairly small. They are characterized by a 'double-box' plan, with occasional variations in the shape of concentric circles or polygons. What this implies by way of superstructure is uncertain: they may have been quite low, with a lean-to veranda surrounding a central *cella* or inner shrine, or they may have been towers with a much lower ambulatory. Sometimes the simpler versions have no veranda, and there is no reason at all to suppose any fundamental difference in religion between the Romano-Celtic temple and the simplest circular shrine, more or less indistinguishable from the native hut. The Romano-Celtic temple itself is a form that sprang from the fusion of Roman and native in the north-western provinces; it is not found outside these provinces, and the two types can exist side by side, for example, inside the old hill-fort of Maiden Castle in Dorset. Both Roman and German dedications are found in circular shrines, as well as purely native cults. It is normal practice in the ancient world to find all sorts of shrine alongside one another, from the greatest classical sanctuaries such as Delphi, through extensive but unpretentious complexes such as Trier or Springhead in Kent, to minor groups such as the adjoining shrines of Mithras, Coventina, and of the nymphs and the *genius loci* outside the fort at Carrawburgh. The last example was unroofed, and it is likely that others were similarly open to the sky. It is perfectly possible that the simple types outlasted the more imposing into post-Roman times, when Roman building materials and architectural skills became scarce, and wealthy patronage less freely available in an increasingly Christianized world. It was wealth and taste, rather than race or religion, that determined the degree of architectural sophistication encountered.

That the Romano-Celtic type evolved from an Iron Age fore-runner is reasonably clear. What is certain is that Roman shrines often overlie Iron Age predecessors. This occurs with both the simple building and the sophisticated. The Romano-Celtic type itself, despite its common occurrence, was almost uniformly mod-est in size throughout the Roman period. Like the shrines of pre-Roman Gaul, they often lie within enclosures, sometimes in pairs or greater numbers, and are frequently dwarfed by the size of the enclosure itself. The idea of a sacred enclosure or precinct, an area extracted from the landscape and specifically holy, was extremely important in both Celtic and classical religion. It sur-vives in the consecrated ground of Christian churches and ceme-teries, a phenomenon that is not simply a legal concept, but still carries with it a sense of awe. The Greek *temenos* (precinct) was literally a piece 'cut' from its surroundings. The Romans cer-tainly regarded the Celtic *nemeton*, a sacred grove or clearing in a forest, as something alien and frightening, since the majority of their own holy places were by classical times either in cities or in open countryside. Yet in the idea of a sanctuary as essen-tially an enclosure rather than a building, Celtic and classical are a great deal closer than might at first appear. Nor is this sur-prising, considering their origins in a common, if very distant, past. In essence, the temples to the deities of the Graeco-Roman pantheon were monuments to the honour in which the partic-ular gods were held. Such a temple served as a symbol of the community or state that the deity protected; it housed his image, and sheltered the votive gifts of people and state. These build-ings were *not* intended to house congregations of worshippers, though rites might be performed inside them by priests or mag-istrates. Public ceremonial and public worship were almost always concentrated on the altar of the god in the forecourt or enclo-sure of the temple, and in the open air. In Britain we have an outstanding example in the great altar of the Imperial Cult in front of the Temple of Claudius at Colchester, within its elabor-ately colonnaded courtyard. This may look very different from the native-style sanctuary at Gosbecks Farm outside the same city, where a tiny temple lies in one corner of another large and elaborate walled enclosure, but the principle is essentially the same. The Gosbecks enclosure has, in fact, the same basic feature—a spacious enclosure—as the classical *temenos*, which was designed for processions, public sacrifices, and public worship, all in the open air. This emphasis on the open air is, of course, apparent not only in the great public altars, but also in the little unroofed shrines we noted earlier. But Gosbecks has a further feature, which almost certainly links it with the pre-Roman world. The temple itself is curiously offset in its enclosure, and it is extremely difficult to explain this unless one assumes that the placing was determined by the presence of a holy object, such as a sacred tree or grove of trees. There was nothing unclassical *per se* in the reverence paid to natural features. The *Lapis Niger*, a black stone in the Forum at Rome, was an object of reverence of great antiquity. Nor was it unknown for the presence of such features to affect the layout of the architecture. The strange shape of the Erechtheum on the Acropolis at Athens owes much to the awesome rock fissures and the holy olive tree within its precinct. The existence of many place-names in the Celtic provinces of the Roman empire that incorporated a *nemeton* element demonstrates at least a local memory, and in many cases probably a continuing cult. 'Vernemeton' occurs as the name of the small Roman settlement at Willoughby on the Wolds in Nottinghamshire; 'Medionemeton' seems to have been somewhere on the Antonine Wall; and 'Aquae Arnemetiae' was the spa town of Buxton, where the tutelary goddess seems to link the concepts of holy springs and groves. In Roman times we may assume any continuing cults to have been relatively innocuous. The Roman sense of horror at native usages comes through Dio's reference to the atrocities carried out by Boudicca's followers on their prisoners 'in the grove of Andate' (whom he describes as the British goddess of victory) and in 'other sacred spots'. A passage in Tacitus, to which we shall return, describes how Suetonius Paullinus had already cut down the sacred groves on the island of Anglesey because of what was practised in them. Nevertheless, religious continuity is established on a number of sites, for example, the temple on Hayling Island. But there may have been many more on which the idea of a holy spot persisted, even to the extent of some taboo on use for secular purposes, without any continuing cult. At Gournay-sur-Aronde in Gaul, for example, a Celtic shrine was meticulously demolished in the first century BC, and the site apparently kept completely free of occupation until the fourth century AD. In that late period it received a temple of Romano-Celtic type. It is not impossible that the demolition was carried out ritually, and it may be that the site was cursed, or otherwise made unusable, but retained its sacred nature.

Another important feature of the Celtic sanctuary is brought to mind by a reference by Strabo to the assembly of the Galatians, a Celtic people settled in north-western Turkey, at a place named Drunemeton, 'the sacred grove of oaks'. In Gaul itself two features of such meeting-places under Roman rule stand out very clearly: the association of the temple or sanctuary with a theatre, and also with a piazza, often conventionally called in the modern literature a 'forum'. The association of temple and theatre is, of course, common in the classical world, both in city and rural contexts. Urban examples include the proximity of the Theatre of Dionysus at Athens to the temples of the Acropolis, or, in a Roman provincial setting, the close architectural linking of a principal temple and the theatre in a single complex at Augst, a Roman *colonia* in Switzerland. At Verulamium there is the interesting juxtaposition of an elaborated form of the Romano-Celtic temple in its own precinct immediately behind the theatre (itself of northern type), though not architecturally linked to it. For the rural equivalent, the great theatre at the sacred site of Epidauros in Greece is perhaps the best-known example; and in Gaul one may quote Sanxay, south-west of Poitiers, where a theatre lies across a small river from the temple and 'forum' complex, or Saint-Cybardeaux, near Angoulême, with its massive theatre built into the hillside, below a complicated group of small temples and other buildings. It is therefore very interesting that the example of a Romano-Celtic sanctuary that we have already noted at Gosbecks Farm outside Colchester also has a theatre alongside. It is much smaller in size, but not all Gallic sanctuaries were on the scale of Sanxay or Saint-Cybardeaux. A small stone theatre at Cherré, in a rural setting near Le Lude, lies close to the site of a temple and probably one of the so-called forums, the whole complex being much more comparable in size to Gosbecks.

The connection of drama with religion is very familiar to us from classical Greece, but the smallness of the stage at Sanxay suggests that, in its religious role, it was perhaps employed as a platform for ritual or speeches to the gathered multitude rather than for dramatic performances. Indeed, we are familiar in modern times with the use of the stadium for the revivalist meeting, and one thinks of the meetings addressed by St Paul and other leaders of the early Church. The forum, too, would have allowed for the gathering of large groups of pilgrims and for open-air ceremonial for those not permitted into the temple enclosure itself.

We have seen how the native religions of north-west Europe and the old classical cults of the Graeco-Roman world shared the tradition of outdoor ritual. The introduction of congregational worship *inside* sacred buildings was largely the responsibility of the mystery-religions from the east. While there were some fairly large buildings in the Greek world that were capable of holding congregations associated with mystery-cults, in the west the cults met at first chiefly in small buildings. In the case of Mithraism, this was because the secrecy and the significance of the dark cave were themselves integral to the ritual; in the case of the Christians, it was for safety against discovery and persecution. When Christianity became lawful and official, it was to the secular buildings of the Roman world that the Church looked for architectural models, not the classical temple.

Another element in religion that became much more important in the classical world with the spread of the mystery-religions was the concept of the professional priest. In traditional Roman religion, every head of a household carried out priestly functions within his own home and family, and, broadly speaking, this was carried over into the public sphere, where the magistrate (and later the emperor) assumed priestly offices along with his political and military career. There were, of course, ancient rules and taboos affecting the choice and behaviour of the holders of these religious offices, but, by and large, there was not a separate priestly caste or profession. In many of the oriental religions this was not so, and the separation was made complete when Christianity became the official religion of the empire, however much the state might interfere in the affairs of the

Church, and vice versa. The Greek world had long held the philosopher in high esteem. The wandering holy man was not unknown under the early Empire, particularly in the east. However, professional priests tended to be equated in the minds of Roman governments with magicians and other political and social undesirables, and were from time to time expelled from Rome. Philosophy, morals, and ethics were proper fields of study for a Roman gentleman, and it was deemed correct that they should inform his public and private life, but the professional priest as such, particularly when preaching a moral code, was alien to the pre-Christian Empire. Since we are pursuing the study of a Roman province, this is the context in which it is appropriate to turn to the Celtic priesthood of the Druids. It is frequently alleged that their political role in focusing and uniting native resistance to Rome was one major reason for Rome's determination to dispose of them, the savagery of their rites being the other. The Romans certainly took them seriously in Gaul. Claudius, for example, whose interest in history and ritual, and whose enthusiasm for promoting the Gallic upper classes in other ways are well known, nevertheless attempted to exterminate the Druids in Gaul. It is difficult to explain this unless the reasons were pressing. Yet we do not have to assume that the same was true in Britain. All the examples of the Druids as a major political force come from the Continent. Claudius boasted of tribes and kings submitting to him in Britain, but he said nothing of Druids, nor do the other sources. Caesar, who could compare Britain—at least the powerful kingdoms of the south and east—with the political structure of Gaul, says of them: 'The Druidic religion is thought to have been found in existence in Britain and taken from there to Gaul. Nowadays those who want to study it deeply still go to Britain.'

In Britain they do not reappear until the year of the Boudiccan rebellion, and then only in the context of Suetonius Paullinus' attack on Anglesey, not specifically in connection with the uprising far away in East Anglia. Tacitus certainly describes Anglesey as 'a source of strength to rebels' and 'heavily populated and a sanctuary for fugitives', but the major reason given for Suetonius' assault is rivalry with his contemporary Corbulo, of whose recent spectacular victory in Armenia he was jealous. The extirpation of Druids is not given as an objective. Tacitus describes the defenders of Anglesey in the following terms:

The enemy was arrayed along the shore in a massive, dense, and heavily armed line of battle, but it was a strangely mixed one. Women, dressed in black like the Furies, were thrusting their way about in it, their hair let down and streaming, and they were brandishing flaming torches. Around the enemy host were Druids, uttering prayers and curses, flinging their arms towards the sky. The Roman troops stopped short in their tracks, as if their limbs were paralysed. Wounds were received while they stood frozen to the spot by this extraordinary and novel sight. However, in the end exhortations from their commander, and an exchange among themselves of encouragement not to be scared of a womanish and fanatic army broke the spell. They overran those who resisted them, and cast them into their own flames. Subsequently, a garrison was imposed on the defeated enemy, and the groves sacred to savage superstitions destroyed (these people regarded it as right (*fas*) to present the blood of prisoners as burnt offerings at their altars, and to consult the wishes of the gods by examining the entrails of humans).

This is more or less the sum of our direct evidence for an active part played by the Druids in British resistance. Caesar, more than a century earlier, did not say that he had come across any Druids himself in Britain, and he leaves us with the impression that he regarded the island as a repository of Druidic lore, giving no hint of contemporary political power or influence. Apart from this passage from Tacitus, Roman references to Druid savagery or subversion are reserved for Gaul, and even in this account of Anglesey Tacitus does not specifically associate them with the groves or human sacrifices, though it is reasonable to assume that they were. But the most surprising feature of his account is that the Roman troops were amazed 'by this extraordinary and novel sight'. If the Druids were well known in Britain, particularly if they were a major element in British resistance to Rome, one can only wonder why the Roman army had not come across them before in the years since the Claudian invasion. We have no record that Claudius extended his measures against the Druids to Britain; and if they had become a significant force in the intervening period, one would have expected the Romans to have heard enough about them not to be surprised when at last they came face to face. There must have been Gauls and Germans—there were almost certainly Batavians—amongst the auxiliary troops included in the assault on Anglesey. Some of these must have been acquainted with Druidic practices on the Continent and been well aware of their reputation in Roman circles there. The only reasonable explanation is that they were not common in Britain—and probably had not been, even in Caesar's time—and that the warlike part they played on this occasion was totally unexpected. It may well have been the 'Furies' that really frightened the Roman troops. In classical legend the Furies were, like the homicidal female devotees of Bacchus, only too familiar. Moreover, the soldiers may have been more chilled by the curses directed at them than by the appearance of Celtic priests themselves. Barbarians were common enough, but ghosts, black magic, and curses were taken seriously in the classical world, and are part of that darker side of classical religion that we shall examine briefly a little later. It is worth noting now that Pliny the Elder, writing perhaps as late as AD 79 and certainly revising his book as a whole well after the taking of Anglesey, talks of the Emperor Tiberius' legislation to exterminate Druidism in Gaul, and then goes on to mention Britain without saying anything about any subsequent action against them there. On the contrary, he emphasizes that at the time of writing (*hodie*) Britain was enthralled by magic, and so obsessed with the elaboration of its ritual that one might suppose that the Persians had learnt their practices from the Britons. Throughout the meagre record of British Druidism, then, we have this emphasis on Druidic lore and ritual, not politics, nor, with the exception of Anglesey, war.

One further piece of evidence is often quoted to support the theory of widespread Druid power in Britain. This is the great hoard of Iron Age metalwork found in the bog of Llyn Cerrig Bach on Anglesey itself, much of it apparently not originating from Wales, but from different parts of south-eastern England. The tradition of depositing votive objects in lakes and wells was certainly prevalent in the Celtic world, and water plays an important part in Celtic religion. This find may therefore provide evidence that the sacred fame of Anglesey had spread far in Britain. On the other hand, it may reflect the local chieftains' dedication to the gods of the place of fine possessions gained in trade, diplomacy, or war. But the most awkward feature for anyone trying to associate this hoard with Tacitus' Druids is that the archaeological dating of the objects puts the hoard well before the Claudian invasion. All in all, we cannot assume a political influence for the Druids in Britain anything like that in Gaul, at least by Roman times. On the other hand, as we shall see, there is every reason to believe Pliny's assertion of British addiction to magic and ritual, and no reason to doubt that Druidic tradition played an important part in the mental climate in which Romano-British religion was to flourish.

It is revealing that Tacitus chooses to make a point of the ritual of human sacrifice in the groves destroyed on Anglesey, and implies—without actually saying so—that it was a regular practice. This is clearly meant to shock the Roman reader, and perhaps to justify the drastic Roman action, but the details described are in themselves significant. The central feature of the public ceremonial in official Roman religion was the sacrificing of *animals* at the altars of the gods. The future was predicted—especially in great matters of state—by the inspection of the entrails of the sacrificial animals by the official *haruspices*. On the other hand, both Greeks and Romans regarded *human* sacrifice as completely barbaric. They could from time to time kill off prisoners of war in a way that most of us would consider unacceptable, but this was done for political or military reasons, not religious ones. The especial horror of what was revealed on Anglesey was that it must have seemed an impious parody of classical religion, perhaps comparable in its way with the revulsion that the Christians felt at the Mithraic rites, which they saw as a Satanic imitation of the Christian sacraments.

Tacitus does not mention the discovery of any severed heads in the groves of Anglesey. The cult of the severed head had been common in Iron Age Gaul, both sculptured and real. It is possible that Tacitus chose the other details as the most effective, for the reasons indicated above, but there are no other literary references to suggest such a cult in Britain, though there is some archaeological evidence. On the other hand, when Tacitus describes what the army of Germanicus found on their arrival at the scene of Quinctilius Varus' defeat in Germany, he goes out of his way to say that they saw human skulls fastened to the trunks of trees, and that in the neighbouring woods were the 'barbaric altars' at which the tribunes and senior centurions captured by the Germans had been slaughtered. The argument—from silence—for what it is worth, suggests that the severed head was not a prominent feature in the cult encountered by the Romans in Anglesey.

Traditional Roman religion, the ancient practice of the Roman state, still meant something in Tacitus' time. Under Trajan, the *gravitas*, simplicity, and integrity that were associated with the aristocratic way of life of the early Republic, and that were inextricably bound up with the traditional religion, seemed to be returning. It is easy to dismiss or deride Augustus' deliberate revival of the old state religion a century earlier as no more than a political sham that only lightly papered over the autocracy and cynicism of his own regime. Nevertheless, whatever Augustus' own inner beliefs may have been, it was part of his elaborate and calculated attempt to restore stability by reviving the outward forms of the Republic. By these means, he hoped both to conciliate the remains of the old conservative aristocracy and to draw in the new men who had risen to senatorial or equestrian rank in the civil wars and were adopting the attitudes of the traditional upper classes. There were enough people ready to be persuaded of the reality of the restored Republic—or willing for the sake of the return of peace at last to go along with what they knew to be a façade—to make this a remarkable success.

It is a compliment both to the strength of Roman tradition and to the cunning with which Augustus went about laying the foundations of this new state that anything of this survived the appalling record of the succeeding Julio-Claudians long enough to revive in the second century. It is perhaps even more surprising that it came through Domitian's attempt to restore it by means of a savagery so bigoted that it did not shrink from burying an unchaste Vestal Virgin alive. Yet it still had a real existence as a symbol of the ancient decencies and the majesty of Rome, a function for which late fourth-century senators were still willing to fight when they struggled with Christian emperors over the Altar of Victory. But in many ways this is symbolic. The old religion was chiefly a symbol or talisman, and by the time Tacitus was writing, personal spiritual needs were beginning to be met in other ways, a point to which we must return later.

In the last years of the old Republic the state religion had fallen into disrepute because of its blatant misuse by Caesar and other politicians to obstruct one another and to promote their own political manœuvres. Augustus employed the machinery of the state religion and all the resources of art, architecture, and literature to promote an appearance of a return to the dignified and honest ways of the earlier Republican past. Linked with this was the close identification of himself and the imperial family with the state religion. This rapidly developed into the Imperial Cult, though it was, with perhaps rare exceptions, only in the eastern provinces that members of the imperial family were actually deified while still alive until well into the first century AD, except in the form of 'the emperor and Rome'. As we have already seen, the provincial aristocracy played an important part in the official religion of the Capitoline triad—Jupiter, Juno, and Minerva—and in the Imperial Cult. At times or in places where it was felt inappropriate to dedicate altars to the emperor direct, it was very common to dedicate them to the emperor's *numen* or *genius*, his presiding spirit, or that of the imperial house as a whole. In fact, it became common to add such a dedication to altars primarily set up to another deity. It also became a frequent practice to erect altars 'for the welfare of the emperor' or in his honour, and a large number of these come from the army. The deliberate cultivation of this devotion to the emperor from the army was one of the ways in which the imperial government tried to ensure the loyalty of the troops. Alongside the parade-ground of the fort at Maryport on the Cumbrian coast have been found a whole series of altars to Jupiter Optimus Maximus that were deliberately buried, apparently representing the dedication, at a military ceremony held at regular intervals, of a new official altar by the current commanding officer. Closely linked with these cults were those of 'Disciplina Augusta', or imperial military discipline, and of the *genius* of the particular unit. The regimental standards were normally kept in a special chapel in the headquarters building, and might themselves be the subject of a cult marked by altars. Dedications to Discipline, and these other manifestations of loyalty were especially common at times of uncertainty and civil war, and underline the essentially political nature of official Roman religion.

The personal religion of Roman Britain can only be described by that overworked word 'kaleidoscopic', for it was not only immensely varied and multi-hued, but also changes shape each time one looks at it, making it exceptionally difficult to describe concisely. Some examples may give a better idea of the situation. On Bollihope Common, near Stanhope on the moors of County Durham, an altar of the Imperial Cult was found in 1747. It had been reused in ancient times, and the following inscription cut on it: 'To the Unconquered Silvanus, Gaius Tetius Veturius Micianus, prefect of the *ala Sebosiana*, auxiliary cavalry, set up this altar in willing fulfilment of his vow, if he were to capture the remarkably fine boar which many predecessors had failed to catch.' In one sense this is remarkably familiar. It combines light-hearted triumph at a sporting victory with the sort of taste that eighteenth-century gentlemen displayed in setting up memorial verses to their favourite hounds. On the other hand, there is a distinct feeling that the power of Silvanus is very considerable: the adjective 'Unconquered' is frequently paralleled in dedications to Mithras and in the imperial religion of the Unconquered Sun. One notes, too, the reference to a vow fulfilled, an extremely common feature. Prayer for a specific objective and to a specific god was a central feature of ancient life. It is very common indeed to find this in the context of closely localized gods. At Greta Bridge, in Yorkshire, for example, a Celtic lady called Brica and her daughter, who bore the Roman name of 'Januaria' and was perhaps the product of a marriage with a soldier in the nearby fort, dedicated an altar to the local nymph by name, again in thanks for a prayer answered. Often the deity has no name and is simply referred to as *genius loci*, the spirit of the place. Sometimes one suspects that the dedicator simply does not know the name of the local god and is playing safe, but one cannot escape the conviction that most people felt that every spot had its own presiding spirit, just as every human being had his *numen*, and every enterprise deserved its prayer. Sometimes the *genius* is on a grand scale, scarcely distinguishable from the 'personification' deities of cities, or provinces, or tribes. Under this heading we may note the dedication to 'The Land of the Batavians' that Ateius Cocceianus, an imperial slave, erected on being released from a vow at the fort site at Old Carlisle in the Cumbrian Plain. Much more direct is the thankful dedication of Claudius Epaphroditus Claudianus, tribune of the First cohort of Lingones, to 'the *genius* of the commandant's house'. This is very close to the ancient Roman family cult of the *lares* and *penates*, the spirits of the home; but the wording once again suggests that a specific prayer had been answered. It is akin to the obvious feeling of relief expressed by whoever set up an inscription at Moresby, 'to record the successful erection of the gable'. One of the most endearing is from Malton: 'Good luck to the *genius loci*! Use this goldsmith's workshop with as much good fortune for yourself as you may, little slave!' Many of these dedications are to deities that occur fairly widely over a particular geographical area, but are nevertheless clearly felt to be essentially of that region. Such, for example, are Cocidius, Belatucader, and Maponus, who are common in the neighbourhood of Hadrian's Wall. In the last case, there is good reason for deducing from the place-name Lochmaben in Dumfries and Galloway that there was a native cult-centre in the region before the Roman army arrived, and that it was felt wise to honour the local deity. At Ebchester we find Virilis, who describes himself as 'a German', fulfilling a vow to Cocidius, whom he describes as 'Vernostonus Cocidius', either a local version of the deity or a conflation with one of his own gods brought from home.

One deity particularly often honoured by the commanders of army units—frequently enough to make it seem like a semi-official cult—is Fortuna. This may perhaps seem unsurprising in that context, particularly in view of the importance attached to the luck of Roman commanders by their troops and themselves. But these dedications occur strikingly often not on the parade-ground, or in the headquarters building, or even in extramural shrines, but in military bath-houses. At Bowes fort there is a particularly interesting example. It records the rebuilding of the bath-house for the First cohort of Thracians under the supervision of the prefect of the *ala equitum Vettonum* (stationed at Ebchester) and by the direct orders of the provincial governor, Virius Lupus. It could thus hardly be more official. At Kirkby Thore another altar seems to have been even more specific about the deity, apparently describing her as 'Fortuna Balnearis'. It has sometimes been conjectured that the bath-house goddess thus commemorated was not primarily the deity of good fortune in war, but was more closely associated with the gaming that was a regular recreation of both soldiers and civilians in bathing establishments. Yet though this may be one aspect, it is difficult to equate it with the obviously official nature of many of the dedications. The Bowes inscription perhaps gives us a different clue. It states that the baths were rebuilt because 'they had been destroyed by the force of fire'. One reason why bath-houses were so often constructed outside forts rather than inside was probably the risk of fire, with furnaces presumably being stoked every day even in summer, and one may suspect that Fortuna was being asked to oversee a potentially dangerous installation. In other words, the motive was fear.

Fear and gratitude are, of course, particularly evident in the healing cults. One finds represented in Britain, as elsewhere, altars to the classical gods of medicine and health, notably Aesculapius, but by far the most striking manifestations are the major centres presided over by native or Romano-native healing deities. The two most notable are of Sulis Minerva around the hot springs at Bath, starting relatively early in the Roman period, and Nodens at Lydney in Gloucestershire, which in its fully developed form is relatively late. The latter was the site of an Iron Age hill-fort and a Roman iron-mine, and developed into a pagan pilgrimage centre of the native healing god Nodens, with temple, baths, extensive guest-house for those seeking help from the god, and a series of rooms that may have been used by patients awaiting visitation by the deity in visions or dreams. Such healing cults, as at many modern saints' shrines, were often adorned with votive models of the part needing cure. The best known of the great healing cults in Britain must be that of Sulis Minerva. The vast monumental complex of temple and baths came into use not very long after the suppression of the Boudiccan revolt, and may have predated by a little the full flowering of urban culture in Britain in the late first century. It continued in use into the fifth. Very briefly described, the sacred spring lay at the heart of the layout. It was linked on one side to an elaborate walled precinct, with a temple of classical type and an outdoor altar, and on the other to the massive bathing establishment. Windows permitted a view directly across the spring from the baths to the main altar.

At various points in its history the complex was extensively modified, the most dramatic change being the provision of a barrel-vaulted roof over the Great Bath, which may or may not have been covered in the earlier phases. This alteration, which necessitated massive strengthening of the structure, seems to have been carried out late in the second century or at the beginning of the third.

As usual, the conflation of Roman and native deities in Bath is unsure and ambivalent. A fine bronze head depicts the classical Minerva, and symbols normally associated with her appear on the temple pediment. Yet the central feature of that pediment is a male gorgon-like head, whose closest parallel in Britain is the Oceanus on the great dish of the fourth-century Mildenhall Treasure. The importance of the complex as a religious centre is underlined by the discovery of a statue-base in the temple enclosure dedicated to Sulis Minerva by L. Marcius Memor, *haruspex*. The *haruspices* represent the Etruscan tradition in official Roman religion, and it is extremely interesting to find one in so distant a province as Britain, honouring a conflated Romano-Celtic deity. Their function was divination by means of inspection of the entrails of sacrificial animals, by interpretation of prodigies (abnormal births and the like), and by the observation of lightning. Not all Romans took the art seriously, but nevertheless, like much in official Roman religion, this did not prevent its acquiring considerable social and political weight. The *haruspices* chiefly operated in Rome and in the Italian cities, which is a measure of the importance of the cult at Bath.

The general social level of Roman Bath, however, is better illustrated from the many dedications by middle-class army officers and the like. A typical example is that to Sulis, for the good health and safety of Aufidius Maximus, centurion of the Sixth legion, erected by his freedman Marcus Aufidius Lemnus. A similar inscription demonstrates both the linking of Roman and native and the practice of including a reference to the emperors: Gaius Curiatius Saturninus, centurion of the Second legion, erected a stone on behalf of himself and his family to Dea Sulis Minerva and to the *numina* of the emperors. As usual, these are in fulfilment of vows, and, one assumes, record a cure gained and the hope of future protection from illness and other misfortune.

Centurions and their like occur, but, with the possible exception of Marcius Memor, no one of more exalted rank. In Roman times the spa was middle class, respectable, and seriously dedicated to healing and recreation. The growth of a comfortable walled town around the great establishment at its centre indicates that these functions brought it solid good fortune.

The personal needs that took people to Bath in Roman days had their darker side. Curses and magic are not unknown in the written remains from Roman Britain, often occurring at the same sites as the appeals for health. Forces that could bestow health could also withhold it. From the reservoir supplied by the sacred spring of Sulis Minerva came a lead sheet with an inscription in handwriting (one of many found there), where each word is written backwards, as is common both in Roman and other magic. It curses someone unknown who has abducted or enticed a girl, and includes the names of the suspects: 'May he who carried off Vilbia from me become liquid as the water. May she who so obscenely ate her lose the power of speech; whether the culprit be Velvinna, Exsupereus, Severinus, Augustalis, Comitianus, Catusminianus, Germinilla, or Jovina.' The range of suspects seems large and is both male and female. It is a commonplace to make sure that a prayer or curse does not overlook the right target, but the range of sexual practices that may have prompted the deed is interesting. At Lydney the target seems less in doubt. A lead plate bears the inscription: 'To the divine Nodens. Silvianus has lost his ring and given half what it is worth to Nodens. Among those who bear the name Senicianus let none enjoy health until he brings it to the temple of Nodens.' This curse does not seem to have worked—at least, not straightaway, for the plaque bears a second inscription: the single word 'renewed' (*rediviva*). A thoroughly unpleasant plaque from Clothall, near Baldock, bears the sentence: 'Tacita is cursed by this and declared putrefied like rotting blood.'

Not all these religious plaques bear such nasty messages. Many are similar to the stone inscriptions we have already considered, and were doubtless often dedicated by those who could not afford anything more expensive. However, even from rural shrines they are often in precious metal, and one may imagine relatively simple structures bedecked with votive offerings, some individually quite costly. A group found at Barkway, near Royston, gives an idea of the contents of a rural shrine: a bronze statuette of Mars; seven silver plaques, six to Mars (one equated with a Celtic god as 'Mars Toutatis'), and one to Vulcan; and part of a bronze *patera* or handled bowl, such as were regularly used in ancient ritual. More obscure ideas are hinted at by a strange inscription on a fragment of gold leaf found in York that has symbols of unknown significance, probably magical, and a Coptic phrase, written in Greek lettering and apparently meaning 'the lord of the gods'. From Stony Stratford comes another silver inscription with the familiar theme of the vow fulfilled: 'To the divine Jupiter and Vulcan, I, Vassinus, their votary, who vowed that if they brought me home safely I would pay six *denarii*, now have remitted what I owed to the gods.' On this occasion, however, a new element is introduced into the archaeology, for the inscription was found along with two plaques to Mars and a number of other metal objects that included a ritual head-dress made up of chains and plates. One recalls Pliny the Elder describing the Britons as being obsessed with ritual.

This piece may be compared with the ceremonial crowns found at another rural shrine, at Wilton, in the parish of Hockwold-cum-Wilton in Norfolk. This lies east of the largest of the southern Fenland settlements, and just across the river from one of the richest of the Fen Edge villa sites. The picture of a multiplicity of relatively small cult-centres in the countryside begins to sharpen, shrines that both acted as a focus for personal hopes and fears and, from the evidence of the ritual dress and equipment, were the scene of ceremonial worship as well as private devotions. There is a strong probability that at least some lay on villa estates. The deities were a mixture of Roman and native, and the occurrence of votive offerings in silver and occasionally gold indicates the participation in the cults of people of means. We are not dealing merely with the religion of the humblest country folk. The following quotation is from a letter that a second-century Roman wrote to a friend, asking if he had ever visited the head of a certain river, named Clitumnus:

The source itself emerges at the bottom of a fair-sized hill, which bears a grove of ancient cypresses. It bubbles out in several separate springs of varying strength. These converge first into a broad, still pool. There the water, clear as glass, allows you to see gleaming pebbles on the bottom and the coins that people have thrown in . . . The banks of the river are lined with ash and poplar, whose reflections appear like objects floating on the limpid surface. The water itself glitters like snow and is icy cold. Hard by, stands the ancient, much-hallowed temple. The image of Clitumnus within it is dressed in the official toga of a Roman magistrate, and from the number of oracular tablets visible it is clear that a god is in truth in the place. Many smaller shrines are dotted around the main one, each to a different deity. Each is named and has its own ceremonial, and some even have their own springs, for the main river is joined by lesser rivulets within the site. A bridge crosses below the point where the streams come together, and this marks the lower limit of the sacred water. Above the bridge only boats are allowed: below one may swim as well. The people of Hispellum, to whom the late deified Emperor Augustus gave the place, have provided public baths and an inn. There are a number of private villas as well that have taken advantage of the superb sites available fronting on to the river. All in all, there is nothing that will not delight you. Indeed, you will even be able to indulge in a little studying, for you will see inscriptions everywhere, emanating from a multitude of people and to be seen on every column and every wall. Many bear sentiments you will applaud, some will make you laugh—but I am being unfair: you are much too kind to make fun of anyone . . .

This could be a description of Roman Gaul or Britain, but in fact it is Pliny the Younger describing a stop on a journey in rural Italy. The affinity between Roman religion and that of the Celtic areas under Roman rule becomes closer and closer the more one looks at the cults that appealed to ordinary people rather than the great public ceremonial of the Roman state. We can usefully turn back now, within this context, to the little Romano-British shrine of Coventina at Carrawburgh, and see how, even in the far reaches of the frontier, one of these local cults, outwardly humble in appearance, could attract large numbers of people over a long period. The shrine itself was the simplest type of structure, similar in plan to a small Romano-Celtic temple, but with the well itself taking the place of the usual central chamber or *cella*. In this well were found more than 13,000 Roman coins, and a mass of pots, altars, carved stones, incense-burners, pearls, a skull, and other objects. Some of these may have been cast in during a period of desecration, perhaps by Christians (the nearby chapel of Mithras was also destroyed), but much seems to have been deposited as votive offerings, and the association of water, a shaft, and possibly the human skull suggests strong links with some of the central characteristics of Celtic religion. Dedicators included officers, soldiers, and possibly civilians, and the coins continue down to the reign of Gratian.

There is good reason, in fact, to suspect a continuation (or reimportation) of the cult of the ritual shaft in Roman Britain. At Ashill, in Norfolk, religious practices involving a shaft were being carried out in the Flavian period, and at Cambridge a site that had previously been occupied by a shrine, possibly going back to the Iron Age, produced nine shafts. In each shaft there was the burial of a dog and one or more babies. These shafts date from the late third century or early fourth. The children were buried with shoes (a practice to which we shall return when we consider burial in general); the presumption is that they had died in infancy and been buried in holy ground, and that the elaborate and sanctified manner of burial in shafts was intended to help the children on their way into the next world, rather than to make the shafts themselves sacred. On the other hand, in late pre-Roman times sacrifice may well have been employed in this connection, for the head of a woman, still attached to the neck, was buried behind the lining of a well at the rural settlement at Odell in Bedfordshire.

For the survival of the severed head cult itself within the Roman period, we have no certain evidence from Britain. The skull from Coventina's well may be accidental, and it is probable that if there had been any such cult active on such a site, where it would be immediately detected by the Roman authorities, it would have been promptly suppressed. The skulls from the site layers corresponding to the Boudiccan destruction in London might at first suggest that the Britons were still head-hunting in war, but the exhibition of the heads of executed traitors was, after all, normal in England as late as the seventeenth century, and in that age it had no religious significance. Indeed, Tacitus' description of the massacres carried out by Boudicca in the captured Roman cities reads in its details like a savage parody of Roman criminal justice at its most cruel. Nevertheless, it is possible that some of the sculpture from Roman Britain—particularly the Towcester head—records the survival of such cults in symbolic form under Roman rule.

Personal religion is, of course, a subject that cannot be separated from death and burial, and the range of burial customs displayed in Roman Britain is wide. The two main rites were cremation and various forms of 'inhumation' or burial of the body unburnt. There is no evidence of exposure of bodies above ground during the Roman period, even though it may have been employed in Iron Age Britain. In very broad chronological terms, cremation, the traditional Roman practice, was the dominant rite during the first and second centuries, and inhumation in the third, fourth, and fifth. This seems to have been partially, but certainly not entirely, due to the spread of Christianity and a literal belief in the resurrection of the body. At Chichester, the St Pancras cemetery, which was used from Flavian times until the fourth century (but less frequently after about AD 200), produced a total of 260 burials from the excavation of 1966–9, all but nine of which were cremations. In contrast, a small rural cemetery at Martyr Worthy in Hampshire, which came into use in the second century and continued into the fourth, contained inhumations only. There are exceptions to the pattern. The large cemetery at Guilden Morden in Cambridgeshire, for example, produced anomalies in the form of a fine first-century inhumation and a cremation of the late third century or early fourth. However, while there is no doubt that pagan funerary fashion was moving in the direction of inhumation elsewhere in the Roman world, concurrently with the rise of Christianity, it was already well established in Britain as part of this general trend before the Christian religion had any real hold here. The depositing of objects with the dead—to help the soul on its journey to the other world, to comfort the dead in the grave, or as a mark of respect and adornment for the corpse at burial—may have become less common with Christian influence, but it did not die out. Their presence does not rule out a Christian burial, nor their absence prove one: the elaborate accompaniments of the body of Maria, wife of the most Christian Emperor Honorius, could hardly make this point more strongly. Similarly, while there was a tendency to place Christian burials with an east–west orientation, it was by no means universal; and pagan cemeteries with regular orientation are not unknown.

Under Roman law it was illegal to bury the dead within a town. At the same time, there was a strong desire not to be overlooked after death, and a fear of loneliness in the grave. Hence we find the main roads leading from cities lined with cemeteries. Here the dead could be sure that the passing traveller would notice their memorials and perhaps stop to read an inscription, and could expect their family and friends to gather on certain festivals. At Winchester, where one of the major town cemeteries lay alongside the road to Mildenhall, the earliest graves lay closest to the city. Sometimes cemeteries went out of use and were not always respected, but on the whole the pattern of cemeteries can be used by the historian to define the outer limits of a settlement. Sometimes renewed urban growth was obliged to site itself beyond the earliest cemeteries. This is particularly true of civil settlements outside major military bases, where one may often suspect that very early army graves prevented civil development occurring close to the fortress itself, even if reasons of tactical prudence did not forbid it.

The same tendency for burial to occur near roads is also observable in the countryside, as, for example, in the Martyr Worthy or Stanton Harcourt groups, which lie alongside country lanes. A type of cemetery well known on the Continent and frequently recognized in a rural context seems to carry through from the pre-Roman Iron Age into the Roman period. This commonly took the form of a rectangular enclosure, like those of the Iron Age mentioned earlier, and is usually marked by a ditch and bank. Some of the Continental examples have evidence for wooden gates at the entrances, and one example from Württemberg is particularly significant, in that its bank overlays one of the shafts with a stake at the bottom noted as a feature of Celtic religion. In the part of the Rhineland around Bonn, some of these enclosures seem to have gone out of use with the arrival of the Romans, but others continued, with an apparent revival in the fourth century of some of those that had been abandoned. Importantly, there is a detectable relationship between the cemeteries and the distribution of Romano-Celtic temples in that region.

While it might appear at first sight that some of the most ancient Christian churches and their associated cemeteries in Continental cities break the rule that prohibited burial within towns, which continued in force even when Christianity became the official religion of the empire, it becomes clear on closer examination that the churches usually originated in chapels set up in cemeteries that, at the time, lay outside Roman cities. In many cases these were over the graves of martyrs, and attracted subsequent burials of Christians who wanted to be as near as possible to the saint. The best-known example is probably that of the Basilica of St Peter at Rome, the result of an enormous engineering operation commissioned by Constantine in order to erect his church over the existing extramural cemetery on the Vatican hillside that was believed to contain the grave of St Peter himself.

Only infant burials seem to have been exempted from the general prohibition, judging from their occurrence within towns and other settlements; and it may be that the classical right of a father to decide whether his new-born child should survive or be exposed affected belief about the necessity to bury outside the inhabited area. Until the baby had been formally recognized by the father and taken into the family, its existence as an individual was perhaps unconfirmed. In country districts, too, where convention, if not law, excluded normal burial within farm or villa precincts, groups of infant burials are not uncommonly found in the corners of farmyards. On the other hand, where adult remains are found in settlements there is a *prima facie* case for suspecting accident or murder. In the Fen Edge settlement at Hockwold the skeleton of a man was found buried in silt in a ditch, and it seems probable that his presence was not known about when the site was reoccupied briefly after a severe flood. However, the couple buried under a new floor in one of the buildings of the civil settlement outside Housesteads, the man having a sword-point embedded in him, had obviously been concealed with intent.

Ghosts were much feared and needed placating, but there was also a more friendly aspect to the cult of the dead. The well-known 'pipe' cremation found at Caerleon, where a tube led from the canister holding the ashes to the surface, is an example of a

Mediterranean practice rare in the northern part of the empire, but it underlines the very common classical belief that the dead could benefit from libations offered at the tomb by the living. Fear that one would not receive proper burial and that one's spirit would wander unregarded encouraged the formation of burial clubs. These were not only responsible for arranging the funeral, but also held regular meetings and commemorative meals, and often purchased plots reserved for the burial of their members, at which they could gather. These societies were particularly popular with slaves and the poor, who might be without the means or surviving relatives to ensure a ritually complete funeral and commemorative rites on anniversaries thereafter. At Halton Chesters on Hadrian's Wall the tombstone of a slave named Hardalio was erected by such an association set up by his fellows. In such cases, the association took the place of the dead man's family. At Ostia a clearer picture of their activities emerges when one contemplates the rows of tombs fronting on to the main road into the city, some with neat enclosures or gardens in front, where offerings might be left, flowers grown, and the funerary or commemorative banquet held. It was not uncommon to portray the dead man himself as present at the banquet. The tombstone of the Moorish freedman Victor, at South Shields, shows him lying comfortably on a dinner-couch, while a small figure offers him wine from a bowl lying beneath the seat. Such representations cannot, of course, be dissociated from ideas of the dead in paradise, or from the ritual meal common to several religions current at the time, though it is often extremely difficult to know what meaning the people who purchased the monuments attached to the scenes portrayed, since gravestones and sarcophagi were often bought from the ready-made stock kept in the mason's yard, awaiting only the addition of a suitable inscription. It is well known that the iconography of one religion was often adapted and given a new meaning by another, and the practices of the funerary masons' trade can only have encouraged the flexibility that we so often encounter.

There is evidence, particularly from the higher levels of society, that the family duty to bury and commemorate the dead was conscientiously carried out generation after generation. In Britain the great earthen burial-mounds at Bartlow, on the border of

Essex and Cambridgeshire, are among the best known instances. There is a similar set at Stevenage, and both probably represent the same social group, the Romano-British aristocracy. Indeed, it is possible that both families were members of the same *civitas*, and were represented on its council. At Holborough in Kent there is a particularly interesting example of behaviour towards the dead. There a barrow had been constructed over an elaborated executive cremation, which can be dated to the beginning of the third century, and a secondary burial, this time the inhumation of a child, had been inserted into it within a few years. Both the initial Holborough burial and one of the Bartlow barrows contained folding stools of the sort that servants carried for their masters, and it is clear that both represent the same high social class. The child's interment at Holborough was, it appeared, carefully inserted, probably with the intention of respecting the original burial. There is a strong chance that this reflects a deliberate family decision. Indeed, it is perhaps not completely fanciful to catch in the change from cremation to inhumation one of those rare echoes of family life. There are signs that the original cremation was already considered rather archaic when it was carried out, for the ashes were deposited in a curious mock coffin, almost as if the wish of an elderly and conservative member of the family to be buried in the old manner had been carried out by his heirs, but with an attempt to make the rite conform to more modern ideas. When the child died a little later, there was no need for such pretence.

The substitution of inhumation for cremation as the more commonly adopted form of burial went deeper than mere fashion, and we should not imagine that the family debate we have imagined at Holborough was about trivialities. It has been argued that the change from cremation to inhumation reflected the triumph of Roman individualism over Greek conceptions of the merging of the soul after death into a universal godhead or divine force. This cannot be sustained. Cremation was not only Greek, it was also the traditional Roman form of funeral. In point of time, the change overlaps with the period when Neoplatonic ideas were modifying traditional Roman philosophy, and when the eastern mystery-religions were winning converts in the west and affecting general ideas about death and the afterlife. It accords more easily with these facts to see Roman respect for the family and for the identity of the individual ancestor as providing an environment in which the new ideas could flourish. Christianity, and to some extent the other religions that had been developing in the eastern part of the known world, where Greek and oriental met, offered individual contact with the divine, salvation, and a life after death. To many Romans this was a creed that was compatible with—indeed, it enhanced—their own ancestral notions of personality. However, there is no reason to think that without the arrival of these outside, predominantly eastern, influences, the Romans would have changed their burial customs. Their innate conservatism, at its most intense in the religion of the family, would almost certainly have held them to their ancient practices to the end.

The emphasis on the individual is reflected more clearly in the obvious importance that was placed in Roman Britain on the grave and on the monuments by which the dead were recorded, however varied their form. They were normally inscribed, and the classic type is a dedication to the *manes* or spirit of the deceased. It records his name, parentage, voting tribe (if a Roman citizen), his career and distinctions, and the name and relationship of the person or persons erecting the monument. Sometimes the dead person is portrayed in relief sculpture, ranging in style and competence from the splendid full-length relief of M. Favonius Facilis, a centurion of the Twentieth legion, erected around the middle of the first century at Colchester by his freedmen, down to the very crude but touching stone commemorating Vacia, *infans*, aged three, buried at Carlisle. It is common to find monuments being built by the heirs of the dead, by spouses, parents, sons, or daughters. Freedman, too, often appear in this role, in many cases doubtless because they had been set free in their master's will—an accepted practice—but often as their late employer's closest associate or man of business. The exact age of the deceased at death is very frequently recorded, though there is a tendency in later inscriptions to adopt the formula 'lived for more or less so many years . . .' (*vixit plus minus*), a custom probably influenced by the spread of Christian notions of the relative unimportance of earthly life and its duration.

The tombstone of Favonius Facilis was originally plastered and painted, in the manner of much ancient sculpture, whether of stone or wood, and it is probable that most of the carved lettering on stone inscription was similarly coloured. In areas where stone was scarce or where the family were too poor to afford it, there were doubtless very many wooden monuments with lettering that was either carved or painted by a signwriter. The ashes from cremation burials in Britain are generally found in pots or glass jars; inhumations were either in wooden, lead, or stone coffins, or were placed straight into the ground. Lead coffins are themselves found enclosed in stone outer cases, sometimes supplied from quarries far away. This could cause unfortunate mistakes. At the Arbury Road cemetery in Cambridge there were clearly some exceptionally incompetent undertakers. Among other errors, the most spectacular resulted in the stone coffin having to be split across its middle to accept the lead inner coffin, which was too long for it. The scene at the funeral can be left to the imagination. We cannot, however, always blame the undertaker, as there was much reuse of funerary monuments. One interesting practice, found, for example, at York and in the the Poundbury cemetery at Dorchester in Dorset, is the pouring into the coffin of liquid gypsum. This set, leaving a mould of the body, and has proved efficient in preserving hair and other materials. In the Poundbury cemetery, for example, the gypsum filling of a stone coffin had kept the outline of a shroud edged with gold wire.

The tomb itself, when it was more than a simple grave, could range from a small stone or tile structure, through unostentatious vaults, to large buildings intended to mark the importance of the deceased or to provide accommodation for generations of dead from the same family or club. The Bartlow Hills, with their flat tops, are mounds closely connected in form with those common in Gallia Belgica, and are probably part of the same cultural tradition. There are a few circular stone, or partly stone, tombs, such as that at High Rochester in Redesdale, which may have been culturally associated with these barrows, but are perhaps more likely to have been derived from the circular monuments fairly common in the classical world. One of the grandest British monuments is the mausoleum on the plateau of Shorden Brae, above the Tyne, which lies between the Roman town of

Corbridge and the site of the Agricolan fort. It consisted of a central structure, probably a tower, containing a pit, and lay within a large walled enclosure, the corners of which seem to have been decorated with impressive stone lions. The monument was dated to the middle of the second century by one pot from the central building. It is not, in fact, absolutely certain that there was ever a body deposited in the monument, as there was no trace of a burial, except for nails in the pit that might have come from a box or coffin. It is not impossible that it was a cenotaph for a very senior officer killed in the Antonine wars in the north. One is reminded of the monument to M. Caelius, centurion of the Eighteenth legion, lost in the disaster of AD 9 in Germany, on which his brother specifically stated that the bones had not yet been recovered. Great importance was attached by the Romans to the proper disposal of the body, and heirs felt it incumbent upon them to make it clear that they were doing the best they could by erecting a cenotaph when an actual burial was impossible. Six years after the defeat, Germanicus made it a particular point of honour to reach the camp of Varus where the bones of his men still lay unburied, and to give them proper burial, marking the spot with a turf monument. The Emperor Tiberius subsequently disapproved, and one of the possible reasons given by Tacitus provides a sudden insight into Roman practices and beliefs: 'It is possible that he felt a Roman commander-in-chief, invested with the powers of an augur and other most ancient religious roles, should not take part in funerary rites.' The underlying concepts are of the sanctity and purity of the priest, and of the ritual defilement associated with contact with death. These are found in many religions. The peculiarly Roman element is that the religious powers, like the secular ones, stemmed from the office of state: once the general or magistrate came to the end of his appointment, he also laid down his priestly powers and the ritual restrictions that they imposed upon his behaviour.

Whilst the correct burial of the dead was felt to be a matter of great importance—a sacred trust laid upon the living—the elaborate precautions that some Romans took to make sure that their tombs were not disturbed suggest that there was less respect for old graves than one might expect. It is common to find threats against the perpetrators of damage to the tomb or those who carry out secondary burial in it being incorporated in funerary inscriptions. Such fears were not groundless. The Roman city walls of Chester, for example, show that in the fourth century large numbers of tombstones were uprooted to provide material for repairs. However, there are sometimes signs that this was done with respect. The Shorden Brae mausoleum was demolished in the late Roman period, but some of the sculptured stone was buried in a pit, like the annual altars on the parade-ground at Maryport.

It is clear that, for some unknown reason, one of the burials in another important mausoleum was removed carefully. This monument provides a contrast to the Shorden Brae example in other ways, for it lies in the south, is associated with a villa, and was certainly not a cenotaph. Its owners, however, may have been officials. Standing alongside the house at Lullingstone in Kent, this mausoleum matches in importance both the pagan and Christian features of the villa itself. In plan and size, it resembled a Romano-Celtic temple, but deep beneath the central room there was a tomb-chamber, which had originally contained two inhumations. The surviving lead coffin was decorated, and each of the burials had been supplied with an identical set of grave-goods. The room above was, like the Christian cult-room in the villa itself, decorated with mural figure-paintings, and was clearly intended to be visited. The construction of the mausoleum was, however, rather earlier in date than the Christian features in the villa—around AD 300—and was probably pagan, though the coffins had been filled with gypsum, which would have been in line with the beliefs of people who expected bodily resurrection.

Sometimes, as here, the burial was intended to be hidden from sight, and one may assume that the decoration on the lead coffin was for the purposes of the funeral and to please the dead. Many stone sarcophagi also were clearly intended to be buried. Others, however, were elaborately decorated and were meant to remain above ground or in a vault, where they could be seen. Sometimes they were free-standing; in other cases they were undecorated on the back and were intended to stand in a niche or against a wall. Some bore inscribed panels very similar to the free-standing tombstones; and a fashion for including portrait busts of the deceased in low relief in a central *tondo* or roundel, often of a married couple, has provided us with some of our most important examples of Roman portrait sculpture. The imperial families of the fourth and fifth centuries indulged in the most extravagant and gigantic sarcophagi of Egyptian porphyry, a stone both difficult to transport and to work, a fitting monument to the deliberate cult of personal grandeur practised by Diocletain and his successors. These sarcophagi were often housed above ground in specially commissioned mausoleums, an imperial taste going back to the very foundation of the Empire. They are extreme examples of the enduring desire of the Roman and provincial nobility for their dignity to be remembered after death.

The funeral itself had long been an important opportunity to display the family distinctions, and in upper-class families images of the ancestors were carried in procession. After the death of Septimius Severus in Britain, an extraordinary ritual was carried out in Rome, where a full-sized image of the dead emperor was displayed for several days and was paid honours as if he were still alive but dying, until the doctors declared the emperor officially dead. In most funerals the body was carried on a litter to the cemetery, where, if cremation was being practised, it was burnt on a pyre. The cremated bones were washed in wine and put into whatever container was being used. Sacrifices were offered to the *lares* or spirits, the mourners were purified from the defilement of contact with death, and a wake was held. The importance of wine in such ceremonial may suggest that the appearance of amphorae in burials even in pre-Roman Britain may not represent mere ostentation or drink for the dead. Certainly, the jug and handled-bowl (*patera*) that appear along with the sacrificial knife in relief on many Roman altars are also found in connection with the dead across the Roman world, including Britain. In the Holborough barrow, in association with the primary burial, several amphorae had been deliberately broken and wine poured over them. It was common to provide the deceased with a coin with which to pay Charon, the ferryman who carried the dead across the river of the Underworld to the realms of Hades in classical mythology. The important cemetery found at Cirencester between the city and the amphitheatre has produced a number of skeletons with a coin in their mouths, and one or more with a coin on each eye, and the same provision is found as late as the middle of the fourth century at Poundbury, despite the generally Christian ethos of that community. We have already noted at several points the placing of treasured objects in the grave. One particularly notable example from York is a folding fan, similar to one held by an elegant Roman lady on a fine tomb relief from Carlisle. That the practice continued in Christian circles is demonstrated by another burial at York, a lady who went to her grave equipped with earrings, bracelets, armlets, a glass jug, a mirror, and a piece of bone-strip pierced with the Christian motto: 'Sister, hail! May you live in God.'

So far the funerary practices have been intelligible, either because they correspond to descriptions by classical authors or clearly stem from beliefs recorded by them, or because they seem to have a rational explanation. The word 'seem' is deliberately used, because there are other practices known archaeologically that would appear to have no literary parallels nor any likely explanation. This must make us think twice before attributing reasons to *any* funerary or religious practice from the ancient world for which we have no written evidence. However, there are degrees of unintelligibility. For example, the fairly common occurrence of pots that have been deliberately drilled or broken may indicate a ritual killing of the object that is to accompany the dead—or it may simply be a way of discouraging the reuse of utensils that have been associated with death and burial. More difficult to understand is the presence of hobnails for boots. These occurred in most of the first-century graves found at Puckeridge, and still appear in the cemetery at Curbridge in Oxfordshire, which is probably late Roman in date. At Puckeridge it appeared that each person buried had been supplied with a pair of boots; in the second case—an inhumation cemetery—the nails were found around the feet of the skeletons. We may perhaps surmise that the dead were felt to need a good pair of boots for their journey to the Underworld. Indeed, the presence of a building at the cemetery near the amphitheatre outside Cirencester that contained a furnace and over 2,000 of these hobnails makes one wonder whether footwear was specially made for funerary purposes—indeed, whether on occasion a few nails may not have been placed in the grave as a symbolic gesture in place of an actual pair of boots.

A much odder practice is the beheaded skeleton. Three from the Guilden Morden cemetery, and four from Dorset are well known. It is now clear that there were considerably more examples of this practice. In many of the cases the head is placed at the feet or between the legs. The bodies were, we may therefore presume, dismembered soon after death: an unusual example from the Dunstable group proves that the limbs were still articulated at the time, for in that case the head had not only been placed between the legs, but the latter had been cut off above the knee and arranged so that the feet lay on either side of the neck. It is interesting, though it may be no more than a coincidence, that the Curbridge cemetery that produced the shoe-nails around the feet also contained three skeletons with their heads between their feet, while Dunstable contained two burials that had had boots laid under the knees. For the present, we seem to have in the decapitation burials a rite that has no easy explanation. If anything, the dating makes it more difficult to hazard a guess. Beginning in the late third century or early fourth, and possibly continuing into the fifth, the practice is too late to be easily associated with the Iron Age severed head cult, yet too early to be obviously associated with the large-scale arrival of barbarians in Roman service. The truth is that we cannot be sure about either the origin of this rite or what it meant. We can only record it, with the observation that it ought to remind us of just how much that is very alien to our ways of thinking lay beneath the superficially modern and familiar appearance of the Roman world.

The sacrifices to the *lares* at the traditional funeral reflect elements at the core of Roman private religion. But we encounter extreme difficulty if we try to define the precise meaning or origins of the underlying beliefs. It is clear that the centre of Roman religion in its strictest sense—the religion of Rome itself, and thence of Italy and the Roman communities abroad—was the cult of the household and the family, living and dead—or rather, of the spirits that oversaw and dwelt within them. Writ large, the core of the state religion was exactly the same—the cults of Vesta, or the sacred hearth of the city and the Forum, and of even older deities. On to this, the Graeco-Roman Olympian religion, with all its myths, was a subsequent graft. The central

Roman cults had no such personified myths, but only a presence and rituals, and were close to pure animism. From such beliefs, the notions of the *numen* of an individual, particularly the emperor, and the cult of the *genius*, of which we have seen examples, could develop naturally and become infinitely flexible. With this background of belief, it is not surprising that, integral to the daily life of the traditional Roman family, were the respects paid to the spirits of the family and household, most notably the *lares*, the *penates* or spirits of the larder, and frequently the slightly more personified Vesta or goddess of the hearth. There is much uncertainty as to the origin and meaning of the *lares familiares* themselves. There is some reason to think that they started as outdoor deities, and *lares* continued to be found as spirits of crossroads in classical times. It is also considered possible that they originated in the cult of the dead, and were thought of as ghosts. Whatever their origin and content, their normal place as gods of the home was in the *lararium* or shrine within the house. There they could also be joined by images of other more personified deities particularly associated with family life and fortune, such as Vesta herself, Venus, Juno Lupicina, goddess of childbirth, and any gods especially venerated by the particular family. The platform for such a household shrine was found at Silchester, a city that has also produced statuettes of a *lar* and of a *genius*. Various forms of the *genius* could represent different aspects of the family and household. Perhaps the most extreme official move that the Christian emperors of the fourth century made against paganism was Theodosius' prohibition of the customary respects to the household gods and the celebration of their festivals. The imperial government was no longer simply requiring public observance of the new state religion, but was striking at what a paterfamilias might do in his own house. The old gods of the Roman state had already been banished from public life. Now the divinities of the family itself were to be denied worship, and in the context of the central place of the family in Roman life, both private and political, the crucial nature of the prohibition becomes obvious. Theodosius was, of course, right in identifying the final target. Until the most ancient cults of the home could be stamped out, there could be no hope of uniform adherence to Christianity in the empire at large, nor could the eventual loyalty of the oldest senatorial families to the policy of the court be hoped for while their children continued to be brought up under the daily influence of the old religion in its most impressive form.

The association of other deities with the *lares* and *penates* in the *lararium* reminds us that Romans frequently included other gods in their family worship. Among the most striking of the local deities in Britain are the *genii cucullati*, usually shown as small figures dressed in heavy cloaks with hoods attached and worn in position, remarkably like representations of medieval peasants. They, like the *matres*, often appear as a triad, and like most other religious reliefs in Roman Britain, there is no reason to doubt that most came from temples or shrines in public places. However, in the *vicus* outside the fort of Housesteads one of the excavated houses had tucked away in its interior a shrine with a relief depicting the *genii cucullati*. It is, of course, possible that the 'house' was in fact a chapel used by a group of devotees to this cult (which was popular in the Wall region), but the situation of the shrine suggests that it was private to that particular family.

It is a moot point to what extent these family cults can be considered *personal* religion. They were certainly private, in that they were inextricably bound up with the closed circle of the household and the family, living and departed. But were they personal, in the sense of communication between individual and deity, a religious experience peculiar to oneself? To many ancients this might have seemed a meaningless question, in that family and state were everywhere involved with the divine. Yet the enormous number of dedications set up in recognition of a prayer answered demonstrates that the individual did feel that his personal needs were noted and heeded by particular pagan gods; and there are occasions where an even closer experience of the supernatural is recorded. An inscription from Bath, for example, quite clearly states that it was erected as the result of a vision (*ex visu*). Other dedications are set up by order of the god (*ex iussu*), presumably the consequence of some similar occurrence, and the practice of the sick sleeping at the temples of the great healing gods was a logical extension of the same belief in the personal appearance of the divinity to an individual.

We noted above, in the context of the gradual change from cremation to inhumation, how Romans turned to the eastern mystery-religions. This was already happening under the late Republic, and gained more and more momentum during the early Empire. Many seem to have felt a need for personal revelation, which was lacking in the old rituals. At the same time philosophy, particularly among the senatorial class, helped to provide an intelligible basis for traditional moral standards, and a consolation in the tribulations through which they passed under the Julio-Claudian and Flavian emperors, the memory of which remained a powerful force in the second century. To understand Tacitus' historical writings, for example, we have to see him against the background of his personal experience of rising in a public career under Domitian, and of the very similar experiences of his relatives, notably Agricola, and his circle of friends and acquaintances. He is not only excusing failure to resist tyranny: some senators had tried, with fatal consequences to themselves, and little apparent effect on the course of events. He is also making the positive point that moral duty requires service to the state, however bad the emperor. Such endurance and persistence in duty was in line with the Stoic philosophy popular in his class; and one might argue that without the combination of this force with family ambition, the mechanism of the Roman government could not have been carried on relatively undamaged for so long. At the same time, there was the countervailing influence of Epicurean philosophy, which argued for the achievement of personal tranquillity by deliberate avoidance of situations that would lead to extremes of pleasure or pain. Epicureanism accorded well with that other powerful tendency we have noted in Roman upper-class attitudes, the desire to withdraw into private life, the high value placed on dignified leisure (*otium cum dignitate*). At its best, this encouraged the quiet cultivation of the arts, friendship, and the enjoyment of the countryside. At its extreme, it fostered the unwillingness of the fourth-century senatorial class to become involved in the burdens of public service even when the opportunity was offered to them once more after the restrictions imposed by third-century emperors. It was a frame of mind that led to the holding of office for the briefest possible time necessary to fulfil family duty, and to the adoption of retirement as a way of life.

Philosophy, however, was not enough for a very large number

of people, particularly in those classes where the conditions of life were a great deal harder; nor, in the end, was it sufficient for many of the senatorial class itself. For Marcus Aurelius, the consolations of philosophy could sustain him to the highest degree as he sought to serve the state; but we already have Hadrian enthusiastically taking part in mystery-religion. At the lowest end of society, among slaves and the urban poor, hope of personal salvation and relief from this world were demanding something more, and Christianity fell on ready ground in the cities of the empire, not least among the proletariat of Rome itself. But as far as Britain is concerned, the first of the major eastern mystery-cults to gain a powerful hold was that of Mithras.

We have already noted Mithraism's attraction for soldiers and merchants. The practice of the cult was exclusively confined to men, and the small size of its chapels underlines the fact that one of the consequences of the rigour of its seven grades of initiation was small congregations. On the other hand, its devotees were persons of consequence: officers and businessmen. It appealed to the same trait in Roman society as Stoicism, the life of discipline and action. One of the altars from the Mithraeum outside the fort at Carrawburgh was dedicated between AD 198 and 211 by the prefect of the First cohort of Batavians, Aulus Cluentius Habitus of Larinum in Italy. It can hardly be coincidence that the man from Larinum who was defended by Cicero on a charge of murder in 66 BC with the speech known as the *Pro Cluentio* was also named Aulus Cluentius Habitus. It is important and significant that this altar, which seems to come from the earliest phase of the temple, confirms that Mithraism could attract a member of one of the few families who still survived in public life from the Italian upper classes of the Republic. The well-known Temple of Mithras in London shows another aspect of Mithraism that may help to explain its popularity with the business community, in addition to the obvious attractions of the cult's Masonic secrecy and insistence on integrity. Some threat to the cult caused the deliberate concealment of a large group of sculpture within the London temple. Together with casual finds from the same site, these demonstrate vividly the ease with which Mithraism seems to have been able to absorb other religions, or at least to offer them tolerant hospitality. As well as the indubitably Mithraic sculptures, the London temple group included a river-god, perhaps the Thames, a *genius*, heads of Minerva and of the Graeco-Egyptian Serapis, a Bacchic scene (reminding us of the popularity of the Dionysiac cult with its joyful afterlife), a circular relief that seems to derive from a cult of Thracian origin, and a fragment of one of the Dioscuri. Such willingness to accommodate other cults may have made Mithraism particularly acceptable to the cosmopolitan business community of London, as well as to army officers, who were themselves gradually being drawn from a wider and wider background.

The evidence for deliberate destruction at both these Mithraea, which are by no means alone in this respect, raises the question of how a cult that had had such powerful backing came to an end. At Carrawburgh there seem to be two periods of destruction, the first occurring at about the end of the third century, the second probably in the fourth, after an extensive refurbishing. It is possible that the first destruction was by enemy action at the time of the fall of Allectus, but it is not entirely impossible that local Christians seized the opportunity presented by the victory of the tolerant Caesar Constantius to attack the detested rival religion. It is certainly very likely that the second and final destruction was due to Christian action, possibly on official orders. The London Mithraeum shows a broadly similar pattern. The dating of its foundation is in dispute, as the major sculptures have been dated, on grounds of style, to the second century, but the pottery suggests construction around AD 240. However, it certainly stood intact until a crisis occurred somewhere about the beginning of the fourth century, when extensive dismantling of the structure took place and the main pieces of sculpture were hidden. Indeed, the head of Mithras seems to have been already damaged by a blow from an implement before the concealment was carried out. Yet, some time not long after the shrine was put out of action, the building was brought back into use and pagan worship was revived, though we do not know whether the congregation was aware of the hidden Mithraic objects beneath their new floor. In fact, it is quite likely that the cult being practised when the temple reopened was one that the Christians found less objectionable than Mithraism. It is not impossible that events connected with the postulated visit of Constantine in 314 had given the London Mithraists reason to believe that a major Christian attack on their chapel was imminent. However, it is the revival of both these chapels for pagan worship in the fourth century that reminds us of the very varied policies of Christian emperors towards such practices. It reminds us, too, of the periods when Britain was under the control of pagans or pagan sympathizers, and of the longevity of paganism in Britain as a whole, to which we shall return.

While it is true that Mithraism presented an especial target for Christian fanatics—there are examples of Mithraic images being destroyed when others are untouched—it would be unfair (or too complimentary, depending on one's point of view) to attribute all such destruction to Christian fanatics. Sometimes one may suspect rivalry between other sects, or mere vandalism. An altar from Bath leaves us completely in doubt about the circumstances—or indeed, the exact religion—but emphasizes the horror felt at sacrilege: 'This sacred spot, which had been wrecked by insolent persons, has been made ritually clean and re-dedicated to the virtue and *numen* of the emperor by C. Severius Emeritus, centurion in charge of a region.' Here it is possible that the place was sacred to the Imperial Cult, though the frequent association of the emperor's *numen* with other deities on inscriptions makes it impossible to be certain. Nevertheless, the position of the dedicator as a *centurio regionarius*, and the possibility that the area around Bath had a special status, make it feasible that the context was a local revolt in which rebels had, like Boudicca, attacked a shrine of the Imperial Cult. We should be very cautious before assuming Christian responsibility for any wrecked pagan shrine. Even the Cirencester column and statue restored by a governor in the name of the 'ancient religion' (*prisca religio*) give no hint that they have been deliberately damaged, let alone that Christians were responsible.

Not all fourth-century Christians possessed the vigorous intolerance of St Martin of Tours, who was not above borrowing troops from the secular authorities in Gaul to assist in the demolition of pagan temples; and even he felt Magnus Maximus was going too far when he proposed to send military forces to root out Christian heretics in Spain. The extremist Maximus, of course, had been raised to the throne in Britain: Britain as a diocese had been thoroughly overhauled and restored a few years earlier by the elder Theodosius, whose own family came from the Christian aristocracy of Spain, which was already developing some extremely rigorous brands of Christianity in the later fourth century, and whose son was the emperor responsible for finally banning the household gods. Yet it is generally agreed that pagan religion survived strongly to the very end of Roman rule in Britain, and probably beyond. This apparent contradiction obliges us to weigh the evidence for the strength and character of the Romano-British Church rather closely.

It is not the task of this book to attempt to chart the rise of the Celtic or 'insular' Church in Britain. This had its roots in Roman Britain, but, in the form in which it is encountered in the later fifth and sixth centuries, it developed largely in regions of Britain that were either not part of the empire at all, or had not been within it for a very long time, or were in the least Romanized areas of the Roman territory. But the enormous importance of Christianity in the life and politics of the later Empire makes it unavoidable that we consider the evidence for the Church in Britain under Roman rule.

The increasing identification of the Roman state religion with the person of the emperor cannot have helped to maintain its credibility. In the course of the first century, the assumption of divine or quasi-divine honours had been accompanied by periods of ludicrous, scandalous, or downright abominable behaviour by emperor and imperial family. The posthumous deification of Claudius was treated as a joke, yet Claudius had been one of those early emperors who resisted divinity for himself as far as possible. By the end of the first century Domitian had insisted on what amounted in practice, if not in law, to the assumption of divinity during his lifetime. This combined with his determined and brutal assault on the position, property, and even the lives of senators to confirm the Imperial Cult as a symbol of oppression, and to strengthen, as we have seen, the hold of ethical philosophy, in so far as it can be dissociated from religion, as the creed of the upper-class opposition to the Principate. However, in the troubles of the later second century and the terrible events of the third, something more than philosophy was widely felt to be needed. The popularity of the mystery-religions increased, and the emergence of a new class of soldier-emperors drawn from the African and eastern provinces, from backgrounds more and more divorced from the traditional world of the aristocratic Roman west, meant that the court itself was ripe for experiments with new forms of official religion. At its worst, this produced the excesses of the Emperor Elagabalus, who made prodigious efforts to introduce his own very peculiar version of sun-worship into Rome itself, but in general it produced a climate in which the eastern religions flourished. A foretaste of fourth-century religious absolutism was provided by the mighty Emperor Aurelian, significantly the restorer of the unity of the empire, who from 274 seems to have intended the worship of the Unconquered Sun to be the exclusive religion of the state. At the time of his death in 275 he was apparently planning a new attack on the Christians, yet, ironically, his own policy encouraged monotheism. A victorious soldier-emperor was moving towards the enforcement of religious unity under his own version of its banner. Compulsory ideology, once confined to the brief reigns of a few eccentric, if not positively mad, emperors, was soon to become a commonplace policy among rational incumbents of the imperial throne.

The overall story of the rise of Christianity is outside the scope of this book, but it should be noted that the periods of active persecution were only brief, and the faith's own almost complete lack of discrimination over admission to its number gave it great advantages over the exclusive cults. Emperors as early as Trajan avoided the deliberate hunting of Christians, and the religion became increasingly respectable. Christian apologists took their faith into the area of philosophical debate and writing, an area traditionally acceptable for a Roman gentleman even if he did not agree with the views being proffered. From the middle of the third century pagan philosophy also took a new and very important turn, which itself influenced Christian thinking. For a considerable time there had been moves towards reconciling the conservative Stoic creed with Aristotelian and Platonic concepts and the more visionary beliefs of the Pythagoreans. Embodied in the work of the philosopher Plotinus and others, this gave new strength to paganism, and became the intellectual core of the opposition to official Christianity in the fourth century.

Diocletian's prolonged attempt to restore the respectable old religion, including a particular emphasis on Jupiter and Hercules, with whom he identified the branches of his new imperial family, has to be seen as part of his general policy of national regeneration through the massive strengthening of the traditional institutions of the state. In this, he was the true heir of Augustus rather than Aurelian. It was only at the very end of his reign that he sanctioned a new persecution of the Christians, for reasons that are uncertain, but possibly because he felt their opposition to the state religion had now, in view of their vastly increased numbers, become a real threat to his programme of restoration. In 313 Constantine's edict of toleration was the first step in the dramatic reversal of official policy towards the Church. For another dozen years Constantine himself combined Christianity with devotion to Sol Invictus, the sun-cult that we have seen was very closely associated with that of Mithras. However, from 324, when the whole empire was at last under Constantine's control, monotheistic Christianity became dominant, and thereafter rapidly assumed the positions in the state formerly occupied by the traditional Capitoline triad and the Imperial Cult.

We have already seen how, for Christians in Britain, the turning of the tide had probably already begun with the recovery of the island by Constantius I as Caesar in 296. There was probably little persecution of Christians in Britain after that date, and from 324 the boot was firmly on the other foot. Henceforth the struggle was, on the one hand, between the new imperial religion and paganism, increasingly illegal as the more extremist Christian emperors passed stricter and stricter measures, with only temporary respites, and, on the other, between the official version of Christianity and heresy, though how these were defined often depended on which emperor was in power. Both paganism and heresy put up a strong fight in the west, and we shall return to the implications of this for Britain and Romano-British archaeology.

However, first we have to look at the evidence for Christianity in Britain *before* the end of the third century. The answer at present has to be that there is very little. Some scholars argue that, while Christianity, like other eastern religions, was carried westward by individuals, it seems to have been particularly strong where there were Jewish communities. Moreover, except when engaged in rebellion in Palestine or civil strife in Alexandria (where hatred between the large Greek and Jewish communities was endemic), the Jews and their faith were protected. Unlike the Christians the very nature of their religion meant that the Jews hardly ever attempted to make converts, and so they posed no threat to the state cults. To many Romans, the Christians were seen as a Jewish sect, even if often disliked by orthodox Jew and Gentile alike. Nevertheless, the presence of Christians in a Jewish community established a potential of growth by external conversion that may not in many cases have been recognized, but existed. Conversely, where there were few Jews—as in Britain —there were likely to be few Christians. The occurrence of a Jewish name as one of the pair of martyrs at Caerleon (SS Julius and Aaron, who constitute two-thirds of the British martyrs known by name) illustrates the point. The earliest literary references to Christianity in Britain do not come until the third century, and even then they sound, at first hearing, rather unconvincing. Tertullian, writing polemic in Carthage around AD 200, claimed that parts of Britain beyond Roman rule had been subdued by the Church. If not a fabrication, the origin of this statement may have been visits by traders to Scotland and Ireland. The fact that even in this century there seems to have been a strong Greek-speaking element in the Christian communities elsewhere in the western provinces supports the notion of the faith being spread to a considerable extent by Christians from the eastern Mediterranean. Eastern merchants were well known in the west, and their mercantile enterprise beyond the bounds of Roman Britain is not inconceivable. The long-established literary stereotype of Britain as the end of the world will have given an edge to Tertullian's point that will not have been lost on his readers. Origen, himself the son of a Christian who died in the Severan persecution and writing around the middle of the century in the eastern Mediterranean, may well have heard similar stories of conversions. It is difficult, though, to credit his claim that Christianity unified the Britons, unless we surmise that he had learnt of martyrdoms in Britain and had judged the strength of the faith in the island in the light of his own experiences of persecution. The literary evidence may well, then, reflect the occurrence of individual conversions and the existence of groups of highly committed Christians, especially in places with cosmopolitan communities, but it cannot be relied on as confirmation of a large Christian presence. It gives no support at all to any notion of an organized Church in Britain before the third century at the earliest.

Though it is generally unsatisfactory to rely upon negative evidence, the archaeology bears this out. Even the famous 'word-square' from Cirencester need not detain us. This is an apparently nonsensical stanza, scratched on Roman wall-plaster of uncertain date, whose letters can be arranged to form a cross composed of the Latin words for 'Our Father' (*Pater Noster*) and the Greek letters alpha and omega. However, it has been demonstrated that it is highly unlikely that this device (known also outside Britain) had a Christian origin—even if subsequently adopted by Christians —and there is no independent evidence to indicate a Christian connection for the British example. A much more important piece of evidence is the hoard of Christian plate found in 1975 within the walls of the small town at Chesterton (Water Newton), which we have already met as the urban centre dependent on the Nene Valley pottery industry. This hoard is certainly Christian, and does contain pieces for which arguments can be produced suggesting a third-century date. It comprises nine vessels of various types and eighteen more or less complete votive plaques, with fragments of a number of others. Many of the pieces bear Christian symbols or inscriptions, and one mentions the word *altare*, almost certainly meaning 'sanctuary' rather than 'altar'. This latter, taken with the plaques that had, like the strikingly similar pagan ones, been attached to some structure, makes it clear that the whole group represents fittings and furnishings deliberately removed from a Christian shrine and carefully buried. The importance of this find is threefold. It is the earliest Church plate from the whole empire. It clearly came from an actual shrine, however small, and was not the travelling equipment of a priest. Finally, the votive plaques show the Christian worshippers adopting one of the commonest forms of religious practice in the ancient world.

Does this constitute evidence for a Christian community at Water Newton, and if so, can it be put into the third century?

It has to be said first that the individual vessels themselves, if one ignores the Christian inscriptions on some of them, could all equally well be secular. There is no specifically Christian form about them. Only two of the vessels are arguably analogous in type with pieces dated elsewhere for the beginning of the third century, and most of them are apparently to be dated stylistically to the second half of the third century or the first half of the fourth. At least one probably comes after the Peace of the Church. On the other hand, there seems nothing in the hoard that is paralleled in work of the later fourth century. It therefore seems on balance that the group as a whole ought to be put in the first half of the fourth century, bearing in mind that precious objects, especially Church plate, are likely to be kept and used long after their date of manufacture. The second question is whether the shrine was at Water Newton itself. Since Water Newton lies on major road and water routes, and the material had to be removed from its home and hidden, there can be no certainty that it did not come from elsewhere. Nevertheless, the unusual nature of Water Newton is worth remembering. In the fourth century the walled town had suburbs covering 250 acres or more (100 hectares). The total complex was thus of the same order of magnitude as the walled area of Roman London—in effect, a rural development amounting in area and perhaps population to an industrial 'city'. It is characteristic of the ancient world that this industrial city is without any sure sign of municipal organization. Even the existence of walls around its centre is no proof. Indeed, the walls may have been erected by the owner of the villa at Castor, whether imperial or private. It could reasonably be argued that a Christian community based on, and perhaps originating from, the semi-urban industrial workers of the potteries is more likely here than in a 'normal' Romano-British country town or among the agricultural peasantry. This is the sort of background that is consistent with much of the social pattern of the early Church before it became respectable and eventually compulsory. Water Newton, exceptional as it seems to be in Britain, is a reasonable setting for a third-century Christian community, but the evidence of the objects themselves, as we have seen, cannot be used to prove it.

There is stronger evidence of third-century Christianity in the story of the martyrdom of St Alban. We have mentioned earlier that Germanus visited this saint's shrine in 429, after routing the Pelagians in public debate. St Alban's judge is described as 'Caesar', which makes it possible that this trial took place when Geta was left in charge of affairs during Septimius Severus' Scottish war of 208–9 (though it may have occurred under Carinus in 282–3, or just conceivably Constantius in 296). The judge is also reported as ordering the cessation of persecution because it was strengthening rather than weakening the Christians. This may indeed have been a general observation, but it would make sense in the particular context of a local Christian community. Moreover, if the great medieval abbey of St Albans really is at or near the site of the shrine visited by Germanus, then its situation just outside the city of Verulamium supports the notion of early Christianity in Britain being an urban phenomenon. Even so, Verulamium may have been unusual—it is, after all, quite possibly the first recorded British martyrdom, and need not reflect the presence of a community founded any appreciable time before that. Its members could well have arrived from abroad in the wake of the Severan victory over Clodius Albinus, rather than represent an indigenous movement. Indeed, the only other pre-Constantinian martyrs that we know of in Britain are the Julius and Aaron already mentioned, who may have been executed by Geta, or in the persecution carried out in the reign of Decius (249–51), or under the Emperor Valerian between 257 and 259. Once again the circumstances may have been exceptional. Legions had always attracted a cosmopolitan civil population, and the unusually grand civil settlement alongside the base at Caerleon may have had municipal pretensions and is atypical of Roman Britain.

We have no martyrs at all recorded for the period of the last great assault on the Church that took place in the final years of Diocletian's reign and under Galerius. The lack of bloodshed can probably be attributed to the control over the north-western provinces exercised by Constantius I, as suggested earlier, and we have no stories of Christian communities being broken up or driven underground. Nevertheless Constantius did permit the destruction of Christian places of worship, while seemingly avoiding the martyrdom of Christians themselves. Yet, for Britain, silence about the Church is paralleled by absence of clear archaeological evidence for such destruction. All in all, the inference must be that apart from individuals and perhaps a few scattered urban groups, Christianity had little hold in Britain before the elevation of Constantine. This is from negative evidence, but there is very little to set on the other side.

The Peace of the Church meant a revolutionary change in circumstances, and we need to look at the evidence for Christianity in Britain in the fourth century to see if this is reflected here. By this time the building block of the organization of the Church was the bishopric. In other provinces the minimum was normally one bishop in each city or *civitas*. Other equivalent units, such as imperial estates and major military bases with their attendant civil populations, might also have bishops. However, the fact that bishops are found in centres of population that were not administratively autonomous—even villa estates—demonstrates that it was the location of population, not the legal status of the settlement, that was decisive. It seems reasonable to go one stage further, and assume that it was the concentration of *Christian* population that determined the need for a bishop—or the presence of influential Christians demanding one—rather than the number of inhabitants overall. There was clearly no automatic allocation of bishoprics on the basis of secular administrative division. In a province where the Church was relatively weak, therefore, we need not assume a bishop for each *civitas* or equivalent unit, but we should expect them in places where there were most likely to be Christian communities or centres of power.

We have seen that in the fourth century the balance in Britain swung away from the old urban centres towards the villa estates. The towns remained important administratively—if increasingly as agents of the central government and as seats for central administrators—but probably with somewhat smaller populations overall, particularly among the commercial classes. We might expect a preponderance of city-based bishops in the earlier fourth century, but after the events of the 340s, 350s, and 360s, anything may have happened. The restoration carried out by the elder Theodosius is likely to have benefited the urban Church at least temporarily, but in the course of the last quarter of the fourth century and the early fifth, as the garrison of Britain was run down, and the centre of economic and political power shifted towards the surviving landed gentry, the organization of the Church is unlikely to have remained unaffected.

Where the Church was predominantly urban, we may expect to find both its bishops and its lower clergy as men of good family and influence; where it was located in a predominantly rural setting, the priests are more likely to have been from the lower orders and, at least in everyday affairs, subject in practice to secular landowners. In the fourth and fifth centuries it could be very much in the interest of Christian landowners to have churches, even bishops, on their estates. This mattered less in the eastern empire, where the aristocracy was often an absentee class, closely associated with the emperor in the capital, than in the west, where it became more and more divorced from the court and was concentrating on building its own separate power base, both in the city of Rome and on its estates. A different sort of Church is implied, as between town and country, and, in the west at least, the weaker the cities, the stronger the power of the secular magnates over it.

Almost as soon as the Church became legal, British bishops appear. In 314 three bishops attended the Council of Arles, and it can be argued that these, together with a priest and a deacon, came from four sees based on the capital cities of the early fourth-century provinces. However, if there were no more than four, and if they came from the four new capitals, one may suspect that the organized Church in Britain was only just being formed, perhaps by imperial command. Bishops from Britain appeared again at the Council of Rimini, under Constantius II, in 359, when their poverty was such that the emperor offered free transport via the Imperial Post. A numerous, powerful, and rich clergy is not the picture that emerges of the British Church. Indeed, one wonders if by 359 the original episcopal organization was already in decline. If the cities were ruined by the troubles of the mid-fourth century, and never recovered—as some would argue —or had only a partial recovery after the Theodosian reconstruction, then it would be possible to explain the non-appearance of later city bishops on this ground alone. But whether or not this happened, there may be another reason, inherent in the social context of the Romano-British Church, which will be examined shortly.

The archaeology of the early Church adds something to the picture. Free-standing churches are almost non-existent in what we know of Roman Britain. The building identified thus at Silchester remains possible, but its date is extremely problematic: it may have been erected early in the fourth century. This modest building is 'basilican' in form (derived from the Roman civil basilica), and the evidence for its identification is persuasive, but not absolute. Hardly any other city churches have been identified yet in Britain, even tentatively. One possibility is a building at Caerwent, and a literary source for St Augustine's arrival at Canterbury in AD 597 states that he found Queen Bertha already using an old Roman building as a church dedicated to St Martin. This may or may not indicate that a specific building had been dedicated as a church in the fourth century, though even then we cannot assume continuity of worship. But a strong case can be made out for maintaining that Queen Bertha's church was not intramural, but should be associated with a site outside the Roman walls. Similarly, a building at Colchester identified as a church also lies outside the city walls, associated with a cemetery. Therein lies a clue to the difficulty. It has been pointed out that there is a notable architectural difference between the cemetery churches (often erected over important Christian graves) and the urban churches of the fourth and fifth centuries. The former were customarily basilican in form—perhaps the grandest being Old St Peter's in Rome. Inside cities the basilican form was relatively unusual. A more normal type comprised a series of rooms set aside for the various liturgical purposes within the bishop's house. While the origins of this scheme may have lain in the need for secrecy in the pre-Constantinian period, the practice continued for a long time on the Continent. It implies that we should expect to find this type of structure more often than basilicas in provincial cities. Yet it is hardly distinguishable from the private house, except by some lucky find of furnishings or decoration, and this fact may go some way towards explaining why we have no indisputable examples of city churches so far in Britain.

Another sort of church is found in the timber structure provisionally identified in the Saxon Shore fort at Richborough. This, however, seems very late in date, is paralleled by examples in late Roman fortifications on the Continent, and has nothing to do with urban Christianity in Britain, except in the sense that it *might* have served a refugee group from a former town community. Like Silchester, however, it was a very modest building. On the other hand, something very different is represented by the splendid chapel above the pagan cult-room in the villa at Lullingstone and was, like it, seemingly adorned with family portraits, though this time as wall-paintings rather than sculptured busts. Other wealthy villa-owners were also Christian—notably those who commissioned the great mosaics in the principal rooms at Hinton St Mary in Dorset and Frampton in Gloucestershire. One may perhaps reasonably suspect that strong Christian communities were found in pockets, rather than being evenly distributed. The occurrence in Dorset, for example, of both the Hinton St Mary villa and the massive Christian town cemetery at Dorchester itself suggests strongly that the religious inclinations of the most influential local landowners were a leading factor in the practices of the whole neighbourhood, particularly where town and country were closely integrated as a result of these landowners being of the curial class—and therefore obliged to serve on the *civitas* council—or taking a direct interest in the town for other reasons. The possibility begins to form that the core of the Romano-British Church lay in a section of the fourth-century landed class. Apart from the occasional third-century urban group whose existence we have conjectured, it seems increasingly likely that the Romano-British Church hardly existed before Constantine. It may well have flourished chiefly in the great new villas, perhaps brought in by rich immigrants from Gaul, and fostered among the supporters of the house of Constantine. How much the older Romano-British gentry was touched by this development is an open question, and any establishment of urban bishoprics may well have been more to do with imperial initiative and the arrival of new officials in the reorganized provinces and their administrative centres than the old interaction between gentry and Romano-British towns. Indeed, it is interesting to speculate whether the concealment of the Water Newton treasure was in the face of a release of pagan resentment against the Church during the short reign of Magnentius from 350 to 353. Certainly, the violence of the subsequent punishment of Britain by Paul the Chain indicates that the outbreak of feeling against the ruling dynasty was regarded as serious. We do not know how widespread it had been, but we have inferred that it had included a significant number of notables. It is perhaps not a coincidence that Water Newton has also produced an important hoard of secular plate and coins, probably buried in AD 350, perhaps by one side or the other in fear of retribution to come. If Paul the Chain left the Christian landowners more powerful, but more isolated from their peers and from the bulk of the common people, the contrast between the occasional rich Christian villa and the general paucity of Christian evidence in Britain is more intelligible. We earlier noted the hypothesis that the main Pelagian opposition to Germanus in 429 lay among a powerful faction within the surviving aristocracy of Roman Britain. It will be remembered that one of the great Roman landowners with estates in Britain was Melania, the benefactress of the Church who sold off her lands for its benefit. She was tolerant of the Pelagian doctrine herself, and we know that she was in possession of property in Britain prior to 404, the date when she decided to realize her assets, and therefore well before the series of revolts that were to sunder Britain from Rome. We may perhaps surmise the existence of a Pelagian land-owning group in Britain both before and after the break with the empire. Christianity had become more acceptable to the western upper classes after the death of Valentinian I in 375, and there are likely to have been rather more Christians among the leading Romano-Britons in the last quarter of the century. On the other hand, we hear no more of city bishops from Britain, and the Church was probably even more firmly in the hands of the land-owning class in this period than before. That must have applied both to the official faith and the various heresies that flourished from time to time. In Spain in the fourth century heresy was rife among the aristocracy, and Melania herself had an estate in Africa with two bishops professing different creeds. In the fourth and fifth centuries the battles were with heresy as well as paganism, and the existence of a Pelagian party may imply that by the early fifth century the British Church had become strong enough to feel that unity in the face of paganism was not the only policy it could afford.

It is interesting to enquire whether the behaviour of their Continental colleagues might tell us how the adoption of Christianity is likely to have affected the behaviour of these aristocrats. Apart from influencing their stand in the various internal political and ideological struggles, one might expect it to change their conduct in what was the most critical area as far as the population at large was concerned—their reaction to the troubles of the times. Yet there is the paradoxical fact that the two main strains in Christian approaches to the barbarian threat and to public duty closely mirrored traditional Roman attitudes, in practice if not in theory. One party in the Christian church regarded contemporary life as a lost cause—even illusory and unimportant—and advocated retreat from the world. The other, typified by the energetic St Ambrose, urged on all Romans a duty to defend the empire and the faith from the heathen or heretical barbarians. Thus we have the two contradictory tendencies in pagan tradition—the Epicurean retreat from the stresses of the world, and the Stoic persistence in public duty—being reproduced in Christian attitudes. It is not therefore surprising to find relatively little difference in the behaviour of pagans and Christians, where we can observe them in better-documented provinces. It may be that the strain in Christian thought that saw the contemporary world as evil and the barbarians as the wrath of God led some to abandon resistance and, at the most extreme, to disappear into one of the earliest monastic communities, which began to develop slowly in the west in the last quarter of the fourth century and spread rapidly in the fifth. But, in general, we may expect no more than a continuation of the traditional dichotomy of behaviour. If there was avoidance of office in fourth-century Britain, and an increased tendency for the nobility to live on their estates in relative ease, it was no more than their contemporaries were practising on the Continent, and a development of a characteristic of their class. In the fifth century we may reasonably assume that there were men in Britain who reluctantly but stoically strove to maintain order and government, like Sidonius Apollinaris in Gaul; others who preferred to come to terms with the situation, retreating to their safest estates and carrying on the life of *otium cum dignitate* as well as they could; and yet others who, having played a prominent part in public life, withdrew into fastnesses, whether their motives were philosophical, religious, or self-preservation—in this world as well as the next. Precedents and moral support could be found for any of these courses of action in both Christian and pagan thought. Roman tradition, in short, once more proved persistent and infinitely adaptable to circumstance.

The contrast in Britain between the occasional rich Christian villa and the general paucity of evidence elsewhere, especially for urban Christianity, does not, of course, mean that there is no other sign of Christian observance at all. The question is how much it adds up to—and to that there is no clear answer. There is a scatter of small personal objects, such as finger-rings or lamps, with certain or possible Christian symbols or phraseology, and a few tombstones similarly distinguished. Then there are the spectacular but rare finds of fourth-century plate, such as Traprain, Mildenhall, or Corbridge, which include some pieces demonstrably of Christian origin. Next there is an interesting group of lead tanks that have been identified as fonts. There are cemeteries and their associated structures. And there is the destruction of pagan monuments.

Taking these categories of evidence one by one, it has first to be said that the quantity of small objects, of graffiti and of tombstones or other inscriptions, is infinitesimal compared with the vast amount that is undeniably pagan. In none of the cases can the major hoards definitely be associated with persons certainly resident in Britain. They are most probably either barbarian treasure (for example, Traprain) lost in transit (as may have been the scattered pieces from the Tyne at Corbridge, which also includes the pagan Lanx), or (as perhaps in the case of the Mildenhall Treasure) personal wealth accompanying a visiting imperial official normally resident elsewhere, even though he might have had some property in Britain.

The lead tanks or troughs are an interesting group. Of the several now known, only some bear Christian symbols, but they are sufficiently similar to suggest that they all had the same purpose. Baptism is a reasonable hypothesis. In the early Church baptism was only performed by a bishop, but we cannot assume that each of these objects marks the centre of a bishop's see. While their physical weight makes it obvious that they are not part of a priest's portable equipment, the presence of light handles on the trough from Ireby in Cumbria indicates that it could be dragged a short distance, for example, into the body of a church, when the bishop arrived to conduct baptism. Where these lead troughs or vats can be associated with a Roman settlement, it seems often to have been a small town, for example, Ashton, in the Nene Valley district, or a villa, such as Wiggonholt in Sussex. Icklingham, just off the Fen Edge in Suffolk, has produced more than one such trough, and is a site with very unusual characteristics. It covers an area of around 37 acres (about 15 hectares), the scale of a small town or of a villa with an exceptionally large group of associated buildings, like some of the great houses in Gaul. It also has an important group of cemeteries that contain features assumed to be of Christian type. There is some evidence that Icklingham had a pagan religious significance before becoming Christian, and the changes may have included deliberate obliteration of its past. One wonders whether it may have been the centre of a Church estate, based on confiscated temple property or on land given to the Church out of Fenland imperial domain. It will bear continued investigation and interpretation.

We looked earlier at Roman attitudes to death, and the way in which the mystery-religions, including Christianity, seem to have influenced changes in burial rite. We have not, however, yet examined Romano-British cemeteries as such for evidence of Christianity in Britain. Of the various sources, they are perhaps the most likely to produce new information on a substantial scale. We have noted some of the difficulties in distinguishing Christian from pagan burials, but there is no doubt that there were certain practices widely adopted in Christian cemeteries in the Roman world: east–west orientation of the burials; avoidance of reuse of previous graves; lack of grave-goods; inhumation in place of cremation. There is sometimes an attempt to preserve the body as completely as possible, and a decided tendency for burials to cluster round a single grave or mausoleum, either that of a martyr, bishop, or other Christian of special significance, or the vault of a family of prominence in the local Christian community. The shrine above a martyr's grave (*martyrium*) was of course a potent attraction for pilgrims. It is clear that many early churches on the Continent, especially those associated with cemeteries outside Roman cities, grew either out of shrines of this type or the mausoleums (*memoriae*) of prominent Christian families, at which communities gathered and, like their pagan counterparts, remembered their dead. At Faversham, in Kent, a Roman mausoleum is incorporated into the chancel of the medieval church. This, and the many other examples where Roman buildings lie beneath later churches, may represent a significant continuity or memory of Christian sanctity. On the other hand, the abundance of ruined Roman buildings that could be reused or employed as quarries in the early medieval period must make us very wary of such speculation. The Poundbury cemetery at Dorchester can fairly be considered a major city graveyard. There are something like 4,000 burials known, apparently starting late in the third century or early in the fourth. The first area has a group of random burials, probably pagan, and a separate, deliberately orientated group lying around a single interment. This was followed in the course of the fourth century by a much larger cemetery, with at least eight mausoleums, including several decorated internally with paintings, and one containing a coffin with an undoubted Christian inscription. This vast assemblage of burials presents a rare opportunity to study a Romano-British community dominated by Christian practices, though not necessarily all subscribing to Christian beliefs. We have to take into account the certain presence locally of powerful Christians. There were, of course, the general effects of Christian practices on the population at large, whether Christian or not, and there could also be an element of compulsion. The latter is particularly likely to have been applied on properties where the master was himself an enthusiastic Christian. The fifth-century compendium of law made since 312 known as the Theodosian Code makes the suggestion that an increase in the number of beatings on estates might help the workers to attend to their devotions more readily.

Our last category of evidence is possible archaeological traces of the exercise of Christian power against the pagans. It is difficult to accept the reuse of second- and third-century coffins and a broken pagan altar in a cemetery at York as signs of Christian disrespect for pagan dead, as has been argued on occasion, for we have seen that such disturbance was common in the ancient world. The destruction of Mithraea, already mentioned, deserves closer attention. In the context of the excavation at Rudchester, it was observed that the damage to the three Mithraea known on Hadrian's Wall had a common feature. In each case the main relief of Mithras slaying the bull had been demolished, but the subsidiary altars had been spared. This suggested to the excavator that it was prompted either by a single order effective throughout the command, or a wave of feeling among the people in the Wall region. The dating evidence pointed to destruction in the late third century or early fourth. The phenomenon could thus have been contemporary with the hiding of the main pieces of sculpture in the London Mithraeum. We may therefore have to reckon with a wider order, issued at one particular moment by someone possessing authority throughout Britain, rather than with any general upsurge of Christian violence.

The military context of the Mithraea on Hadrian's Wall must lead us to consider the position of the army in fourth-century religion. Constantine's order to his army at the Milvian Bridge to bear the Christian symbol, and his subsequent victory, undoubtedly conferred immediate military prestige on Christianity. Later it was soldier-emperors, notably Valentinian I, and the Pannonian officers risen from the ranks who were rigid and enthusiastic Christians. Yet, for Britain, there is hardly any evidence at all for Christian sentiment in the Roman army. All we have is a few small objects, such as those we have been considering in the general context, plus one Christian symbol on a single stone in the bath-house at Catterick, another from an unknown context at Maryport, and the desecration of the Mithraea.

This picture for the army is not out of line with the general pattern for fourth-century Britain. The evidence for the use of pagan shrines extends as far as for other categories of Roman site—in other words, to some unspecifiable period in the fifth century. Like the villas, for example, the evidence from individual religious sites is very variable. Some pagan shrines went out of use in the early or mid-fourth century, others continued throughout it, some were actually built after the war of 367, and some certainly continued in use into the fifth century. The Carrawburgh Mithraeum was not repaired and had become a tip by about the middle of the fourth century; the rural shrine at Brean Down in Somerset was converted for some industrial purpose in about AD 370, and the temple behind the theatre in the centre of Verulamium was abandoned about 380. Yet the coins do continue at many pagan shrines after that, and the economic explanation for the decline in the quantity of offerings may be as good as the religious one. The Hockwold ritual crowns were hidden in a hole cut in the floor of a temple that had certainly remained in use to the very end of the fourth century. It would, of course, be very surprising if the general advance of Christianity had no effect on the popularity of the pagan cults, but none of this allows us to accept an overwhelming decline in pagan belief or, which is even more surprising, in pagan practices. Indeed, since we can find no evidence for a dominant observance of Christianity among the army, where, as always, the official religion was compulsory, we cannot be disappointed if evidence for it elsewhere in Britain is sparse and, for the collapse of paganism by AD 400, unconvincing.

This conclusion is quite contrary to the commonly held assumption that, by the early fifth century, Roman Britain was a Christian country in which paganism had largely ceased to be a real issue. That notion led to a view of Church history that includes a universally established Romano-British Church that was broken by the 'Arrival of the Saxons'—or some other catastrophe —in the middle of the century, and forced back into the monasticism and tribal bishoprics of the Celtic hinterland. Yet such a picture of the Romano-British Church can only be built on implied evidence—the vigour with which neighbouring barbarians were converted (for example, in Ireland by St Patrick), or the emergence of Pelagianism as a formidable heresy—combined with an assumption that the empire at large was by now wholly Christian.

Both these arguments are weak. Neither St Patrick nor Pelagius can be used to demonstrate a thoroughly Christian country. We have already touched on the possibility that British Christianity flourished chiefly among a very influential, but possibly quite small group, in the Romano-British aristocracy. There were certainly heretics among this class: we may strongly suspect that there were plenty of pagans as well. The empire in the west was in fact anything but solidly Christian. In Rome itself we have seen the struggle between senatorial pagans and Christian emperors, symbolized by the disputes over the Altar of Victory, continuing late in the fourth century. In 388 Theodosius the Great himself was formally met at the Balkan city of Aemona by pagan priests, officials of the corporation. Later, as we noted, Theodosius prohibited even the private celebration of pagan rites—but how successful was he? One may perhaps explain away an incident like the martyrdom of a Christian group in the Tyrol in about AD 400 for attempting to destroy a cult of Saturn at a holy well as being the exceptional result of rural isolation and superstition. But how does one account for the fact that at Cosa in Italy a building in the decayed town forum that had been taken over for use as a shrine of Dionysus in the course of the fourth century continued to house a flourishing cult apparently well into the fifth? If that could happen in Italy, is it surprising that pagan shrines survived to the end of Roman Britain? In fact, they fall into place in a much wider picture, one that is not difficult to substantiate. In the Italian countryside paganism was still active in the second half of the fifth century. Further north, archaeological evidence from the intensely Romanized Rhineland indicates that the temple complex at Pesch was still in use under Honorius, and literary evidence has been used to demonstrate a lively pagan survival at an even later date in the western provinces at large.

There can be little doubt, of course, that Roman religious and political conservatism did much to prolong the life of the pagan cults. But there is a further factor that has yet to be introduced in this context: the increasing Germanic element in the late Roman army. Doubtless, many officers found it expedient to follow imperial Christianity from the days of Constantine onwards, though we should not forget about the reign of Julian and the later interlude between AD 392 and 394, when the pagan *magister militum* Arbogast ruled with the Christian but compliant Eugenius and the temporary support of the Roman aristocracy. In the ranks, however, many Germanic troops must have remained pagan, if privately. They are likely to have found that in Britain many of those Germanic and Celtic cults which had long been established among the armies were still being practised. As Roman armies came increasingly to rely on barbarian allies, even the appearance of an army religiously united under the official imperial faith must have become less and less convincing, since barbarians, even if Christian, were likely to be Arian rather than Catholic.

The replacement after AD 375 of Valentinian's crude Pannonian associates as the dominant party at court by the Gallo-Roman aristocrats of Ausonius' circle not only helped the process of reconciling the western upper classes with the militant Church, it also must have greatly increased the prestige of the Christian provincial nobility at home. It is perhaps not entirely accidental that in the last part of the fourth century these aristocrats felt able to indulge in the luxuries of ecclesiastical controversy. The most notable were perhaps the Priscillianists, whom Magnus Maximus persecuted, but in the 390s Victricius, bishop of Rouen and pupil of St Martin, visited Britain to settle some unspecified ecclesiastical disputes. There is no evidence, however, to suggest that either St Martin himself or Victricius carried out a programme of vigorous evangelization of the lower rural population in Britain, as they did in northern Gaul. Even for Gaul, Victricius' claim that the north-western part of the country was more or less completely Christian was probably overstated. For Britain, we may recall that in 429 Germanus had to resort to mass baptism to acquire a Christian army. Fourth- and fifth-century paganism in Britain has to be seen in the light of surviving paganism on the Continent. Furthermore, the break with Roman rule may have given new opportunities to Romano-British pagans as well as to anti-imperial Christians, for without a secular central power to back up the Church, it is unlikely that any action against either pagans or heretics could be taken, other than where some local magnate or churchman chose to act of his own accord and had sufficient local power or support to carry it out.

This pagan persistence may explain two sorts of 'sub-Roman' cemeteries that occur chiefly in those western parts of Roman Britain that were late to come under Saxon occupation. One group seems to be associated with sites that had certainly been religious (mainly pagan) in the Roman period. The other seems to be associated with hilltop occupation, mostly hill-fort sites, in the post-Roman period. It has been suggested that some of these may have been religious centres at that time, and did not take on a renewed military role, though, of course, the two functions are not mutually exclusive. Certainly, some Iron Age hill-forts, such as Maiden Castle, had become temple sites under Roman rule, when they had ceased to be native military strongholds. The religious associations of such places may well have lingered on, whether with a pagan or a Christian connotation.

There is, altogether, good reason to suppose that the Saxons encountered a strong indigenous pagan element in Britain as well as the Christian Church, and we should take into account the probability that religious beliefs among the Germanic troops of late Roman armies closely resembled their own. We cannot simplify the conflicts around and after the end of Roman rule in Britain as being Christian against pagan any more than we can see them purely in terms of Romano-Briton against barbarian. However, in the context of the collapse of the structure of Roman Britain, it is perhaps significant that the Britons who appear in Gaul in the middle and later fifth century have their own bishops. Bishop Mansuetus is recorded at the Council at Tours in 461, and a possible British bishop, Riochatus, is mentioned by Sidonius Apollinaris in about 476, in the very period when the imperial court collapsed in Italy but independent Roman authority survived in northern Gaul. With all its uncertainties, the movement of a substantial population from Britain to the Loire and Brittany had probably coincided with the collapse of the last remnants of the Romano-British way of life in the major part of the old province. That way of life had depended on the provincial gentry and the system of landed estates and towns, never so much as when the imperial government had been expelled and the army had disintegrated. Such evidence as there is points to the organized Roman Church in Britain having depended on the same structure. The Church that endured was very different, but one factor in its eventual survival in the unconquered western parts of Britain may have been that, in the course of the fourth century, its centre of gravity had already moved from the towns to the landed gentry and their estates. In the first half of the fifth century, after the break with Roman rule, it is not difficult to imagine bishops and clergy as clients of local 'tyrants' and lesser notables throughout the old provinces. Some may even have emerged as leaders of secular communities themselves, though, except in cases where existing secular notables were pressed to take orders and become bishops, this is perhaps only likely where no secular leader remained. As order progressively collapsed in Britain, some seem to have crossed to Gaul, others may well have retreated gradually westwards.

In western Britain itself it is reasonable to expect that something of the old pattern persisted for a long time, particularly where estates were left undisturbed, as appears likely in south Wales. However, the Church's survival probably owed just as much to the monastic groups existing in remote places, and to the fact that the insular Church turned outward and proceeded to convert the barbarians of Ireland and Scotland. Some of these were indeed now settled in the western part of what had been Roman Britain, but they were not by any means necessarily (or even probably) in social and political sympathy with Rome. The British Church, we may conjecture, now contained highly disparate elements. As a distinctive political and social structure, the old Church had gone down with the old Romano–British world.

FURTHER READING

General

Breeze, D. J., *Roman Scotland: A Guide to the Visible Remains* (Newcastle upon Tyne, 1979).

Clayton, P. A. (ed.), *A Companion to Roman Britain* (Oxford, 1980), an elegantly produced and illustrated series of essays, with gazetteer.

Collingwood, R. G., and Richmond, I. A., *The Archaeology of Roman Britain*, revised edn. (London, 1969), the classic survey of the material evidence, now out of date in many respects, but still useful.

Frere, S. S., *Britannia: A History of Roman Britain*, 3rd edn. (London, 1987), a straightforward narrative history based on an encyclopaedic knowledge of the period.

—— and St Joseph, J. K. S., *Roman Britain from the Air* (Cambridge, 1983), a selection of the best Cambridge aerial photographs, with detailed discussion.

Greene, K. T., *Archaeology, an Introduction: The History, Principles, and Methods of Modern Archaeology* (London, 1983), an excellent introduction to the discipline.

Hartley, B. R., and Wacher, J. S. (eds.), *Rome and the Northern Provinces: Papers Presented to Sheppard Frere* (Trowbridge, 1983), includes G. A. Webster on Magnentius, and other interesting essays.

Jones, G. D. B., and Mattingly, D., *An Atlas of Roman Britain* (Oxford, 1990), more a thematic study, illustrated by a large number of new maps and diagrams.

Keppie, L. J. F., *Scotland's Roman Remains* (Edinburgh, 1986), a museum publication, useful introductory survey.

Maxfield, V. A., and Dobson, M. J. (eds.), *Roman Frontier Studies 1989: Proceedings of the XVth International Congress of Roman Frontier Studies* (Exeter, 1991), contains essays on a wider variety of topics than the title suggests, including useful surveys of recent work in Britain.

Maxwell, G. S., *The Romans in Scotland* (Edinburgh, 1989), sound and well written.

Millett, M. J., *The Romanization of Britain: An Essay in Archaeological Interpretation* (Cambridge, 1990), applies analytical methods currently in use among prehistorians to Roman Britain.

Munby, J. T., and Henig, M. E. (eds.), *Roman Life and Art in Britain:*

A Celebration in Honour of the 80th Birthday of Jocelyn Toynbee (Oxford, 1977), a broad collection of essays, chiefly on art and religion.

Nash-Williams, V. E., *The Roman Frontier in Wales*, ed. M. G. Jarrett, 2nd edn. (Cardiff, 1969), records the sites as known in the 1960s, classic large-scale publication.

Todd, M., *Roman Britain 55 BC–AD 400* (London, 1981), an excellent short account.

—— (ed.), *Research on Roman Britain, 1960–1989* (London, 1989), an important round-up of progress in, and the present state of, the principal areas of study.

Toynbee, J. M. C., *Art in Roman Britain* (London, 1962), the learned and magnificently illustrated catalogue of a major exhibition.

—— *Art in Britain under the Romans* (Oxford, 1964), a magisterial survey.

Wacher, J. S., *Roman Britain* (London, 1978), sound and well illustrated.

SITES AND FINDS

De la Bédoyère, G., *The Finds of Roman Britain* (London, 1989), a patchy but well-illustrated introduction.

Wilson, R. J. A., *A Guide to the Roman Remains in Britain*, 3rd edn. (London, 1988), a visitor's guide to the visible and accessible antiquities.

For more detailed information on sites and finds, see the annual reports entitled 'Roman Britain in 19xx' in the *Journal of Roman Studies* (until 1969) and *Britannia* (from 1970).

WRITTEN SOURCES

Bowman, A. K., and Thomas, J. D., *Vindolanda: The Latin Writing-Tablets* (London, 1983), original letters and documents from the turn of the first and second centuries.

Collingwood, R. G., and Wright, R. P., *The Roman Inscriptions of Britain*, i (Oxford, 1965), Index to vol. i (Gloucester, 1983), ii/1 (Gloucester, 1990), ii/2 (Gloucester, 1991). Generally referred to as *RIB*, this is the standard collection of epigraphic material, not yet completed. Finds subsequent to a particular section are recorded in the epigraphic reports in *Journal of Roman Studies* (to 1969), and *Britannia* (from 1970).

Ireland, S., *Roman Britain: A Sourcebook* (London, 1986), a convenient collection of most of the literary sources in translation, other than the longest (notably Caesar, *Gallic Wars*, and Tacitus, *Agricola*).

Mattingly, H., and Handford, S. A. (trans.), *Tacitus: The Agricola and the Germania* (Harmondsworth, 1970).

Ogilvie, R. M., and Richmond, I. A., *Cornelii Taciti: De vita Agricolae* (Oxford, 1967), text and detailed notes.

Wiseman, A., and Wiseman, T. P., *Julius Caesar: The Battle for Gaul* (London, 1980), a fresh translation, with illustrations chosen by B. W. Cunliffe.

CLASSICAL BACKGROUND

Boardman, J. (ed.), *The Oxford History of the Classical World* (Oxford, 1986).

Braund, D. C., *Rome and the Friendly King* (London, 1984), explores the relationship between Rome and the client kingdoms.

Casey, P. J., *Understanding Ancient Coins* (Oxford, 1986).

Cunliffe, B. W., *Greeks, Romans, and Barbarians: Spheres of Interaction* (London, 1988), particularly stimulating on Roman contacts with Britain through Gaul before and after Caesar.

Foss, C., *Roman Historical Coins* (London, 1990), an illustrated catalogue of coins referring to contemporary incidents and policies, underlining the role of coins as propaganda.

Grant, M., *The Roman Emperors: A Biographical Guide to the Rulers of Imperial Rome, 31 BC–AD 476* (London, 1985), useful brief biographies.

Hammond, N. G. L., and Scullard, H. H., *The Oxford Classical Dictionary*, 2nd edn. (Oxford, 1970), an indispensable work of reference.

Henig, M. E. (ed.), *A Handbook of Roman Art* (Oxford, 1983), concise and beautifully produced.

Howatson, M. C. (ed.), *The Oxford Companion to Classical Literature*, 2nd edn. (Oxford, 1989).

McManners, J. (ed.), *The Oxford Illustrated History of Christianity* (Oxford, 1990).

Matthews, J. F., and Cornell, T., *Atlas of the Roman World* (Oxford, 1982).

Millar, F. G. B., *The Emperor in the Roman World (31 BC–AD 337)* (London, 1977), a magisterial and illuminating study of the central institution of the Empire.

—— et al., *The Roman Empire and its Neighbours* (London, 1967), essays on external relations in various parts of the Roman world.

Salmon, E. T., *A History of the Roman World from 30 BC to AD 138*, 6th edn. (London, 1968), a standard short narrative history of the early Empire.

Todd, M., *The Northern Barbarians, 100 BC–AD 300*, 2nd. edn. (Oxford, 1987), highly relevant to Roman policy on Britain.

Wacher, J. S. (ed.), *The Roman World* (London, 1987), a grand general survey.

The First Roman Contacts

Bradley, R. J., *The Prehistoric Settlement of Britain* (London, 1978), studies change in prehistory through forms of farming activity.

—— *The Social Foundations of Prehistoric Britain* (London, 1984), applies sociological methods to the study of relationships in and between communities.

Cunliffe, B. W. (ed.), *Coinage and Society in Britain and Gaul: Some Current Problems* (London, 1981).

—— *Iron Age Communities in Britain*, 3rd edn. (London, 1991), a standard general work.

—— and Miles, D. (eds.), *Aspects of the Iron Age in Central Southern Britain* (Oxford, 1984), essays that bring together many of the main issues.

Darvill, T. C., *Prehistoric Britain* (London, 1987), an up-to-date general introduction.

Dyer, J. F., *The Hillforts of England and Wales* (Princes Risborough, 1981), a brief but useful handbook.

Harding, D. W., *The Iron Age in Lowland Britain* (London, 1974).

Macready, S., and Thompson, F. H. (eds.), *Cross-Channel Trade between Gaul and Britain in the Pre-Roman Iron Age* (London, 1984), an excellent set of essays.

Piggott, S., *The Druids*, 2nd edn. (London, 1975), a lively but immensely level-headed study of a topic that has attracted more than its share of nonsense.

Powell, T. G. E., *The Celts*, 2nd edn. (London, 1980), a classic account of the Celts across Europe.

Thomas, N. de l'E. W., *A Guide to Prehistoric England*, 2nd edn. (London, 1976), a visitor's guide to the principal monuments.

Van Arsdell, R. D., *Celtic Coinage of Britain* (London, 1989).

The Roman Conquest

Bishop, M. C., and Coulston, J. C., *Roman Military Equipment* (Princes Risborough, 1989), a brief but useful account that, unusually, does not neglect the late Roman army.

Breeze, D. J., *The Northern Frontiers of Roman Britain* (London, 1982), studies the fluctuating dispositions in northern Britain from the first arrival of the Roman army in the region.

—— and Dobson, B., *Hadrian's Wall*, 3rd edn. (London, 1987), a modern critical study of the evidence.

Bruce, J. Collingwood, *Handbook to the Roman Wall*, 13th edn. by C. M. Daniels (Newcastle upon Tyne, 1978), the standard handbook, feature by feature.

Daniels, C. M., *The Eleventh Pilgrimage of Hadrian's Wall* (Newcastle upon Tyne, 1989), an important summary of the evidence, and a guide to the visible remains as at the date of publication.

Hanson, W. S., *Agricola and the Conquest of the North* (London, 1987), a minimalist view of Agricola's contribution.

—— and Maxwell, G. S., *Rome's North-West Frontier: The Antonine Wall* (Edinburgh, 1983).

Holder, P. A., *The Roman Army in Britain* (London, 1982), includes a catalogue of all units known to have been in Britain.

Johnson, A., *Roman Forts of the 1st and 2nd Centuries AD in Britain and the German Provinces* (London, 1983).

Johnson, J. S., *Hadrian's Wall* (London, 1989), a well-illustrated account for the general public.

Lepper, F. A., and Frere, S. S., *Trajan's Column: A New Edition of the Cichorius Plates* (Gloucester, 1988), the most important visual record of the army of the early Empire in action, in photographs taken from casts made before modern pollution damaged the Column.

Ordnance Survey, *The Antonine Wall* (Southampton, 1969), fine mapping, like the 1972 Hadrian's Wall map, and on a base at the full 1:25,000 scale.

—— *Map of Hadrian's Wall*, 2nd. edn. (Southampton, 1972), superb mapping of the whole Wall on a base slightly reduced from the 1:25,000 sheets of the region.

—— *Historical Map and Guide: Hadrian's Wall* (Southampton, 1989), selective mapping, intended as a visitor's guide, but a poor substitute for the 1972 edition, even for the tourist.

Robinson, H. R., *The Armour of Imperial Rome* (London, 1975).

Starr, C. G., *The Roman Imperial Navy, 31 BC–AD 324*, 2nd edn. (Cambridge, 1960), the standard work.

Wacher, J. S., *The Coming of Rome* (London, 1979), a general account from Caesar onwards.

Watson, G. R., *The Roman Soldier* (London, 1969), investigates the life of the individual soldier.

Webster, G. A., *Boudica: The British Revolt against Rome, AD 60*, 2nd edn. (London, 1978).

—— *The Roman Invasion of Britain* (London, 1980).

—— *Rome against Caractacus: The Roman Campaigns in Britain, AD 48–58* (London, 1981).

—— *The Roman Imperial Army of the First and Second Centuries AD*, 3rd edn. (London, 1985), the standard work.

Imperial Crisis and Recovery

Brown, P., *The World of Late Antiquity: From Marcus Aurelius to Muhammed* (London, 1971), the best general introduction.

Goodburn, R., and Bartholomew, P. (eds.), *Aspects of the* Notitia Dignitatum (Oxford, 1976), essays on a number of significant topics related to this difficult but important document.

Johnson, J. S., *The Roman Forts of the Saxon Shore*, 2nd edn. (London, 1979), a general study.

—— *Later Roman Britain* (London, 1980), a useful general study, complementing J. S. Wacher's *The Coming of Rome*.

Johnston, D. E. (ed.), *The Saxon Shore* (London, 1977), a set of essays.

Jones, A. H. M., *The Later Roman Empire, 284–602: A Social, Economic and Administrative Survey* (Oxford, 1964), the standard work.

Kent, J. P. C., and Painter, K. S., *The Wealth of the Roman World: Gold and Silver, AD 300–700* (London, 1977), an exhibition catalogue that surveys the subject of plate in precious metals, and offers valuable insights into politics and society in the late Empire.

King, A. C., and Henig, M. E. (eds.), *The Roman West in the Third Century: Contributions from Archaeology and History* (Oxford, 1981), a collection of essays on a period often neglected.

Matthews, J., *The Roman Empire of Ammianus* (London, 1989), a comprehensive historical study of the Roman world in the middle of the fourth century, built around the surviving text of Ammianus Marcellinus.

—— *Western Aristocracies and Imperial Court, AD 362–425*, 2nd edn. (Oxford, 1990), an important study of the relationships between people in positions of power in this critical period.

Maxfield, V. A. (ed.), *The Saxon Shore: A Handbook* (Exeter, 1989), an extremely useful collation of the evidence.

Painter, K. S., *The Mildenhall Treasure: Roman Silver from East Anglia* (London, 1977), a museum publication describing the hoard, and offering some ideas on its possible context.

Ritchie, A., *The Picts* (Edinburgh, 1989), brief museum publication that usefully summarizes the evidence for the origins and character of this northern people.

Williams, S., *Diocletian and the Roman Recovery* (London, 1985).

The End of Roman Britain

Alcock, L., *Arthur's Britain: History and Archaeology, AD 367–634* (London, 1971), drew attention to the then recent work in the archaeology of the later fifth century, previously largely unknown to the wider public.

Arnold, C. J., *Roman Britain to Saxon England* (London, 1984), contro-versial.

Brown, P. D. C., *Anglo-Saxon England* (London, 1978), a short but use-ful survey.

Campbell, J. (ed.), *The Anglo-Saxons* (Oxford, 1982), a splendid series of studies that includes much of importance to the end of Roman Britain.

Casey, P. J. (ed.), *The End of Roman Britain* (Oxford, 1979), useful essays on various related topics.

Dixon, P. W., *Barbarian Europe* (London, 1976), an excellent and beau-tifully produced introduction.

Esmonde Cleary, A. S., *The Ending of Roman Britain* (London, 1989), a clear and largely convincing new look at the subject.

Ferrill, A., *The Fall of the Roman Empire: The Military Explanation* (London, 1986), controversial analysis.

Myres, J. N. L., *The English Settlements* (Oxford, 1986), replaces his section of the Oxford History of England volume by himself and R. G. Collingwood, *Roman Britain and the English Settlements*, 2nd edn. (Oxford, 1937).

Thomas, A. C., *Celtic Britain* (London, 1986).

Thompson, E. A., *Saint Germanus of Auxerre and the End of Roman Britain* (Woodbridge, 1984).

Britain under Roman Rule

THE ASSIMILATION OF BRITAIN

Allason-Jones, L., *Women in Roman Britain* (London, 1989), an impor-tant and balanced contribution.

Birley, A. R., *The People of Roman Britain* (London, 1979), investigates what can be deduced about a large number of the people known by name.

—— *The Fasti of Roman Britain* (Oxford, 1981), individual studies of the holders of important posts in Roman Britain.

Blagg, T. F. C., and King, A. C. (eds.), *Military and Civilian in Roman Britain: Cultural Relationships in a Frontier Province* (Oxford, 1984).

Burnham, B. C., and Johnson, H. B. (eds.), *Invasion and Response: The Case of Roman Britain* (Oxford, 1979), essays on the interaction be-tween Roman and native in the light of analogous situations else-where and in other periods.

Salway, P., *The Frontier People of Roman Britain*, 2nd edn. (Cambridge, 1967), examines the civil settlements outside the military stations in the north, and their population.

P. R. V. Marsden, *Roman London* (London, 1980); R. Merrifield, *London: City of the Romans* (London, 1983); B. Hobley, *Roman and Saxon London: A Reappraisal* (London, 1986); J. Hall and R. Merrifield, *Roman London* (London, 1986), all summarize thinking on the capital, and have much of relevance to the organization of Roman Britain. Further evidence continues to appear.

THE HISTORICAL GEOGRAPHY OF ROMAN BRITAIN

Evans, J. G., *The Environment of Early Man in the British Isles* (London, 1975).

—— Limbrey, S., and Cleere, H. F. (eds.), *The Effect of Man on the Landscape: The Highland Zone* (London, 1975).

Fox, C. F., *The Personality of Britain*, 4th edn. (Cardiff, 1943), the classic study of the historical geography of Britain, now out of date in important respects, but still stimulating.

Gelling, M. J., *Signposts to the Past: Place-Names and the History of England* (London, 1978), a stimulating introduction to place-name studies.

Jones, M. K., and Dimbleby, G. W. (eds.), *The Environment of Man: The Iron Age to the Saxon Period* (Oxford, 1981).

Limbrey, S., and Evans, J. G. (eds.), *The Effect of Man on the Landscape: The Lowland Zone* (London, 1978).

Ordnance Survey, *Historical Map and Guide: Roman Britain*, 4th edn. (revised) (Southampton, 1991).

Phillips, C. W. (ed.), *The Fenland in Roman Times: Studies of a Major Area of Peasant Colonization, with a Gazetteer Covering All Known Sites and Finds* (London, 1970), first mapping of a whole region, which was followed by others not restricted to Roman period, including a group of independent but complementary studies, consisting of: D. Benson and D. Miles, *The Upper Thames Valley* (Oxford, 1974); T. Gates, *The Middle Thames Valley* (Reading, 1975); R. H. Leech, *The Upper Thames Valley in Gloucestershire and Wiltshire* (Bristol, 1977); J. C. Richards, *The Archaeology of the Berkshire Downs* (Reading, 1978). In 1976 the Royal Commission on Historical Monuments (England) published (as volume 1 of their survey of Gloucestershire) *Iron Age and Romano-British Monuments in the Gloucestershire Cotswolds.*

Rivet, A. L. F., and Smith, C., *The Place-Names of Roman Britain* (London, 1979), combines an important study of the ancient geographers and topographical documents with a dictionary of known place-names.

Thompson, F. H. (ed.), *Archaeology and Coastal Change* (London, 1980), essays exploring the important changes that have affected sea-levels and coastline.

Union Académique Internationale, *Tabula Imperii Romani: Condate—Glevum—Londinium—Lutetia* (London, 1985), maps southern Britain and northern Gaul on a single sheet, and includes a detailed gazetteer.
—— *Tabula Imperii Romani: Britannia septentrionalis* (London, 1987), maps northern Britain on similar principles.

TOWN AND COUNTRY

Burnham, B. C., and Wacher, J. S., *The 'Small Towns' of Roman Britain* (London, 1990).

Clack, P. A. G., and Haselgrove, S. (eds.), *Rural Settlement in the Roman North* (Durham, 1982).

Davey, N., and Ling, R. J., *Wall-Painting in Roman Britain* (London, 1982), contains analysis and catalogue, with colour microfiche.

Esmonde Cleary, A. S., *Extra-Mural Areas of Romano-British Towns* (Oxford, 1987), reminds us that towns were not confined to the areas defined by their walls.

Fowler, P. J., *The Farming of Prehistoric Britain* (Cambridge, 1983).

Grew, F. O., and Hobley, B. (eds.), *Roman Urban Topography in Britain and the Western Empire* (London, 1985).

Hingley, R., *Rural Settlement in Roman Britain* (London, 1989), employs current methods of archaeological analysis to take a new look at the countryside.

Johnson, P., *Romano-British Mosaics* (Princes Risborough, 1982), a brief introduction.

Maloney, J., and Hobley, B. (eds.), *Roman Urban Defences in the West* (London, 1983).

Miles, D. (ed.), *The Romano-British Countryside* (Oxford, 1982), essays on related topics.

Morris, P., *Agricultural Buildings in Roman Britain* (Oxford, 1979).

Museum of London, *Londinium*, 2nd edn. (Southampton, 1983), combines mapping of the principal monuments and find-spots of Roman London with a visitor's guide. The physical remains are located in very welcome fashion by superimposition on a modern street map. The Ordnance Survey, Royal Commission on Historical Monuments (England), and York Archaeological Trust, *Historical Map and Guide: Roman and Anglian York* (Southampton, 1988); OS, RCHME, and Bath Archaeological Trust, *Historical Map and Guide: Roman and Medieval Bath* (Southampton, 1989); and OS, RCHME, and Canterbury Archaeological Trust, *Historical Map and Guide: Roman and Medieval Canterbury* (Southampton, 1990) perform the same function for their respective cities.

Neal, D. S., *Roman Mosaics in Britain* (London, 1981), an analytical monograph based on the author's collection of paintings of mosaics.

Percival, J., *The Roman Villa: An Historical Introduction* (London, 1976), an important general survey of the villa in the Roman world.

Rees, S., *Agricultural Implements in Prehistoric and Roman Britain* (Oxford, 1979).

Reynolds, P. J., *Iron-Age Farm: The Butser Experiment* (London, 1979), describes research through actual farming that has fundamentally changed our understanding of many aspects of ancient agriculture in Britain.

Rivet, A. L. F. (ed.), *The Roman Villa in Britain* (London, 1969), essays that summarized the state of research at the end of the 1960s.

Smith, R. F., *Roadside Settlements in Lowland Roman Britain* (Oxford, 1987).

Sommer, S., *The Military* Vici *in Roman Britain* (Oxford, 1984).

Todd, M. (ed.), *Studies in the Romano-British Villa* (Leicester, 1978), further essays on various topics, recording substantial advances and new theoretical approaches.

Wacher, J. S., *The Towns of Roman Britain* (London, 1974).

Webster, G. A. (ed.), *Fortress into City: The Consolidation of Roman Britain, First Century* AD (London, 1988), separate studies by individual authors of the origins and early development of six of the principal cities.

White, K. D., *Agricultural Implements of the Roman World* (Cambridge, 1967), a reference work.

—— *Country Life in Classical Times* (London, 1977), splendid anthology of Greek and Roman writing on the countryside.

THE ECONOMY

Chevallier, R., *Roman Roads* (London, 1976), a classic general study.

Cleere, H. F., and Crossley, D. W., *The Iron Industry of the Weald* (Leicester, 1986), explores a major industry that tells us much about Roman technology and organization.

Greene, K. T., *The Archaeology of the Roman Economy* (London, 1986), an excellent introduction both to the subject and its methodology.

Margary, I. D., *Roman Roads in Britain*, 2nd edn. (London, 1967), the magisterial catalogue, not yet superseded.

Milne, G., *The Port of Roman London* (London, 1985), provides description and analysis, leading to significant conclusions on the history and nature of London.

Peacock, D. P. S., *Pottery in the Roman World* (London, 1982).

—— and Williams, D. F., *Amphorae and the Roman Economy: An Introductory Guide* (London, 1986), tackles one of the principal archaeological indicators of contact and trade.

Swan, V. G., *Pottery in Roman Britain*, 3rd edn. (Princes Risborough, 1980), a brief but helpful introduction.

—— *The Pottery Kilns of Roman Britain* (London, 1984).

Taylor, J. du Plat, and Cleere, H. F., *Roman Shipping and Trade: Britain and the Rhine Provinces* (London, 1978).

Wild, J. P., *Textile Manufacture in the Northern Roman Provinces* (Cambridge, 1970).

RELIGION AND SOCIETY

Barley, M. W. C., and Hanson, R. P. C., *Christianity in Roman Britain, 300–700* (Leicester, 1968), a set of conference papers that was for a long time the standard accessible work on the subject.

Cunliffe, B. W. (ed.), *The Temple of Sulis Minerva at Bath*, ii. *The Finds from the Sacred Spring* (Oxford, 1988), includes a large number of curse-tablets, a contemporary written source for religious and social attitudes.

Green, M. J., *The Religions of Civilian Roman Britain* (Oxford, 1976).

—— *The Gods of the Celts* (Gloucester, 1986).

Harris, E., and Harris, J. R., *The Oriental Cults in Roman Britain* (Leiden, 1965).

Henig, M. E., *Religion in Roman Britain* (London, 1984), a splendid survey.

—— and King, A. C. (eds.), *Pagan Gods and Shrines of the Roman Empire* (Oxford, 1976).

Johns, C. M., and Potter, T. W., *The Thetford Treasure: Roman Jewellery and Silver* (London, 1983), catalogues and discusses this hoard, whose mixture of symbolism raises important doubts about the conventional identification of some Romano-British material as Christian.

Lewis, M. J. T., *Temples in Roman Britain* (Cambridge, 1966).

Merrifield, R., *The Archaeology of Ritual and Magic* (London, 1987), explores the often neglected or misinterpreted material remains that record human activity rooted in belief and superstition.

Painter, K. S., *The Water Newton Christian Silver* (London, 1977), a museum guide to this undoubtedly Christian hoard.

Pearce, S. M. (ed.), *The Early Church in Western Britain and Ireland* (Oxford, 1982).

Reece, R. M. (ed.), *Burial in the Roman World* (London, 1977), essays that include much of relevance to Britain.

Rodwell, W. J. (ed.), *Temples, Churches, and Religion in Roman Britain* (Oxford, 1980), a large collection of essays, many on, or directly relevant to, Britain.

Thomas, A. C., *Christianity in Roman Britain to AD 500*, 2nd edn. (London, 1985), detailed, learned, and often ingenious.

Toynbee, J. M. C., *Death and Burial in the Roman World* (London, 1982), a survey of the topic by one of the leading authorities.

Webster, G. A., *The British Celts and their Gods under Rome* (London, 1986).

Note: Articles in journals have not been included in this list, but readers interested in pursuing particular topics in the specialist literature will find the following classified bibliographies useful:

Bonser, W., *A Romano-British Bibliography* (55 BC–AD 449) (Oxford, 1964), includes publications to the end of 1959.

Council for British Archaeology, *Archaeological Bibliography* (London, 1949–87): originally entitled *Archaeological Bulletin for the British Isles*, this covered work published in the years 1940–80 inclusive.

—— *British Archaeological Abstracts* (London, 1967–91): with a pilot volume published in 1967, this appeared in two parts for each year from 1968 to 1991, with comprehensive coverage from 1980, when the record in the *Archaeological Bibliography* ceased. From 1992 it is replaced by the *British Archaeological Bibliography*, a computerized service based at the Institute of Archaeology, University College, London.

CHRONOLOGY

Entries in italics give the names and dates of Roman governors of the British provinces, where they are known or can be reasonably conjectured.

77/8–83/4 *Gnaeus Julius Agricola*

   83/4 Battle of Mons Graupius

   83/96 *Sallustius Lucullus*

   85/92 *Leg.* II *Adiutrix* transferred to Danube

   ?87 Inchtuthil evacuated

   90/100 Foundation of Lincoln and Gloucester *coloniae*; at London stone fort constructed, second basilica started; Richborough victory monument built

   by 98 *Publius Metilius Nepos?*

?97/8–?100/1 *Titus Avidius Quietus*

   c.100 Frontier on Tyne–Solway line, Scotland largely abandoned

?100/1–3 (or later) *Lucius Neratius Marcellus*

   108/130s Final withdrawal of *leg.* IX from Britain

   c.115/18? *Marcus Appius (or Atilius) Bradua*

   117/38 Hadrianic fire of London

   118–22 *Quintus Pompeius Falco*

   122 Hadrian visits Britain, the Wall begun, revival of public building in cities; *leg.* VI posted to Britain

122–4 (or later) *Aulus Platorius Nepos*

130/1–2/3 *Sextus Julius Severus*

132/3–5 (or later) *Publius Mummius Sisenna*

138/9–?42/3 *Quintus Lollius Urbicus*

   140–2/3 Antonine conquests in Scotland, by 143 Antonine Wall begun

?142/3–?5 *Cornelius Priscianus?*

   by 146 *Gnaeus Papirius Aelianus*

   150s Serious trouble in the north, Antonine Wall evacuated, Hadrian's Wall recommissioned

   c.155 Verulamium extensively damaged by fire

   by 158 *Gnaeus Julius Verus*

158/9–61 . . . . *anus*

   c.160/3 Second occupation and evacuation of Antonine Wall

   161/2 *Marcus Statius Priscus*

   161–80 Reign of Marcus Aurelius, major wars on Danube and in east, serious pressure on empire from outside begins

162/3–?6 *Sextus Calpurnius Agricola*

   c.163 Hadrian's Wall restored

   169/80 *Quintus Antistius Adventus; Caerellius Priscus?*

   175 Surrendered Sarmatian cavalry sent to Britain

   180/250 Land walls of London built

   c.182/3 Major warfare breaks out on northern frontier of Britain

   c.182/4 *Marcus Antius Crescens Calpurnianus (acting governor)*

   184/5 *Ulpius Marcellus*, victories in Britain

mid-180s Earthwork defences begin to be provided for previously unwalled British towns

185 Army in Britain sends delegation to demand dismissal of Perennis, praetorian prefect

185/?7 Publius Helvius Pertinax

191/2–?3 Decimus Clodius Albinus (193 proclaimed in Britain as emperor)

193–7 Britain under rule of Clodius Albinus as emperor

197 Victory of Septimius Severus at Lyons, Britain falls to Severans

197 Restoration of forts in northern frontier region begins

197–?200/2 Virius Lupus

?202/3–5 Gaius Valerius Pudens

205/7 Lucius Alfenus Senecio

205 Restoration of Hadrian's Wall begun

?208/13 Gaius Junius Faustinus Postumianus

?211/12 Ulpius Marcellus

by 213 Gaius Julius Marcus

197/213 Britain divided into two provinces

197/c.250 Pollienus Auspex (*Britannia Superior*); *Rufinus* (*Brit. Sup.*); *Marcus Martiannius Pulcher* (*Brit. Sup., acting*)

208–11 Campaigns of Septimius Severus and Caracalla in Scotland, imperial court in Britain, Geta effectively regent

?208/11 (or later) Martyrdom of St Alban

211 Death of Septimius Severus at York

211–13 Caracalla makes frontier dispositions in Britain, possibly finalizes division into two provinces

212 Murder of Geta by Caracalla in Rome

212 *Constitutio Antoniniana* (Roman citizenship extended to almost all free citizens of empire)

by 216 Marcus Antonius Gordianus (*Britannia Inferior*)

by 219 Modius Julius (*Brit. Inf.*)

220 Tiberius Claudius Paulinus (*Brit. Inf.*)

221–2 Marius Valerianus (*Brit. Inf.*)

222/35 Calvisius Rufus (*Brit. Inf.*), *Valerius Crescens Fulvianus* (*Brit. Inf.*)

223 Claudius Xenophon (*Brit. Inf.*)

by 225 Maximus (*Brit. Inf.*)

c.235 Claudius Apellinus (*Brit. Inf.*)

235–70s Civil wars and invasions in east and west of empire

by 237 (T)uccianus (*Brit. Inf.*)

by 237 York receives title of *colonia*

238/44 Maecilius Fuscus (*Brit. Inf.*), *Egnatius Lucilianus* (*Brit. Inf.*)

by 242 *Nonius Philippus* (*Brit. Inf.*)
?after 244 *Aemilianus* (*Brit. Inf.*)
253/5 *Titus Desticius Juba* (*Brit. Sup.*)
255/70 Riverside wall of London built
259/60 Revolt of Postumus in Gaul; Gallic Empire (*Imperium Galliarum*) formed
259/60–74 Britain under rule of Gallic emperors
263/8 *Octavius Sabinus* (*Brit. Inf.*)
270s Renewed growth in Britain; Saxon Shore system first formed?
274 Surrender of Tetricus, end of Gallic Empire
after 274 *Lucius Septimius* (*Brit. Sup.?*)
275–6 Germanic invasions of Gaul
c.277 Probus repeals restrictions on viticulture in Gaul and Britain
277/9 Burgundian and Vandal troops settled in Britain used in suppression of a governor's revolt
282–5 Britain under control of Carinus
284 Accession of Diocletian
286 Maximian's campaign in Gaul
287 Carausius seizes Britain
287–93 Britain under rule of Carausius; last certain record of *leg.* XX (coinage of Carausius)
293 Tetrarchy formed; Carausius' forces expelled from Boulogne, Carausius assassinated by Allectus
293–6 Britain under rule of Allectus
294 Palatial building work in London
296 Britain retaken by Constantius I as Caesar
after 296 Britain becomes a civil diocese of four provinces
296/305 *Aurelius Arpagius* (*Brit. Inf. or Brit. Secunda*)
late 3rd/early 4th c. *Hierocles Perpetuus* (*province unknown*)
297/8 Constantius I sends skilled tradesmen from Britain to restore Autun
before 305 Reconstruction work begins on the northern frontier
306 Campaign of Constantius I in Scotland, Constantine the Great proclaimed at York
311 Persecutions of Christians end
312 Battle of the Milvian Bridge (defeat of Maxentius by Constantine)
313 Edict of Milan, Peace of the Church confirmed
314 British bishops at Council of Arles
by 319 *Lucius Papius Pacatianus* (*vicarius*)
324 Constantine sole emperor, foundation of Constantinople
340 Defeat of north-western Roman armies at Aquileia by Constans

398/400 Victories over Picts, Scots, and Saxons

400/2 Possible troop withdrawals from Britain by Stilicho

402 Official import of new bronze coinage to Britain ceases

404 Western imperial court withdrawn from Milan to Ravenna

406 Proclamation of usurper Marcus in Britain, Germans cross Rhine

407 Gratian and Constantine III successively proclaimed in Britain

407–11 Constantine III rules from Arles

409 Britain revolts from Constantine III, end of Roman rule in Britain

410 Sack of Rome by Alaric; 'Rescript of Honorius'

411 Fall of Constantine III

416 Pelagianism officially condemned as heresy

417 First recorded exercise of Roman authority in northern Gaul since end of Constantine III's rule

418 Visigothic kingdom of Toulouse established

by 420/30 Regular use of coinage ceases in Britain, factory-made pottery no longer available

425–9 Aetius in Gaul as *magister militum per Gallias*

429 Visit of St Germanus to Britain

431 Episcopate of Palladius in Ireland

432 Episcopate of St Patrick in Ireland begins (traditional date)

440s/50s Traditional dates for Saxon take-over in Britain, probable final end of recognizable Romano-British society

446/54 Appeal of Britons to Aetius (Gildas)

451 Battle of Catalaunian Plains, advance of Attila halted by Aetius

454 Murder of Aetius, regular Roman army in west subsequently run down

460s Britons recorded in Brittany

476 Romulus 'Augustulus' deposed by Odoacer at Ravenna

480 Julius Nepos, last western emperor, murdered in Dalmatia

LIST OF ROMAN EMPERORS

This list gives the dates of reigns down to the death of the last western emperor. The dates are those of the effective reign (many emperors designated their sons or other intended successors as co-emperors, but these are only shown when there was a real sharing of the supreme power). The list does not attempt to differentiate between 'legitimate' emperors and 'usurpers', or to list every minor usurper, particularly after the end of Roman rule in Britain. Appointments to the late Roman junior imperial rank of *Caesar* are only shown where they are relevant to Britain. Names are given in the forms in which they are commonly encountered in modern works in English.

Julio-Claudians

Augustus (Octavian)	27 BC–AD 14 (sole ruler from 30 BC)
Tiberius	14–37
Gaius ('Caligula')	37–41
Claudius	41–54
Nero	54–68

'Year of the Four Emperors'

Galba	68–9
Otho	69
Vitellius	69
Vespasian	69–79 (see also below)

Flavians

Vespasian	69–79
Titus	79–81
Domitian	81–96
Nerva	96–8
Trajan	98–117
Hadrian	117–38

Antonines

Antoninus Pius	138–61
Marcus Aurelius	161–80
Lucius Verus	161–9 (with M. Aurelius)
Commodus	180–92
Pertinax	193
Didius Julianus	193

Severans and their rivals

Septimius Severus	193–211
Pescennius Niger	193–4
Clodius Albinus	193–7
Caracalla	211–17
Geta	211–12
Macrinus	217–18
Elagabalus	218–22
Severus Alexander	222–35
Maximinus ('Thrax')	235–8
Gordian I	238
Gordian II	238
Pupienus	238
Balbinus	238 (with Pupienus)
Gordian III	238–44
Philip I ('the Arab')	244–9
Pacatian	248
Jotapian	249
Decius	249–51
Gallus	251–3
Aemilian	253
Valerian	253–59/60
Gallienus	253–68
Macrianus	260–1
Quietus	260–1
Regalianus	260/1
Aemilianus ('Aegippius')	261–2
Aureolus	267–8
Laelianus	268

Gallic Empire

Postumus	260–9
Marius	268

Victorinus	269–71
Tetricus	271–3
Claudius II ('Gothicus')	268–69/70
Quintillus	269/70
Aurelian	269/70–5
Domitian II	270/5
Vaballathus	270–1
Tacitus	275–6
Florian	276
Probus	276–82
Saturninus	280
Carus	282–3
Julian I	283
Carinus	283–5 (*Caesar* 282–3)
Numerian	283–4

The Tetrarchy

Diocletian	284–305
Maximian	286–305, 307–8 (*Caesar* 285–6)
Constantius I ('Chlorus')	(*Caesar* 293–305, *Augustus*, see below)
Galerius	305–11 (*Caesar* 293–305)
Carausius	287–93 (in Britain and Gaul)
Allectus	293–6 (in Britain and Gaul)
Domitius Domitianus	297 (in Egypt)
Flavius Severus	306–7 (*Caesar* 305–6)
Maximin Daia	309–13
Maxentius	307/8–12
Alexander	308–9/10 (in Africa)
Licinius	308–24
Valens I	316

House of Constantius and their rivals

Constantius I (*Augustus*)	305–6
Constantine I ('the Great')	306–37
Constantine II	337–40
Constans	337–50
Constantius II	337–61
Nepotian	350
Vetranio	350
Magnentius	350–3
Silvanus	355 (in Gaul)

Julian II ('the Apostate')		360–3 (*Caesar* 355–60)	
Jovian		363–4	

House of Valentinian and their rivals

Valentinian I		364–75	
Valens		364–78	
Procopius		365–6	
Gratian		375–83	
Valentinian II		375–92	

House of Theodosius and their rivals

Theodosius I ('the Great')		379–95	
Magnus Maximus		383–8	
Eugenius		392–4	
In the West		*In the East*	
Honorius	395–423	Arcadius	395–408
Marcus (in Britain)	406		
Gratian (in Britain)	407		
Constantine III	407–11	Theodosius II	408–50
Maximus (in Spain)	409–11		
Jovinus (in Gaul)	411–13		
Johannes (John)	423–5		
Constantius III (Flavius Constantius)	421		
Valentinian III	425–55		
		Marcian	450–7
Petronius Maximus	455		
Avitus	455–6		
Majorian	457–61	Leo I	457–74
Libius Severus	461–5		
Anthemius	467–72		
Olybrius	472		
Glycerius	473		
Julius Nepos	473–80	Leo II	474
Romulus ('Augustulus')	475–6	Zeno	474–91 (*etc.* to 1453)

INDEX

Notes: 1. Pages referring to captions of maps are shown in *italics*. There are occasionally also textual references on these pages. 2. Subentries are arranged *chronologically* where necessary. 3. Although the names of Roman citizens in the period before AD 284 are (except for those otherwise very familiar under another name) entered under the second of the three names (*praenomen, nomen, cognomen*), some cross-references (or double entries) have been supplied, e.g. *Agricola* see *Julius Agricola*. 4. The qualification 'emperor' in brackets after a name includes usurpers as well as legitimate emperors. Other names are qualified when there are two or more people with the same name, e.g. *Suetonius*.